Jonathan Edwards's Moral Thought and Its British Context

The Institute of
Early American History and Culture
is sponsored jointly by
The College of William and Mary
and The Colonial Williamsburg Foundation.

Norman Fiering

Jonathan Edwards's Moral Thought and Its British Context

PUBLISHED FOR THE INSTITUTE OF

EARLY AMERICAN HISTORY AND CULTURE

WILLIAMSBURG, VIRGINIA

BY THE UNIVERSITY OF NORTH CAROLINA PRESS

CHAPEL HILL

© 1981 The University of North Carolina Press

Library of Congress Cataloging in Publication Data

Fiering, Norman.
Jonathan Edwards's moral thought and its British
context.

Bibliography: p.
Includes index.
1. Edwards, Jonathan, 1703–1758. 2. Christian
ethics—History. I. Title.
BX7260.E3F53   241'.0458   80-26755
ISBN 0-8078-1473-3   AACR1

In memory of my father,

who loved ethics

Preface

The importance, the rarity, of Jonathan Edwards was first impressed upon me in one of Eugen Rosenstock-Huessy's extraordinary lecture courses at Dartmouth College in the 1950s. I did not begin intensive reading of Edwards's work and the literature about him, however, until 1962 when I started research on a doctoral dissertation. That dissertation, completed in 1969, was on the general topic of moral philosophy in colonial America and in fact never got as far as Edwards, despite my original ambitions. It began with the Cambridge Platonists, covered the British moralists Shaftesbury, Hutcheson, and Wollaston, and then the Americans Benjamin Franklin and Samuel Johnson. Edwards more or less remained to be "done."

I began another period of intense engagement with Edwards's thought in 1969 under the auspices of a postdoctoral fellowship at the Institute of Early American History and Culture. In 1970, with the aid of the American Philosophical Society's Penrose Fund, as well as Institute support, I was privileged to spend the summer studying the Edwards manuscripts and the excellent collection of eighteenth-century books at the Beinecke Library, Yale University, that mecca for Edwards scholars. But most of this research I ended up storing away for later use, as it turned out, for I came to feel during the course of my fellowship at the Institute that my time could be more valuably spent studying seventeenth-century moral philosophy than continuing to work on Edwards and that Edwards's thought would be that much better grasped as a result of this digression backwards in time.

The first draft of this book, then, was not written until the academic year 1975–1976, during a period of leave as a National Endowment for the Humanities fellow. The manuscript was finally revised and enlarged in the fall of 1978 at the National Humanities Center in Research Triangle Park, North Carolina. I am grateful to all of the institutions named here for giving me the leisure time and other resources needed to study and write on Edwards.

The actual composition of this book took no more than eighteen months in all, but the preparation for it, as I have tried to indicate, was stretched out over a much longer period of time. My debts to teachers and fellow scholars

can be similarly divided into those owed for long-term help and those owed
for specific assistance with this book. Regarding the latter type of aid, William
Breitenbach, David Hall, Thomas Schafer, and John E. Smith each gave the
manuscript a close reading when it was near completion, and to them I am
grateful for the kinds of suggestions and criticisms that enable an author to
avoid at least the very worst errors and faults concerning his subject. I am
particularly indebted to Tom Schafer, who has been at the hub of serious
research on Edwards for twenty years, and whose unfailing generosity to
fellow students of Edwards, young and old, deserves a special place of honor
in the records of scholarship.

Parts or chapters of the manuscript were also read and criticized by David
Ammerman, Sacvan Bercovitch, Bruce Kuklick, and James Smiley, with
valuable benefits for me.

More generally I would like to acknowledge the aid, comfort, and stimulating companionship I have received from my colleagues at the Institute of
Early American History and Culture since 1969, Michael McGiffert, John E.
Selby, and particularly Thad W. Tate, the director, who has been consistently
helpful in enabling me to sustain some degree of scholarly research and
writing while I am employed full-time as an editor.

Since this book was originally written as a continuation of *Moral Philosophy at Seventeenth-Century Harvard: A Discipline in Transition* (Chapel Hill,
N.C., 1981), many names listed in the acknowledgments to that volume could
with equal appropriateness be mentioned here. I shall forgo that temptation,
but it gives me pleasure to note several others to whom I owe much for encouragement at crucial times: Thomas Vance, Margaret Stuart, and Alan Sklar.

Final preparation of the manuscript was done at the Institute of Early
American History and Culture by Cynthia Austin Carter, who has been a
challenging and assiduous editor, and Doris M. Leisch.

My deepest gratitude is owed to my wife Renée, who has always cared, and
to my children, Benjamin, Jason, and Cassie, for their inspiring trust.

In his thoughtful book *The Perfectibility of Man*, John Passmore exposes
the fallacy of Pelagianism by referring to the nature of the accomplishment involved in writing a scholarly book. The writing of a book, Passmore observes,

> is made possible only by a series of "graces," gifts from others, gifts the
> author has done nothing to deserve. These graces are manifold, and
> highly diversified in their origin. . . . In the case of a learned work they
> would include the tradition of scholarship which the author inherits; the
> encouragement, the criticisms, the suggestions, of teachers, pupils, and
> colleagues; the contributions of his predecessors. It is not an author's
> own doing, not a reward for his merit, that he lives in a country and at a

time when he is free to write as he will, and that is the greatest grace
of all.

For an author to feel proud of himself for what he has done would
therefore be absurd. In relation to any single one of these graces he is, no
doubt, a co-operator: no one of them, by itself, explains why he has
written as he has written. To that extent, he can rightly speak of "his
contribution" in relation to, let us say, the existing tradition of scholarship or the culture of his country; he can think of himself as "saying
something original," so long as he realizes that his "originality" is, in
relation to what he has learnt from others, extremely slight in extent. A
deeper exploration of the situation, however, soon reveals how dependent even that "originality" is on other sources of grace, on genetic
inheritance, on upbringing, on the accidents of history.

Scholarly work takes place in a rich world of prior and ongoing achievement.
Since one of the points I try to make in this book is that Edwards's writing on
moral philosophy occurred within a cultural context made up of his reading of
British and Continental authors, it would perhaps not be out of place here for
me to acknowledge my own sense of dependence on the free gifts of others.

Contents

CHAPTER SEVEN
MORAL THEOLOGY
322

APPENDIX
363

BIBLIOGRAPHICAL NOTE
371

INDEX
381

Jonathan Edwards's
Moral Thought and
Its British Context

Moral Philosophy or Divinity was
his favorite study. . . .

He confined not himself to authors
of any particular sect or denomination;
yea took much pains to come at the books
of the most noted writers, who advance
a scheme of divinity most contrary to
his own principles.

SAMUEL HOPKINS
The Life and Character of . . . Jonathan Edwards (1765)

Introduction

These chapters on the moral thought of Jonathan Edwards were originally written for inclusion in a much larger work on moral philosophy in America from *ca.* 1630 to *ca.* 1750. When that work, as originally planned, became impractically elephantine, I decided to publish my studies on Edwards as a single volume, and the material included here has been accordingly revised to enable this book to stand on its own. The volume does remain, however, something of a sequel to my previously published *Moral Philosophy at Seventeenth-Century Harvard: A Discipline in Transition*, and the reader who has already come upon that book will, perhaps, find the analysis of Edwards presented in the following pages more convincing than might otherwise be the case.

To compensate a little for the absence of sufficient preparatory material in this volume, I will review quickly the history of moral philosophy in Anglo-America, as I conceive of it, up to the time of Edwards's involvement. Moral philosophy, along with natural philosophy, had been part of the European university curriculum since the late Middle Ages. Its study was centered almost invariably on Aristotle's *Nicomachean Ethics*, usually presented in the form of a commentary that neutralized Aristotle's paganism. Other works of moral thought were read, of course, notably Cicero's *Offices*, but not strictly within the framework of the academic discipline of moral philosophy, or ethics.

The use of a pagan source as the main text for a subject as important as ethics was continuously controversial, as might be expected, and various forms of reconciliation were devised. It was said, for example, that pagan ethics remained useful in preparing people for civil life and external behavior; but the guidance of Holy Scripture was essential for leading mankind to salvation and for developing a sanctified interior life. Yet this kind of uneasy peace between the secular and the religious realms, based upon specious reasoning, was inherently unstable, and during the Reformation it was profoundly challenged. Martin Luther in particular was a bitter foe of the study of the *Nicomachean Ethics* in any guise, and many Calvinists took up the same cry. The consequences of this challenge can be seen in microcosm in the history of the ethics course taught at Harvard during the first hundred years of the college's existence. Harvard seemingly could not make up its mind how to teach moral philosophy or whether to teach it at all as a subject separate from divinity. The young college was caught in the dilemma of desiring, on the one hand, to be a Christian seminary, but also longing, on the other hand, to have a curriculum that would qualify it as a full-fledged participant in the grand European university tradition.

This tension was relieved ultimately by the revolution in university curricula that occurred everywhere in the West in the seventeenth century, namely, the overturning of Aristotelianism in natural philosophy, in logic, and in moral philosophy. In the latter subject, as part of the rejection of Aristotelianism, a new synthesis of considerable complexity was forged, which made the university teaching of moral philosophy in 1750 nearly a different subject from the moral philosophy of 1650. After about 1680 one must speak of the "*new* moral philosophy" in order to avoid confusion with the old course based so heavily on Aristotle alone.

The formation of the new moral philosophy is a subject deserving in itself of independent book-length treatment, especially when one considers that this course became preeminent over all others in the curricula of American colleges, more important than divinity, and capable of making tributary, for a time, even logic and natural philosophy.[1] The magical hold of the new moral philosophy in American colleges was fed by a series of outstanding achievements in the field in the course of the eighteenth century, culminating in the classic works of Hume, Adam Smith, Rousseau, Kant, and others, which equaled the stunning advances made in natural philosophy in the seventeenth century.

It is possible here to mention only summarily the ingredients of this new discipline, which flourished until the latter part of the nineteenth century. As with so much else in modern philosophy, its beginnings are traceable first of all to the Cartesian emphasis on starting afresh with an axiomatic method. The Scholastic and Classical inheritance of ethical ideas was to be tested for the clarity and distinctness of its first principles in the light of critical reason. Although the method was rationalistic at its core, in that the phenomena of mere sense experience were to be treated with skepticism, the Cartesians also stressed the importance of close observation of human nature. In any case, the writings of Montaigne, Pierre Charron, and others had already started a definite movement toward the naturalistic reexamination of human nature.

---

1. For background and substantiation, see Norman Fiering, *Moral Philosophy at Seventeenth-Century Harvard: A Discipline in Transition* (Chapel Hill, N.C., 1981), and Fiering, "President Samuel Johnson and the Circle of Knowledge," *William and Mary Quarterly*, 3d Ser., XXVIII (1971), 199–236.

The impact of Cartesianism on moral philosophy was matched by the startling originality and brilliance of Hobbes's work in the field, which was itself a product, to some extent, of the influence of Continental thought. In England at least, Hobbes's writing launched a new era of speculation in moral philosophy. The sharpness of his challenges to conventional opinion demanded a more comprehensive reevaluation of assumptions than had been called for in any preceding era. Hobbes insisted on direct observation without preconceptions, including the use of introspection, and in order to answer him English moralists were required to become his equals as moral psychologists. Mere citations of old texts would no longer do.

Cartesian dualism was conducive to intensive study of the operations of mind, of soul, and of self, and this preoccupation, as it happened, coincided with the growth of religious concern with the inner man, evident in both Catholic and Protestant pietism. Puritans and Jansenists labored hand in hand with Hobbesians and anti-Hobbesians, Cartesians and anti-Cartesians, in the investigation of all facets of the inner life of human beings. Looking only at the study of the passions and the investigation of their role in behavior, it seems clear that there was an unprecedented increase in psychological knowledge. The period from, let us say, 1649, when Descartes's treatise on the passions was published, to 1759, when Adam Smith's *Theory of Moral Sentiments* appeared, may have been the most fruitful epoch of psychological investigation in the history of the West, with the exception only, perhaps, of our own century. Locke, of course, was a major figure in this progress in philosophical psychology, although he had but slight interest in the passions.

These new ingredients in moral philosophy did not totally displace Classical and patristic influences, but the older influences diminished in importance in relation to the whole enterprise of moral philosophy. The Stoics, particularly Seneca and Plutarch, were more deeply studied in the seventeenth century than at any previous time, and aspects of Neostoicism underlay much of eighteenth-century ethical thought. Aristotle lost his central and unique place, but Aristotelianism remained a permanent contribution. In addition, through the work of Pierre Gassendi and others there was a significant revival of Epicurean philosophy, the effects of which may be seen in both Locke and Hume. The traditional topics studied in Classical moral philosophy, such as the determination of man's highest end, the definition of happiness, the nature of moral strength and moral weakness, the place of reason and judgment in moral decision, and the role of habit, all continued to be of interest in the new moral philosophy. But combined with the old Classical ethics, as we have indicated, was a renewed religious concern with the whole man, an immersion in the problems of the inner life, the realm of appetites, affections, passions, and inclinations, which the pagan moralists, by comparison, had only touched on. So great was the energy applied to this investigation that by the middle of the eighteenth century the most pressing problem in ethics had become that of the relation between sentiment and reason in moral judgment, a question that before 1600 had hardly been addressed at all, at least not in the same terms.

Added to this complex of factors was the continuing Christian influence on all questions of philosophical anthropology. Along with Neostoicism, the seventeenth century also spawned that doctrine's powerful arch rival, Neo-Augustinianism. Both Jansenist and Puritan, as bearers of the Augustinian tradition, examined with great acuteness such questions as the moral status of self-love and the possibility of disinterested action, adding new depth and complexity to the concept of original depravity. One of the salient characteristics of the new moral philosophy, in fact, was its close reconsideration of the philosophical anthropology of Christianity in the light of nonreligious experiential evidence. Thus, the problem of the will, which had been peripheral at best in Classical ethics, was actively explored in the eighteenth century not only in relation to systems of divine determinism, such as predestination, but also in relation to full-scale analyses of human nature and to formal considerations of moral agency and responsibility.

In addition to the novel study of the passions and affections, the use of an experiential and critical method, and the complex integration of certain Christian assumptions, the new moral philosophy was also characterized by sophisticated and innovative analyses of conscience and obligation, by a preoccupation with the moral criterion of benevolence (a criterion foreign to Classical and Scholastic ethics), and by a notable admixture of moral exhortation that made the subject more than merely academic. Despite Hume's reputation as a dry skeptic, for example, all of his work in ethics is pervaded with moral preaching. The "new moral philosophy," in other words, combined descriptive and prescriptive ethics to a degree seldom attempted in the twentieth century. It was also, obviously, a course of study far broader than the technical philosophical ethics practiced at mid-twentieth century, since in addition to much theology or divinity it included in nascent form the social sciences of a later period—psychology, sociology, economics, anthropology—that are now distinct from philosophy.

Finally, the amalgam of the new moral philosophy included a sense of mission. At its very base was an awareness that the twin institutions of clergy and Holy Scripture were losing their previously unqualified claim to authoritative utterance, and that libertinism, skepticism, and nihilism were real threats to Western civilization. Neoclassicism and neopaganism were in themselves inadequate solutions to the crisis in values, and in consequence it was the responsibility of philosophy to reconstruct in (for the most part) secular and naturalistic terms ethical foundations and values for a new age. The guiding assumption behind almost all of the new work was the belief that God's intentions for man, His expectations of human beings as moral creatures, could be discovered independently of the traditional sources of religious authority, through a close investigation of human nature. Through the study of human behavior and endowments, and of human potentialities, both intellectual and emotional, direction could be gained about how people *ought* to conduct themselves. It was the faith in this methodological assumption—that the discovery of "facts" could decisively confirm moral values—that above all energized the grand moral philosophy enterprise of the eighteenth century.

Jonathan Edwards is usually thought of as primarily a theologian and a metaphysician, insofar as he was more than a working Christian minister in the New England Puritan tradition. But his most lasting and developed writings may also be seen as contributions to the new moral philosophy, a field that is not so easily recognized today because, as we have noted, it had disintegrated before the end of the nineteenth century. Edwards's treatises on the will, on the affections, and on virtue are not readily classifiable in twentieth-century categories, but they can be comfortably fitted into the context of eighteenth-century moral philosophy debates. Even Edwards's treatise on Original Sin was at one point designed to be part of a single vaster work akin to the new moral philosophy. Edwards's initial plan, as he described it, had been to prepare a "treatise" in two parts, the first of which would deal with "the nature of true virtue" and "God's end in creating the world." The second was to be an inquiry into the truth of the doctrine of Original Sin, "both as to corruption of nature and imputation and in the next place concerning the manner in which man's nature came to be corrupt and in total corruption and then concerning infused habits and concerning the saving grace's differing from common grace in nature and kind and concerning that moral taste that natural men [have?] to show that there is nothing of true virtue in it."[2]

Most of the elements in this plan for a book were treated by Edwards at some length in one work or another, but the single unified treatise on virtue and human nature considered from the viewpoints of both religion and natural experience was never written. The most convincing evidence of Edwards's deep involvement in moral philosophy projects of this sort is his list of fifty-odd "Subjects to be handled in the Treatise on the Mind," which is printed as an appendix to this book.[3] Judging from the range of topics covered in the list, the questions raised, and the suggestions Edwards gave of how he in-

2. Edwards's manuscript "Book of Controversies," 102 (Beinecke Library, Yale University, New Haven, Connecticut), as quoted in Jonathan Edwards, *Original Sin*, ed. Clyde A. Holbrook, in *The Works of Jonathan Edwards* (New Haven, Conn., 1957–), III, 22–23.

3. See pp. 363–369, below. This list, which has received little attention from students of Edwards, should not be confused with Edwards's famous "Notes on the Mind," written much earlier and with quite different intent.

tended to handle these questions, it seems evident that Edwards's "Natural History of the Mental World," had he ever had the leisure to write it, would have been one of the major works of moral philosophy in the eighteenth century.

As in the case of his American contemporary Samuel Johnson, there was an evolution in Edwards's philosophical work toward recognition of the centrality of moral philosophy as a concern of thinking men. With the diminution of clerical and scriptural authority among intellectuals, the rhetoric of serious discourse about man and his relations to other men and to God became increasingly the property of the moral philosophers, who were not part of a discredited dogmatic tradition but who sustained, for the most part, the moral values of Judaeo-Christian institutions. In other words, despite his essentially theological interests, Edwards was thrust into a dialogue with some of the major voices of early eighteenth-century British moral thought, writers such as Samuel Clarke, the third earl of Shaftesbury, William Wollaston, Francis Hutcheson, Bishop Joseph Butler, and, eventually, David Hume. Others in early America who attempted serious writing on human nature and conduct— Benjamin Franklin, Samuel Johnson, mentioned earlier, James Logan, and Thomas Clap—were caught up in the same colloquy, whatever their religious denomination and regardless of whether they were clergymen or laymen. Edwards was exceptional in his skills, but his philosophical preoccupations were fairly typical of his time.

Edwards's engagement with the eighteenth-century moralists has never been studied in detail, nor has there been an effort to assess the impact upon him of his extensive reading in nonreligious philosophy. It is one contention of this book that Edwards's study of eighteenth-century moral thought affected him profoundly and presented him with a major intellectual problem, which his dissertation on the nature of true virtue, written quite late in his life, was an attempt to resolve. The new gospel of benevolence and optimism preached by Shaftesbury and Hutcheson was not simply old-fashioned Christian moralism or a doctrine of salvation by works against which Edwards could hurl the sola fide and his conviction that true virtue is a matter of inner disposition; this new gospel was itself based on a theory of the affections and of human nature that directly rivaled some of the basic tenets of Christian anthropology. It was, in effect, a Christian heresy, a counter-religion. "In our nature," one of the proponents of the Shaftesbury-Hutcheson gospel asserted, "religion and virtue are one and the same thing: it is the same natural disposition of the mind, employed *contemplatively* in admiring and loving supreme virtue, and *actively* in imitating that model."[4] A good heart, or sound charitable dispositions issuing in benevolent practice, was put forward as the equivalent of traditional

4. George Turnbull, *The Principles of Moral Philosophy: An Enquiry into the Wise and Good*

religion in nearly all respects. Within this counter-religion there were schools that disagreed on such matters as whether reason, sense, sentiment, or instinct provides the key to moral judgment and action, but all of the membership were unified in their virtue-devotion. John Taylor, for example, the author of *The Scripture-Doctrine of Original Sin Proposed to Free and Candid Examination* (London, 1740), which Edwards vigorously attacked in his own work on the subject of Original Sin, opposed Hutcheson on the matter of the place of reason in morality, but it would be hard to distinguish him from Hutcheson in some of his other convictions. Why does Jesus save us from death? Taylor asked. "It was his *Obedience* to God, and *Good-Will* to men; it was his consummate *Virtue*. . . . It is *Virtue*, Obedience to the Truth, or to the Divine Will, and Benevolence to his Creatures, that wins every Prize, that carrieth every Cause in Heaven. *Virtue* the only Price which purchaseth every Thing with God."[5]

Hutcheson and his followers were particularly difficult for Edwards to deal with because the foundations of their thought mirrored Edwards's exactly. There is a direct evolution from seventeenth-century Puritan piety to eighteenth-century sentimentalist ethics, which meant that, ironically, Edwards confronted in much of the new moral philosophy familiar ideas in secular garb.

In the face of this counter-religion, Edwards more and more came to realize that traditional polemics and apologetics were an ineffective response to the decline in the status of orthodox Christianity in the middle of the eighteenth century. To return revealed religion to the central role it had held in Western thought for so many centuries, it would be necessary to construct a new philosophical anthropology that would meet naturalism on its own ground and serve as a foundation for thought about man in both secular life and religion without inconsistency. Edwards's attempt to assimilate and utilize contemporary secular philosophy for purposes of Christian restoration may be seen as comparable to the self-conscious mission of the Cambridge Platonists, but it is, perhaps, even more akin to Leibniz's efforts at synthesis in the late seventeenth century.[6] Edwards's dissertation on *The Nature of True Virtue* is about God, to be sure, but it is an extraordinary fact that Scripture is never cited in the work, nor does Edwards draw on the theological tradition for support. Thus, although at an earlier stage in his life Edwards was determined

---

Government of the Moral World, I (London, 1740), 214. The title of vol. II of this work is slightly different: *The Principles of Moral and Christian Philosophy.* . . .

5. John Taylor, *The Scripture-Doctrine of Original Sin Proposed to Free and Candid Examination*, 2d ed. (London, 1741 [orig. publ. 1740]), 72.

6. For Leibniz's program and the many parallels between his ideas and Edwards's, see Leroy E. Loemker's pioneering work, *Struggle for Synthesis: The Seventeenth Century Background of Leibniz's Synthesis of Order and Freedom* (Cambridge, Mass., 1972).

"to shew how absurd for Xtians to write treatises of Ethicks distinct from Divinity as Reveald in the Gospel,"[7] his plans for a "Natural History of the Mental World" are an indication that he changed his mind and came to believe, at least in part, that he would have to be something of a moral philosopher himself.

The terminology I have used in this book is mostly that found commonly in scholarly work on the history of philosophy, but two or three words not found in general dictionaries may require special comment. "Sentimentalism" refers to the emphasis in early eighteenth-century British literary and philosophical culture on the constructive role of the affections and passions (in French, *sentiment*, feeling) in the moral life. "Benevolism" is a more precise word for a closely related idea, that man is inherently benevolent and this benevolence is rooted in natural feeling. I use "benevolism" as the antonym of "egoism." The word "altruism" might do as well, but it lacks the connotation of "goodness based on feeling" that attaches to "benevolism." "Sentimentalism" is usually used to mean *benevolent* feeling, but it is a word so general that even an egoist, who argues that the human personality is dominated by *feelings* of self-love, might correctly be called a sentimentalist. "Intellectualism" refers to the opinion in moral psychology that cognitive faculties—understanding, intellect, reason—are determinative in the moral life, not feelings. "Intellectualism," then, is the opposite of "sentimentalism." Sentimentalism, of course, should not be allowed to suggest the idea of sentimentality, which is an entirely different notion.

I have had four goals in mind in writing this book that together distinguish it, I trust, from other studies of Edwards's thought. I have tried, first, to keep reasonably separate Edwards's work in critical ethics and his work in synthetic ethics. In an effort to demonstrate the inadequacy of all secular moral schemes, Edwards did a considerable amount of writing in opposition to British moralists such as Hutcheson, George Turnbull, and Hume. This critical or analytic work is easily put into the context of British moral thought between 1700 and 1750. Edwards also attempted, however, to formulate his own system of moral philosophy, which might more appropriately be called a moral theology. This synthetic work belongs properly in a context made up not of the eighteenth-century British moralists but of the late seventeenth-century Continental rationalists, such as Spinoza, Malebranche, and Leibniz. After the Cambridge Platonists, none of the British moralists, perhaps because

7. Quoted by Thomas A. Schafer, "The Concept of Being in the Thought of Jonathan Edwards" (Ph.D. diss., Duke University, 1951), 79, from Edwards's "Preface to the 'Rational Account,' " MS, Beinecke Lib., Yale Univ.

they were intimidated by Locke, seem to have ventured as far as Edwards did in attempting to establish an ethics founded on ontology.

Second, in addition to keeping Edwards's critical ethics and his synthetic ethics distinct, I have also tried to avoid or evade entanglement with his more strictly theological views. Given Edwards's abiding and deep religious commitments, such an approach is possible only to a degree. In four chapters of this work, however, I concentrate exclusively on Edwards's concept of the natural (non-regenerate) man in relation to ethics, an exercise in selectivity that is less artificial in the case of Edwards than some historians may realize.

A third goal has been to study Edwards's moral thought developmentally. So far as possible I have tried to present Edwards's ideas chronologically, moving from his earliest notions to those held shortly before his death.

Finally, as is perhaps implicit in all that I have already said, I have constantly tried to keep Edwards's thought in its proper intellectual context, which has meant reading much of what Edwards read and working toward some degree of precision in understanding his concerns at the moment of his writing. Of course, any such enterprise is inherently hazardous. The relationships between ideas, between reading and writing, between thought and its stimuli are so many and so diverse that there is no hope of exhaustiveness. We speak of the ramifications and the roots of ideas as though nice, neat trees of thought existed, but in truth the world of ideas is more like a thicket that one can enter but never definitively sort out. One is happy enough to trace accurately a few of the twigs to the right branches and a few of the branches to the right trunks.

The first chapter is the least substantively engaged with Edwards's philosophy, but concentrates instead on the historical and intellectual context in which he came to maturity as a thinker. Chapters 2 through 4 are a survey of all that Edwards said about the moral powers of the natural man, that is, the person unaided by special grace. These powers, Edwards believed, are reducible to two basic human qualities: the faculty of natural understanding and the moral possibilities of self-love as a motive, or, in other words, intelligence and egoism. The fifth chapter looks at Edwards's assessment of other traits of the natural man that might be thought to indicate a natural potentiality for virtue, particularly the emotions of pity and compassion. Chapter 6 is an attempt to establish a context in moral philosophy, rather than theology, for Edwards's writing on the free will problem. Chapter 7 summarizes Edwards's moral theology, that is, his synthetic ethics.

The book as a whole may be said to revolve around the question: What is the specific contribution of religion and grace to moral conduct? In an age when naturalism began its great conquest of modern thought, this question was the major one Edwards was compelled to wrestle with. How successfully he answered it and what he had to offer in response to it is my theme.

Although several highly competent studies of Edwards's moral philosophy have been published—recently, for example, works by Roland Delattre and Clyde Holbrook[8]—the present book is the first that has consistently tried to read Edwards in the context of British and Continental moral philosophy and the first that has made an effort to trace his thought developmentally. I am convinced that only through such an approach can real sense be made of Edwards's non-theological writing.

8. For my general criticisms of Roland André Delattre, *Beauty and Sensibility in the Thought of Jonathan Edwards: An Essay in Aesthetics and Theological Ethics* (New Haven, Conn., 1968), and Clyde A. Holbrook, *The Ethics of Jonathan Edwards: Morality and Aesthetics* (Ann Arbor, Mich., 1973), see my reviews in *WMQ*, 3d Ser., XXVIII (1971), 655–661, XXXII (1975), 139–141.

I

An Intellectual Context

9. To be very moderate in the use of terms of art[.]
Let it not look as if I were much Read or
were conversant with books or the learned world.[1]

Friday, Jan. 10. *Remember to act according to Prov. xii. 23,*
A prudent man concealeth knowledge.[2]

Jonathan Edwards is the culminating thinker in early American moral philosophy. He was both more profound and original, and more acute in philosophical reasoning, than any other American in the eighteenth century. This
truth seems to be widely agreed upon. It is easy, however, to exaggerate
Edwards's stature and his originality, for in the midst of a rather barren
colonial intellectual scene his figure necessarily looms all the greater. Although it is true that the social, economic, and cultural conditions that are
usually needed to underpin and stimulate first-rate indigenous work in philosophy did not exist in colonial America, a fact that does make Edwards
extraordinary, it also must be emphasized that New England was well within
the orbit of the cultural centers of Britain and the Continent, and that the eager
student or clergyman-intellectual could learn more about current ideas than
has sometimes been suspected. Edwards has been too often pictured as an

1. This is one of 21 rules of style that Edwards wrote on the "cover" of his manuscript "Notes
on Natural Science." The rules contain a great deal of shorthand, which was deciphered by William P. Upham, "An Account of the Short-Hand Writings of Jonathan Edwards," Massachusetts
Historical Society, *Proceedings*, 2d Ser., XV (1902), 514–521. The rules were probably written
after 1722, since there is a reference in rule number 12 that is intelligible only if it is assumed that
Edwards was writing after that date. See n. 16, below.

2. Edwards kept a diary fairly regularly throughout 1723 and 1724. This entry is from 1724.
The manuscript is lost, but the diary is printed in Sereno E. Dwight, *The Life of President Edwards*, in Dwight, ed., *The Works of President Edwards: With a Memoir of His Life* (New York,
1829–1830), I, hereafter cited as Dwight, *Life of Edwards*. I am quoting from the reprinting of
the diary in Clarence H. Faust and Thomas H. Johnson, eds., *Jonathan Edwards: Representative
Selections* . . . (New York, 1935), 48. Dwight preceded this entry with an editorial note that
misinterpreted the diary, as Upham observes in the paper cited in n. 1, above.

isolated mental giant, nourished only by the near-miraculous circumstance of his early exposure to Locke and Newton. Instead he ought to be seen in the larger context of the Atlantic intellectual community in the first half of the eighteenth century. This requirement entails more than simply referring to the great impression Locke and Newton made upon Edwards (as though they were themselves isolated figures); it means attempting to reconstruct the intellectual context to a degree that at least suggests its full density.[3]

From the viewpoint of later centuries Locke, for example, stands out as a seminal thinker in a way that he could not possibly have appeared to clerical intellectuals in early America. Locke had warm admirers but also sharp critics in his time and after. Very few thoughtful men in the early eighteenth century were as ready as some historians have been to discount the force and respectability of the intellectual traditions that preceded Locke and helped to shape him.[4] Many historians seem to have little awareness of the extent to which Locke himself was dependent upon his predecessors, both Scholastic and Cartesian. The consequence of this unawareness is that various ideas held by Edwards and other thinkers who happen to have read the *Essay Concerning Human Understanding* are automatically attributed to the influence of Locke, when in fact these ideas were the common coin of philosophical scholarship in the late seventeenth century.

The Republic of Letters

The nursery of Jonathan Edwards's major philosophical ideas was not the intellectual environment created by Locke and Newton alone. That environment in any case is largely a retrospective construct of historians duly impressed by Newton's tremendous scientific achievement and somehow convinced, in accordance with the prevailing myth, that Locke's empirical method was the perfect philosophical complement to Newton's science. The writings of Locke and Newton point in contrary directions from each other, however, as much as, or more than, they programmatically agree, and the effects of their independent influence in early America (it is meaningless to speak of a joint influence) were generally more limited and more paradoxical than has commonly been recognized, especially in the case of Edwards. Edwards's thought was rooted in the great watershed period in British and Continental thought

3. For a general discussion of the state of philosophy in early America, see Fiering, "Early American Philosophy vs. Philosophy in Early America," Charles S. Peirce Society, *Transactions*, XIII (1977), 216–237.

4. A good study of Locke in his own context is John W. Yolton, *John Locke and the Way of Ideas* (London, 1956). See also for context, Richard A. Watson, *The Downfall of Cartesianism, 1673–1712: A Study of Epistemological Issues in Late 17th Century Cartesianism* (The Hague, 1966).

that extended from about 1675, when Nicolas Malebranche's *Search after Truth* was first published in French (two separate English translations followed by 1694), to 1711, when the third earl of Shaftesbury's *Characteristics* appeared in full. This period of about thirty-five years, which includes Locke and Newton but was not dominated by them, was one of great fertility and interchange in ideas.[5] England, France, and Holland composed a remarkably well-integrated republic of letters, and New England shared many common borders with these countries in the realm of thought. The extent of the correspondence and the personal relationships among men of ideas at this time must seem astonishing if one has made the mistake of allowing national frontiers to confine one's thinking. Within this period, it seems that nearly all of the major intellectual figures were in some sort of contact. One can step into this circle of philosophers almost anywhere and be led around its entirety.

Beginning with Cartesianism, for example, well known to seventeenth-century American scholars both directly and through the writings of disciples such as Antoine LeGrand and Adrian Heereboord,[6] one can move to Malebranche, who directly influenced George Berkeley; to Locke, who wrote against Malebranche but also learned from him; to Antoine Arnauld who engaged with Malebranche in a famous controversy over the nature of ideas and whose *Logique, ou l'art de penser* was translated into English in 1685 and again in 1717 and was used by Jonathan Edwards in college; or to John Norris, Malebranche's most devoted English disciple who, not surprisingly, wrote one of the earliest and best critiques of Locke's *Essay Concerning*

---

5. Cf. the summary comments of Ira O. Wade, *The Intellectual Origins of the French Enlightenment* (Princeton, N.J., 1971), 656–660: "Never, in fact, had there been in Europe in a single century a dozen or so eminent philosophers comparable in excellence to the philosophers of that period: Montaigne, Bacon, Hobbes, Descartes, Gassendi, Pascal, Spinoza, Leibniz, Malebranche, Locke, Newton, Bayle, and Fontenelle. . . . The sudden growth in the importance of philosophy can be attributed in large part to a desire to bolster the weaknesses now apparent in theology with the findings of philosophical speculation." See the excellent chapter entitled "Crisis in the Republic of Letters" in Loemker, *Struggle for Synthesis*, 28–52.

6. Solomon Stoddard already owned Descartes's works in 1664 when he was a postgraduate student at Harvard. See Fiering, "Solomon Stoddard's Library at Harvard in 1664," *Harvard Library Bulletin*, XX (1972), 255–269. The notes to this article cite several other studies that give detailed information on reading and libraries in 17th-century New England. Of particular value is Arthur O. Norton, "Harvard Text-Books and Reference Books of the Seventeenth Century," Colonial Society of Massachusetts, *Transactions*, XXVIII (1935), 361–438. Samuel Eliot Morison, *Harvard College in the Seventeenth Century*, 2 vols. (Cambridge, Mass., 1936) also has material on Cartesian books and reading. A number of copies of books by Descartes with Harvard student signatures survive from the 17th century. In *Moral Philosophy at Seventeenth-Century Harvard*, I discuss the importance of LeGrand, Heereboord, and others, and address the general question of Cartesianism in early America. See also Fiering, "The Transatlantic Republic of Letters: A Note on the Circulation of Learned Periodicals to Early Eighteenth-Century America," *WMQ*, 3d Ser., XXXIII (1976), 642–660.

Human Understanding. Norris was also an admirer of Henry More, the English philosopher with probably the greatest influence in America between 1675 and 1720, and corresponded with him shortly before More's death in 1687. More himself, in his youth, had corresponded with Descartes and at first publicized the French philosopher's ground-breaking achievements, but later became an opponent. More had a profound influence on Shaftesbury, as did all the Cambridge Platonists. John Locke was Shaftesbury's tutor. Shaftesbury was a close friend of Pierre Bayle's, whose great *Dictionary* was already in use in America only a few years after it appeared in English translation in 1710. Bayle was extremely interested in Malebranche and Arnauld. And so on. Such a list is intended to be only suggestive. A number of other figures could easily be fitted in, such as Pierre Gassendi, Newton and his disciple Samuel Clarke, Leibniz, and Addison and Steele.[7] Some of the work of each of these figures, except possibly Leibniz, was known to Edwards before his twenty-fifth birthday.

It was a period when translations into Latin still served to bring new scholarship to the attention of learned men in every country, and when international journals sprang up whose reason for being was solely to report on current activities in the entire world of learning. We know that Cotton Mather, for one, was familiar with both the *History of the Works of the Learned*, an English periodical that flourished from 1699 to 1712, and the *Nouvelles de la République des Lettres*, a journal that was under Pierre Bayle's editorship from 1684 to 1687 and ran until 1718. The Leipzig journal *Acta eruditorum*, published in Latin under Leibniz's influence, was in continuous existence from 1682 to 1731 in its first series and can be found in a number of early American libraries.[8] The *History of the Works of the Learned*, which was a monthly of about sixty pages, undertook to report on every new book published in England as well as to review and abstract foreign language publications. It would be difficult to summarize adequately the huge variety of works

7. Leibniz not only had a famous correspondence with Samuel Clarke but was also personally acquainted with Malebranche, whom he had met in Paris in 1672 and corresponded with thereafter. Steele was deeply influenced by Clarke, his pastor.

8. See Fiering, "Transatlantic Republic of Letters," *WMQ*, 3d Ser., XXXIII (1976), 642–660. In Mather's earliest extant letter to a foreign correspondent, written when he was in his twenties to the English bookseller Richard Chiswell (Nov. 7, 1683), he commented, "I have met with *The Weekly Memorials for the Ingeniose*; as far as August 7, 1682, I have already; be pleased to let me have what of them have come out since" (Kenneth Silverman, comp., *Selected Letters of Cotton Mather* [Baton Rouge, La., 1971], 6, 12). The *Weekly Memorials for the Ingenious; or, an Account of Books Lately Set Forth in Several Languages* . . . (London, 1682–1683) was possibly the first of the English review journals for scholars. See George Watson, ed., *The New Cambridge Bibliography of English Literature*, II (Cambridge, 1974), 1291–1294, and Walter Graham, *The Beginnings of English Literary Periodicals: A Study of Periodical Literature, 1665–1715* (New York, 1926).

noticed in this periodical; they included Latin, French, and English books from every publishing center in Europe and on every conceivable topic of interest to the erudite. The journal was not just philological, not just Classical, not just theological. It contained reviews and discussions of recent works in military engineering, ornithology, and medicine, as well as abridgments of finds and speculations of greater interest to humanists. Any American able to acquire copies would have been almost completely au courant.

Jonathan Edwards's first references to the learned periodicals of his day do not occur, apparently, until 1732, when his "Catalogue" of reading, in which he noted books he wanted to read or intended to buy, begins to include phrases like: "exceedingly commended in the Republick of Letters, vol. 17"; "of which the Republick of Letters gives a very agreeable Idea vol. 18"; and "see an account of it Repub. of Lett., vol. 12."[9] Yet he may have used such journals somewhat earlier, since his contemporary Samuel Johnson of Stratford, Connecticut, owned copies of some of them by 1726. It has recently been argued that Edwards's famous description of "flying" spiders, written in 1715 when he was not yet twelve years old and often pointed to with extravagant praise for its precocity and originality, "is one specimen only . . . of a well-established genre of whose existence Edwards was probably aware . . . , and his essay shows marked similarities to earlier examples of the genre." The *Philosophical Transactions* in 1710 contained François-Xavier Bon's "Discourse upon the Usefulness of the Silk of Spiders," which may have influenced Edwards.[10] The *Memoirs of Literature*, another English scholarly journal, also discussed Bon's work in 1710. It seems highly probable that a variety of conduits of British and Continental thought were available to Edwards from his earliest years, which makes it safe to assume that Edwards grew up in a more cosmopolitan intellectual milieu than is usually recognized.

We cannot review here at any length Edwards's "Catalogue" of reading, which he began to keep in the early 1720s.[11] But his interest in London periodicals, in dictionaries and encyclopedias, and in compilations is evident in this manuscript, which itself is an indication of his powerful drive to escape

9. The *Present State of the Republick of Letters* was published in London from Jan. 1728 to Dec. 1736. It was a successor to the *New Memoirs of Literature* . . . , which ran from Jan. 1725 to Dec. 1727. For the use of these journals in early America, see Fiering, "Transatlantic Republic of Letters," *WMQ*, 3d Ser., XXXIII (1976), 655–659.

10. See David S. Wilson, "The Flying Spider," *Journal of the History of Ideas*, XXXII (1971), 447–458.

11. Edwards's MS "Catalogue" is in the Beinecke Lib., Yale Univ. It has not yet been adequately transcribed or studied. James S. Caskey, "Jonathan Edwards' 'Catalogue'" (B.D. thesis, Chicago Theological Seminary, 1931) is useful but contains many inaccuracies. Also helpful but not entirely reliable is Thomas H. Johnson, "Jonathan Edwards' Background of Reading," Col. Soc. Mass., *Trans.*, XXVIII (1935), 193–222.

provincial isolation. Some of these publications deserve mention here. Edwards early read the *Spectator* and retained a serious respect for it all of his life.[12] Richard Steele's writings appear to have been particularly fascinating to him, and Edwards apparently owned bound copies of the *Guardian* (published from December 1715 to June 1716), to which George Berkeley was a contributor, and of the *Freeholder*.[13] Edwards also mentioned in his "Catalogue" three other short-lived journalistic efforts of Steele's, the *Englishman*, the *Lover*, and the *Reader*, published mostly between 1713 and 1715.[14]

In the twenty-one rules of style that Edwards set down about 1722,[15] there is a reference to a book that exemplifies the importance and utility of compilations and collections in early America, *The Ladies Library*.[16] This volume, also edited by Steele as it happens, was one of a number of anthologies published at the time that brought the reader quickly into touch with current ideas. It contained excerpts from Jeremy Taylor's *Holy Living*, William Fleet-

12. It is remarkable that in a solemn publication concerned with the benefits of simultaneous prayer everywhere in the Christian world, written 25 years after he first discovered Addison and Steele, Edwards cited "the *Spectator* (whom none will call a whimsical author)" as confirmation of the value of unity and simultaneity in such devotions. Edwards, *An Humble Attempt to Promote Explicit Agreement and Visible Union of God's People in Extraordinary Prayer* . . . (Boston, 1747), 96.

13. Walter Graham, *English Literary Periodicals* (New York, 1930), discusses the *Guardian* on pp. 80–84. Berkeley's contributions are printed in A. A. Luce and T. E. Jessop, eds., *Works of George Berkeley, Bishop of Cloyne* (London, 1948–1957). See also A. A. Luce, "Berkeley's Essays in the *Guardian*," *Mind*, N.S., LII (1943), 247–263. Berkeley wrote numbers 27, 35, 39, 49, 55, 62, 70, 77, 83, 88, 89, and 126. As late as the 1730s and 1740s Edwards was lending out his volumes of the *Guardian* to friends and parishioners.

14. Richard Steele's anti-Stoic, book-length essay, *The Christian Hero* . . . (London, 1701), is another very early entry in Edwards's "Catalogue," and in 1724 Edwards noted that he was eager to read Steele's "Account of the State of the Romish Religion" and his "History of the Duke of Marlborough's Life." The first was either *An Account of the State of the Roman-Catholick Religion throughout the World* (London, 1715), of which Steele was the editor, or *The Romish Ecclesiastical History of Late Years* (London, 1714), which was mainly a compilation. The entry for the duke of Marlborough's biography enables us to determine for certain that Edwards not only noted the *Reader* (London, 1714) in his catalog but also read it, for only in no. 6 of the *Reader* did Steele announce his intention to prepare a history of Marlborough's campaigns in Flanders (a book that in fact he never wrote). See George A. Aitken, *The Life of Richard Steele*, II (New York, 1968 [orig. publ. 1889]), 29.

15. See n. 1, above.

16. "In writing," Edwards told himself in rule 12, "let there be much compliance with the [readers] weakness and according to the Rules in the Ladies Library Vol. 1 p. 340 & seq." The word in brackets was in shorthand in the original. Edwards could not have used the first edition of *The Ladies Library* (London, 1714), since the reference to p. 340 does not conform in content. The next English edition was in 1722, and there was a third in 1723. Either of these fits Edwards's reference, which indicates that the rules of style were composed several years later than is usually assumed. There were at least seven English and three French editions of *The Ladies Library* in the course of the 18th century. See Aitken, *Life of Steele*, II, appendix 5.

wood's *Relative Duties of Parents and Children*, *The Whole Duty of Man*, *The Government of the Tongue*, *The Ladies Calling*, Locke's *Thoughts on Education*, Richard Lucas's *Practical Christianity* and his *Enquiry after Happiness*, John Scott's *Christian Life*, John Tillotson's *Sermons*, Mary Astell's *Serious Proposal to the Ladies*, Halifax's *Advice to a Daughter*, and Fénelon's *Education of a Daughter*.[17] The copy Edwards read may have belonged to his mother or one of his sisters, which is incidental to the point that ideas and attitudes circulated in the eighteenth century, as in the twentieth, not only in original volumes but also in compilations, popularizations, condensations, and periodicals. A volume like *The Young Students Library*, to take another instance, compiled by the bookseller and publisher John Dunton in 1692, contained an abridgment of Locke's *Essay Concerning Human Understanding* as well as reviews and abstracts of works or collections of works by Lightfoot, Barrow, Usher, Jurieu, Stillingfleet, and Boyle, much Cartesian and anti-Cartesian material, scores of pages on the Greek fathers Gregory Nazianzen and Irenaeus, and a number of travel accounts, to give only a sample. A listing of borrowers from the Harvard College library in 1764 shows that *The Young Students Library*, although by then nearly three-quarters of a century old, was still actively circulating. Similarly, Edwards thought well enough of *The Ladies Library* to be regularly lending it out to parishioners as late as the 1740s.[18]

Edwards's "Catalogue" shows also that he depended on encyclopedia-type reference books. It is uncertain whether he ever actually used Pierre Bayle's enormously stimulating *Dictionary*, a treasury of philosophical argument that was raided by many British writers in the early eighteenth century, but Edwards mentioned it twice in the early pages of his "Catalogue," and he also noted Jeremy Collier's *Great Historical, Geographical, Genealogical, and Poetical Dictionary*, published in four volumes between 1701 and 1721.[19] Collier's was a translation of Louis Moréri's *Le Grand Dictionnaire* of 1674,

17. Aitken, *Life of Steele*, II, 39–41, tracked down these sources; all are printed in the volume anonymously.

18. On *The Young Students Library*, see Fiering, "Transatlantic Republic of Letters," *WMQ*, 3d Ser., XXXIII (1976), 650–651. For Edwards's lending of books, see his MS "Account Book," July 1733–Dec. 1757, discovered only recently by Professor George Claghorn and now housed in the Beinecke Lib., Yale Univ. I am grateful to Thomas Schafer for allowing me to read his transcription of it and to Claghorn and the Beinecke Lib. for permission to use it. *The Ladies Library* was in other New England libraries. The Rev. Thomas Weld read it in 1727. See Evan A. Evans, Jr., "Literary References in New England Diaries, 1700–1730" (Ph.D. diss., Harvard University, 1934), 107.

19. See the 1724 correspondence between the Harvard College corporation and Thomas Hollis concerning editions of Bayle's *An Historical and Critical Dictionary* (London, 1710 [orig. publ. Rotterdam, 1697]), described in Josiah Quincy, *History of Harvard University*, 2 vols. (Cambridge, Mass., 1840), I, 433. See also chap. 5, n. 70, below.

and is found widely in colonial American libraries. Edwards's reliance on Ephraim Chambers's *Cyclopedia: or, an Universal Dictionary of Arts and Sciences* . . . , published in London in 1728 and unquestionably the best work of its kind before the famous French *Encyclopédie*, is more explicit. After 1737, when Edwards acquired his own copy of Chambers, numerous entries in his catalog refer to it. Thus, for example: "An Inquiry into the Original of our Ideas of Beauty[,] that seems a very ingenious thing by the specimans of that Book in Chambers under the word *Common Places* where tis mentioned as a Book in octavo. & the 199 page is Refered to also under the word Evil."[20]

In attempting to recreate the intellectual context of Edwards's early years, it is often necessary to look for the presence in America of works by authors whose names are now obscure but who in *circa* 1700 were influential middlemen in the transmission and circulation of thought. Most important for early America, perhaps, was Jean LeClerc, who working from Amsterdam (Holland was then the publishing center of the international network of scholars) seems to have published more in one lifetime, as one of his eulogists said, than some scholars are able to read in theirs. In addition to editing several of the best journals in French, which meant doing most of the writing in them, revising Moréri's *Dictionnaire*, translating Thomas Stanley's famous *History of Philosophy* and Henry Hammond's *Paraphrase and Annotations on the New Testament* into Latin,[21] and editing Erasmus's letters, which is only a sampling of LeClerc's industry, he was also, without question, the leading publicist of Locke's work in Europe. LeClerc's *Logica, sive Ars Ratiocinandi* and his *Ontologia et Pneumatologia*, first published in 1692 and again in 1697 and 1710 in his *Opera Philosophica*, were some of the earliest texts to attempt to integrate Robert Boyle's and Locke's ideas into the received academic traditions and are typical of the eclecticism of the time. Samuel Johnson of Connecticut probably read LeClerc's philosophical work before he read Locke himself.[22]

20. The reference is, of course, to Francis Hutcheson's *An Inquiry into the Original of Our Ideas of Beauty and Virtue* (London, 1725). Cadwallader Colden in New York and James Logan in Philadelphia were original subscribers to the printing of the *Cyclopedia*. Chambers extracted heavily from Shaftesbury and Hutcheson in the philosophy sections of the work. Benjamin Franklin's journalistic rival in Philadelphia, Samuel Keimer, put weekly excerpts from Chambers in his newspaper, a practice that Franklin continued after he had driven Keimer out of business.

21. LeClerc's notes to Hammond were then published in English as a *Supplement* (London, 1699); copies of the book were in a number of early American libraries.

22. LeClerc's Arminianism limited his influence in America as a religious writer. On Samuel Johnson and LeClerc, see Fiering, "President Samuel Johnson and the Circle of Knowledge," *WMQ*, 3d Ser., XXVIII (1971), 199–236. On LeClerc, see: Gabriel Bonno, ed., *Lettres Inédites de LeClerc à Locke* (*University of California Publications in Modern Philology*, LII [Berkeley and Los Angeles, Calif., 1959]); Annie Barnes, *Jean Le Clerc (1657–1736) et la République des*

Among the numerous student précis that circulated at Harvard College in the seventeenth century, prepared by the tutors and intended to serve in lieu of printed textbooks, one was entitled "Theses quaedam extractae potissimum ex Enchiridio Metaphysico Domini Johannis Clerici." Several Harvard student notebooks from the early eighteenth century contain copies of this précis —for example, those of Obadiah Ayer (A.B., 1710), James Varney (A.B., 1725), and Marston Cabot (A.B., 1724)—and there is a separately bound copy, transcribed in 1718, that was owned successively by Richard Dana (A.B., 1718), Rozewell Saltonstall (A.B., 1720), and Ezra Carpenter (A.B., 1720). As all of the copies indicate, the précis was made by Jonathan Remington, a tutor from 1703 to 1711 who also prepared a short summary of Henry More's *Enchiridion Metaphysicum* (1671) that is found in many student versions. But it has not been observed before, I think, that the metaphysical propositions attributed variously in these student "ponies" to "J. Clerici," "Joannis Clark," and "Johannis Clerici" come from Jean LeClerc's *Ontologia et Pneumatologia*, a work that Remington obviously admired. Like these students, Jonathan Edwards's early education in metaphysics and epistemology probably came from such sources, directly or indirectly, even before he had read John Locke's *Essay* or Malebranche's *Search after Truth*.[23]

Given the paucity of detailed information on Edwards's early intellectual development, it may be impossible ever to discover exactly which of his ideas came from where and exactly when he first articulated or encountered an idea. But if we think in terms of a milieu, rather than individual influences, and begin to appreciate its unities, it becomes less urgent to know the specifics. It is clear that Edwards was an independent and highly creative thinker; it is also indisputable that at an early age, directly or indirectly, he learned much from his older contemporaries overseas.

On the matter of the availability of books, two questions are always at

---

Lettres (Paris, 1938); Rosalie L. Colie, *Light and Enlightenment: A Study of the Cambridge Platonists and the Dutch Arminians* (Cambridge, 1957); Samuel A. Golden, *Jean LeClerc* (New York, 1972); *An Account of the Life and Writings of Mr. J. Le Clerc . . .* (London, 1712); and Jean Barbeyrac, "Eloge historique," *Bibliothèque Raisonnée . . .* , XVI (1736), 344–418. Other editors, translators, and writers, mostly Huguenots, who were carriers and critics of leading ideas were Michael de la Roche, Pierre Desmaizeaux, Jean-Pierre de Crousaz, Pierre Coste, and Jean Cornand (de la Crose). James O'Higgins, *Anthony Collins: The Man and His Works* (The Hague, 1970), 77, 209–210, uses the term "literary middlemen" to refer to some of the Huguenots in Holland.

23. There is a similar précis of Henry More's *Enchiridion Ethicum . . .* (London, 1667), which was drawn up by John Leverett, tutor from 1685 to 1697, with copies surviving from 1694 at the latest. All of these manuscripts and notebooks are housed in the Harvard University Archives, Cambridge, Massachusetts. Morison, *Harvard in the Seventeenth Century*, 258, refers to abstracts of More's *Enchiridion Ethicum* and *Enchiridion Metaphysicum . . .* (London, 1671) made by tutor William Brattle.

issue: how were the authors and titles of the truly significant books recognized and selected from the dross, and how were the books themselves acquired? The learned journals and compilations such as we have already mentioned certainly were of great assistance in dealing with the first problem, as were the publishers' advertisements printed in the back of books. In addition, there was a "guide" literature, aimed particularly at young candidates for the ministry, that appraised authors and books. Edwards frequently cited, and obviously learned from, Cotton Mather's *Manuductio ad Ministerium* published in 1726, and there were several other such sources, like Daniel Waterland's *Advice to a Young Student* (1730) and John Clarke's *An Essay upon Study* . . . (London, 1731). Issues of the *Spectator* often commented informatively on books and reading, such as number 37 (April 12, 1713), which listed some titles from the library of "Leonora," who "has turned all the passions of her sex into a love of books and retirement." Among other items, "Leonora" owned Newton's works, Locke on human understanding, and Malebranche's *Search after Truth*. Edwards's evident interest in Pierre Bayle may have come from the *Spectator*, since Addison borrowed freely from Bayle's amazing dictionary and did not hesitate to show his respect for the author. He called Bayle "one of the most learned Men of the present age" (no. 90) and a man "of exquisite Learning and Judgment" (no. 451). Most important, undoubtedly, for the identification of good books was the personal recommendation, with the chain beginning in a letter from an overseas correspondent and extending from one American to another. Individual lending and borrowing of books was also ubiquitous, as becomes evident to any researcher who studies the correspondence and diaries of New England clergymen.[24]

Historians have paid a good deal of attention to the Dummer gift of books to the Yale College library in 1713, and deservedly. Amounting to nearly five hundred titles amassed by Jeremiah Dummer through donations in England (Richard Steele and Isaac Newton were among the donors), the collection constituted a massive updating of Yale's then meager resources. Samuel Johnson testified to his own great benefit from the availability of this excellent literature, and Edwards had access to it probably by 1719 or 1720.[25] Through

24. See Thomas Goddard Wright, *Literary Culture in Early New England, 1620–1730* (New Haven, Conn., 1920); Evans, "Literary References"; and Samuel Eliot Morison, *The Intellectual Life of Colonial New England* (New York, 1956 [orig. publ. 1936 as *The Puritan Pronaos: Studies in the Intellectual Life of New England in the Seventeenth Century*]); all comment on the importance of the informal circulation of books.

25. The titles are printed in Louise May Bryant and Mary Patterson, eds., "The List of Books Sent by Jeremiah Dummer . . . ," in *Papers in Honor of Andrew Keogh, Librarian of Yale University*, ed. Staff of the [Yale University] Library (New Haven, Conn., 1938), 423–492. See also Franklin Bowditch Dexter, ed., *Documentary History of Yale University, 1701–1745* (New York, 1969 [orig. publ. New Haven, Conn., 1916]), 173, on the use of the library. The Dummer library may not have been entirely available for anybody's use until the school year 1718–1719. Prior to

the Dummer gift, if not from other sources, the determined student had within reach most of the writings of Henry More, Robert Boyle, John Locke, Jean LeClerc, Isaac Newton, the third earl of Shaftesbury, and Descartes; Malebranche's *Search after Truth*, Bayle's *Dictionary*, and Fénelon's *Demonstration of the Existence, Wisdom, and Omnipotence of God*, all in English; John Norris's *Essay towards the Theory of the Ideal or Intelligible World*; and several significant works by Samuel Clarke.

The Dummer gift was a great boost for an infant institution, but it would be a mistake to assume that the contents descended upon New England like a revelation of literature never dreamed of. It must be emphasized that the books were more important to Yale in particular than they were to New England as a whole, or even to the Connecticut Valley as a whole. When the Reverend Ebenezer Pemberton died in Boston in 1717, at age forty-five, his personal library contained among its 678 titles most of the writings of Henry More, John Norris, and Descartes, Locke's *Thoughts on Education* and his *Reasonableness of Christianity*, although not his *Essay Concerning Human Understanding*, Malebranche's *Search after Truth*, one volume of Bayle's *Dictionary*, and Collier's translation of Moréri's *Dictionnaire*.[26]

The American Setting

The first intellectual influence upon Edwards was probably his father, Timothy, pastor of the church in East Windsor, Connecticut. It is certain that Timothy Edwards received a master's degree from Harvard in 1694, but it is unknown how much time he actually spent at Harvard between 1686, the year he apparently matriculated, and 1694, when he appeared at commencement and responded in the negative to the *quaestio*, "Whether indifference is the essence of free will?"[27] If we knew that he had been in residence at Harvard for some of those years prior to 1694, a number of assumptions could be safely made, such as that he was familiar with Cartesianism in physics,

---

that time it was at the Buckingham house in Saybrook. A library was built for the books in New Haven in the fall of 1717, but in Nov. 1718 most of them were still in Saybrook.

26. *A Catalogue of Curious and Valuable Books, Belonging to the Late Reverend and Learned Mr. Ebenezer Pemberton* . . . (Boston, 1717). Pemberton was a tutor at Harvard between 1697 and 1700.

27. Timothy may have been rusticated in 1688 and educated privately until 1694, when he returned to get his M.A. and was granted at the same time, "as of 1691," a B.A. Clifford K. Shipton discusses the problem in *Sibley's Harvard Graduates: Biographical Sketches of Those Who Attended Harvard College* . . . (Cambridge, Mass., 1873–1970), IV, 92–99. For the philosophical problems implicit in Timothy Edwards's *quaestio*, see Fiering, *Moral Philosophy at Seventeenth-Century Harvard*, chap. 3.

metaphysics, logic, and ethics, that he was tutored by John Leverett or William Brattle, that he was aware of some of Charles Morton's lectures, that he had been introduced to Henry More's ethics and metaphysics, and that in general he had experienced firsthand some of the forces in the anti-Peripatetic revolution in the last half of the seventeenth century.[28] Being away from Cambridge, however, his thinking may have been somewhat less au courant than that of his peers. Tradition has it, in any case, that he was a very good scholar, especially in the learned languages. His choice of a master's *quaestio* suggests an interest in philosophical questions no less than in theological ones. In the same year that Timothy Edwards got his degrees from Harvard he married Esther Stoddard, a daughter of Solomon Stoddard of Northampton, Massachusetts. Esther apparently had more education than many colonial wives and may have brought to the marriage some of her own intellectual culture.

We know relatively little about the books in the Edwards household. In a surviving memorandum book the elder Edwards listed the "Books, and papers" in his "Trunk" in September 1722, but it seems improbable that this record of sixty titles represented his entire library at that date.[29] Until the list is transcribed and annotated, no selection of titles from it can be altogether sound. Most of the works are theological treatises or sermons. Others are such as were found widely in American libraries at the time: John Ray's *Wisdom of God*, one of the best studies of natural divinity and a work wide ranging in its speculations, and John Newton's *The English Academy, or a Brief Introduction to the Seven Liberal Arts* (1677; 2d ed., 1693), the work of a well-known mathematician and education reformer. *The English Academy* aimed to present higher learning in the vernacular and included logic and rhetoric

28. The importance of tutors Leverett and Brattle on the liberalization of studies at Harvard has been recognized since the publication of Morison's *Harvard in the Seventeenth Century* and Perry Miller's *The New England Mind: The Seventeenth Century* (New York, 1939). On the influence of Charles Morton, who came to Massachusetts in 1686 with a distinguished reputation as a teacher at English dissenting academies, see Morison, "Charles Morton," Col. Soc. Mass., *Collections*, XXXIII (1940), vii–xxix, and Fiering, *Moral Philosophy at Seventeenth-Century Harvard*, chap. 5.

29. People do not usually keep their entire library in a trunk. Moreover, of the four titles published before 1722 that we know definitely Timothy Edwards owned (these are now in the Yale University Library with Edwards's signature in them), some at least do not appear to be listed in this memorandum. The manuscript memorandum book is in the Beinecke Lib. There is miscellaneous information about Timothy Edwards and the household in which Jonathan was raised in John A. Stoughton, *"Windsor Farmes." A Glimpse of an Old Parish* . . . (Hartford, Conn., 1883). One of Timothy's diary entries, transcribed in this volume, reads: "June 6 [1726] Lent Bro. Whitman One of Jonathan's books concerning True Christianity, or some such subject by a German divine" (p. 89). This would be Johann Arndt's classic work, *Of True Christianity* . . . (see chap. 4, n. 10). Stoughton also gives a list of the students whom Timothy Edwards prepared for college by training them in Latin and Greek.

texts as well as arithmetic, astronomy, and so on. There were many works by the Mathers, by Solomon Stoddard, by Ebenezer Pemberton, and, especially, by Benjamin Colman. Colman and Pemberton were Timothy Edwards's contemporaries at Harvard. If Timothy Edwards was in close touch with Colman, it is another sign of the wider philosophical world reaching to the Edwards home, for Colman was one of the most intellectually aware of New England clergymen.

Jonathan entered Yale College in September 1716, shortly before his thirteenth birthday, having been conscientiously prepared in Latin by his father. Even before he went to New Haven, however, he must have had some exposure to the young Harvard scholars Elisha and Stephen Williams, kinsmen through his mother, Esther Stoddard.[30] Elisha had entered college at a very young age, as Jonathan would, and received a B.A. degree from Harvard in 1711, when he was seventeen. From February 1714 until 1726 Elisha lived in Wethersfield, Connecticut, about ten miles from the Edwards parsonage in East Windsor. Stephen Williams was in the Harvard class of 1713. After graduation he was schoolmaster for a while at Hadley, Massachusetts, and then permanently at Longmeadow, near Springfield, Massachusetts. Timothy Edwards's diary entries for 1715 and 1716 show that he was in fairly close touch with "cousin" Stephen. In January 1715, Edwards "Lent Cousin Stephen Wms Roberts Discourse of the State of a Natural Man, with his Directions to Seek, etc. in the same book." In March, he "Lent Cousin Stephen Williams" another book. A year later Timothy noted that he had been lent a book by Stephen.

Although later there would be destructive quarrels with members of the Williams family, during these years Jonathan was doubtless well acquainted with his brilliant cousin Elisha in nearby Wethersfield. Elisha would one day be Jonathan's teacher at the Wethersfield "branch" of "Yale," and between 1726 and 1739, rector (or president) of the college at New Haven. A series of rather technical philosophical letters from Elisha to Stephen has survived, beginning in December 1711, the year that seventeen-year-old Elisha had graduated from Harvard and Stephen was entering the junior class. From these letters, which run until October 28, 1714, some impression may be gained of the extent of Elisha's philosophical learning when he was fresh out of Harvard and still very young, and therefore of the kind of education that was circumstantially available to Jonathan Edwards before he ever left the Connecticut River Valley.

30. Elisha Williams was not a blood relation, but his stepmother, Christian Stoddard Williams, was Esther Stoddard Edwards's sister. Stephen Williams was the son of Eunice Mather Williams, half-sister of Esther Stoddard Edwards. Eunice Williams and Esther Edwards had the same mother, Esther Warham, who was married first to Eleazer Mather and then to Solomon Stoddard.

The letters are mostly concerned with logic and metaphysics, with the prevailing tone being the anti-Aristotelianism found in Antoine Arnauld and Pierre Nicole's *Art of Thinking*, the celebrated Port Royal logic we have already mentioned, from which at times Elisha Williams virtually quotes. Thus, on the Aristotelian predicaments or categories, Elisha wrote to Stephen:

> Even those who most loudly cry up their predicaments do assert . . . that under Ens [i.e., Being] are comprehended all substances and accidents. And then having minced out poor accident into nine, they must of necessity allow that these nine predicaments are comprehended under accidents. And therefore since accident is so general as to comprehend in its extent those nine it is impossible for us otherwise to conclude than that accident is their genus. And then since Ens comprehends in its extent both substance and accident, the same conclusion we have to make that they are to be referred to Ens as to their genus. And since we have found such a genus as comprehends in its extent all the predicaments, the predicaments then must disclaim the thought of being each of them a highest genus.[31]

As had the Port Royal logic, Elisha Williams condemned the predicaments as "things meerly arbitrary." There are other ways to dispose "the objects of our thoughts," he wrote, and the Aristotelian categories have the defect of allowing men to believe they "know all things when they are only able to say by rote names of arbitrary signification which yet imprint no clear ideas in our minds." The predicaments "have been of very little service to the world. (I think I might have said does it a mischief.)"[32]

Since Ramist logicians had been assaulting the Aristotelian predicaments for a century, there was perhaps nothing new in Elisha Williams's attitude. But the effect of the Cartesian logic was, as in Locke later, to lead philosophers away from preoccupation with the forms of reasoning for their own sake and more toward the problem of how useful knowledge and factual truth could be attained.

Most of Elisha's letters address academic questions, such as whether "arguments"—a technical term in Ramism—are properly considered real or notional; and a long list of theses he proposed to Stephen for use at a forthcoming Harvard commencement contains little that could not have appeared fifty years before. But Elisha showed a particular interest in the nature of "ideas" as objects of intellect, which was characteristic of the period between

31. Elisha Williams to Stephen Williams, Nov. 29, 1712. The letters are at the Beinecke Lib.

32. *Ibid.* There is a similar criticism in Pierre Gassendi's *Exercitationes paradoxicae adversus Aristoteleos* . . . (Grenoble, 1624), 3d exercise, "That It Is Foolish to Distinguish Ten Categories As Sorts of Reality" (see Craig B. Brush, ed. and trans., *The Selected Works of Pierre Gassendi* [New York, 1972], 47). Gassendi's work was well known in 17th-century New England.

Descartes and Berkeley. Is a genus (or presumably any abstract term) the object of the imagination? Elisha asked. Those who take the imagination "to be the forming of images upon their brain" will say that "there can be no material image (a better term I [haven't]) of a genus formed in their brain," for "nothing but bodies are the objects of imagination."

> That there is upon the brain all material object[s] painted where the soul views them and that these images are kept distinct and that the soul can call them to view, etc. I wish they could tell me the painter. Why can't they allow the soul to form ideas of material beings after the same manner as it does of other things. I know not why there is a greater necessity that the soul should have the image of a material being painted on the brain that it may view it than that it should have the idea of an argument (or the like) there painted to see that. Then let imagination be called the souls forming ideas (for other imagination there is none).[33]

Implicit in Elisha Williams's comments is the rejection of a vast legacy of Scholastic speculation concerning so-called intentional and intelligible species, the entities that served as intermediaries between external objects and mental representations of the world. Descartes and his followers had blasted this doctrine, substituting the term "idea," which was intended to refer to an entirely subjective modification of mind that, however the process occurred, was the means of our knowing both the external world and our interior sensations. As Williams undoubtedly realized, to assume that the mind in any way duplicated the image of an external object required that the soul itself have eyes to view the image in the brain, which rather than solving the problem of perception simply relocated it. Arnauld and others regarded sensations as the *occasion* of the formation of ideas in human consciousness, but not as material causes, since the latter would suggest a materialist connection between matter and spirit. Ideas represented external objects, but they in no way resembled them. Since as *ideas* there is no ontological difference between the idea of a physical body and the idea of an abstract concept, Williams could argue that the old theory of the imagination, as the repository of concrete images, was defective. In Cartesian terms, all ideas are mental (or spiritual) substance, unextended in space.[34]

If Elisha Williams's early letters are any measure, there may have been more stimulating philosophical discussion in the vicinity of East Windsor than has hitherto been recognized. He wrote to Stephen, who had complained of melancholy, that he lived at Wethersfield partly because of the "extraordinarily good conversation" available to him in the persons of Stephen Mix, the

33. Elisha Williams to Stephen Williams, May 19, 1713.
34. See Watson, *Downfall of Cartesianism*, *passim*.

minister at Wethersfield (a graduate of Harvard in 1690 and like Timothy Edwards the husband of one of Solomon Stoddard's daughters), and William Burnham, the minister at Kensington, Connecticut (a 1702 Harvard graduate). Such conversation, Elisha wrote to Stephen, "you can hardly know unless you experienced it."[35] If Esther Stoddard ever came to see her sister Mary Mix in Wethersfield, Jonathan Edwards at the same time might have taken the opportunity to converse with his impressive cousin Elisha, nine years his senior.

A Yale Education?

The correspondence of Elisha and Stephen Williams was heavily collegiate in that they devoted so much of it to talking about commencement theses. Scholastic wrangling over theses was explicitly condemned in one of Elisha's letters, but a college education in the eighteenth century commonly emphasized disputation, and Elisha had not escaped this influence. The commencement theses of any given year revealed to the knowing reader the state of philosophical education at the time. In the exchange of letters from 1714 to 1716 between two young Yale graduates, Samuel Johnson and Daniel Browne, which has something of the character of the Williamses' letters, Browne reported that he had "of late gained some sort of friendship with one of the Cambridge [i.e., Harvard] scholars, now Senior Sophister, Mr. Thomas Pain of Barnstable," and from Paine he "received the master's questions and the bachelor's theses." Browne copied out three of them for Johnson and asked, "How do you like 'em?"[36] Similarly, Elisha told Stephen Williams in a letter of February 7, 1714, that he had procured "Mr. Fisks Metaphysicks of Seabrook, I intend to peruse them and remark of his notions to you."[37]

Mr. Fisk was a Yale tutor from 1706 to 1713 whom Samuel Johnson, as a student, greatly admired and to whom he effusively dedicated his early manuscript "encyclopedia" of the academic arts. Later, after he had read more modern philosophy, Johnson was chagrined by his excessive praise of Fisk and wrote next to the original dedication: "Oh! dismal, intollerable, an hundredth part of this would be enough for him."[38] In fact, Fisk was probably not an outstanding scholar, and whatever his natural abilities he was certainly

35. Elisha Williams to Stephen Williams, Dec. 18, 1713.

36. Browne to Johnson, Aug. 3, 1716, in Herbert Schneider and Carol Schneider, eds., *Samuel Johnson, President of King's College: His Career and Writings* (New York, 1929), II, 196.

37. Yale did not begin to print its commencement theses until 1714. The first surviving list is from 1718. "Seabrook" is Saybrook, where the college was first located.

38. For Johnson's comments on Phineas Fisk, see Schneider and Schneider, eds., *Samuel Johnson*, II, 57.

handicapped by having attended Yale College in its earliest infancy, graduating in 1704 when it was far behind Harvard in the assimilation of modern learning. Yale was founded by Harvard graduates (clergymen naturally), but almost all of them had taken their bachelor degrees before 1670, that is, before the Cartesian revolution had effectively changed higher education in Cambridge, Massachusetts. As a result, in the original dialectic between the two schools, which was based on an active and conscious rivalry, Yale was expected to serve as a refuge from the pace of philosophical change at Harvard in the last quarter of the century. Yale was intended "to provide for the youth of [Connecticut] colony what Harvard had given the trustees in their undergraduate years," a recent historian of the New Haven school has commented.[39] In the early years, before about 1720, some of Yale's conservative trustees were expressly opposed to hiring Harvard graduates as tutors,[40] a crippling reservation that perpetuated backwardness. This restriction also helps to explain the persistent dissatisfaction Yale students found with their tutors in this period. Eighteenth-century students simply did not want a mid-seventeenth-century education, especially if earlier they had gotten to know any recent Harvard graduates, as Jonathan Edwards certainly had. Since the tutors were invariably only a year or two past the baccalaureate themselves and usually ventured to teach only what they had learned as undergraduates, it was the system itself, not the tutors, that was faulty in this era of rapid intellectual expansion. Thus, if one inquires about the state of academic culture in New England *circa* 1710, the answer must in part depend upon whether Harvard or Yale is the main reference.

Two great errors have long been perpetuated about Jonathan Edwards's early intellectual growth: one is that Samuel Johnson's well-known description of Yale as it was in his student days also tells us something about Edwards's Yale education; the other is that Samuel Hopkins's recollections about the impression John Locke's *Essay Concerning Human Understanding* made upon Edwards ought to be taken as definitive. For the moment it is only the first fallacy we are concerned with. "The condition of learning (as well as everything else)" at Yale between 1710 and 1714 "was very low," Samuel Johnson wrote in his autobiographical memoir, ". . . indeed much lower than in the earlier time while those yet lived who had had their education in England and first settled the country."

> These were now gone off the stage and their sons fell greatly short of
> their acquirements. . . . It was nothing but the scholastic cobwebs of a
> few little English and Dutch systems . . . , some of Ramus and Alsted's

39. Richard Warch, *School of the Prophets: Yale College, 1701–1740* (New Haven, Conn., 1973), 40.
40. *Ibid.*, 49.

> Works was considered as the highest attainments. They heard indeed in
> 1714, when he [Johnson] took his Bachelor's Degree of a new
> philosophy that of late was all in vogue and of such names as Descartes,
> Boyle, Locke, and Newton, but they were cautioned against thinking
> anything of them because the new philosophy, it was said, would soon
> bring in a new divinity and corrupt the pure religion of the country. . . .
> Indeed, there was no such thing as any book learning to be had in those
> times under a 100 or 150 years old, such as the first settlers of the
> country brought with them 70 or 80 years before.[41]

Johnson's autobiography was written fifty years after he left college and can
be shown to be inaccurate on several points. Furthermore, he had reason to
exaggerate the intellectual poverty of Congregational New England as compared to the culture of the Anglican church that he converted to in 1722.
However, it does seem to have been the case that when Johnson was a student
at Yale early in the second decade of the eighteenth century, not even William
Brattle's compend of Cartesian logic was yet in use there.[42] But whatever
truth Johnson's comments do possess must certainly be restricted to education
at Yale specifically and not applied to all of New England, or even all of the
hinterland. Above all, Johnson's estimation of the condition of learning must
not be used as a foil to set off the marvel of Jonathan Edwards's brilliance and
originality as a youth, prodigy though he was, since Edwards's experience at
Yale was markedly different from Johnson's.[43]

When Edwards entered Yale in the autumn of 1716 the college, temporarily
housed at Saybrook, did not yet have a permanent location. One faction
wanted the school to locate in Hartford and another preferred New Haven.
Moreover, partly as a result of its inadequate plant, but also because of the
poor training of its tutors, since the institution's founding in 1701 there had
been a history of student dissatisfaction and discontent. The situation was so
bad in the spring of 1716 that the trustees temporarily dissolved the school.

---

41. Schneider and Schneider, eds., *Samuel Johnson*, I, 4. See also Johnson's brief memoir on
the history of Yale in Dexter, ed., *Documentary History of Yale*, 148*ff*.

42. After circulating for many years in manuscript in student copies, William Brattle's *Compendium Logicae Secundum Principia D. Renati Cartesii* was published in book form in Boston
in 1735 and in a second edition in 1758. Student copies exist in both Latin and English from the
1680s and 1690s. See Morison, *Harvard in the Seventeenth Century*, 192–193, and Elizabeth
Flower and Murray G. Murphey, *A History of Philosophy in America* (New York, 1977), I, 365–
373. There is a great deal of confusion about the teaching of logic in early America and even mis-
understanding of the definition of the subject as it was understood in the 17th and 18th centuries.
Precise monographic treatment of the history of the teaching of logic in early America is needed.

43. Johnson's tutors at Yale were Joseph Noyes, Yale B.A., 1709, tutor 1710–1715; Phineas
Fisk, tutor 1706–1713; William Russel, Yale B.A., 1709, tutor 1713–1714. None of these men
achieved any intellectual distinction in later years or published significantly.

The students were allowed to disperse, continuing their education under whatever ad hoc arrangements they could work out, with the understanding that the college would reconvene the following September. Some of the students remained at Saybrook and others went home, but a small group assembled in Wethersfield, Connecticut, where Elisha Williams was the obvious magnet.[44] This state of disintegration, despite the trustees' hopes, was to continue for three years, Jonathan Edwards's first three years of college, and he spent all of them, except for one brief interlude, under Elisha Williams's tutelage at Wethersfield. When the rifts in the college were finally mended in the spring of 1719, and Edwards returned to the main body, which was then settled at New Haven, the rector was Timothy Cutler, a Harvard graduate of 1701. In other words, unlike Samuel Johnson and others who attended Yale in its first quarter century, Edwards had the benefit of having as mentors recent Harvard graduates rather than Yale graduates like Phineas Fisk.[45]

What then can we surmise about Edwards's undergraduate college education between the years 1716 and 1720? I think we can say with confidence that with regard to texts and curriculum it would be equivalent at least to a Harvard education between about 1700 and 1710. Teaching at Harvard during those years was mainly in the hands of the tutors Jonathan Remington and Henry Flynt. It would not be hard to reconstruct the curriculum in detail, but to do so would carry us beyond the purposes of this chapter. Roughly, instruction in logic would have been eclectic, with George Downame's Ramist logic, Heereboord's revision of Burgersdyck's logic, and Brattle's compend based on Arnauld and LeGrand all in evidence. Locke's *Essay*, which was considered a logic text, was known about but not assimilated into academic training. In metaphysics, Henry More, Heereboord, and LeClerc were the dominant figures, and More and Heereboord were also the main sources for the teaching of ethics at this time. The teaching of natural philosophy, which was still very philosophical in the sense that the subject included a lot of theoretical psychology and other topics pertaining to the nature of man, would also have been a mixture of Aristotelianism and Cartesianism. But in addition, Jacques Rohault's Cartesian physics in Samuel Clarke's Latin translation with

44. Warch, *School of the Prophets*, excellently summarizes the problems at Yale in this period.
45. Precisely speaking, for most of Edwards's years at Wethersfield, Samuel Smith, Jr. (Yale B.A., 1713) was Edwards's tutor, and during the second year Samuel Hall (Yale B.A., 1716) helped out. (I am grateful to Thomas Schafer for this information, which is based on Timothy Edwards's payments to the tutors as recorded in his account book.) However, Smith and Hall were both working under Elisha Williams's leadership, and it seems certain that Williams's own learning would be the major force at the school. The senior Edwards's account book shows that during Edwards's third year at Wethersfield, Williams was definitely his instructor. Samuel Smith, like Samuel Johnson, had been taught by Phineas Fisk, who resigned in 1713, the year Smith graduated.

Clarke's Newtonian notes might also have been an influence. In almost all subjects—logic, ethics, metaphysics, and physics—Charles Morton's syncretic teaching texts would have been used along with the other materials.[46]

It is often stated that Samuel Johnson was Jonathan Edwards's tutor during Edwards's last year, and that Johnson introduced the younger scholar to Newton and Locke. The origin of this belief seems to lie with some remarks in Johnson's own autobiographical memoir, but it is incorrect or doubtful on two counts. First of all, Johnson had already resigned his Yale tutorship by the time Edwards came to New Haven and entered his senior year.[47] Second, it is probable that Johnson's account of the introduction of Newton and Locke had become somewhat distorted in the fifty-year interval before he wrote his memoir. According to Johnson, in the school year 1718–1719, when he and Daniel Browne were tutors together, "they joined their utmost endeavors to improve the education of their pupils by the help of the new lights they had gained. They introduced the study of Mr. Locke and Sir Isaac Newton as fast as they could."[48] The study of Locke they supposedly introduced was almost certainly not directly from the *Essay Concerning Human Understanding* but from LeClerc and John Brightland, that is, textbook writers of logic who admired Locke but did not intend to rashly alter academic training. In short, despite Johnson's comments about the influence of the Dummer gift upon his intellectual development, it probably never influenced his tutoring very much, and his knowledge of Locke was not gained through that collection. Johnson himself left a most illuminating catalog "Of Books read by me from year to year since I left Yale College, i.e., after I was Tutor of the College." The list begins in October 1719. Not until June 1720 is Locke's *Essay* entered, and Johnson's special markings in the catalog indicate that he *owned* the copy he read. It is possible this was a second reading, but unlikely, for Johnson always noted it on his list if he was reading a work for the second time. Moreover, the surviving Yale commencement theses from Samuel Johnson's days as a tutor

---

46. The manuscript notebook of Obadiah Ayer or Ayers, 1708–1716, in the Harvard Univ. Archives is a good source of material on Harvard in this period. Ayer graduated in 1710.

47. Dexter, ed., *Documentary History of Yale*, 198. There were two brief periods when Johnson and Edwards did overlap at Yale, as Prof. Thomas Schafer has pointed out to me in a personal letter. Johnson was a tutor from Sept. 1716 to Sept. 1719. Edwards returned to New Haven for his senior year in late June 1719 and thus was there a month or two before Johnson left. In addition, Edwards did begin his junior year at the New Haven location, and as Schafer notes, he may have been exposed to Johnson for a week or two at that time, before Edwards and other students seceded to Wethersfield. However, Schafer generally concurs with my main point that, as he put it, "Johnson is likely to have had very little influence on JE."

48. Schneider and Schneider, eds., *Samuel Johnson*, I, 8. Johnson's autobiographical memoir must in general be used with caution. For example, Johnson says that Browne was made a tutor in Sept. 1717, but he was not made a tutor until Sept. 1718. See Dexter, ed., *Documentary History of Yale*, 173.

do not show evidence of Locke's influence. Johnson's reliability in the early section of his autobiographical memoir is thus questionable.[49]

Edwards probably first began actively to use the new books in the Yale library during the school years 1720–1722, when he was at Yale as a post-graduate student reading in theology. During most of the year 1722–1723 he was in New York City as a pastor at a Presbyterian church. In September 1723, Edwards was awarded his master's degree, and for part of the succeeding school year he may have been in New Haven again. Then, from the summer of 1724 until the summer of 1726 he was a tutor at Yale.[50] Thus, for a total of more than four years after attaining his bachelor's degree, Edwards had fairly easy access to a good library. Most of the titles noted in the early pages of his "Catalogue" of reading were also titles in the Dummer collection, which may indicate that Edwards was making good use of the opportunity.

Locke and Arnauld

On July 21, 1719, when Edwards was preparing to begin his senior year at college, he wrote to his father about the books needed for the forthcoming session. "I have enquired of Mr. Cutler, what books we shall have need of the next year," Jonathan wrote. "He answered he would have me get against that time, Alstead's Geometry and Gassendus' Astronomy . . . ; and also, the *Art of Thinking*, which, I am persuaded, would be no less profitable, than the other necessary, to me."[51] The geometry by Johann Alsted was traditional,

49. Johnson's catalog is printed in Schneider and Schneider, eds., *Samuel Johnson*, I, 496–526. A month after reading Locke's *Essay*, Johnson for the first time read More's *Enchiridion Ethicum*, of which he also owned a copy. For a review of the Yale curriculum in the college's first 25 years, see Warch, *School of the Prophets*, 186–249. See also the letter from Benjamin Lord (Yale B.A., 1714) to Ezra Stiles, May 28, 1779, in Franklin Bowditch Dexter, *Biographical Sketches of the Graduates of Yale College . . .* (New York, 1885–1912), I, 115–116, in which Lord recounts his studies at Yale between 1710 and 1714.

50. For the first half of the school year 1725–1726, however, Edwards was perilously ill and did not serve as tutor.

51. Dwight, *Life of Edwards*, 31–32. Arnauld's and Pierre Nicole's *La Logique ou l'art de penser* was first published in French in 1662. The Latin translation, *Logica, sive ars cogitandi*, was known as the *Ars Cogitandi* and was published in London in 1674 with subsequent printings in 1677, 1682, and 1687. The first English translation, *Logic; or The Art of Thinking . . .*, appeared in London in 1685, followed by at least three additional printings before an entirely new English translation, by Jacques Ozell, was published in London in 1717. The book was widely dispersed in both English and Latin editions in early American libraries. The first copies of *The Art of Thinking* must have been available at Harvard by the early 1690s, if not before. In 1700 Samuel Sewall ordered from London two copies of the *Ars Cogitandi*, along with three copies of Heereboord's *Meletemata Philosophica . . .*, rev. ed. (Amsterdam, 1680 [orig. publ. Leiden, 1654]), and single copies of LeGrand's *Institutio Philosophiae . . .* (London, 1672), Henry

but the use of Gassendi's *Institutio Astronomica* and the Arnauld logic represented advances over the old learning, both Aristotelian and Ramist.[52] The assignment of *The Art of Thinking*, a logic text, during the senior year is puzzling (logic was usually taught during the first two years only), although it was a work that, like Locke's *Essay* written almost thirty years later, deliberately touched on many matters of general philosophical and theological importance. Arnauld believed that a logic text should add to one's moral education as well. It is also puzzling that Edwards had not read the book before, *if* he had not. (His letter could be construed to mean that *once more* going through *The Art of Thinking* would be profitable.) In 1712 Elisha Williams, writing from Hadley, Massachusetts, asked Stephen Williams if he could get some copies of Arnauld, presumably because Elisha wanted to use it with his grammar school students.[53] And two years later Elisha wrote again asking for the "Art of Thinking . . . and any choice books that you can spare me, or any papers from Europe that I have not seen, The Crisis if you have it."[54] Given Elisha Williams's interest in *The Art of Thinking*, it seems likely that under his tutelage Edwards would have used the book earlier at Wethersfield. Edwards was, in any case, undoubtedly familiar with the spirit of the Port Royal logic, since he owned a manuscript version of William Brattle's logic compendium that had formerly belonged to William Partridge, a Harvard graduate in 1689 who lived in Hadley, Massachusetts.[55] Edwards's autograph and notes in the Partridge book indicate that he was using it by 1718.[56]

More's ethics and metaphysics and his *The Immortality of the Soul* . . . (London, 1659), Collier's dictionary, plus several other titles, all known to be Harvard texts in this period. The order was apparently for books needed at Harvard. See Sewall to John Love, a London merchant, June 10, 1700, *Letter-Book of Samuel Sewall* (Mass. Hist. Soc., *Collections*, 6th Ser., I–II [Boston, 1886–1887]), I, 237.

52. On Alsted, see Miller, *New England Mind*, 102–103; on the significance of Gassendi's astronomy, see Mel Gorman, "Gassendi in America," *Isis*, LV (1964), 409–417, and Warch, *School of the Prophets*, 208–218.

53. Elisha Williams to Stephen Williams, Mar. 16, 1712. The 1685 translation may have been hard to come by 20 years later. A copy of Ozell's 1717 translation survives with Edwards's signature in it.

54. Elisha Williams to Stephen Williams, Oct. 14, 1714. *The Crisis* . . . was a political pamphlet written by Richard Steele in defense of the Hanoverian succession, first published in London in Jan. 1714.

55. Partridge died prematurely in 1693, and his student logic notebook, which contained other logic systems besides Brattle's (see n. 56, below), was passed on to Warham Mather, who in turn gave it to Timothy Edwards, a relation through Esther Stoddard.

56. Partridge's manuscript notebook is in the Beinecke Lib., Yale Univ. It dates from 1686, with material in it also from 1688. In addition to Brattle's logic, it has a logic system prepared by Charles Morton in the vernacular and George Downame's Ramist logic. The book also contains a good deal of natural philosophy. The following statement in Latin precedes the transcription of Brattle's "Compendium of Logick, according to the modern philosophy, Extracted from Legrand and others their systems":

The exact dating of Edwards's familiarity with Cartesian logics like Le-Grand's or Arnauld's is not of itself a question of great importance, except insofar as it may be useful in correcting certain misimpressions and exaggerations concerning the foundations of Edwards's thought. Since we are concerned in this book with Edwards's moral philosophy only, we are spared the necessity of a close investigation of the sources of Edwards's youthful metaphysical idealism, that perennially intriguing problem in American intellectual history. Yet even an understanding of Edwards's moral thought can be seriously skewed if the myth that Edwards began his career as a disciple of John Locke is not laid to rest.

It has been taken as accepted fact now for more than two hundred years that Edwards read Locke's *Essay Concerning Human Understanding* at Wethersfield during his second year of college, that is, during the school year 1717–1718, when he was fourteen years old. This piece of information, which is not in itself altogether implausible, derives from Samuel Hopkins's biography of Edwards, first published in 1765.[57] The reference to Locke is almost the only mention of specific intellectual influences upon Edwards that Hopkins makes in his short biography, and perhaps for that reason Locke's *Essay* has always been an overly conspicuous part of the story of Edwards's growth as a philosopher. According to Hopkins's recollection, Edwards took a volume of Locke's *Essay* into his hands "not long before his death" in 1758, and said to some of his "select friends who were then with him," that "he was beyond expression entertain'd and pleas'd with it, when he read it in his youth at college; that he was as much engaged, and had more satisfaction and pleasure in studying it, than the most greedy miser in gathering up handfulls of silver and gold from some new discovered treasure."[58] It is as important to note

---

To the Reader

Good reader, you have in the first part of this book G. Downame's Exposition, set out in question and answer form, of Ramus' Dialectic. In the second part is included another treatise of logic. If you read through this (and indeed it is not of great extent) I venture to say that you will find in it nothing which is in disagreement with right reason. And indeed this short work is no less praiseworthy on account of its author, D. Legrand, a man exceedingly learned and experienced, whose bright name will scarcely ever fade into oblivion.

Warning

Before your perusal of this summary of logic, dear reader, remember this one thing: to read, and not understand, is to forget.

57. Samuel Hopkins, *The Life and Character of the Late Reverend Mr. Jonathan Edwards* (Boston, 1765). See the modern edition in David Levin, ed., *Jonathan Edwards: A Profile* (New York, 1969), 5. Sereno E. Dwight repeats Hopkins's statement in his authoritative biography. Hopkins said Edwards was 13 at the time.

58. Hopkins, *Life of Edwards*, in Levin, ed., *Jonathan Edwards*, 5–6.

what we do not learn from this account as it is to recognize what we do. Hopkins did not say—nor could he possibly have said, given the profound differences between Edwards's views and Locke's—that Edwards thereupon was convinced by all that Locke wrote. Indeed, given the diversity of material in the *Essay*, it is not clear from Hopkins's comment what it was specifically that gave Edwards such pleasure. It was surely not Locke's empiricism or his tendencies toward skepticism and positivism, nor could it have been the materialist implications of his work. For if one thing is certain, it is that Edwards remained a philosophical rationalist, a supernaturalist, and a metaphysician all of his life.

Perry Miller, the great historian of New England Puritanism, has been the most influential purveyor of the tradition that has emphasized Locke's influence on Edwards. Before Miller, more balanced interpretations prevailed.[59] Miller called Edwards's reading of Locke "the central and decisive event in his intellectual life," and went on to say:

> History cannot scrape together out of all America as early as 1717 more than a handful of men who had read the *Essay*, and none with any such realization that the "new way of thinking by ideas" would determine the intellectual career of the eighteenth century. The boy of fourteen grasped in a flash what was to take the free and catholic students of Professor Wigglesworth [at Harvard] thirty or forty years to comprehend, that Locke was the master-spirit of the age, and that the *Essay* made everything then being offered at Harvard or Yale as philosophy, psychology, and rhetoric so obsolete that it could no longer be taken seriously.[60]

On several grounds this dramatic picture of the relationship between Edwards and Locke must be rejected. It is misleading to think of Locke himself

59. Alexander V. G. Allen, *Jonathan Edwards* (Boston, 1889) remains one of the best general studies of Edwards's thought. Of Locke's *Essay*, Allen wrote, "The impression it left upon [Edwards's] mind was a deep and in some respects an abiding one." But "Locke was . . . rather the occasion than the inspiring cause of his intellectual activity. Had he read Descartes instead, he might have reached the same conclusion" (p. 5). Allen did not realize how much exposure to Cartesianism Edwards might have had. H. N. Gardiner, "The Early Idealism of Jonathan Edwards," *Philosophical Review*, IX (1900), 573–596, wrote: "If now, discarding the hypothesis of Berkeleyan influences, we raise the question of where then, Edwards got the suggestions for his ideas, I am inclined to answer: Mainly from three sources: from Locke with his doctrine of ideas; from Newton with his doctrine of colors; and from Cudworth with his diffused Platonism. Three authors we know he read. If we go beyond these, I would as soon include hypothetically Descartes, with the problematical idealism of the early part of the *Meditationes*, or John Norris, whose *Theory of the Ideal or Intelligible World*, published in 1701, reproduced ideas of Malebranche . . . , as I would include Berkeley."

60. Perry Miller, *Jonathan Edwards* (New York, 1949), 52–53. In general, Miller's discussion of Locke and Edwards on pp. 52–68 is probably the worst piece of writing he ever did, judged in terms of substance and interpretative accuracy.

as writing in isolation from the currents of thought in his day and during the preceding decades.[61] It is erroneous to place so much emphasis on the term "idea" and imagine that every use of it reveals the hidden presence of Locke. A similar mistake has been made in the interpretation of Samuel Johnson's early thought. Locke's analysis of the nature of ideas was written in response to the widespread discussion about ideas that had been generated by Descartes. Malebranche, Arnauld, and others wrote about ideas at great length, and there are many occasions when Edwards refers to "ideas" in ways that are by no means distinctively Lockean. It was pointed out almost immediately by Locke's critics that his use of the term "idea" was inconsistent and unclear, especially given the degree of precision that had been achieved in the writings of the Cartesians and of Gassendi in both Latin and French.

One even sees the assumption in Miller that Locke was the inventor of the distinction between secondary and primary properties; so that when Edwards notes that the pain is not in the needle and the color is not in the leaf, he was necessarily borrowing from Locke. The notion of the subjectivity of sensory experience has an ancestry going back to Galileo, and possibly even to Democritus, but it was again Cartesian speculation that made interest in this epistemological problem so alive in the late seventeenth century. Malebranche has a long discussion of it, for example, and it was discussed by LeGrand.[62] It is erroneous to assume that for Edwards or Professor Wigglesworth's students (or for a twentieth-century philosopher) Locke's *Essay* rendered all that came before as obsolete. To use an American example, Thomas Clap, president of Yale from 1740 to 1766, was devoted in philosophy above all to John Norris's *Theory of the Ideal or Intelligible World*. Norris was a disciple of Malebranche and a sharp critic of Locke. Here Locke made hardly a dent in the continuity from the past. Samuel Johnson turned to Bishop Berkeley rather than to Locke. And Edwards himself was no Lockean. On hardly any single point in moral philosophy does he follow Locke, and in logic and metaphysics his differences from Locke are fundamental. In moral philosophy Locke's initial effect was to stimulate certain adjustments in theory rather than to inaugurate any school of his own. His greatest influence was in logic in the broadest sense.[63] But the fact is, the revolt against Scholasticism and Aristo-

61. Miller seems to have made of Locke a symbol of modernity, just as in *The New England Mind* he used Calvin as a symbol of authoritarian and obscurantist theology. In neither case is the picture accurate. On the other hand, Miller gained much from these symbols in the way of literary or rhetorical structure.

62. Dugald Stewart believed that Addison's reference in the *Spectator* to the distinction between qualities that inhere in the objects themselves and those that are dependent upon human perception was based on his reading of Malebranche, not Locke. William Hamilton, ed., *The Collected Works of Dugald Stewart*, I (Edinburgh, 1854), 583.

63. See Wilbur Samuel Howell, "John Locke and the New Logic," in Theodore K. Rabb and Jerrold E. Seigel, eds., *Action and Conviction in Early Modern Europe: Essays in Memory of E.*

telianism in logic, ethics, psychology, physics, and metaphysics, that is, the really shattering changes, had already begun before Locke. Locke was the decisive contributor in certain areas of this revolt, but he did not accomplish the job single-handedly, his views were not entirely surprising or novel to any student of the philosophical thought of the late seventeenth century, and his ideas did not effectively dominate the outcome of the great revolt, least of all in America.

Finally, though it would be wayward to dispute that the *Essay Concerning Human Understanding* was a work of extraordinary cogency and that Edwards was enormously excited by it, it must be questioned whether Edwards's reading of Locke was the central and decisive event in his intellectual life. Perry Miller's beliefs on this point are challenged by William Sparks Morris in a nine-hundred page dissertation completed in 1955, "The Young Jonathan Edwards: A Reconstruction." Morris argues, correctly I think, that academic philosophy in early eighteenth-century America was necessarily eclectic. Men took the best of what they saw going on around them, and no one, not even Jonathan Edwards, could predict where the thought of the day was heading or could arrive at an entirely satisfactory synthesis. Locke at the time was one more luminary whose brilliance had somehow to be added to the other lights of the day. Morris points specifically to the continuation into the eighteenth century of the influence of the Dutch philosophers Franco Burgersdyck and Adrian Heereboord. In this he is certainly correct, for Heereboord's work was in use at Yale until at least 1714 and at Harvard into the 1720s.[64] "It must again be stressed," Morris wrote, "that, precocious though [Edwards] was, he did not read or meditate upon Locke's *Essay* in isolation either from others who had read Locke, or from other literature germane to the problems with which Locke, and himself as a student of Locke, were struggling."[65]

H. Harbison (Princeton, N.J., 1969), 423–452, and Howell's two-volume history of logic and rhetoric in England from 1500 to 1800.

64. Heereboord's texts, particularly in logic, ethics, and metaphysics, were among the most widely dispersed in the American colonies, prior to about 1725. Timothy Cutler's copy of Heereboord's *Meletemata Philosophica*, a work that brought together most of the Leiden professor's writings, is in the Boston Public Library. See Fiering, *Moral Philosophy at Seventeenth-Century Harvard*, chap. 2, for additional discussion of Burgersdyck and Heereboord.

65. William Sparks Morris, "The Young Jonathan Edwards: A Reconstruction" (Ph.D. diss., University of Chicago, 1955), 188. Morris's dissertation remains the most comprehensive investigation of the intellectual influences upon Edwards in his youth. Morris asks the essential questions: "What did Edwards bring to his reading of Locke, and what did he take away from [it]?" (p. 174), and answers: "In his early readings in . . . Bayle, Malebranche, and Norris, in Newton, and probably in Henry More (and perhaps John Smith and Ralph Cudworth), Burgersdicius and Heereboord, Edwards would have had more than sufficient stimulation to make the inferences from Locke which seem to be parallel to those of Berkeley" (p. 195). See the summary of Morris's view in his "The Genius of Jonathan Edwards," in Jerald C. Brauer, ed., *Reinterpretation in American Church History* (Chicago, 1968), 29–65.

In 1963 another rebuttal was launched against the thesis that Locke was the principal influence on the formation of Edwards's philosophical thought. Leon Howard attempted a chronological reconstruction of Edwards's early "Notes on the Mind" and concluded from his investigation that the traditions that these notes "were begun during [Edwards's] sophomore year in college" and that Edwards was an "enthusiastic follower" of John Locke were both "myths." Like Morris, Howard perceived that in the "Notes on the Mind," rather than favoring Locke, Edwards "consistently attacked" the *Essay*. Howard also readjusted the date of Edwards's reading of Locke (as had Morris) from 1717 to the period between 1720 and 1724, that is, during Edwards's senior year or after his graduation, an assumption that in itself totally alters the usual characterization of Edwards's intellectual development. But Howard was less conversant than Morris was with the intellectual milieu at the beginning of the eighteenth century and in some respects he perpetuated the view that there was a single decisive influence on Edwards's early thought. Howard proposed that Arnauld's *Art of Thinking* "was the one other reference book [Edwards] had always at hand, in addition to Locke's *Essay*, while composing his notes on 'The Mind.' "[66] Such a statement creates the misleading impression that Edwards's early philosophical speculations were composed over a period of a few days, rather than over a period of months or more probably years, and that these speculations related to only two books rather than to a wide range of stimulating literature, past and contemporary. If it is assumed that Edwards was nurtured in a desert, then of necessity one must search for the single source of nourishment.

Since Howard's study, the new research that has most deeply undercut the thesis that John Locke's *Essay* is the master key to comprehending Jonathan Edwards is Wallace Anderson's retracing of the logic behind Edwards's metaphysical idealism. The traditional interpretation has been that Edwards moved from Locke's empiricism to a subjective idealism, which is also the path, it was once believed, that Bishop Berkeley followed. With regard to Berkeley, it is now better understood that his earliest inspiration was from Malebranche and Bayle,[67] and Anderson has argued convincingly that Edwards, too, may have adopted the idealist or immaterialist position from premises in Henry More and in Newton, quite independent of his reading of Locke.[68] But it

66. Leon Howard, *"The Mind" of Jonathan Edwards: A Reconstructed Text* (Berkeley and Los Angeles, Calif., 1963), ix, 7.

67. A. A. Luce, *Berkeley and Malebranche: A Study in the Origins of Berkeley's Thought* (Oxford, 1934).

68. Wallace E. Anderson, "Immaterialism in Jonathan Edwards' Early Philosophical Notes," *Jour. Hist. Ideas*, XXV (1964), 181–200. It seems that Edwards first denied the existence of matter on rationalist grounds. Somewhat later he developed an argument in favor of idealism on the basis of reasoning from empirical phenomenalism, or sensationalism. See also the careful

should also be noted that on the basis of the evidence in Edwards's "Catalogue" of reading, it is not improbable that like Berkeley he read Malebranche's *Search after Truth* at a young age, and that in New England as in Ireland, Malebranche's suasive vision was a crucial ingredient in a young philosopher's growth.

Malebranche

To assert that the writings of the great French philosopher-monk Nicolas Malebranche were a major influence on Edwards's development as a thinker undoubtedly strikes twentieth-century American historians as highly improbable, since everybody assumes that Locke and Newton were the master-spirits of the age, and Malebranche seems exceedingly esoteric by comparison. But such skepticism is misguided, for time and circumstance have played tricks on Malebranche's huge reputation at the end of the seventeenth century and have blinded scholars of colonial thought to his significance. In the middle of the eighteenth century Bishop William Warburton tried to explain what had happened: "All you say of Malebranche is strictly true," he wrote to Richard Hurd,

> he is an admirable writer. There is something very different in the fortune of Malebranche and Locke. When Malebranche first appeared, it was with general applause and admiration; when Locke first published his Essay, he had hardly a single approver. Now Locke is universal, and Malebranche sunk into obscurity. All this may be easily accounted for. The intrinsic merit of either was out of the question. But Malebranche supported his first appearance on a philosophy in the highest vogue [*Cartesianism*]; that philosophy has been overturned by the Newtonian, and Malebranche has fallen with his master. It was to no purpose to tell the world, that Malebranche could stand without [Descartes]. The public never examines so narrowly.

Warburton also believed that Malebranche "debased" his "noble work with his system of *seeing all things in God*." When a "great author" proposes a notion that appears so paradoxical, "one half of his readers out of folly, the other out of malice, dwell only on the unsound part, and forget the other, or use all their arts to have it forgotten." Edwards would not have agreed with Warburton that Malebranche's theological idealism was unsound, of course, since his own position, ultimately, was so much like Malebranche's. As for

---

analysis by George Rupp, "The 'Idealism' of Jonathan Edwards," *Harvard Theological Review*, LXII (1969), 209–226.

Locke, Warburton concluded, he "supported himself by no system on the one hand; nor, on the other, did he dishonour himself by any whimsies; the consequence of which was, that, neither following the fashion nor striking the imagination, he at first had neither followers nor admirers: but being every where clear, and every where solid, he at length worked his way; and afterwards was subject to no reverses."[69]

One of the leading modern authorities on George Berkeley has proposed a different explanation for Malebranche's peculiar eclipse. In the early eighteenth century, A. A. Luce observes, Berkeley was rightly regarded as a disciple of Malebranche. Subsequently he came to be regarded as a Lockean. "The new opinion was a natural growth. In the course of time British acquaintance with Malebranche sank, and the fame of Berkeley rose. National sentiment adopted him as the English philosopher in succession to Locke." Moreover, Luce suggests that Berkeley avoided advertising the influence Malebranche had on him because "in some quarters 'Malebranche' spelled enthusiasm, and enthusiasm was literally a sin. . . . A Roman Catholic monk who wrote bitterly of 'heretics', and who called the English 'those wretched people, those children of the world', attacking the English Crown, the Church, and the State, would not be the most profitable patron for Berkeley's first important venture in authorship."[70] It is not improbable that Edwards suffered from similar constraints, perhaps even more than Berkeley did.

As Luce cautions, there is no need to depreciate the influence that Locke also had on Berkeley. But in the case of both Berkeley and Edwards—their philosophical development is closely parallel—there is need to right the balance.[71] The need is all the greater because Locke himself, who also was a close reader of Malebranche's writings, suppressed this influence upon his work, as he did almost all Scholastic and Cartesian influences.[72] Locke even-

69. Warburton to Hurd, Mar. 3, 1759, Warburton [Bishop of Gloucester], *Letters from a Late Eminent Prelate to One of His Friends* (Boston, 1809), 210.

70. Luce, *Berkeley and Malebranche*, 10, 40. The kind of nearsightedness that Luce is talking about is evident in the following comment from Henry Sidgwick's otherwise useful volume, *Outlines of the History of Ethics for English Readers*, 6th ed. enlarged (London, 1931 [orig. publ. 1886]), xxiii: "For the century and a half that intervenes between Hobbes and Bentham the development of English ethics proceeds without receiving any material influence from foreign sources."

71. Like Edwards, Berkeley was a provincial and became an immaterialist by the time he was 21, in 1706. His early notebooks resemble Edwards's early notes. Again like Edwards, he was influenced by the writings of Jean LeClerc, who himself had borrowed from Malebranche, and profoundly so by Bayle's *Dictionary*.

72. Locke bought the two volumes of Malebranche's *De la Recherche de la Vérité* . . . in Mar. 1676, when he was in France. They had been published successively in Paris in 1674 and 1675. See Gabriel Bonno, "Les Relations intellectuelles de Locke avec la France (D'après des documents inédits)," *University of California Publications in Modern Philology*, XXXVIII (1963), 58, 170, 243–244.

tually wrote a well-known essay against Malebranche, his *Examination of Malebranche's Opinion*, published posthumously, which he withheld from the press because, he said, "I like not controversies, and have a personal kindness for the author." It is said that Locke was moved to attack Malebranche directly only because of his detestation of Malebranche's greatest English disciple, John Norris of Bemerton, who, as we earlier noted, was one of the earliest critics of Locke's *Essay*.[73]

Dugald Stewart, who was a penetrating student of seventeenth- and eighteenth-century thought, had the greatest respect for *The Search after Truth*, commenting that "Few books can be mentioned, combining in so great a degree, the utmost depth and abstraction of thought, with the most pleasing sallies of imagination and eloquence; and none, where they who delight in the observation of intellectual character may find more ample illustrations, both of the strength and the weakness of the human understanding."[74] Like Warburton, Stewart reflected on the precipitate decline of a writer "formerly so universally admired, and, in point of fact, the indisputable author of some of the most refined speculations claimed by the theorists of the eighteenth century," attributing this decline to his "strong disposition to blend his theology and his metaphysics together." Yet Stewart believed that Malebranche "contributed a greater number of remarks than Locke himself" to our fund of "practical knowledge of the human understanding," that is, the habits and manners of the way people think and act.[75]

Stewart may be considered an objective observer, writing a century after Malebranche's death in 1715. Earlier, the praise waxes more eloquent and the direct influence of Malebranche is more obvious. Chambers's *Cyclopedia* (1728) used *The Search after Truth* as a principal authority on many philosophical and psychological subjects; Alexander Pope placed Malebranche in the company of Locke and Bolingbroke, both of whom he exceedingly admired.[76] Francis Hutcheson's theory of the passions, the most important work on the subject in English in the first half of the eighteenth century, is a development of Malebranche's own investigation of the subject, as Hutcheson acknowledged; and we have already mentioned Berkeley.

It is surely one of the most astonishing indications of the contemporary importance of an author that two separate and independent English translations of *The Search after Truth* appeared in the same year, 1694. The

---

73. John Locke, *An Essay Concerning Human Understanding*, ed. Alexander Campbell Fraser (New York, 1959 [orig. publ. Oxford, 1894]), I, xlvii; Charlotte Johnston, "Locke's *Examination of Malebranche* and John Norris," *Jour. Hist. Ideas*, XIX (1958), 551–558.

74. Hamilton, ed., *Works of Stewart*, I, 150.

75. *Ibid.*, 150–155. Stewart gives several examples of Locke's indebtedness to Malebranche.

76. Pope to Jonathan Swift, Sept. 15, 1734, in George Sherburn, ed., *The Correspondence of Alexander Pope*, III (Oxford, 1956), 433.

coincidence may be attributed to some failure of communication in London intellectual circles, or more likely to a wasteful publishing rivalry between John Dunton and Thomas Bennet,[77] but it is still indicative of Malebranche's fame at the time. Bennet was the publisher of Thomas Taylor's translation, which sold well enough to go into a second edition in 1700. It is the version most commonly found in libraries today, but it is probably not the version Edwards read. Although Taylor was sympathetic enough to Malebranche to be described by Georges Lyon, the historian of English idealism, as a disciple, one does not find in Taylor's version to the same degree the anticipation of Edwardsian phrasing and vocabulary that is unmistakable in the other translation, that by Richard Sault.[78] Indeed, it is possible that Edwards's borrowing from Malebranche has been obscured because copies of the Sault translation are relatively rare.

The likelihood that Edwards read Sault's version is reinforced by reasons other than those dependent upon internal comparison of texts. The publisher of this translation, John Dunton, had been to New England in the 1680s and was interested in cultivating the American book market. Moreover, his curious literary circle, the Athenian Society, composed principally of John Norris, Samuel Wesley, a minor poet and the father of John and Charles Wesley, and Sault, who was a professor of mathematics at Cambridge, had various connections to New England, not least the popularity of Norris's books in America.[79] Norris's *Theory of the Ideal or Intelligible World*, which was mainly an exposition of Malebranche for English readers, survived long enough in American esteem to be the favorite book, as we have noted, of Thomas Clap. Norris was a writer and thinker of considerable stature, and although there is no indication that Edwards read *The Ideal or Intelligible World*, he must certainly have read other works by Norris.[80]

Norris has been called "the English Malebranche," and his biographer comments that the description is just in the main: "the later books of the

77. Stephen Parks, *John Dunton and the English Book Trade: A Study of His Career with a Checklist of His Publications* (New York, 1976); "John Dunton and *The works of the learned*," *Library*, 5th Ser., XXIII (1968), 13–24.

78. Georges Lyon, *L'Idéalisme en Angleterre au XVIIIe siècle* (Paris, 1888), 176–178. In London in 1704 Taylor published *The Two Covenants of God with Mankind; . . . an Essay Design'd to Shew the Use and Advantage of Some of Mr. Malebranch's Principles in the Theories of Providence and Grace, etc.* He was associated with Oxford University during his early years, and the British Museum Catalogue distinguishes him from others with the same name by calling him Taylor of Magdalen College. Lyon treats Taylor at length but barely mentions Sault.

79. For some of this evidence, see Fiering, "Transatlantic Republic of Letters," *WMQ*, 3d Ser., XXXIII (1976), 642–660.

80. Edwards's "Catalogue" of reading mentions Norris's *A Collection of Miscellanies . . .* (Oxford, 1687) and his *A Practical Treatise Concerning Humility . . .* (London, 1707). Norris titles were in many early American libraries.

Englishman are little else than a reproduction of the Frenchman's writings."[81] Norris's esteem for Malebranche may be measured by these laudatory remarks in a letter addressed to his children:

> If you would have a book that is alone a library, and an ever-rising and flowing spring of knowledge, that ought never to be out of your hands, but always to be read, studied, felt and fed upon till it be digested, made your own, and converted as it were into the very substance of your souls, let me recommend to you Mr. Malebranche "de la Recherche de la Verite.". . . I take it to be one of the best books that is in the world; and of all human composures, that does better serve the interests of truth and of true religion.[82]

It is, of course, one thing to show, as I have tried to do here, that there would not have been the slightest anomaly in Edwards's having read and learned from Malebranche, and quite another to prove that he did in fact read *The Search after Truth*. The external evidence is not great. Edwards's "Catalogue" of reading mentions Malebranche twice in its earliest pages. First, there is a reference to "Some of Malebranche's writing," and then later appears the entry "Malebranches Search After Truth," which is crossed out, indicating, I believe, that Edwards got the book and read it.[83] Exact dating is not possible, but it is almost certain the entries were made before 1726.

Before leaving Malebranche, a word should be said about the possibility that Malebranche was the stimulus for Edwards's metaphysical idealism as he was for Berkeley's. The problem is that of finding the exact date not only of Edwards's reading of Malebranche but also of his essay "Of Being" and his "Notes on the Mind." These are subjects too difficult and complicated for analysis here, but the skeptical attitude of Georges Lyon toward some of the more improbable assertions of earlier Edwards scholars continues to deserve respect. Lyon, not realizing that there was any mention of Malebranche in Edwards's papers, was convinced that before Edwards had engaged in his idealist speculations he had read Berkeley. Be that as it may, it is not so much

---

81. Frederick J. Powicke, *A Dissertation on John Norris of Bemerton* (London, 1893), 141. See also, by the same author, *The Cambridge Platonists: A Study* (Cambridge, Mass., 1926).

82. Powicke, *John Norris*, 17. The letter appears in Norris's *Spiritual Counsel: or, the Father's Advice to His Children* (London, 1694). John H. Muirhead, *The Platonic Tradition in Anglo-Saxon Philosophy: Studies in the History of Idealism in England and America* (New York, 1931), 307, comments: "What seems most likely is that [Edwards's idealistic metaphysics] came rather . . . from a subtle air wafted across the Atlantic from the Malebranchean mysticism of which his English contemporaries John Norris and Arthur Collier had drunk so deeply than from what he found in any individual writer."

83. There are no other direct references to Malebranche in Edwards's books or manuscripts that I know of.

the soundness or unsoundness of Lyon's guess that I want to call attention to, but his healthy, metropolitan incredulity.

> This sketch of idealist philosophy [*Edwards's "Notes on the Mind"*], which would do honor surely to a mature writer, was put on paper [it is said] by a schoolboy of sixteen or seventeen years! Neither Sereno Dwight in his biography, nor Moses Coit Tyler in his history of American literature, has the least doubt about this. But metaphysical precocity is not sufficient for their admiration. They want the Notes on Natural Science to be hardly later than the Notes on the Mind. Yet to enumerate the incredible scientific insights that make up these remarks one must outstrip the list of discoveries that make up the glory of the age. Ethereal matter, the compressibility of the air, fixed stars compared to suns, an explication of electrical phenomena close to Franklin's theories, the diverse refrangibility of light rays, the laws of sound, the origin of colors, etc.: on all these matters and more, this child prodigy showed a marvelous divination. A comparison to Pascal is altogether too modest. He contained several Pascals in himself, this young student who invented metaphysics, astronomy, physics, the science of nature, the science of the future. And, by a double miracle, it happened that such a genius, whose intellectual gifts surpassed Galileo's and Newton's combined, suddenly changed direction [i.e., gave up natural science completely].[84]

Other Reading

It would be laborious to review here all of the external evidence of Edwards's reading in moral philosophy. In most cases I have indicated in the text or footnotes the relevant sources. Usually, the record in Edwards's "Catalogue" of reading or in his other manuscripts or printed books provides positive proof of what he read, and we can often be quite certain of when he read a particular work. Generally speaking, uncertainty about Edwards's reading exists only for the early years of his life, that is, the period prior to his move to Northampton in 1726 at age twenty-three. As the years go by, his "Catalogue" and the private notebooks known as his "Miscellanies" become absolutely explicit about his sources. Of course, the absence of evidence in Edwards's manuscripts cannot prove that he had *not* read a particular work, but there are grounds for confidence in what we know about what he did read.

As for the early years, it is all too easy to mistakenly attribute the source of an idea in Edwards's work to a book that he had not yet read, or to attribute

84. Lyon, *Idéalisme en Angleterre*, 429–430.

the origin of an idea to the wrong book of several that Edwards read with that same idea in it. To take one example, Edwards wrote in his "Notes on the Mind":

> Place of Minds. Our common way of conceiving of what is spiritual is very gross and shadowy and corporeal—with dimensions and figures, etc.—though it be supposed to be very clear, so that we can see through it. If we would get a right notion of what is spiritual we must think of thought, or inclination, or delight. How large is that thing in the mind which they call thought? Is love square or round? Is the surface of hatred rough or smooth? Is joy an inch or a foot in diameter? These are spiritual things.

In Ralph Cudworth's monumental *True Intellectual System of the Universe* (1678), we find:

> It is certain that we have notions of many things, which are . . . altogether unimaginable, and therefore have nothing of length, breadth, and thickness in them, as virtue, vice, etc. . . . We cannot conceive a thought to be of such a certain length, breadth, and thickness, measurable by inches and feet, and by solid measures. . . . And the same must be affirmed of volitions likewise, and appetites or passions, as fear and hope, love and hatred, grief and joy. . . . But if . . . these things . . . be unextended, then must the substances of souls and minds themselves be unextended also.[85]

In *The Search after Truth* there is the following passage:

> Is it so difficult a task to distinguish the difference there is between the Soul and the Body, between what thinks, and what is extended? Do's it require so great an Attention of Mind to discover that a Thought is neither Round nor Square: That Extent only is capable of different Figures and different Motions, and not Thought and Reasoning: And consequently, that what Thinks, and what is Extended, are two Beings directly opposite to one another? . . . But how could any Body imagine that the Mind were Extended and Divisible? We may by a right Line cut a Square into two Triangles, . . . But by what Line can it be conceiv'd, that a Pleasure, a Pain, or a Desire can be Cut?[86]

There are, indeed, dozens of passages in Edwards's early philosophical notes that sound like Cudworth, yet Edwards almost certainly did not read *The True*

85. Cudworth, *True Intellectual System*, II, 827.
86. *Malebranche's Search after Truth* . . . , trans. R. Sault (London, 1694–1695), I, Bk. iv, chap. ii, 14.

Intellectual System until late in life, since he refers to it in his "Catalogue" in the 1750s as a work he would like to read. A quotation from Cudworth in Edwards's early notes seems to have been copied from another source, or possibly added much later.

Similarly, the resemblance between much of Leibniz's writing and Edwards's ideas is sometimes marked, but aside from Leibniz's correspondence with Samuel Clarke, and possibly an article or two in one of the scholarly journals, it is unlikely that Liebniz was much known in colonial New England.[87] Yet we must insist here that even though Edwards probably never read a single word written by Leibniz and had probably not read much about him, a knowledge of Leibniz can be more helpful in understanding Edwards than hours devoted to reading Locke's *Essay*, which Edwards had definitely closely studied.[88]

Finding the right context for a thinker, placing him in a school or a tradition or a circle, even when one cannot demonstrate definitively the exact influences, is extremely important for getting the right "feel" of a man. In the case of Edwards, it is evident he is not comprehensible in terms of his New England Puritan background alone. He was too much of a philosopher for that context; his speculations carried him beyond the immediate concerns of the ministry to an engagement with metaphysics and ethics that was more than a collegiate exercise. He has, of course, been widely considered some sort of a descendant of John Locke, but Edwards's mind was profoundly antithetical to Locke's on most matters of importance. There is a need, then, to direct research more broadly into the background and milieu of Edwards's thought.

87. Most of Leibniz's writing was not published until long after his death. The *Essais de Théodicée* . . . (Amsterdam, 1710) was not translated into English in the 18th century.

88. The following sequence of manuscript notes from Leibniz, to take one example, can hardly be distinguished from Edwards's ideas:

"The end or aim of God is his own joy or love of himself.

God created creatures, and especially those endowed with mind, for his own glory or from love of himself.

God created all things in accordance with the greatest harmony or beauty possible. . . .

God loves to be loved or loves those loving him.

God loves souls in proportion to the perfection which he has given to each of them. . . .

He who obeys God from fear is not yet the friend of God. . . .

He who at the same time seeks the glory of God and the common good obeys God. . . .

Whoever does not delight in the contemplation of the divine perfection does not love God."

Philip P. Wiener, ed., *Leibniz Selections* (New York, 1951), 568.

2

The Moral Achievements of "Natural Understanding"

Besides the two sorts of Assent of the mind,
called Will and Judgment, there is a third,
arising from a sense of the General Beauty
and Harmony of things, which is Conscience.[1]

Both Catholic and Protestant Scholastic moralists typically justified the study of natural ethics—that is, ethics without foundation in scriptural authority and revelation—by resorting to a distinction. Natural ethics or moral philosophy, these writers said, could not get one to heaven, but the study of the subject could nevertheless help people to know how virtue and happiness can be attained in this world. Moral philosophy could point out what was obligatory for civilized life on earth and what is morally incumbent on man as a natural creature.

Implicit at the same time in this self-limiting notion of moral philosophy was the reciprocal idea of a moral theology (or supernatural ethics), which also considered how happiness might be attained through the practice of virtue but included in its scope the next world as well as this one. In moral theology there was no need to divorce from the natural man's capabilities the additional possibility of divine assistance through grace and revelation.[2] The distinction was a convenient one for those who despaired of harmonizing

[margin notes: Natural ethics; Supernatural ethics (moral theology)]

1. Jonathan Edwards, "Notes on the Mind," no. 39. There are three published versions of these early notes. Sereno Dwight's *Life of Edwards*, 668–702, is the primary source, since the original manuscript is lost. The version in Harvey G. Townsend, ed., *The Philosophy of Jonathan Edwards from His Private Notebooks* (Eugene, Ore., 1955), 21–68, and the one in Howard, *Edwards's Notes on "The Mind"* are both based on Dwight's. Since the textual differences between these versions are insignificant (they differ primarily in their ordering of the notes), in the course of my research I have turned to whichever version was conveniently reached at the moment.

2. On the distinction between moral and theological virtues, see, for example, St. Thomas Aquinas, *Summa Theologica*, trans. Fathers of the English Dominican Province, 3d ed. (London, 1938), Pt. II (first part), Q. 62, art. 2.

Christian doctrine with the conclusions of secular ethics, but it was subjected to constant adverse pressure from both sides. Many eighteenth-century moral philosophers looked upon their enterprise as a replacement for theology, rather than a complement to it, at least insofar as theology had anything to say about man. From the other direction, pietists from the time of the Reformation had been attempting to abolish moral philosophy.

It was the latter tradition to which Jonathan Edwards was heir. According to seventeenth-century Protestant reformers such as William Ames and Peter van Mastricht, moral philosophy had virtually no usefulness and no claim to autonomy. These theologians argued, as did Cotton Mather, that moral philosophy, with its pagan origins, is essentially superfluous. Only through Christian theology can one arrive at rules of conduct that encompass all of life and at the same time prepare one for salvation. The moral philosophers could talk interminably of virtue, but from the standpoint of the highest truths it was necessarily counterfeit virtue and unworthy of serious attention.

Edwards's Method

Edwards was in agreement with the pietists in that he believed in a unified Christian life in which piety and virtue would be interchangeable terms. Yet he also differed from Ames and Mather. These men eschewed moral philosophy. They refused to soil their hands with it any more than was absolutely required. Certainly neither Mather nor Ames engaged in any extended critical work in the field. Edwards, on the contrary, tried to have it both ways. Rather than shunning the subject, he was willing to contend on fine points with the naturalistic moral philosophers of his day, dedicating himself especially to demonstrating—in vigorous opposition to the rampant benevolism and psychological optimism of the eighteenth century—that the doctrine of Original Sin is valid; that natural men are moved principally by selfishness; and that the so-called "moral sense" of the secular philosophers was simply old-fashioned conscience in a new guise. All the while, however, Edwards kept in reserve his moral theology, for he had no intention of allowing these philosophical contests to decide matters regardless of intellectual consequences. Edwards regarded his engagements with secular philosophy as debates on the steps of the temple, merely interesting preliminaries to the sacred truths inside, which he held to undeviatingly.

Yet Edwards's real immersion in philosophy was recognized even before he had published his major philosophical works. As early as 1743 Charles Chauncy noticed that although Edwards quickly accused others of making "philosophy" rather than Holy Scriptures their rule of judging religious experience, especially "the philosophical notions . . . of the nature of the soul, its faculties and affections," Edwards himself had "made use of more philosophy . . . than anyone that I know of, who has wrote upon the times."[3] Chauncy's observation went straight to the mark. However reluctantly and unwittingly, Edwards was inevitably drawn into philosophical debate. Reliance on the theological tradition alone, on scriptural exegesis, on pietistic affirmations, or on pre-Cartesian thought would have been tantamount to excluding oneself from the terms in which the central issues of the time were being fought out. But at the same time, Edwards's moral *theology* flatly posited that no matter what could be shown about the so-called virtuous capacities of unredeemed human nature, natural virtue *must* fall short of "true virtue," if for no other reason than that it is natural rather than divinely inspired. On this point Edwards was quite explicit: "It is evident," he wrote, "that true virtue must chiefly consist in *love to God.*"[4] True virtue is, "in other words, true *grace* and real *holiness.*"[5] In the end, therefore, in Edwards's moral theology true virtue is indistinguishable from the state of grace or regeneration.

This unacknowledged double standard spread confusion in Edwards's own time and continues to do so. In the face of the epochal religious crisis of the eighteenth century, Edwards sometimes seems to have been inventing his own rules of debate and evidence. For the pietists such as Ames and Mastricht, compartmentalization of moral knowledge into natural and supernatural (or into philosophy and theology) was unacceptable in principle. Morality in theory and in practice was simply the unified Christian life. But by Edwards's day the expansion of philosophical speculation and understanding both in the physical and the moral sciences had been tremendous, and the task of integration had become so complicated and difficult that few thinkers even attempted to hold religious and secular learning together, except in the vaguest and most general terms. With the Aristotelian synthesis in ruins, it was far easier to take refuge in a loose syncretism. Yet a work like Bayle's *Dictionary* pitted religion and philosophy against each other in paradox after paradox, contradiction after contradiction, driving readers either toward fideism or skepticism.

Edwards's efforts at integration, at system building, as it were, made him an anomaly in the mid-eighteenth century. His intertwining of metaphysics

3. Charles Chauncy, *Seasonable Thoughts on the State of Religion in New England . . .* (Boston, 1743), 384.

4. Edwards, *The Nature of True Virtue* (Boston, 1765), ed. William K. Frankena (Ann Arbor, Mich., 1960). Similarly in Edwards's *[Treatise Concerning] Religious Affections* (Boston, 1746), ed. John E. Smith, *Works of Edwards*, II: The "moral excellency of an intelligent being, when it is true and real, and not only external, . . . is holiness. . . . Holiness comprehends all the true moral excellency of intelligent beings: there is no other true virtue, but real holiness" (p. 255).

5. *True Virtue*, ed. Frankena, 25–26.

and Scripture, his evangelical ambitions, indeed, the very foundation of his work in the experience of man's dependence upon God, are reminiscent of a period in philosophy earlier even than that of the great Anglican bishops Joseph Butler and George Berkeley. As we have earlier noted, Edwards belongs properly in the company of Leibniz, Malebranche, and Pascal fifty years earlier, figures who like him philosophized freely, but did so *within* a dogmatic tradition. It is a moot point whether this kind of relation to religious dogma excludes one from the Enlightenment.

That Edwards shared the faults and virtues of Malebranche, for example, should be no surprise. On many specific questions the two can be found to differ, but both were inspired by a vision of the immediate divine government and sustenance of the world, of the harmonious ordering of the creation, and of its fundamental intelligibility to man; and both considered themselves orthodox Christians within their own denominational traditions and were unwilling to depart from dogmatic teaching on scarcely any point. Edwards's distance from earlier American Puritanism lay in his use of modern philosophy and in his full acceptance of the post-Cartesian intellectual world, yet he did not renounce his dogmatic heritage as it was expressed in the Westminster Confession. Such a combination of limits and freedom often promotes brilliance and imagination. It may also encourage sophistry and evasiveness. All of these traits are evident in Edwards's work.

Edwards shared with Malebranche the dictum, "La religion c'est la vraie philosophie." For Malebranche, according to one commentator, "the data of religious experience furnished by revelation and the tradition of the Church were on a level with all other data of experience and had to be included and interpreted in any rational philosophical system."[6] In this respect, as well as in others, both Malebranche and Edwards differed decisively from Descartes and Locke, especially the latter. In the introduction to his *Essay Concerning Human Understanding* Locke had lectured other philosophers on the dangers of "meddling with things exceeding" human understanding and on the folly of letting "loose our thoughts into the vast ocean of Being." Locke, above all, contributed to the isolation of theology with his powerful contention that philosophical investigation should be restricted to the technicalities of logic and epistemology. Edwards was working in quite the opposite direction.

Malebranche and Edwards confused and irritated opponents precisely because they loved God more than philosophy. They preferred always to reason toward previously revealed ends, rather than to philosophize with no other avowed end in mind but the abstraction "truth," no matter what the results.[7]

6. Nicolas Malebranche, *Dialogues on Metaphysics and on Religion*, trans. Morris Ginsberg (New York and London, 1923), preface, 62.

7. John Herman Randall, Jr., *The Career of Philosophy*, I: *From the Middle Ages to the En-*

Truth, for Edwards, was the consistency and agreement of one's ideas with the ideas of God.

Some of Edwards's philosophical work is not only apologetical but also slightly casuistical in character. In a lesser thinker the defect would be condemnable. The eighteenth century had many would-be philosophers whose premises were completely arbitrary and varied from argument to argument; who cited Scripture where convenient but used natural evidence when they could; and who were capable at any time of reasoning in a perfect circle from dogmatic principles. Edwards, however, was unquestionably a first-rate thinker, reasonably well informed, acute in logic, and nearly always profound. Yet he is not easily pinned down. His thinking was never open-ended and therefore subject to reversal. He was not above a sophistry or two for the sake of the heavenly cause; after all, the truth had already been unveiled in Scripture. The task of the philosopher in Edwards's eyes, it would seem, is to reduce to absurdity all counterclaims to final knowledge; and, second, to explicate as well as can be done God's meaning and purposes for man.

A case in point is Edwards's *The Great Christian Doctrine of Original Sin Defended* . . . , published in Boston in 1758.[8] Here we find the most unpredictable and ad hoc interweaving of theological dogma and philosophy. Perry Miller's characterization of the book as "a strictly empirical investigation and induction, in the manner of Boyle and Newton of a law for phenomena" is manifestly contrary to its real nature.[9] Edwards did flourish words to this effect (by which Miller may have been misled), but he never delivered on the promise. Aside from scriptural quotations and a few entirely commonplace reflections on *homo homini lupus*, Edwards in *Original Sin*, if anything, avoided the inductive method, and where he did use it there were no consistent rules of what constitutes evidence. John Taylor, author of *The Scripture-Doctrine of Original Sin, Proposed to Free and Candid Examination* (London, 1740), who was Edwards's chief object of attack on the topic of Original Sin, proved himself much the better empiricist in one sentence that Edwards, because of his theological commitment, could never have written: "I do not think," Taylor wrote, "that we, who are not capable of precisely deciding in what Degree any person, even of our intimate Acquaintance, is either virtuous or vicious, are qualified to pass a true Judgment upon the moral State of the

---

lightenment (New York, 1962), 460–497, has described the peculiar susceptibility of the English mind at the end of the 17th century to forms of rationalist idealism from the Continent. Edwards's work is one of the greatest expressions of this tendency, which was antithetical to the empiricism and utilitarianism spawned by Locke.

8. I am using the Yale edition prepared by Clyde Holbrook, which is volume III of the *Works of Jonathan Edwards*.

9. Miller, *Jonathan Edwards*, 266–267.

whole World."[10] I do not mean to suggest that Taylor was right and Edwards wrong about human nature, but only to point out that the true empiricist would be more reserved in his judgment on the subject than Edwards could ever even consider being.

In *Original Sin* we find Edwards at his weakest as a philosopher, for reasons that will be explained later. But even though this book is not representative of Edwards's greatest powers, there is value in our pausing briefly to examine it, for in it some of the peculiarities of his method were most clearly exposed. The basis for Perry Miller's assessment lies in several passages in *Original Sin* wherein Edwards seemingly announced the rules he would follow in the debate.[11] We are attempting to discover the predominant propensity or tendency in men, Edwards said, and this can be done only by "observation" of "events." The "commonness or constancy of events" will reveal such a tendency. "Thus we judge of the tendencies or propensities of nature in minerals, vegetables, animals, rational and irrational creatures." Any tendency that truly belongs to the nature of man will be observed "in mankind in general, through all countries, nations and ages, and in all conditions." The proposition to be proved, of course, is that there is in human nature an innate tendency to wickedness, and this, Edwards stated, may be proved through proceeding "according to such rules and methods of reasoning, as are universally made use of . . . in experimental philosophy."[12]

An innocent participant in this debate might think the rules were relatively clear. It would be necessary only to arrive at some working definition of "wickedness" and "goodness" as they are represented in "events" or in the actions of men, and then begin some review of the human story. Of course, the magnitude of the required induction is far too great for real agreement ever to be reached, but at least the discussion could proceed along understood lines.

Edwards did some of this. The epigraph to *Original Sin Defended* is taken from Juvenal: "*Ad Mores natura recurrit damnatos, fixa et mutari nescia . . . Dociles imitandis turpibus et pravis omnes sumus*" ("Nature, firm and changeless, returns to the ways which it has condemned. . . . For we are all of us teachable in what is base and wrong").[13] A. O. Aldridge has noted that this was the only time Edwards ever put a Classical quotation on a title page.[14]

---

10. *Supplement*, 2d ed. (London, 1741), 50–51. On *homo homini lupus*, see Arthur O. Lovejoy, *Reflections on Human Nature* (Baltimore, 1961), 3–4, and n. 17, below.

11. *Original Sin* is divided into two parts: the first considers the question of "innate sinful depravity of heart"; the second, the question of the "imputation of Adam's sin." It is the first part with which we are immediately concerned.

12. *Original Sin*, ed. Holbrook, 121–125, 167.

13. See *Juvenal and Persius*, trans. G. G. Ramsay (London, 1930), Loeb Classical Library Edition, Satire XIII, 239, XIV, 38.

14. Alfred Owen Aldridge, *Jonathan Edwards* (New York, 1964), 59.

Edwards's point, of course, was that the testimony of mankind in all ages, including the pre-Christian, supports the Christian dogma. And in the text itself the doctrine of Original Sin is reinforced with some historical allusions:

> Notwithstanding what some authors advance concerning the prevalence of virtue, honesty, good neighborhood, cheerfulness, etc. in the world, Solomon, whom we may justly esteem as wise and just an observer of human nature, and the state of the world of mankind, as most in these days . . . judged the world to be so full of wickedness, that it was better never to be born, than to be born to live in such a world. (Eccles. 4 at the beginning).

"If we consider the various successive parts and periods of the world," Edwards continued, "it will, if possible, be yet more evident, that vastly the greater part of mankind have in all ages been of a wicked character."[15] Sacred history makes this clear: Adam; Cain and Abel; Noah; the whole postdiluvian period; Jacob's family; and so on. "Wickedness was the generally prevailing character in all the nations of mankind, till Christ came. And so also it appears to have been since his coming, to this day."[16]

In this same vein Edwards poured out a string of rhetorical commonplaces on human nature. Consider, he said, "the degree to which mankind have from age to age been hurtful to one another. Many kinds of brute animals are esteemed very noxious and destructive, many of 'em very fierce, voracious, and many very poisonous . . . : but have not mankind been a thousand times as hurtful and destructive as any one of them, yea, as all the noyous beasts, birds, fishes, and reptiles in the earth, air and water, put together." Men exceed the beasts in wickedness, because they are destructive to their own species, which is true of no other animal.[17] Finally, this time more in his

---

15. *Original Sin*, ed. Holbrook, 163–164.

16. *Ibid.*, 166.

17. *Ibid.*, 168. This last observation in particular appears very widely in all periods of Western literature. Shaftesbury had earlier questioned the meaning of *homo homini lupus*: "To say in disparagement of man 'that he is to man a wolf' appears somewhat absurd, when one considers that wolves are to wolves very kind and loving creatures. . . . The meaning, therefore, of this famous sentence (if it has any meaning at all) must be, 'That man is naturally to man as a wolf is to a tamer creature'; as, for instance, to a sheep. But this will be as little to the purpose as to tell us that 'there are different species or characters of men; that all have not this wolfish nature, but that one half at least are naturally innocent and mild' " (*Characteristics of Men, Manners, Opinions, Times* [London, 1711], ed. John M. Robertson, 2 vols. bound as one [Indianapolis, Ind., 1964], II, 83). Cf. William Wollaston, *The Religion of Nature Delineated*, 2d ed. (London, 1724), 201*ff*: "Indeed the history of mankind is little else but the history of uncomfortable, dreadful passages: and a great part of it, however things are palliated and gilded over, is scarcely to be read by a good natured man without amazement, horror, tears."

own original accent, Edwards impressively summarized the "facts" about universal evil:

> Mankind has been determined to evil, in like manner before the flood, and after the flood; under the law, and under the gospel; among both Jews and Gentiles, under the Old Testament; and since that, among Christians, Jews, Mohametans; among Papists and Protestants; in those nations where civility, politeness, arts and learning most prevail, and among the Negroes and Hottentots in Africa, the Tartars in Asia, and Indians in America, towards both the poles, and on every side of the globe; in greatest cities, and obscurest villages; in palaces, and in huts, wigwams and cells under ground.[18]

Now the critical point to be made here about Edwards as a philosopher has nothing to do with the limited extent of his inductive survey, or with whatever naiveté the reader may find in his examples. In the instances quoted Edwards was arguing along conventional lines in order to defend the teaching under question. George Turnbull, the other moral philosopher besides John Taylor whom Edwards had particularly singled out for rebuttal, had complained about the common tendency to "magnify" and "multiply" the vices of mankind, whereas, in fact, he argued, "very great villainies have been very uncommon in all ages."[19] Edwards was simply responding in kind. Nor would it be fair to Edwards to challenge the relevance of his use of sacred history, which represented for him supreme wisdom about human nature. The peculiar, elusive character of Edwards's argumentation is apparent not in his use of empirical, or what he called "experimental," data, but in what he said otherwise that simply negates the validity of all such data. For throughout *Original Sin*, in the form of several premises, Edwards firmly indicated that no evidence of any kind from history or social science could possibly alter his conviction about universal innate human depravity. An examination of these premises will reveal the problems posed to the reader by Edwards's method of utilizing moral philosophy in his arguments, but ultimately relying on moral theology for his conclusions.

Edwards presumptively settled the question of Original Sin through the use of two major principles. First, he divided the world into the realm of nature ⓵ and the realm of grace, or spirit, and then intimated strongly that whatever good qualities do happen to be found on earth should be credited automatically to the assistance of divine grace, not to mere nature. Although the

18. *Original Sin*, ed. Holbrook, 194.
19. Quoted by Edwards, *ibid.*, 109, from Turnbull, *Principles of Moral Philosophy*, I, 289–290.

question of human depravity presumably refers to the realm of nature, Edwards believed that at any time grace may be, and often is, "introduced [into the world] to oppose the natural tendency, and reverse the course of things." Moreover, we do not always know when we have been aided by "common" grace, which is pervasive in its benefits to the natural world. For Edwards, however, the presence of grace in the world is virtually proven by the simple datum that things are not much, much worse than they are. All sin, he stated, "deserves and exposes to utter and eternal destruction . . . , and would end in it, were it not for the interposition of divine grace to prevent the effect."[20] In short, Edwards could not help but presuppose the very fact that he set out to defend in the first place. Since the world in Edwards's view is an indissoluble mixture of nature and both common and redemptive grace, what is actually "natural" will always be open to dispute. Predictably, Edwards's piety led him to assign to nature most of what he found bad, and to grace most of what he found good. Turnbull's or Taylor's observations, then, about the apparent prevalence of virtue and goodness in history are invalid because all that is good in the world is the result of God's saving interventions, which cannot be relied upon as though they were natural laws. All that can be certainly relied upon in nature is the persistence of sin.

②   A second principle of Edwards's that strongly biased his response to the doctrine of Original Sin and made his handling of the question definitely non-empirical, was his introduction of a radical distinction between vice and sin. On the basis of this distinction, all inductive evidence about the ostensible or apparent behavior of men becomes irrelevant, telling the observer only about the relative quantities of virtue and vice in the world without revealing anything about the measure of holiness and sin. Thus, in Edwards's terms, even if it could be demonstrated empirically that the quantity of virtue in the world outweighs the quantity of vice it would still be impossible to show that *sin* is outweighed.[21]

In good sentimentalist fashion,[22] Edwards opened his treatise on Original Sin with the assertion that "all moral qualities, all principles either of virtue or vice, lie in the disposition of the heart." And at first, as we have seen, he

---

20. *Original Sin*, ed. Holbrook, 110, 114. On the role of common grace, see pp. 61–62, below, and Fiering, *Moral Philosophy at Seventeenth-Century Harvard*, chap. 1.

21. Edwards could speak as follows about sin, but his dissertation on *True Virtue* makes clear that he would never have said the same about human immersion in vice: "Sinful men . . . are *full* of *sin*; full of principles of sin, and full of acts of sin. . . . They are totally corrupt in every part, in all their faculties; and all the principles of their nature, their understandings and wills; and in all their dispositions and affections . . . ; all their senses, hearing, tasting, etc., are only inlets and outlets of sin, channels of corruption." *A Divine and Supernatural Light, Immediately Imparted to the Soul by the Spirit of God . . .* (Boston, 1734), 205.

22. Edwards's relationship to the sentimentalist movement is discussed more fully below. See pp. 107–149.

appeared to be adhering to the view that a "disposition" or a tendency is something that can be discovered by "observation" of the "events" or actions that reveal the disposition.[23] But before long, the seemingly empirical question of "disposition" became in *Original Sin* a deep psychological mystery penetrable only by religious intuition: "The question to be considered . . . is not whether [man] is not inclined to perform as many *good deeds* as *bad ones*, but, which of these two he preponderates to, in the frame of his heart, and the state of his nature."[24] Edwards had first given the reader reason to think that the key to discovering a person's underlying "disposition" is the ratio of good to bad deeds. But then he asserted that it is the "determination or the tendency" of man's heart and nature that must be looked at "in order to determine whether his nature is good or evil." Therefore, it follows, according to this logic, that "it is wholly impertinent, to talk of . . . innocent and kind actions . . . surpassing . . . crimes in numbers; and of the prevailing innocence, good nature, industry, felicity and cheerfulness of the greater part of mankind." And it is "absurd," Edwards claimed, to decide whether nature is good or bad "under a notion of men's doing more honest and kind things, than evil ones." This is as absurd as it would be to deem an ocean-going ship that is certain to founder and sink along the way a "good" ship only because the vessel will have sailed more hours than it takes to sink.[25]

From one point of view, this analogy to a ship is pure sophistry. Edwards seems to have meant by it that death is the ultimate punishment for sin, or, in general terms, that with regard to the question under consideration it is the end result only that matters. Since more lives end in hell than in heaven and the afterlife is infinitely longer than life on earth, it is clear that sin predominates in human affairs. The moral philosopher would put the end result in the context of life on earth. The moral theologian puts the end result in eternity.

By Edwards's reckoning, any sin, any transgression of God's law, is infinitely heinous, for God is infinite and therefore deserving of infinite respect. Compared to infinity, no human deed can count as anything at all. Compared to the wickedness of sin, "all the virtuous acts that ever [a man] performs, are as nothing to it." There is "an infinite demerit in all sin against God, which must therefore immensely outweigh all the merit which can be supposed to be in our virtue." Obviously, Edwards so confounded vice and sin in his discussion of human nature that two entirely different questions were at issue. And,

---

23. *Original Sin*, ed. Holbrook, 108, 121.

24. *Ibid.*, 128. Edwards's reasoning was dependent on certain traditional notions regarding the relationship between habits and acts (particularly infused habits), which cannot be addressed here. See below, chap. 6, pp. 308–313, and for additional discussion of the technical meanings of habit in the 18th century with some reference to Edwards, see Fiering, "Benjamin Franklin and the Way to Virtue," *American Quarterly*, XXX (1978), 199–223.

25. *Original Sin*, ed. Holbrook, 128–129.

as we saw in his use of the distinction between nature and grace, the empirical anthropological question about the validity of the doctrine of Original Sin was prejudged. It is the hidden crimes that must decide, according to Edwards's final reasoning. For man's crimes against God may not be as visible or conspicuous as his apparent virtues, but they are too heinous to be atoned for, and in the end overbalance all the contrary evidence of innocent and kind actions.[26]

One extenuating point should be noted, however, that somewhat absolves Edwards from the sheerest inconsistency in his debate with Taylor and Turnbull. He stated that the question of Original Sin was to be decided by the method of "experimental philosophy."[27] Perry Miller incorrectly assumed that this term meant the method of Newton and Boyle. But Edwards's idea of the experimental method was expressly like that of George Turnbull, which incorporated more than the observation of external phenomena alone. "Experimental philosophy" for Edwards was comparable to "experimental" religion: the former "brings opinions and notions to the test of fact"; the latter "brings religious affections and intentions, to the like test."[28] In short, for Edwards the experimental definitely included the experiential. Throughout the eighteenth century—indeed, beginning with Descartes—moral philosophers had hoped to achieve fixed results in the study of human nature such as were being discovered in natural philosophy. Since the positivist distinction between subjective and objective evidence was not yet widely accepted, "experiment" in moral philosophy included personal experience. It would have occurred to no moral philosopher in this period to exclude introspection from the study of human nature. Searching into oneself was vital and necessary for evidence. Turnbull was explicit on this point. "The study of nature," he said, articulating a widespread premise, "whether in the constitution and economy of the sensible world [i.e., the world of physical nature], or in the frame and government of the moral, must set out from the same first principles, and be carried on in the same method of investigation, induction, and reasoning; since both are enquiries into facts or real constitutions."[29] Moral philosophy, however, as distinguished from "phisiology," said Turnbull, "enquires chiefly about objects not perceivable by means of our outward organs of sense, but by

26. *Ibid.*, 130, 133, 139. Holbrook, *Ethics of Edwards*, 49, has pointed out that Edwards's argument that the "degree of hatefulness or demerit in sin is to be measured by the being against which it is committed" was a criterion employed by Anselm. Holbrook appropriately calls it "feudalistic." For full discussion, see chap. 5, below.

27. *Original Sin*, ed. Holbrook, 167.

28. *Religious Affections*, ed. Smith, 452.

29. Turnbull, *Principles of Moral Philosophy*, I, 2.

internal feeling experience; such as are all our moral powers and faculties, dispositions and affections."[30] Edwards would have agreed totally.

The ultimate unspoken premise in Edwards's *Original Sin* was his own religious experience, in particular his conversion experience. From the vantage point of *regenerate* nature, it may indeed be empirically true that most purported virtue is removed from sin hardly at all. Edwards's own heart, struggling for purity with the assistance of the Spirit, was his conclusive experimental reference to test the doctrine of Original Sin. Thus, the philosophical or quasi-scientific inductive investigations pursued by natural men could be only a side issue. As for a more extended induction than the examination of his own heart, Edwards simply offered to others the same opportunity:

> And now I must leave it to everyone to judge for himself, from his own opportunities for observation and information concerning mankind, how little there is of this disinterested love to God, this pure divine affection, in the world. How very little indeed in comparison of other affections altogether diverse, which perpetually urge, actuate and govern mankind, and keep the world, through all nations and ages, in a continual agitation and commotion![31]

There are an infinite number of ways to err, but only one path to God.

It is obviously difficult, and perhaps artificial, to separate out Edwards's moral philosophy from his moral theology. Most of his work in moral philosophy was critical or destructive, that is, an effort to poke holes in some of the prevalent assumptions of his time, and thus to leave standing only a pietistic edifice. However, it is extremely valuable for an understanding of Edwards, even as a moral theologian, to attempt to delineate his moral philosophy, and this for two reasons: it can help us to see him in the context of an important body of thought that he studied closely and with great interest; and

---

30. *Ibid.*, 9. Cf. the subtitle of David Hume's *A Treatise of Human Nature: Being An Attempt to Introduce the Experimental Method of Reasoning into Moral Subjects* (London, 1739).

31. *Original Sin*, ed. Holbrook, 144–145. Even before Edwards published *Original Sin* he had earlier in *Religious Affections* (1746) made plain the underlying basis of man's knowledge of Original Sin. The assent to gospel truth, Edwards said in the earlier volume, depends upon "the special influence and enlightenings of the Spirit of God." Once a person's eyes are opened by conversion "a multitude of most important doctrines of the gospel . . . are at once seen to be true." Among these, of course, is "what the Word of God declares concerning the exceeding evil of sin." A man comes to see "his own sinfulness and loathsomeness; for he has now a sense to discern objects of this nature. . . . He now sees the dreadful pollution of his heart, and the desperate depravity of his nature, in a new manner . . . and this shows him the truth of what the Scripture reveals concerning the corruption of man's nature." *Religious Affections*, ed. Smith, 300–301. See also, pp. 207–213, 259–260, below.

it can help us to view his moral theology in better perspective, for this higher ground of Edwardsian thought was deeply interpenetrated with the moral philosophy he avidly absorbed and put to use for his own ends.

Edwards was not a reactionary; he certainly made no effort merely to reiterate seventeenth-century or earlier ideas. His goal, if it can be put in one sentence, was to give seventeenth-century Puritan pietism a respectable philosophical structure, which would make it rationally credible and more enduring than it could be without the aid of philosophy. Edwards seems to have felt personally offended by the progressive spirit of the age insofar as it boasted of its critical learning yet failed in his eyes to bring about vitality in religion and vigorous moral reform. "Great Discoveries have been made in the Arts and Sciences, and never was human Learning carried to such a Height, as in the present Age; and yet never did the Cause of Religion and Vertue run so low." He resented that the supposed "Weakness and Bigotry," the alleged "Folly and Absurdity," of the eminent divines of former generations were held up to scorn in the eighteenth century because it was "imagined" that the principles of these divines (such as those of strict Calvinism) "did destroy the very Foundations of Vertue and Religion, and ennervate all Precepts of Morality." Yet vice and wickedness now prevail "like an overflowing Deluge," Edwards believed. In the mid-eighteenth century there were alleged to be "more free, noble, and generous Thoughts" than in earlier ages, but at the same time, in what Edwards saw as a contradiction to this claim, "Religion in general" was "despised and trampled on."[32]

Yet eighteenth-century British moral philosophy, though secular, was itself profoundly indebted to the Protestant thought of the preceding one hundred years. Therefore, ironically, Edwards found ready-made in the new moral philosophy certain conceptual structures that corresponded very closely to his own religious predilections. In the late seventeenth century moral philosophers had begun the process of converting into secular and naturalistic terms crucial parts of the Christian heritage. Edwards in a sense reversed the ongoing process by assimilating the moral philosophy of his time and converting it back into the language of religious thought and experience. He can be considered retrogressive only if one interprets as retrogressive every step in the eighteenth century not directly aimed toward secularism or naturalism. On the other hand, his progressivism must be seen not so much as a vision of a radically different future for society, but as a remarkable receptivity to the philosophical speculation of his own era insofar as it bore on the well-being of religion. Edwards was an Enlightenment figure only in the limited sense that he entered fully into dialogue with some of the philosophers of the British

32. Edwards, *Humble Attempt to Promote Union*, 71. Shaftesbury and Hume in particular maintained that many of the tenets of orthodox Calvinism were adverse to the cultivation of virtue.

Enlightenment; his purpose, contrary to that of the *philosophe*, was to turn the best thought of his time to the advantage of God. ⇐

It seems justified, then, to begin an exploration of Edwards's ethics with the question: What for Edwards was the moral capacity of the natural man, or the man without special spiritual assistance? From this analysis, which runs from the present chapter through chapter 6, we will move in chapter 7 to Edwards's moral theology, to see how the world of mere nature could, with divine assistance, be transcended.[33]

Common Grace

Any discussion of the powers of nature as conceived of by Edwards must presuppose the role of common grace. No part of the creation, in Edwards's view, could survive for a moment without God's sustaining will, and human nature, too, is ordinarily saved from its worst inclinations by the help of God. "There are many in this World, who are wholly destitute of saving Grace, who yet have common Grace: They have not true Holiness, but nevertheless, have something of that which is called *moral virtue*; and are the subjects of some Degree of the common Influences of the Spirit of God."[34] Common grace differs from special redeeming grace, according to Edwards, in that it influences "only by assisting nature, and not by . . . bestowing anything *above* nature. The light that is obtain'd, is wholly natural, or of no superior kind to what meer nature attains to." In other words, "*Common grace* only assists the faculties of the soul to do that more fully, which they do by *nature*."[35] Thus, in a sense, there was no entirely natural world for Edwards, as we have already noted. Certainly all of human life on earth is something more than natural. Mankind depends utterly upon God's goodness for a daily existence free of the greatest misery, whether we know it or not. To find the tendencies of bare nature one would have to descend into hell, where the

33. The present chapter analyzes Edwards's theory of natural understanding up to *ca.* 1746. Chapter 3 concentrates on Edwards's later interpretation of natural understanding, especially as expounded in *True Virtue*, which he was writing in 1755. Chapter 4 addresses the permutations of self-love and instinct as a source of alleged natural virtue. Chapter 5 treats the significance of Edwards's hell preaching and his critical response to the humanitarianism of the age, particularly the question of the significance of the emotion of pity as evidence of natural virtue. Chapter 6 concerns the background and philosophical context of Edwards's theory of the will. Finally, chapter 7 summarizes Edwards's theory of *true* virtue, i.e., the virtue that flows from divine grace.

34. Edwards, *True Grace, Distinguished from the Experience of Devils* . . . (New York, 1753), 6.

35. *Divine and Supernatural Light*, 5–6. This theory regarding common grace is found also in nos. 471 and 626 of Edwards's Miscellanies. The latter number was probably written in 1733 and extracted for the sermon just quoted from.

damned are "deprived forever of all good."[36] In the condition of hell, "when God has done waiting on sinners, and his spirit done striving with them, he will not restrain their wickedness" as He does on earth for all. Sin will therefore "rage" in the hearts of the condemned like "a fire no longer restrained or kept under."[37] Indeed, one of the defining characteristics of devils is that they are bereft of common grace.[38] "In hell all those principles will reign and rage that are contrary to love, without any restraining grace to keep them within bounds."[39]

Common grace assists the natural powers of men and women to an indeterminate degree. But since, like the air we breathe, it is always present, it need not require further attention from us. After the hypothetical peeling away of common grace two qualities are left that even devils in hell possess: natural understanding and self-love.[40] These may seem like weak pillars upon which to build a structure of ethical order, but no one was more ingenious than Edwards in demonstrating that all of the vaunted natural human virtue in the world was a product principally of these two unedifying qualities. The source of most of what is accounted virtue in the world has nothing whatsoever to do with virtue, Edwards believed, but is rooted essentially in cunning and vanity.

Synteresis

According to Edwards, the most important function of natural understanding or intellect in the moral life is the exercise of conscience. Indeed, virtually all of the moral uses of natural understanding could be comprised within the broad meaning of conscience. Edwards's early speculation included in the idea of conscience at least three components: (1) synteresis; (2) knowledge of the will of God and the threat of His retribution or vengeance; and (3) an innate sense of balance, symmetry, and proportion, which in turn leads to a sense of accountability and a sense of desert, or to the idea of retributive justice.

Synteresis Synteresis, or the power of understanding the first principles of morality without prior instruction, was widely acknowledged in the Scholastic tradition, for the authority of Rom. 2:14–15 made it almost unthinkable to reject its existence: "When Gentiles who do not possess the law carry out its precepts by the light of nature, then, although they have no law, they are their

---

36. Miscellanies, no. 427.

37. *True Virtue*, ed. Frankena, 73.

38. *True Grace Distinguished*, 6.

39. Edwards, *Charity and Its Fruits: or, Christian Love as Manifested in the Heart and Life*, edited from the original manuscripts by Tryon Edwards (New York, 1851), 518.

40. *True Grace Distinguished*, 31.

own law, for they display the effect of the law inscribed on their hearts. Their conscience is called as witness." We do not have any extended statements by Edwards on synteresis, only one or two vague allusions. The medieval idea of a storehouse of fundamental law in the mind, more or less innate or connate, merged imperceptibly in the seventeenth century into Natural Law theory. Edwards seems to have taken this theory for granted, but he nowhere showed a great deal of interest in it. Natural conscience, Edwards said in an early note, can "give an apprehension of right and wrong," and "suggest to the mind the relation that there is between right or wrong and a retribution. Sin and sensuality . . . greatly hinders conscience in doing this work[.] It clogs and lames it but don't destroy its power so that it shall not be able to do it."[41] Samuel Pufendorf, the German historian and Natural Law theorist, about fifty years earlier had expressed the basic idea that was carried into the eighteenth century, largely undamaged by Locke's criticisms of innatism:

> The common saying that that law is known by nature, should not be understood, it seems, as though actual and distinct propositions concerning things to be done or to be avoided were inherent in men's minds at the hour of their birth. But it means in part that the law can be investigated by the light of reason, in part that at least the common and important provisions of the natural law are so plain and clear that they at once find assent, and grow up in our minds, so that they can never again be destroyed, no matter how the impious man, in order to still the twinges of conscience, may endeavor to blot out the consciousness of those precepts. For this reason in Scripture too the law is said to be "written in the hearts" of men.[42]

But this kind of moral awareness is, at best, rather superficial, according to Edwards. The notion of evil or wrong that it conveys to the natural man is only "the relation or adaptedness there is between such things and . . . being hated by others and having evil brought upon [him]." It is ratiocinative; at least in part a deductive process. What it cannot give is an immediate, sensory, nondiscursive or intuitive response to right and wrong. It is syllogistic and sequential. "The notion that natural conscience gives of wrong is not of something deformed and loathsome," Edwards wrote. "Natural men in strictness see nothing of the proper deformity of wrong, but only they see an agreeableness between such certain things and being hated or being the object of displeasure or suffering ill."[43]

41. Miscellanies, no. 471. See also *Religious Affections*, ed. Smith, 207.
42. Samuel von Pufendorf, *De Officio hominis et civis juxta legem naturalem Libri Duo* (Cambridge, 1682), trans. Frank Gardner Moore (New York, 1927), 20.
43. Miscellanies, no. 372, written about 1731. A good example of what Edwards was talking

It is clear that in the early 1730s when Edwards wrote these words distinguishing between natural conscience and the moral perceptions of the regenerate, he had not yet read Francis Hutcheson. And though he probably knew Henry More's thinking, and the third earl of Shaftesbury's, where adumbrations of Hutcheson's ideas could be found, Edwards apparently was not yet familiar enough with this thinking to be compelled to come to grips with the concept of a "moral sense," the intuitive, immediate apprehension of the deformity and loathsomeness of vice that the benevolists maintained (by an analogy to aesthetics) was a universal trait of men who are not wholly corrupt. Shaftesbury in his *Characteristics* had already directly opposed the Scholastic idea of conscience as an internal judge that convicted men according to the law of God. "To have awe and terror of the Deity does not, of itself, imply conscience," Shaftesbury argued. "Nor does the fear of hell or a thousand terrors of the Deity imply conscience, unless where there is an apprehension of what is wrong, odious, morally deformed, and ill-deserving. . . . And thus religious [conscience] supposes [i.e., presupposes] moral or natural conscience."[44] What Edwards in 1731 considered to be the exclusive property of the supernaturally inspired, namely, an awareness of the essential deformity of vice, Shaftesbury called the very presupposition of any conscience whatsoever. In Shaftesbury, the natural power was made the foundation of the religious, or rather, the reputedly exclusive religious sensitivity was universalized.

To some extent Edwards's analysis rested on a standard distinction in Christian theology, seen in both Catholic and Protestant works in the seventeenth century and much earlier, between the workings of a good conscience and a bad one. The latter was characteristic of the unregenerate; it was a conscience that served to convict without guiding one to right doing. It was a conscience of remorse only, bringing one to judgment. A good conscience, on the other hand, enabled its possessor to judge good and evil antecedently and was a

---

about here is found in William Ames's well-known *Conscience with the Power and Cases Thereof, Divided into Five Books* (Latin, 1630; English, 1643). Conscience "is a man's judgement of himselfe, according to the judgement of God of him," Ames wrote. Conscience "stands in the place of God himselfe." Its function is divided into three parts: a law, a witness, and a judge to the sinner. The general law, which states the major proposition in universal terms, is technically the *synteresis*. For example, "He who lives in sin shall die." Then follows the application to the individual, the witness, sometimes called *syneidesis* (the Greek equivalent of the Latin word "conscience"): "I live in sin." Finally, the judgment, which Ames called the crisis: "I shall die" (see *Cases of Conscience*, I, 2–6). For the complex history of the concept of *synteresis* in the Middle Ages, see Odon Lottin, *Psychologie et Morale aux XIIe et XIIIe Siècles*, II (Louvain, 1948), 103–349. See also Fiering, *Moral Philosophy at Seventeenth-Century Harvard*, chaps. 1 and 2.

44. *Characteristics*, ed. Robertson, I, 305–306. The *Characteristics*, really a collection of individual essays and pamphlets, first appeared as a single work in 1711.

bearer of the Holy Spirit. Such notions may be found, for example, in William Perkins's *Discourse of Conscience*, published in 1596.

In number 732 of his Miscellanies (composed about 1736), Edwards implicitly accepted that it would no longer be as easy to depreciate the moral powers of the natural man as it had been for Puritans in the early seventeenth century. His reading in ethics undoubtedly began to broaden by the mid-1730s: the third dialogue in Berkeley's *Alciphron* with its careful discussion of Shaftesbury; Samuel Clarke's *Discourse*;[45] various volumes of the *Republick of Letters*. Synchronously with Benjamin Franklin, Samuel Johnson of Connecticut, and James Logan, in the 1720s and 1730s Edwards was beginning to be reached by the ingenuity and vigor of the new moral philosophy. (Edwards's full education in the new moral philosophy did not come, however, until after 1746.) In number 732 we find the following significant concession: The natural man "is capable of a sense of heart of . . . evil, i.e., he is capable of a deeply impressed and lively and affecting idea and sense of these things which is something more than a mere conviction in the judgment concerning their truth." In addition to intellectual assent, there could also be a degree of emotional consent. And common grace assists not only the reason or judgment but also "the sense of the heart" against the stupefying effects of sin. The mind and heart of the normal man, then, even without the introduction of special supernatural principles, is capable to some degree of an intuitive, nondiscursive sense of good and evil, which is something beyond the recognition of law and punishment or of disobedience and retribution. However, as we will see, Edwards eventually rejected this view. His grand strategy in ethical thought, as it developed, was to interpret the moral knowledge of the natural man as essentially and inescapably intellectual and "secondary," thereby crippling it with the limitations that a purely intellectualist mode of moral understanding must have. As Edwards's thought matured, he came to reserve for the graciously regenerate alone the possession of an inner affective sense of the intrinsic nature of good and evil, a position that would set him in direct opposition to the Hutchesonian school.

There could be no doubt, of course, that all persons, regenerate and unregenerate alike, sinners and saints, have the common faculties of understanding, will, and sentience. Edwards rejected intellectualism in religion, since it so easily led to the heterodoxies of legalism, moralism, Pelagianism, and illuminationism. Although he accepted divine illumination of the understanding as an intrinsic part of the redemptive process on earth, his emphasis in

45. Edwards's Diary or Account Book, July 1733 to Dec. 1757, MS, Beinecke Lib., Yale Univ., shows that in the middle 1730s Edwards was already lending out Samuel Clarke's *A Discourse Concerning the Unchangeable Obligations of Natural Religion, and the Truth and Certainty of the Christian Revelation*, 2d ed. (London, 1708), to his parishioners and colleagues.

describing this process was always on the alteration in the dispositions, not the understanding. Now in secular moral thought there were also those who rejected intellectualism and worked to establish the principle that real virtue is seated in the heart and dispositions, not in cerebral knowledge. Edwards's problem was to demonstrate, in opposition to these sentimentalists, that natural morality is necessarily always a function of intellect alone (with the exceptions of self-love, which is immoral judged by the highest standards, and of certain "instincts," which Edwards considered to be non-moral), thus keeping exclusively for religion the ethics of the heart. Such a demonstration was exceedingly difficult to effect, especially since the secular moralists during the preceding seventy-five years had preempted so much of Christian pietistic teaching.

Edwards understood perfectly well the close parallel between the problems he faced in religion and those under discussion in secular moral thought. He wrote in 1734,

> As with God, so with *good*. There is a twofold understanding or knowledge of Good, that God has made the mind of man capable of. The first, which is merely *speculative* or *notional*: As when a person only speculatively judged, that any thing is, which by the agreement of mankind, is called good or excellent, *viz.* that which is most to general advantage, and between which and reward there is a suitableness. . . . And the *other* is that which consists in the sense of the heart: As when there is a sense of the beauty, amiableness, or sweetness of a thing; so that the heart is sensible of pleasure and delight in the presence of the *idea* of it.

Speculative or notional knowledge of God as of goodness requires only the exercise of the speculative faculty, "or the understanding strictly so called, . . . in distinction from the will or disposition of the soul." A sense of the heart, however, always involves the will or inclination and necessarily leads one into practice, that is, piety toward God and real virtue, not merely detached understanding of what is required without complementary action.[46]

Edwards did not suppose that the structure of motivation in the natural man was different from that in the saint. Sinners and saints both are led by the delectation of the soul in any given case, not by reason. The difference is only that the saint takes pleasure in Christ above all; the natural man in the gratification of the self. Moreover, both have aesthetic sensibility in the broadest meaning; but the natural man's response to beauty, though equally nonintellectual with that of the saint, by lacking divine grace is trapped forever in the

46. *Divine and Supernatural Light*, 12.

perception of material formal relations and cannot ascend to an appreciation and delight in the beauty of the harmony of wills.

Edwards's position on the nature of synteresis may have wavered between the Thomist view, which was intellectualist, and the view of Henry of Ghent and others, which located synteresis in the will. According to this latter view, which originated with Bonaventure, no process of syllogistic reasoning is required for the recognition of the moral law; man is endowed with an instinctive disposition toward its fundamental principles. But in the end, Edwards's conviction about natural conscience was one with St. Thomas's: the moral capacities of the unregenerate person are limited to *knowing* the good, without his having any substantial inclination or relish for it. Edwards spoke of a "rational will" that cannot give rise to consistent holiness or virtue, for it is unable to control the disposition of the soul and therefore is always subject to perversion by lower appetites.

God's Retribution

The concept of synteresis could not alone account for the functioning of conscience. The syllogism of moral self-condemnation via conscience presupposed a middle term that was required for completeness, namely the certain knowledge by the sinner that God will take revenge against transgressors of the law. In an explication of Rom. 2:14–15, Edwards noted that not only must the law be known, so that one's duty is clear, but it must also be apparent in conscience that " 'tis the will of God" that certain things be done and that one "shall incur his displeasure by the contrary."[47] Edwards maintained that natural conscience suggests to every man "the relation and agreement there is between that which is wrong or unjust and punishment." People

47. Miscellanies, no. 533. The sense of obligation created by conscience can be either that which arises from the realization that the moral law is God's will, that He has provided a rule, or that which arises from a rational grasp of the principles of equity and justice. Both notions are present in John Wise, *A Vindication of the Government of New-England Churches* . . . (Boston, 1717), 34–35: "By a Law immutable, Instampt upon his Frame, God has provided a Rule for Men in all their Actions, obliging each one to the performance of that which is Right, not only as to Justice, but likewise as to all other Moral Vertues, the which is nothing but the Dictate of Right Reason founded in the Soul of Man. . . . That which is to be drawn from Mans Reason, . . . when unperverted, may be said to be the Law of Nature; on which account, the Holy Scriptures declare it written on Mens hearts . . . Rom. 2. 14. . . . When we acknowledge the Law of Nature to be the dictate of Right Reason, we must mean that the Understanding of Man is Endowed with such a power, as to be able, from the Contemplation of humane Condition to discover a necessity of living agreeably with this Law: And likewise to find out some Principle, by which the Precepts of it, may be clearly and solidly Demonstrated."

normally expect punishment for their sins and expect that others, too, will be punished when they transgress. So strong is the mental association that develops between crime and punishment that it is "shocking to men's minds," Edwards said, to witness great wrong and injustice going unpunished.

In the twentieth century it has become a trite gibe at religious theism to point out with Freud and others that the image of God is often simply a projection of comforting infantile fantasies. Curiously, Edwards saw this phenomenon quite clearly, but rather than interpreting it as inimical to mature belief in God, he considered such psychological projections one of the deliberate means chosen by God for allowing knowledge of Himself to be received in the world before one gains the assurance furnished by revelation. Men are "naturally averse to thinking that there will be no punishment," Edwards observed, "especially when they themselves are great sufferers by injustice, and have it not in their power to avenge themselves." And this comforting feeling has sustained in the world "among all nations the doctrine of superior power that would revenge iniquity." Along with synteresis, the rational storehouse of fundamental moral law, there is also a "sense of conscience" upholding the notion of God as the "Revenger of evil."[48]

By its very nature, according to Edwards, law includes the threat of severe sanctions if it is breached. Without the threat of punishment one has only "counsel or advice; or rather . . . a request," but not law. An expression of will without the danger of punishment for disobedience lacks "authority."[49] Edwards's God, as is well known, did not rule by love alone. Edwards was not persuaded by the humanitarian tendency of his era to reduce God to loving impotence. An understanding of the undeviating connection between sin and divine punishment was, by his lights, an essential part of the proper and normal functioning of natural conscience.

When speaking of God's justice, Edwards easily slipped into the old-

---

48. Miscellanies, no. 533. Cf. Pufendorf, *De Officio hominis*, trans. Moore, 20: "We have evidence that the social life has been enjoined upon men by God's authority. . . . Hence in the minds of men not entirely corrupt a very delicate sense is born, which convinces them that by sin against the natural law they offend Him who holds sway over the minds of men, and is to be feared even when the fear of men does not impend." It should be observed that Edwards assumed that conscience not only brings self-judgment but also moral judgment of others. One of the ways that the 18th-century notion of the "moral sense" differed from the traditional idea of conscience was that the latter was often explicated in such a way that it seemed to have little function in judging others, whereas the moral sense existed particularly for that purpose.

49. Edwards's comments on the general nature of law in no. 779 of his Miscellanies expressed the traditional understanding. His words are almost identical, for example, to Alexander Hamilton's half century later in *Federalist* no. 15: "It is essential to the idea of a law that it be attended with a sanction; or, in other words, a penalty or punishment for disobedience. If there be no penalty annexed to disobedience, the resolutions or commands which pretend to be laws will, in fact, amount to nothing more than advice or recommendation."

fashioned rhetoric of absolute monarchism, which must have seemed, even to himself, more and more anomalous in mid-eighteenth-century America. The "justice of God obliges him to punish sin," Edwards wrote, for "it belongs to God, as the Supreme ruler of the universality of things, to maintain order and decorum in his kingdom." It "does not become the Sovereign of the world . . . to suffer such a thing as sin, an infinitely uncomely disorder . . . to appear in the world subject to his government, without his making an opposition to it, or giving some public manifestations and tokens of his infinite abhorrence of it."[50] The picture of God as an autocratic deity governing by personal will was out of phase with the development of both politics and science in the eighteenth century. One can see in Edwards's philosophical theology definite adjustments and adaptations that reflected the pressing need at the time to refine the image of God so that it would better conform to Enlightenment preconceptions. In metaphysics, for example, Edwards's idealism and his occasionalist theory of causation made possible an accommodation between his belief in God's personal sustenance of the universe and the idea of a world governed by universal, fixed, mathematically related laws. Although, as we will see, Edwards hardly compromised at all with the humanitarianism and benevolism of the age, he did alter his political theology, so to speak, in that he emphasized more and more the impersonality of the moral laws of the universe, under the influence, it seems, of the teaching of Samuel Clarke. Furthermore, Edwards's vision of the healthy universe roughly paralleled the Lockean conception of the healthy state: both were consensually ordered, though the analogy does not hold much beyond that. Edwards's *mature* political theology resembled a constitutional monarchy rather than an absolute government. The laws were severe, but fixed and intelligible, and not arbitrary. The best citizens consented wholeheartedly to the regime in its entirety. Dissent was crushed unmercifully, as it would be in any ideal kingdom, for instance, Plato's Republic.

One further reflection is necessary. What we have divided into two parts of natural conscience, (1) synteresis, and (2) the individual's sense of God's retribution, were one in function. Synteresis is static, intellectualist, and only superficially internalized. The sense of God's retribution, on the other hand, is actively threatening, voluntaristic in that it reflects God's will, and sufficiently internalized to produce the emotion of guilt.[51]

<hr/>

50. Miscellanies, no. 779, in *The Works of President Edwards in Four Volumes* . . . (New York, 1879), I, 582–611, hereafter cited as *Works*.

51. Edwards's belief that a sense of desert, or a sense of the appropriateness of reward and punishment, was essential even in a system of natural ethics (i.e., a system without God), finds support in A. O. Lovejoy's criticism of David Hume's opinion that ethical judgments are only forms of approbation and disapprobation. When a man calls Hitler wicked, Lovejoy observed, he means something more than "I am very unpleasantly affected when I think of it." The "something

As with the old notion of synteresis, Edwards fairly quickly ceased to speak in terms of man's natural anticipation of God's retribution for wrongs committed. Both of these conceptions had innatist connotations, which were unfashionable after Locke. Early in the seventeenth century, Lord Herbert of Cherbury had listed as one of the five indisputable common notions of humankind that "there are rewards and punishments after this life." For Lord Herbert, as for others, this statement was not so much an article of religious faith as an innate axiom taught by conscience. Edwards moved from this position to that suggested already by Shaftesbury and Clarke of a sense of retribution and desert that was less Hebraic and monarchist and more formally rationalist. Without much elaboration, Shaftesbury, for example, asserted in his *Inquiry Concerning Virtue*: "No creature can maliciously and intentionally do ill without being sensible at the same time that he deserves ill. And in this respect, every sensible creature may be said to have conscience."[52] The theological notion had become a psychological principle.

Conscience and Symmetry

The connection between sin and punishment and, in fact, the functioning of conscience in general, had yet another basis, more sophisticated than either the notion of God's personal vengeance or the legalism of synteresis: namely, the tendency of human beings to be influenced by a sense of balance, symmetry, proportion, reciprocity, and similar formal relationships in their moral judgments. Edwards came to appreciate the value of these concepts for ethical analysis very early, possibly sometime between 1724 and 1726 when he was tutoring at Yale. It is not unlikely that he was influenced by Shaftesbury or a Shaftesburian, though as Leroy Loemker has shown, Neoplatonism, which was an important force in seventeenth-century New England, was imbued with concepts of harmony and order, with analogies drawn in particular to music.[53] John Henry Bisterfeld's ideas seem to have been particularly akin to

---

more" is the conviction that the wicked deserve punishment, and it is the sense of desert that makes ethical judgments distinctive. In fact, to make an ethical judgment and to say that punishment or reward ought not to follow leaves that judgment something less than a moral judgment. This is also the point at which ethical and aesthetic judgments diverge. Joseph Butler's "Dissertation on the Nature of Virtue," appended to his *The Analogy of Religion . . . to the Constitution and Course of Nature* (London, 1736), considered the "sense of good and ill desert" fundamental to moral judgments, but Edwards apparently did not read Butler until the early 1750s.

52. Cf. Basil Willey, *The Seventeenth Century Background: Studies in the Thought of the Age in Relation to Poetry and Religion* (New York, 1950 [orig. publ. London, 1934]), 135. Shaftesbury, *Characteristics*, ed. Robertson, I, 306, also p. 259.

53. Loemker, *Struggle for Synthesis*, 187.

Edwards's, and it is possible that Edwards knew something of him. Bisterfeld was a pupil of Alsted's, whose *Encyclopaedia Scientiarium Omnium* was a standard source in New England,[54] and a model to Adrian Heereboord, who put together a two-volume posthumous edition of Bisterfeld's writings.[55] However, although Heereboord's own books were among the most widely distributed academic texts in early America, one rarely finds Bisterfeld's writings. In any case, Bisterfeld's frequent use of the terms of harmony, *"convenientia," "congruentia," "consensus,"* and *"conspirare,"* was also characteristic of Jonathan Edwards's vocabulary, as Loemker notes, although Heereboord is an equally likely source.[56] In his *Meletemata*, Heereboord advanced the view that all goodness is a matter of "fittingness" or *convenientia*. Before the Creation, God's goodness consisted in His befittingness or harmony with Himself. And the goodness of the Creation lies in its befittingness to God. Thus, man's happiness on earth and his capacity for goodness are part of a larger metaphysical relationship, the essential quality of which is harmony or fittingness.[57]

The earliest record we have of Edwards's interest in this geometrical or aesthetic idea of conscience may be number 39 in his "Notes on the Mind."[58] It reads as follows, with a minor deletion:

Besides the two sorts of Assent of the mind, called *Will* and *Judgment*, there is a third, arising from a sense of the General Beauty and Harmony

54. (Herborn, 1630). See Miller, *New England Mind*, 102–103: With Alsted's encyclopedia, "Cotton Mather said, you can 'make a short Work of all the Sciences,' for it is a veritable 'North-West Passage' to them."

55. *Bisterfeldius Redivivus. Seu Operum Joh: Henrici Bisterfeldii . . . posthumorum*, ed. Adrian Heereboord (The Hague, 1661); also, Bisterfeld, *Philosophiae primae seminarium*, ed. Adrian Heereboord (Leiden, 1657). Cotton Mather referred to Bisterfeld in his *Manuductio ad Ministerium* . . . (Boston, 1726). See Kennerly M. Woody, "Bibliographical Notes to Cotton Mather's *Manuductio ad Ministerium*," *Early American Literature*, Supplement to VI (Spring 1971), 58.

56. Loemker, *Struggle for Synthesis*, 177–203. See in Bisterfeld such statements as the following, quoted by Loemker, p. 192: "Out of the goodness of being flows its convenience, by which one being is congruent, or unitable, with another. . . . From this flows all *society* [i.e., all harmony among things]. . . . This congruence is between all consentient beings." Like Edwards, Bisterfeld believed that the highest reality is the social order of consenting beings, culminating in the Holy Trinity. Physical nature is a pale reflection of this order and harmony of spirit. On virtue Bisterfeld wrote, *"Actio honesta* is that action which is produced with convenience [i.e., fittingness], or which fits congruously into the excellence, nature, and state of things."

57. *Meletemata Philosophica*, 159–160.

58. There is internal evidence that the "Notes on the Mind" correspond roughly to some of the themes in Edwards's Miscellanies, nos. 175 to 235. The "Notes" consist of about 72 entries of greatly varying length and should not be confused with another manuscript, also first published by Dwight, entitled "The Natural History of the Mental World," which was obviously written at least 10 years later, in the late 1730s at the earliest, after Edwards had read more extensively in

of things, which is *Conscience*. . . . These Assents of Will and
Conscience have indeed a common object, which is Excellency. Still
they differ. The one is always General Excellency: that is Harmony,
taking in its relation to the Whole System of beings. The other, that
Excellency which most strongly affects, whether the Excellency be more
general or particular. But the degree wherein we are affected by any
Excellency, is in proportion compounded of the Extensiveness, and the
Intensiveness, of the Excellency.[59]

Edwards's meaning in this rather difficult passage has not been generally
understood. Analysis of it requires some background in metaphysics. According to traditional Scholastic doctrine, the three transcendent aspects of being
are the one, the true, and the good (*unum, verum, and bonum*). Through
intellect and judgment, man knows and assents to being as it is true; through
the will, he assents to being as it is good. All being is true in that it is what it
is; any true proposition must begin with the principle of identity and is thus
grounded in being itself. All being is also good, not only because all of God's
creation and He himself are good by definition, but also because all human
striving, beginning with the struggle for life itself at the moment of birth, is a
striving for the goodness in things, however the good is conceived of. Whatever people desire, no matter what, is sought insofar as it is believed to be
good in some sense. Thus, all being is good as well as true. Finally, the unity
or oneness of being is self-evident since being is the most fundamental
concept the mind can arrive at by which existence itself is unified. These three
"transcendentals," then, are convertible with being because they apply to all
of being, yet each is limited in that each applies to being considered in only
one of its relations, either that of truth, that of goodness, or that of unity.

Man ordinarily relates to being, however, not in terms of universals but in
particular cases, and these transcendental attributes of being are attributes of
individual things also. For along with the concrete properties of things, which
are limited to specific qualities and quantities and are not convertible with
being itself, the individual objects of human consideration partake also of the
transcendentals. When a person confronts an object, in addition to perceiving
where it is in space, its dimensions, its color and uses, it may also be
categorized in terms of the transcendentals of being, that is, in terms of its
goodness, or lack thereof, its truth, and its unity.

In the passage quoted, Edwards's first two "sorts of Assent of the mind"
refer to the familiar teaching that goodness and truth are responded to by man

---

British moral philosophy. It may even have been written in the 1750s. Both manuscripts are now
lost. A copy of the "Natural History" is appended to this volume, for it is an outline of the great
synthetic book in moral philosophy that Edwards never wrote.

59. "Notes on the Mind," no. 39, in Dwight, *Life of Edwards*, 698.

through will and judgment. We desire the good and exercise our will toward it, with or without the specification of intellect; and we exercise our judgment, which is a faculty or power of intellect, in that we require knowledge of reality, or truth, for sanity: that what is, is. Edwards then added a third "assent," which was not traditional, an assent to the "General Beauty and Harmony of things." The specific power of the mind that responds in this case is conscience. It may be deduced from the absent element of the traditional triad of the good, the true, and the one, that conscience responds to being as *one*, as unity. Will and conscience are alike, Edwards noted, in that they both have being itself as an object, which Edwards here calls excellency (being, when considered in its perfect totality, is supreme excellence). But will and conscience also differ in that the will assents to being mainly as it "most strongly affects," that is, as particular things attract it by their individual goodness, whereas conscience remains unmoved by the liveliness of objects and is in constant relation to being only as it is the whole. Thus conscience takes in the whole harmonious system of beings, and is always attuned to the transcendental of unity. The will, too, on occasion may be moved by being in its extensiveness, the good of the whole; but it is also highly susceptible to being in its intensiveness, that is, as represented by particular goods. Because the will is moved by some combination of intensive and extensive aspects of the goodness of being, it cannot serve as a reliable moral criterion. A curious feature of Edwards's analysis is that conscience, which is a moral category, conforms not to the transcendental of goodness, but to that of unity. That ethics shades in this way into ontology is typical of all of Edwards's moral theology. It is a fundamental principle of Edwards's thought (as in Malebranche, Leibniz, and Shaftesbury) that the *whole*, the harmonious system taken as one, has the highest value. For Edwards, the transcendental attribute of being that expresses this supreme value is unity, even more than truth and goodness.

The meaning of "excellency" for Edwards, a term used six times in the brief passage quoted above, has always been difficult to understand, but it is a key concept in Edwards's moral thought.[60] Although the "Notes on the Mind"

60. The word "excellency" was widely used in both secular and theological writing before Edwards, but one does not find it often with quite Edwards's emphasis. Cf. these instances in Shaftesbury, *Characteristics*, ed. Robertson, I, 266–268: "Now as to the belief of a Deity, and how men are influenced by it, we may consider, in the first place, on what account men yield obedience, and act in conformity to such a supreme Being. It must be either in the way of his power, as presupposing some disadvantage or benefit to accrue from him; or in the way of his *excellency* and worth, as thinking it the perfection of nature to imitate and resemble him. . . . If there be a belief or conception of a Deity who is considered as worthy and good, and admired and reverenced as such, being understood to have, besides mere power and knowledge, the highest *excellence* of nature, such as renders him justly amiable to all" (my italics). There are many other instances in Shaftesbury.

contains a lengthy exposition of the term, it is still surrounded by obscurity. Excellency, Edwards posited, "consists in the *Similarness* of one being to another—not merely Equality and Proportion, but any kind of Similarness—thus Similarness of direction." Excellency resembles harmony, symmetry, equality, and proportion, but if one attempts to discover even what underlies the sensory pleasantness or satisfyingness of these relationships, it will be found, according to Edwards, that the common irreducible ingredient can be given no other name but excellency, which appears to be some sort of unity in variety, although Edwards never says this directly. The concept of beauty, which is nearly synonymous with that of excellency, is itself finally reducible to excellency, since the latter, according to Edwards, is the more comprehensive term. The "universal definition" of excellency that Edwards proposed is as follows: "The Consent of Being, or Being's Consent to Entity." Entity in this context may be defined as *positive existence*. "The more the Consent is," Edwards added, "and the more extensive, the greater is the Excellency,"[61] that is, the greater is the perfection and the unity within diversity. The dynamic concept of consent absorbs the mere "similarness" in the first definition. Excellency, which Edwards perhaps intended to rank with the classical transcendental attributes of being, may be defined as the dynamic (that is, the willing or consenting) unity of the diverse elements of existence, God and all of His creation.

In the preface to Alexander Richardson's *Logicians School-Master* (1629, 1657), which students at seventeenth-century Harvard all studied, *Ens*, or being, was distinguished into *ens primum* and *ens à primo*, first being, who is God, and being from a first, which is the entire creation. Edwards's comments on being rarely leave it clear whether he is talking about God, about the creation, or about both together. It seems probable, however, that by the consent of being to being, Edwards had in mind the consent of the creation to God, the Creator, particularly the consent of men and angels, who are the potentially and the actually disruptive elements, and also the consent of created beings to each other. In addition, as we will see, within the Godhead there is a consent of the Persons.

It is remarkable that the concept of "consent," and its general designation as excellency, which Edwards hit upon apparently when he was in his early twenties, would not appear in print until thirty years later in his treatise on

61. "Notes on the Mind," no. 1, in Dwight, *Life of Edwards*, 696. See also p. 697, no. 14: "Excellence, to put it in other words, is that which is beautiful and lovely. That which is beautiful . . . only with respect to itself and a few other things, and not as a part of that which contains all things—the Universe—; is false beauty and a confined beauty. That which is beautiful, with respect to the university of things, has a generally extended excellence and a true beauty." Also no. 64: "Excellency may be distributed into *Greatness* and *Beauty*. The former is the Degree of Being; and the latter is Being's Consent to Being."

True Virtue. In that treatise, true virtue also is defined as the consent of being to being, with the result that, ultimately, in Edwards's mature system, excellency and true virtue become identical. And it is apparent, too, finally that conscience in the highest and most refined sense is consciousness of and consent to excellency, or consciousness of and consent to the perfect unity of being in general, though there will, of course, be degrees of conscientious awareness. As W. S. Morris correctly observed in his study of the young Edwards, in his early unpublished notes Edwards established the basis of morals, psychology, aesthetics, and religion in the one common metaphysical principle of consent to being.[62]

When Edwards was reflecting in his early years on the nature of conscience, the problem of distinguishing precisely and finally between the capacities of the natural man and the regenerate was not yet an acute concern. But in his treatise on *Religious Affections* published in 1746, and in *The Nature of True Virtue*, written during Edwards's last years, this distinction was always present in his mind, and one of his chief aims in the latter book was to demonstrate once and for all the limitations of nature, even after he had acquiesced to much of the psychological optimism of his age. In the early "Notes on the Mind," however, Edwards was not on guard, nor was he especially polemical. Yet there can be no doubt that what he had to say at this stage about conscience pertained in his mind to the moral capacity of all men, not just to those aided by supernatural grace. After all, conscience must to some degree be a universal human possession, otherwise it is not conscience.

The explication of conscience Edwards advanced in number 45 of his early "Notes" (as also in number 39) is largely in naturalistic terms. He stated that conscience is "the Sense the Mind has," however faint or ruined, of God's love for Himself, a love that necessarily includes His entire creation. Conscience is the sense we retain of the "Divine Excellence," especially at those moments when "our idea of that tranquility and peace, which seems to be overspread and cast abroad upon the whole Earth, and Universe, naturally dissolves itself into the idea of a General Love and Delight, everywhere diffused." Or, in somewhat different words, conscience consists in "the Consent of the Perceiving Being [that is, men and angels] to such a General Consent; . . . and the Dissent of [the perceiving being] to a Dissent from Being in general."[63]

But how does this idea explain the pangs of conscience, the reflexive function of conscience as a moral judge and prosecutor in the natural man? Edwards's reasoning is ingenious: it is "naturally agreeable" to men, as higher perceiving beings, to consent to being. (This is much like Malebranche's

---

62. Morris, "Young Edwards," 574.
63. "Notes on the Mind," no. 45, in Dwight, *Life of Edwards*, 701.

positing a basic "natural inclination to the good in general," comparable to the force of gravity in natural bodies.) Similarly, dissent from the great harmony and mutuality of general being is naturally disagreeable. Therefore, when "a particular and restrained love [or consent] overcomes this General Consent, the foundation of that [general] Consent *yet remaining in the nature* exerts itself again, so that there is a contradiction of one consent to another."[64] This "contradiction" of a higher natural principle (or rather the "foundation" in human nature of such a principle) with a lower one—in effect, the contradiction of universal love with particular or restrained private love—is painful and disturbing.[65]

Pain arises when a human being dissents from universal love or from being in general because in consequence of such an act, one is inevitably left with a sense that "Being in general" reciprocally "dissents from him, which is most disagreeable. . . . And as he is conscious of a dissent from Universal Being, and of that Being's dissent from him, wherever he is, he sees what excites horror." Any action or inclination that is against man's "*natural inclination* [my italics] as a Perceiving Being . . . must necessarily cause uneasiness, inasmuch as that natural inclination is contradicted." This uneasiness is the "Disquiet of Conscience." It follows that the simple acceptance of being in general, and the absence of internal "contradiction," bring a degree of reconciliation and the "Peace of Conscience," although one may not altogether lose "a remembrance of past dissentions with nature." This formulation of the nature of conscience appears to be a metaphysical version of the idea that man has a natural awareness of God's intention to punish sin, yet it is clearly an advance over that older idea.

Finally, if one has a sense not only of *not* dissenting but also of positively consenting to being in general, "or Nature," and acting accordingly, "he has a sense that Nature, in general, consents to him." A person then has "not only *Peace*, but *Joy, of Mind*, wherever he is."[66] At the end of this note Edwards indicated unmistakably that he was speaking in purely naturalistic terms, for he observed that "these things are obviously invigorated by the knowledge of God and his Constitution about us, and by the light of the Gospel."[67] "These things," then, do not in themselves depend upon knowledge of God or special

64. *Ibid.* My italics.
65. Cf. Malebranche, *Treatise Concerning the Search after Truth* . . . , trans. T[homas] Taylor (London, 1694), I, Bk. iv, 138–143. There is also a close parallel to the distinction in Shaftesbury between "entire affection," which lives "according to Nature, and the dictates and rules of supreme wisdom" and is "morality, justice, piety, and natural religion," and its contrary, "partial affection." *Characteristics*, ed. Robertson, I, 300ff.
66. "Notes on the Mind," no. 45, in Dwight, *Life of Edwards*, 701–702. Cf. William Ames on the "joy" of good conscience in *Conscience*, Bk. I, chap. 11.
67. "Notes on the Mind," no. 45, in Dwight, *Life of Edwards*, 701–702.

grace; they are merely "invigorated" by them. By the time Edwards started to write his dissertation on *True Virtue*, however, he had come to believe that this logic of consent applied to spiritual processes only, and he treated natural conscience in the more intellectualistic terms of "fitness" and "suitability" rather than "consent," which unlike fitness connotes affectional involvement. In short, it seems that as Edwards gave more thought to differentiating natural and supernatural virtue, he retracted some of his early opinions about conscience. From the perspective of his later work, these early notes on conscience described only the highest spiritual processes, not a universal characteristic of human nature.

The bare outlines, then, of Edwards's early theory of conscience are simple enough. The innate general principle (functionally, though not substantively, resembling synteresis) is the standard by which particular acts of the will are measured. When there is a contradiction with the general law, that is, an infringement or a trespass (in Edwards's terms, dissent), there is a crisis of conscience, self-judgment, conviction, and disquietude.

The underlying structure of Edwards's formulation resembled Natural Law theory but with some important modifications. According to Richard Cumberland, for example, writing in the last quarter of the seventeenth century, moral decisions must always be made with reference to the good of the whole system of which one is a part, and not from a self-centered point of view; and men have a natural awareness of self-censure when they ignore the whole. "He, who, with respect to a like right, determines otherwise in another man's case than in his own, contradicts himself in a most known matter," Cumberland wrote. Such a contradiction "greatly hurts the soundness, peace, and contentment, of the mind in its actions; as uniformity in these matters produces the greatest tranquillity." Cumberland also described the "joy arising from the harmony and agreement of our actions. For it is more pleasing to the mind of man, to observe agreement in itself and its own actions, than in musical notes and geometrical figures."[68] In works by Samuel Clarke and Shaftesbury these same ideas are repeatedly stated. Edwards's contribution at this early stage of his philosophical ethics was to transfer this pattern of reasoning to the ontological level and also to imbue it with the voluntarist idea of consent, rather than to frame it in intellectualist terms.

Some of his inspiration undoubtedly came from Alsted and his disciples, as Loemker has observed. Alsted attributed human knowledge of the transcendentals of being not to a rational process of inference, but to a "universal natural intuition," and he brought secondary transcendentals such as beauty and order into a close relationship "not merely to the intellect, but to the affec-

---

68. Richard Cumberland, *A Treatise of the Laws of Nature*, trans. John Maxwell (London, 1727 [orig. publ. in Latin, 1672]).

tions of men." His follower Bisterfeld asserted similarly to Edwards, "No being is solitary: all being is symbiotic"; "the notion of being united with being is reciprocal"; and "all things are essentially related to other things."[69] None of these notions, moreover, nor Edwards's idea of conscience, was very far removed from the important role given to conscience in the "covenant theology" characteristic of much Calvinist thought in the seventeenth century. Through conscience, according to the Dutch theologian Johan Cocceius, man knows innately that "communion with God is the supreme essential good," and that he must strive for this communion with God by living in accordance with His will. Conscience makes man aware of his covenant with God and informs him that if he acts righteously he will receive God's friendship and fellowship. Conscience bears witness that "God cannot put off those who seek Himself or refuse to satisfy and fulfill a right and holy desire." Thus, conscience reveals man's claim on God's love. Although the process is described in the personalistic or paternalistic terms of a covenant, it may be reduced to the rational principle inherent in all Calvinism that God does not act erratically or unpredictably. The innate knowledge of the fundamentals of moral law with which God endowed man at the Creation are an expression of God's own holiness. For God to turn away man's righteousness would be contradictory.

At the same time, just as conscience assures man of God's support of his righteousness, so it also informs him of the consequences of his dissent from God. Conscience bears witness that by disobedience to God's will man loses the love of God and "covenant fellowship with God."[70] Although it is sometimes assumed that Edwards abandoned covenant theology, his theory of conscience could be interpreted as a continuation of it.

In Malebranche also there are some close parallels, though the French Catholic thinker apparently had relatively little interest in conscience, that is, in the self-censure that inevitably follows from disagreement with the divine order. "That which makes a Man Just," Malebranche wrote, "is that he loves Order, and conforms his Will to it in all things: . . . the Sinner is only so, because he does not approve of Order in all things, and that he would fain have it to be conformable to what he wishes." Ordering is necessary because although all beings in the universe have a necessary existence in God they are

---

69. Loemker, *Struggle for Synthesis*, 141–144.

70. See Heinrich Heppe, *Reformed Dogmatics . . .* , ed. Ernst Bizer, trans. G. T. Thomson (London, 1950), 286–288, hereafter cited as Heppe, *Reformed Dogmatics*. Covenant theology was a rationalist theory disguised as theological voluntarism. Descartes's religious philosophy was, in that respect, similar to it. Interestingly, the Cocceians and the Cartesians in Holland were allies. For a discussion of this affinity, see Thomas McGahagan, "Cartesianism in the Netherlands, 1639–1676: The New Science and the Calvinist Counter-Reformation" (Ph.D. diss., University of Pennsylvania, 1976), 364–374.

not equally perfect. It is evident, therefore, Malebranche said, "that there must be an immutable and necessary Order among them . . . , by reason of the relations of Perfection [*Edwards would say excellency*] which are among the same Beings." God's love for Himself, therefore, is an ordered love, in that He loves better in Himself (which is to say in the universe as a whole) that which includes more perfection than that which includes less. And this same "immutable Order which has the force of a Law in respect to God himself, has visibly the force of a Law in relation to us. Order is known to us, and our natural love suits itself to it, when we look into our selves, and when our Senses and Passions leave us free: In a word, when our Self-love does not corrupt our natural Love."[71]

Edwards may have derived his vision of the dynamic unity that informs conscience from his reading of Malebranche, who maintained that God has imprinted in the hearts of all men a natural and invincible inclination toward Himself. Some years before Newton had published a word, Malebranche conceived of the spiritual universe as analogous to the gravitational motion of corporeal bodies. "God cannot Will the Existence of any Mind which cannot love him," Malebranche wrote, "because he cannot Will that any Mind should not love that which is most Amiable, or love it more than that which is less Amiable. . . . Thus it is requisite that a Natural Love should carry us to God, since it comes from him; and that there is nothing that can stop the Motions of it, only God himself who imprinted them. Every[body's] Will therefore necessarily follows the Motions of this Love. The Righteous and Wicked, the Happy and the Damned, Love God with this Love." The inevitable love to God that all men have innately is the same, Malebranche said, as their "Natural Inclination . . . to Good in General," a concept that is close to Edwards's idea of conscience, because it goes beyond mere knowledge of God as the ultimate good and speaks in terms of a motion, an inclination, a consent to Him.

Malebranche also posited that "the Love of Good in General" is the underlying principle of our particular affections, "since that Love really is nothing but our Will." In other words, as in Edwards, the one term "will" could be used to describe both a basic inclination of the soul toward the highest general good and also inclinations toward particular limited choices. For even those lesser loves that detain and distract the soul in its perpetual quest for God are chosen only because they are images of the highest good. The power of love itself comes only from God, though men abuse it by misplacing it on finite and false goods.[72]

The next step for Edwards, however, as we have already remarked, was to

71. *Search after Truth*, trans. Sault, 466–468.
72. *Ibid.*, Bk. III, chap. iv, 20–22.

deny that love and consent are forces in natural conscience, or the conscience of the unregenerate, and to treat it instead as primarily an intellectual reflexive process. The most important influence on him in the formulation of this doctrine was probably Samuel Clarke. But before we turn to Clarke it is necessary first to bring in three other elements in Edwards's early theorizing about ethics, namely, his conceptions of beauty, of the Trinity, and of nature.

Beauty

The moral elements in Edwards's theory of natural conscience must be clearly distinguished from the purely aesthetic, although it is easy to slip into the fallacy of believing that beauty in some sense is the ultimate standard of conscience for Edwards, at least for the regenerate if not for those in a natural state. Does he not say directly that "Excellence . . . is that which is beautiful and lovely?"[73] And indirectly the connection between excellence, virtue, and beauty is made a number of times. A recent influential study of Edwards's thought asserts that "beauty is the reality in terms of which the Divine Being and the moral and religious life of human beings as well as the order of the universal system of being, both moral and natural, can best be understood."[74] Beauty, this author holds, is for Edwards "the highest good and the measure of goodness."[75] The notion is attractive and simplifying, but it erroneously biases Edwards's metaphysics.

In the "Notes on the Mind," written early in his life, Edwards did not discuss beauty as extensively as he did later in *True Virtue*; missing in particular from the early work was the distinction Edwards drew later between "spiritual" and "secondary" beauty. Nevertheless, Edwards did establish in rudimentary form in his early writings a hierarchy of beauty that is comparable to the later distinction. The secret of all physical beauty, Edwards argued, "the beautiful shape of flowers, the beauty of the body of man, and of the bodies of other animals," and even the beauty known through the sense of hearing, is the underlying consent of being to being. Thus, when a "perceiving Being," or a person, is pleased by beauty, this state of "pleasedness" always arises, Edwards believed, from the perceiving being's sense of the consenting relations between things. The beauty even in material things, then, is

---

73. "Notes on the Mind," no. 14, in Dwight, *Life of Edwards*, 697.

74. Delattre, *Beauty and Sensibility in the Thought of Edwards*, 1.

75. *Ibid.*, 79. Delattre's assertion is somewhat qualified by the following comments on the same page: "It is not necessary to insist that beauty is somehow higher than goodness in Edwards' vision of things." But the author does not concede much, for he concludes with the words: "And yet the principles of beauty do emerge as the more central and critical ones," and it is "ultimately beauty that is the measure of goodness, and not the other way around."

a form of society and is reducible to the idea of consent. Consent itself, however, is a *moral* potentiality of souls, not an aesthetic property. Edwards was emphatic in maintaining that when speaking of "Excellence in Bodies" he was *"borrowing"* [my italics] the word "consent" from "Spiritual things." In its "prime and proper sense," being's consent to being refers to the relations between spirits, Edwards asserted. For "there is no other proper consent but that of *Minds*, even of their Will; which, when it is of Minds towards Minds, it is *Love*, and when of Minds towards other things, it is Choice."[76] It seems clear that the consenting relation of minds described here is not in itself essentially aesthetic, even though this relation may underlie beauty. Thus, the phenomenon of beauty is derivative from moral or spiritual relations; beauty is not itself an ultimate category. The moral perfection of willing (or loving or consenting to) the diversity of existence created and unified by God (called by Edwards excellency) is the primary quality in Edwards's ethical ontology, not beauty.

Any doubts one may have about the dependency of beauty upon moral virtue, and about the unquestionable primacy of the latter, are dispelled in *Religious Affections*. "The true beauty and loveliness of all intelligent beings," Edwards wrote, "does primarily and most essentially consist in their moral excellency or holiness." Without *moral* perfections, all of the *natural* perfections of angels, for example, their strength and knowledge, would make them no more lovely than devils. " 'Tis moral excellency alone, that is in itself, and on its own account, the excellency of intelligent beings: 'tis this that gives beauty to, or rather is the beauty of their natural perfections and qualifications. . . . Holiness [or moral excellency] is in a peculiar manner the beauty of the divine nature."[77]

The dynamic, conscious consent or love that higher beings (such as humans and angels) feel toward one another may, *by analogy*, be conveniently used for understanding aesthetics, Edwards explained, because "sensible things, by virtue of the harmony and proportion that is seen in them, carry the appearance of perceiving and willing being." Physical objects, whether in nature or made by man, "show at first blush, the action and governing of understanding and volition."

> The Notes of a tune or the strokes of an acute penman, for instance, are placed in such exact order, having such mutual respect, one to another, that they carry with them, into the mind of him that sees or hears, the conception of an understanding and will exerting itself in these appearances; and were it not that we, by reflection and reasoning, are led to an

76. "Notes on the Mind," no. 45, in Dwight, *Life of Edwards*, 696–699.

77. *Religious Affections*, ed. Smith, 257. Delattre, I believe, did not take note of these definitive statements by Edwards.

extrinsic intelligence and will, that was the cause, it would seem to be in the Notes and Strokes themselves. They would appear like a society of so many perceiving beings, sweetly agreeing together. I can conceive of no other reason why *Equality* and *Proportion*, should be pleasing to him that perceives, but only that it has an appearance of *Consent*.[78]

These comments reveal that for Edwards all that is ordinarily meant by "beauty" was to be understood only as a *symbolic* counterpart to a higher kind of correspondence, that of wills. For, obviously, "sensible things" cannot really consent one to another except by "equality or by likeness or by proportion," Edwards observed. But the resulting beauty, nonetheless, is the "image of mutual love."[79]

The Trinity

The best model, perhaps, by which to comprehend Edwards's conception of excellency and the "consent of being to being" is the idea of the Trinity. The Trinity for Edwards was never an inert dogma. His entire moral theology is logically deducible from his theory of the Trinity alone, although unquestionably it worked the other way, too, and some of Edwards's insights into moral psychology contributed to his understanding of the Trinity. It is possible that Edwards arrived at a profound understanding of the Trinity only after formulating the salient ideas of his moral thought, but in terms of logical order in Edwards's system, the Trinity comes first.[80]

Edwards's point about the Trinity as an example for ethics is simple: there can be no more perfect model of the consent of being to being. The Trinity, of course, is infinitely excellent and beautiful. Edwards's reflections on the Trinity are rich and ingenious; only a small part of them can be referred to here. The three persons of the Godhead are made up of God, His idea of Himself, and the love or delight that God feels in the idea of Himself. On each of these Edwards expounded at length. What is particularly relevant here is one aspect of the defense of the Trinity that Edwards introduced into his Miscellanies in the early 1720s. "It appears," Edwards stated, that "there

78. "Notes on the Mind," no. 63, in Dwight, *Life of Edwards*, 698–699. Cf. Shaftesbury, *Characteristics*, ed. Robertson, II, 60–69, for similar remarks.

79. "Notes on the Mind," no. 1, in Dwight, *Life of Edwards*, 698. In terms of typology, the consent underlying all beauty is only a "type" or shadow; moral excellency is the antitype or substance.

80. For an extended early discussion, see Edwards's Miscellanies, no. 94, printed in Townsend, ed., *Philosophy of Edwards*, 252–258. See also, George P. Fisher, ed., *An Unpublished Essay of Edwards on the Trinity, with Remarks on Edwards and His Theology* (New York, 1903).

must be more than a unity in infinite and eternal essence, otherwise the goodness of God can have no perfect exercise." For to be perfectly good "is to incline to and delight in making another happy, in the same proportion as [one] is happy [oneself]; that is, to delight as much in communicating happiness to another, as in enjoying of it himself." In other words, the goodness of God absolutely requires an object, or better, a correspondent. But it is impossible that God could incline to communicate happiness to any mere finite being to the same degree that He inclines to His own happiness. And yet as a perfect being He must be exercising perfect goodness in some way. Therefore, Edwards concludes, God must have "the fellowship of a person equal with himself." Indeed, Edwards wrote, "No reasonable creature can be happy . . . without society and communion; not only because he finds something in others that is not in himself, but because he delights to communicate himself to another. This cannot be because of our imperfection, but because we are made in the image of God; for the more perfect any creature is, the more strong this inclination. . . . Jehovah's happiness consists in communion, as well as the creature's."[81] The Trinity is the very model of a morally ideal human society, with perfectly mutual communication of happiness, love, and delight.[82]

In another note in his Miscellanies, written shortly after the one quoted just above, the connection of the Trinity to the doctrine of consent is confirmed. God, Edwards wrote, as He is infinitely perfect and happy, also has infinite

---

81. Miscellanies, no. 96. According to Heppe, *Reformed Dogmatics*, 106, most Reformed theologians rejected efforts at describing the Trinity by way of similes. Edwards was thus an exception, although the tradition went back to Augustine and Richard of St. Victor. (See, e.g., the treatment in Anders Nygren, *Agape and Eros*, rev. ed., trans. Philip S. Watson [Philadelphia, 1953], 541–542, 629–630, 654.) Two of Edwards's predecessors in this type of speculation were Melanchthon and Bartolomaeus Keckermann, and Edwards's description of the Persons is very close to that in Keckermann's *Systema S[acro] S[anctae] Theologiae* . . . (Geneva, 1611), 72. George Cheyne's *Philosophical Principles of Religion* . . . , Pt. II (London, 1716, 1725), 128–129, contained speculation on the representations of the Trinity in nature, which were cited by Cotton Mather in *The Christian Philosopher* . . . (London, 1721) and may have been known to Edwards. But that Edwards published very little of his philosophizing on the Trinity, confining his thoughts to private manuscripts, is not surprising given Peter van Mastricht's strong denunciation of such exercises: "The dogma of the Trinity is the basis of the whole Christian faith: hence, if it is resolved into reason, it thereby degenerates from faith into philosophy; no natural reason can be set up which impregnably concludes that God is therefore one in essence, trine in persons." Mastricht reviewed the various previous attempts at such systematizing and then declared himself one with Thomas Aquinas in holding that all such attempts of reason "derogate from faith." Heppe, *Reformed Dogmatics*, 108.

82. In the Aristotelian formulation, the human inclination to live in society was a sign of incompleteness, a deficiency. One of the perfections of Aristotle's God was His complacency in solitude. For Edwards, man's sociality is not a weakness or imperfection but one more way in which man is made in God's image.

love, for love is "the perfection as well as the happiness of a spirit." God must have an object for His infinite love. And we know, according to Edwards, that "all love arises from the perception, either of consent to being in general or a consent to that being that perceives." God's infinite love, therefore, can only be toward infinite-love-to-being-in-general, or toward infinite love or consent to Him. Yet these are the same, in fact, "because God is the general and proper entity of all things." It is necessary, then, that "that object which God infinitely loves must be infinitely and perfectly consenting and agreeable to Him."[83] In sum, "one alone cannot be excellent, inasmuch as, in such a case, there can be no consent."[84] God's excellence requires that there be in Him a plurality, otherwise there can be no consent, and harmonious mutual consent is the essence of excellency.

Conscience, then, in the highest sense, is not only some kind of mental awareness of excellency, or of the consent of being to being, but also, implicitly, an instinctive awareness of the Trinity, which is the ultimate paradigm of excellency and mutual consent. Edwards later denied that this notion of conscience applies to the capacities of unregenerate persons, that is, those lacking in saving grace, yet it may be correct to say that even on the natural level of existence there is implicitly throughout a person's life an innate and instinctive craving for participation in the Trinity. When one acts discordantly with its inner law, one is conscience stricken. When, in conformity with the intrinsic excellency of the Trinity, one loves being in general, one may experience the joy of real peace.

The Morality of Nature

In order to plumb deeper the character of human awareness of the divine order of things, an awareness that underlies natural conscience, we must recognize, too, that the entire physical universe had moral overtones for Edwards, as it did for many other eighteenth-century philosophers and theologians. In Edwards's case, of course, the relation between the physical world and the continuous creative activity of God was not simply a matter of analogy. There

83. Miscellanies, no. 117, printed in Townsend, ed., *Philosophy of Edwards*, 258. Some of these early notes were incorporated into Edwards's "Dissertation on the End for Which God Created the World," published 30 years later.

84. Miscellanies, no. 117, printed in Townsend, ed., *Philosophy of Edwards*, 258. Here, as in so many other places in Edwards's work, one thinks of Emerson: "Nothing is quite beautiful alone; nothing but is beautiful in the whole. A single object is only so far beautiful as it suggests this universal grace. . . . Beauty in nature is not the ultimate. It is the herald of inward and eternal beauty, and is not a solid and satisfactory good." Emerson, *Nature* (Boston, 1836), in Brooks Atkinson, ed., *The Complete Essays and Other Writings of Ralph Waldo Emerson* (New York, 1940), 13.

is an actual metaphysical connection between the perceived world and divine activity, explicable in terms of Edwards's philosophical idealism. "When we behold a beautiful body, a lovely proportion, a beautiful harmony of features of face, delightful airs of countenance and voice, and sweet motion and gesture," he wrote in 1724, "we are charmed with it, not under the notion of a corporeal, but a mental beauty."[85] A statue with all of these same characteristics would not impress us in the same way, Edwards maintained. "We should not fall entirely in love with the image, if we knew certainly that it had no perception or understanding." Missing in the statue would be the agreement of physical perfections with mental. Similarly, there is a "consent between the beauty of the skies, trees, fields, flowers, etc. and spiritual excellencies, though the agreement be more hid, and requires a more discerning, feeling mind to perceive it. . . . These have their airs, too, as well as the body or countenance of man, which have a strange kind of agreement with such and such mental beauties." For the Son of God created the world to "communicate himself in an image of his own excellency," which He does, not only to intelligent perceiving beings who are capable themselves of becoming "proper images of his excellency," but He communicates also "a sort of shadow or glimpse of his excellencies to bodies, which . . . are but the shadows of being, and not real beings." In some respects the union between the mental or ideal world and physical nature is more perfect than is the corresponding union in man of mind and body. For though the beauties of face and sweet airs in men and women "are not always the effect of corresponding excellencies of mind" (we are often deceived by a beautiful face), "the beauties of nature are really emanations, or shadows, of the excellencies of the Son of God."[86] Nature, unlike man, does not deceive us—a typically Romantic conception. Yet Edwards did not generally think like a Romantic, one who opposed unsullied nature to human failing.

To apprehend or sense in all fullness that the created universe is but an

85. Miscellanies, no. 108. Cf. Shaftesbury, *Characteristics*, ed. Robertson, II, 127–144. A superb exposition of this important union of natural and moral philosophy is Earl R. Wasserman, "Nature Moralized: The Divine Analogy in the Eighteenth Century," *ELH: A Journal of English Literary History*, XX (1953), 39–76.

86. Miscellanies, no. 108. Cf. Malebranche, *A Treatise of Nature and Grace*, bound into *Search after Truth*, trans. Taylor, 6–7: "Jesus Christ is the Model by which we are made. . . . We were fram'd after His Image and Similitude, and have nothing comely in us any farther than we are the Draft and *Ectypon* of Him. . . . We judge of the Perfection of a Work by its Conformity with the Idea afforded us by Eternal Wisdom: For there is nothing Beautiful or Amiable, but as related to Essential, Necessary, and Independent Beauty. Now that Intelligible Beauty, being made sensible, becomes even in this capacity the Rule of Beauty and Perfection. Therefore all Corporeal Creatures ought to have the same Thoughts and the same Inclinations as the Soul of *Jesus*, if they would be agreeable to those who see nothing Beautiful, nothing Amiable, save in what is conformable to Wisdom and Truth."

emanation of God's idea of Himself, one needs spiritual assistance through grace, and we are not concerned here with the special experiences of the regenerate. Still, Edwards, like any Shaftesburian, in his early writings accepted that natural euphoric transports alone could convey an appreciation of the harmony of the Whole. One of the earliest entries in Edwards's Miscellanies seems to echo Shaftesburian strains: "The greatness, distance and motion of this great universe, has almost an omnipotent power upon the imagination; the blood will even be chilled with the vast idea. . . . When we think of the sweet harmony of the parts of the corporeal world, it fills us with such astonishment that the soul is ready to break."[87] Edwards went on to insist in this piece that such corporeal wonders omnipotently breaking in upon the imagination remain "worthless, except as they conduce to true and real greatness and excellency, and manifest the power and wisdom of God," for the "vast expanse, immense distance, prodigious bulk and rapid motion" of the universe is "trivial and childish greatness" in comparison with "spiritual greatnesses." In short, one must never lose sight of the excellencies of spirit of which the physical world is but a shadowy copy. Nonetheless, it was the very power of the natural experience that demanded Edwards's depreciation of it in comparison to spiritual understanding. The significance for our immediate purposes of this natural awe of the harmonious order of the universe is that it is one of the ways that mundane conscience may be informed of the great tendency of things. The holy man or the saint differs from the natural man in that he is truly and literally attuned to the harmony of the spheres. In contrast to the unregenerate, the saint "distinguishes as a musical ear." His holiness consists in inner "spiritual harmony; and whatever don't agree with that, as a base to a treble, the soul rejects."[88] But no such perfect pitch forms

---

87. Miscellanies, no. 42. The American Samuel Johnson's first recorded reading of Shaftesbury was specifically the second volume of the *Characteristics*, or the treatise known as "The Moralists," which was the work of Shaftesbury's that was most appealing and least offensive to orthodox Christians. It is unlikely that Edwards could have read all of the *Characteristics* and not have been disturbed by its skepticism and urbanity. But he may well have read volume two, and the early reference in his manuscript notes to the advantage of writing dialogues for philosophical presentation, which refers to Shaftesbury, was probably a reference to "The Moralists," Shaftesbury's great philosophical dialogue. In "The Moralists" there are many passages closely akin to Edwards's thinking. For example: "Whatever in Nature is beautiful or charming is only the faint shadow of that first beauty." "Nothing surely is more strongly imprinted on our minds, or more closely interwoven with our souls, than the idea or sense of order and proportion." "I am resolved to enter again into cool reason with you and ask if you admit for proof what I advanced yesterday upon that head, 'of a universal union, coherence, or sympathising of things'?" To which is answered, "By force of probability . . . , you overcame me. Being convinced of a consent and correspondence in all we saw of things, I considered it as unreasonable not to allow the same throughout." *Characteristics*, ed. Robertson, II, 126, 63, 107.

88. Miscellanies, no. 141. For an erudite discussion of the background of this traditional comparison between metaphysics, morals, and music, see Leo Spitzer, *Classical and Christian Ideas*

part of the endowment of merely natural conscience, which must follow an imperfect score with imperfect hearing. Precisely lacking in natural, or unredeemed, men and women is the "beautiful symmetry and proportion" of soul that affords a near perfect correspondence to the moral character of the universe.[89] Yet despite these limitations, Edwards sometimes appears to have believed, as did Emerson a century later, that there is a moral message for every man, not just the regenerate, in the structure of physical nature.

Clarke

Edwards was profoundly indebted, I believe, to Samuel Clarke above all for providing him with an up-to-date intellectualist theory of ethics that accounted for the moral understanding of the natural man. After Edwards read Clarke there is a detectable shift in his thinking. From early in his career Edwards believed that the religious life, or the truly moral life, is centered in the affections. Natural men, too, may be emotionally moved by religion and virtue, but they are guided ultimately by mercenary considerations—fear of punishment and hope of reward—not by real love of God and hatred of sin as an offense against God. The countless subterfuges of self-love determine the conduct of natural men, making their motivations different from those of the regenerate. But leaving aside these forms of motivation that could dissemble true virtue, Clarke's Boyle lectures showed Edwards how one could explain almost everything else about the natural moral life in purely intellectualist terms. Thus, the natural *understanding* of unregenerate persons could be expanded indefinitely—this was after all part of the rational structure of the universe—but still be interpreted as essentially non-moral, a form of natural knowledge rather than of moral character.

Previous interpretations of Edwards's thought have not given sufficient attention to the rationalism with which he imbued the universe and God *at the level of nature*. The better-known sentimentalism in Edwards's thinking, those areas where his motivational psychology appears to be so much like Hutcheson's, for example, in his later writings applies almost exclusively to the realms of grace.

As we have already noted, in Edwards's analysis there is a perfect parallel between the two basic types of religious experience and the two basic types of moral experience. On the one side, in religion, are book knowledge, observances, theological principles, speculative notions, and other products and

---

of World Harmony: Prolegomena to an Interpretation of the Word "Stimmung," ed. Anna Granville Hatcher (Baltimore, 1963).

89. *Religious Affections*, ed. Smith, 365.

exercises of the understanding or intellect; on the other side, there is the inward religious life, which is a matter of dispositions, inclinations, affections, and, in sum, what Edwards called the "sense of the heart." In different terms, the division may be understood as that between ratiocinative and practical religious knowledge, with the latter necessarily God-given. In ethics the situation is exactly the same. The natural man is capable of a high degree of moral understanding, of comprehension of the truth of the basic propositions of ethics, and even of assent to them up to a point. The rational structure of God's moral universe is manifested in the mind of man, as Clarke assumed. True virtue, however, is not a matter of "assent," Edwards said, but of "consent," that is, of dispositions, affections, and sense knowledge that can occur only when one has been touched by the Spirit. Propositional knowledge, natural conscience, the logic of contradiction, any utilitarian computations, are of a much lower order of moral perception and no more to be considered representative of true virtue than mere conversancy with Scriptures, however detailed and knowledgeable, would be representative of true religion.

This parallel between Edwards's religious thought and his ethics is very apparent in number 539 of his Miscellanies, which concerns principally the function of the means of grace, otherwise known as "works," in the quest for salvation. Calvinists were perennially faced with this question: Since grace is not attainable directly through means or works, what is the role or purpose of means? Edwards responded to the problem very solidly. He noted, first, that outward means can usefully "supply the mind with notions or speculative ideas of the things of religion"; second, they may have an "effect upon meer natural reason in a measure to gain the assent of the judgment"; and third, they may have an effect "upon the natural principles of heart to give in a degree a sense of the natural good or evil of those things that the mind has a notion or speculative idea of and so may accordingly move the heart with fear and desire, etc." All three reasons have applicability to the question of the relation between academic knowledge of ethics and a moral life. The third justification suggests in particular the potential of a crossover from understanding to affect, but the resulting affections are only fear and desire, not love and hate. One may *desire* to be saved, in the sense that one would like to be so blessed in the future, and yet lack a saving love in the heart.

Once a person is genuinely moved by a practical love of virtue, or love of God, rather than fear, divine infusion *must* be assumed to have occurred. After such an infusion, one's acquired background in purely intellectual growth becomes extremely useful. The prior intellectual development makes the "actings of the soul . . . greater and more suitable" than they would have been without it. Edwards clearly was no seventeenth-century "enthusiast." The new principles of heart, whether one is talking about holiness or moral virtue, add no specific content to the mind. Knowledge either preexists the conversion or is subsequently acquired in the conventional way. Means are important, Edwards said, because without means, "there could be no opportunity for grace to act, there could be no matter for grace to act upon. God gives grace immediately, but he doesn't give immediately and by inspiration those ideas and speculative notions that are the matter that grace acts upon."[90]

With this basic division established for both religion and ethics, Edwards could freely expand on either side of the equation, the natural or the gracious, provided the proper place of each was recognized. But here, too, he sometimes confused his listeners. After reading Clarke, Edwards in his personal notes began to reflect on the predominantly "natural" fittingness of certain relations between God and man, particularly justification and reprobation. His goal apparently was to show how the natural order and congruity of the universe provides a rational foundation for religious and moral principles that is logically independent of God's providential judgment. Of course, in one sense this rational order is not truly an independent foundation, or truly independent of God's special judgment, since it is all part of the creation and, thus, from the beginning is part of God's deliberately chosen design. Yet even with this qualification, Edwards's notes reveal that the rationalism of these formulations troubled those he communicated them to, for the sovereign will of God seemed greatly minimized in Edwards's reasoning.[91]

Beginning in number 647 of his Miscellanies, which was composed about 1734, Edwards spoke of two different types of fitness for a particular state: moral and natural. (The distinction was, of course, not original with Edwards.) It was Protestant dogma that no man was *morally* fitted for salvation. "Whatever qualifications, therefore, . . . by which we are justified or saved . . . must be understood as natural fitness." A natural fitness exists, Edwards wrote, when there is "a good natural agreeableness or accord between the person or his qualifications and the state; or that there is a good capacity for the state, or that he is so qualified for such a state that there will be . . . good effects of his being in such a state, or such as will render it of good and not ill

---

90. "Inspiration" for Edwards, and generally in the 18th century, meant the infusion of substantive notions without any rational foundation, and was usually used pejoratively. Those who claimed "inspiration" were dangerous antinomians and enthusiasts in Edwards's eyes.

91. Some of Edwards's ideas on natural fitness were presented in his *Discourses on Various Important Subjects* . . . (Boston, 1738), for which he seems to have received some criticism. Clarke's influence is manifest: "The wisdom of God" is apparent in the constitution of the universe, "so that those things are established to be done that are fit to be done" and things are connected in his constitutions "that are agreeable one to another." Men are justified because it is "a fit" thing "that such should be justified" (p. 11). Another 20 years passed before Edwards was able to pen a definitive commentary on the balance of natural law and special providences in God's rule. This was no. 1263 of his Miscellanies, which assumes a gradation between so-called "arbitrary" actions and regular actions in the constitution of the universe. See below, pp. 93–103.

consequence for him to be in such a state." He noted that often in "secular affairs" we speak of persons as fit or unfit for some state "when 'tis no moral but some natural fitness" that we mean. Edwards continued to develop this distinction in many subsequent notes. "When it is said Forgive and ye shall be forgiven Blessed are the merciful for they shall obtain mercy, . . . There is no necessity of supposing that 'tis out of respect to the moral fitness there is between one that forgives and a being forgiven, or between one that shews mercy and receiving mercy." It is not the special moral merit or worthiness of forgiving someone that *earns* divine forgiveness in return. Rather, "there is a natural fitness and suitableness between these things. 'Tis acknowledged that God has a respect to a natural suitableness between the subject and the gift. In a person's forgiving of injuries there is a special manifestation of a natural suitableness and concord between his soul and the benefit of forgiveness."[92]

Many ostensibly moral relationships, then, may be understood in natural terms, Edwards argued, natural in the sense that they do not require description in ethical terms and are actually sub-moral, on the order of physical relationships in nature, which are governed by universal laws of regular occurrence. Since Edwards had long been an occasionalist, he was not bothered by problems of cause and effect in these relationships.[93] The reward for good works and the punishment of sin are not the consequence of God's love for particular acts, but of His impersonal love for order, for fixed relationships, for beauty and harmony. The constitution of the universe is a testimony, Edwards said, to God's "love of order," for He "delights in order and not confusion." The first assumption above, that God rewards particular acts, erroneously "supposes this divine constitution to [be] a manifestation of his

92. Miscellanies, no. 670. No. 647 of Edwards's Miscellanies contains almost a direct quote from Clarke's *Discourse Concerning the Unchangeable Obligations of Natural Religion* (1706), 47–48. It is difficult, of course, to show the direct influence of Clarke on Edwards. I treat the frequent recurrence of the terms "suitability" and "fittingness" or "fitness" as fairly reliable clues in the early 18th century to Clarke's influence. On the other hand, in the 1640s Thomas Shepard was preaching as follows: How does a man see Christ? " 'Tis [as] in marriage, there is a respect to Beauty and feature, and that draws. Now a woman some times appears to one so, that though Portion be great, etc., yet he cannot like[;] another can because God hath a hand in it, and what fits the fancy, that's beauty: there is a sutableness every way. So Christ is presented with a rich Portion to many, and yet they cannot like, cannot see a Beauty, because they cannot see a fitness and sutablenesse to them, and for them: another man can, because he sees a fitnesse and sutablenesse in the Lord Jesus for him." *The Parable of the Ten Virgins* . . . (London, 1660), 77.

93. Cf., for example, Miscellanies, no. 629: "In natural things means of effects in metaphisical strictness are not the proper causes of the effects, but only occasions[.] God produces all effects but yet he ties natural events to the operation of such means or causes them to be consequent on such means according to fixed, determinate, and unchangeable rules which are called the laws of nature." For the dispersion of occasionalism after Descartes in other thinkers besides Malebranche, who was by far the most famous occasionalist, see Randall, *Career of Philosophy*, I, 403–406, and n. 104, below.

regard to the beauty of the act of faith"; the second, correctly, "only supposes it to be a manifestation of his regard to the beauty of that order there [is] in uniting those things that have a natural agreement and congruity the one with the other."[94] Thus, God does not reward the act of faith specifically in itself; rather, He has so constituted the world that the act of faith is particularly suitable, fit, and orderly and thus normally receives a reward.

Of course, a specifically moral order exists, too, in addition to the natural rational order, though it is best discussed with reference to grace and supernature, for it is only in that context that it emerges clearly. The true moral order is not as obviously governed by fixed laws, and it presupposes the natural order of the universe in the same way that a miracle presupposes nature governed by regular laws. Authentically "moral" as opposed to merely "natural" relations occur relatively infrequently between God and man, just as saints are rare individuals in the midst of thousands of merely conscientious or "good" men and women. "A moral suitableness or unsuitableness includes a natural, but a natural don't include a moral," Edwards wrote.[95]

The connection between these theological considerations and the conscience of unregenerate persons is close. The natural man, after all, is not assisted by special grace; he is not a consenting member of the universe of saints all of whom are infused with divine love, which is the only true moral order for Edwards. Yet the world is governed by a natural order as well, not only in physics and astronomy, but also in morals where there are fixed congruities. The mind of man, in traditional rationalist theory, has access to these natural laws of morality, which sufficiently explains the grasp of conscience. The mind of man, Samuel Clarke held, "naturally and necessarily Assents to the eternal law of Righteousness." "Virtue and true Goodness, Righteousness and Equity, are things so truly noble and excellent, so lovely and venerable in themselves, and so necessarily approve themselves to the Reason and Conscience of Men," that all men commend them in others, even if in practice they allow themselves to be led away from the strict path of virtue.[96] For Clarke, however, this intellectual system was the zenith of

94. Miscellanies, no. 712. For Malebranche on God's love of order, see pp. 78–79, above, and pp. 341–345, below.

95. Ibid.

96. Clarke, *Discourse Concerning the Unchangeable Obligations of Natural Religion* (1706), 75–76. This was Clarke's second series of Boyle lectures. The earliest date that we can be sure Edwards read Clarke's *Discourse* is 1734. However, Clarke's work was so famous and so often discussed that the main ideas could have come to the New England philosopher from a dozen different sources. We know that Cotton Mather first heard of Clarke's *Discourse* in an abridgment in the Jan. and Feb. 1706 issues of the *History of the Works of the Learned: or, an Impartial Account of Books Lately Printed in All Parts of Europe* (London, 1699–1711). See Fiering, "The Transatlantic Republic of Letters," *WMQ*, 3d Ser., XXXIII (1976), 654n. The commonplace book of Nicholas Sever, a Harvard tutor in the first decade of the 18th century, contains summaries of Clarke's two published Boyle lectures that may have been recorded as early as 1708. Even so

the moral life; for Edwards it is all pre-moral, comparable to "works" or "means" in the religious life. But the entire rationalist structure was available for Edwards to borrow for his own ends.

The proposition that "suffering is suitable and answerable to the quality of sinful dispositions and actions," or that it is "suitable that they that will evil and do evil, should receive evil in proportion to the evil that they do or will," described for Edwards not only a natural process in the universe, one of God's laws, but also a clear declaration of intellectual conscience. "There is nothing that men know sooner, after they come to the exercise of their reason, than that, when they have done wickedness, they deserve punishment." Both Christians and heathens have such an awareness, Edwards believed, which he once described, in a memorable phrase, as "a sense of obligation to punishment."[97] The question of whether such innate principles truly exist was never an important problem for Edwards. He was content, it seems, to rely on the authority of Clarke (and perhaps other reasoners like Clarke both before and after him) to uphold the validity of conscience in this sense.

The adoption of Clarke's theories as a sufficient explanation of natural conscience is evident in Edwards's work because after Edwards had read Clarke he never recurred to using the logic of consent as a description of the processes of conscience in the natural man. Edwards came to believe not only that the life of true religion and true virtue is centered in the affections, but also that consent to being or holy love (which are obviously affects) are to be found exclusively in the spiritually reborn. Whatever ostensibly moral powers are manifest in natural persons are all reducible to the following five natural capacities, either in combination or singly: intellectualist conscience, which Clarke described; the perception of "secondary" beauty; self-love; instinct; and acquired habits of thought and action. But the one quality that is most certainly not present in unregenerate men and women is the ability to have truly moral affections.

Instead of "dissent" from being, which connotes an aversion, that is, an emotional response, Clarke spoke in rationalist terms of a "contradiction" to the general principles of morals. The norm is agreement, congruity, or fittingness. Indeed, Clarke wrote, not even the "congruity or proportion" found in the uniform order and disposition of physical bodies (such as, for example, the solar system), nor even the "fitness or agreement" supremely evident in the geometrical relations of figures, is "so visible and conspicuous as is the Beauty and Harmony of the exercises of God's several Attributes, meeting

years later Clarke was a major figure. Benjamin Wadsworth, a graduate of Harvard in 1769, entered in his commonplace book in his senior year about Clarke's *Discourse Concerning the Being and Attributes of God* (see chap. 6, n. 40): "N.B. This was the most excellent Piece I ever read upon the subject." Both of these manuscript books are in the Harvard Univ. Archives.

97. Miscellanies, no. 779, reprinted in *The Works of President Edwards*, I (Worcester, Mass., 1808).

with suitable returns of Duty and Honour from all his rational Creatures throughout the Universe."[98] For "suitable returns" and "agreement" in this passage, one could easily read "consent," but the psychological basis would then be quite different.

Clarke did use the term "self-will," but in an intellectualist setting. Men perversely obey or consent to their self-will "in opposition to the nature and reason of things . . . : Which is . . . the greatest Absurdity imaginable; an acting contrary to that Understanding, Reason and Judgment which God has implanted in their Natures on purpose to inable them to discern the difference between good and evil; an attempting to destroy that Order, by which the Universe subsists." The result is iniquity, Clarke said, which is the "very same in Action, as falsity or Contradiction in Theory."[99] Clarke emphasized repeatedly the *logical* inconsistency of vice with the inherent principles of virtue. Emotional considerations such as a sense of guilt or shame hardly entered into his thinking. "He that wilfully refuses to Honor and Obey God, from whom he received his Being, and to whom he continually owes his preservation; is really guilty of an equal absurdity and inconsistency in Practise, as he that in speculation denies the Effect to owe anything to its cause, or the Whole to be bigger than its Part. . . . He that refuses to deal with all Men equitably, and with every Man as he desires they should deal with him; is guilty of the very same unreasonableness and contradiction in One case; as he that in Another case should affirm one Number or Quantity to be equal to another, and yet That other at the same time not to be equal to the first."[100] The weight of conscience here is not a felt "uneasiness," a disturbing and frightening personal inconsistency that forbodes ostracism by the source of all love, a casting out from the harmony of the creation; it is simply a contradiction in reasoning.

The Depersonalization of Providence

Edwards's recourse to considerations of structure and intrinsic relations rather than to the sovereign will of God as a means of understanding the moral order of the universe was not a distinctively post-Newtonian approach. It is important to recognize that Newton's discoveries reinforced an already existing philosophical trend. Edwards was deeply influenced, I believe, by Samuel Clarke's formulations and before that by Malebranche's.[101] Although Clarke

98. Clarke, *Discourse Concerning Natural Religion*, 83.
99. *Ibid.*, 65.
100. *Ibid.*
101. David Hume believed that Clarke himself derived this rationalist approach to the moral

is often automatically classified as a Newtonian, his ideas can be traced to other influences besides the great inspiration of Newton's scientific work. In his *Treatise on Nature and Grace* Malebranche maintained that divine grace is not a particular providence but a general law. Some may suffer under it just as some suffer under the physical laws of nature. The rain falls on everyone and everything equally, helping some while hindering others, although the general end is universal good. "Such as ascribe to God particular Designs and Wills, for all the particular Effects produc'd in Consequence of General Laws, commonly employ the Authority of Scripture to justifie their Opinion." But Scripture, Malebranche said, was written for the simple as well as for the learned, and it "abounds with *Anthropologies*," that is, anthropomorphisms.[102]

Malebranche's goal, like Edwards's later, was not to reduce the texture of the universe to a clocklike mechanism with an indifferent or dormant God presiding. On the contrary, Malebranche wanted to break down the artificiality of the distinction between nature and grace in order to enlarge the domain of the latter. "Natural effects," he wrote, "are complicated and mix'd a thousand ways with the Effects of *Grace*." The order of grace is strengthened or weakened in its efficacy or effects by the order of nature "according as these two Orders variously combine together." In other words, it is more proper to think of an interpenetration of grace and nature rather than of an antithesis between them. The "Nature" referred to by the heathen philosophers is a "Chimera," Malebranche insisted, for the name of grace may be given to all natural effects; "God works in all things."[103] It was necessary to eliminate anthropomorphisms in the images of God's acts because they served falsely as "exceptions" against which to set off a machinelike cosmos. But the universe is not a natural machine, for the miracle of God's handiwork is present in everything, not simply in the uncanny or the unique.

In a universe sustained in all of its parts by the will of God, and in which operations are connected not by mechanical causation but by the constant

---

law from Malebranche, not from Newtonianism: "[Montesquieu] supposes all right to be founded on certain *rapports* or relations. . . . Father Malebranche, as far as I can learn, was the first that started this abstract theory of morals, which was afterwards adopted by Cudworth, Clarke, and others; and as it excludes all sentiment, and pretends to found everything on reason, it has not wanted followers in this philosophic age." Clarke was, of course, an ardent Newtonian, but the aspect of his thought presented here did not owe its origin to Newton. Hume, *Enquiries Concerning the Human Understanding and Concerning the Principles of Morals* (London, 1777), ed. L. A. Selby-Bigge, 2d ed. (Oxford, 1927), 197n, hereafter cited as *Enquiry Concerning the Principles of Morals*, ed. Selby-Bigge.

102. *A Treatise of Nature and Grace* was bound into the Oxford 1694 translation of the *Search after Truth* by Thomas Taylor of Magdalen College. Here and subsequently I have quoted from the 2d ed. (London, 1700), p. 11. The *Treatise of Nature and Grace* in Taylor's translation was also published separately in 1695.

103. Malebranche, *Treatise of Nature and Grace*, trans. Taylor, 19.

exercise of God's conservatory will, even the so-called laws of nature become immediate effects of special grace. Malebranche's famous theory of causation did not change the appearance of things; but metaphysically it eliminated simple mechanistic models as appropriate descriptions of how the universe functions. God's will makes everything happen from instant to instant. Theoretically this leaves open the possibility of erratic and unpredictable behavior, but, however that may be, no miracles can occur in such a world, since there are no mechanically necessitated sequences of events to form a backdrop against which a miracle would be distinguishable. The continued existence of things as they are every moment is the one perpetual miracle. Miracles make sense only in a setting of regular "natural" occurrences.[104]

The world is not erratic and unpredictable under Malebranche's theory because God governs and conserves in accordance with rules or laws determined by His perfect wisdom, and He does not alter or go against this wisdom. Thus, though every event is in fact the product of God's personal sustenance, it is appropriate to interpret the world only in accordance with principles of order, harmony, and beauty.[105]

According to Samuel Clarke, the alleged "arbitrary" will of God is present in the act of Creation, for God can "create things when he pleases, and destroy them again whenever he thinks fit." But once the world was created, and so long as it pleases God to keep it in being, its proportions and relations are "absolutely unalterable." God disdains to act in discord with His own prior wisdom.[106] ("This immutable order has the force of law in respect to God Himself," in Malebranche's words.) The will of God always determines itself to act according to the eternal reason of things, Clarke believed. The na-

---

104. Occasionalist teaching was rather widespread among the Cartesians. It followed in part from the doctrine of the continuous creation or conservation of the universe, which Edwards adhered to along with many 17th-century Puritans, which was held by Descartes, and which had theological roots going back to the patristic period. Since God is the cause of a corporeal thing's existence at any given time, its changed character from moment to moment or place to place must be the result of divine influence, not the effect of an antecedent corporeal event. See Morris Ginsberg's preface to his translation of Malebranche, *Dialogues on Metaphysics*, 52–55.

105. Cf. *ibid.*, 129, 245–246: "[God] always follows the laws which He has established in order to keep His procedure perfectly uniform; God never performs miracles; He never acts according to particular volitions against His own laws, for the order does not demand or permit it. . . . But God . . . does not remain idle, with arms folded, as certain philosophers maintain." Note, however, that Malebranche specifically allowed for the mediation and intercession of Jesus. "God does not act as men do, as particular causes and limited intellects. The reason of His choice comes from the wisdom of His laws, and the wisdom of His laws from the relations in which they stand to His attributes, from their simplicity, their fruitfulness, their divinity. The choice which God makes of men in the distribution of His grace is thus reasonable and perfectly worthy of the wisdom of God, though it is based neither upon differences of nature nor upon inequality of merits."

106. Clarke, *Discourse*, 110–111.

ture of the world may be said to be arbitrary in the sense that it is not the result of a necessity upon God to act this way or that way; but it is a world based on wisdom and goodness. The laws of the Creation are necessary in the sense that things "could not have been otherwise than they are, without diminishing the Beauty, Order, and well Being of the Whole."[107]

In Shaftesbury's theodicy, *The Moralists*, the problem of evil is dealt with in a fashion similar to that found in Malebranche. God rules in accordance with general principles that are designed for the optimum good of the whole. Inevitably, there is some suffering. We see "in the several orders of terrestrial forms a resignation is required, a sacrifice and mutual yielding of natures one to another." Plants by dying sustain animals, and animal bodies die and decompose, thereby enriching the earth in order to recreate the vegetable world. Insects are eaten by superior kinds of birds and beasts, and "these again are checked by man, who in his turn submits to other natures, and resigns his form a sacrifice in common to the rest of things." These cycles are representative of the greater order of the world, which requires the subjection of inferior natures to the higher principles governing the Whole. "The central powers, which hold the lasting orbs in their just poise and movement, must not be controlled to save a fleeting form, and rescue from the precipice a puny animal, whose brittle frame, however protected, must of itself so soon dissolve."[108] God sees the sparrow fall, but this does not deflect Him from His purposes. The grace of God is evident in the beauty and order of the entire system, not in erratic manifestations of power.

Shaftesbury contemptuously dismissed the evidence of miracles as both unnecessary to sustain the faith of a real believer and insufficient to overcome the incredulity of the nonbeliever. Moreover, a miracle can prove only "power," not goodness, not intelligent design. "Power can never serve as proof of goodness, and goodness is the only pledge of truth."[109] Miracles lead people superstitiously to look for divinity in the bizarre rather than in the harmony of the whole system. All this religious "labouring to unhinge Nature, . . . searching heaven and earth for prodigies and studying how to miraculise everything" brings "confusion on the world," breaks its uniformity, and destroys "that admirable simplicity of order from whence the one infinite and perfect principle is known."

> After all this mangling and disfigurement of Nature, if it happens (as oft it does) that the amazed disciple, coming to himself and searching leisurely into Nature's ways, finds more of order, uniformity, and

107. Clarke, *A Demonstration of the Being and Attributes of God* . . . , 2d ed. (London, 1706), 107. See below, pp. 341–345.

108. Shaftesbury, *Characteristics*, ed. Robertson, II, 23.

109. *Ibid.*, 92.

constancy in things than he suspected, he is, of course, driven into atheism; and this merely by the impressions he received from that preposterous system which taught him to seek for Deity in confusion, and to discover Providence in an irregular disjointed world.[110]

The blending of grace and nature, of God's arbitrariness and His regularity, of His will and His wisdom, was a theme of consistent interest to Edwards, culminating in the magisterial statement of number 1263 of his Miscellanies, written in the 1750s.[111] Edwards, like Malebranche, Clarke, and Shaftesbury, held that God always acts according to strict laws in the realm of nature. Of course, these laws are not necessarily deducible a priori. They must be discovered by experience (although the human mind, which does the experiencing, is itself part of the evidence for rationality in nature). In this sense God is always the arbitrary sovereign. The rational laws of nature must be accepted for what they are, the laws of God. The Creation was not anticipated by reason. Yet the laws are fixed, and God does not capriciously intervene in particular cases. Thus, Edwards explicitly denied the efficacy of petitionary prayer to bring about external change in the world. The value of prayer lies primarily in its effects upon the souls of the prayerful, particularly in that it prepares them to receive humbly God's blessings.

Number 1263 of Edwards's Miscellanies is ostensibly a defense of miracles, but the total effect of it is to diffuse the idea of a miracle along a graded scale, as in Malebranche, so that one can speak in the end only of *the more or less miraculous* in a natural world that is one great miracle in all of its parts. Edwards began by rejecting out of hand, as had Malebranche, the exaggerated notion of secondary causation, or the belief that God acts upon the world only "mediately." This concept leads only to infinite regression, Edwards said. There are other writers, he noted, who willingly accept the *im*mediate operation of God in the universe—as in the mysterious and clearly nonmechanical force of gravity—but who are yet averse to allowing that "God acts any otherwise than as limiting Himself by . . . invariable laws, fixed from the beginning of the creation." This would be the clockmaker God of the deists, who never departs from His original plan.[112]

---

110. *Ibid.*, 93. Many of these themes in Malebranche, Clarke, and Shaftesbury were classically stated later in Alexander Pope's *An Essay on Man* (London, 1732–1734). For example: "Remember, Man, 'the Universal Cause/Acts not by partial, but by gen'ral laws;'/And makes what Happiness we justly call/Subsist not in the good of one, but all. . . ./ORDER is Heav'n's first law. . . ." In Maynard Mack's edition (London, 1951), William Wollaston, Clarke's disciple, is cited as part of the background of Pope's reasoning. See pp. 131–140, and notes 125–130.

111. For an early comment, see Miscellanies, no. 177: "Nothing else is the rule of [God's] influence, but only harmony and general proportion."

112. No. 1263 of Edwards's Miscellanies is printed in Townsend, ed., *Philosophy of Edwards*, 184–193.

We must begin, however, with the recognition, Edwards said, that the two notions, that of the arbitrary God, and that of the God who is always limited by fixed laws, are not altogether separable. The arbitrary act "is the first and foundation of the other and that which all divine operation must finally be resolved into, and which all events and divine effects whatsoever primarily depend upon." For an "arbitrary" action, in Edwards's definition, should not be understood as an action opposed to the exercise of wisdom. The original establishment of the laws of nature is in itself an instance of arbitrary operation. Without "arbitrary" acts there could be no divine operation at all, no Creation, and "nothing besides God could ever exist." God's arbitrariness appears in His supreme originality, not in whimsicalness. "Originally He, in all things, acts as a being limited and directed in nothing but His own wisdom, tied to no other rules and laws but the directions of His own infinite understanding."

It is important to note that Edwards's definition of "arbitrary" enabled him to slide over the questions of whether God can act in contradiction to the laws of reason or logic and whether the moral law, the definition of the good and the just, is simply a product of God's will or if God Himself is, in a sense, defined by these ideals. "Whoever thinks there is a God, and pretends formally to believe that he is just and good, must suppose," Shaftesbury wrote, "that there is independently such a thing as justice and injustice, truth and falsehood, right and wrong, according to which he pronounces that God is just, righteous, and true. If the mere will, decree, or law of God be said absolutely to constitute right and wrong, then are these latter words of no significancy at all."[113] This posed what had been the central question for theologians and moralists since the early seventeenth century, but Edwards avoided facing it squarely, preferring perhaps to leave the problem an insoluble mystery. But he was implicitly more aligned with the rationalists than is sometimes recognized.[114]

A parallel may be drawn between God's arbitrariness in the Creation and man's freedom in comparison to the lower animals, plants, and dead matter; for man, made in God's image, has "a secondary and dependent arbitrariness" in that he is not limited in his actions to the laws of matter and motion. Human beings act in accordance with what pleases them and govern the

---

113. Shaftesbury, *Characteristics*, ed. Robertson, I, 264.

114. Cf., for example, this comment from Edwards's [*Enquiry into . . .*] *Freedom of the Will* (Boston, 1754), ed. Paul Ramsey, *Works of Edwards*, I, 166: "God's actions . . . are morally good in the highest degree. They are most perfectly holy and righteous; and we must conceive of him as influenced in the highest degree by . . . the moral good which he sees in such and such things. . . . The essential qualities of a moral agent are in God, in the greatest possible perfection; such as understanding, to perceive the difference between moral good and evil; a capacity of discerning that moral worthiness and demerit, by which some things are praise-worthy, others deserving of blame and punishment."

motions of their bodies by their will. The bodies of all lower forms of created life, in descending order, are governed by physical laws of impulse, attraction, and so on. It seems, then, that rather than making a rigid distinction between arbitrariness and fixed laws, it is necessary to speak of a scale or gradation, as we have already indicated. The higher one ascends in the scale or chain of created existence, Edwards notes, the more and more arbitrary are the divine operations, "or those communications and influences" with which God maintains "an intercourse with the creature." Divine operations are themselves "more or less arbitrary," depending upon their approach to the absolutely arbitrary, where "no use is made of any law of nature, and no respect had to any one such fixed rule or method." Almost the only absolutely arbitrary action was the original creation "of the matter of the material world out of nothing."

It becomes clearer as Edwards proceeds that the meaning of "arbitrary" for him is the "new," the "unique," the "unprecedented," and the "particular," not the unconditioned. Thus, the first act in any series is arbitrary in a sense, or it is more arbitrary than the subsequent acts. This conception of the arbitrary moves it very far from the popular image of the Calvinist God, whose sovereignty, it was alleged, was tantamount to capriciousness. As Edwards explains arbitrariness, it is perfectly compatible with the strictest exercise of scientific reason. After the Creation ex nihilo the so-called arbitrary actions of the deity differ from fixed laws only in that they are generally less common.

Edwards suggested several ways that the arbitrary and the "fixed" might be combined.

(1) An event may be a mixture of something that is arbitrary ("tied to no fixed rule or law") and something else wherein the laws of nature are made use of. An example of this would be the gradual bringing of the formless matter of the world into order and harmony. When the primary particles of matter were put into motion, this operation was not "so absolutely, purely, and unmixedly arbitrary as the first creation out of nothing," since certain laws of nature were established, such as the laws of inertia, gravity, resistance, and so on, "that are essential to the very being of matter, for the very solidity of the particles of matter itself consists in them." Similarly, the whole of the Creation was effected in seven days by "a mixed operation partly arbitrary and partly by stated laws."

(2) A second kind of combination occurs when "though some law or rule is observed, the rule is not general or very extensive," and "some particular rule makes an exception to the general laws of nature." The particular or exceptional rule covers very few instances, however. Supposing, Edwards suggested, that on an island somewhere a certain kind of matter disagreed with the general laws of gravitation and tended to fly away from the center of the earth. Such a phenomenon, because of its rarity, would approach nearer to the

arbitrary and the "miraculous" than other divine operations. It is notable that Edwards did not naively consider such an event an exception to the general principle of divine government of nature by fixed laws. He saw such rare occurrences simply as instances of laws with less extensive operations. Edwards used the word "miraculous," but as Hume pointed out in his essay on miracles published in 1755, in such a case, the word "miracle" is hardly applicable. It might be said, then, that in the light of Hume's criticism Edwards had defeated his own purpose, which was avowedly to establish the possibility of genuine miracles.[115] On the other hand, by viewing natural occurrences in a continuum from the most commonplace to the most rare Edwards succeeded in making all of nature arbitrary and miraculous to a degree.

(3) Finally, Edwards did leave open the possibility of situations in nature wherein laws might "fail" in their fixity, a suggestion that is probably inconsistent with the second type of divine operation described just above. Although God "generally keeps" to the method of establishing fixed laws of greater or less extent, He "ties not Himself to it," Edwards said, and sometimes departs from it "according to His sovereign pleasure." In other words, God does not consistently exclude strange exceptions to the uniformity of His laws, exceptions that cannot be categorized simply as cases of exceedingly rare laws in operation. Edwards did not answer the question of how mortal men can tell when an unprecedented event is an instance of a comparatively rare law, or when it is an actual interruption in a law otherwise assumed to be fixed. Hume reasoned that once men commit themselves to a belief in the government of nature by fixed laws, they are logically bound to interpret uncanny events as instances of unknown laws rather than as miraculous interventions in the operations of known laws. By this third reservation, then, Edwards fell short of a consistently modern philosophy of nature, but it may be surprising to some readers to see how close he came.

Given the continuum from the arbitrary to the fixed, or from grace to nature, a wonderful harmony and symmetry is observable. We have already noted that in the scale of created existences there is a descent from the absolutely arbitrary to the exercise of government more and more by fixed law, with man in an intermediate position. The same applies, Edwards said,

115. Hume, of course, knew almost nothing of Edwards's writings, but the following anecdote is told in E. C. Mossner's *Life of David Hume* (New York, 1954), as reported in Antony Flew, *Hume's Philosophy of Belief: A Study of His First "Inquiry"* (New York, 1961), 163: "A clerical companion happened to mention [to Hume] a sermon published by Jonathan Edwards under the curious title *The Usefulness of Sin.* 'The usefulness of sin!' echoed Hume. 'I suppose,' he went on musingly, 'Mr. Edwards has adopted the system of Leibniz that all is for the best in this best of all possible worlds.' Then he burst out: 'But what the devil does the fellow make of Hell and damnation?' " As for Edwards's reading of Hume's works, there is evidence only that the New England minister read Hume's *Enquiry Concerning the Principles of Morals*.

with respect to time. "If we ascend with respect to time, and go back in the series of existences or events in the order of their succession to the beginning of the Creation, and so till we come to the Creator, . . . after we have ascended beyond the limits and rise of the laws of nature, we shall come to arbitrary operation." Throughout the eons there is a "mixing of arbitrary with natural operations," although in decreasing degree as one approaches the beginning. The highest order of creatures, "viz., intelligent minds, . . . were wholly created, complete in their kind, by an absolutely arbitrary operation." The creation of the mind of man totally transcended the natural order. Because of man's specialness in this respect, there can never be a complete moral science, or what we would today call a behavioral or social science. Human nature in its entirety is not wholly reducible to fixed laws, not even in theory. The mind of man is the closest thing on earth to a perpetual miracle, with the exception of the extraordinary operations of the Holy Spirit.

The balance of number 1263 in Edwards's Miscellanies consists of a remarkable application of these premises to Christian eschatology, which reveals Edwards's unusual powers as a synthetic thinker. If we proceed in the succession of existences in the other direction, not toward the beginning of things, but toward the end of the world, and gaze into the future until we come to the Supreme Being and the end of time, we again arrive at "a disposition of the world by a divine arbitrary operation," similar to circumstances at the beginning. At the end of time God will "arrest" the laws of nature everywhere, in all parts of the visible universe, and "by an entire new disposition" change "all things at once." The end and the beginning, then, are the most arbitrary. One might conceive of Edwards's history of the universe as a great parabola. From the middle of the curve one may ascend in either direction to the unique and singular actions of God, whereas in the middle most of existence is governed by regular and familiar occurrences, no less divinely ordered and continuously created than at the beginning and the end, but lacking in the qualities of the miraculous because of their invariable repetition.

The same model holds if we ascend toward God along the scale of existence according to "degrees of excellency and perfection," rather than time. The nearer we come to God, the nearer we shall come to the "arbitrary influence of the Most High on the creature, till at length, when we come to the highest rank [i.e., the angels], we shall come [to] an intercourse that is, in many respects, quite above those rules which we call the laws of nature." The lowest rank of material things is governed completely by the most general laws of matter and motion. Plants are governed by more particular laws, some of which are distinct from the laws governing sub-biological things, and these laws, according to Edwards's formulation, are therefore more akin to an arbitrary influence. When we come finally to humankind, "and particularly the mind of man, by which especially he is above the inferior creatures, and consider the laws of the common operations of the mind, they are so high above such a kind of general laws and are so singular that they are altogether untraceable. (The more particular laws are the harder to be investigated and traced.)'' Beyond even these normal operations of human faculties, but still confining our view to earthly happenings, there are the motions of the Spirit, especially the processes of conversion and salvation.

Both election and reprobation are treated by Edwards as mixtures or combinations of fixed laws and special grace, but the former, the election of saints to eternal happiness, is much higher on the scale of the arbitrary. The spiritual relations between God and man, Edwards wrote, do not altogether occur "without use made of means and some connection with antecedents" in the manner of second causes, but the operation may still "properly be said to be arbitrary and sovereign." As in the case of an immutable law of nature, the sequence of events in the saving operation of God will be in strict relation to the "degree and exact measure, time, and precise state of the antecedent." The difference between God's communication with angels and that with men is that in the case of the angels, "who behold the face of the Father which is in Heaven," no natural means of communication, such as sense organs or language, are required. The meeting of mind to mind is nearly complete and exact. If we rise to the "highest step of all," to Christ Jesus who is "united personally to the Godhead," there is a "constant intercourse, as it were, infinitely above the laws of nature."

Spiritual relations are rare and refined occurrences, and in that sense arbitrary, God's will in these matters being largely unknowable on earth. But Edwards pointedly rejected the notion that they are amorphous and fuzzy. Their precision is not below that of mathematical physics, but above it, and hence unmeasurable with man's rough calibrators.

Edwards completed this superb sketch of the hierarchy of creation with the observation that by conjoining the order according to perfection or excellency and the order according to time, and ascending with both in mind, the degree of arbitrariness along the way is heightened. Thus, if we first ascend up to intelligent creatures, that is, men and angels, and then go back in time to the Creation, "we shall find more of an arbitrary operation in their creation, and being brought to perfection in their kind, than in the creation of any other particular species of creatures." When the angels were created out of nothing, by an absolutely arbitrary operation comparable to the creation of the primary particles of matter, or when the first man was created by an only slightly less arbitrary action, it was necessary for God to intervene in daily existence much more arbitrarily than He does now. For these new beings "could not be left to themselves and to the laws of nature to acquire that knowledge and exercise of their faculties by contracted habits and gradual association of ideas, as we do now, gradually rising from our first infancy." God had to grant directly to the first man, lest he perish, "immediate instincts enlightening and conducting him, and arbitrarily fixing those habits in his mind which now are gradually established through a great length of time." For the same reason, in the early years of the world God continued this miraculous intercourse with mankind, which explains the prevalence of miracles in scriptural times as compared to their virtual cessation afterward.

It is easy to see, too, that at the end of the world, again proceeding conjointly according to both time and degree of excellence, God acts most arbitrarily at the judgment day in His relations with the souls of angels and men. "In the execution of the sentence on both the righteous and the wicked, the glorious powers of God will be wonderfully and most extraordinarily manifested, in many respects, above all that ever was before in the arbitrary exertions of it." Thus, Edwards summarized, "proceed which way we will in the series of things in the creation, still the higher we ascend and the nearer we come to God in the gradation or succession of created things, the nearer it comes to this, that there is no other law than only the law of the infinite wisdom of the omniscient first cause and supreme disposer of all things."

The significance of this essay of Edwards's goes beyond its address to the problem of miracles. It is a statement on the meaning and limits of all natural knowledge. Despite Edwards's association with a deterministic philosophy, which we will be discussing in a later chapter, the theory presented here espouses an open and creative universe, pregnant always with the possibility of new beginnings and unique events. Ultimately, both God and man are free, not in the sense that their choices are liable to be gratuitous or beyond the grasp of reason, but in the sense that they can never be wholly reduced to fixed laws. Both science and religion, or the proponents of nature and the proponents of grace, are given latitude to explore the universe indefinitely, the one in search of uniform laws, the other in search of unique evidence of the spirit. The one God is reflected in both.

To summarize the essential findings of this chapter. Long before Edwards wrote his dissertation on true virtue, he had given careful thought to the meaning and function of conscience and to its foundations in both human psychology and the moral order of the universe. By the 1740s he had considerably progressed toward differentiating what he believed were the natural moral attributes of men and women from what he believed were purely supernatural attributes, arguing ultimately that moral knowledge in unregenerate persons is necessarily intellectualistic. Even God's moral order is maintained at its mundane level merely by rational principles of fittingness and congruency that are far below the level of spiritual consent to the harmony of the whole with God at its head, which defines true virtue. Far from manifesting an interest in minimizing the moral capacity of natural men and women,

Edwards was deeply appreciative of this capacity and benefited from Samuel Clarke's analysis of the rational foundations of ethics. On the other hand, without special spiritual assistance natural persons are necessarily limited in their ethical development, since natural understanding alone, Edwards argued, cannot be reliably transferred into conduct. For the whole man to be ethical— in will, or affections, as well as in understanding—nature is not enough.

3

Final Thoughts on "Natural Understanding"

*As to the arguments made use of by
many late writers, from the universal moral
sense, and the reasons they offer from experience,
and observation of the nature of mankind, to shew that we
are born into the world with principles of virtue; with a natural
prevailing relish, approbation, and love of righteousness, truth, and
goodness, and of whatever tends to the public welfare; with a prevailing
natural disposition to dislike, to resent and condemn what is selfish, unjust,
and immoral; a native bent in mankind to natural benevolence, tender
compassion, etc.[,] those who have had such objections against the
doctrine of original sin, thrown in their way, and desire to see
them particularly considered, I ask leave to refer them to
a* Treatise on the Nature of True Virtue, *lying by me
prepared for the press, which may ere long
be exhibited to public view.*[1]

The entire body of Jonathan Edwards's thought has a notable consistency. Ideas he sketched out in the 1720s were given full treatment thirty years later with relatively little change in substance. It is nearly futile to look for major shifts or leaps, let alone retractions or reversals. Of the elements of natural moral understanding we have already examined, all of which may be comprehended under the generic term "conscience," none was explicitly rejected in Edwards's later thought. Synteresis, the most Scholastic of his early ethical notions, seems to have been superseded altogether, but it was never an important concept in his thinking. The logic of consent, as we have noted, became the central idea in his metaphysics of morals, but with application only to the regenerate, or as a supernatural standard. The sense of desert and the awareness of suitability or fitness, as two basic elements in natural conscience, re-

1. Edwards, *Original Sin*, ed. Holbrook, 433.

ceived additional refinement. The major change was prompted by Edwards's reading of Hutcheson, Hume, and other British moralists, and involved closer psychological scrutiny of natural conscience. In addition, the distinction between primary and secondary, or moral and natural, beauty was fully elaborated.[2] In this chapter we will extend our examination of Edwards's ideas on the natural foundations of morality, taking into account for the first time his most mature views, in particular, his responses to his increased reading in British moral philosophy.

After the 1730s the stakes in the contest with the secular moralists rose considerably. As Edwards became better acquainted with the persuasive psychological optimism of British moral philosophy, it was more difficult for him to dogmatically attribute to the converted a superior form of virtue. Thus, his principal endeavor in *True Virtue* was to demonstrate that the "moral sense" posited by Hutcheson and others was in fact inferior to the spiritual illumination and taste of the divinely regenerated and that it was no more than old-fashioned natural conscience in a new guise. Specifically, Edwards undertook to show that nothing the benevolists could bring forth as an endowment of the natural man was of the quality of true virtue, and that all of the traits they cited were reducible in the end to intellectualist conscience, to the perception of natural or secondary beauty, or to some subtle variety of self-love. Edwards was willing to allow the use of the term "moral sense," but the thing itself was drained of vitality compared to the enthusiasm of Hutcheson's presentation. It became in Edwards's hands a dead and insignificant principle for personal morality. If I am correct in suggesting that Hutcheson himself was an heir to Puritan enthusiasm (as was Shaftesbury via the Cambridge Platonists), which is what brought conviction to his ethics and made it a kind of new gospel, then it may also be true to say that Edwards retrieved what had been expropriated from religion in the first place, leaving the naturalistic ethics of benevolism without a soul. The result for ethics could only be Benthamite utilitarianism. Stated in positive terms, Edwards's goal was to transfer the idea of holiness from its isolation in the temples of religion and make of it a philosophically credible notion in the forums of enlightenment. The substance of holiness was not changed, but its new name, in conformity to the age, would be "true virtue."[3]

2. Edwards's strictly philosophical interests emerged in two phases. The first began in his earliest college days, extended through his tutorship at Yale, and lasted until he assumed pastoral duties in Northampton in 1727. The second phase began about 1746 and lasted until his death in 1758. The 20 years between 1727 and 1746 were in large part absorbed in working out the questions for the religious life posed by the Great Awakening, as well as by pastoral problems and responsibilities.

3. Edwards did leave standing and untouched the system of intellectualist ethics proposed by Samuel Clarke, confining it to the description of moral judgments characteristic of the natural

By 1755, when he began to write *True Virtue*, Edwards had read Hutcheson's *Inquiry into Beauty and Virtue* and his *Essay on the Passions*; Bishop Butler's *Analogy*, which included the brief but closely reasoned "Dissertation of the Nature of Virtue," though he had probably not read Butler's *Fifteen Sermons*; George Turnbull's two-volume *Moral Philosophy*, which was mainly a compendium of the ideas of Shaftesbury and Hutcheson; David Fordyce's *Dialogues on Education*, a Hutchesonian work that had also greatly interested Samuel Johnson of Connecticut; and Hume's *Enquiry Concerning the Principles of Morals*.[4] This course of study in sentimentalist ethics made a deep impression on Edwards, which accounts for the emergence of the concept of the moral sense as a factor in his work. But even where the Northampton minister did make real concessions to the discoveries of the secular moralists, he strove to scale these findings down to the level of mere preliminaries to the truly virtuous life. When he did not deny them altogether, he relegated the discoveries of naturalistic ethics in the eighteenth century to the world of "types," incomplete forms, foreshadowings only of the eternal truth.

A comparison could be made to the traditional Christian evaluation of heathen moral philosophy, a subject that intensely interested Edwards. Such evaluations typically argued that heathen moral philosophy represented an incomplete development of what was fulfilled only later in Christ's ethical teaching and that heathen philosophy of itself was incapable of consummation into absolutes, which could occur only with the aid of divine revelation. Edwards's very first entry in his philosophical Miscellanies, "Of Holiness," written probably in early 1723, dilated on the superiority—the "sweet, pleasant, charming, lovely, amiable, delightful, serene, calm, and still nature"—of holiness above "all the heathen virtues."[5] On dozens of occasions thereafter in his private notes Edwards returned to this theme of the "defects of heathen morality." "It may be worthy of consideration," he conceded in about 1750, "whether or no some of the heathen philosophers had not with regard to some things some degree of inspiration of the Spirit of God. . . . Inspiration is not so high an honour and priviledge as some are ready to think." Nevertheless, at best God provided these truths to the heathens "without giving with them any certain evidences by which others to whom they declared them might determine them to be such or by which they might be

---

man. In a subsequent publication I hope to elaborate more fully on the religious origins of Shaftesbury's and Hutcheson's moral philosophy. For a preliminary investigation, see Fiering, *Moral Philosophy at Seventeenth-Century Harvard*, chaps. 4 and 6.

4. Edwards's reading can be deduced more or less tentatively from his "Catalogue," MS, Beinecke Lib., Yale Univ., and with greater certainty from the explicit references in his manuscript notes and published works.

5. Miscellanies, letter "a."

obliged to regard and receive them as such." Therefore, such knowledge, lacking the authority of revelation, could not serve as an absolute rule for the heathen, though it could help "prepare the Gentile nations" to receive the Gospel at the appropriate time.[6]

Eighteenth-century secular ethics was not as susceptible as ancient heathen morality to this kind of neat categorizing, however, for as a body of thought it was inherently Christian and incorporated many of the same values to which Edwards was devoted. Under these circumstances, an alleged deviation from orthodoxy could easily be interpreted as an advance on the old truths rather than as a reversion to paganism. Thus Hutcheson, who was a third-generation Presbyterian minister, once casually referred to the beliefs of the "*old* Protestants."[7] Hutcheson himself, then, by implication was a new Protestant, not a heretic.

Edwards occasionally complained that the humanitarians and utilitarians reversed the proper order of ends by putting service to mankind ahead of devotion to God; if they did not remove God from the picture altogether, they spoke of such service to humanity as though it were perfectly equivalent to true holiness. In similar fashion Hutcheson's close comparison of the aesthetic sense and the moral sense, according to Edwards, reversed the order of the Creation and erroneously made the perception of material relations, such as regularity, equality, proportion, and symmetry, the prototype for the perception of intelligent ethical relationships. Both Edwards and Hutcheson found in the experience of beauty an essential key to understanding and describing moral perceptions and moral conduct. But Edwards believed that the "moral sense" school, at least after Shaftesbury, was concerned with an essentially inferior phenomenon. Its followers mistook elementary ethical relations for the highest reaches of virtue.

Hutcheson and Shaftesbury are commonly treated as agreeing on what may be called the aesthetics of morals, but they were worlds apart in one respect. The aesthetics of Neoplatonism pervaded Shaftesbury's discussions of beauty, as it did Edwards's, whereas few if any Neoplatonic notions, such as the concept of transcendent "plastic power," are present in Hutcheson's work. Edwards, it seems, was much more a Shaftesburian in philosophy than a Hutchesonian—how much we will never know since there is reason to suspect that Edwards's first editors suppressed whatever evidence of this connection

6. *Ibid.*, no. 1162. For an extensive statement on this widely discussed question, see John Maxwell, "Concerning the Imperfectness of Heathen Morality," printed as a preface to his translation of Richard Cumberland's *Laws of Nature*, xxxvii–clxviii.

7. Francis Hutcheson, *An Essay on the Nature and Conduct of the Passions and Affections. With Illustrations on the Moral Sense*, 3d ed. (London, 1742), 293. My italics.

may have existed, after Shaftesbury's reputation in later years made him anathema to American clerics.[8] Shaftesbury's famous paean to Beauty in *The Moralists* would have gone straight to Edwards's heart, as it did to the heart of anyone with idealist proclivities. "If we may trust to what our reasoning has taught us," Shaftesbury wrote, "whatever in Nature is beautiful or charming is only the faint shadow of that first beauty. . . . Can the rational mind rest here, or be satisfied with the absurd enjoyment which reaches the sense alone?" One was never to admire the "representative beauty except for the sake of the original." The quest of the philosopher or the poet is to penetrate to a "deep view of Nature and the sovereign genius," which would prove "the force of divine beauty" and provide an object capable and worthy of real enjoyment. It was a discovery only to be reached by the "enthusiasm" that is characteristic of all sound "love and admiration." And just as there are "senses by which all . . . graces and perfections are perceived," such as in painting and music, can it not be assumed that there is a special sense by which "this higher perfection and grace is comprehended? Is it so preposterous to bring that enthusiasm hither, and transfer it from those secondary and scanty objects to this original and comprehensive one?"[9]

The lover of divine beauty discovers, according to Shaftesbury, that it is the "beautifying, not the beautified, [that] is really beautiful." In material things, beauty comes and goes. There is no inherent principle of beauty in any physical body. "The beautiful . . . [is] never in the matter, but in the art and design; never in body itself, but in the form or forming power." What is it that we admire but "mind, or the effect of mind? 'Tis mind alone which forms." Thus, three degrees of beauty emerge: (1) Dead forms or objects, which are made by man or nature, but lack forming power themselves; (2) The creative capacity to make something beautiful—or the forms that form, which have intelligence, action, and operation, and which are, in effect, "double beauty," since they are at the same time the product of higher mind (and thus a created

8. Mid-century works like Philip Skelton's *Ophiomaches: or, Deism Revealed* . . . (London, 1749; 2d ed. 1751) and John Leland's *A View of the Principal Deist Writers . . . in England in the Last and Present Century* (London, 1754–1756), both of which Edwards read, contributed to Shaftesbury's bad name. As late as 1748, however, when Ezra Stiles read the *Characteristics*, he failed to realize, as he said later, that he was reading the "deists' Bible, or their favourite author," and read the work with admiration, though he was shocked in places. Stiles was impressed by the "sublime views of Nature" and with Shaftesbury's treatment of the "moral government of the Most High." Quoted in I. Woodbridge Riley, *American Philosophy: The Early Schools* (New York, 1907), 213, and Edmund S. Morgan, *The Gentle Puritan: A Life of Ezra Stiles, 1727–1795* (New Haven, Conn., 1962), 66.

9. Shaftesbury, *Characteristics*, ed. Robertson, II, 125–130. Shaftesbury's belief in special "senses" of divine things may have influenced Edwards's formulation of the idea of a spiritual sense, though the notion was already widely current in the 17th century.

form) and the possessors of mind (or a forming power themselves). This second order of beauty includes the beauty that may be found in human character and ethics; (3) Finally, the highest order of beauty creates "not only such as we call mere forms but even the forms which form." This third order "contains in itself all the beauties fashioned by [other] minds, and is consequently the principle, source, and fountain of all beauty."[10] "Thus the improving mind, slightly surveying other objects, and passing over bodies and the common forms (where only a shadow of beauty rests), ambitiously presses onward to its source, and views the original of form and order in that which is intelligent."[11] Contrary to his reputation in some circles both in the eighteenth century and now, Shaftesbury was a passionate enemy of materialism, skepticism, and egoism, which threatened, he believed, to drive "pure" religion out of the world. At a preliminary level, he and Edwards could easily agree.

Edwards's treatment of "secondary beauty" in *True Virtue* can be accurately described (in Shaftesbury's categories) as an effort to distinguish thoroughly the natural forms from the ultimate forming power. For Edwards, however, the discovery of the forming power, the highest order of beauty, was possible only with the aid of grace, that is, by providential assistance. With this assistance, one can become an enthusiast of supernature, which is quite different from being merely an intellectual admirer of the natural order.

Secondary Beauty and Conscience

The notion that virtue is beautiful has, of course, ancient Platonist roots and was a concept current among seventeenth-century philosophers. In Henry More's analysis, the proposition referred to the beauty of symmetrical or balanced passions. "Virtue," More said, "for the most part, is but a mere Symmetry of the Passions, in reference to their Degree and Objects," and in the same way, "Beauty it self is made up from a due proportion of external Parts."[12] In support of this idea, More quoted from Cicero's *Tusculan Questions* a similar statement describing the beauty of virtue. At the same time, among seventeenth-century Puritans the "beauty of holiness" was a commonly used figure of speech. In December 1654 Michael Wigglesworth of Massachusetts recorded in his diary that "this 2d. day at a private conference, the Lord hath in some measure shew'd me the bewty of holiness and fired my heart with desires after it . . . especially seeing the bewty of an heavenly

10. *Ibid.*, 130–137.
11. *Ibid.*, 144.
12. Henry More, *An Account of Virtue: or, Dr. Henry More's Abridgment of Morals, Put into English* (New York, 1930 [orig. publ. London, 1690]), 62.

mind, of affections weaned from this world."[13] In Puritan sermon literature beauty was one of a number of descriptive terms that a preacher could use to impress upon his listeners the special qualities of divinity. Thus in 1674 Samuel Torrey told a Boston audience, "If ever we do hope, or intend to make thorough work in *Reformation*, we must recover Order, the Beauty, the Harmony, the Peace and Tranquility, the Regularity, the Purity and Simplicity, the Power and Efficacy, Life and Spirit of Order, Gospel-Order."[14]

On the Continent, J.-P. de Crousaz, a Swiss scholar whose work was known in America in the 1730s and after, published his *Traité du Beau* in 1715 with ideas akin to Shaftesbury's and later Hutcheson's. "It is beautiful," Crousaz wrote,

> to see as many different wills as there are men in a society, all capable of freely choosing differently, uniting themselves as though they were incapable of diversity. It is *beautiful*, I say, to see a multitude of men live as if they had one will and were parts of one person by their continual attention to the common good. It is *beautiful* to see each individual forget his own interests in order to give his care and application to the common interest, and to find repaid usuriously his own interests when he had looked only to those of the society to which he had devoted himself.[15]

13. Edmund S. Morgan, ed., "The Diary of Michael Wigglesworth," Col. Soc. Mass., *Trans.*, XXXV (1951), 396.

14. Samuel Torrey, *An Exhortation unto Reformation* . . . (Cambridge, Mass., 1674), 40. Cf. John Norris, *A Collection of Miscellanies*, 3d ed. (London, 1699), 18–19, 107, which Edwards may have read in the 1720s. In the poem "Seraphick Love" Norris wrote: "Through Contemplation's Optics I have seen/Him who is Fairer than the Sons of Men:/The source of good, the light Archetypal;/Beauty in the Original./The Fairest of ten thousand, He,/Proportion all and Harmony./All Mortal Beauty's but a Ray/of his bright ever-shining Day." Also, in the poem "Beauty": "All his Perfections Beauties are,/Beauty is all the Deity." Beauty declined as an important theological term in the course of the 18th century, Edwards's work being perhaps the last vestige of what had been a characteristic trait of 17th-century theology. The decline is associated with an apparent change in the meaning of the word "beauty." Judith F. Hodgson, "Satan Humanized: Eighteenth-Century Illustrations of *Paradise Lost*," *Eighteenth-Century Life*, I (1974), 41, argues that earlier, beauty was an "all-purpose aesthetic term denoting perfection, God, Nature's harmonic order, and the personal comeliness of both sexes of the human species." Later, as in Edmund Burke's *A Philosophical Enquiry into the Origin of Our Ideas of the Sublime and Beautiful* (London, 1757), beauty connoted "love, virtue, smoothness, delicacy, timidity, amiability, weakness, imperfection, and feminine characteristics, completely separating it from sublimity, power, awesomeness, and masculine characteristics."

15. Jean-Pierre de Crousaz, *Traité du Beau* . . . , 2d ed. (Amsterdam, 1724), I, 36–38. James Logan, the learned Philadelphia Quaker, believed that Hutcheson had simply copied his theory of beauty from Crousaz. Ideas like Crousaz's were common enough earlier, however, for Hutcheson to have gotten the rudiments of his theory elsewhere.

For Crousaz, beauty is variety reduced to some unity, very much like Hutcheson's famous definition of beauty as uniformity amidst variety, or like Edwards's conception of excellency, as we have interpreted it, as the mutual loving consent of all the diverse elements of being, such that they form a transcendental unity. Crousaz also anticipated Edwards's views when he saw in human affairs the beauty of "variety . . . unified by a foundation of generosity and goodness of heart."[16]

Crousaz himself was anticipated by St. Francis de Sales, who is quoted by Theophilus Gale as holding that "union establisht in distinction makes order: order breeds convenance, agreament, and proportion: and convenance in things entire and accomplisht makes Beautie." Like Crousaz later, de Sales saw beauty in such things as the individual parts of an army reduced to "that agreament, which they ought to have together." In the same way, music is beautiful because of the consonance and harmony that is brought out of its distinctive parts. Thus, beauty can be called a "discordant Accord, or rather an accordant Discord."[17]

The typical eighteenth-century analysis of the "beauty of virtue" sought to find in virtuous conduct, or in the character of "the good" as an abstraction, those qualities of symmetry, proportion, and harmony that were the time-tested criteria for aesthetic evaluation.[18] Edwards partially accepted this approach, especially with regard to the perception of justice, which has often been understood as roughly analogous to a sense of balance and order. However, he broke from tradition and categorized all such notions of moral beauty as inherently "secondary," or inferior, reserving for *primary* moral beauty alone the occurrence of "consent, agreement, or union of being to being, . . . the union or propensity of minds to mental or spiritual existence."[19]

16. *Ibid.*, 65. See, e.g., Edwards's *Humble Attempt to Promote Union*, 79: "*Union* is one of the most *amiable* Things, that pertains to human Society; Yea, 'tis one of the most beautiful and happy Things on Earth. . . . A civil Union, or an harmonious Agreement among Men in the Management of their secular Concerns, is amiable; but much more a pious Union."

17. Theophilus Gale, *The Court of the Gentiles* . . . (London, 1669–1677), Pt. IV, 16ff. This work of Gale's was widely read in New England. See Fiering, *Moral Philosophy at Seventeenth-Century Harvard*, chap. 6.

18. The comparison between beauty and virtue was often so indefinite as to make exact interpretation impossible. One can speak somewhat more precisely about the comparison between *moral judgments* and *aesthetic judgments*. The analogy is discussed philosophically in D. Daiches Raphael, *The Moral Sense* (London, 1947), 71ff, and Raphael cites E. F. Carritt, "Moral Positivism and Moral Aestheticism," *Philosophy*, XIII (1938), 131–147. Raphael observes that the analogy makes some sense with reference to feelings about moral intentions, but has no applicability at all to our recognition of moral obligation. There is a rough kind of parallel in both cases, however. With regard to the latter, awareness of obligation may have a quasi-aesthetic component in perceptions of balance, equality, and symmetry, at least enough of a similarity to aesthetics to make sense of the traditional analogies.

19. Edwards, *True Virtue*, ed. Frankena, 27.

What was unusual in Edwards's theory was not so much this division into two qualitatively different kinds of beauty, with one subordinate to the other, but his belief that secondary or natural beauty, which constitutes all the humanly perceived beauty in the universe short of the loving union of spiritual creatures to universal being, is simply a "type," that is, an inferior material symbol, of primary beauty. Rather than the beauty of true virtue being reducible somehow to the ordinary aesthetic criteria, or explicable by them, Edwards turned the Classical notion on its head and argued that the ordinary aesthetic criteria were themselves merely shadows of divine love, resonances of the mutual love of the persons of the Trinity, or afterimages of primary beauty.

Edwards spoke of beautiful "inanimate things" as exemplifying a "mutual consent" within their parts. "Such is the mutual agreement of the various sides of a square, or equilateral triangle, or of a regular polygon. . . . Such is the agreement of the colors, figures, dimensions, and distances of the different spots on a chessboard. Such is the beauty of the figures on a piece of chintz or brocade. Such is the beautiful proportion of the various parts of the human body or countenance. And such is the sweet mutual consent and agreement of the various notes of a melodious tune."[20] Hutcheson's hypothesis that beauty is essentially uniformity amidst variety was not rejected by Edwards, but Edwards subsumed this idea under his own broader law of consent or agreement: "The more there are of different mutually agreeing things, the greater is the beauty."[21] Hutcheson's analysis was not fundamental enough, for it treated natural or secondary beauty, which is merely a by-product of certain spiritual relations, as the be-all and end-all.

It would be easy to take issue with Edwards's reasoning, however. Can the idea of "consent" be applied equally to conscious, intelligent willing and to inert, impersonal, formal harmony? Is the "agreement" of parts in a design comparable to the "agreement" of souls, except as a metaphor? Yet Edwards's apparent stretching of the idea of consent to include both secondary and primary beauty was probably not exceptionable to him, since in the eighteenth century the word "consent" still retained associations with the term used in logic, "consentaneous," meaning simply an agreement or consistency between propositions. The confusion also ran the other way, for in some logics the descriptions of the relations between propositions were remarkably personalized and anthropomorphic. "Consentaneity" and "dissentaneity" were looked upon as living attributes of arguments.[22] Originally, it

20. *Ibid.*, 28.

21. *Ibid.*

22. A student at 17th-century Harvard copied into his notebook the following description, probably from Alexander Richardson's *The Logician's School-Master* (1629), which was widely circulated in 17th-century New England: "Dissentanys have as much affection to the things they argue as consentanys; but they have not the same. Consentanys have an affection of love, these of

seems, the application to arguments in logic of the idea of consent, which etymologically means "to feel together," was by way of metaphorical comparison to human experience of agreement and unity. Edwards thus extended the term "consent" to its maximum breadth. The highly flexible denotation of "consent" in the eighteenth century led him into arguing, with assurance, that the idea of consent could be used univocally to describe both spiritual love and triangles.[23]

Edwards's encompassing of the more tangible aesthetics of Hutcheson by his own aesthetics of consent, which stretched from the spiritual unity of the Trinity down to the beauty of the humblest daisy in the field, was one more expression of a general principle in his thought, namely, the interpretation of the entire material world in terms of spiritual reality. His well-known "typology," as represented, for example, in *Images or Shadows of Divine Things*, is a similar instance.[24] "The system of created being," Edwards wrote, "may be divided into two parts, the typical world, and the antitypical world. The inferior and carnal, i.e., the more external and transitory part of the universe, that part of it which is inchoative, imperfect, and subservient, is typical of the superior, more spiritual, perfect, and durable part of it which is the end, and as it were, the substance and consummation of the other. Thus the material and natural world is typical of the moral, spiritual, and intelligent world, or the City of God."[25]

To the modern reductionist mind Edwards's reasoning appears to be upside-down. Rather than looking for the simplest and smallest number of material antecedents with which to account for the whole creation, Edwards began with the Spirit and saw the material world as derivative from it—in structure, in time, in essence, and in intelligibility. Instead of interpreting man by reference to lower animals, Edwards was inclined to interpret and understand lower animals as lesser analogues of man. "It pleases God to observe analogy in his works," Edwards argued, and ". . . especially to establish inferiour things with analogy to superior." God first made man in His own image. He then went on to form the brutes in analogy to the nature of mankind, and plants in analogy to animals "with respect to the manner of their generation,

---

hatred and anger; agreers and disagreers do both agree, in that they both *sentire*, but they do *con*, and these do *dissentire*." Abraham Pierson, "Notes of Lectures Attended at Harvard College," MS, Beinecke Lib., Yale Univ. This notebook contains lecture notes from a number of Harvard students between 1647 and 1667 other than Pierson himself. See n. 26, below, for an example from Edwards.

23. See n. 56, below, for examples from Henry Grove and George Turnbull.

24. Edwards, *Images or Shadows of Divine Things*, ed. Perry Miller (New Haven, Conn., 1948).

25. Miscellanies, no. 1069, "Types of the Messiah," in Dwight, ed., *Works of Edwards*, IX, 494.

nutrition, etc."[26] And by the same law, the "uniformity and mutual correspondence of a beautiful plant, and the respect which the various parts of a
regular building seem to have one to another, and their agreement and union,
and the consent or concord of the various notes of a melodious tune, should
appear beautiful; because therein is some image of the consent of mind, of the
different members of a society or system of intelligent beings, sweetly united
in a benevolent agreement of heart."[27] As we noted earlier, human society is
thus the paradigm of all lower or secondary beauty, just as the Trinity is the
ultimate standard for human love and society.

In his *Images or Shadows of Divine Things* Edwards copied out a long
excerpt from George Turnbull's *Moral Philosophy* (which he was reading in
1752 or thereabouts) on how external things are intended to be images of
things spiritual, moral, and divine. "There is a much more exact correspondence and analogy between the natural and moral world than superficial
observers are apt to imagine or take notice of," Turnbull wrote.[28] But like
his mentor Francis Hutcheson, Turnbull fell short of Edwards's Augustinian
idealism and never attempted as Edwards did to erect a system of ethics with a
foundation and a prototype in the sacred love of the persons in the Trinity. Yet
when Edwards confronted secular moralists such as Hutcheson, William Wollaston, or Turnbull, he rarely dogmatically rejected their insights in toto.
Usually he expressly recognized the special truth and usefulness on this earth
of their intuitions. Edwards maintained, for example, that the resemblance between primary beauty and secondary beauty ("especially in those kinds of it
which have the greatest resemblance [to] primary beauty, as the harmony of
sounds and the beauties of nature") can "assist those whose hearts are under
the influence of a truly virtuous temper to dispose them to the exercises of
divine love, and enliven in them a sense of spiritual beauty."[29] And just as
secondary beauty may serve to remind the regenerate of spiritual beauty and
lead them to appropriate devotions, so secondary morality may contribute to
the life of true virtue. Rather than rejecting secular ethics, Edwards assigned
it to the arena of mere nature, or the city of man. But he did not believe that
for practical purposes secular morality was necessarily discontinuous with

---

26. *True Virtue*, ed. Frankena, 30. Cf. also Edwards, *Images or Shadows*, ed. Miller, no. 8:
"It is apparent . . . that there is a great and remarkable analogy in God's works. There is a won-
derfull resemblance in the effects which God produces, and consentaneity in His manner of
working in one thing and another throughout all nature. . . . He makes the inferiour in imitation
of the superiour, the material of the spiritual, on purpose to have a resemblance and shadow of
them."

27. *True Virtue*, ed. Frankena, 30–31. See also Wasserman's "Nature Moralized," *ELH*, XX
(1953), 39–76.

28. *Images or Shadows*, ed. Miller, 131.

29. *True Virtue*, ed. Frankena, 31.

higher reality. The secular moralist such as Hutcheson perceives something real, but it is only what God has implanted in man for the preservation of life on earth; he altogether fails to see the higher principle of virtue that subordinates his limited perceptions.

One power in which the man of merely natural morality is always deficient is that of deep perception into the real sources of the beauty that he respects and responds to. Just as a person may be pleased with the harmony of the notes in a tune, Edwards said, and "yet know nothing of that proportion or adjustment of the notes, which by the law of nature is the ground of the melody," so the secular moralist is confined to a merely superficial apprehension of the underlying laws of ethics.[30] He may indeed see something of the proper formal relationships, as well as the consequences of certain types of behavior, and these will help him. Moreover, God has endowed all persons with the capacity to feel instinctive pleasure when perceiving secondary beauty, and this beauty is often one of the attributes of virtuous conduct; but the natural man will still lack "the immediate view of that wherein the beauty fundamentally lies."[31] Such an "immediate" view is, of course, not attainable by human effort, but depends upon the gift of grace.

Here again we come upon Edwards's rationalist approach to the natural world. Secondary beauty is a mental phenomenon that arises as a result of the interrelation between certain forms in the material world (both animate and inanimate) and fixed, inbuilt human responses to those forms. (It is parallel, in fact, to the concept of "secondary qualities" of matter, like color or taste, which inhere in the relationship between the object and the percipient.) This connection between the observer and the phenomena is already structured, established by God, and exactly comparable to the determined and involuntary responses of conscience to fitness or unfitness, to suitability or unsuitability.

Although the capacity of the natural mind for perceiving the primary spiritual relations that underly all beauty is limited, persons without the aid of special grace can still see and respond to the beauty that is a consistent attribute of virtue. Just as natural conscience, despite its limitations, that is, its inability to get to the essence, usually responds justly and appropriately to sin and vice, so the perception of secondary beauty is an accurate guide to the beauty of morality, although the percipient does not comprehend its true moral basis. But in both cases the possession of these merely natural powers does not represent the possession of true moral character, and such powers,

30. *Ibid.*, 32. This comparison of musicology to deep moral understanding was misleading, for it suggests that spiritual grace primarily bestows intellectual enlightenment, that is, gives one a kind of esoteric *knowledge*. This was hardly Edwards's opinion. It would follow from that suggestion that anyone who had read Edwards's book on *True Virtue*, wherein he explained the inherent nature of virtue, would then be virtuous merely by understanding the book.

31. *Ibid.*, 33.

Edwards believed, ought not to be considered intrinsically moral traits at all. They are representative only of God's natural organization of the world, more a matter of physics, in a sense, than ethics. "The cause why secondary beauty is grateful [i.e., pleasing] to men, is only a law of nature which God has fixed, or an instinct he has given to mankind." In establishing this relation between human perceptions and secondary beauty, God desired to duplicate in some faint way "the resemblance there is in such a natural agreement, to that spiritual, cordial agreement, wherein original beauty consists." But it is not because of a real understanding of this profound resemblance between secondary beauty and primary beauty that any particular form or state of objects appears beautiful to natural men. "Their sensation of pleasure, on a view of this secondary beauty, is immediately owing to the law God has established, or the instinct he has given," that is, to a principle of perception imbedded in nature of which man is basically unconscious.[32] The foundation, or what Edwards called the "ground or rule," of this law of nature is hidden from those who are not joined with God in spirit.

Edwards's approach to both conscience and the sense of natural beauty (he considered them to be closely related faculties) was in line with the general trend in the eighteenth century toward the development of a psychology independent of ethics and theology. It is clear that Edwards, at least in certain moods, welcomed an empirical anthropology and psychology, for he was confident that the realm of supernature was an elite fortress immune from damaging criticism or reductionism. Whatever could be discovered about the faculties of the natural man and the laws of behavior could only serve to magnify the grand design and rational order of the created universe.

Although the analogy between beauty and virtue was ancient, Hutcheson made more of it than any previous philosopher. By putting moral perceptions in the same category as aesthetic perceptions—indeed, by the very assumption that moral judgments *are* a form of perception—Hutcheson was able to shed new light on the moral faculties of human beings, particularly to explain the apparent involuntariness, disinterestedness, and swiftness of moral judg-

32. *Ibid.* Edwards's understanding of the response to secondary beauty was exactly like Hume's. Cf. Hume, *Enquiry Concerning the Principles of Morals*, ed. Selby-Bigge, Appendix I, 291–292: "It is on the proportion, relation, and position of parts, that all natural beauty depends; but it would be absurd thence to infer, that the perception of beauty, like that of truth in geometrical problems, consists wholly in the perception of relations, and was performed entirely by the understanding or intellectual faculties. . . . Euclid has fully explained all the qualities of the circle; but has not in any proposition said a word of its beauty. The reason is evident. The beauty is not a quality of the circle. . . . It is only the effect which that figure produces upon the mind, whose peculiar fabric of structure renders it susceptible of such sentiments." Hume, of course, did not distinguish between this kind of natural perception and a higher form, as did Edwards.

ments. Like Edwards, Hutcheson believed that the moral sense was part of the divinely instituted laws of nature. But Edwards differed from Hutcheson on two major points, on which there could be no accommodation. First, as we have seen, Edwards considered Hutcheson's criteria for beauty, whether in physical things or in morals, to be applicable only to a relatively low order of beauty or goodness. This difference arose because Hutcheson began with certain formal physical relationships, such as symmetry and equality, and moved upward to moral relationships, whereas Edwards began with spiritual relationships and descended to the material world. The difference was that between a typologist, like Edwards, who began with spiritual reality, and a naturalist, like Hutcheson, who argued from material reality.

Second, Edwards maintained, in the face of all Hutcheson's and even Hume's arguments, that the so-called moral sense was solely an intellectual capacity and not psychologically related to affect. By thus classifying the moral sense, Edwards was treating it as a faculty incapable of moving a person to action. He agreed with the Scots that all motivation springs from feelings or passions, but he denied that the perceptions of the moral sense necessarily gave rise to virtuous action or that its perceptions were tied to dispositions at all. The apparent motivating power of the moral sense, in Edwards's analysis, was resolvable into merely selfish choices or into amoral innate instincts or habits. In other words, Edwards believed that the moral sense, such as it was, could be disengaged from virtue in conduct and that it was not, in itself, a motivating power toward virtue. The first difference with Hutcheson, concerning the ultimate criterion of virtue and beauty, may be considered metaphysical and thus inherently resistant to final proof. But the second difference was a matter of psychological analysis, and the whole validity of Edwards's philosophical ethics hung on the power of his arguments against Hutcheson on this point.[33]

33. Aldridge, *Jonathan Edwards*, 138–139, has pointed to another significant difference between Edwards and Hutcheson: "Edwards' most fundamental departure from Hutcheson concerns the connection between natural objects and a sentiment of beauty. Hutcheson maintained that the connection was arbitrarily imposed by God, who could have formed us so as to receive no immediate pleasure from the regular forms, actions and theorems that we now account beautiful, and could have united pleasure to quite contrary objects. Edwards emphatically denied that the temper or disposition 'whereby the mind is disposed to delight in the idea of true virtue, is given *arbitrarily*, so that if he had pleased he might have given a contrary sense and determination of mind, which would have agreed as well with the necessary nature of things.' Edwards, like Shaftesbury, regarded beauty as an absolute quality, conforming to an invariable law in nature in consequence of which all rational beings perceive beauty in certain relationships and deformity in the contrary." It is apparent from this difference how much more of a rationalist metaphysician the Calvinist Edwards was as compared to the secular philosopher Hutcheson. On the restricted meaning of "arbitrary" for Edwards, see pp. 98–103, above. Aldridge correctly points out that "the theory of an arbitrary connection contradicts Edwards' principle that the essence of virtue consists in agreement or consent of being to being, for it implies that there is nothing in the nature of

To pause for a summary, Edwards was contending with the secular moralists on three main issues: What are the a priori criteria of true virtue? What is the psychological basis of moral choice leading to action? What is the epistemological or psychological basis of moral judgments, or of moral approbation and disapprobation? The first question, which concerns norms, we will not consider here any further, since it will be taken up again in our discussion of Edwards's moral theology in chapter 7. With regard to the second question, Edwards denied (in opposition to Hutcheson) both that the natural man is capable of acting out of disinterested benevolent affections and that this kind of moral disposition is commonly found in the world. With regard to the third question, Edwards denied (again in opposition to Hutcheson) that the so-called moral sense (which allegedly apprehends and approves of the benevolent dispositions and tendencies of agents in moral situations) is a non-intellectual power or a unique and irreducible characteristic of human nature. According to Hutcheson, the moral sense, not reason, perceives the rightness and wrongness of actions, though reason is often needed to determine the facts. Paradoxically, Edwards could agree with Hutcheson's description of the moral sense *insofar as the moral experience of the regenerate is concerned; that is,* Edwards's concept of an irreducible spiritual sense was exactly comparable to Hutcheson's moral sense. But for the natural man, Edwards rejected all of this and sided with the intellectualists like Clarke, or Hutcheson's opponent Gilbert Burnet. For both levels of moral experience, the natural and the spiritual, Edwards believed that the analogy to aesthetics is valid. The person with divinely renewed spirit, however, perceives and approves of primary beauty, which is an attribute of true virtue; the natural, unregenerate person perceives only secondary beauty, which is an attribute of such natural relations as "regularity, order, uniformity, symmetry, proportion, harmony, etc." In such relations, no will, disposition, or affection plays a part. The preeminent model of secondary moral beauty is that found in the virtue of justice, which consists, Edwards said, "in the agreement of different things, that have relation to one another, in nature, manner, and measure; and therefore is the very same sort of beauty with that uniformity and proportion which is observable in those external and material things that are esteemed beautiful."[34] But not all morality can be understood as a form of justice.

In *Religious Affections* Edwards had stressed that the spiritual knowledge

---

things to hinder an exactly contrary temper of mind agreeing as well with the nature of things." However, it should be noted that as far as Edwards was concerned, what Hutcheson was talking about referred only to the level of common natural occurrence and therefore would be normally interpreted in terms of regular, nonarbitrary, laws of nature. God's "arbitrariness," according to Edwards's definition, becomes evident only at the level of grace and spirit, although there, too, Edwards's God, like Malebranche's and Leibniz's, is a logician, not an oriental despot.

34. *True Virtue*, ed. Frankena, 28, 36.

of the regenerate was a form of immediate apprehension, or sense knowl-edge as opposed to discursive knowledge of propositions and their relations. "Spiritual knowledge primarily consists in a taste or relish of the amiable-ness and beauty of that which is truly good and holy: this holy relish is a thing that discerns and distinguishes between good and evil, between holy and unholy, without being at the trouble of a train of reasoning." In the same way, "He who has a true relish of external [secondary] beauty, [also] knows what is beautiful by looking upon it: he stands in no need of a train of reasoning about the proportion of the features, in order to determine whether that which he sees be a beautiful countenance or no: he needs nothing, but only the glance of his eye."[35] But the similarity between the perception of "exter-nal beauty" and the perception of true virtue and holiness lies only in the immediacy by which the knowledge is gained, that is, the absence of the necessity of a "train of reasoning." No substantive resemblance exists, ac-cording to Edwards.

Even with regard to the act of perception the similarity is not total, but neither Edwards nor Hutcheson showed a consistent awareness of the ambi-guities lurking in the concept of a taste for beauty. The words "relish" and "taste" may convey disinterested appreciation of an object, that is, apprecia-tion without an orectic component, or they may convey not only appreciation but also desire for possession, including the desire to embody beauty in one's own conduct. Indeed, it was on this score that much of the discussion of the beauty of virtue became fuzzy, since the peculiar nature of at least some aesthetic experience is that of love without desire.[36] The aesthetic sense,

35. *Religious Affections*, ed. Smith, 281–282.

36. Nietzsche, in his *Genealogy of Morals*, trans. Francis Golffing (New York, 1956), 238, ridiculed much of the academic speculation about beauty in the 18th century: "Kant had thought he was doing an honor to art when, among the predicates of beauty, he gave prominence to those which flatter the intellect, i.e., impersonality and universality. . . . Kant, like all philosophers, instead of viewing the esthetic issue from the side of the artist, envisaged art and beauty solely from the 'spectator's' point of view. . . . This would not have mattered too much had that 'spec-tator' been sufficiently familiar to the philosophers of beauty, as a strong personal experience, a wealth of powerful impressions, aspirations, surprises, and transports in the esthetic realm. But I am afraid the opposite has always been the case, and so we have got from these philosophers of beauty definitions which, like Kant's famous definition of beauty, are marred by a complete lack of esthetic sensibility. 'That is beautiful,' Kant proclaims, 'which gives us disinterested pleasure.' Disinterested! Compare with this definition that other one, framed by a real spectator and artist, Stendhal, who speaks of beauty as 'a promise of happiness.' Here we find the very thing which Kant stresses . . . [is] rejected and canceled [in the esthetic condition]. Which is right, Kant or Stendhal?—When our estheticians tirelessly rehearse, in support of Kant's view, that the spell of beauty enables us to view even *nude* female statues 'disinterestedly' we may be allowed to laugh a little at their expense. . . . Let us honor our aestheticians all the more for the innocence reflected in such arguments—Kant, for example, when he descants on the peculiar character of the sense of touch with the ingenuousness of a country parson!"

unlike the moral sense, is properly contemplative rather than active. Edwards assumed, however, that at the level of spiritual perception, which is characteristic exclusively of the regenerate, a moral taste for primary beauty is absolutely inseparable from the temper of a virtuous nature. Without the existence of true virtue in the soul of the observer, he believed, that observer could never recognize truly virtuous conduct in others, or truly virtuous relations. True virtue, then, unlike the possession of the secular moral sense, necessarily entails both an intellectual and a practical "habit" or disposition. In the character of a saint no separation is possible between the powers of moral judgment and the bases of conduct.

Such ideas about virtue were common in the seventeenth century in Puritan thought and also among the Cambridge Platonists. Henry More had written, "All pretenders to philosophy will indeed be ready to magnify reason to the skies, to make it the light of heaven, and the very oracle of God: but they do not consider that the oracle of God is not to be heard but in his holy temple, that is to say, in a good and holy man, thoroughly sanctified in spirit, soul, and body." Knowing what is good and doing what is good are unified in the saved, for grace brings about integration of judgment and will, or a harmony of moral perceptions and approbation with inner prevailing dispositions.[37] Hutcheson had argued similarly that the moral sense was a kind of sentiment of benevolence to observed benevolent affections, and thus it was both a basis for judgment and an active source of right conduct. This similarity is another instance of Hutcheson's Puritan background emerging unwittingly in his secular moral thought. Edwards strove to demonstrate, however, that without divine assistance a person would necessarily lack the psychological integration that assured the union of a cognitive grasp of the elements of morals (or secondary beauty) with a constant inclination to goodness. Of course, he first had to prove that Hutcheson's moral sense was cognitive, and not a sentiment.

"The disposition," Edwards said, "which consists in a determination of mind to approve and be pleased with [secondary] beauty, . . . has nothing of the nature of true virtue, and is entirely a different thing from a truly virtuous taste."[38] Carrying the point so far that he was attacking a rather ludicrous straw man, Edwards asked: "Who will affirm that a disposition to approve of

37. Cf., for example, the *Discourses* of John Smith, in Gerald R. Cragg, ed., *The Cambridge Platonists* (New York, 1968), 115: "Grace doth more and more reduce all the faculties of the soul into a perfect subjection and subordination to itself. . . . The life of a good man is under the sweet command of one supreme goodness and last end. This alone is that living form and soul which, running through all the powers of the mind and actions of life, collects all together into one fair and beautiful system, making all that variety conspire into a perfect unity." The More quotation is from *A Collection of Several Philosophical Writings of Dr. H. More . . .*, 4th ed. (London, 1712), viii.

38. *True Virtue*, ed. Frankena, 40.

the harmony of good music, or the beauty of a square or equilateral triangle, is the same with true holiness, or a truly virtuous disposition of mind?"[39] The constituents of beauty in these material things, notably uniformity and proportion, are found also in intangible things, particularly in the ordering of society and the relations of justice, and therefore it requires no "higher" or "diverse" faculty (such as a moral sense) to perceive, approve of, and be pleased with these common forms of morality. But what do these things have to do with the "virtue of the heart," Edwards asked? Both reason and experience show that "men's approbation of this sort of beauty [*which is found in natural morality*] does not spring from any virtuous temper, and has no connection with virtue." A taste for this "inferiour beauty in things immaterial" has been mistakenly understood as "a true virtuous principle . . . implanted naturally in the hearts of all mankind." There are no essential differences, Edwards argued, among any of the forms of secondary beauty, whether manifested in the regularity of architecture or in the regularity of human relations; thus if it were true that virtue consisted in delight in these forms, virtuous conduct and aesthetic appreciation would increase in tandem. The taste for beauty would be "raised to a great height in some eminently virtuous or holy men" and "wholly lost in some others that are very vicious and lewd."[40] One is tempted to respond to this criticism that Edwards unfairly attributed to the secular moralists the belief that beauty and virtue are *literally* identical, rather than analogically or metaphorically identical. Yet his criticism had some validity in the face of the common and, perhaps, casual abuses of the Platonic tradition that united the good and the beautiful without careful discrimination.

To summarize, Edwards rejected the prevailing secular belief that in the characteristics of conscience, or in the analogy between the perception of beauty and the perception of virtuous conduct, or in the notion of the moral sense, real grounds may be found for attributing intrinsic moral dispositions to the unassisted human being. Insofar as morality has a perceivable aesthetic dimension, it is reducible, Edwards argued, to the secondary characteristics of beauty, such as order, regularity, and symmetry. Such characteristics the natural person may, on intellectual grounds alone, indeed recognize as good and beautiful, since God has endowed human understanding with instinctive responses of this type. But these perceptions fall short of true insight into the actual foundations of moral beauty, which is essentially spiritual. In addition, none of these natural, instinctive perceptions are necessarily connected to dispositions or inclinations in the perceiver that lead to virtuous conduct. They remain fundamentally cognitive and inert.

39. *Ibid*.
40. *Ibid*., 41.

Spiritual Sense

Edwards believed that the intrinsic unity of goodness and beauty is fully recognizable only by those who are aided by divine grace. In *True Virtue* and in *Religious Affections* he repeatedly took note of that "certain divine spiritual taste, which is in its whole nature diverse from any former kinds of sensation of the mind"; this taste is given to the regenerate and enables them to perceive uniquely "the beauty of holiness." This kind of beauty, Edwards wrote, "is the quality that is the immediate object of this spiritual sense."[41] Unlike the moral sense, which in Edwards's construction is likely to be detached and impassive at best, the spiritual sense is a vital principle of conduct as well as of perception. It is given only by special providence or grace and thus is a more "arbitrary" operation of God's relationship to man than the moral sense, which is wholly resolvable into certain natural laws having to do with the human mind in a fixed relation to the design and structure of the universe.

In a fashion similar to Hutcheson's deployment of the moral sense, Edwards attempted to stretch out "spiritual sense" to cover a huge range of psychological and moral phenomena. It was a means of sensation, and thus analogous to other senses like sight and hearing; it was a form of intellectual illumination, and thus analogous to rational intuition or the perception of relations; it was an affection or emotion that was passively experienced, like pleasure or delight; it was a passion or desire that led to action; and it was a habitual disposition that inclined the soul to seek holiness with constancy. In the face of such an ambiguous and multifaceted concept, it is legitimate to ask: Does this complex have a center out of which its properties radiate?

Although Edwards's concept of the spiritual sense is properly part of his moral theology (which we will discuss in more detail in chapter 7), it seems appropriate to comment on it here in close connection with his critique of the moral sense. For nearly everything that Edwards denied about the moral sense he was willing to grant to the spiritual sense in a different context. The origins of the idea of the spiritual sense in Edwards's thought have nothing to do with Hutcheson directly, but both the Scottish philosopher and the New England minister were subject to many of the same shaping intellectual forces—Puritan piety, Cambridge Platonism, Malebranche, Locke, and Shaftesbury—an ironic fact that cannot be insisted on too much. Both men also were completely aware of the Aristotelian discussions, carried along in Scholasticism into the seventeenth century, of the inward or internal sense (also sometimes called the common sense) that was posited to account for the human awareness of certain phenomena not directly traceable to particular external sensations, such as, for example, the sense of time. Hutcheson commented directly

41. *Religious Affections*, ed. Smith, 259–260.

on the perniciousness of Lockean naive empiricism in this regard in the preface to his *Essay on the Passions*:

> Whatever confusion the Schoolmen introduced into philosophy some of their keenest adversaries seem to threaten it with a worse kind of confusion by attempting to take away some of the most immediate simple perceptions and to explain all approbation, condemnation, pleasure, and pain, by some intricate relations to the perceptions of the external senses. . . . We have multitudes of perceptions which have no relation to any external sensation, if by it we mean perceptions immediately occasioned by motions or impressions made on our bodies, such as the ideas of number, duration, proportion, virtue, vice, pleasures of honor, congratulation, the pains of remorse, shame, sympathy, and many others. It were to be wished that those who are at such pains to prove a beloved maxim, "that all ideas arise from sensation and reflection," had so explained themselves that none should take their meaning to be that all our ideas are either external sensations or reflex acts upon external sensations.

In Puritan literature spiritual "sensations" were more matters of metaphor than formal psychological hypotheses, but the writings of Thomas Hooker, John Flavel, Thomas Shepard, and others are full of references to the new taste, the new sight, and so on. Once the "affections" gain a "taste and relish of the sweetness that is in Christ, and his Truth," Hooker wrote, one's thoughts "will never wander from him." "Saints have an experimentall knowledge of the work of Grace," according to Shepard, "by virtue of which they come to know it as certainly . . . as by feeling heat, we know fire is hot, by tasting honey, we know 'tis sweet."[42] The source of such typical expressions was ultimately the Bible. Edwards himself cited I Corinthians 2:14 as well as many other scriptural passages that refer to special powers of spiritual discernment given to the elect. And long before the time of the Puritans, in the Catholic pietistic tradition, exemplified by figures like St. Bonaventure and St. Bernard, metaphors of sensation were used to describe the unique characteristics of religious belief and experience.

The *Discourses* of the Cambridge Platonist John Smith have been particularly singled out as influential upon Edwards's notion of a spiritual sense, but Smith's kind of psychological rhetoric was common among the Cambridge group as a whole. Smith spoke of "an Inward Sense in Man's Soul," which once it is "awakened and excited with an inward taste and relish of the divinity" can better "define God . . . then all the world else."[43] Henry

42. Perry Miller and Thomas H. Johnson, eds., *The Puritans*, rev. ed. (New York, 1963 [orig. publ. 1938]), I, 307; Shepard, *Parable of the Ten Virgins*, Pt. I, 142.

43. C. A. Patrides, ed., *The Cambridge Platonists* (Cambridge, Mass., 1970), 182. I find John E. Smith's statement about Edwards's concept of spiritual sense, in his introduction to the Yale

More, also, knew of a "boniform sense" and of the taste and relish of divine virtue, and Peter Sterry's *Discourse of the Freedom of the Will* (London, 1675), a defense of Augustinian voluntarism, contains passages such as the following:

> We are taught in metaphysicks, that being, truth and goodness, are really one. How sweet a rest now doth the spirit, with its understanding, and its will, find to it self in every being, in every truth, in every state or motion of being, in every form of truth. When it hath a *sense* of the highest love, which is the same with the highest goodness, designing, disposing, working all in all, even all conceptions in all understandings, all motions, in every will, humane, angelical, divine? With what a joy and complacency unexpressible doth the will, the understanding, the whole spirit now lie down to rest everywhere, as upon a bed of love, as in the bosom of goodness it self?[44]

There was then a "terminological heritage"[45] that blended smoothly into the Lockean stress on sensation and direct experience as the basis of all knowledge. Yet it must be emphasized once more that, contrary to Perry Miller's views and those of many others, both the moral sense and the spiritual sense, especially the latter, are outright repudiations of Lockean empiricism, not imitations of it. Both Hutcheson and Edwards circumvented Locke by borrowing enough of his fashionable language to satisfy empiricist critics. But except for the accidental parallel to Lockean simple ideas, such as the taste of honey or the sight of the color red, Edwards's spiritual sense has little resemblance to anything in Locke, and the English philosopher, had he been alive, would undoubtedly have dismissed Edwards's idea of a special sensation of divine things as "enthusiastick" nonsense.[46] Nor did Edwards need

---

edition of Edwards's *Religious Affections*, too strong: "This new sense represents the unique contribution of the *Affections*; no idea in all of Edwards' works is more original and no doctrine was more far reaching in its influence upon the course of Puritan piety" (p. 30). Edwards did not formulate a clear doctrine of the spiritual sense until the 1730s. Before that one finds in his work at most only the typical Puritan notions of the uniqueness of grace expressed in sensual metaphors. For Edwards's early discussion of the spiritual sense, see his Miscellanies, no. 782, and the published sermon *Divine and Supernatural Light* (1734). The best treatment of the historical background of Edwards's "spiritual sense" or "sense of the heart" is Terrence Erdt's *Jonathan Edwards: Art and the Sense of the Heart* (Amherst, Mass., 1980). See also Fiering, *Moral Philosophy at Seventeenth-Century Harvard*, chaps. 4 and 6.

44. Vivian de Sola Pinto, *Peter Sterry: Platonist and Puritan, 1613–1672* (New York, 1968 [orig. publ. Cambridge, 1934]), 140. My italics. Original italics have been eliminated and capitalization has been modernized in this quotation.

45. Morris, "Young Edwards," 371, uses the quoted phrase.

46. In *Religious Affections*, ed. Smith, 215–216, Edwards disparaged Locke's sensations as sources of knowledge in much the same fashion as Malebranche disparaged sense impressions: "The external ideas men have are the lowest sort of ideas. These ideas may be raised only by im-

Locke to give him the idea of an irreducible sensation or experience, since Puritans and mystics had been talking about such experiences for generations. "The experience of the work of grace [and only that] makes men savingly to know what grace is," Thomas Shepard wrote.[47] Solomon Stoddard repeated the same idea years later, which he could understand without Locke's guidance: "There is no infallible sign of grace, but grace. Grace is known only by intuition."[48]

The first step in gaining a clear understanding of Edwards's "spiritual sense" must be the realization that in this instance the term "sense" is something of a misnomer. Edwards meant by spiritual sense not only a new capacity for being affected by the things of God, but also a new inclination or a new will directed toward those things. The new sense of the heart brought about by the workings of grace is also a new disposition or an infused habit that is identical to holy love or holiness. Which comes first? Does love toward the object alter its appearance and clothe it with delight for the beholder, or does the ability to see with unveiled eyes precede and thus induce the love? This is an ancient philosophical question, and one not easily answered in the case of Edwards. He seems to have believed that the taste for the beauty of divine things springs initially from God's infused love, and that thereafter the regenerate soul sees beauty in what it has first been induced to love. Edwards implicitly rejected the Platonist assumption (at least insofar as it was based on intellectualist premises) that the recognition of the beauty precedes the emotion of love. In interpreting Edwards's thought one must always begin with his concept of love.[49] Love is the key to comprehending his theory of the

---

pressions made on the body, by moving the animal spirits, and impressing the brain. . . . These external ideas are as much below the more intellectual exercises of the soul, as the body is a less noble part of man than the soul."

47. *Parable of the Ten Virgins*, Pt. II, 79, quoted in Michael McGiffert, ed., *God's Plot: The Paradoxes of Puritan Piety Being the Autobiography and Journal of Thomas Shepard* (Amherst, Mass., 1972), 23. Shepard's *The Sound Beleever* . . . (London, 1670) is full of references to spiritual senses and related ideas.

48. Solomon Stoddard, *The Defects of Preachers Reproved* . . . (New London, Conn., 1724), 17. A Yale College commencement thesis from 1733 shows how Locke was absorbed into the pietist tradition, rather than reshaping it: "*Ad ideam simplicem producendam, immediata Dei exertio requiritur*" (To produce a simple idea, the immediate work of God is needed). It is rarely pointed out that even the terms "simple idea" and "complex idea" do not originate with Locke, although he gave them a new definition. The terms were used with a different meaning in 17th-century logic before Locke, as in the following example from Malebranche, *Search after Truth*, trans. Taylor, II, 57: "We must never meddle with the Enquiry of compound things before the simple, on which they depend, have been carefully examin'd. . . . The ideas of compound things, neither are, nor can be clear, as long as the most simple, of which they are compos'd, are but confusedly and imperfectly known." On p. 58 the phrase "simple Ideas" is used directly.

49. See the discussion in Conrad Cherry, *The Theology of Jonathan Edwards: A Reappraisal* (Gloucester, Mass., 1974 [orig. publ. Garden City, N.Y., 1966]), 39–41, concerning the priority

will as well as his notion of the spiritual sense. Since the spiritual sense included at once intellectual illumination, aesthetic delight, and a new inclination toward God, Edwards could comfortably speak about this sense in diverse ways. But the logical foundations of the spiritual sense (and of Hutcheson's moral sense, too, I believe) lie in the idea of a disposition of the soul.[50] For Edwards, as contrasted with Hutcheson, this special moral disposition is not innate—human infants are little vipers—but comes about through the direct physical (as opposed to moral) influence of God upon the will or the affections. "The immediate seat of grace, is the will or disposition," Edwards wrote in *Charity and Its Fruits*.[51]

---

of love versus the priority of "seeing and judging" in the act of faith. Cherry cites Thomas A. Schafer, "Jonathan Edwards and Justification by Faith," *Church History*, XX (Dec. 1951), 55–67, in favor of the first view, which Cherry himself adheres to in only a qualified sense. An analysis of Edwards's discussion of "spiritual understanding" in *Religious Affections*, ed. Smith, 270–272, shows that by "understanding" Edwards means only nonintellectual sensations, or rather a taste for the "loveliness of divine things." In other words, the kind of knowledge that Edwards is talking about is sense knowledge that necessarily affects one's inclinations at the same time.

50. Cf., however, Allen, *Jonathan Edwards*, 358: "Among the characteristics of the Treatise on Grace [published in Alexander B. Grosart, ed., *Selections from the Unpublished Writings of Jonathan Edwards, of America* (Edinburgh, 1865)], one of the foremost to arrest attention is the abandonment of the ethical principle laid down in the Nature of True Virtue. Edwards had there asserted in his most positive manner that virtue primarily consists in love to being in general; in the propensity, as he calls it, in the impulsion or gravitation, as it were, of the infinitely smaller fragments of being to the infinitely larger mass of being. Or, as he had there said: 'True virtue primarily consists, not in love to any particular Beings because of their virtue or beauty, nor in gratitude because they love us, but in a propensity and union of heart to Being simply considered.' But in the Treatise on Grace he writes: 'The main ground of true love to God is the excellency of His own nature.' These two kinds of love Edwards had designated as the 'love of benevolence' and the 'love of complacence.' In his dissertation on Virtue he placed love of benevolence first, as the primary ground of virtue, to which the love of complacence was secondary or subordinate. He now asserts [in the treatise on grace]: 'Of these two, a love of complacence is first, and is the foundation of the other; *i.e.* if by a love of complacence be meant a relishing, a sweetness in the qualifications of the beloved, and a being pleased and delighted in his excellency. This in the order of nature is before benevolence, because it is the foundation and reason of it. A person must first relish that wherein the amiableness of nature consists, before he can wish well to him on account of that loveliness.'" I am not certain there is a real issue here, because as long as it is understood that God must make the first move, by changing the constitution of the soul, the love of benevolence and complacence are coordinate and occur in no sequence.

51. *Charity and Its Fruits*, ed. T. Edwards, 327. Since the process of regeneration as described by Edwards is supernatural and cannot be fitted into modern scientific categories, there is a tendency for historians, as for many of Edwards's opponents in his own day, either to ignore or explain away his reasoning on the subject, as though it were an embarrassment. Edwards himself was apparently genuinely puzzled by this resistance. "No good reason can be given," he wrote, "why men should have such an inward disposition to deny any immediate communication between God and the creature, or to make as little of it as possible. 'Tis a strange disposition that men have to thrust God out of the world, or to put Him as far out of sight as they can. . . . There-

Hutcheson's moral sense and Edwards's spiritual sense were similar, however, in their dependence on ratiocination to compensate for sensory errors.
The will or disposition of the soul is not dependent on intellectual deliberation
in order to incline this way or that, but intellect is needed as an occasional
corrective to error. Neither of these senses was held to be infallible, in other
words. Edwards believed that divine inclinations in the soul are always right
in themselves, even infinitely perfect, but although the "disposition in general
may be good, . . . the particular determination of that disposition, as to particular actions, objects and circumstances may be ill," and rather than emanat-
ing from the spirit of God "may be from the intervention or interposition of
some infirmity, blindness, inadvertence, deceit, or corruption of ours." Holy
affections, like Hutcheson's benevolent affections, must be tempered by rational consideration of the circumstances. "A good disposition," Edwards
wrote, may "strongly incline a person to that, which if he saw all things as
they are, would be most contrary to that disposition." Edwards adverted
specifically to a concern that was also Hutcheson's and that in fact compelled
Hutcheson to bring in the utilitarian criterion of the greatest happiness for the
greatest number, namely, the problem of determining the future consequences
of an action as opposed to knowing the immediate and direct benefits. "Our
views must be extensive," Edwards believed; "we must look at the consequences of things." However, with regard to duties clearly required by moral
rules or by the positive commands of God, these must be done regardless of
future consequences, which must then be "left with God."[52]

---

fore so many schemes have been drawn to exclude or extenuate, or remove at a great distance,
any influence of the Divine Being in the hearts of men, such as the scheme of the Pelagians, the
Socinians, etc. And therefore these doctrines are so much ridiculed that ascribe much to the immediate influence of the Spirit, and called enthusiasm, fanaticism, whimsey, and distraction; but
no mortal can tell for what" (quoted by Allen, *Jonathan Edwards*, 362, from Edwards's *Treatise
on Grace* in Grosart, ed., *Unpublished Writings of Edwards*). Edwards's teaching on this point is
unmistakable, however. In his sermon on *Divine and Supernatural Light*, 4, he explained: God
uses no secondary cause or intermediate means of conveying "spiritual knowledge." "He imparts
this Knowledge immediately, not making use of any intermediate natural Causes." Cf. also Miscellanies, no. 138: "I, for my part, am convinced of an immediate communication between the
Spirit of God and the soul of a saint." Perry Miller, *Jonathan Edwards*, 139, was totally in error
on this point when he wrote: "The Arminians [according to Edwards] were using an obsolete
psychology when they said that conversion had to be either a reasonable persuasion or a physical
influx; the Northampton experiment proved that grace comes not as argumentation or as interposition, but as idea. Conversion is a perception, a form of apprehension, derived exactly as Locke
said mankind gets all simple ideas, out of sensory experience." On the contrary, Edwards believed that converting grace was a physical influence on the will that changed the will's delectation from self to God. This "fact" cannot be broken down into simpler elements. The influence of
Locke is simply an extraneous supposition in the interpretation of Edwards's thought on this matter. See chap. 6, n. 108, below.
  52. Edwards, *Some Thoughts Concerning the Present Revival of Religion in New-*

Eighteenth-century British moralists used the term "sense" loosely. Thomas Reid found fault with Hume on this matter, and his remarks would apply as well to Edwards: "When Mr. Hume derives moral distinctions from a moral sense, I agree with him in words, but we differ about the meaning of the word *sense*. Every power to which the name of a sense has been given, is a power of judging of the objects of that sense. . . . The moral sense therefore is the power of judging in morals. But Mr. Hume will have the moral sense to be only a power of feeling, without judging: This I take to be an abuse of a word."[53] It is difficult, however, to think of a more accurate word than "sense" that Edwards or Hume could have used.

Wollaston, Hutcheson, and the Moral Sense

When Edwards wrote *Religious Affections* (published in 1746) he was not yet fully acquainted with the benevolist school. It was sometime after 1746 that he first read Hutcheson's *Inquiry*, although through the medium of Ephraim Chambers's encyclopedia and other secondary sources he had already learned something of Hutcheson's key ideas. The longest single quotation in *Religious Affections* is cited from "Chambers, *Cyclopedia*, Vol. 2, under the word 'Taste.' " It has not been noticed before that here as elsewhere in his two massive volumes Chambers was drawing from Shaftesbury and Hutcheson. In fact, Chambers's major authority on several topics in ethics and moral psychology was Hutcheson.[54] But despite this indirect, preliminary acquaintance with the benevolist school, Edwards could only have been amazed and dismayed when he first read Hutcheson's *Inquiry* and discovered in it arguments for a natural and universal moral sense that paralleled almost exactly what Edwards had been claiming exclusively for spiritual sense, especially Hutcheson's description of the moral sense as a capacity for immediate, involuntary (or, in theological terms, irresistible), nonpropositional recogni-

---

England . . . (Boston, 1742), 243–246. Comparable statements by Hutcheson may be found throughout his books, increasingly so as he modified his earlier claims about the moral sense as compared to reason. See *Inquiry into Beauty and Virtue*, 162, 183–185; *Essay on the Passions*, 107; and Hutcheson's later works.

53. Quoted from Thomas Reid's *Essays on the Intellectual Powers of Man* in R. F. Brissenden, " 'Sentiment': Some Uses of the Word in the Writings of David Hume," in Brissenden, ed., *Studies in the Eighteenth Century: Papers Presented at the David Nichol Smith Memorial Seminar* . . . (Toronto, 1968), 107.

54. See *Religious Affections*, ed. Smith, 282–283. Smith notes that "no other work of Edwards' is so heavily dotted with footnotes containing long extracts from the works of other theologians and divines" (p. 52). Edwards probably read Hutcheson's *Inquiry into Beauty and Virtue* in 1749. About 1738, however, he began to use Chambers regularly. See chap. 1, n. 20.

tion of virtue. Not only in the work of the master, Hutcheson, but also in that of his disciples George Turnbull and David Fordyce, which Edwards also eventually read, there were dozens of comparable passages, ascribing to nature what Edwards for years had been insisting belonged to grace alone. Turnbull, for example, paraphrasing Hutcheson, spoke of

> the wisdom and goodness of nature . . . , in giving us a rule to guide us in our moral conduct, distinct from and antecedent to all our knowledge acquired by reasoning, which is a moral sense of beauty and deformity in affections, actions and characters, by means of which, an affection, action, or character, no sooner presents itself to our mind, than it is necessarily approved or disapproved by us. . . . Reason must be grown up to a very great maturity, and be very considerably improved by exercise and culture, before men can be able to go through those long deductions, which shew some actions to be in the whole advantageous to the agent, and their contraries pernicious. But the Author of Nature has much better furnished us for a virtuous conduct than many philosophers seem to imagine . . . by almost as quick and powerful instructions as we have for the preservation of our bodies.[55]

Turnbull dwelt on the beauty found in human "affections, actions, and characters," which is analogous, he said, to our "natural sense of beauty and harmony in material objects." And everyone feels, he noted, "that beauty of the moral kind is yet more charming and transporting than any corporeal beauty." Just as in corporeal beauty we look for unity, simplicity, and "consent of parts," Turnbull continued, so in moral beauty "we are prompted and directed to enquire after the goodness and fitness of general laws, that is, their tendency to the good of the whole to which they belong."[56] His *Principles of Moral and Christian Philosophy* (1740) was uncannily like a direct

---

55. George Turnbull, *Principles of Moral Philosophy*, I, 39. Typically in this passage there is no clear distinction made between the power of judging moral behavior and the ground of motivation.

56. *Ibid.*, 51. It is notable that Turnbull, like Edwards, spoke of the "consent of parts" in material things as a precondition of beauty. An even more distant perspective on Edwards's use of the term "consent" is provided by Henry Grove's *A System of Moral Philosophy*, ed. Thomas Amory, 2 vols. (London, 1749), an academic ethics text largely written before 1715, which Edwards read in about 1750. Grove spoke of the peculiar delight that arises from the contemplation of beauty, which should not be confined to objects of sense, however. "There is such a thing as *intellectual* Beauty. Virtue is so, being nothing else than the symmetry, proportion, and good order of the powers and passions of the mind, and actions of the life, *consenting* [my italics] among themselves, and with the Law of Reason and of God" (I, p. 357). Like many other authors in this tradition, Grove cited Cicero on the beauty of virtue. Many anticipations of Edwards's theory of "consent" can also be found in the Latin literature of Protestant Scholasticism, such as that studied by Loemker, *Struggle for Synthesis*.

challenge to Edwards's *Religious Affections* (although, of course, this would have been chronologically impossible). "As high as the virtue is which is set before us in Scripture as our duty," we shall find, Turnbull asserted, if we look into human nature, that "we have all the affections, dispositions, powers and faculties, which progress towards it pre-supposes or requires." Quite without any help from supernatural grace, according to Turnbull,

> we have not only a benevolent disposition; but a sense of beauty and order; a strong sense of the beauty of holiness, and of the deformity and vileness of vice; and together with this we have strength of mind, if we will but exert it, which is able to cleave to virtue in spight of all temptation and opposition. What therefore is wanting to us, in order to our making immortal advances in virtue, if we are not wanting to ourselves.[57]

Such remarks must have struck Edwards as profoundly threatening to Christian orthodoxy as he understood it, far more dangerous than atheism. The Shaftesbury-Hutcheson gospel was in fact a heresy, a rival religion.

We have called Hutchesonian aesthetics "tangible" in order to contrast it with Edwards's aesthetics of consent, which depended upon vital intangible unities rather than formal relationships. But this distinction does not do full justice to the secular moralists, since they readily extended their principles to spiritual entities. Thus, the uniformity and proportion of which material beauty consists was extended as a criterion to judge whole societies and many human relationships. In this regard intellectualists such as Samuel Clarke and William Wollaston found common cause with Hutchesonian sentimentalists, differing only on the epistemology of moral knowledge. Clarke and Shaftesbury, though antagonists on the place of reason in moral judgments, could agree that virtue partakes primarily of order, balance, and proportion.

Although Edwards accepted this contention, he held that the resulting picture was still incomplete. There may be beauty in the order of society not unlike that in the regularity of a beautiful building, Edwards admitted, as when the different members of society "have all their appointed office, place and station, according to their several capacities and talents, and everyone keeps his place, and continues in his proper business."[58] Above all, this similarity between material and immaterial beauty applies in the consideration of justice, as we have noted. The idea of retributive justice, as well as standards like the golden rule of Christian ethics, is akin to material symmetry, which is in turn related to equality and proportion. And "most of the duties incumbent on us," Edwards was prepared to accept, ". . . will be found to

---

57. Though with a modified title page, this is vol. 2 of Turnbull's *Principles of Moral Philosophy*, 44, 63–64, 87–88, 160–161, 303–304.
58. *True Virtue*, ed. Frankena, 35.

partake of the nature of justice." Edwards conceded, it seems clear, that most of the everyday moral responsibilities of life are adequately explained in the terms of the secular philosophers. Justice consists in "the agreement of different things, that have relation to one another, in nature, manner, and measure; and therefore is the very same sort of beauty with that uniformity and proportion, which is observable in these external and material things that are esteemed beautiful."[59] But just as secondary beauty is only a corollary of primary beauty, justice in this sense is no more than a corollary of true virtue.

It was in the context of the elaboration of the idea of justice in relation to aesthetics that Edwards first found occasion to comment on Wollaston's *Religion of Nature Delineated*, a work with a remarkable vogue in early America as well as in Britain. Edwards first heard of Wollaston's famous book in the early 1730s, a few years after arriving in Northampton, when "Mr. Williams of Lebanon" reported to him that *The Religion of Nature Delineated* was "the best Piece on the subject that ever he read."[60] Edwards himself may have read Wollaston before 1735, and before sitting down to write his dissertation on the nature of true virtue, he studied intensively the work of Wollaston's mentor, Samuel Clarke, even going to the trouble of compiling a short index to Clarke's *Discourse Concerning the Unchangeable Obligations of Natural Religion*.

Wollaston's *Religion of Nature* was as much a work in ethics as in natural theology. The author believed that he had made an original discovery in ethics, namely that the criterion of *truth* applied as much to actions as to words, which meant that one could prove the rightness or wrongness of any deed by processes of logic and observation no different from those employed to determine the facts of a case. To be immoral, Wollaston held, was to act as if things were true that were not true, or to act as if those things were not true

59. *Ibid.*, 36–37.
60. Edwards, "Catalogue." At about this same time, Ebenezer Parkman (1703–1782, a minister in Westborough, Massachusetts, about 35 miles from Boston) entered in his diary, Aug. 16, 1727: "I read in Wollastons Religion of Nature. I take it to be a very Excellent Piece" (Francis G. Walett, ed., *The Diary of Ebenezer Parkman, 1719–1728*, 1st part [Worcester, Mass., 1974]). Although now considered a work of minor significance and little originality, in the middle third of the century Wollaston's *Religion of Nature Delineated* was rivaled only by Hutcheson's books in popularity in America among moral philosophy texts. It was used as a text at Yale beginning in the 1740s at the latest; in 1750 Samuel Johnson of Connecticut recommended it to Benjamin Franklin for use at the College of Philadelphia; James Logan, the polymath Philadelphia Quaker, read the book in 1726 and considered it "a piece for which one may justly . . . congratulate the age" (Edwin Wolf 2nd, *The Library of James Logan of Philadelphia, 1674–1751* [Philadelphia, 1974], 525). Wollaston has the unique honor of being the only British philosopher criticized at length by the three greatest minds in 18th-century America: Franklin in 1725; Edwards at mid-century; and Jefferson in a letter to Thomas Law at the late date of 1814. Such was the harmonizing power of the new moral philosophy in the 18th century.

that were true. In other words, the proposition that can be framed with regard to any immoral act, that agent "A" performed act "B," is always in logical contradiction to the previously existing true state of things, to prior reality itself. Immorality is thus a denial of reality. For example, Wollaston wrote: "If *A* should enter into a compact with *B*, by which he *promises* and ingages never to do some certain thing, and after this he does that thing: in this case it must be granted, that his act *interferes* with his promise, and is *contrary* to it. Now it cannot interfere with his promise, but it must also interfere with the truth of that *proposition*, which says there was such a promise made." "A"'s breaking of the contract amounts to a denial of its existence, according to Wollaston. This denial in action is as "inconsistent" with the former agreement as if "A" had verbally stated that no agreement existed, or had said there is and at the same time there is not an agreement. Morality is to be judged, Wollaston said, in accordance with the following dictum: "No act (whether word or deed) of any being, to whom moral good and evil are imputable, that interferes with any true proposition, or denies anything to be as it is, can be right."[61]

The difficulties and fallacies in Wollaston's system are many. Benjamin Franklin, with his usual wit, got to perhaps the central one. Wollaston writes, Franklin said, that "every action which is done according to *Truth*, is good; and every Action contrary to *Truth*, is evil: to act according to *Truth* is to use and esteem every thing as what it is, etc. Thus if *A* steals a Horse from *B*, and rides away upon him, he uses him not as what he is in *Truth*, viz. the Property of another, but as his own, which is contrary to *Truth*, and therefore, *evil*." Unfortunately, however, the truth of the case can be extended in ways that Wollaston might not find desirable. Supposing, Franklin continued, "that *A* is naturally a *covetous* Being, feeling an Uneasiness in the want of *B*'s horse, which produces an Inclination for stealing him stronger than his Fear of Punishment for so doing. This is *Truth* likewise, and *A* acts according to it when he steals the Horse."[62] The point is that any number of propositions can be framed about any single action. In order to make a statement relevant to the

61. Wollaston, *Religion of Nature Delineated*, 10–13. (The book was originally published privately in 1722. The first sizable printing was in 1724. Nine editions were published before 1760.)

62. Franklin learned of Wollaston's book when he was working at Palmer's printing house in London in 1725 and was assigned to typeset the third edition. Franklin's *Dissertation on Liberty and Necessity, Pleasure and Pain* (London, 1725), from which these quotations are taken, was in part a response to Wollaston. See Leonard W. Labaree *et al.*, eds., *The Papers of Benjamin Franklin* (New Haven, Conn., 1959–), I, 61. Wollaston's ethics lends itself to satire. See Leslie Stephen, *History of English Thought in the Eighteenth Century* (New York, 1927 [orig. publ. 1876]), I, 130: "Thirty years' profound meditation had convinced Wollaston that the reason why a man should abstain from breaking his wife's head was, that it was a way of denying that she was his wife. All sin, in other words, was lying."

morals of an action rather than to, let us say, the pertinent psychology, or the pertinent biology, or even to the weather, one must already have in mind some moral categories. Wollaston's theory, in short, begs the question.

Edwards was more tolerant of Wollaston than many other critics in the eighteenth century and after were.[63] The intellectualism of *The Religion of Nature* did not threaten the exclusive preserve of true religion, in Edwards's view. According to Edwards's understanding of Wollaston, the author had only secondary beauty "in his eyes when he resolved all virtue into an agreement of inclinations, volitions and actions with truth."[64] Wollaston appraised correctly the "natural regularity" in the universe, Edwards believed, the inbuilt reciprocity that establishes tit for tat. "He whose heart opposes the general system, should have the hearts of that system, or the heart of the ruler of the system, against him; and . . . should receive evil, in proportion to the evil tendency of the opposition of his heart," Edwards wrote.[65] But Wollaston erred, because justice, in this sense, is not the whole of virtue. It is significant —indeed it is extraordinarily revealing about Edwards—that unlike most of Wollaston's critics, the New England philosopher-theologian found no quarrel with the validity of the comparison of logical relations to ethical ones. "Expressing such affections and using such a conduct towards another, as hath a natural agreement and proportion to what is in them, and what we receive from them" is as much a "natural conformity of affection and action with its ground, object, and occasion, as that which is between a true proposition and the thing spoken of in it."[66] A moral act conforms to the underlying reality, to rational categories intrinsic to nature, in the same way that a proposition, in order to be true, must be descriptive of reality. So Edwards did not find the thrust of Wollaston's ideas exceptionable, particularly concerning natural justice. However, encompassing Wollaston as he had Hutcheson, Edwards maintained that his own synthetic ethics was more fundamental and comprehensive. Benevolence to being in general, that is, true or primary virtue in Edwards's terms, as part of its nature will automatically "incline to justice, or proportion. . . . He who loves being, simply considered, will naturally, other things being equal, love particular beings in a proportion compounded of the degree of being, and the degree of virtue, or benevolence to being, which they have. And that is to love beings in proportion to their dignity." This "first and most general kind of justice" will "produce all the subordinate kinds." Wollaston's theory of moral judgments had the defect, then, of being derivative rather than fundamental, although it was not an incorrect theory.

63. For Thomas Jefferson's critique of Wollastonian ethics, see his 1814 letter to Thomas Law, quoted in Riley, *American Philosophy*, 283–284.

64. *True Virtue*, ed. Frankena, 37.

65. *Ibid.*, 36.

66. *Ibid.*, 37.

Edwards differed from Wollaston not only in the level of generality he introduced or in his having found a higher abstraction to set up as the norm of virtue. The very perception of virtue, as well as the motivation to it, was of a different quality in Edwards's view than in Wollaston's. Wollaston observed the formal relationships, the uniformity, the equality, and so on. But the man of holy virtue "relishes and delights" in good acts that are grounded in love to being in general. He perceives the agreement of such acts to both general benevolence and to the glory of God, and this agreeable tendency makes them beautiful and pleasing "to a virtuous taste, or a truly benevolent heart."[67] The difference is mainly that between the sentimentalist who discriminates with the heart and the intellectualist who discriminates with the head. In *Charity and Its Fruits* Edwards invoked the traditional distinction between *assent* and *consent* to describe how a "speculative faith" may be distinguished from a "saving faith." The former consists in the "assent of the understanding," the latter in the "consent of the heart."[68] Edwards's case against Wollaston could be reduced to a similar distinction. In addition, with regard to the definition of virtue, Edwards believed that his criterion of "benevolence to being" contained within itself a principle of distributive justice to which Wollaston's theory could be reduced.

Given Edwards's predispositions, Wollaston's theory was, perhaps, easily dismissed on the grounds of intellectualism. A logic of moral relations, such as Wollaston proposed, could at best have only a subordinate place in an adequate theory of the constitution of virtue. Edwards's pietist background in the Augustinian voluntarism of Ames and Mastricht would inevitably leave him dissatisfied with any theory of ethics that failed to unite moral judgments with moral conduct inseparably. The sources of moral conduct were coiled in the affections, not in logical propositions. The secular sentimentalists also asserted that moral judgments must imply a disposition or inclination to particular forms of conduct, which brought this school of thought into formal kinship with Edwards, though Edwards denied authenticity to their theories. Yet up to the point of specifying the essential nature of "the deformity of vice and the beauty of virtue," Edwards and David Hume agreed on what was wrong with Wollaston's ethics. As Hume said, "The end of all moral speculations is to teach us our duty. . . . Extinguish all the warm feelings and prepossessions in favour of virtue, and all disgust or aversion to vice; . . . and morality is no longer a practical study, nor has any tendency to regulate our

---

67. *Ibid.*, 39. In no. 1123 of his Miscellanies Edwards also criticized Wollaston on the grounds that if moral virtue consisted primarily in truth, "love could not properly be said to be the sum of all the moral commands of God and of all moral duties; all moral virtues could not be ultimately resolved into love as their common fountain."

68. *Charity and Its Fruits*, ed. T. Edwards, 19.

lives and actions."[69] For any moral ideal to be effective in life, "it is requisite," Hume believed, "that there should be some sentiment which it touches, some internal taste or feeling, or whatever you may please to call it, which distinguishes moral good and evil, and which embraces the one and rejects the other."[70]

The central problem Edwards confronted in *True Virtue*, as we have already noted, was not that of replying to Wollaston's ideas, but that of differentiating his own position from statements such as Hume's. Could the Hutchesonian moral sense—"so much insisted on in the writings of many of late," as Edwards observed—be as easily refuted as Wollaston's intellectualism? Edwards expressed concern that some moralists had been misled into believing that the moral sense is convincing "evidence of a disposition to true virtue, consisting in a benevolent temper, naturally planted in the minds of all men."[71] We have seen that Edwards's strategy was to deny that the moral sense had a capacity for recognizing anything other than the formal qualities of secondary beauty, such as uniformity and proportion, which are essentially amoral relations. He thus made the moral sense merely a variety of natural conscience and a faculty of moral recognition that Clarke and Wollaston could have accepted. In short, Edwards maintained that fundamentally there was no real choice between the ethical theories of Wollaston and Hutcheson. All natural morality is intellectualist in Edwards's analysis, when it is not simply an expression of self-love. Yet Hutcheson had claimed for all human beings the possession of "a moral sense of excellence in every appearance, or evidence of benevolence" and a "universal determination to benevolence in mankind, even toward the most distant parts of the species." "From the very frame of our nature," Hutcheson said, "we are determined to perceive pleasure in the practice of virtue."[72]

Edwards seems to have detected well enough in Hutcheson's work the ambiguities that many other critics pointed to in the eighteenth century and later. The moral sense was presented at one and the same time as an organ of sensation; a principle of motivation; a judge of the motivations of others; a utilitarian calculating machine that rapidly assessed consequences for good or ill; a form of love or an inclination to benevolence that also, necessarily, loved and approved the benevolence of others; and a rationalist judge of the fitness and suitability of certain actions in relation to ends. Edwards noted particu-

---

69. Hume, *Enquiry Concerning the Principles of Morals*, ed. Selby-Bigge, 172.

70. *Ibid.*, 294. Despite Hume's reputation for skeptical detachment as a philosopher, about half of his *Enquiry Concerning the Principles of Morals*, which was his own favorite among his works, is simply exhortation. Moral philosophers in the 18th century on all sides of the issues were still half-preachers and unashamedly preached as well as analyzed virtue.

71. *True Virtue*, ed. Frankena, 70.

72. Hutcheson, *Inquiry into Beauty and Virtue*, 248, 193, 138.

larly a confusion in Hutcheson over the question of whether the moral sense was a form of reflexive conscience, that is, a power of arriving at moral judgments concerning one's own conduct (and possibly that of others), or whether it was an expression of the inclination of the heart, that is, in Edwards's words, a "natural disposition and determination of the mind to love and be pleased with virtue."[73] Edwards's intention was to force Hutcheson's theories into one or the other of these positions, which would then make the concept of the moral sense more vulnerable to critical analysis.

Conscience and moral dispositions are not necessarily identical, Edwards argued. If they were, a person with the most active conscience would also have the most virtuous heart. And vice versa, in a person who has a "high degree of virtuous temper," the "testimony of conscience in favour of virtue would be equally full."[74] Yet in practical experience, the opposite is often true.

> Some men, through the strength of vice in their hearts, will go on in sin against clearer light and stronger convictions of conscience than others. If conscience, approving duty and disapproving sin, were the same thing as the exercise of a virtuous principle of the heart in loving duty and hating sin, then remorse of conscience will be the same thing as repentance; and just in the same degree as the sinner feels remorse of conscience for sin, in the same degree is the heart turned from the love of sin to the hatred of it, inasmuch as they are the very same thing.[75]

Edwards sought to establish with these few words more than simply the claim that virtue is in the will or the inclination, whereas conscience is a judgment of the intellect. He was suggesting that conscience and the virtue of the heart function independently, even inversely, not in tandem as the moral sense school seemed to assume. People with an acute conscience may yet compulsively ignore it in actions. Are they exemplars of the moral sense? There may be those of saintly purity of soul and innocence of heart who act rightly without the judgments of conscience to guide them. Are they also exemplars of the moral sense? At work here once more was Edwards's well-known fondness for the reductio ad absurdum. *True Virtue* is in large part a dissection into primitive elements of the unexamined assumptions of the benevolists. If the moral sense consists of intellectual judgments, it becomes simply "speculative" or "notional" morality, which the natural man is quite capable of, but which is a far cry from *lived* virtue. On the other hand, if the moral sense is benevolent inclinations, even including benevolence to be-

73. *True Virtue*, ed. Frankena, 71.
74. *Ibid.*
75. *Ibid.*, 72.

nevolence, it is closer to true virtue, but it is still suspect; it must then prove itself immune from the subtle encroachments of self-love and the other natural affections that may create only the illusion of disinterested and universal benevolence.

As a dramatic example of the difference between the exercises of an intellectual moral sense and the exercises of a virtuous heart, Edwards presented the case of the Last Judgment. On that day God will perfectly enlighten all consciences so that sinners will see fully the justice of their condemnation. "Their consciences will approve the dreadful sentence of the judge against them; and seeing that they have deserved so great a punishment, will join with the judge in condemning them." But this recognition, this assent of the conscience, is obviously not the same as repentance, not the same as a heart "perfectly changed to hate sin and love holiness." For if sinners could feel this, they would not be sinners. On the contrary, at the very moment that the sinner has the clearest possible *intellectual* conviction of his own wickedness, that same sin and wickedness of his heart, functioning inversely to his conscience, also "will come to its highest dominion and completest exercise," and God will give up the sinner to his wickedness, "even as the devils are!"[76] Conscience "may see the natural agreement between opposing and being opposed, between hating and being hated, without abhorring malevolence from a benevolent temper of mind, or without loving God from a view of the beauty of his holiness. These things have no necessary dependence one on the other."[77]

That the moral sense was a confused notion of the secular moralists, Edwards could easily show. Much of what was claimed for it was reducible to self-love, Edwards believed, rather than virtue. And after self-love was removed, only the processes of natural understanding remained, which Edwards considered to be moral phenomena of so elementary a kind as hardly to deserve the designation of virtue. His chief conclusion, then, was that one cannot attribute to the natural man the pure inclinations of heart that constitute true virtue, even though the natural man may be admitted to have a largely intellectualist moral sense.

Conscience and Sympathy

Given that the moral sense could be considered only a dimension of common intellectualist conscience rather than a new discovery of moral psychology, what were Edwards's mature thoughts on the foundations of conscience? In

76. *Ibid.*, 72–73.
77. *Ibid.*, 74.

True Virtue Edwards added to his earlier analyses mainly the concept of sympathy as an integral component of the working of conscience. Edwards noted, as a natural fact (if such it is), the "uneasiness" of mind that follows from "consciousness" of doing unto others what one would resent others doing unto oneself. This uneasiness arises "in some sort" from self-love understood as "self-union," or as the need for unity with oneself. As Richard Cumberland, Samuel Clarke, and others before Edwards had observed, natural conscience is an expression of the general uneasiness that follows upon self-contradiction.[78]

According to this theory, the golden rule (Matthew 7:12) is based on a natural psychological principle. It is not just a normative precept without relation to personal experience of pain and pleasure. Rather than being a historically unique Judaeo-Christian doctrine, the golden rule in Edwards's thinking is a perennial discovery in human experience and is supported by the usual "consistence and harmony of nature's laws."[79] Edwards accepted implicitly the principle enunciated with various degrees of precision by Cumberland, Butler, and others, that nature itself through the imposition of pleasure and pain provides real support for virtue. The uneasiness or discomfort that a person may feel when acting inconsistently with the psychologically self-evident golden rule, plus the often lamentable practical consequences, is nature's way of encouraging elementary social ethics. Butler's *Analogy* in particular had emphasized the moral government inherent in nature in a variety of forms.[80]

78. *Ibid.*, 61. Cf. Richard Cumberland: "The cultivation of the happiness of any one person, or of a few . . . cannot have any probable grounds of hope for the future, so long as it is sought by opposing or neglecting the happiness of all other rational beings. . . . The mind that is so disposed lacks a certain element essential to its perfection, namely the internal peace that comes from a uniform, continually *self-consistent* [my italics] wisdom. For it is in conflict with itself when it decides that it should act in one way concerning itself and another way concerning others who share the same nature" (D. D. Raphael, ed., *British Moralists, 1650–1800* [Oxford, 1969], I, 87–88, translating portions of *De Legibus Naturae* [1672]). Cf. also chap. 2, p. 77, above. Edwards probably never read Cumberland's *Laws of Nature*, in either the Latin or the English version, but Cumberland's influence on the work of later moral philosophers was enormous.

79. Locke specifically excluded the golden rule from self-evidence or the status of an "innate principle." "Should that most unshaken rule of morality and foundation of all social virtue, 'That one should do as he would be done unto', be proposed to one who never heard of it before, but yet is of capacity to understand its meaning; might he not without any absurdity ask a reason why? And were not he that proposed it bound to make out the truth and reasonableness of it to him? Which plainly shows it not to be innate; for if it were it could neither want nor receive any proof; but must needs . . . be received and assented to as an unquestionable truth, which a man can by no means doubt of." *Essay Concerning Human Understanding*, ed. Fraser, Bk. I, chap. ii, sec. 4.

80. "God has appointed satisfaction and delight to be the consequence of our acting in one manner; and pain and uneasiness of our acting in another, and of our not acting at all" (Butler, *Analogy of Religion*, in W. E. Gladstone, ed., *The Works of Joseph Butler* [Oxford, 1896], I, ii, 6). Butler was thinking primarily of the consequences of imprudence, e.g., sloth, rashness, etc.,

The mere "inclination to agree with ourselves," or the uneasiness that follows from disagreeing, is a natural principle. But this need for self-agreement differs altogether, Edwards claimed, from the "agreement or union of heart to the great system, to God the head of it, who is all and all in it," for this latter kind of agreement, Edwards said, "is a divine principle."[81] Edwards did not insist, however, that the practical results of these two independent sources of virtue were necessarily incompatible or diverse. On the contrary, both lead to fair dealing and even benevolence. Edwards was sufficiently convinced by the arguments of the secular moralists to recognize as legitimate a natural as well as a divine foundation for morality. In practice, the results were complementary; the foundations, however, were inherently antithetical, like two curved lines that appear to run together for a short space but that having begun at different angles will ultimately diverge. Or, to use a different simile, natural morality was like Euclidean geometry: practical for this world but insufficient for the realms of the infinite.

Edwards's assumption, that the uneasiness of natural conscience is the result of *felt* self-contradictory behavior, implies that the conscience-stricken person can project himself in imagination into the aggrieved state of the wronged party and by this means can feel the anomaly of his immoral action. Without this psychological identification, which is in effect to reverse the moral situation ceteris paribus and put oneself in the place of the other and vice versa, there could be no internal sense of inconsistency. This ability or human tendency to imagine oneself in another's place was investigated with extraordinary energy in the eighteenth century, generally in terms of the idea of sympathy.[82] From the time of Henry More to 1759 when Adam Smith published his masterly study of the subject, sympathy and its role in the moral life had been given increasing attention. Though Edwards had indirectly touched on the phenomenon in some of his earlier writings, he did not give the subject of sympathy extended treatment until *True Virtue*.

It seems probable that the attention Edwards paid to the role of sympathy in ethics was prompted by his reading in 1754 or 1755 of Hume's *Enquiry Concerning the Principles of Morals*, just before he started to write *True Virtue*. The principle of sympathy was useful to him because, as Edwards conceived of it, it was non-moral in substance and yet could be shown to be one more natural mechanism by which the superficial appearance of virtue gained undeserved applause in the world. Hume's purposes were, of course,

---

as was Locke in his comments on the natural supports for virtue, rather than the pain of conscience that Cumberland, Clarke, and Edwards stressed, but the principle of cosmic feedback established by divine design is similar. Cf. also Shaftesbury, *Characteristics*, ed. Robertson, I, 306.

81. *True Virtue*, ed. Frankena, 63.

82. See Fiering, "Irresistible Compassion: An Aspect of Eighteenth-Century Sympathy and Humanitarianism," *Jour. Hist. Ideas*, XXXVII (1976), 195–218.

quite different, but the fact of sympathy was there, ready for Edwards's exploitation. "In general, it is certain," Hume wrote, "that wherever we go, whatever we reflect on or converse about, everything still presents us with the view of human happiness or misery and excites in our breast a sympathetic movement of pleasure or uneasiness. . . . The very aspect of happiness, joy, prosperity gives pleasure; that of pain, suffering, sorrow, communicates uneasiness." Sympathy, Hume allowed, "is much fainter than our concern for ourselves." But without its continuous operation there could be no public exchange or social intercourse. "We every day meet with persons who are in a situation different from us, and who could never converse with us were we to remain constantly in that position and point of view which is peculiar to ourselves."[83]

Edwards's few remarks before the 1750s on sympathetic identification all dealt with the problems of mankind's relationship to the deity. One of the very first notes in his Miscellanies, written some thirty years before his treatise on true virtue, observed that the incarnation of Christ made it possible for men to understand God's love for mankind, for Christ loves us with "such a sort of love as we have to him, or to those we most dearly love." "So that now when we delight ourselves at the thought of God's loving us[,] we need not have that allay of our pleasure which our infirmity would otherwise cause that tho' he loved us[,] yet we could not conceive of that love."[84] In number 238 of the Miscellanies, written probably in the winter of 1724/1725 when Edwards was a tutor at Yale, he reflected on the peculiarities of our conceptions of "acts of the mind (as the ideas of thought, of choice, love, fear, etc.)." It is impossible, he observed, "to have an idea of thought or of an idea, but it will [be] the same idea repeated." In order to think of love, for example, either of a love now vanished or of the possibility of loving someone not presently loved, "we either so frame things in our imagination that we have for a moment a love to that thing . . . , or we excite for a moment that love which we have, and suppose it in another place."[85] The same is true of all "spiritual

83. Hume, *Enquiry Concerning the Principles of Morals*, ed. Selby-Bigge, 221, 220, 229. Aside from the unmistakable internal evidence, we know that Edwards read Hume from a 1755 entry in his "Catalogue" as follows: "Concerning a Book entitled *L'Esprit des Loix* Mr. Hume in his Enquiry concerning the Principles of Morals p. 54 55 calls Him a Late author illustrious writer of great Genius as well as extensive Learning." But Edwards does not seem to have read Hume's *Treatise of Human Nature*, though he referred to it in his "Catalogue" twice, once in 1750 and once in late 1754. See the "Catalogue," MS, 22, 37, and Paul Ramsey's edition of Edwards's *Freedom of the Will*, 14n.

84. Miscellanies, letter "z."

85. Townsend, ed., *Philosophy of Edwards*. Edwards added that in those cases when we cannot somehow recreate the experience itself, we make use of the "antecedents, concomitants, and effects of loving" that are known, and then imagine "something unseen, and govern our thoughts about [it] as we have learned how by experience and habit."

ideas," Edwards said. If we are to have a clear idea of the idea, it must be "repeated, perhaps very faintly and obscurely, and very quick and momentaneously."[86] To examine our own feelings, or the feelings of another, we must in some degree reproduce the feeling itself in our minds, otherwise the feeling cannot be clearly understood.

The concept of sympathetic identification was therefore not wholly new to Edwards's own reasoning. But after reading Hume, Edwards was prepared to speak on the subject with a definiteness that is seldom found in any literature before the publication of Adam Smith's *Theory of Moral Sentiments* in 1759.

> We have no other ways to conceive of anything which other persons act or suffer, but by recalling and exciting the ideas of what we ourselves are conscious we have found in our own minds; and by putting the ideas which we obtain by this means in the place of another; or as it were, substituting ourselves in their place. Thus, we have no conception, what understanding, perception, love, pleasure, pain, or desire are in others; but by putting ourselves as it were in their stead, or transferring the ideas we obtain of such things in our own minds by consciousness into their place. . . . It is thus in all moral things that we conceive of in others.

Indeed, Edwards said, harking back to letter "z" of his Miscellanies, "this is the only way that we come to be capable of having ideas of any perception or act even of the Godhead."[87]

Yet this essential capacity is not itself distinctively moral, Edwards held, nor is there any deliberation in it. Human beings put themselves in the place of others "habitually, instantaneously, and without set purpose." "In all a man's thoughts of another person, in whatever he apprehends of his moral conduct to others or to himself, if it be loving or hating him, approving or condemning him, rewarding or punishing him, he necessarily, as it were, puts himself in his stead; and therefore the more naturally, easily, and quietly sees whether he, being in his place, should approve or condemn, be angry or pleased as he is."[88] The capacity for sympathetic identification serves in Edwards's theory as a kind of sensor for guiding moral judgments, both about oneself and about others. The judgments themselves are based mainly on the sense of desert or other related rational and aesthetic criteria in nature.

In summary, natural conscience consists of two things: (1) an internal awareness of self-contradiction, or the disposition to approve or disapprove "the moral treatment which passes between us and others" out of the deter-

---

86. See also Miscellanies, no. 621: "A clear idea of sorrow or joy or any act, exercise, or passion of the mind is the very same thing in a degree existing in the mind that it is an idea of."
87. *True Virtue*, ed. Frankena, 64.
88. *Ibid.*, 64–65.

mination of the mind to be easy or uneasy according to our self-consistency or lack of it, with the processes of sympathy acting as the necessary middle term in the equation; and (2) the principles of reciprocity and retribution, or the sense of desert, consisting in "natural agreement, proportion and harmony, between malevolence or injury, and resentment and punishment; or between loving and being loved, between shewing kindness and being rewarded, etc." The first has application mainly to self-judgment. The second is the norm of goodness and virtue as these are known to the natural man. Concern for purity of intentions in moral relations, which is usually a large part of ethical evaluation, is conspicuously absent in this analysis of what occurs without the aid of special grace.

Both the sensitivity to inconsistency and the sense of desert are necessary to the functioning of natural conscience. The sense of desert, however, comes first and is the foundation of the uneasiness resulting from self-contradiction,[89] because the need for self-union, or man's liability to the pains of self-contradiction, cannot by itself explain the anger we feel when we ourselves are unjustly condemned or injured. In such cases, something more primitive is operative. But both kinds of approving or disapproving "concur" in the ordinary actings of conscience, "the one founded on the other." For example,

> when a man's conscience disapproves of his treatment of his neighbour, in the first place he is conscious, that if he were in his neighbour's stead, he should resent such treatment from a sense of justice, or from a sense of uniformity and equality between such treatment, and resentment, and punishment. . . . And then in the next place, he perceives that therefore he is not consistent with himself, in doing what he himself should resent in that case; and hence disapproves it, as being naturally averse to opposition to himself.[90]

From this example we see that sympathy is a prerequisite for a conscientious response, for only through sympathy can we transfer our sense of desert to the situation of another. But the pain or uneasiness of conscience comes not from the mere psychological fact of sympathy but from the affront to our sense of desert.

Edwards's theory of natural conscience was in some respects a synthesis of the theories of the intellectualists and the sentimentalists. Clarke and Wollaston were drawn upon in his emphasis on the sense of desert, which Edwards treated as a principle based ultimately on formal relations such as fitness

89. *Ibid.*, 66. Bishop Butler's "Dissertation of the Nature of Virtue," appended to his *Analogy of Religion* (1736), may have influenced Edwards toward making the sense of desert a fundamental category of ethical perception. In *Freedom of the Will*, ed. Ramsey, 358, Edwards asserted that children develop a sense of desert as soon as they can speak or act at all as rational creatures.

90. *True Virtue*, ed. Frankena, 66–67.

and suitability. Hutcheson and Hume received their due in his recognition of the importance of sympathy. On the other hand, Edwards's stress on self-disagreement as the basis of the uneasiness produced by natural conscience was an expression of his belief that the natural man is primarily egoistic and hedonistic. Writing from a standpoint outside of the secular schools of thought, and removed from the thick of controversy by his location in the provinces, Edwards felt free to pick and choose from the available theories in order to reconstruct the foundations of the moral life. Yet this was no academic exercise. He took the results very seriously, since the "moral sense" or "natural conscience . . . is indeed the general natural rule which God has given to all men, whereby to judge of moral good and evil."[91] It is easy to forget how far Edwards went in accepting the conclusions of the secular ethicists. "The moral sense," he wrote, "—if the understanding be well informed, exercised at liberty, and in an extensive manner, without being restrained to a private sphere—approves the very same things which a spiritual and divine sense approves; and those things only; though not on the same grounds, nor with the same kind of approbation."[92]

Edwards took it for granted that his analysis of natural moral understanding was not an investigation of a subjective psychological principle. It was, on the contrary, an investigation of the fundamental structure of the universe, in which the role of the moral sense or natural conscience was as fixed and definite as the laws of physics. The difference between moral philosophy and moral theology was not at all that the former was somehow subjective and the latter objective, as is sometimes assumed by historians who are not sufficiently familiar with Hutcheson's thought, or that moral philosophy was relativist whereas Edwards's ethics is absolutist. The moral sense, in both Hutcheson's view and Edwards's, is as firmly lodged in the "necessary nature of things" as the spiritual and divine sense ("by which those who are truly virtuous and holy perceive the excellency of true virtue"). Both are "established in agreement with the nature of things," Edwards believed. Indeed, since the spiritual sense by definition is agreeable to the necessary nature of things (although it is infused by a special divine dispensation), so this "inferior moral sense, being so far correspondent to that [divine sense], must also so far agree with the nature of things."[93]

---

91. *Ibid.*, 104.
92. *Ibid.*, 103.
93. *Ibid.*, 103–105. A principal error in Clyde A. Holbrook's *Ethics of Edwards* is the assumption that the sentimentalist ethicists, unlike Edwards, were caught in subjectivism. In fact, the concept of subjectivism would have had no meaning for them. God, as the author of nature, framed all, man and the world.

Sentiment versus Reason

In the last chapter of *True Virtue*, entitled "In What Respects Virtue or Moral Good Is Founded in Sentiment; and How Far It Is Founded in the Reason and Nature of Things," Edwards took up directly the central question of David Hume's *Enquiry Concerning the Principles of Morals*. "There has been a controversy started of late," Hume observed at the beginning of his work,

> . . . concerning the general foundation of Morals; whether they be derived from Reason, or from Sentiment; whether we attain the knowledge of them by a chain of argument and induction, or by an immediate feeling and finer internal sense; whether, like all sound judgement of truth and falsehood, they should be the same to every rational intelligent being; or whether, like the perception of beauty and deformity, they be founded entirely on the particular fabric and constitution of the human species.[94]

It has been overlooked that, despite Edwards's strong rejection of Hume's utilitarianism, both men answered this question in the same way, namely by affirming a correspondence between the moral sense and the structure of the universe, for are not both man and nature the creation of one supreme maker? The moral standard that reason uncovers, "founded on the nature of things, is eternal and inflexible, even by the will of the Supreme Being," Hume said. The standard of taste, sentiment, internal sense, or whatever, "arising from the eternal frame and constitution of animals," is also "ultimately derived from that Supreme Will, which bestowed on each being its peculiar nature, and arranged the several classes and orders of existence."[95]

Edwards also pleaded that sentimentalism per se, whether in relation to religion or to natural ethics, did not imply subjectivism or arbitrariness in moral relations. It is true, he said, that they who see the beauty of true virtue do not perceive it by argumentation based on its connections and consequences. But they perceive it, nonetheless, "by the frame of their own minds, or a certain spiritual sense given them of God." And this frame of mind or inward sense is not given "arbitrarily, so that if [God] had pleased he might have given a contrary sense and determination of mind, which would have agreed as well with the necessary nature of things."[96] Such a belief, Edwards showed, results in a string of absurdities, for "God, in giving to the creature such a temper of mind, gives that which is agreeable to what is by absolute necessity his own temper and nature."[97]

94. Hume, *Enquiry Concerning the Principles of Morals*, ed. Selby-Bigge, 170.
95. *Ibid.*, 294.
96. *True Virtue*, ed. Frankena, 99. Cf. n. 33, above.
97. *Ibid.*, 100.

We can put aside for the moment Edwards's metaphysical proofs for the unity of natural conscience (or the moral sense) with the nature of things, since this question would bring us prematurely into the tenets of his moral theology. But an empirical question still remains concerning the relativity of moral judgments. Admitting that a great variety of moral sentiments can be found in the world, "especially in different nations," how therefore can the discrimination of virtue and vice "be any other than arbitrary," that is, determined not "by the nature of things, but by the sentiments of men with relation to the nature of things?"[98] Edwards's response to this important question was taken expressly from Hutcheson: "What has been said by others, Mr. Hutchison in particular, may abundantly show, that the differences which are to be found among different persons and nations concerning moral good and evil, are not inconsistent with a general moral sense, common to all mankind."[99] The central idea in Hutcheson's and Edwards's answer to the relativist challenge is that in the internal structure of moral responses we do find universality, though disagreement may exist about specific applications. All people consider some acts deserving of esteem and others of reprobation; they view things in a moral framework, or from a moral point of view, though they may disagree strongly about what in particular is deserving or undeserving. The moral sense is everywhere "the same thing in general," Edwards said, "—a suitableness, or natural uniformity and agreement between the affections and acts of the agent, and the affection and treatment of others some way concerned." Nevertheless, the responses of different persons to moral situations will vary according to "a variety of apprehensions about them, and the various manner in which they are viewed, by reason of the partial attention of the mind."[100] The elements are the same; the view may change. Other influences on the perception of a moral situation will be example, custom, education, and mental association.

Finally, perhaps remembering Locke's assertion that the terms of ethics— virtue and vice, good and evil, right and wrong—are merely arbitrarily applied and can follow only the force of social custom when there is no absolute standard provided by divine law,[101] Edwards replied with an argument as ancient as Socrates: "Mankind in general seem to suppose some general standard, or foundation in nature, for an universal consistence in the use of the terms whereby they express moral good and evil. . . . This is evidently supposed in all their disputes about right and wrong; and in all endeavours used to prove that any thing is either good or evil." Disputes about morals

---

98. *Ibid.*, 105.
99. *Ibid.*, 106.
100. *Ibid.*, 105.
101. Locke, *Essay Concerning Human Understanding*, ed. Fraser, Bk. II, chap. xxviii, sec. 10.

presuppose a standard, however elusive. As Hutcheson had asked, "Did ever blind men debate whether purple or scarlet were the finer colour?"[102]

The main elements in Edwards's analysis of the *intellectual* bases of natural morality have now all been isolated. The *affectional* sources of natural goodness will be addressed in the next two chapters. In the case of both the intellectual factors and the affectional, however, Edwards maintained that the resulting morality was commonplace and thin, rooted in self-regard or involuntary psychological structures lacking in moral substance. The highly touted moral sense is reducible to natural conscience, which is itself reducible to a primitive sense of desert and the natural desire for logical self-consistency, or rather, to the discomfort resulting from self-contradiction. Human beings tend to be pleased by moral conduct because such conduct often partakes of certain elements of formal beauty, but in such cases, too, the appreciation of virtue is more the pleasure of geometry than morality. Finally, whatever capacities are found in the natural man for properly judging himself and others in moral terms, Edwards was convinced that this ability was not translatable into consistent virtuous conduct without the inner transformation that only divine grace can effect. Without the aid of grace, men and women are too disintegrated psychologically to be inwardly moral, although they may have much of the intellectual equipment necessary for valuing moral behavior in both themselves and others.

In Edwards's work, the pietist impetus in American Calvinism, which had begun under the leading influence of William Ames, was both enhanced in some areas and checked in others. Edwards's belief in and defense of the notion that God's grace has a direct physical influence upon the will, his lengthy demonstrations that the will is an affection, his emphasis upon the affections and dispositions as the necessary core of a holy life, and his concern for preserving man's sense of dependency upon divine power undoubtedly added rigor to existing notions in evangelical theology in need of clarification and strengthening. On the other hand, the persistent striving in pietist ranks, to keep moral philosophy dependent upon theology or, more precisely, to fuse the moral life with Christian theology[103] suffered a surprising setback, in Edwards's dissertation on true virtue. Although *True Virtue* portrayed the supreme religious ideal of "living to God" in some of its sections, an ideal that was claimed to be completely inaccessible to the natural man, other parts

---

102. *True Virtue*, ed. Frankena, 107; Hutcheson, *Inquiry into Beauty and Virtue*, 84.

103. Cf., for example, John Wesley's journal for July 1739: Faith, holiness, and good works are the root, the tree, and the fruit, which "God hath joined, and man ought not to put asunder." For further discussion of the pietists' ambitions, see Fiering, *Moral Philosophy at Seventeenth-Century Harvard*, chaps. 1 and 3.

of the book unquestionably endorsed and gave free rein to naturalistic ethics in both theory and practice. The absorption by the new moral philosophy of so many of the ideas and principles of seventeenth-century religious thought, particularly from Puritanism and Continental Augustinianism, and the transmutation of these ideas and principles into secular form made it exceedingly difficult for Edwards to differentiate effectively a Christian moral philosophy from what was already being asserted by the moral philosophers without specifically Christian intentions. William Ames could fairly easily distinguish a Christian ethics from Aristotle's; Edwards faced the much harder task of distinguishing Christian ethics from Hutcheson's. This explains the relative intellectual poverty of Edwards's 1758 publication, *The Great Christian Doctrine of Original Sin Defended*, which he was composing simultaneously with *True Virtue*. After so many concessions to natural human virtue, Original Sin as a *psychological* concept was approaching the vanishing point. The way was prepared for Channing, Emerson, and Parker to affirm expressly that nature itself is redeemed. There would still remain the infinite distance between the saint and the common man, but the whole level of appreciation of the intrinsic benignity of the common man had been momentously, perhaps irreversibly, raised. Only the two great wars of the twentieth century and the Holocaust have been able to shake into ruins, at least temporarily, the psychological optimism of the Shaftesbury-Hutcheson gospel of the innate goodness of man.[104]

As we will see in the next chapter, Edwards was not slow to make use also of the new insights into human psychology that revealed the baseness of human motives. Here, too, there was a remarkable merging of Puritan and Augustinian thought with naturalistic theories of egoism and psychological pessimism, so that by the time of Edwards's work it is impossible to differentiate so-called Calvinist theories from those of the libertines and the cynics. The subtle permutations of self-love were never explored in more depth than in the seventeenth and eighteenth centuries. But Edwards knew, no less than Calvin, that in the hands of the Christian, cynicism is a weapon that can explode in one's face. Carry these pessimistic psychological analyses too far,

---

104. It is surely one of the great ironies in the history of American thought that William Ellery Channing was "converted" by reading Hutcheson. As his son recounts the story, "It was while reading, one day in [Hutcheson] some of the various passages in which he asserts man's capacity for disinterested affection, and considers virtue as the sacrifice of private interests and the bearing of private evils for the public good, or as self-devotion to absolute, universal good, that there suddenly burst upon his mind that view of the dignity of human nature which was ever after to 'uphold and cherish' him, and thenceforth to be 'the fountain light of all his day, the master light of all his seeing.' " "The place and the hour" of this conversion were thereafter sacred in Channing's memory. "It seemed to him that he then passed through a new spiritual birth, and entered upon the day of eternal peace and joy." *The Works of William E. Channing* . . . (Boston, 1886), introduction.

and the outcome is bound to be a skepticism even toward the possibility of real holiness. Due recognition has to be given to what is ostensibly good in the world, lest this life be confused with hell. Thus, Edwards's writing on self-love was necessarily bridled. The theory of egoism had to be asserted with caution: it could be used to demolish pride in and pretensions to moral goodness; but it had to be carefully contained when its explosive power threatened even the alleged evidences of redemption.

4

The Permutations of Self-Love

He that trusts his own heart is a fool.[1]

If it is sometimes true that philosophical debates fail to achieve any real advancement of knowledge, a contrary example is the history of the great debate over self-love, which in some respects was at the center of discussion in moral philosophy for more than a hundred years. From about the middle of the seventeenth century, when the problem of self-love was propelled into the main arena of learned discussion—in secular studies by Hobbes and in religious studies principally by the Jansenists—there was impressive progress in subtlety and clarity of reasoning on the subject and in general understanding. If interest in the problem of self-love declined by the end of the eighteenth century, it was surely in part because it had been so thoroughly analyzed, both as to the questions that could be raised and the solutions that could be given; literally, almost nothing more could be said about it.

The nature of self-love was a subject of study that any Puritan or heir of Puritans gravitated to with as much ease as he picked up his Bible; so it is not surprising that Edwards would be interested in the problem. But beyond this general concern, Edwards was particularly intent, first, upon counteracting the prevalent psychological optimism of the eighteenth century, which in his estimation tended to minimize the potency and ubiquity of basic human selfishness; second, Edwards carefully scrutinized the workings of self-love because, like his seventeenth-century Puritan ancestors, he believed it was important for salvation that the faithful test the authenticity of their love of God and of neighbor. The first of these concerns was polemical and philosophical; the second was personal and religious.

It is convenient to divide into three questions the problem of self-love that Edwards confronted: (1) What is the meaning of self-love, or how is the term to be precisely defined and distinguished in its parts? (2) In either religion or ethics is there an acceptable role for self-love, or is it to be entirely discounte-

---

1. Edwards, *Thoughts Concerning the Revival*, 201.

nanced? This question was of long-standing importance to those responsible for giving pastoral advice on matters relating to sanctification, as well as to philosophers intent on defining true virtue. (3) To what extent and degree does vicious self-love underlie the apparent virtues and religious observances of this world, covertly feeding hypocrisy, insincerity, and counterfeit morality? This third question was most dangerous to handle because it was double-edged. It was necessary, on the one hand, for a religious thinker to explore all of the secret ways of the heart's deception of both oneself and others in order to expose the limited and amoral basis of much of the world's ostensible virtue; on the other hand, Edwards considered it vital also to prove that there was a holy virtue that had its foundation in a divine principle altogether different from narrow self-love. The danger was that in the hands of cynics, the subtle encroachments of self-love could just as well be used as evidence against the existence of holy virtue as against natural virtue. The three problems that Edwards confronted, then, may be designated that of the definition, that of the legitimacy, and that of the inroads of self-love. In each of these areas he made perceptive contributions.

The Definition of Self-Love

An anxious and searching concern for the purity of one's motivations was a part of daily life in New England, as many surviving diaries reveal. Edwards's own youthful journal contains the familiar signs of this characteristic scrupulosity: July 30, 1723, "Have concluded to endeavour to work myself into duties by searching and tracing back all the real reasons why I do them not, and narrowly searching out all the subtle subterfuges of my thoughts . . ."; August 6, 1723, "Very much convinced of the extraordinary deceitfulness of the heart, and how exceedingly affection or appetite blinds the mind, and brings it into entire subjection. . . . How doth the Appetite stretch the Reason, to bring both ends together."[2] And so on.

Beyond this general cultural inheritance, Edwards's maternal grandfather, Solomon Stoddard, had a particular interest in the manifestations and significance of self-love and wrote on the subject in some detail. In a note written only about four or five years after the diary entries quoted above, Edwards tes-

---

2. Printed in Dwight, *Life of Edwards*, 91–92. The last sentence, beginning "How doth," is probably a quotation from somewhere, though the text gives no indication of this. Cf. Benjamin Franklin's remark in his *Autobiography* after describing how he came to break his vegetarian regimen: "So convenient a thing is it to be a *reasonable creature*, since it enables one to find or make a reason for every thing one has a mind to do."

tified to Stoddard's influence on him in interpreting the relationship between Original Sin and self-love:

> The best philosophy that I have met with of original sin and all sinfull inclinations, habits, and principles [is] undoubtedly that of Mr. Stoddards of this town of Northampton[;] that [is], that it is self love in conjunction with the absence of the image and love of God, that natural and necessary inclination that man has to his own benefit together with the absence of original righteousness, or in other words the absence of the influence of God's Spirit whereby love to God and to holiness is kept up to the degree that this other inclination [self-love] is alwaies kept in its due subordination.

Once the superior regulating principle, "the governour and guide," is removed, "self love governs alone and . . . breaks out into all manner of exorbitancies, and becomes in innumerable cases a vile and odious disposition and causes thousands of unlovely and hatefull actions."[3] In the absence of restraining grace self-love is the norm.

There is much in this statement of Edwards's that immediately brings us into some of the main issues concerning self-love, but for our present purposes, we need only note the definition: "that natural and necessary inclination that man has to his own benefit." The emphasis on the necessity of selflove already declared Edwards's commitment to what may be called an *analytic* position on the question of self-love, as compared to the *rigorist* view that all manifestations of self-love must be purged from the soul. "Necessary" inclinations cannot be purged. We will see that for Edwards, self-love, properly defined, is an irremovable and acceptable substratum in human motivation.[4]

---

3. Edwards, Miscellanies, no. 301, written in about 1727. Solomon Stoddard's *Three Sermons Lately Preach'd at Boston* (Boston, 1717) contained as one of the sermons, "That Natural Men Are under the Government of Self-Love," which was probably his most extensive written statement on the subject, but, in addition, he and Edwards would have had many opportunities for face-to-face discussion. The theory presented here as Stoddard's was not at all unique to him.

4. The rigorist view was usually based on the Augustinian distinction between the two antithetical loves possible in the soul of man—that toward God and that toward the city of man. As Anthony Levi, *French Moralists: The Theory of the Passions, 1585–1649* (Oxford, 1964), 228, has observed, in this tradition it was not always clear whether by self-love was meant primarily a psychological motive or a physical state of the soul from which acts proceed. The analytic view was clearly based on psychological analysis, as opposed to the essentially theological view of the rigorists. On pp. 225–233, Levi gives an excellent brief discussion of the theory of self-love in the 17th century. I am borrowing the term "rigorism" from F. B. Kaye's classic introduction to his edition of Bernard Mandeville's *The Fable of the Bees: or, Private Vices, Publick Benefits*, 2 vols. (Oxford, 1924).

In his sermon on self-love Stoddard had distinguished between a "lawful self-love, an holy self-love, and a sinful self-love."[5] Although godly men are under the influence of a higher principle than self-love, namely the spirit of love to God, yet "much of a spirit of self-love" remains in them. The difference is that the godly are released from the *preponderant* power of natural self-love. The basis of Stoddard's distinctions lay in an analysis of the functional role of self-love, its place in relation to the other powers or possibilities in the soul. This dynamic approach was shared by Edwards and underlay his taxonomy of the forms of self-love. That which is "often called" self-love, Edwards noted, is "exceedingly improperly called love," for the term "self-love" is used to describe two quite different things; a delight in what is amiable in oneself, on the one hand (sometimes called self-esteem), and an inclination to pleasure or aversion to pain, on the other. The latter meaning, the hedonic or eudaemonic, is so general it serves to describe the self-love of angels and saints as well as of devils and damned spirits. Devils love themselves "not because they see anything in themselves which they imagine to be lovely, but merely because they do not incline to pain but to pleasure, or merely because they are capable of pain or pleasure." Yet in what sense is such an inclination called *love*? All sentient beings prefer what is agreeable to them to what is disagreeable (by definition). Exercising preference is choosing what is agreeable or pleasing. Thus, we might say, the masochist chooses pain because it is agreeable to him, but in such a case his pain *is* his pleasure. In order to resolve this paradox, it is clear (and this was apparently one of Edwards's points) that one must differentiate between the self-love of the monk and the self-love of the sybarite. Self-love in this second sense "is not affection," Edwards wrote, "but only the entity of the thing, or [a person's] being what he is."[6] The eudaemonic principle, then, is not properly classified as a distinguishing form of self-love.

Edwards did not, in this early note, draw out all of the implications of the distinction between self-esteem and eudaemonism; but we can see that the foundation was laid in it for establishing the difference between, on the one side, a commendable and proper self-love, which is, in effect, the love of what is worthy or truly lovable in oneself, and, on the other side, that form of so-called self-love that necessarily underlies all human choice. The choice of what is agreeable to oneself can only rightly be called an act of self-love when that choice is shown to be selfish. To make a moral judgment on the case we must know what particular thing is judged agreeable or disagreeable by the agent in any given instance, for the same psychological law of "self-love" is

5. Stoddard, *Three Sermons*, 35.
6. "Notes on the Mind," no. 1, in Dwight, *Life of Edwards*, 692–697.

operative in the person who finds benevolence most agreeable and the person who finds, let us say, miserliness most agreeable.[7]

Edwards's refinement of the meaning of self-love in this early note followed from a traditional metaphysical principle that he adopted from the start of his serious reflections, namely, that God necessarily loves only Himself. God cannot but love the highest good and is perfect in all His doings; therefore, He can only love Himself, who is the sum of love in the universe and comprehends all goodness within Himself.[8] Edwards warned, however, that "when we meditate on this love of God to himself as being the thing wherein His infinite excellence and loveliness consists," there is the danger "of some alloy to the sweetness of our view, by its appearing with something of the aspect and cast of what we [*pejoratively*] call self-love."

> But we are to consider that this love includes in it, or rather is the same as, a love to everything, as they are all communications of Himself. So that we are to conceive of divine excellence as the infinite general love, that which reaches all proportionally, with perfect purity and sweetness; yea, it includes the true love of all creatures, for that is His spirit or, which is the same thing, His love.[9]

God's self-love is thus a model of proper self-love. Men, too, as part of the creation, may properly love themselves provided that their love is *proportional* to that which is good in themselves. This is simply appropriate self-esteem.

7. It is notable that Edwards introduced these distinctions without having read Bishop Butler's sermons, where some of the same points were classically made. Edwards's remarks are merely suggestive, however, as compared to the completeness of Butler's analysis. Edwards's distinction is not quite the same as the difference between *amour propre* and *amour-de-soi*, which was introduced in 17th-century France and later popularized by Jean-Jacques Rousseau. In his *A System of Moral Philosophy* (London, 1755), Bk. I, 39, Hutcheson drew the usual distinctions. Self-love is a universal principle in human nature, he said, if it means "desire for one's own happiness." On the other hand, "self-esteem," or "the preference of our moral character and accomplishments to those of others," is not universal, for it is plainly contrary to "what the modest and self-diffident continually experience" (quoted from Paul McReynolds, ed., *Four Early Works on Motivation* [Gainesville, Fla., 1969]). Devils are not modest and self-diffident, and therefore they lack *proper* self-esteem (or dis-esteem), since they know themselves to be truly hateful. Yet like all sentient creatures, they desire their own happiness.

8. See Nygren, *Agape and Eros*, trans. Watson, 653–655, for discussion of the medieval treatment of God as *amor sui*.

9. "Notes on the Mind," no. 45, in Dwight, *Life of Edwards*, 700–701. I have rather freely inserted bracketed material in quotations, either to complete an author's statement or to interpret it. When these bracketed interpolations are italicized it signifies that I am interpreting or commenting on the text, perhaps even extending the author's meaning. Bracketed interpolations in roman are more conventional editorial additions.

It is notable that despite Edwards's close resemblance in many of his ideas to the Jansenists in France and to Lutheran pietists like Johann Arndt in Germany, the tendency of his philosophical mind (as opposed, perhaps, to his theological commitments) was to reduce rather than to exaggerate the dichotomy between Augustine's famous two loves. "Love is the efficient Cause of all Things," Arndt wrote in a typical passage, "and as there are two Sorts of Love, the Love of God, and the Love of ourselves, and these *directly opposite to each other*, it follows, that the one must be extremely Good, and the other extremely Evil."[10] Anders Nygren has spoken of the "campaign against self-love" undertaken by Luther, who recognized "no justifiable self-love" whatsoever, a campaign that in fact went beyond conventional medieval interpretations of Augustine on the question.[11] Jansenius took a position very similar to Luther's.[12] A Jansenist disciple, Jacques Esprit, whose work was widely known in English translation, wrote: "The best insight into our religion shows that love, far from being innocent, is guilty of the most enormous crimes; since it cannot exist in man without depriving God of his right. For by stifling his love for God, it hinders him from paying that due honour, admiration and service which the creator requires."[13] The French Quietists, though in profound disagreement with the Jansenists in their treatment of Original Sin, yet were like them in their emphasis on utter disinter-

10. Johann Arndt, *Of True Christianity . . .* , trans. Anthony William Boehm, 2d ed. rev. (London, 1720), II, 564. Arndt's well-known work was republished in London in Latin in 1708 and in English in 1712. It appeared first in German in 1609. Edwards almost certainly read it in his youth, and he was probably influenced by it in several ways. Arndt's great importance for the pietist movement is treated in F. Ernest Stoeffler, *The Rise of Evangelical Pietism* (Leiden, 1971 [orig. publ. 1965]), 202–212.

11. Nygren, *Agape and Eros*, trans. Watson, 709–716.

12. For Jansenius, "self-love stands in radical theological opposition to the love of God: it is incompatible with it and incapable of being compounded with it in any degree." Levi, *French Moralists*, 226.

13. Quoted by John Passmore, *The Perfectibility of Man* (London, 1970), 120, from Esprit's *Discourses on the Deceitfulness of Humane Virtues*, trans. William Beauvoir (London, 1706), 264. For a good summary of Esprit's thinking, see *History of the Works of the Learned*, VIII (May 1706), 310ff. Passmore argues that in the course of the 18th century the disfavor attached to self-love generally diminished. He suggests that one of the reasons for this change was that motives were no longer considered to be of such overwhelming importance in ethics. The only qualification that needs to be added to this explanation is that until the rise of the new moral philosophy in Britain, which was so heavily influenced by Puritanism, motives had never been considered very important by secular ethicists. The emphasis on purity of intentions is one of the factors that distinguishes the psychologizing of 18th-century moralists from Classical and Scholastic moral philosophy. The emergence of utilitarianism, which was indifferent to motives, is a sign of the decline of the religious energy that had informed much ethical thought in the 18th century. The moral acceptance of self-love (whether sanctioned directly or indirectly) probably has some relation to the social change that brought bourgeois individualism into dominance as a public philosophy in the West.

estedness as an essential criterion of acceptable love to God.[14] In some seventeenth-century Puritan texts there are comparably rigorous sentiments, although it is easy to misinterpret them. What sometimes appears initially to be an outright condemnation of self-love is later qualified so that, as in the case of Edwards, it becomes clear that only a particular kind of self-love— carnal, or concupiscent, or whatever—is under attack.

Self-love was a conception so vague it was easily and often manipulated into paradox. A Harvard student notebook dating from the middle of the seventeenth century contains the outline of a disputation defense of the thesis, "Man in his fallen, corrupted and depraved estate hates himself, has no true love for himself." Usually, of course, it was argued that in the fallen state man is peculiarly the captive of self-love, as Solomon Stoddard had maintained. But this student went on to argue that in his fallen estate, man loves his "corrupted being," which he attempts to preserve in accordance with the natural principle of self-preservation; "[there]fore he loves the preservation and continuance of his corruptions, and his being in them and is exceeding averse from the . . . destroying himself as he is corrupted." But, if a man does not desire and love "a being in grace, and the continuation of this being; he is justly said not to love himself," because "he does not love himself as he is sprunge up out of principles which give being to him [and] as he is a plante that grows in nature's garden." He loves, instead, an unnatural self. "A love of the being of sin, and a love of a being in grace are incompatable; the loving of one implies the non loving of the other." If a man is corrupted and does not love a being in grace, he hates it. "[There]fore it may now be said man [in his fallen state] does not love, but hates himself."[15] By implication it was permissible to love oneself in a redeemed state, insofar as one was redeemed. Along the same lines, a moderate self-love was often considered an allowable ingredient in human love to God. William Ames, for example, allowed subordinate ends, such as self-interest, to be *part* of one's love to God and also to be part of one's quest for salvation, and his opinion reflected a long tradition of such moderation.[16]

Writing in about 1732, Edwards maintained that the very asking of the

14. Pope Innocent XII's condemnation of Quietism was reprinted in English in *History of the Works of the Learned*, I (Mar. 1699). Condemned propositions IV and V were: "In a State of Holy Indifference, The Soul no longer retains any Voluntary and Deliberate Desires for its own Interests. . . . In the same State of Holy Indifference, we Will nothing for our Selves, but all things for God. We desire nothing that may be perfect and happy for our own proper Interests."

15. Abraham Pierson, "Notes of Lectures Attended at Harvard College," MS, Beinecke Lib., Yale Univ. The basic idea of this argument goes back to Augustine: "The love wherewith a man truly loves himself is none other than the love of God. For he who loves himself in any other way is rather to be said to hate himself." Quoted in Passmore, *Perfectibility of Man*, 90.

16. Ames, *Conscience*, Bk. III, chap. 17.

question "Whether or no a man ought to love God more than himself?" is invalid when the question is left uninterpreted. Self-love, "taken in the most extensive sense" (i.e., as the eudaemonic law), and love to God "are not things properly capable of being compared with one another," Edwards wrote. "For they are not opposites or things entirely distinct, but one enters into the nature of the other." Following up on the earlier discussion in his unpublished notes, Edwards observed again that in the broadest meaning self-love is no more than "a man's love of his own pleasure and happiness, and hatred of his own misery, or rather 'tis only a capacity of enjoyment or suffering." To say that a person loves his own happiness or pleasure is to say only that he delights in what he delights in; and to say that a person hates his own misery is to say only that he is "grieved or afflicted in his own affliction." In this meaning, then, self-love is only "a capacity of enjoying or taking delight in any thing." It thus makes no sense for a person to declare that his or her love to God is superior to self-love, if by self-love is meant the human capacity to delight in anything, since equivalent to one's love to God is one's disposition to delight in Him and His good. Moralists who ask people to do away with concern for their own happiness in favor of love to God are speaking nonsense. Again, therefore, we are brought back to the necessity for more precise definition.

Self-love is a person's love to his or her own good, according to Edwards, yet this definition may be taken in two senses. First of all, whatever a person delights in can be understood broadly as one's "own" good, "whether it be a man's own proper and separate pleasure or honour, or the pleasure or honour of another." It is nonsense to say that a man should delight in any good that is not his own, which would be tantamount to demanding that he delight in that in which he does not delight. Love to God cannot possibly be superior to this type of self-love, which is misnamed as a form of love. However, in another sense, we may speak of self-love as delight in a "separate good" that is *exclusively* one's own, and "love to God can and ought to be" superior to this. Love that is directed to one's "own proper single and separate good" Edwards designated "simple" self-love, and he considered it truly "entirely distinct" from love to God. "Simple" self-love is man's preponderant natural inclination. Somewhat removed from it, however, but also natural (rather than gracious) in origin is another form of self-love, which Edwards called "compounded" self-love. This latter form is "exercised in the delight that a man has in the good of another." Compounded self-love is not identical to proper love to God, but it is not entirely distinct from it like simple self-love is. Compounded self-love seems to be in an intermediary position in Edwards's theory, and represents the highest possible reach of natural love. It is called "compounded" because although like simple self-love "it arises from the necessary nature of a perceiving and willing being, whereby he loves his own pleasure or delight," it includes also "another principle that determines the exercise" of simple self-love (or, we might say, regulates it) and "makes that to become its object which otherwise cannot, a certain principle uniting this person with another that causes the good of another to be its good."[17]

Edwards left unexplained at this stage in his thinking the source, the nature, and even the name of the "certain principle" that transforms simple self-love into compounded and unites one person with another in a sense of common good.[18] He undoubtedly had in mind, however, several mechanisms at the level of common grace—natural affection or *storgé*,[19] conscience as described in Natural Law theory, and perhaps other passions or intellectual processes such as were delineated in Malebranche, Shaftesbury, and others.

It was already commonplace when Edwards was writing for moralists to speak of the necessary *balance* between self-love and social love. In 1714 in a *Spectator* essay the dissenting minister Henry Grove affirmed in opposition to Hobbes: "The Contriver of Human Nature hath wisely furnished it with two Principles of Action, Self-love and Benevolence; designed one of them to render Man wakeful to his own personal Interest, the other to dispose him for giving his utmost Assistance to all engag'd in the same Pursuit." Grove argued that "kind and benevolent Propensions were the original Growth of the Heart of Man."[20] In 1704 in his long critique of Locke, Leibniz argued that "God has given to man *instincts* which prompt at once and without reasoning to some portion of that which reason ordains; just as we walk in obedience to the laws of mechanics without thinking of those laws." Although such instincts are not invincible—"passions may resist them, prejudices obscure them"—yet "we agree most frequently with these instincts of conscience,"

17. Miscellanies, no. 530.

18. The word "principle" in Edwards's moral psychology should be understood in the sense of the Latin *principium*, meaning "foundation," or "groundwork." In *Religious Affections*, ed. Smith, 206, Edwards referred to the spiritual perceptions or spiritual sense of the sanctified as "new principles of nature. . . . By a principle of nature . . . , I mean that foundation which is laid in nature, either old or new, for any particular manner or kind of exercise of the faculties of the soul; or a natural habit or foundation for action, giving a person ability and disposition to exert the faculties in exercises of such a certain kind." Later, on p. 242, he spoke of self-love as a "principle entirely natural." On p. 381 he quoted Thomas Shepard's *Parable of the Ten Virgins* as follows: "There is never a hypocrite living, but closeth with Christ for his own ends: for he cannot work beyond his principle."

19. "*Storgé*," a Greek word referring principally to the affection of parents for their children, which appears in the New Testament in the negative, *astorgos*, meaning brutal inhumanity, was used by most 17th- and 18th-century moralists, but it lost currency in the 19th century. See n. 110, below.

20. *Spectator*, no. 588, Sept. 1, 1714.

Leibniz continued, "and we follow them also when stronger impressions do not overcome them." In addition, "nature gives to man and also to most of the animals affectionate and tender feelings for those of their species. . . . Besides this general instinct of *society*, . . . there are some more particular forms of it, as the affection between the male and female, the love which father and mother bear toward the children, which the Greeks call Στοργή and other similar inclinations."[21] Edwards's conception of compounded love was distinctive only in his insistence that what others might call a separate and independent principle of social love or benevolence was still a species of self-love.[22] But more analysis would clearly be needed in order to demonstrate this proposition, which in its Hobbesian form had provoked an enormous amount of opposition. How difficult the battle against psychological optimism was to be, Edwards did not know in the early 1730s, since he had not yet encountered in his reading the full development of benevolism.[23]

To summarize thus far, Edwards's early writing took note of four forms of self-love: (1) a universal psychological principle of seeking happiness defined as that which is agreeable to oneself, true of all creatures in heaven and hell and of God Himself; (2) the seeking of one's own exclusive good, which necessarily is at the cost of other people, called "simple self-love" (and in common language, selfishness); (3) an enlarged sense of one's own good, which may include others to a greater or less degree, called by Edwards "compounded self-love"; this could be the result of a process of reasoning

21. G. Leibniz, *New Essays Concerning Human Understanding*, ed. and trans. A. G. Langley (New York, 1896), 89, 91. These essays were first published posthumously in French in 1765.

22. Malebranche distinguished three major natural inclinations: (1) toward the good in general (or God); (2) toward the preservation of our own being or welfare; and (3) toward other creatures whom we either love or who are useful to us (*Search after Truth*, trans. Taylor, I, 139). Shaftesbury dropped the first of these and began with (1) "the natural affections, which lead to the good of the public"; followed by (2) the "self affections, which lead only to the good of the private"; and (3) the "unnatural affections," which tend to neither public nor private good. Edwards's schema included the holy love to God possessed by the regenerate, and then two species of self-love, simple and compounded, the latter of which resembled what others called social love.

23. It is notable that Edwards's grandfather, Solomon Stoddard, appears to have accepted the irreducibility of both compassion and conscience. The persistent self-love of natural men is sometimes "over-ruled by a spirit of compassion," Stoddard said. "Men that are devoted to themselves, are so overborn sometimes with a Spirit of Compassion that they forget their own Interest." Conscience also can overrule self-interest, Stoddard believed. "Some things," he said, "are so manifestly good, that they cannot but give an approbation to them, and some are so manifestly evil, that Men must disapprove them. . . . Conscience will bear its testimony for some things and against others, though it thwarts their own interest." This approval or disapproval can also lead to disinterested action. For "some times carnal Men will stand up in a cause from the meer dictate of conscience, though he doth expose himself to great calamities thereby." Stoddard, *Three Sermons*, 37.

(such as is meant by the term used later in the century, "enlightened self-interest") or be the result of natural instincts that propel men into caring for others; (4) a measured and proportional esteem for oneself in relation to the created universe of goods, whereby one loves oneself as a creature of God, which may be called limited self-regard.

Perhaps the most important corollary that Edwards drew from this set of definitions was the anti-Quietist proposition (which he held to all of his life) that it is "impossible for any person to be willing to be perfectly and finally miserable for God's sake." The teaching that the saint is or ought to be willing to be damned for the glory of God supposes that love to God can be superior to self-love "in the most general and extensive sense of self love" (the first definition above), but self-love in this sense must be part of love to God. A man may indeed be willing to be deprived of all his own separate good for God's sake, "but then he is not perfectly miserable but happy in the delight that he hath in God's good."[24] Love to God, Edwards held, necessarily includes both a love of benevolence (that is, benevolent love, or good will) and a love of complacence (that is, passive love, or delight in the loved object).[25] The love of complacence was particularly inconsistent with a willingness to be utterly miserable (or damned) for God's sake, "for if a man is utterly miserable he is utterly excluded the enjoyment of God. . . . The more a man loves God, the more unwilling will he be to be deprived of this happiness."[26]

There are obvious parallels between the theological question of whether love to God must be altogether superior to self-love, and the ethical question of how far self-love may enter into the performance of one's duties to society before one's acts are no longer deemed meritorious. In the 1720s and 1730s several Harvard master's *quaestiones* touched on these issues: "Is it lawful for any one to do good works with a view to reward in heaven?" (Affirmed, 1727, 1737). "Would any one embrace virtue for itself, if its rewards were

---

24. Edwards stated his opposition to the "willing to be damned" test in *A Faithful Narrative of the Surprising Work of God in the Conversion of Many Hundred Souls in Northampton . . . ,* 3d ed. (Boston, 1738), 31, and in *Religious Affections*, ed. Smith, 411. Stoddard, *Three Sermons*, 59, also rejected the notion. Samuel Hopkins, Edwards's disciple, who espoused this mystical doctrine, may have read the idea into Edwards's thinking from such passages as that on p. 222 in Edwards's *Discourses on Various Important Subjects*. On Hopkins, see Frank Hugh Foster, *A Genetic History of the New England Theology* (New York, 1963 [orig. publ. Chicago, 1907]), 129–188. Stoddard, like Edwards later, maintained that accepting and loving God's judgment of the wicked is a test of faith, but this is quite different from being willing to be damned oneself; it is being willing that others will be damned. For discussion of hell and damnation in Edwards's thought, see chap. 5, below.

25. The distinction between love of benevolence and love of complacence was a commonplace of Scholastic discussions.

26. Miscellanies, no. 530.

taken away?'' (Negated, 1731).[27] The answers to both questions allowed for some admixture of self-love. As occurs so often in our period, theological discussions were frequently interchangeable with the questions debated in ethics. The discussion of the dogma of Original Sin by religious thinkers, for example, was replicated by secular philosophers studying the nature of man, the place of self-love, and related questions. But there are also limits to this parallelism. In the case under consideration here, it should be noted that disinterested love to God, who is the source of all good, here and hereafter, is a very peculiar kind of disinterested love, if it can exist at all. God is the source of all love, as Malebranche among others had emphasized, which means that even Edwards's "simple" or exclusive self-love is dependent on God's agency, because love is a continuum. In Malebranche's conception, which was similar to Edwards's, disinterested love to God is impossible because the desire for happiness is intrinsic to all willing or loving whatsoever, and God is the necessary end of the search for happiness. Logically, one cannot be disinterested about the source or basis of all interest. Yet at the same time action for social ends can very well be disinterested, which is simply a matter of sacrificing one's personal, exclusive good, or any lesser good, to the higher end. Love to God and love to humanity may sharply conflict in the hierarchy of duties, as Edwards knew. Rather than being always parallel, they can easily be antithetical. But God is the highest end of desire, and love for Him cannot meaningfully be sacrificed to anything else.

In seventeenth-century England Giles Firmin, a Puritan who had lived in Massachusetts for a number of years, replied to the "willingness to be damned" teaching of Thomas Hooker and Thomas Shepard along the lines just indicated. "It is contrary to man as man," he said. "To require such a duty . . . destroys the very nature of man, as he is rational creature." The will, Firmin said,

> is determined by a natural inclination to its ultimate end, that is *blessedness*; it can not but necessarily . . . desire and court blessedness: so that it is impossible for any man to *will* not to be happy; he must cease to be a rational creature in so doing. . . . To be content without the love of God, to be cast out from him and damned forever . . . is for a man to be willing to be separated from his *chief* good; make a man will not to be happy; make a man will the *summum malum*, the greatest evil that can befall a rational creature; things impossible; there is no *suspension* of the acts of the *will* about its ultimate end, *blessedness*.[28]

27. Edward J. Young, "Subjects for Master's Degree in Harvard College from 1655 to 1791," Mass. Hist. Soc., *Procs.*, XVIII (1881), 119–151.
28. Quoted from Giles Firmin, *The Real Christian, Or A Treatise of Effectual Calling* (Lon-

About the same time, the Cambridge Platonist John Smith in his *Select Discourses* (1660) also repudiated the teaching that "in a perfect resignation of our Wills to the Divine will a man should be content with his own Damnation . . . if it should so please God." This is as impossible, Smith said, as for heaven to be hell. Though it is true that to attain union with the Holy Spirit one must overcome "Self will," the denial of self-interest in this endeavor cannot possibly at the same time result in self-love, pride, and arrogance, which are the personal traits that flourish in hell.[29] In other words, the type of self-love that is overcome in finding union with God is specifically selfishness, not the self-love that seeks the consummation of happiness. It is precisely the hell of selfishness that is vanquished in finding God, and thus conditions exactly opposite to damnation are created. A hell populated by those willing to be damned would be transformed into heaven.

Just as certain secular moralists, such as Shaftesbury, preached that the only true virtue is pure and disinterested, so religious mystics for centuries had sought a love of God that is pure and disinterested. The problem was, as D. P. Walker has observed, that the doctrine of rewards and punishments in the afterlife—meted out unerringly by a just God—made it a virtual psychological impossibility for a believer to perform any good act on earth without the consciousness that it would be rewarded ultimately by God. Thus, even the most zealous striving for holiness was frustrated by the unwanted awareness that such striving also happened to be expedient.[30] A Shaftesbury could achieve the desired moral purity by dismissing the doctrine of the future life from consideration in ethics. One must be virtuous without regard to future rewards. For an orthodox moralist or a saint, who could not ignore heaven and hell, the problem of maintaining an intention altogether free of mercenary overtones imposed by the doctrine of the afterlife could be solved only by boldly asserting one's willingness to be damned for the glory of God. Religious thinkers who made this claim took it very seriously, but it was a teaching inevitably caught in a web of paradoxes as soon as it was closely analyzed.

Whatever assumptions scholars may have about a mystical strain in Edwards's theology, on the matter of purity of intentions his position was very down-to-earth. The affections true Christians feel toward God, he said, are

---

don, 1670; Boston, 1742), in "Hopkinsianism Before Hopkins," *American Presbyterian Review*, II (1870), 687–699, III (1871), 110–112. This useful article deals mainly with Hooker and Shepard.

29. John Smith, "The Excellency and Nobleness of True Religion," which was Discourse IX in Smith's *Select Discourses* (London, 1660), reprinted in Patrides, ed., *Cambridge Platonists*, 183.

30. D. P. Walker, *The Decline of Hell: Seventeenth-Century Discussions of Eternal Torment* (Chicago, 1964), 172–177.

"not always purely holy and divine." And Christian virtues are adulterated not only by a mixture of self-love and of what is common and natural with gracious influences, but also by "that which is animal, that which is in great measure from the body, and is properly the result of the animal frame."[31]

In *Religious Affections* (1746) Edwards addressed himself once more to the question of whether there could be a totally disinterested love of God, but on this occasion he approached the problem from a different point of view, that of an apologist for the doctrine of special grace. The admixture of self-love in holy love to God was not denied—Edwards here spoke of self-love as a "handmaid" to the saints' disinterested recognition of God's glory, for the saints' direct or personal interest in God's goodness "serves the more to engage his mind, and raise the attention," and thereby heightens the joy and love. But Edwards's focus in *Religious Affections* was on the select refinements of holy love to God as opposed to various natural affections, and therefore he was now required to combat and oppose those who claimed "that *all* love arises from self-love; and that it is impossible in the nature of things, for any man to have any love to God, or any other being, but that love to himself must be the foundation of it."[32] Here was the point at which the pessimistic interpretation of human nature had gone too far and had to be cut off.[33]

It is true, Edwards observed, that whoever loves God and desires His glory finds happiness in it; yet this fact does not necessarily mean that the desire for personal happiness is the motive or foundation of the love. For we must first inquire "how the man came to place his happiness in God's being glorified," and how he came to place his happiness "in contemplating and enjoying God's perfections." It will then be found that only *after* God's glory is agreeable to the person will he desire it "as he desires his own happiness." This happiness is "the fruit of love," not the cause of it. "A man must first love God, or have his heart united to him, before he will esteem God's good his own, and before he will desire the glorifying and enjoying of God, as his happiness."[34] Then, after a man loves God and "has his heart so united to him," it is natural that "even self-love, or love to his own happiness, will cause him to desire the glorifying and enjoying of God." But it does not follow that the self-love preceded the love to God, or that the love to God was "a consequence or fruit" of the self-love.

Edwards's argument was of a form widely used by benevolists in opposition

31. Edwards, *Thoughts Concerning the Revival*, 271.

32. *Religious Affections*, ed. Smith, 240, 248. My italics.

33. Edwards's goal here was the same as that at the center of much medieval discussion: how a person can move from self-love to pure love for God. See Nygren, *Agape and Eros*, trans. Watson, 641–658.

34. *Religious Affections*, ed. Smith, 240.

to egoist theory. In considering the immediate motives for virtuous actions—the parallel case in ethics to Edwards's investigation of the possibility of disinterested love to God—Francis Hutcheson delivered the classic analysis, and he was quite conscious of the parallel to theology: "All the actions counted *religious* in any country, are supposed, by those who count them so, to flow from some affections toward the Deity; and whatever we call *social virtue*, we still suppose to flow from affections toward our fellow creatures: for in this all seem to agree, that external motions, when accompanied with no affections toward God or man . . . can have no moral good or evil in them."[35] In both cases, Hutcheson argued, genuine disinterest is far from impossible. It is especially apparent in love of complacence or esteem, when we are "entirely excited by some moral qualities, good or evil, apprehended to be in the objects, which qualities the very frame of our nature determines us to approve or disapprove, according to the moral sense." People are involuntarily moved to actions or to moral judgments by inbuilt passions or affections that are focused on specific types of objects. The predisposition to act or to judge in accordance with, for example, love or hate, exists independently of hope or fear concerning the consequences, and independently of anticipated pleasure or pain.

Edwards had ready and waiting his own theory of the predetermined excitation that conduces to love for God, an excitation different from Hutcheson's "frame of our nature" and the "moral sense." The only motive that can determine a disinterested response to God, according to Edwards, is the infusion of grace, bringing about "a change . . . in the views of [a person's] mind and relish of his heart; whereby he apprehends a beauty, glory, and supreme good, in God's nature, as it is in itself. This may be the thing that first draws his heart to [God], and causes his heart to be united to him, prior to all considerations of his own interest or happiness."[36] The saint loves God not because he *wants to*, in the sense that he *would like to*, but because he *has to* as a result of an altogether changed disposition. Self-interest, or the prospect of future pleasure, is not the motive of what is in actuality a necessary bent of the soul, although the pleasure of self-pleasing is one of the results.[37]

35. Raphael, ed., *British Moralists*, I, par. 315.

36. *Religious Affections*, ed. Smith, 241. Such spiritual sensations, Edwards said, require a "peculiar, inimitable and unparalleled exercise of the glorious power of God, in order to their production." *Ibid.*, 215.

37. More precisely, God so changes man's nature in conversion that the new man takes pleasure in divine things. The basic change is in that in which one finds pleasure, *away* from the things of this world and *to* the things of God. According to Malebranche, when God converts a person He creates in him a "pre-ingaging delectation" to obey religious duties, which is necessary to counteract the pleasures we take in selfish and sensual things. *Search after Truth*, trans. Sault, II, 385.

It is in this context that the analogy with aesthetic experience, which Edwards embraced, is especially fruitful. We do not love a beautiful sunset or the glimmering refulgence of the sunlight on green fields because of previous benefits bestowed or benefits expected. The response to beauty is involuntary and disinterested. A holy love to God, then, must be clearly distinguished from the kind that arises when there is a "preconceived relation" between the agent who loves and the object of that love, such as exists in family relations typically or in one's self-sacrificing regard for the welfare of groups that one *belongs* to. Self-love (simple or compounded) is actually operative in these latter cases, Edwards believed, for there is usually some benefit already received or depended on. And the anticipated or expected benefit "precedes any relish of, or delight in the nature and qualities inherent in the being beloved."[38] In sum, there is a great difference between loving another because the first thing "is the beholding those qualifications and properties . . . which appear . . . lovely in themselves," and on this account alone worthy of esteem and goodwill, and loving another when the love that arises is "from some gift bestowed." The "first foundation of a true love to God [i.e., the objective foundation, the ontological foundation], is that whereby he is in himself lovely. . . . What chiefly renders God lovely, and must undoubtedly be the chief grounds of true love, is his excellency."[39] A person whose love to God is founded primarily on God's profitableness for him or her is no different from the dog who loves his master for his kindness.[40]

Edwards carried this theological argument even a step further, with shattering implications for the ungodly and the mercenary. In reality, he said, there are no grounds for a self-interested love of God, that is, a love given in expectation of benefit or reward, or out of natural gratitude. Those who love God in this spirit are terribly deluded and ipso facto will be condemned to hell. Their insidious self-love produces in them an altogether "false notion of God . . . ; as though he were only goodness and mercy, and no revenging justice; or as though the exercise of his goodness were necessary, and not free and sovereign; or as though his goodness were dependent on what is in them, and as it were constrained by them." Thus, on misguided grounds like these, people will love a God "of their own forming in their imaginations," but they do not love the God that "reigns in heaven." In other words, self-seeking natural men, if they faced the truth, would realize, devastatingly to themselves, that they have no real reason to love God and can do so only by delud-

38. *Religious Affections*, ed. Smith, 241.

39. *Ibid.*, 242. For excellency, see pp. 73–74, above; on love to God, see pp. 126–127, above.

40. The distinction goes back to Augustine's love that "enjoys" (*frui*) and love that "uses" (*uti*), or an object loved for itself as compared to one loved for the ends it may serve. God, of course, is to be enjoyed as an absolute end in Himself; everything else is to be seen as a means to God. For discussion, see Nygren, *Agape and Eros*, trans. Watson, 503–512.

ing themselves into the belief that God will not deal with them severely. Indeed, when they are brought to trial and condemned, they will rage against Him for what they consider to be a betrayal of their expectations, which in any case were false. This self-delusion is then a particularly deadly form of self-love or self-centeredness. Edwards's reasoning on this point is akin to the old religious wisdom that the hater of God is closer to His reality than the lukewarm (and, perhaps, optimistic) sinner who has never in fact confronted the God of justice and judgment. From hatred there can be an inversion to love; but the lukewarm or indifferent unregenerated person is living in a fool's paradise, a fantasy world of his or her own devising, and does not know God at all.

> Self-love may be the foundation of an affection in men towards God, through a great insensibility of their state with regard to God, and for want of conviction of conscience to make 'em sensible how dreadfully they have provoked God to anger; they have no sense of the heinousness of sin, as against God, and of the infinite and terrible opposition of the holy nature of God against it: and so having formed in their minds such a God as suits them, and thinking God to be such a one as themselves, who favors and agrees with them, they may like him very well.[41]

The difference ultimately is that "the saint's affections begin with God," since they are directly caused by God, whereas "false affections begin with self." The passage in 1 John 4:19, "We love him, because he first loved us," is not an endorsement of self-love, that is, a description of a quid pro quo, but a pronouncement, Edwards believed, that God, through love, gives the regenerate a capacity for love that becomes the foundation of their love to God in return. Therefore, in the saint, even gratitude to God for bounties received can be spiritual, for it is from "a stock of love already in the heart, established in the first place . . . [out of] God's own excellency; and hence the affections are disposed to flow out, on occasion of God's kindness." False affections, on the other hand, are founded on self-love. The natural man "lays himself at the bottom of all, as the first foundation, and lays on God as the superstructure." It is true that self-love can be exceedingly far-reaching, making a person concerned for the interest of the whole "world of mankind." After Shaftesbury, Edwards could not well deny the great range of what he had earlier called "compounded self-love." But no matter how incorporative or encompassing the embrace of natural benevolence, its foundation in self-love remains unchanged if there is no infusion of special grace.[42] Gracious or holy affections, on the other hand, issue in holy practice, or, we might say, Chris-

41. *Religious Affections*, ed. Smith, 245.
42. *Ibid.*, 247–249.

tian virtues, for no other reason than that "a love to holiness, for holiness's sake, inclines persons to practice holiness. . . . Those acts which men delight in, they necessarily incline to do." The "Spirit of God . . . gives the soul a natural relish of the sweetness of that which is holy . . . and excites a disrelish and disgust of everything that is unholy."[43] The parallel here with what was claimed for the moral sense by the secular philosophers is exact.

The Legitimacy of Self-Love

We have already at numerous points touched on the question of the legitimacy of self-love, as Edwards saw it. Defined as an innate propensity to seek happiness or to choose what is agreeable to self, there is no logical way self-love can be eradicated. In the life of the godly self-love is present, in this sense, in the delight and joy they take in their union with God, although it is not the foundation or motive of their turning to God in the first place, which occurs despite simple self-love or self-centeredness and is the effect of grace. Moreover, Edwards admitted that his description of the disinterested affections of the regenerate was an ideal more than a reality, for "we do not dwell in a world of purity and innocence and love, but in one that is fallen and corrupt. . . . The principle of divine love that was once in the heart of man, is extinguished and now reigns in but few, and in them in a very imperfect degree."[44] But these harsh, empirical facts do not themselves, of course, legitimize self-love.

In his sermons on charity, composed in 1738 though not published until the nineteenth century, Edwards expounded at greater length than anywhere else his position on the question of whether the spirit of Christian love is contrary to all self-love. The emphasis in these sermons is on proportion and order as the proper criteria for assessing the place of self-love, an emphasis that put Edwards much in tune with his age. If the medieval spirit concentrated on the Neoplatonic sublimation of self-love, and the Reformation spirit on the eradication of self-love as the antithesis of piety, the typical motif of the eighteenth century was the balancing of self-love by countervailing social love.[45] The emergence of full-fledged bourgeois individualism in the eighteenth century perhaps made inevitable the philosophical acceptance of self-love as an in-

43. *Ibid.*, 394. In *True Virtue* Edwards noted: "Men who have benevolence to others have pleasure when they see others' happiness, because seeing their happiness gratifies some inclination that was in their hearts before." When they see some others happy that they care about, "their inclination is suited, and they are pleased." *True Virtue*, ed. Frankena, 44–45.
44. *Charity and Its Fruits*, ed. T. Edwards, 124.
45. The first two generalizations are drawn from Nygren, *Agape and Eros*, trans. Watson, the last is mine. All three are easily exceptionable but have a useful rough truth.

dependent and necessary force in human relations of all kinds. The idea of balancing this socially sanctioned selfishness with an equal emphasis on social love, benevolence, or altruism was the only available approach for moralists to take, once self-love was given such license.

Edwards's reasoning on the exact nature of the Fall of Man, which we have seen was like that of his grandfather Solomon Stoddard's, led him necessarily to an acceptance of self-love as an ineradicable part of human nature. For the Fall did not infuse man with sin, it left him with it. As Edwards described the situation in the last book he saw to press, *Original Sin Defended* (1758), when God first made man, He implanted in him two kinds of principles: "an *inferior* kind, which may be called *natural*, being the principles of mere human nature; such as self-love. . . . [And] *superior* principles, that were spiritual, holy and divine, summarily comprehended in divine love; wherein consisted the spiritual image of God, and man's righteousness and true holiness; . . . the *divine nature* . . . called *supernatural*."[46] The latter principles depend immediately on man's union and communion with God, or the "divine communications and influences of God's spirit." The Fall consisted in the withdrawal of the superior principles from the soul as a result of man's sin, and divine influences ceased as "light ceases in a room, when the candle is withdrawn." Human nature remained, but the proper order of things was catastrophically altered.[47]

This argument gave great sanction to the ordinary characteristics of human nature, which were assumed to be continuously in existence in all three states of man: the natural or Adamic, the fallen, and the redeemed. In *Charity and Its Fruits* Edwards described the process dramatically. As God created man he was "exalted and noble, and generous; but now he is debased, and ignoble,

46. *Original Sin*, ed. Holbrook, 381. Cf. also Malebranche, *Search after Truth*, trans. Sault, I, 271: "The principal Change which happen'd to [Adam], and which caus'd all the Disorders of his Senses and Passions, is, that God forsook him by way of Punishment, and would no longer be his Good, or, rather, would not any longer make him sensible of that Pleasure which assur'd him that he was his Good: So that Sensible Pleasures, which do but incline a man to Corporeal Good, remaining only, and being no longer Counterballanc'd by these, which formerly carry'd him to his true Good, the strict Union which he had with God is strangely weaken'd, and that which he had with his Body is much strengthened. . . . But after all, we cannot say that there was any great Change in respect of the Sense, 'tis as if two Weights hang'd in Aequilibrio in a Ballance, and I should take something from one of them, the other would weigh down, without any Change in its self." Cf. Edwards's use of the balance metaphor in *Freedom of the Will*, ed. Ramsey, 298.

47. *Original Sin*, ed. Holbrook, 383. No. 290 of Edwards's Miscellanies, written before 1727, cited Mastricht as the source of the following: "If it be enquired how man came to sin seeing he had no sinfull inclinations in him except God took away his grace from him that he had been wont to give him and so let him fall[.] I answer there was no need of that[.] There was no need of taking away any that had been given him, but he sin'd under that temptation because God did not give him more." God withheld his "confirming grace." "This was the grace Adam was to have had if he had stood when he came to receive his reward. This grace God was not obliged to grant him."

and selfish. Immediately upon the Fall, the mind of man shrank from primitive greatness and expandedness, to an exceeding smallness and contractedness. . . . Before[,] his soul was under the government of that noble principle of divine love, whereby it was enlarged to the comprehension of all his fellow-creatures and their welfare. . . . It was not confined within such narrow limits as the bounds of the creation, but went forth in the exercise of holy love to the Creator, and abroad upon the infinite ocean of good, and was, as it were swallowed up by it." But sin, the first transgression, caused the loss of this "excellent enlargedness of man's soul . . . [and] like some powerful astringent, contracted his soul to the very small dimensions of selfishness."[48]

The great result of this sudden contraction of soul was a breakdown in the proper ordering of man's loves. Self-love, good in its place, was cast in the role of master, for which it is badly fitted. The selfishness that charity, or a Christian spirit, is contrary to, Edwards said, is therefore "only an *inordinate* self-love."[49] Edwards's arguments in support of this proposition ran as follows. First, as we have already noted, self-love defined as a tendency to one's own happiness is part of human nature and cannot be destroyed. The saints and angels in heaven love their own happiness. Second, Edwards maintained that Christ's command to love thy neighbor as thyself (Matt. 19:19) "certainly supposes that we may and must love ourselves. It is not said *more* than thyself, but *as* thyself."[50] Moreover, the Scriptures, Edwards said, "from one end of the Bible to the other, are full of motives that are set forth for the very purpose of working on the principle of self-love. Such are all the promises and threatenings of the word of God, its calls and invitations, its counsels to seek our own good, and its warnings to beware of misery." It is plain, Edwards concluded, "that charity, or the spirit of Christian love, is not contrary to *all* self-love,"[51] but only to inordinate self-love.

Edwards's exploitation of the scriptural basis for the legitimacy of self-love was prominently anticipated by John Clarke, master of the grammar school at Hull, in the *Foundation of Morality* (1726), a well-known refutation from the standpoint of strict hedonism of the ethical theories of both Samuel Clarke and Hutcheson. According to John Clarke, God has instilled into mankind self-love or the constant desire for pleasure or happiness as a means of enforc-

---

48. *Charity and Its Fruits*, ed. T. Edwards, 227–228.

49. *Ibid.*, 231. My italics.

50. Augustine and many later commentators had argued similarly from the golden rule, that it contained a commandment to love thyself. Luther categorically rejected this interpretation, arguing that the love for oneself was only a "type" of the proper love to others, as Adam is a "type" for Christ. "Thou doest ill in loving thyself. From this evil thou art delivered only when thou lovest thy neighbour in like manner—that is, when thou ceasest to love thyself." See Nygren, *Agape and Eros*, trans. Watson, 709–714, quotation on p. 712.

51. *Charity and Its Fruits*, ed. T. Edwards, 231.

ing divine morality. Thus in Scripture the greatest reward is promised to virtue, and vice is threatened with the greatest of punishments. "The language of the New Testament . . . everywhere inculcates the Rewards and punishments of a future State, on purpose to excite Men to such a Conduct as is called Virtuous."[52] Edwards never read Clarke's *Foundation*, though he took note of it in his "Catalogue" in about 1750 when he was reading Clarke's popular *Essay on Study*. Similarly, Bishop George Berkeley's *Alciphron, or the Minute Philosopher* (1732), which Edwards read in the early 1730s, took issue with Shaftesbury's contemptuous dismissal of fear as an acceptable motive for virtue. "Whatever may be the effect of pure theory upon certain select spirits, of a peculiar make [*such as Shaftesbury himself*], . . . I do verily think," Berkeley wrote, "that in this country of ours, reason, religion, laws are all together little enough to subdue the outward to the inward man." Berkeley doubted that the ideal of virtue was alone adequate "to engage sensual and worldly-minded men in the practice of it," and he maintained that the "hope of reward and fear of punishment are highly expedient to cast the balance of pleasant and profitable on the side of virtue."[53]

Edwards resembled Shaftesbury in believing that at its highest reaches virtue must stand independent of simple self-love or the contracted self-interest of fear of punishment, yet he endorsed also the realistic assessments of Locke, John Clarke, Berkeley, and others that fear of punishment is part of a divinely ordained system to bring men to moral obedience and could not be spurned. Edwards's respect for the natural order of morality, an order that in itself is as much an expression of God's plan as the special grace of true virtue, is apparent here. "God [hath so] contrived and constituted things, in his dispensations towards his own people," Edwards surmised, "that when their love decays, and the exercises of it fail, or become weak, fear should arise; for then they need it to restrain them from sin, and to excite 'em to care for the good of their souls, and so to stir them up to watchfulness and diligence in religion." But it is also established by God that "when love rises, and is in vigorous exercise, then fear should vanish, and be driven away; for then they need it not, having a higher and more excellent principle in exercise to

52. John Clarke (of Hull), *The Foundation of Morality in Theory and Practice* . . . (York, England, [1726]), 48–49.

53. Luce and Jessup, eds., *Works of George Berkeley*, III, 131–132, 118–119. The same hardheaded view is in *Cato's Letters*, no. 61, Jan. 13, 1721: "The most reasonable Meaning that can be put upon this Apothegm, that *Virtue is its own Reward*, is, that it seldom meets with any other. God himself, who having made us, best knows our Natures, does not trust to the intrinsick Excellence and native Beauty of Holiness alone, to engage us in its Interests and Pursuits, but recommends it to us by the stronger and more affecting Motives of Rewards and Punishments." Jonathan Trumbull (1710–1785), governor of Connecticut during the Revolution, copied this exact passage and others from *Cato's Letters* into his notebook when he was a student at Harvard in 1725. Trumbull's notebook is in the Harvard Univ. Archives.

restrain 'em from sin, and stir 'em up to their duty. There are no other principles, which human nature is under the influence of, that will ever make men conscientious, but one of these two, fear or love. . . . Like the two opposite scales of a balance; when one rises, the other sinks."[54] Edwards believed, therefore, that self-love, expressed as fear of punishment, was a respectable ingredient in the moral life of unregenerate persons, and even of saints in their weaker moments.

Whether Edwards would agree with St. Paul, "If the dead rise not, let us eat and drink, for tomorrow we die" (1 Cor. 15:32), as Locke and John Clarke did, is another matter, however. Edwards believed, of course, that God provided a unique inducement to holy virtue through the agency of special grace. But even on the level of the natural virtues, Edwards, more than Locke, gave credence to motives other than the fear of eternal torment that served to keep men on the strait and narrow path.[55]

To return to the original question, Edwards concluded on the basis of the evidence of Scripture alone that Christian charity, while not contrary to all self-love, is contrary to an inordinate self-love, or "selfishness." The next question is, then, "in what does this inordinateness consist?" It is not a matter of degree in any absolute sense, Edwards argued, but only the comparative strength of self-love in relation to love to others. As long as it is balanced by love to God and to fellow creatures, there cannot be such a thing as too much self-love. When a man is converted and sanctified, his love for happiness is not diminished, Edwards said, but becomes "regulated."[56] Like Bishop Butler, Edwards pointed out that "in some respects wicked men do not love themselves enough—not so much as the godly do; for they do not love the way of their own welfare and happiness."[57]

54. *Religious Affections*, ed. Smith, 179.

55. Locke also emphasized that the concern for reputation, or the shame and pride induced by society, is a mechanism that tends to support good morals. The more advanced moralists of the age, including Edwards, nevertheless found Locke's moral psychology quite limited. Thus Lord Kames (Henry Home), *Essays on the Principles of Morality and Natural Religion* (Edinburgh, 1751), 14–15: "We see how imperfect the description is of human nature, given by Mr. Locke. . . . [He acknowledges] no motive to action, but what arises from self-love; measures laid down to attain pleasure, or to shun pain. Our particular appetites and affections, and the desires and aversions involved in them, are left entirely out of the system. And yet we may say, with some degree of probability, that we are more influenced by these than by self-love." Edwards read Kames's *Essays* late in 1754 or early in 1755. See *Freedom of the Will*, ed. Ramsey, 14n and 443ff.

56. *Charity and Its Fruits*, ed. T. Edwards, 232.

57. *Ibid.*, 236. The observation that the wicked do not love themselves enough has a long literary tradition behind it, though it was rarely expertly analyzed before Butler. Thus, in Milton: "Oft-times nothing profits more than self-esteem, grounded on just and right"; and Lord Halifax's "Moral Thoughts and Reflections": "Self-love rightly defined is far from being a fault. A man that loveth himself right will do everything else right." A Harvard commencement thesis

The inordinateness of self-love consists also in a person's placing his happiness "in things that are confined to himself." Here the error is not in the comparative degree of love, but in the "channel in which it flows." If love for one's own happiness brings benefits to one's friends, family, and community, indicating that happiness is found by that person in more than his own confined good, this form of self-love is not what is called "selfishness, but is the very opposite of it."[58] Similarly, it is allowable to long for the happiness of enjoying God. "And so, persons may place their happiness considerably in the good of others, . . . and [in] desiring the happiness that consists in seeking their good, they may, in seeking it, love themselves, and their own happiness. And yet this is not selfishness, because it is not a confined self-love, but the individual's self-love flows out in such a channel as to take in others with himself." The self that is loved in this case is, as it were, "enlarged and multiplied, so that in the very acts in which he loves himself, he loves others also."

In some of these passages from *Charity and Its Fruits* it appears as though Edwards had forgotten about his earlier differentiation of three types of love: simple, compounded, and holy. The "enlarged and multiplied" self-love described above was surprisingly called by Edwards, at one point, "the Christian spirit, the excellent and noble spirit of the gospel of Jesus Christ." This, he said, "is the nature of divine love."[59] In these remarks Edwards seems to have recognized only the difference between confined or simple self-love (selfishness) and the extension of self whereby more than one's own exclusive happiness is intended (compounded self-love). Absent in particular is Edwards's familiar argument that true virtue (or holy love, or Christian charity—the terms all have the same meaning) has an altogether distinct foundation, that there is a *qualitative* difference between it and all merely natural social benevolence. In *True Virtue*, for example, written nearly twenty years after *Charity and Its Fruits*, Edwards went so far as to make the audacious claim, in opposition to the Shaftesburian description of universal benevolence, that no natural love to humankind whatsoever, even if it comprehends the whole created world, can be considered virtuous. Benevolence to humankind is as nothing compared to the infinity of being that is God; therefore, such an extended love, when it does not arise from "a temper of mind wherein consists a disposition to love God supremely," is not only not virtuous, it is inimical to virtue.[60] In the later book, Edwards is unmistakably aligned with the more

---

in 1647 proposed: *"Vera Philautia est virtus foecunda"* (True self-esteem is a fruitful virtue). See also p. 156, above.

58. *Charity and Its Fruits*, ed. T. Edwards, 237.
59. *Ibid.*, 239.
60. *True Virtue*, ed. Frankena, 19–23.

extreme Jansenist and Quietist views on the baseness of all forms of self-love, no matter how incorporative. And late in life Edwards showed much approval of the work of the Quietist Fénelon's greatest British disciple, the Chevalier Andrew Ramsay. Edwards copied from Ramsay's *Philosophical Principles of Natural and Revealed Religion* (1748) passages on the insuperable difference between merely natural self-love and that capacity for obedience to the law of eternal order that is given to man only through supernatural grace.[61] Reading Ramsay probably helped Edwards to tighten his system in the 1750s.

In general, *Charity and Its Fruits* has peculiarities that are inconsistent with nearly all the rest of Edwards's extant writings. It may be that Edwards chose not to publish these sermons because of some doubts he had about them, or even that the text prepared by Tryon Edwards in the nineteenth century is corrupt. Nowhere else in Edwards's writing pertaining to morals is he as prudential and "pragmatic" as here, although one would expect to find more of this approach in unpublished homilies than in philosophical texts written for the reading public.[62] Self-love, or, better, compounded self-love, is legitimated in this text, at least momentarily, to a far greater degree than was customary for Edwards, and made nearly equivalent to the charity of the regenerate.

Before concluding, however, Edwards returned from these apparent compromises with compounded self-love and stressed again "the peculiar nature of Christian or divine love." All love, in general, "is of a diffusive nature, and espouses the interests of others."[63] But only Christian love is "above the selfish principle." The love of parents to children, the closest friendships, the love between blood relatives, all have self-love (or sometimes instinct) as the mainspring. "It is because men love themselves, that they love those persons and things that are their own, or that they are nearly related to, and which they

---

61. See, e.g., Edwards's Miscellanies, no. 1254.

62. Passages such as the following from *Charity and Its Fruits*, ed. T. Edwards, 265–266, are so unrepresentative of Edwards's usual position on moral questions that it is hard to believe he wrote them: "If you are selfish, and make yourself and your own private interests your idol, God will leave you to yourself, and let you promote your own interests as well as you can. But if you do not selfishly seek your own, but do seek the things that are Jesus Christ's, and the things of your fellow-beings, then God will make your interest and happiness his own charge, and he is infinitely more able to provide for, and promote it, than you are. The resources of the universe move at his bidding, and he can easily command them all to subserve your welfare. So that not to seek your own, in the selfish sense, is the best way of seeking your own in a better sense. It is the directest course you can take to secure your highest happiness." Edwards's recommendation here goes against the Augustinian principle that is usually a baseline of his reasoning in moral theology: God is to be enjoyed (*frui*) not used (*uti*). It is also unusual for Edwards to espouse a kind of Stoic ethics in defense of reason (as he does on p. 280), and on p. 327 he uses the phrase, "the great author of our being," in reference to God, which was very unlike him in the 1730s.

63. *Charity and Its Fruits*, ed. T. Edwards, 248.

look upon as belonging to themselves, and which, by the constitution of society, have their interest and honor linked with their own." Nature, Edwards said, "cannot go beyond self-love." Yet he had shown already that nature can go far beyond mere *selfishness* by a process of incorporating in one's own good the welfare of very large groups. And, as we noted, for a moment Edwards had intimated that this expanded selfhood was true Christian virtue. But here, once more, he recurred to the theological principle that informed so much of his thinking and radically divided it from secular philosophy: "Divine love is the offspring of supernatural principles" and is "something of a higher and nobler kind, than any plant that grows naturally in such a soil as the heart of man. . . . It is a plant transplanted into the soul out of the garden of heaven, by the holy and blessed spirit of God; and so has its life in God and not in self."[64] Out of this love, more "free and disinterested" than any other love, "men are loved not because of their relation to self, but because of their relation to God as his children." The expanded form of natural love, on the one hand, and Christian love, on the other, may both be contrary to practical selfishness; yet the former is inescapably imbued with a "selfish spirit," because if we "follow it up to its original, it arises from the same root, viz: a principle of self-love."[65] We are thus brought to a discussion of how self-love, concealed at the roots, can emerge in the flower as goodness and virtue. In other words, it is necessary now to look at the subtle inroads of self-love. For Edwards this task meant unmasking much of what the world too easily accepted as real virtue.

The Inroads of Self-Love

Though Edwards remarked on the deviousness and subterfuges of self-love or selfishness on a number of occasions before the 1750s, his most complete exposition occurs in *True Virtue*. It was only in the wake of the failure (in his eyes) of the evangelical revival of the 1730s and 1740s that Edwards began to study the subject in earnest. In fact, the deepest lesson he took from the Great Awakening may have been a renewed appreciation of the labyrinth of the human heart. "I once did not imagine that the heart of man had been so unsearchable as I find it is," he wrote in 1741. "I am less charitable, and less uncharitable than once I was. I find more things in wicked men that may counterfeit, and make fair shew of piety, and more ways that the remaining corruption of the Godly may make them appear like carnal men, formalists,

64. *Ibid.*, 249–251.
65. *Ibid.*, 251–252.

and dead hypocrites, than once I knew of."[66] It was a lesson he knew from his own anxious self-examination in his youth, but one he perhaps had momentarily forgotten in the promise and jubilance of the Awakening. It was after the Awakening, too, that he first encountered with full force the new optimistic psychology of the age, and thus in his critique of the benevolism of the Shaftesbury-Hutcheson gospel, he was also attacking his own earlier delusions, the incautious hope he had for mankind in the late 1730s, when he dared to imagine for a moment that he would be the leader of a worldwide redemptive movement.[67]

However that may be, Edwards's uncovering of the deceptive masks of self-love was an essential part of his ethics. For unless this negative or critical work was accomplished, the positive and synthetic elements of his philosophy would remain vulnerable to naturalistic reductionism. His goal of formulating a moral theology that was demonstrably superior to anything set forth by the secular moralists—whether ancient philosophers or eighteenth-century benevolists—required first that he uncover the flaws and deficiencies, that is, the impurities, of alleged natural morality. Although there was a long tradition in Christian thought of showing the inferiority of pagan moral virtue,[68] dealing with the eighteenth-century optimists was a more original and more difficult challenge. The proofs of natural goodness adduced in Edwards's time were sometimes quite sophisticated and not easily dismissed as *splendida peccata*, especially since Edwards and his opponents in this controversy accepted some of the same premises, notably that virtue was essentially a matter

66. Edwards, *Distinguishing Marks of a Work of the Spirit of God* . . . (Boston, 1741), 102. There are similar confessions of a new humility toward discerning the state of the soul in the conclusion to *Religious Affections*, ed. Smith, 460, and in Miscellanies, no. 821, written in about 1740. In the "Account of His Life," also written in about 1740, Edwards said of himself: "It is affecting to me to think, how ignorant I was, when I was a young Christian, of the bottomless, infinite depths of wickedness, pride, hypocrisy and deceit left in my heart." Hopkins, *Life of Edwards*, in Levin, ed., *Jonathan Edwards*, 38.

67. Strict periodization of Edwards's thought is exceedingly difficult, however. Some of his sharpest insights into self-love are in Miscellanies, nos. 473 and 534, both written between 1730 and 1735.

68. This was also a lifelong interest of Edwards's that clearly intensified in the 1750s, as his Miscellanies reveal. The topic under which Edwards covered the subject in his incomplete index to the Miscellanies was "The Defects of Heathen Morality." The subject was of prime interest in the 18th century because the revival of natural morality depended to some extent on the authority and cogency of the ancient moralists. Edwards wrote in *Charity and Its Fruits*, ed. T. Edwards, 76–78: "Many of the heathen have been eminent for their great performances; some for their integrity, or for their justice, and others for their great deeds done for the public good. . . . Many have done great things from fear of hell, . . . and many have done great things from pride, and from a desire for reputation and honor among men. . . . It is hard to say how far such natural principles may carry men in particular duties and performances."

of inclinations or affections, rather than of intellectual deliberation and cool judgment. How well Edwards succeeded in undermining Hutcheson, Turnbull, Fordyce, Hume, and others without falling into skeptical and cynical argumentation, or into an intellectualism that was incompatible with his religious predispositions, is the question that we must face here.

We have established already that Edwards's goal in exposing the selfish foundations of natural virtue was not entirely proscriptive or censorious. He was one with Locke and Berkeley in accepting the usefulness and the practical benefits that flowed from God's natural laws of psychology. He was not a rigorist like Jacques Esprit or like the imaginary moral judge in Bernard Mandeville's *Fable of the Bees*, who would eradicate from the world all of the operations of self-interest. But notwithstanding this moderation, Edwards was determined to draw an impassable line between the virtues of the regenerate, which existed solely by special grace, and everything else the world could offer of moral worth, which he believed could be only "imitations" of true virtue.

Yet these imitations, counterfeit though they might be in a sense, were not all condemnable. God Himself was not a rigorist in Edwards's eyes. He governed the world on two levels: continuously supporting the laws of nature in mind and matter (or in psychology and physics) by common grace, and continually pouring forth special graces by which persons in the world could be redeemed from their fallen and sinful state. We might say, then, that Edwards's investigation of the ramifications of self-love was descriptive in intent, an effort directed primarily toward identifying and preserving the exclusiveness of Christian revelation and divine grace in morals, not toward abolishing self-love. It was necessary to know the enemy with as much accuracy as possible in order to prevent distinctive Christian virtue from being swallowed up by that voracious eighteenth-century naturalism that would make of such divinely given virtue just one more historical variety of natural virtue found commonly in the world, rather than a unique consequence of special grace. This difference from the aims of the rigorists, however, did not bar Edwards from borrowing some of their insights into the machinations of self-love.

In the middle of the seventeenth century, Pascal had asserted: "The Greatness and the Misery of Man being alike conspicuous, it is necessary the true Religion should declare, that he contains in himself some Noble Principles of Greatness, and at the same time, some profound Source of Misery."[69] Yet the prevailing philosophies, Pascal continued, other than the Christian, stressed

---

69. Blaise Pascal, *Thoughts on Religion, and Other Subjects* (London, 1704). Edwards read Pascal's *Thoughts* in ca. 1733. Its great popularity in Britain and America was enhanced by translators and editors who elided from the work "Lines which directly favour'd the distinguishing Doctrines of those of the *Roman* Communion" ("The Translator to the Reader").

only one or the other of these "contrarieties." There were those who would "equal [man] with God," and those who would "bring us down to the level of Beasts." The constant employment of philosophers was to emphasize only one or the other of these disorders. Some "gratifie . . . Pride; by vainly insinuating, that [human] Nature was constituted under a parity with the Divine." Others, seeing "the extravagance of such Pretensions, . . . set [man] upon the other Precipice; by tempting [him] to believe that [his] Nature was of-a-piece with that of the Beasts."[70] But once take into account the teaching of Christian revelation, Pascal said, that "Humane Nature is deprav'd, and fallen from God, this clears up my Sight, and enables me to distinguish, throughout, the Characters of so Divine a Mystery." Those who know the "Excellency of Man" are "ignorant of his Corruption." And those who are "sensible of the Infirmity of Nature" are "Strangers to its Dignity." Only the Christian religion has cured these "opposite Distempers: not so as to drive the one out by the other, according to the Wisedom of the World; but so as to expel them both by the Simplicity of the Gospel." The "Philosophers," by which Pascal meant the ancient schools (though his discussion has precise bearing on the eighteenth century as well), "never furnished Men with Sentiments agreeable to these two Estates. They either inspired a Principle of pure Grandeur; and this cannot be the true Condition of Man: or else of meer Abjectness; and this Condition is as ill proportion'd as the former."[71] Edwards's strategy was exactly like Pascal's: to show the contrarieties that the secular philosophers in their one-sidedness failed to account for—both man's divinity *and* his corruption.

The most intricate means by which exclusive self-love metamorphoses into benevolence, its apparent opposite, is through the intermediary affections of pride, self-esteem, and what A. O. Lovejoy has termed "approbativeness," or the need for the approval of others.[72] Long before Edwards began to publish, the complex functioning of these mechanisms was well understood. Pascal, Pierre Nicole, Jacques Abbadie, Mandeville, and others had dilated

70. *Ibid.*, 36.

71. *Ibid.*, 43–47.

72. Lovejoy, *Reflections on Human Nature*, 88: Approbativeness is that "peculiarity of man which consists in a *susceptibility to pleasure in, or a desire for, the thought of oneself as an object of thoughts or feelings, of certain kinds, on the part of other persons*." There is an entire graded vocabulary, Lovejoy notes, to describe the levels of approbation all men seek, from mere "notice," "interest," "respect," and "consideration," to "esteem," "praise," "admiration," "honor," and "veneration." And there is a similar vocabulary to describe the levels of disapprobation men fear and try to escape from, including terms like "indifference," "disrespect," and "contempt." So persistent is this trait in men, Lovejoy observes, that "to *proclaim* your freedom from approbativeness is plainly to manifest approbativeness—to make it evident that you wish to be admired by others for your indifference to their admiration" (pp. 101–102).

on the efficacy of pride, shame, and other such feelings as substitutes for inherent virtue,[73] and in the Puritan tradition a similar understanding was not uncommon.[74] It is one limitation of Edwards's writings on the hidden encroachments of self-love, however, that he devoted relatively little attention to these complex mechanisms. He noted in *True Virtue* that there is a "natural disposition in men" to be pleased when they are objects of the honor and love of others, and to be displeased when they are objects of hatred and contempt. God has so "constituted our nature," he asserted, that self-love is exercised in "no one disposition more than in this." Moreover, men are probably "capable of much more pleasure and pain through this determination of the mind, than by any other personal inclination or aversion whatsoever." The contempt of others is dreaded more than death itself.[75] But the exposure in detail of the

73. See Lovejoy's exposition of this tradition, *ibid.*, 153–193, and F. B. Kaye's introduction to his edition of Bernard Mandeville's *Fable of the Bees*. Malebranche observed that "those very Inclinations which seem most repugnant to Society, are the most useful to it when they are somewhat moderated. . . . The Desire, for Instance, which All Men have of *Greatness*, directly tends to the Subversion of all Societies. Nevertheless, this Desire is so temper'd by the *Order of Nature*, that it conduces more to *Publick* Welfare than many other weak and languid Inclinations." *Search after Truth*, trans. Taylor, I, 166–167.

74. See, e.g., Shepard, *Parable of the Ten Virgins*: The principle of seeking "external applause and praise of men . . . will carry a man beyond all the best Examples: Nay, sometimes to be singular, and a man alone. . . . Men forsake their friends, and trample underfoot the scorns of the world, [in order to] . . . have credit elsewhere: To maintain their interest in the love of godly men they will suffer much. . . . Men in the ministry pray for grace to beautifie and perfect their parts, that so they may preach and convert and have credit. . . . Hence the Lord is neglected secretly, yet honored openly. . . . Hence many men keep their profession, when they lose their affection[;] they have by the one a name to live, and that is enough, though their hearts be dead. . . . I have wondered that the opinion of men, nay, [the] dream of men's thoughts should act men" (p. 183). "I pray, but self-love sets me a work; I profess, but praise of men acts me; I observe duties in secret, but natural conscience only carries me" (p. 187). See also Fiering, *Moral Philosophy at Seventeenth-Century Harvard*, chap. 4.

75. *True Virtue*, ed. Frankena, 46. Edwards drew an object lesson here about the terrors of hell, for if men suffer so from rejection merely by their peers, consider how terrible is the state of being despised and abhorred by God, the source of all goodness. John Locke commented frequently on the importance of praise and blame, concern for reputation, and shame as motives, but emphasized mainly the fear of contempt and disgrace. See, e.g., *Essay Concerning Human Understanding*, ed. Fraser, Bk. II, chap. xxviii, secs. 10–12: "He who imagines commendation and disgrace not to be strong motives to men to accommodate themselves to the opinions and rules of those with whom they converse, seems little skilled in the nature or history of mankind. . . . The penalties that attend the breach of God's laws some, nay perhaps most men, seldom seriously reflect on. . . . And as to the punishments due from the laws of the commonwealth, they frequently flatter themselves with the hopes of impunity. But no man escapes the punishment of their censure and dislike, who offends against the fashion and opinion of the company he keeps, and would recommend himself to. Nor is there one of ten thousand, who is stiff and insensible enough, to bear up under the constant dislike and condemnation of his own club. He must be of a strange and unusual constitution, who can content himself to live in constant disgrace and disrepute with his own particular society. . . . This is a burden too heavy for human sufferance."

processes by which concern about shame and praise could result in a perfect semblance of virtue did not seem to interest Edwards. Instead, he concentrated on what he considered to be a more direct expression of self-love: *gratitude*, or doing good to others because they have benefited or can benefit the doer.

Both in his earlier writings and later in *True Virtue* more fully, Edwards relied on the concept of "natural gratitude" to account for most conventional morality. That men reciprocate with good will those actions that have *tendencies* toward their benefit is simply a form of generalized self-interest. From a love of pleasure and a "love of being loved," and from a hatred of pain and "an aversion to being hated," one may come to feel benevolence toward persons and even inanimate things that have been the occasion of much delight and pleasure. Beyond the respect and benevolence we may feel toward those who do us direct good, the same goodwill may be extended even to those who show "qualifications of mind" that are only potentially beneficial. The degree of this love will depend partly upon how "considerable and honorable" (that is, how politically or socially important) the potential benefactor is. Finally, at the most abstract level, there may be, Edwards said, a love to certain virtues, such as justice and generosity, that tend "directly to man's good." In the same way we reject the contrary vices because of their ill consequences.[76] These observations appear convincing, but the ongoing debate had made them obsolete, for Hutcheson had already pointed out (though when Edwards wrote the above he had not yet read Hutcheson) that if social or personal benefit alone was the source of moral approbation, then people would feel the same gratitude toward a fruit-bearing tree as they do toward the *intentionally* beneficial conduct of a goodwilled individual. Hutcheson had pioneered in establishing that there was a specifically moral mode of perception such that men were aware of the subtle, but vital, shade of difference between moral approval and mere gratitude from self-interest. By claiming that the love of justice could be simply self-interest, Edwards was ignoring the moral approbation that takes place independently of direct or even indirect benefits.[77] It is precisely because human beings know the difference between

76. Miscellanies, no. 473, written in about 1730. On gratitude as a selfish emotion, see also *Religious Affections*, ed. Smith, 243.

77. Cf. Hutcheson: "Can any one say he only loves the Beneficent, as he does a Field or Garden, because of its Advantage? His Love then must cease toward one who has ruin'd himself in kind Offices to him, when he can do him no more. . . . And then again, our Love would be the same towards the worst Characters that 'tis towards the best, if they were equally bountiful to us, which is also false. Beneficence then must raise our Love as it is an amiable moral Quality: and hence we love even those who are beneficent to others" (L. A. Selby-Bigge, ed., *British Moralists: Being Selections from Writers Principally of the Eighteenth Century* [Oxford, 1897], I, par. 99). Everyone knows the difference, Hutcheson said, between "pleasing the man in power who can promote us," and the "inward joy from the approbation of the judicious or ingenious" who can do us no practical good other than bestow praise. We value the praise of others not in

the fruit dropped from a tree and the generous benefactions of a person that Hutcheson could speak of a moral sense. We will return to the problem of gratitude shortly.

Aside from his conclusion that forms of "natural gratitude" are frequently taken for virtue when, in fact, they are only a species of self-love, Edwards introduced in this same manuscript from the 1730s two other ideas that were more enduringly perceptive concerning the inroads of self-love. Rather than showing signs of being pre-Hutcheson, they presciently leaped ahead of Hutcheson to Hume, Bentham, and beyond. Edwards suggested, first, that natural gratitude (based on self-love) for direct or indirect benefits could be enormously extended by processes of mental association and yet remain all the more masked. Second, he suggested that zealous rectitude in moral judgments and conduct could be the result (partially, at least) of repressed envy of those who are uninhibitedly licentious.

Regarding the first, it is usually assumed that John Gay, in his *Dissertation Concerning the Fundamental Principle of Virtue or Morality* published in 1731, was the first to show explicitly how the association of ideas could be used to explain away most instances of apparently "disinterested" approval of moral deeds, including those that have no direct or indirect benefits for the person making the judgment. Hutcheson had earlier pointed out, in answer to the egoists, that we morally approve or disapprove of heroes and villains in ancient history whose actions cannot possibly have a practical effect upon us, and similarly we respond with moral judgments to characters in stage plays, which are entirely imaginary. Such judgments do not appear to be the result of calculated self-interest, and Hutcheson believed their existence proved that the exercise of the moral sense is independent of any assessment of direct benefits derived from the moral conduct of others, or, in other words, that moral approval is not reducible to self-love. Gay's reply brought out the role of mental association in such apparently disinterested judgments:

> We first perceive or imagine some real good, i.e. fitness to promote our natural happiness, in those things which we love and approve of. Hence . . . we annex pleasure to those things. Hence those things and pleasure are so tied together and associated in our minds, that one cannot present itself, but the other will occur. And the association remains even after that which at first gave them the connection is quite forgot, or perhaps does not exist, but the contrary.[78]

---

proportion to how much they can serve our interests but on the basis of our respect for their authority in moral judgment. See Hutcheson's *System of Moral Philosophy*, Bk. I, 27, reprinted in McReynolds, ed., *Four Early Works on Motivation*.

78. John Gay, *Dissertation Concerning the Fundamental Principle of Virtue or Morality*, in Selby-Bigge, ed., *British Moralists*, par. 884. Gay's *Dissertation* was published as a prefix to

In effect, people tend to give moral approval to those *classes* of actions that they know from experience bring them happiness and pleasure; when they see such actions performed, as in a stage play, they judge them to be virtuous and morally worthy because of the strong connection already established in the mind between these classes of action and personal benefit in the present. But the original selfish basis of the approval is forgotten and has been replaced instead by an unconscious association that leads one to regard such actions as independently laudatory.

Gay had probably come to a realization of the explanatory power of the doctrine of association after reading John Locke's *Some Thoughts Concerning Education*, which placed considerable emphasis on mental association or habit. Before Gay, however, it had been more common to cite mental association as the source of error, rather than as the acquired basis of valuable moral responses. Descartes and Locke both had referred to the destructive influences of early nurses who implant in children certain mental associations that remain the basis of lifelong superstitions. Gay's argument showed how mental association could also be the source of socially useful traits, and following his work George Turnbull and Hume made extensive use of the theory of association in ethical analysis. Gay's essay was the wedge of the utilitarian critique of Hutcheson's theory of the disinterested moral sense. The theory of mental association made it possible eventually to bypass the eighteenth-century debate over whether human motives are predominantly altruistic or selfish, since motives did not figure in the theory at all. Whether speaking of the development of the moral standards of an individual or of an entire culture, the principle was the same: at an early stage one becomes habituated to the approval of this or that virtue because at some earlier time it was seen to be broadly useful. Thereafter, it is approved by mental habit without close consideration of its effects and without any unique moral feeling. As opposed to the quite different notion of moral habituation that assumed a transfer from outward habit to an inward disposition, which disposition might truly be called virtuous, mental association was a mechanical intellectual process without any apparent foundation in the affections or inner life. To some extent the theory of association transferred moral accountability to the nurturing society or culture and removed individual moral conscience from center stage.[79]

It seems that Edwards posited the associationist or utilitarian argument against the benevolists almost simultaneously with Gay, and probably inde-

---

Edmund Law's translation of William King's *An Essay on the Origin of Evil* (London, 1731 [orig. publ. Dublin, 1702]). There is no evidence that Edwards read this work, but it was very well known in its time.

79. For some discussion of the theory of habit and mental association in the 18th century, see Fiering, "Franklin and the Way to Virtue," *Am. Qtly.*, XXX (1978), 199–223, and the literature mentioned in the notes to the article.

pendently. Edwards's comment was made only as an aside: he noted rather obscurely that a person "may have a kind of benevolence and complacence in an immediate thing that has been the occasion of much delight and pleasure to him, by a certain kind of association of ideas and inclinations and acts of the mind. Ideas that are habitually associated together do partake of one another's love and complacence and benevolence, i.e., in the benevolence and delight the soul exercises towards them."[80] In *True Virtue*, written twenty-five years later, Edwards expanded this argument considerably, though by that time he had read Hume and others.

In addition to making use of associationist theory to undercut optimism about man's moral condition in the natural state, Edwards also noted how much of alleged righteousness had false foundations in repressed envy. Historians of ideas know how many of the insights now assigned only to Freud were in circulation hundreds of years before, though Freud is rightly credited for his systematic use of them. Shakespeare's lines in *King Lear*,

> Thou rascal beadle, hold thy bloody hand!
> Why doest thou lash that whore?
> Strip thine own back;
> Thou hotly lusts to use her in that kind
> For which thou whipst her . . . ,

show considerable understanding of the twisted consequences of unconscious repression.[81] Edwards noted that a person may "habitually" hate a particular vice, and yet inwardly desire it. Restrained from such vicious acts himself the person's disapproval will be all the greater since "he is not an actor but only a sufferer by such vices, and so he has no benefit but only injury by 'em," that is, because of their ill social consequences. A man may scorn certain vices only out of concern for the shame and contempt he would suffer if he gave in to the temptation they offer. With only a weak habit of restraint and the fear of social ostracism to bolster his virtue, a man "may dislike [other] men for some vices from envy, for he is restrained and . . . has not the pleasure of 'em[;] and his envy in such a case is without restraint, for he looks upon his zeal as good, and gives it the reins."[82] The unmitigated envy is concealed in, or even transformed unconsciously into, a zealous righteousness.

Whereas natural gratitude as a form of self-love could exist in a world with only two people, a giver and a receiver, "approbativeness" (the human need for social approval) and related passions of the soul imply the existence of an extensive social setting. The zeal that may spring from repressed envy is

80. Miscellanies, no. 473. This manuscript note is printed in Townsend, ed., *Philosophy of Edwards*, 238–239.

81. *King Lear*, Act IV, sc. v.

82. Miscellanies, no. 473.

similar to approbativeness in that it, too, requires a comparative measure—such as degrees or strata of freedom, eminence, privilege, or whatever—in society. As Edwards's sophistication in matters of the heart expanded, he paid more attention to these complexities. Early in the 1740s, probably as a result of discouraging experiences during the Awakening, he penned a long note on pride, a word that he now precisely defined for the first time. Pride, he said, is something diverse from self-love, though it is properly included among its manifestations. Pride is "a habit or state of a persons heart whereby he is inordinately disposed to exaltation amongst other beings as to his comparative dignity or worthiness of esteem and value."[83] The immediate object of pride is "not a mans sensual pleasure nor is it a mans own excellency considered absolutely." Indeed, Edwards observed, a person cannot desire too much to be excellent in an absolute sense, that is, "to have those qualifications that will render him a just object of esteem." But pride has no consideration of excellency as such. " 'Tis only a comparative dignity that pride affects or the height that one is in or may be conceived to be in amongst other beings." It is not even the love and esteem of others absolutely considered that is sought by pride, but instead a comparative esteem and value. "It don't content pride to be esteemed and loved by others and to be so much valued by them, but to be highly valued and esteemed comparatively."[84] In other words, pride or approbativeness, both forms of self-love, may drive a person to extraordinary acts of virtue, all for the sake of social distinction. In a different place, Edwards added to these thoughts the observation, familiar to seventeenth-century students of the heart, that pride is particularly difficult to eliminate, since it "lies deepest, and is most active, [and] is most ready secretly to mix it self with everything." Since its nature consists in a person's having too high a regard for himself, it is the excessiveness of this regard that he is least aware of, "for he necessarily thinks that the opinion he has of himself, is what he has just grounds for."[85]

83. *Ibid.*, no. 950, written in *ca.* 1741. Edwards was also reading carefully at this time Theophilus Gale's *Court of the Gentiles*, a Jansenist work that had been popular in New England since its publication in the 17th century. Gale wrote: "That which makes self-love more potent to promote sin is its policie and many artifices to concele its self and sin. . . . There is a great resemblance between spiritual self-love and carnal: whence the latter oft conceles it self under the vizard of the former. The more a man loves himself, the lesse he conceits he loves himself: as the more mad a man is, the lesse he judgeth himself so. Self-love is so artificial in its colors, as that it can discolor virtue with the face of vice, and vice with virtues face. Thus by its fraudes and deceits in conceling it self and sin, it greatly advances sin. The members of self-love are principally three. (1) Concupiscence, or adherence to the Creature as our last end. (2) Carnal confidence, or dependence on self as the first cause. (3) Spiritual pride, or an over-valuing estime of self-excellences" (Pt. IV, Bk. I, 121).

84. Miscellanies, no. 950.

85. *Thoughts Concerning the Revival*, 199, 201, which was written about the same time as no.

Edwards's analysis of pride, it should be noted, was primarily theological in intent. His purpose was to expose the corruptions of the heart that lay in wait for the pilgrim on his road to sanctification. While discoursing on the hazards of pride, Edwards was expressly more interested in the problem of attaining true humility. Many anchorites and recluses, he commented, have abandoned "the wealth, and pleasures, and common enjoyments of the world, who were far from renouncing their own dignity and righteousness." They "sold one lust to feed another. . . . 'Tis inexpressible, and almost inconceivable, how strong a self-righteous, self-exalting disposition is naturally in man; and what he will not do and suffer, to feed and gratify it."[86]

Edwards did not give thought to the uses pride may have in civil society as a positive mechanism for sustaining the outward practice of virtue. Although pride could contribute to religious hypocrisy, some writers considered it a divinely instituted device for maintaining social order, a consideration that John Adams would ponder a little later.[87] Once this vital contribution that pride made to civil virtue was faced, it was necessary to speak about pride and self-love (in the sense of "approbativeness") with somewhat more detachment and, perhaps, even admiration for the beneficial subtlety of God's natural laws.

The Meaning of Gratitude

In *The Nature of True Virtue* a slight change is evident in Edwards's approach to self-love from that in his earlier writing. He spoke in this work more as a secular moral psychologist and philosopher, and he had to extend his arguments to combat Hutcheson, Turnbull, Hume, and others whose books he read in the 1740s and 1750s. He continued to argue that "natural gratitude" is the principal mechanism by which self-interest is transformed into benevolence, but he had to demonstrate also that gratitude was not itself, in fact, an example in support of the natural "moral sense."

---

950 of Edwards's Miscellanies. See also *Religious Affections*, ed. Smith, 315–319: "It seems to be the nature of spiritual pride to make men conceited and ostentatious of their humility."

86. *Religious Affections*, ed. Smith, 315.

87. Adams's most extensive commentary on the uses of vanity or self-love for public good is in his "Discourses on Davila," written in the late 1780s. "There is in human nature, it is true, simple *Benevolence*, or an affection for the good of others; but alone it is not a balance for the selfish affections. Nature then has kindly added to benevolence, the desire of reputation, in order to make us good members of society." "Nature" has imposed the law of promoting the good and respecting the rights of mankind through the rewards of the "*esteem* and *admiration* of others," and the punishments of "*neglect* and *contempt*," etc. (*The Works of John Adams*, ed. Charles Francis Adams, VI [Boston, 1851], 234). Adams's reflections on the subject relied heavily on Adam Smith's *The Theory of Moral Sentiments*, published in London in 1759.

In *True Virtue* Edwards spoke of the "natural disposition in men" to be pleased when they are objects of honor and love and displeased when they are objects of hatred and contempt, as a fixed law of nature, a law, he believed, as real and determined "as any of the pleasures and pains of external sense." The psychological foundation of this human characteristic is the same as that mentioned earlier: "Man's love to himself will make him love love to himself, and hate hatred to himself." In consequence, a person will love those he believes are broadly like himself, "who are warmly engaged on his side, and promote his interest." This tendency is the "natural consequence of a private self-love." There is no more true virtue in a man thus loving his friends, Edwards wrote, "than there is in self-love itself, the principle from whence it proceeds."[88]

Edwards took special care to state that, although the connection between a person's self-love and his love of others who love him and promote his interest is an instituted law of nature, it carries with it no metaphysical or logical necessity; that is, to suppose things otherwise would not be an internal contradiction. In the same way, in the system of the universe a reversal of the natural laws of physics, such as a cessation of universal gravitation, would contradict only that "beautiful proportion and harmony, which the Author of Nature observes in the laws of nature he has established."[89] It would not be inherently illogical. Self-love, with its natural ramification into benevolence via the extension of gratitude, is a regular and orderly occurrence in human motivation and behavior. But it is not one that cannot be interrupted by God at will, as when He makes a saint, that is to say, a person whose benevolence is not rooted in self-love. The uncovering of the psychological law of self-interest, the human tendency to judge good and bad in accordance with benefits to self, left Edwards with more than cynicism or utilitarianism to choose from. For in individual cases, God changes the entire foundation of natural human psychology and makes Himself the ground of moral judgment.

There persisted, however, certain questions about gratitude, for the benevo-

---

88. *True Virtue*, ed. Frankena, 46–47. Edwards gave a shrewd example of deceptive self-love for one's own party masquerading as benevolence, in *Distinguishing Marks of a Work of the Spirit*, 55–56: "There is a Counterfeit of Love, that often appears amongst those that are led by a Spirit of Delusion: There is commonly in the wildest Enthusiasts a Kind of Union and Affection that appears in them one towards another, arising from Self-Love, occasioned by their agreeing one with another in those Things wherein they greatly differ from all others, and for which they are the Objects of the Ridicule of all the rest of Mankind; which naturally will cause them so much the more to prize the Esteem they observe in each other, of those Peculiarities that make them the Objects of others Contempt: So the ancient *Gnosticks* and the wild *Fanaticks*, that appeared in the Beginning of the Reformation, boasted of their great Love one to another: One Sect of them in particular calling themselves the *Family of Love*. . . . 'Tis only the working of a natural Self-Love, and no true *Benevolence*."

89. *True Virtue*, ed. Frankena, 47.

lists were using it, Edwards learned, not as an explanation of how self-love is converted into the appearance of benevolence, but, on the contrary, as a proof in itself of disinterested virtue. By the middle of the century a rather diffuse debate had come into focus over the question of whether disinterested gratitude and disinterested moral indignation, or anger, could possibly exist. Hutcheson, writing in 1725, had no doubts that gratitude was disinterested (or could be) and viewed it as a divinely implanted affection for regulating man's generalized benevolence by guiding it toward those who most directly affect each individual's well-being. Without the guidance provided by the emotion of gratitude, man's benevolence would be "quite distracted with a multiplicity of Objects, whose equal Virtues would equally recommend them to our regard."[90] Moreover, the predictability that gratitude will go to immediate benefactors rather than going arbitrarily or randomly to any goodwilled souls whatsoever, no matter how distant, also serves to keep alive benefactions, and thus benefits society in general. Gratitude, like gravity, Hutcheson said, points universal benevolence to the nearest bodies, and helps to maintain order and regularity in the moral world.[91]

Hume, also, had rebuked those "superficial reasoners" who, "observing many false pretenses among mankind," draw the hasty conclusion that because men sometimes are moved by selfishness, everyone is at all times

---

90. Selby-Bigge, ed., *British Moralists*, par. 146. In *The Moralists* Shaftesbury had already argued that gratitude and resentment, pride and shame, were intrinsic proofs of moral sensibility. Has a man "gratitude or resentment, pride or shame? Whichever way it be, he acknowledges a sense of just and unjust, worthy and mean. . . . As long as I find men either angry or revengeful, proud or ashamed, I am safe. For they conceive an honourable and dishonourable, a foul and fair, as well as I" (*Characteristics*, ed. Robertson, II, 140–141). Thomas Burnet (the Master of the Charterhouse), who was one of the originators of the idea of the moral sense, wrote at the beginning of the 18th century: "This I am sure of, that the Distinction, suppose of Gratitude and Ingratitude, Fidelity and Infidelity, . . . and such others, is as sudden without any Ratiocination, and as sensible and piercing, as the difference I feel from the Scent of a Rose, and of Assafoetida. 'Tis not like a Theorem, which we come to know by the help of precedent Demonstrations and Postulatums" (quoted from Burnet's *Remarks upon an Essay Concerning the Humane Understanding* . . . [London, 1697], in Ernest Lee Tuveson, *The Imagination as a Means of Grace: Locke and the Aesthetics of Romanticism* [Berkeley and Los Angeles, Calif., 1960], 48). See also Tuveson, "The Origins of the 'Moral Sense,'" *Huntington Library Quarterly*, XI (1947–1948), 241–259.

91. Selby-Bigge, ed., *British Moralists*, par. 146. See above, n. 77. Aside from the issue in philosophy over the nature of gratitude, and the question of whether its existence proved the existence of a moral sense, the considerable amount of attention focused on this emotion in a number of contexts was symptomatic of a social order that necessarily placed an extremely high value on it. In a society organized in large part along lines of patronage, gratitude, which meant loyalty and reciprocity as needed, was of vital importance. Gratitude, Descartes said, is one of the "bonds of society." On the other hand, ingratitude was for centuries condemned by moralists as one of the worst crimes not punishable by law. Edwards's cynical discussion of gratitude may have touched some exposed nerves.

equally corrupted by private interest. "What heart one must be possessed of who professes such principles, and who feels no internal sentiment that belies so pernicious a theory, it is easy to imagine," he said. The testimony of the heart, then, or internal sentiment, is enough to prove that the theory of universal egoism is false. How could anyone in the grip of such false opinions about the nature of man have any degree of affection or benevolence toward mankind, Hume asked? It is represented "under such odious colors" and supposed to be "so little susceptible of gratitude or any return of affection." Clearly, in this example of what is good about mankind, Hume did not mean that gratitude was merely self-interested reciprocity. "The most obvious objection to the selfish hypothesis," Hume wrote, "is that as it is contrary to common feeling and our most unprejudiced notions, there is required the highest stretch of philosophy to establish so extraordinary a paradox. . . . To the most careless observer there appear to be such dispositions as benevolence and generosity, such affections as love, friendship, compassion, gratitude. These sentiments . . . [are] plainly distinguished from those of the selfish passions."[92] "Is gratitude no affection of the human breast," Hume asked, "or is that a word merely without any meaning or reality? Have we no satisfaction in one man's company above another's, and no desire of the welfare of our friend, even though absence or death should prevent us from all participation in it? Or what is it commonly that gives us any participation in it, even while alive and present, but our affection and regard to him?"[93]

With regard to anger, or more specifically resentment or indignation, similar reasoning was advanced. George Turnbull maintained that "the only way in which our reason and understanding can raise anger or resentment, is by representing to our mind, injustice, or injury of some kind or other. Its object is not natural but moral evil: it is not suffering, but injury [that is its object]." We do not feel anger toward one who appears to the suffering person "to have been only the innocent occasion of his pain or loss"; but we do feel it toward "one who has been in the moral sense injurious either to ourselves or others." Resentment, like gratitude, is plainly a response to the intentional exercise of moral good or evil. "The indignation raised by cruelty and injustice, and the desire of having it punished, which persons unconcerned feel, is by no means malice. No, it is resentment against vice and wickedness."[94]

92. David Hume, *An Inquiry Concerning the Principles of Morals* . . . , ed. Charles W. Hendel (Indianapolis, Ind., 1957), 113, 115–116.

93. *Ibid.*, 117–118.

94. Turnbull, *Principles of Moral Philosophy*, II, 313–314. Turnbull, as was typical of his writing, was borrowing heavily from others, in this case from Bishop Butler's eighth sermon, "On Resentment." Thus, Butler, *Sermons*, in Gladstone, ed., *Works of Butler*, II, 139: "The only way in which our reason and understanding can raise anger, is by representing to our mind injustice or injury of some kind or other." The balance of Turnbull's statement is also taken here and

Edwards gave a detailed response to these ideas, under the assumption that if gratitude and anger could be demolished as examples of disinterested moral perceptions and conduct and reduced to expressions of self-love, two of the mightiest pillars of alleged natural virtue would have been removed.[95] His rebuttal took advantage of the evident confusion in the moral sense school regarding the criteria by which people are assumed to judge good and bad. (Even Hume's *Enquiry Concerning the Principles of Morals*, it may be observed, leaves the reader uncertain as to how far utility, or immediate perceptions, or sympathy, form the basis of moral judgment.) Edwards's first objection pointed to the ambiguity of Hutcheson's analysis of gratitude as a quality illustrative of the moral sense. Hutcheson asserts, on the one hand, Edwards argued, that the moral sense provides the capacity for discrimination between those benefits received from persons, who have the capacity for good *intentions*, and those benefits received from things without life, such as a timely rainfall or a fruit tree. On the other hand, the moral sense is said to be "the effect of that principle of benevolence or love to others, or love to the public, which is naturally in the hearts of all mankind." Can the moral sense (or its representative, in this case, gratitude) be both a discriminating faculty for distinguishing moral intentionality and a faculty guided only by concern for general utility or the public good? A conception of gratitude as a disinterested, morally significant emotion depends upon the assumption that the above faculties or qualities operate together. Edwards took them singly and doubted that either one was illustrative of moral virtue.

"According to [the benevolists'] own way of arguing," Edwards said, if the moral sense is essentially a sentiment of benevolence, would not gratitude arise even toward inanimate things "such as sun and clouds, that do good to the public," and anger arise toward "mildew, and an overflowing stream, that does hurt to the public?" If gratitude is founded on disinterested public

---

there from Butler. On p. 141 Butler continued: "The indignation raised by cruelty and injustice, and the desire of having it punished, which persons unconcerned would feel, is by no means malice. No, it is resentment against vice and wickedness: it is one of the common bonds, by which society is held together; a fellow-feeling, which each individual has in behalf of the whole species, as well as of himself." But Butler, like Edwards, saw moral indignation as proof of a "sense of desert," not a "moral sense" in Hutcheson's terms. Cf. also Butler's "Dissertation on the Nature of Virtue," *ibid.*, I, 398–399, on gratitude and anger as proof of a "moral faculty."

95. In his "Book of Controversies," MS, Beinecke Lib., Yale Univ., Edwards wrote: "As there appears in brute Creatures some taste of this external Beauty that is an Image of moral Beauty[,] so there appears some degree even of that natural sense it self which our new Philosophers call moral Taste in Men and assert to be a virtuous Principle. These Philosophers insist that the natural Principles of Anger and Gratitude which are in all mankind are evidences of a moral Taste. They say these cant arise merely from self-love but suppose a moral sense or sense of desert that in the exercise of these assertions is prior to self-love" (p. 181). This section of the manuscript dates from about 1753.

affections, we ought to be as "affected toward inanimate things that are beneficial or injurious both to us and the public, . . . as to them that are profitable or hurtful to both on choice and design, and from benevolence or malice."[96] That gratitude is limited to special cases of public benefits suggests that it does not proceed from a general concern for the public good, but from something more refined.

Looking at the ability of people to discriminate between natural benefits and moral benefits, or natural good and moral good, Edwards questioned whether there was anything distinctively moral in this ability. The "Author of Nature, who observes order, uniformity, and harmony" in all of His laws, has so ordered things that it is "natural for self-love to cause the mind to be affected differently towards exceedingly different objects"; it is natural for "our heart to extend itself in one manner towards inanimate things, which gratify self-love without sense or will, and in another manner towards beings which we look upon as having understanding and will, like ourselves." Moreover, Edwards implied, the capacity for distinguishing a moral situation from a merely natural one is actually better explained by self-love than by any other fact. "No wonder, seeing we love ourselves, that it should be natural to us to extend something of that same kind of love which we have for ourselves, to them who are the same kind of beings as ourselves, and comply with the inclinations of our self-love, by expressing the same sort of love toward us."[97] We give moral value to the deliberate good deeds of a person and not to random acts of nature or to acts without benevolent intent because, out of self-love, we love the recognizable expression of love to ourselves.

In sum, natural gratitude underlies many allegedly disinterested moral acts, and it is itself embedded firmly in self-love. Gratitude in Edwards's analysis becomes simply the granting of love to the mirror image of our own self-love, as it is reflected in the love of others to us. And it follows that anger, or indignation, is a response to the recognition of the emotion of hatred that we know internally and that our self-love cannot tolerate. The conception of a moral sense is not required as an explanation of gratitude.

In arguing against intellectualists such as Wollaston, who believed that mere contrariety in relations was enough to trigger a moral response, Hume, without reference to a moral sense, had also pointed to the difference between a person's perception of relations between inanimate things and his perception of relations between beings with understanding and will. But Hume did not explain this difference with the same profundity that Edwards brought to it. "The crime of ingratitude," Hume noted, "is not any particular individual *fact*, but arises from a complication of circumstances which, being presented

96. *True Virtue*, ed. Frankena, 49–50.
97. *Ibid.*, 50–51.

to the spectator, excites the *sentiment* of blame by the particular structure and fabric of his mind." Thus, "inanimate objects may bear to each other all the same relations which we observe in moral agents, though the former can never be the object of love or hatred, nor are consequently susceptible of merit or iniquity. A young tree which overtops and destroys its parent [from whose seed it sprung] stands in all the same relations with Nero when he murdered Agrippina."[98] But we do not blame the young tree for matricide, according to Hume, because the sentiment of blame is not excited. Edwards's analysis is more fruitful and, indeed, opens the way to some of Adam Smith's ideas in *The Theory of Moral Sentiments*.

Edwards maintained that even if gratitude and anger do include the exercise of "some kind of moral sense—as it is granted there is something that may be so called—all the moral sense that is essential to those affections, is a sense of *Desert*."[99] By "some kind of moral sense," Edwards had in mind in part that judgment of measure and proportion in the exercise of gratitude and anger that distinguishes these particular emotions from certain excesses that have a family resemblance to them, such as sycophantic fawning or blind rage. The sense of desert, it will be remembered, is rooted, according to Edwards, in man's natural apprehension of "that secondary kind of beauty that lies in uniformity and proportion." The love and kindness of others, as well as their ill will and injuriousness, naturally appear to "deserve" a reciprocal response. "It seems to us no other than just, that as they love us and do us good, we also should love them and do them good. And so it seems just, that when others' hearts oppose us, and they from their hearts do us hurt, our hearts should oppose them, and that we should desire themselves may suffer in like manner as we have suffered." This, Edwards concedes, is a "kind of" moral sense, or "sense of beauty in moral things." But he had already made clear that this apprehension of secondary beauty in things was not essentially a moral taste, and, of course, he insisted, fell far short of true virtue. When the moral sense is dissected into its elements, and its vague if attractive connotations stripped away, it is, Edwards held, either a self-contradictory notion or a non-moral faculty. Certainly, according to Edwards, it is not the same as a love of virtue, or even "a disposition and determination of mind to be pleased with true virtuous beauty, consisting in public benevolence."[100]

Edwards had two last criticisms of the assumptions of benevolist theory. First, gratitude and anger (if accepted as implying the existence of a moral sense grounded in universal benevolence) very often are expressed with no reference whatsoever to the public good or public injury. Second, the passion

---

98. Hume, *Inquiry Concerning Principles of Morals*, ed. Hendel, 108–111.
99. *True Virtue*, ed. Frankena, 51.
100. *Ibid.*, 51–52.

of anger in particular seems as often connected to general irascibility and bad temper as to a fine sense of public good. On the first point, Edwards's example went back at least to Augustine, even to Socrates. There is gratitude and anger amongst pirates and thieves. A gang of brigands who are helped by a sympathetic onlooker to escape arrest will be very grateful to their benefactor, but their gratitude is only in relation to themselves, not the public good. It is easy to produce similar examples of indignation or resentment that refer in truth only to private benefits. Such examples do not prove, of course, that *all* gratitude or anger is unconcerned with universal welfare, but only that sometimes these affections are self-centered.

In these cases, as in some other of Edwards's arguments, what has been shown is only that human behavior is easily subject to contradictory interpretations. Fifty years earlier Shaftesbury had used the evidence of pirates and thieves to demonstrate the ineradicable persistence of social affections in mankind. The problem, Shaftesbury said, was only that men usually failed to extend their social affections broadly enough. Thus, paradoxically, international warfare proves both the strength of human love, loyalty, disinterested self-sacrifice, public benevolence, and social affections of all kinds *within* a nation, and at the same time, selfishness, hatred, malice, and destructive self-interest *between* nations. Which of these alternative descriptions, after all, is to be the measure of man? The optimists envisioned a community of mankind based upon his most noble feelings; the pessimists, like Edwards, saw only constantly changing social and political unities, always limited in extent to a small portion of mankind, always based ultimately on compounded self-love at best.[101]

Turning to Edwards's final argument, concerning the ill uses of anger, it must be said that he prejudiced the case by the lack of precision in his definitions. Edwards maintained that if the moral sense that is exercised in anger "were that which arose from a benevolent temper of heart, being no other than a sense or relish of the beauty of benevolence," there ought to be a regular, positive correlation between a disposition to anger and the growth of "a sweet, benign, and benevolent temper."[102] But this, he observes, is entirely contrary to experience. Usually it is the other way around: a bad temper and little benevolence go together. It is easy to see, however, that if the emotion of indignation is substituted for anger, such a correlation does not seem impossible. Herman Melville's *Billy Budd*, for example, is about this exact relationship between extraordinary goodness of soul and overwhelming indignation in the face of evil.[103] Edwards's conclusion to his brief discussion

---

101. Like Pascal, Edwards was a pessimist about the capacities of unaided nature, an optimist about the promises of grace.

102. *True Virtue*, ed. Frankena, 54.

103. Cf. the brilliant analysis in Hannah Arendt, *On Revolution* (New York, 1963), 68–83.

of the fallacies in benevolist claims about gratitude and anger was surprisingly, perhaps even excessively, modest: "Not all" gratitude, and not all anger, he said, "arises from a truly virtuous benevolence of heart."[104]

Natural Affection

In addition to gratitude and anger, sentimentalist moral philosophy in the eighteenth century placed great emphasis on the evidence of certain other affections that seemed to prove that men were influenced predominantly by motives other than selfishness. The most important of these by far was compassion or pity, which will be treated in the next chapter.[105] But among others often cited were *storgé*, usually translated "natural affection," meaning particularly love between parents and children; the mutual love between the sexes; and several motives that Edwards preferred to call "instincts." Shaftesbury's *Inquiry Concerning Virtue and Merit* had already cataloged these emotions or instincts under the general designation of the "social affections." "In the passions and affections of particular creatures there is a constant relation to the interest of a species or common nature," Shaftesbury wrote. "This has been demonstrated in the case of natural affection, parental kindness, zeal for posterity, concern for the propagation and nurture of the young, love of fellowship and company, compassion, mutual succour, and the rest of this kind. . . . This we know for certain, that all social love, friendship, gratitude, or whatever else is of this generous kind, does by its nature take place of the self-interesting passions, draws us out of ourselves, and makes us disregardful of our own convenience and safety."[106]

Edwards's tack in relation to these claims is predictable. He did not deny their existence, but he also maintained that they had little to do with virtue. There is no question, Edwards said, that men have various natural dispositions and inclinations that depend on particular laws of nature and that determine their minds to certain affections and actions toward particular objects. These laws seem to be established chiefly for human self-preservation and for mankind's "comfortably subsisting in the world."[107] These "instincts" are of several kinds. Some contribute to the individual's personal sustenance; others are social and extend to other persons, such as the "mutual inclinations between the sexes." They are also classifiable in another way. Some are sensitive appetites, such as the desire for meat and drink or for sexual rela-

104. *True Virtue*, ed. Frankena, 54–55.
105. See chap. 5, pp. 247–259, below.
106. Shaftesbury, *Characteristics*, ed. Robertson, I, 280–281.
107. *True Virtue*, ed. Frankena, 75.

tions. Others are more "internal and mental," Edwards wrote, and consist of the affections men have toward others as "fellow-creatures," or in some cases toward mankind in general. Finally, Edwards noted, human instincts may be divided into "kind affections" having in them something like benevolence; and affections akin to anger, such as the passion of jealousy. This last division is obviously a vestige of the old Scholastic distinction between concupiscible and irascible passions. Edwards's interest was only in the kind, social, and unsensual affections that are expressed in the appearance of benevolence, which he intended to show could not be "of the nature of true virtue."[108]

It is notable that Edwards accepted with little question the achievement of moral psychology over the preceding one hundred years in establishing that benevolent and social affections were irreducible elements in human nature, equivalent to the most well-known passions and instincts. The concept of man's sociality was hardly new (it was a commonplace of ancient thought) but this fact had been enlarged enormously in its details and given major philosophical standing by the middle of the eighteenth century.[109] The issue between Edwards and the benevolists was how this information was to be interpreted.

Edwards first considered "natural affection," meaning particularly the love of parents to their children and often called "storgé" by eighteenth-century moralists, though Edwards did not use this term.[110] Edwards denied, though

---

108. *Ibid.*

109. Cf. R. S. Crane, "Suggestions toward a Genealogy of the 'Man of Feeling,'" *ELH*, I (1934), 207: The complex of doctrines supporting the man of feeling "was something new in the world," according to Crane. "Neither in antiquity, nor in the sixteenth century, nor in the England of the Puritans and Cavaliers had the 'man of feeling' ever been a popular type." See also Fiering, "Irresistible Compassion," *Jour. Hist. Ideas*, XXXVII (1976), 195–218. In no. 864 of his Miscellanies, printed in *Works*, I, 565–572, which is the closest thing that Edwards ever wrote to a systematic natural theology, he represented his century's view: "God has so made and constituted the world of mankind, that he has made it natural and necessary, that they should be concerned one with another, linked together in society, by the manner of their propagation, their descending one from another and their need one of another, and their inclination to society. We see, that in other parts of the creation, wherein many particulars are dependent and united into one body, there is an excellent harmony and mutual subserviency throughout the whole; as in all bodies natural. How then can we believe, that God has ordered so much of the contrary in the principal part of his creation [i.e., mankind]?" Cf. also William Gould's sermon, *The Generosity of Christian Love* (London, 1676), 12–13: "God hath fastened on all the Creatures not onely a private desire to satisfie the demands of its own Nature, but a general Charity and feeling of Communion as sociable parts of the Universe or Common Body." Quoted in Lois Whitney, *Primitivism and the Idea of Progress in English Popular Literature of the Eighteenth Century* (Baltimore, 1934), 24.

110. More, *Account of Virtue*, 48, refers to that "noble and natural sort of Love, which the Greeks termed *Storgé*, and which we may call natural Affection." Wollaston, *Religion of Nature Delineated*, 165: "That ς[τ]οργή or affection on both sides, which naturally and regularly is in parents towards their children, and *vicissim*, ought to be observed and followed, when there is no

not strongly, that the "instinct" toward "natural affection" is properly considered antithetical to self-love. In his thinking it belonged under the category of private affections or compounded self-love, whereby one incorporates others into the love of self insofar as they are part of one's own group. Yet he was willing to concede that natural affection may exist independently of self-love, the question being hardly "worthy of any controversy or dispute." It was not impossible, he said, for both opinions to be true. Natural affection "may be said to arise from instinct, as it depends on a law of nature. But yet it may be truly reckoned as an affection arising from self-love; because, though it arises from a law of nature, yet that is such a law as according to the order and harmony every where observed among the laws of nature is connected with, and follows from self-love."[111] In other words, natural affection could be considered a corollary of Edwards's first principle of social psychology: men love love to themselves and hate hate to themselves. The exponents of *storgé* as a key article in benevolist ethics concluded that it was both natural and irreducible. Edwards agreed that it was natural, in the sense that it was not humanly contrived, conventional, or artificial, but he saw this kind of love as a subsidiary of a more fundamental law that was rooted in self-love. The workings of the fulcrum and the lever, for example, are as natural as the principle of universal gravitation, but they can be used to work against the direct force of gravity; nevertheless, the mechanics of the first depend for explanation upon the second. This was not Edwards's example, nor was he explicit on this point, but it is clear he was moving toward the recognition seen more commonly in nineteenth-century philosophy, that the elemental forces of nature are detectable in paradoxical forms. Yet how remote must a trait be from its primitive foundations before it is considered to be qualitatively different?

In any case, Edwards's real dispute with the benevolists concerning "natural affection" was simply that it cannot be of the nature of true virtue because it is by its nature "particular," directed to a "private system," and therefore so infinitely small in relation to universal existence as to bear no proportion to it. "Such limited private benevolence, not arising from, not being subordinate to benevolence to being in general, cannot have the nature

---

reason to the contrary." Turnbull, *Principles of Moral Philosophy*, I, 73: "Our bodily appetites being for good reason accompanied with uneasy sensations, our moral desires and affections are strengthened in like manner by uneasy strong sensations to maintain a just balance; so is plainly the Στοργή or natural affection to children." This is a small sample. Since higher education everywhere required familiarity with the Greek New Testament, the use of "*astorgos*" (i.e., ruthlessness, or the want of natural affection) in Rom. 1:31 and in 2 Tim. 3:3 brought the root word into currency. It is surprising the Greek word was not eventually absorbed into English, given its extraordinarily wide usage in philosophy.

111. *True Virtue*, ed. Frankena, 76.

of true virtue." Most of his opponents, Edwards said, agreed that virtue is "general benevolence or public affection." Yet these particular affections "do not arise from this principle, whether one assumes they are rooted in self-love or independent instincts."[112]

By treating natural affection in isolation from other social affections, Edwards evaded, perhaps, the main argument of the benevolists. Natural affection was for them simply one fact in a whole pattern of evidence that demonstrated man's essential good nature, his innate inclination to benevolence. Obviously *storgé* could not stand alone as entire proof that all natural virtue was not derivative from self-love. Bishop Butler in his *Sermons* had been particularly emphatic on the point that it was the pattern of evidence that mattered, and it is tempting to believe that Edwards would not have taken some of the positions he did had he read Butler's *Sermons*.[113]

Edwards had a further objection that was more tied to his own synthetic ethics. These "private affections," he said, if they do not arise from general benevolence and are "not connected with it in their first existence," can have no tendency to produce universal benevolence. Not being directly dependent on the only principle of heart that can constitute true virtue, "their detached and unsubordinate operation rather implies opposition to being in general, than general benevolence."[114] Particular loves, according to Edwards's thinking, do not merge into authentic general love; they are its enemy. Here again Edwards was in direct opposition to Shaftesbury and Hutcheson. As we noted above, Shaftesbury had persuasively argued that man's very social nature— which was in itself evidence of his essential goodness—paradoxically stood in the way of universal peace. In his effort to refute Hobbesianism, Shaftesbury had brilliantly shown that the cause of war and social conflict was not individualist egoism but something more like group egoism, man's tendency to join with and love his circle exclusively. And now Edwards was using this same insight to prove that all particular affections, such as *storgé*, not only fell short of true virtue, that is, of universal benevolence, but were among the main obstacles to its realization. No simple leap or extension was possible, in

112. *Ibid.*, 77.

113. *Sermons*, in Gladstone, ed., *Works of Butler*, preface, 8*ff*: Butler made the central point that human nature must be interpreted as an integer, a complex whole with reciprocal relations; none of the parts should be interpreted without reference to the functioning of the whole. It is the organization of the personality, or what Butler called the "constitution of human nature," that matters. "Appetites, passions, affections, and the principle of reflection, considered merely as the several parts of our inward nature, do not at all give us an idea of the system or constitution of this nature; because the constitution is formed by somewhat not yet taken into consideration, namely, by the relations which these several parts have to each other."

114. *True Virtue*, ed. Frankena, 78.

Edwards's estimation, from a person's private loves to a sentiment of general benevolence. In this area, grace does not perfect nature; it totally eradicates the selfish basis of natural love and refounds love again on a different principle. True virtue stands against the parochiality of the world, the comforting alliances of like souls and common blood. This parochiality is exposed as opposition to God's demand upon man to turn his back on mother and father and to love from heaven down. Edwards drove home this point with an extreme example: "If there could be a cause determining a person to benevolence towards the whole world of mankind, or even of all created sensible natures throughout the universe, exclusive of union of heart to general existence and of love to God—not derived from that temper of mind which disposes to a supreme regard to him, nor subordinate to such divine love—it cannot be of the nature of true virtue."[115] There could be no more categorical denial of utility (or the greatest happiness principle) as the ultimate criterion of ethics.[116]

We may admire the audacity of such a statement, which dismissed love to "all created sensible creatures throughout the universe" as merely particular, private, limited, and insignificant in the eyes of God. But it is also open to obvious criticism. Edwards's position introduced a dubious discontinuity into the nature of love. All true love is surely homogeneous. In the light of developmental psychology, we know that human beings learn first about love from infantile experience with the mother. Then later this primitive and egoistic love is refined and chastened in the family constellation with father and brother and sister. By the time the child leaves the nurture of the family, he must already have the ingredients of mature and unselfish love, in some state, in his personality. Further integration and refinement will be needed, but not total erasure of all of this early emotional experience, unless from the beginning it was profoundly disturbed. One's earliest experiences with love in the family may need to be transcended, but the seed of natural love remains at the core of spiritual love.

Edwards undoubtedly understood this, for much religious metaphor from the most ancient times drew upon family experience: the "fatherhood" of God is an effort to express God's relationship to humankind as protecting, con-

---

115. *Ibid.*, 78–79. In the last section of his *Illustrations on the Moral Sense* (London, 1728), Hutcheson took up the question of "how far a Regard to the Deity is necessary to make an Action virtuous," and, of course, disagreed with Edwards in his conclusions. See below, pp. 339–340.

116. As some of Edwards's critics were to point out after his death, the combination of a standard of ethics pitched as high as Edwards's was, plus the depreciation of utility as a criterion of good works, can lead to indifference to lower order morality and even encourage license for want of a practical standard of action at any level below the highest. See below, pp. 353–356.

cerned, guiding, authoritative—all part of divine love; similarly, men should
be as brothers, we say; we hope for the brotherhood of men, which is not an
abstract ideal but a concrete one that resounds in the experience of every
person with a brother or sister. The brotherhood of man obviously does not
contradict the experience of brotherly love in the family; it universalizes it.[117]

In an earlier work, *Some Thoughts Concerning the Present Revival of
Religion* (1742), Edwards made clear that he would never be a party to any
Stoic virtue, even in Christian guise. He warned against the endeavor "utterly
to root out and abolish all natural affection or respect to . . . near relations,
under a notion that no other love ought to be allowed but spiritual love . . .
and that it becomes Christians to love none upon the account of anything else,
but the image of God." One might as well argue, Edwards said, that a man
ought "utterly to disallow of, and endeavor to abolish all love or appetite to
their daily food, under a notion that it is a carnal appetite." Why would it be
desirable for the saints to strive for a kind of holiness that "the Apostle in
Rom. 1:31, mentions as one instance wherein the heathen had got to the most
horrid pass in wickedness, viz., a *being without natural affection?*"[118] God
has put natural affections in man for the good of mankind, Edwards continued,
and they are "of great use when kept in their proper place." To try to root
them out is "a reproach" to the wisdom and goodness of the Creator. Finally,
Edwards stated here, the existence of these natural inclinations, if well regulated, is not "inconsistent with any part of our duty to God, or any argument
of a sinful selfishness."[119]

The apparent contradiction between Edwards's disparagement of natural
love in *True Virtue* and his favorable comments in the earlier work is easily
resolved. His method in *True Virtue* was not pastoral, but philosophical. His
goal was to prevent the optimists from using the concept of "natural affections" to support their philosophy. In *Some Thoughts* he was defending the
validity of the existence of these feelings, even in a saint.

If *storgé* was altogether remote from true virtue, so also, Edwards believed,
was that "mutual affection which naturally arises between the sexes," al-

---

117. Cf. Milton, *Paradise Lost*, IV, ll. 754–757:

Through wedded love,
Founded in reason, loyal, just and pure,
Relations dear, and all the charities
Of father, son, and brother, first were known.

118. *Thoughts Concerning the Revival*, 286. In the Greek New Testament the italicized phrase
is the word "*astorgos.*" See n. 110, above. On the conflict with Stoic ethics in this period, see
Fiering, *Moral Philosophy at Seventeenth-Century Harvard*, chap. 4.

119. *Thoughts Concerning the Revival*, 287.

though in the case of this latter "particular" instinct Edwards gave up trying to prove that it was properly classified as a species of self-love or sensitive appetite. "I agree with Hutchison and Hume in this," he wrote, "that there is a foundation laid in nature for kind affections between the sexes, diverse from all inclinations to sensitive pleasure, and which do not properly arise from any such inclination." Edwards had too good a marriage himself to believe anything different. "There is doubtless a disposition," he said, "both to a mutual benevolence and mutual complacence, that are not naturally and necessarily connected with any sensitive desires."[120] However, he did continue to argue that in this case, as with natural affection, the inclination is ipso facto private and particular and does not arise from a principle of general benevolence. He saw in the love between man and woman a great divine design, including its sexual components. These inclinations were the means by which "persons become willing to forsake father and mother, and all their natural relations in the families where they were born and brought up, for the sake of a stated union with a companion of the other sex, in bearing and going through that series of labours, anxieties, and pains, requisite to the being, support, and education of a family of children; and partly also for the comfort of mankind as united in a marriage relation." But still, these important and lovely natural dispositions "cannot be of the nature of true virtue."[121]

How then to summarize Edwards's position on the important questions surrounding self-love in relation to morality? We have seen that he was too shrewd a psychologist to accept any blanket condemnations of self-love insofar as the most fundamental human inclinations are concerned, such as the desire for happiness or the desire for what is agreeable to self. He was also less of a purist than might be supposed, in his full acceptance of admixtures of fear and animality in even the most elevated relations of man with God. When Edwards spoke as a comforting student of the human heart, he told people to cease to believe that either total disinterest or total purity of inclination could be achieved. When, however, he spoke as an enemy of secular complacency and philosophical optimism he made use of every weapon of psychological analysis to demonstrate that what the world generally accepted as signs of virtue or morality were merely elaborations of self-interest. In fact, he argued, there was no escaping the blight of self-interest by any natural means. God gives mankind by nature or by common grace a modicum of social or moral regulatory principles in order to save us all from rapid descent into hell on

120. *True Virtue*, ed. Frankena, 79.

121. *Ibid*. Cf. Edwards's lovely parting message to his wife, Sarah: "Give my kindest love to my dear wife, and tell her that the uncommon union that has so long subsisted between us has been of such a nature as I trust is spiritual and therefore will continue for ever."

earth. Those who want more can depend only on supernatural aid, which can bring about a new principle, a new starting point in the soul with a new orientation. The difference from the internal condition of the natural person is entirely qualitative, not quantitative, such that no form of natural benevolence, no matter how extensive, can equal the effects of divine grace in instilling disinterested universal love.

5

Hell and the Humanitarians

It will be found, that there will be
no satisfying the infidel humor, with anything
that is very contrary to men's inclinations:
any thing that they are very averse to bear,
they would be averse to believe.[1]

It is sometimes considered an irony that Jonathan Edwards, the greatest theologian and philosopher in eighteenth-century America, of whom it was said by Dugald Stewart that "in logical acuteness and subtility, [he] does not yield to any disputant bred in the universities of Europe," should be remembered most for fanatical preaching of the terrors of hell.[2] We may be grateful that this narrow image of the great man as primarily a hell preacher has been largely repudiated by scholars. Yet often the popular view of a person contains a germ of truth that deserves serious attention. What does it mean that *Sinners in the Hands of an Angry God*, Edwards's notorious hellfire sermon at Enfield, Connecticut, outsold all of his other American publications?[3] At the least this fact may suggest that despite the efforts of some modern interpreters to make the doctrine of hell merely a footnote to Edwards's other speculations,[4] there

1. Edwards, "Concerning the Endless Punishment of Those Who Die Impenitent," *Works*, I, 642.

2. Dugald Stewart, *Dissertation First: Exhibiting the Progress of Metaphysical Ethical and Political Philosophy; since the Revival of Letters in Europe*, ed. William Hamilton (Edinburgh, 1854), 424. This is volume I of Hamilton's edition of the *Works of Stewart*.

3. The Shipton and Mooney *Short-Title Evans* lists eight editions from 1741, when it was first published in Boston, to 1797. No other American publication of Edwards's was reprinted more than half so often, and I am assuming from this fact that more copies were sold as well. Only Edwards's *Faithful Narrative of the Surprising Work of God*, which saw four editions by 1744 and many printings, and his *Account of the Life of . . . David Brainerd . . .* (Boston, 1749) are likely to have had more readers in the 18th century.

4. Perry Miller, *Jonathan Edwards*, 149: "Of course, Edwards never doubted that a hell exists to which sinners go after death, but that consideration was a footnote." Douglas J. Elwood, *The Philosophical Theology of Jonathan Edwards* (New York, 1960), 3: "If this mystical strain in his thought and experience is taken seriously it must be adjudged that his imprecatory sermons are not

is good reason to treat the traditional image respectfully and to consider closely all that the reality of the inferno meant to the Northampton minister.

Such an investigation reveals that the eternal torment of the damned was for Edwards a matter of central importance theologically, philosophically, and even, perhaps, personally. His own conversion appears to have revolved around this very question, and thereafter he made it a requirement of faith that one not just believe in hell but also lovingly accept its existence. Most important, the existence of hell (in the orthodox conception) became a key issue in Edwards's struggle with the sentimental humanitarianism of the age, which led to his formulation of one of the few effective critiques of the ethics of compassion in the eighteenth century. In defending the doctrine of hell, Edwards was also demonstrating the inadequacy of merely natural ethics. In sum, Edwards clung tenaciously to the dogma of strict reprobation in all its horrendous and fanciful details. It was for him both a functional and a fruitful belief, not simply an incidental tenet in a larger theological system.

Edwards's personal involvement with the idea of hell is woven into all of his discussions of the subject. Yet anyone who knows the bulk of his writings is inevitably faced with the question: How could a man as deeply sensitive and tender as he appears to have been, as enchanted with beauty and order, and as aware of the latest developments in thought, dwell so unflinchingly upon the most excruciating and unimaginable horrors? We see in Edwards some of the traits of the eighteenth-century man of sensibility, and in his psychological theory he was aligned with the sentimentalists. In his later years he read and enjoyed the novels of Samuel Richardson, in which, despite some gloom and morbidity, delicacy of sentiment was highly prized. From the perspective of these aspects of Edwards's personality, the ruthlessness of his hell preaching may seem on the surface to be incompatible with the whole man.

Of course, historically speaking, belief in some sort of hell was overwhelmingly the dominant view in the first half of the eighteenth century, and we should not be surprised therefore by Edwards's conviction. Given the context of his thought, it would be much more startling if he had not believed in a hell. But Edwards did more than passively believe; as James Carse has pointed out, he appears to have rather frequently dwelt on this terrifying subject mat-

---

necessarily integral to his philosophy, but may simply reflect the mind-set of colonial New England." Many other recent commentators attempt to extenuate in one way or another the charge that Edwards was obsessed with hell. James Carse's *Jonathan Edwards and the Visibility of God* (New York, 1967), 150–151, is an exception: "Edwards delivered the most searing maledictions in the memory of the American church. . . . There is no way of avoiding this fact. . . . The eternal torment of the damned was a subject to which he repeatedly and tirelessly turned in his preaching, and even in his miscellaneous notes. There is no item in this vivid explosion of metaphoric carnage on which his imagination could not feed at length. Indeed, we might well argue that his creative powers are nowhere more in evidence than in these astonishing pages."

ter, whereas he could easily have minimized it, as many others prudently chose to do. When the Reverend James Hervey, the eighteenth-century British author of cemetery "Meditations," alarmed his audience with a sermon on the imminence of hell, the *Monthly Review* expressed the opinion that Hervey would have done better to convince "his auditors by appealing to their reason and by representing to them the beauty of holiness rather than by terrifying them." Even in the seventeenth century the important Protestant Scholastic Francis Turretin, whose authority in exposition of doctrine Edwards rated second only to Peter van Mastricht's, taught that unlike the mystery of election, which needed to be preached frequently because it tended to "comfort believers," reprobation "ought to be mentioned more sparingly, not only among common folk but among the initiates in schools also."[5] The Edwards biographer Alexander Allen was convinced that Edwards taught the doctrine of endless punishment in an "extreme form" that was "unsurpassed, if not unequalled in the whole range of Christian literature." But as Allen rightly asked, why Edwards of all other men?[6]

That this kind of preaching was effective in bringing sinners around is obvious enough (although some ministers believed it drove people away). Edwards was of the school that maintained the preacher had to conjure up vivid images if he was to reach the heart more than the head, for "the soul is more strongly inclined to near than distant good." Because of the intensity and liveliness of immediately present sensations, the transient pleasures of the moment tend to affect the will more powerfully than the prospect of an eternity of heaven.[7] The problem at Sunday service partly was to rectify this perceptual distortion and to make one's auditors feel heaven and hell with an intensity equivalent to their more proximate concerns.

Moreover, it was axiomatic in this age, as it had been for centuries, that hell was an essential deterrent against vice and sin. Any relaxation in adherence to the strict doctrine was interpreted as a danger not only to religion but to society as well.[8] This concern was so compelling that the learned generally

5. Flora McLaughlin Kearney, *James Hervey and Eighteenth-Century Taste*, Ball State Monograph no. 14 (Muncie, Ind., 1969); Francis Turretin, *Institutio Theologiae Elencticae . . .* (Geneva, 1688), printed in John W. Beardslee III, ed. and trans., *Reformed Dogmatics: J. Wollebius, G. Voetius, F. Turretin* (New York, 1965), 335.

6. Allen, *Jonathan Edwards*, 116.

7. Edwards reflected on this problem in his early "Notes on the Mind," no. 60, in Dwight, *Life of Edwards*, 692. Locke, *Essay Concerning Human Understanding*, ed. Fraser, Bk. II, chap. xxi, secs. 29–45, had earlier discussed the question at length. "Were the will determined by the views of good, as it appears in contemplation greater or less to the understanding . . . —I do not see how it could ever get loose from the infinite eternal joys of heaven, once proposed and considered as possible."

8. E.g., the marquess of Halifax in *The Character of a Trimmer* (first circulated in manuscript in 1684): "Without the help of religion the laws would not be able to subdue the perverseness of

kept frank discussion of the doctrine of future rewards and punishments away
from the ears of laymen, who, it was believed, would draw encouragement
for licentiousness from any hint of skepticism toward future punishment. It is
particularly significant about Edwards that in addition to his forceful public
preaching of hell, which was perhaps to be expected, he also showed unusual
interest in the subject in his private reflections. Edwards's personal manuscript notes concerning hell are more revealing than his notorious imprecatory
sermons, for the notes prove that he was not preaching hell's torments merely
for reasons of expedience.

The Doctrine of Hell in the Early Eighteenth Century

Edwards was the most famous fire and brimstone preacher in the eighteenth
century, and possibly the most famous in the entire history of Western civilization. But this judgment gives us no hard information about the frequency or
prevalence of hell preaching in the early eighteenth century in America and
Britain. While we can gain a fairly accurate sense of the place occupied by the
doctrine of hell in the corpus of Edwards's writings, it is almost impossible,
on the other hand, to say anything definite about the preaching of this doctrine
in the period as a whole. One could read every sermon published in Britain
and America in the seventeenth and eighteenth centuries and still know only
what percentage of *published* sermons dwelt on the eternal torment of the
damned. There is no way of knowing on how many hundreds of other occa-

---

men's wills, which are wild beasts, and require a double chain to keep them down. . . . The consideration of religion is so twisted with that of government that it is never to be separated"
(*Halifax, Complete Works*, ed. J. P. Kenyon [Baltimore, 1969]). John Locke, borrowing from
Scripture, expressed the prevailing reasoning: "For if there be no prospect beyond the grave, the
inference is certainly right—Let us eat and drink, let us enjoy what we delight in, for to-morrow
we shall *die*" (*Essay Concerning Human Understanding*, Bk. II, chap. xxi, par. 35 [1690 ed.]).
Pierre Bayle's assertion in his *Miscellaneous Thoughts on the Comet of 1680* (1682) and
elsewhere, that there was no good reason to assume that atheists could not be excellent citizens,
even though they lacked the fear of divine judgment, started up a tremendous controversy that
was not practically resolved until the passage of the Virginia Statute for Religious Liberty a century later, the first attempt in the Western world to eliminate direct state support of religion. In
1778 the South Carolina Constitution still required belief in an afterlife of reward and punishment
as a condition of toleration by the state. In a sermon on "The Eternity of Hell Torments" delivered by George Whitefield in 1738, he censured in particular those "who go about to dissuade
others from the belief of such an important truth. . . . For if the positive threats of God, concerning the eternity of hell-torments, are already found insufficient to deter men from sin, what higher
pitch of wickedness may we imagine they will quickly arrive at, when they are taught to entertain
any hopes of a future recovery . . . , or, what is worse, that their souls are hereafter to be annihilated, and become like the beasts that perish" (*Sermons on Important Subjects* . . . [London,
n.d.], 314). Hundreds of other examples of this fear could be given.

sions ministers preached hell's torments without leaving any printed record of it and no way of knowing what were the causes behind the publication of these particular sermons rather than others that addressed completely different subjects. Even in the case of Edwards himself, of the hundreds of his sermons that still survive in manuscript, perhaps less than 2 percent pertain to the afterlife of the damned. Yet of his sermons that have been published over the course of the past two centuries, maybe 15 percent are of the imprecatory type, a fact that tells us more about Edwards's various editors than about the author.[9] In short, in generalizing about Edwards's *peculiar* devotion to hell-fire, if such it is, any historian is on treacherous ground as soon as he attempts to make comparative statements about other places, other times, or other preachers and theologians. Nevertheless, it will be useful to essay some rough surmises, keeping in mind always the inadequacy of the evidence and the limited research that has been done on the subject.

We cannot be sure that the doctrine of hell was preached more in seventeenth-century Britain and America than in the first half of the eighteenth century.[10] Judging from the existing bibliographies, it appears that hell preaching grew in frequency when the orthodox doctrine of the afterlife was seriously challenged. During those brief times when no new universalist, Origenist, or Socinian tracts were stimulating controversy, the tendency of the orthodox ministry may have been to keep hell rather quietly in the background, since it was widely recognized that congregations preferred not to hear about it. One could make a passing reference to the "awful state of the damned" and move on quickly to other things, leaving aside the many questions and complications associated with the doctrine of hell that inevitably arose as soon as the subject was ventilated at any length. What seems to have been unusual about Edwards was neither his skill at invoking the torments of hell in scarifying images (other passages in the contemporary literature are easily equivalent to Edwards's best efforts), nor the relative frequency with which he addressed the subject of damnation (which cannot be accurately measured, in any case),

9. Edwards's hellfire sermons seem to have been delivered mostly during the period of the Great Awakening, when he felt peculiarly driven to compel the recalcitrant to come around. Edwards seems to have seen himself during this period literally in a revolutionary situation, and like a Robespierre or a Lenin, he strove to make his victory total, all-inclusive, and to cast into ruin the stubborn and the oppositional who somehow lacked the same vision of Zion in New England. Yet Edwards's concern with hell clearly went beyond homiletics and bringing sinners to Christ; it went beyond this teaching's usefulness (real or alleged) as a deterrent against sin. It had metaphysical importance for him.

10. For a still earlier period, see G. R. Owst, *Preaching in Medieval England: An Introduction to Sermon Manuscripts of the Period, c. 1350–1450* (New York, 1965 [orig. publ. Cambridge, 1926]), 321–322, 334–338, with examples: "Long before black-gowned Calvinists started to gnash teeth in the pulpit . . . threatening of sinners was almost a commonplace of religious instruction."

but simply the theological and philosophical completeness of his treatment of the subject, including both published and unpublished writings.[11] In other words, it is the stature of Edwards's writings on hell that make him unusual. In addition to his major books on free will and Original Sin, his various writings on hell complete the story of man's reprobation, making the entire presentation exceedingly thorough.[12]

Edwards's sermons on reprobation and hell stand out among similar lectures by American contemporaries in the same way that his writings stand out in general in early American religious and philosophical literature. Edwards's preaching was exceptional for its intellectual force, psychological penetration, thoroughness, and ingenuity, but his urge to preach sermons on hell was not exceptional. Samuel Moodey's *Doleful State of the Damned*, for example, a collection of several sermons preached in 1710 at York, Maine, is certainly not inferior to any of Edwards's sermons in its *effort* at terrifying the audi-

11. I can see no evidence for Perry Miller's claim that Edwards developed a new rhetoric that is manifest in his hellfire sermons. For this claim, see Miller, "The Rhetoric of Sensation," in *Errand into the Wilderness* (Cambridge, Mass., 1956). William Rounseville Alger, the greatest 19th-century authority on the history of theories of the afterlife, and the author of the standard study, asserts that "all other paintings of the fear and anguish of hell are vapid and pale before the preternatural frightfulness of those given at unmerciful length and in sickening specialty in some of the Hindu and Persian sacred books. . . . One who is familiar with the imagery of the Buddhist hells will think the pencils of Dante and Pollok, of Jeremy Taylor and Jonathan Edwards, were dipped in water" (Alger, *A Critical History of the Doctrine of a Future Life* [New York, 1867], 510). A preacher with the literary genius of John Donne could undoubtedly make his auditors quake at will. See "Sermon LXXVI" in *LXXX Sermons* (London, 1640): "That God should let my soul fall out of His hand into a bottomless pit, and roll an unremoveable stone upon it, and leave it to that which it finds . . . and never think more of that soul, never have more to do with it; that of the providence of God, that studies the life of every weed and worm and ant and spider and toad and viper, there should never, never, any beam flow out upon me . . . ; that that God . . . should so turn Himself from me, to his glorious Saints and Angels, as that no Saint nor Angel, nor Christ Jesus Himself, should ever pray Him to look towards me, never remember Him that such a soul there is," and so on with extraordinary power. Donne was reputedly preoccupied with hell.

12. C. A. Patrides opens a learned and useful article, "Renaissance and Modern Views on Hell," *Harvard Theol. Rev.*, LVII (1964), 217–236, with the observation that Jonathan Edwards was not so unusual in his conception of hell as is sometimes believed, and then goes on to cite dozens of examples from the 17th century and earlier of hell images and preaching comparable to Edwards's. Cf., for example, Michael Wigmore's *The Way of All Flesh* . . . (London, 1619): "If all the agonies of the spirit of man, that ever were since life was first; if all the tyrannies of humane invention: as hot glowing ovens; fiery furnaces; chaldrons of boyling oyle; roasting upon spits; nipping of the flesh with pincers; parting of the nayles and finger ends with needles and the like; if all these tortures were joyned in one, to shew their force upon one wretched soule, yet they were all as the biting of a flea, a very nothing in respect of hel, where God hath shewne the power of his vengeance, in preparing that infinite, endlesse, ineffable, insufferable place of torments." But Patrides mentions no other *series* of sermons comparable to Edwards's that attempted to represent the orthodox doctrine in all of its aspects.

ence.[13] Similarly, Israel Loring's *Serious Thoughts on the Miseries of Hell*, preached at Sudbury, Massachusetts, and William Cooper's *Three Discourses Concerning the Reality, the Extremity, and the Absolute Eternity of Hell Punishments*, both published in Boston in 1732, were not reticent in defending and representing the state of those cast off by God. Solomon Stoddard, Edwards's maternal grandfather and his predecessor in the Northampton pulpit, strongly recommended the preaching of hell, for he believed that people were able to continue in sin so blithely only because they were insufficiently afraid of damnation. One of the characteristics of a sinner's heart, according to Stoddard, is its indifference to the threat of hell. Men in "a natural estate" ought to fear hell, Stoddard said, and the message of his published sermon on the subject was that ministers should do more to bring home hell's terrors and to break through sinners' indifference. Stoddard himself, however, judging only from his published works, did not spend much time describing the tortures awaiting the damned.[14] Twenty years later Israel Loring, in the sermon mentioned above, quoted Stoddard on the point that Jesus Christ himself was the greatest preacher of hell in the Gospels and that ministers should follow his example.[15]

Edward Wigglesworth, the distinguished Harvard professor of divinity, lectured in defense of the orthodox doctrine of hell at least twice, though in a rather detached and academic fashion quite different from Moodey's evident desire to win souls for Christ.[16] Nevertheless, Wigglesworth shared the conviction of Moodey, Stoddard, and others, expressed by Wigglesworth in philosophical terms, that the fear of hell is a necessary motive for maintaining moral and religious order on earth. Arguments from reason and nature are "too faint and lifeless to be opposed to sense and passion," according to

13. Samuel Moodey, *The Doleful State of the Damned; Especially Such as Go to Hell from under the Gospel; Aggravated from Their Apprehensions of the Saints Happiness in Heaven . . .* (Boston, 1710).

14. Solomon Stoddard, *The Efficacy of the Fear of Hell, to Restrain Men from Sin . . .* (Boston, 1713), preached in 1712. "The miseries of hell will be exceeding great." Those in hell will be "standing monuments of the vengeance of heaven." "If their strength were the strength of stones, or their flesh of brass, they could not endure the misery." Observations of this type were quite conventional.

15. Israel Loring, *Serious Thoughts on the Miseries of Hell* (Boston, 1732), 1: "Of all Preachers that we read of in Scripture, none was so frequent in warning the people to avoid Hell, as Jesus Christ."

16. Edward Wigglesworth, *A Discourse Concerning the Duration of the Punishment of the Wicked in a Future State* (Boston, 1729) and *The Sovereignty of God in the Exercises of His Mercy and How He Is Said to Harden the Hearts of Men* (Boston, 1741). Of Moodey, Clifford Shipton has said: Living 50 years hemmed in between the sea and the Indian menace (at York, Maine), Moodey's "religious attitude was more primitive than that of more sheltered contemporaries." Shipton, *Sibley's Harvard Graduates*, IV, 358.

Wigglesworth.[17] Therefore, God in "tender mercy" has presented mankind "with objects of fear and desire, so much greater than any thing the world can do, as one would think enough even to deride temptations." Israel Loring agreed that the lesson of hell is an expression of God's mercy and compassion, for it is a way of powerfully forewarning sinners of the need to repent. In short, however improbable the reasoning, it was widely believed that the minister who preached hell's torments was himself engaged in a merciful activity, unpleasant though it might be. Thus, even though, as George Whitefield said, "there is something so shocking in the consideration of eternal torments . . . that men (some at least of them) can scarcely be brought to confess it as an article of their faith, that an eternity of misery awaits the wicked in a future state,"[18] the context in which Edwards was serving as a minister generally encouraged teaching of the doctrine to its full extent.[19]

Edwards's Personal Involvement

There is some evidence that Edwards adhered to the doctrine of hell with the fanaticism of the new convert who had once been a doubter. In the autobiographical "Account of His Conversion," written in about 1740, Edwards explained, "From my childhood up, my mind had been wont to be full of objections against the doctrine of God's sovereignty, in choosing whom he would to eternal life, and rejecting whom he pleased; leaving them eternally to perish, and be everlastingly tormented in hell. It used to appear like a horrible doctrine to me."[20] The chronology is hard to pin down exactly, but it seems that Edwards was quite unreconciled to predestination and everlasting torment until he was about eighteen or nineteen and had already graduated

17. Wigglesworth, *Duration of the Punishment*, 2. Cf. William Cooper, *Three Discourses Concerning the Reality, the Extremity, and the Absolute Eternity of Hell Punishments* (Boston, 1732), 27: "Hope and fear are the most active passions of humane nature: And the blessed God having made us with them, deals with us according to our frame, and makes use of these affections, to bring us to himself." Hence the promise of heaven and the threat of hell.

18. Whitefield, "Eternity of Hell Torments," in *Sermons*, 1.

19. Cf. Cooper, *Three Discourses*, 4: "This is indeed no pleasing subject for us to insist upon, but a necessary one for you to hear of, which we, who are put in trust with the gospel, must not baulk." See also Samuel Whittelsey, *The Woful Condition of Impenitent Souls in Their Separate State* (Boston, 1731). A spate of hell sermons was delivered in New England between 1729 and 1732, but I am uncertain about what prompted it. The 17th-century Puritan minister Thomas Shepard could occasionally invoke the terrors of hell in detail equivalent to Edwards's, as could the 18th-century minister-poet Edward Taylor.

20. This account was first printed in 1765 in Samuel Hopkins's *Life of Edwards*, reprinted in Levin, ed., *Jonathan Edwards*, from which I have quoted, p. 25.

from Yale College.[21] His youthful defection resembles the process by which several of the Cambridge Platonists, most notably Henry More, emancipated themselves from Calvinist orthodoxy, though in the case of these men the liberation did not stop there.[22] In Edwards's case a total reversal of these earlier doubts occurred, a change that he later came to believe was truly spiritual. Thereafter these new convictions were continuously solidified. His autobiographical account relates that at first he was merely "convinced, and fully satisfied, as to this sovereignty of God, and his justice in thus eternally disposing of men, according to his sovereign pleasure." He put an end, he said, "to all those cavils and objections, that had 'till then abode with me, and the preceding part of my life." There was a "wonderful alteration" in his mind, so that he "scarce ever found so much as the rising of an objection against God's sovereignty, in the most absolute sense, in showing mercy to whom he will show mercy, and hardening and eternally damning whom he will." Later, a further metamorphosis took place, and Edwards had "quite another kind of sense of God's sovereignty": not just a conviction of God's goodness and justice in the damnation of sinners, but "a delightful conviction." From the time of that greater appreciation, "The doctrine of God's sovereignty has very often appeared, an exceeding pleasant, bright and sweet doctrine to me: and absolute sovereignty is what I love to ascribe to God."[23] This account in itself might not be very significant if we did not know that Edwards also began to imply at this time that a delight in the spectacle of hell could serve as a test of conversion for others and if we did not find in his manuscript notes repeated intellectual justifications for the everlasting torments of the damned.

Edwards's increasingly elaborate and sometimes brilliant defenses of the doctrine were undoubtedly a reaction to the rising skepticism shown toward it in the eighteenth century from several different quarters. For Edwards, important theological issues hung in the balance. Eternal torment for the damned was a stone in the arch of his system that could not be removed without causing collapse of the structure. It would not be far wrong to say, for example, that Edwards's *Enquiry into the Modern Prevailing Notions of That Freedom of Will, Which Is Supposed To Be Essential to Moral Agency, Virtue*

---

21. Edwards graduated from Yale with a bachelor's degree in 1720 at age 17.

22. See Cragg, ed., *Cambridge Platonists*, 11, and Richard Ward, *The Life of the Learned and Pious Dr. Henry More* . . . (London, 1710). Nearly all of the Cambridge Platonists had been Calvinists in their childhood training and later modified the doctrine, emphasizing in their new beliefs human responsibility, man's essential goodness, and God's benevolence and mercy.

23. Hopkins, *Life of Edwards*, in Levin, ed., *Jonathan Edwards*, 26. Samuel Moodey, *Doleful State of the Damned*, 88, quoted John Norton as follows: "It is an Effect of Election . . . to be Affected with the Decree of Election. . . . They that love to see the Shining Face of God in Christ, delight in no Truth more than this."

and Vice, Reward and Punishment, Praise and Blame, his most widely respected work, was written in part to buttress the Calvinist theory of reprobation, as the conclusion to the book suggests. Edwards felt compelled to
demonstrate that even though sinners are predestined to be cast into eternal
hell, they are still fully responsible for their unregenerate state, and their
punishment, therefore, is just and appropriate. The book also attempted to
deal with one of the most common evasions of belief in the everlastingness of
misery in hell, namely the proposal, identified with the Greek father Origen,
that punishment in the afterlife is reformatory, and therefore through it all the
sinner retains the moral freedom to repent. Eventually, according to this
teaching, all sinners will be saved. In addition to these vital philosophical
and theological concerns, it also seems probable that Edwards was strongly
enough affected by the humanitarian pull of his age to often feel the desire to
return to the intellectual grounds of the everlasting punishment of the wicked,
impelled by the need not only to convince others of the "beauty of vindictive
justice" in God's decrees, but also to convince himself.[24]

Edwards's earliest manuscript notes on the problem of hell have a rather
impatient tone when they address doubters. "It is but a foolish piece of
nonsense," he wrote, to "cry out upon" infant damnation "as blasphemous"
or contrary to God's mercy. Is it "contrary to his mercy to inflict punishment
upon any according to their Deserts?" Was it "contrary to God's mercy to
damn the faln Angels? There was no mercy shewed to them at all, and why is
it blasphemous to suppose that God should inflict upon infants so much as
they have Deserved. . . . Who shall determine just how much sin is sufficient, to make Damnation agreeable to the Divine Perfections . . . ?"[25] This
comment, probably written when Edwards was about twenty-one and certainly
not yet a parent himself, may have something in it of the dogmatism of youth.
Of all the elements in the Calvinist doctrine of hell, infant damnation was the
most unassimilable in the eighteenth century and after and was probably
responsible for more covert disaffection with orthodox church teaching than
any other article of faith.[26] It was perhaps the one article on which some years

24. The quoted phrase occurs in Edwards's early "Notes on the Mind," no. 45, par. 11, in
Dwight, *Life of Edwards*, 700–701. Perry Miller has asked with regard to Edwards's conception
of hell: "Was this the recoil of a sensibility that could not endure the spectacle of agony . . . ?
Was . . . there engendered [in his youth] a dread of soul that could be assuaged only by being
shared?" Miller, *Jonathan Edwards*, 146.

25. Miscellanies, letter "n."

26. Doctrine concerning infants was often mitigated, beginning with Thomas Aquinas, if not
before, by the suggestion that those condemned suffered only the *poena damni*, or deprivation
from God, not the *poena sensus*, or hellfires. A good example of the *poena damni* is given in the
quotation from John Donne in n. 11 above. Normally, damned adults would suffer both, though
deprivation from God was always considered the greater punishment. Cf. the Harvard master's
degree *quaestio* in 1730, answered in the affirmative by Solomon Prentice: *"An Poenae Infer-*

later Edwards was willing to compromise even a mite, by suggesting, at least privately, and maybe also in his pastoral counseling, that " 'tis generally supposed to be a common thing that the infants of the godly that die in infancy are saved."[27] In the seventeenth century, among the Reformed the Remonstrants were particularly concerned about the welfare in the afterlife of the dead children of believers, arguing that they would all be saved. The Contra-Remonstrants rejected this position because it was inconsistent with rigorous predestination, though the idea expressed in Michael Wigglesworth's *Day of Doom* (1662), that damned infants will occupy only "the easiest room in hell," was probably widely accepted. Unfortunately, Protestant dogma did not allow for an infants' circle in the afterlife, such as the Roman Catholic limbo. In any case, even at best it was only for the children of Christians that the doctrine was moderated. Hardly anyone in the seventeenth century bothered to worry about the dead children of heathens and infidels. Yet Edwards's beliefs became increasingly out of step as the eighteenth century progressed.

A note written by Edwards only a few years after his early defense of infant damnation, probably in about 1726, reads like a confession of faith: "I am convinced that the torments of hell are literally as great as they are represented. . . . I am ready [to] think that such agonies of mind as are sufficient to put nature into such violent commotion and ferment so as to cause the blood to strain through the pores of the sk[in] are as great affliction as one

---

nales, magis in damno, quam in sensu consistant? " (Does the punishment of hell consist more in deprivation than in sensible pains?) In the controversy over the subject of infant damnation and Original Sin in mid-18th-century New England between Samuel Webster and Peter Clark, *both* men denied that infants in hell suffered the *poena sensus*. See the discussion in H. Shelton Smith, *Changing Conceptions of Original Sin: A Study in American Theology since 1750* (New York, 1955), 37–50, and in Joseph Haroutunian, *Piety versus Moralism: The Passing of the New England Theology* (New York, 1932), 21–42. Clark, like Lyman Beecher in the next century, went so far as to deny that it had *ever* been Calvinist teaching that reprobated infants suffered all the pains of the damned, in which belief he was, of course, in error. In the 17th century the Remonstrants tended to reject the belief that there was wholesale damnation of the offspring of professing Christians when such offspring died before the opportunity to convert, whereas the Contra-Remonstrants or Calvinists took the hard line seen in Edwards. The subject was reviewed in detail by Francis Jenks, the editor of the *Christian Examiner*, in *A Reply to Three Letters of the Rev. Lyman Beecher, D.D. against the Calvinistic Doctrine of Infant Damnation* (Boston, 1829). The greatest bibliographical source pertaining to the whole subject of hell is that monument of 19th-century scholarship, Ezra Abbot's *Literature of the Doctrine of a Future Life: or, a Catalogue of Works Relating to the Nature, Origin, and Destiny of the Soul* (New York, 1867), which is usually found appended to Alger's *Critical History of the Doctrine of a Future Life*.

27. Quoted from Miscellanies, no. 849, by Clyde Holbrook in the introduction to his edition of Edwards's *Original Sin*, 27n. Holbrook, in a useful short comment, observes that Edwards "agonized over the problem of the sinful nature and punishment of infants, as his extensive notes on the subject in the [manuscript] 'Book of Controversies' show."

would endure if they were all over in a fiery furnace."[28] These words suggest some sort of psychological resolution about the extreme pains of the damned.

In his manuscript notes thereafter Edwards periodically returned to the theme of the difficulty of accepting the doctrine of everlasting excruciating punishment. "I know it will be ready to [be] objected that such an extreme degree of suffering is incredible, that 'tis incredible that [God] should ever make any creature so miserable." But his answers now were steady and determined rather than impatient. "There is no argument from hence, for God will have no respect or consideration at all of the welfare of those that are damned, nor any concern least they should suffer too much."[29] Those that are damned, Edwards wrote, "are entirely lost and utterly thrown away by God as to any sort of regard that he has to their welfare. Their very existence is for nought else but to suffer; the wicked are made for the day of evil. They are on purpose that God may shew the dreadfulness of his wrath upon them."[30]

Edwards's accentuation of the tortures of hell necessarily brought to the foreground the problem of evil in general. Ever since theologians began to discuss the existence of hell, two broad questions have been raised concerning it: Why should there be a hell at all? or differently expressed, Why did an omnipotent God have to make sin and punishment? Second, What are the nature and the duration of the punishment in hell, if such a realm does exist?

28. Miscellanies, no. 280. Edwards also seems to be explaining here that the metaphor of the furnace is apt even if the punishments of hell do not require the resurrection of the body. There was a millennia-old controversy over how much of the doctrine of hell was to be interpreted metaphorically, though it should be noted that those on both sides of the issue agreed completely that the pains would be not one jot less even if the lake of fire, etc., was a metaphor. In New England, Israel Loring in 1732 argued that "it seems probable, that as the Bodies of the Damned are of a *material substance*, so God will make use of some *material instrument* for its torture in Hell. . . . We cannot tell how far [the lake of fire and brimstone] may be a literal account. . . . These Expressions (at least many of them) may be taken in their literal and proper sense, for real *fire* and *brimstone*." Echoing a theory of William Whiston's, Loring suggested that the earth may be turned into a fiery comet to hold the damned (Loring, *Miseries of Hell*, 14–15). Whiston's theory in *Astronomical Principles of Religion, Natural and Reveal'd* . . . (London, 1717), is discussed in D. P. Walker, *Decline of Hell*, 100. Samuel Moodey, on the other hand, writing in 1710, argued (as had Origen in the 3d century and many others subsequently, including Calvin, *Institutes of the Christian Religion* [1536], Bk. III, chap. 25, par. 12) that hell is "Metaphorically, and in Scripture Language a prison; a Lake of Fire and Brimstone; a Bottomless Pit; a Furnace of Fire; Everlasting Fire Prepared for the Devil and his Angels. . . . For, whatever the Body could Suffer in these Material Flames, the Sufferings of Immortal Souls must needs be Greater." Moodey, *Doleful State of the Damned*, 32–35.

29. Miscellanies, no. 545, written in *ca.* 1733. Similarly, a little earlier, in no. 491: "Some may be ready to think that it's incredible that God should bring miseries upon a creature that are so extreme and amazing and also eternal and desperate."

30. *Ibid.*, no. 491.

The first question is the hardest to deal with, since it verges immediately into the problem of theodicy, and eventually becomes insoluble. Yet some sort of answer to it is needed if one expects to go on and develop the second, since the justification for the very existence of a hell provides the essential framework for any discussion of its specific nature. Edwards's response concerning the more general question was quite traditional: the fullest possible manifestation of God's glory requires the existence both of condemnation and of election to salvation.

> 'Tis necessary that God's awful majesty, his authority and dreadful greatness, justice and holiness should be manifested. But this could not be unless sin and punishment had been decreed. . . . The shining forth of God's glory would be very imperfect, . . . and also the glory of his goodness, love and holiness would be faint without them. . . . [Without sin] there could be no such thing as justice in punishing because there could be no such thing as punishing. . . . We little consider how much the sense of good is heightened by the sense of evil, both moral and natural.[31]

> The terribleness of God is part of his glory, and that a sense of it should be kept up in the minds of the creatures, is needful in order to their right and just apprehensions of his greatness and gloriousness. . . . That awful and reverential dread of God's majesty that arises from such a sense is needfull, in order to the proper respect of the creature to God and the more compleat happiness in a sense of his love.[32]

If many people were saved, rather than just a few, it would appear as though mere nature were the underlying cause, not the specific bestowment of a divine "exception," Edwards wrote. "By reason of there being so few saved the grace and love of God towards those that are saved will be the more valued and admired."[33]

In later years, under the influence of the English philosopher Samuel Clarke, Edwards paid significantly less heed to these psychological effects upon men (such as the usefulness of the doctrine of hell for evoking gratitude and praise of the Lord) and stressed instead the constancy of the general laws and "fitnesses" by which God rules His domain. Thus, the salvation of a few may be exceptional, but in Edwards's eyes it was not arbitrary, and the mean-

---

31. *Ibid.*, no. 348.
32. *Ibid.*, no. 407.
33. *Ibid.*, no. 520. This theme appears frequently in Edwards's sermons. See, e.g., "The End of the Wicked Contemplated by the Righteous: Or, The Torments of the Wicked in Hell, No Occasion of Grief to the Saints in Heaven," in *Works*, IV, 291: "God glorifies himself in all that he doth; but he glorifies himself *principally* in his eternal disposal of his intelligent creatures: some are appointed to everlasting life, and others left to everlasting death" (my italics).

ing of both election and reprobation was to be understood in terms of the inherent relationship of congruity between sin and punishment and between holiness and reward even more than in terms of God's self-glorification. A lawful God could have it no other way.[34]

By and large, however, from the time of his conversion, Edwards considered it a symptom of faithlessness to be asking too many questions about God's eternal judgments. The true sense of God's "glory and excellency and loveliness" will make a person "leave off quarreling and objecting." It is typical of the damned in hell, on the other hand, that they will not be freed "from a disposition to quarrel, and doubtless they will spend their eternity in blaspheming," raising such objections as:

> Why did God give me a being when he knew I must perish forever[?] Why did he decree my damnation, and decree my sin in order [to] it[?] Why was I born with a corrupt nature, and under a necessity of sinning[?] How could I help my own corrupt nature[?] I had not the making of myself. . . . Why did God withhold from me his assistance and let me fall into sin when it was impossible that it should be otherwise, and then punish me for it[?][35]

Of course, there were no fully satisfactory answers to these grander questions. Edwards could achieve greater success in polemics by concentrating on the specific objections to the Calvinist conception of the nature and duration of hell punishment, and by attempting to demonstrate the truth of the orthodox teaching in that more limited area.

The Finer Points of the Doctrine

When the doctrine of hell was fully elaborated, it was more complex and variegated than is sometimes realized, presenting challenging intellectual problems in several different areas. Edwards became fully engaged with almost all of these problems, and many of his answers brought him directly into contention with some of the most fundamental assumptions of eighteenth-century secular philosophy. In general, no other tenet of Edwards's theological system put him more at odds with the tendencies of benevolist moral philosophy than his convictions about the reality of eternal hell punishment.

A prominent element in the traditional doctrine of hell was the belief that

34. Edwards's mature thinking on the relation between natural laws and special divine interventions is set forth with clarity and brilliance in Miscellanies, no. 1263, printed in Townsend, ed., *Philosophy of Edwards*, and discussed above, pp. 93–103. Damnation, he believed, was much more a part of the natural order than election.

35. Miscellanies, no. 470.

the blessed in heaven continuously witness the agony of the damned, and, vice versa, the damned are onlookers to the bliss of the saved. This arrangement, by the opportunity it afforded for comparison, heightened both the bliss of heaven and the pain of the condemned. The locus classicus for this teaching was the last chapter of Tertullian's *De Spectaculis*, but it was supported also by St. Augustine and St. Thomas Aquinas, to mention only the most distinguished of many other later adherents.[36] The logic of the doctrine of hell required this belief, as Edwards knew, although by the eighteenth century humane emotions were running against it. Human compassion, according to the traditional teaching, though a legitimate virtue on earth, became disaffection with God if exercised in heaven toward the misery of those in hell. "When we think of the extreme degree of hell torments," Edwards wrote, "we are ready to be shocked by it and are ready to say within our selves[,] how can such an infliction consist with the merciful nature of God. But the saints in heaven tho they'll have a more adequate and lively idea of the greatness of [the] misery [of the damned], yet will not be at all shocked by it and very much because they'll also at the same time have a truer and more lively apprehension of the evil of sin. . . . It will seem no way cruel in God to inflict such extreme sufferings on such extremely wicked creatures."[37] The punishment witnessed by the saints and angels should be fully agreeable to the

36. Edward Gibbon's use of the *De Spectaculis* in chap. 15 of *The History of the Decline and Fall of the Roman Empire* (London, 1776–1778) as an example of early Christian ruthlessness has made Tertullian's passage well known. Nietzsche also cited it in his *Genealogy of Morals*. For a brief discussion of this so-called "abominable fancy," as it was termed by Dean F. W. Farrar in the 19th century, see Walker, *Decline of Hell*, 29–32. It is notable with reference to Edwards that Walker in his excellent and compact book wrongly believes that this aspect of hell was "almost obsolete by the late 17th century" and was seldom mentioned in the 18th century.

37. *Miscellanies*, no. 558. The standard teaching was that no one had pity for the eternally condemned, neither their fellow sufferers in hell nor those in heaven. Compassion or pity, absent in both heaven and hell, was uniquely a terrestrial emotion. Cf. Cooper, *Three Discourses*, 37: "In their most piteous state, [the damned] are absolutely unpitied. . . . Their fellow sufferers don't pity them; for all humane tender affections are lost in hell. . . . The holy angels and the blessed spirits in heaven don't pity them; for they are not the objects of pity. . . . The saints in heaven will not pity their nearest relations in hell. For they now know them no more after the flesh. The love which they once bore to them is now swallowed up in the love of God." Many writers, not least Jonathan Edwards, made special note of this indifference of the saints in heaven to the excruciating pain of their nearest kin, including parents' indifference to their children. Cf. Edwards's sermon "End of the Wicked Contemplated by the Righteous," in *Works*, IV, 296: When your parents see you in hell, and you have a "frightened, amazed countenance, trembling and astonished, and shall hear you groan and gnash your teeth; these things will move them not at all to pity you, but you will see them with a holy joyfulness in their countenances, and with songs in their mouths. . . . They will praise God, that his justice appears in the eternity of your misery." Increase Mather, among others, used the theme of the parent joining with God in condemning the sinful child to hell. See Emory Elliott, *Power and the Pulpit in Puritan New England* (Princeton, N.J., 1975), 67–68.

sense they have of God's glory and of the evil of sin, otherwise "there will be a visible defect[,] an unharmoniousness[,] [an] unanswerableness in the things which they see." Such a weakness in their consciousness would "tend to depress that idea of God's majesty that other things tend to raise"; the whole purpose of the punishment, after all, is "to raise their idea of God's power and majesty[,] to impress it with exceeding strength [and] liveliness upon their minds and so to raise their sense of the riches and excellency of his love to them."[38] Thus, any objections that might arise—"Why would the great author and orderer of all things suffer things to come to this?" "Why would [God] be the author of the work when he knew that his work would come to such a dreadfull issue?"—lead one "much to . . . suspect," Edwards said, "that notwithstanding the plausibleness of such an objection the very principal reason of such thoughts arising in the mind is a want of a sense of the horrible evil of sin."[39] The raising of humanitarian objections was a symptom, Edwards believed, of continued devotion to carnal standards.

Yet the pleasure of identification with God in surveying the state of the damned could be carried too far. Samuel Moodey in 1710 was among those who stressed that "the damned in hell will have such apprehensions of the saints happiness in heaven, as shall dreadfully aggravate their own eternal misery."[40] But Moodey also warned that although glorified saints "shall find their everlasting joyes proportionably heightened, while they consider the sorrows of the tormented," it would not be proper for them to "*rejoice in that misery of their fellow-creatures* which themselves have deserved as well and as much, and many of them, more than most of the damned." The rejoicing of the blessed shall be for deliverance "from so great a death as the second death

38. Miscellanies, no. 866. If the saint is united in heart and mind to God, it follows that he will delight in God's justice and abhor the evil of sin. John Dunton's popular *Athenian Oracle*, first issued in London in 1703, discussed the question of whether the damned are visible to the saints and vice versa, as follows: "We cannot will any Good to [devils and damned spirits], as not being capable of any. For we cannot exert any Act of Love, which we know to be in vain and to no purpose at all. . . . And besides, if we could possibly wish well to such Beings, yet I don't see how we may do it *lawfully* and *Regularly*, for our Will would not be then conformable to God's, but directly opposite to it; and besides, we should disapprove, at least tacitly and interpretatively, the *Justice* of his Ways, by thus loving them whom he extremely hates, and blessing them whom he curses and abandons for ever" (*The Athenian Oracle: Being an Entire Collection of All the Valuable Questions and Answers in the Old Athenian Mercuries* . . . , 3d ed. [London, 1728], 4). This comment was probably written by John Norris of Bemerton, who expressed a related point of view in *The Theory and Regulation of Love* . . . , 2d ed. (London, 1694 [orig. publ. Oxford, 1688]), 99–100. *The Athenian Oracle* was in a good number of early American libraries. Edmund Berkeley of Middlesex County, Virginia, had a copy in 1718; a copy of the second edition was sent to the Yale library in 1713; and Judge Samuel Sewall discovered a copy in a Boston bookstore in 1704.

39. Miscellanies, no. 866.

40. Moodey, *Doleful State of the Damned*, 29, 40.

is.''[41] According to the theory, the blessed will rejoice in the substantial evidence of God's justice, though not so inhumanely as to take personal pleasure in witnessing the intrinsic suffering itself. The suffering is praised for what it means, not for what it is. Yet vindictive pleasure, or at least triumphant self-satisfaction, was always a latent factor in this conception of heavenly bliss, a factor that became an increasingly important consideration as the humanitarian emphasis on the virtue of compassion grew.

Writing thirty years later, Edwards felt compelled to take even more care than Moodey to distinguish this joy in heaven from the perverse emotions of the devil, "who delights in misery, for its own sake, from a malicious disposition." It is true that the "saints in glory," Edwards said, will see the damned in hell and their misery and "be far more sensible of it than now we can possibly be," and that this vision will be "no occasion of grief to them." Rather than being sorry for the suffering of the damned, "it will excite them to joyful praises." But the delight of the saints will be based on "exceedingly different principles" from those that inspire the joy felt by a devil contemplating human misery. "It will not be because they delight in seeing the misery of others absolutely considered [that they rejoice]," Edwards wrote. "The damned suffering divine vengeance will be no occasion of joy to the saints merely as it is the misery of others, or because it is pleasant to them to behold the misery of others merely for its own sake." Writing with obvious awareness of humanitarian protests, Edwards continued: "The rejoicing of the saints on this occasion is no argument, that they are not of a most amiable and excellent spirit. . . . It is no argument that they have not a spirit of goodness and love reigning in them in absolute perfection."[42] Nevertheless, in the eyes of those in heaven, "the glory of God" is of "greater consequence than the welfare of thousands and millions of souls." When they "shall see the smoke of [the damned ones'] torment, and the raging of the flames of their burning, and hear the dolorous shrieks and cries, and consider that they in the meantimes are in the most blissful state, and shall surely be in it to all eternity; how will they rejoice!"[43]

In direct contrast to the blessed, those in hell hate God with raging intensity, since they are eternally unwilling to identify emotionally with the righteousness of His decrees. Similarly, the wicked on earth, resenting God for His power over them, hate Him implicitly, if not overtly. Long before Nietzsche, Edwards, in one of his most psychologically perceptive sermons, "Men Naturally God's Enemies," attempted to cut through the veneer of conventional social respectability and charged that natural men (that is, the unregenerate)

41. *Ibid.*, 115. My italics.
42. "End of the Wicked Contemplated by the Righteous," in *Works*, IV, 290–291.
43. *Ibid.*, 292.

would "pull [God] down out of heaven, and dethrone him if they could! . . . [They] would be glad if there was no God, and therefore it necessarily follows, that they would kill him . . . if they could."[44]

> You object against your having a mortal hatred against God; that you never felt any desire to kill him. But one reason has been, that it has always been conceived so impossible by you, and you have been sensible how such desires would be in vain, that it has kept down such a desire. But if the life of God were within your reach and you knew it, it would not be safe one hour.[45]

Such thoughts as these would surely arise: "Now I have opportunity to set myself at liberty. . . . I need not be kept in continual slavery by the strict law of God. . . . And God has not done well by me in many instances. . . . He has shown mercy to others, and refused it to me. I have now an opportunity to deliver myself, and there can be no danger of my being hurt for it: God will not be alive to revenge it."[46] The natural man would thus remove the one source of absolute justice and throw the entire world into permanent chaos, creating a hell on earth, simply to save himself. It was on these grounds that Edwards could claim in *Sinners in the Hands of an Angry God*: "There is laid in the very nature of carnal men a foundation for the torments of Hell."[47]

The concealment in the world of such monstrous and monumental egoism is, of course, very artful, and sometimes even unconscious. People hide their hatred of God and dissemble love for Him because they fear Him. Edwards gave the example of a person under the control of a hated enemy. Such a person "would be afraid to exercise his hatred in outward acts, unless it were with great disguise." And if it be supposed that the enemy could see into the heart of the one he controlled and know all his thoughts, and the powerless one felt that he would be put to a terrible death if the enemy saw the workings of malice there, "how greatly would this restrain!" A person so intimidated, so much under the power of an enemy, "*would be afraid so much as to*

44. Edwards, "Men Naturally God's Enemies," *ibid.*, 41.

45. *Ibid.*, 48. Cf. also, p. 58: "If you continue in your enmity a little longer, there will be a mutual enmity between God and you to all eternity. . . . If you should die an enemy to God, there will be no such thing as any reconciliation after death. . . . As you are a mere enemy to God, so God will then appear a mere enemy to you; he will appear in perfect hatred without any love, and without any pity. . . . God will continue an enemy to you to all eternity. . . . You will find that you cannot move the heart of God by any of your cries. . . . Then you will appear as you are, a viper indeed. . . . Then you will as a serpent, spit poison at God, and vent your rage and malice in fearful blasphemies."

46. *Ibid.*, 48.

47. *Sinners in the Hands of an Angry God*, 7. "There are in the Souls of wicked Men those hellish *Principles* reigning, that would presently kindle and flame out into Hell Fire, if it were not for God's Restraints."

believe himself, that he hated his enemy; but there would be all manner of smothering, disguise, and hypocrisy, and feigning even of thoughts and affections."[48] Hell was thus, for Edwards, an unmasking of the existing tendencies of unredeemed human nature.

The perceptiveness of Edwards's imprecatory sermons would be unexplainable unless we assume that he scrutinized carefully his own inner workings and those of his parishioners. Yet it would be an exaggeration to claim that all of the elements of the dogma of hell accepted by Edwards had psychoempirical foundations. His literal interpretation of Scripture counted for as much as or more than any empirical knowledge. Edwards's thinking was governed primarily by the received interpretations of Scripture that accepted as literal truth all of the pronouncements about the nature and the duration of punishment for the damned, including the image of a vengeful deity. It is true that in the seventeenth century the notion was already current that heaven and hell are simply natural and ineluctable extensions of earthly states of mind. Origen had said that "every sinner kindles for himself the flame of his own fire"; he suggested that when the soul parts from that "order and connexion and harmony in which it was created by God for good action and useful experience" and is not "at concord with itself in the connexion of its rational movements, it must be supposed to bear the penalty and torture of its own want of cohesion and to experience the punishment due to its unstable soul and disordered condition."[49] The advantage of such a conception, as D. P. Walker has pointed

48. "Men Naturally God's Enemies," in *Works*, IV, 49 (my italics). The process by which "thoughts" are unconsciously "feigned" is what we would call rationalization, which is the result of being afraid to confront one's real emotions and the thoughts necessarily connected to those emotions. Such insights were commonplaces of Augustinian as well as libertine thought in the 17th century.

49. Origen, *De Principiis*, trans. G. W. Butterworth (London, 1936), II, x, 4, quoted in Patrides, "Renaissance and Modern Views on Hell," *Harvard Theol. Rev.*, LVII (1964), 232. Patrides gives many other examples of this kind of interpretation. Paul C. Davies, "The Debate on Eternal Punishment in Late Seventeenth- and Eighteenth-Century English Literature," *Eighteenth-Century Studies*, IV (1970–1971), 257–276, calls attention, for example, to *Spectator*, no. 447, Aug. 2, 1712, where Addison writes: "We must, in this World, gain a Relish of Truth and Virtue, if we would be able to taste that Knowledge and Perfection, which are to make us happy in the next. . . . Heaven is not to be looked upon only as the Reward, but as the natural Effect of a religious Life." Similarly, the torments of hell have already taken root in the wicked in the present world. "They may, indeed, taste a kind of malignant Pleasure in those Actions to which they are accustomed, whilst in this Life, but when they are removed from all those Objects which are here apt to gratifie them, they will naturally become their own Tormentors." John Scott's *The Christian Life, from Its Beginning to Its Consummation in glory* . . . (London, 1681), according to Addison, shows "how every particular Custom and Habit of Virtue will, in its own Nature, produce the Heaven . . . in him who shall hereafter practise it: As on the contrary, how every Custom or Habit of Vice will be the natural Hell of him in whom it subsists." Donald F. Bond, ed., *The Spectator* (Oxford, 1965), IV, 72–73.

out, is that it spares God from the charge of actively and positively punishing people for their sins. God establishes only the general laws and conditions by which men entrap or save themselves.[50] Edwards used his psychological skill, however, not to explain away the objective reality of hell or to reduce it to a series of symbols, but to pick out the evasions and escapes that he believed were behind the recurrent drive to weaken the dogma in its incredible details. To some degree he may have been guilty of the fallacy of believing that to show the "corruption" of the opposition was proof in itself of the truth of the dogmas.

The extent to which the debate over eternal punishment was interwoven with scriptural evidence throughout most of the eighteenth century as well as earlier is hard for us to understand today. Hundreds of pages were devoted to proving that the Greek word αιων (aion) meant literally "eternity," rather than simply "age" or in the plural, "ages," as Origen and others had claimed.[51] The weight of biblical evidence appeared to uphold everlasting torment; therefore, the task of the minister, the Christian philosopher, or the theologian was to justify it rationally. The sophistries that could ensue were many. In some cases ingenious arguments that originally had been devised only to bolster the dogmatic authority of scriptural texts took on a life of their own and made the existence of hell a matter of self-evident truth. In other words, it reached the point with a reasoner as vigorous as Edwards that the orthodox conception of hell was a necessary part of his system whether or not the Bible supported it! If the Bible did not tell him that hell existed, he would have had to invent a hell in order to complement his sense of the enormous crime of sin. Yet at the same time, his concept of the enormity of sin was also based in large part on the dogma that God punished some people by sentencing them to incalculable misery for eternity. Surely, Edwards and others inferred, the crime must be very great to justify such stupendously malign treatment. It was a commonplace in the various expositions of hell doctrine that one of the purposes of eternal punishment was to show men how greatly God despised sin. The existence of hell, in other words, proved the enormity of sin; yet, on the other hand, sin so great justly deserved an eternity of hell. The whole argument was circular.

50. Walker, *Decline of Hell*, 63.

51. At the end of a short essay, written in about 1707, on "Reason and Philosophy No Enemies to Faith," published in his *Sermons and Essays upon Several Subjects* . . . (London, 1709), William Whiston suggested that "punishments shall continue the whole duration of the wicked who are the subjects of it; or through all those αιωνες των αιωνων long and undeterminate periods of being, to which their lives shall be preserved by the Divine Power." In other words, rather than being eternal, punishment would simply continue for as long as the soul of the sinner existed, which was a matter God could control as He saw fit. This collection of essays was reviewed in *History of the Works of the Learned*, XI (Aug. 1709), 492–504, where in particular Whiston's unorthodox interpretation of *aionios* was noted.

Perhaps the biggest challenge facing the orthodox theologian on the subject of hell was the problem of justifying an "eternity" of torment for the sins of a brief terrestrial life. The eternity of it was the very "hell of hell," as many commentators observed, the incomprehensible and stupefying fact that the torture would never, never end.[52] For centuries advocates of this doctrine had vied with each other in trying to impress its full impact on finite minds:

> Do but consider what it is to suffer extreme torment for ever and ever; to suffer it day and night, from one day to another, from one year to another, from one age to another, from one thousand ages to another, and so adding age to age, and thousands to thousands, in pain, in wailing and lamenting, groaning and shrieking, and gnashing your teeth; with your soul full of dreadful grief and amazement, with your bodies and every member full of wracking torture, without any possibility of getting ease.
> . . . After you shall have worn out the age of the sun, moon, and stars, in your dolorous groans and lamentations, without any rest day or night, or one minute's ease, yet you shall have no hope of ever being delivered . . . ; you shall know that you are not one whit nearer to the end of your torments; but that still there are the same groans, the same shrieks, the same doleful cries, incessantly to be made by you. . . . The more the damned in hell think of the eternity of their torments, the more amazing will it appear to them; and alas! they are not able to avoid thinking of it, they will not be able to keep it out of their minds. Their torture will not divert them from it, but will fix their attention to it.[53]

The perennial question in the face of such truly amazing religious fantasies was, Can such punishment be consistent with divine justice and mercy? Again and again in contending with this central objection, Edwards fell back on an argument so common and ancient that Pierre Bayle called it "la règle ordinaire des Théologiens."[54] The evil of sin is infinite, Edwards claimed, because it is a transgression against an infinite being. God is infinitely worthy of love, honor, and obedience; therefore our "obligation to love, honor, and obey him is infinitely great." The violation of that obligation is therefore an infinite evil, which deserves an infinite punishment.[55] Edwards considered this an

---

52. Both William Cooper and Israel Loring used the quoted phrase. Or cf. Tobias Swinden, *An Enquiry into the Nature and Place of Hell*, 2d ed. (London, 1727 [orig. publ. 1714]), 15: "And this is that which consummateth the torments of hell, that they must be undergone to all eternity, that they must never have an end, although they are each moment intolerable."

53. Edwards, "The Eternity of Hell Torments," in *Works*, IV, 278–279.

54. Walker, *Decline of Hell*, 43, quotes Bayle.

55. "Eternity of Hell Torments," in *Works*, IV, 267. Edwards also used this argument in Miscellanies, nos. 1348 and 1356. Every American apologist for eternal hell also used it.

impregnable argument, unless one were willing to deny the infinity of God.[56] Yet it has all the earmarks of its origins as a Scholastic defense of scriptural texts. No one would conceive of such a principle of punishment a priori, as an axiom upon which to found a theory of penal law, for example. It is a sophistical argument molded strictly to accommodate the dogma. But Edwards and scores of other theologians before him developed their own calculus of infinities that made eternal punishment sound like a law of physics.

Edwards's sequence of sermons on hell attempted to seal off any possible escape from the totality of the orthodox teaching. Human beings are naturally God's enemies. God is just in His utter condemnation of them. They will suffer eternally, the purpose of which is above all God's glorification, as represented by the heightened bliss of the souls in heaven no less than by the just retribution for infinite sin. Finally, this punishment is certain; it is absolutely unavoidable for those who are condemned. There is no hope of escape through "sinking into nothing at death, like brute creatures." The Socinian doctrine of annihilation is false.

> All such wishes are vain. . . . There is no hope that God, by reason of the multiplicity of affairs which he hath to mind, will happen to overlook them, and not take notice of them, when they come to die; and so that their souls will slip away privately, and hide themselves in some secret corner, and so escape divine vengeance. . . . Neither is there any hope that they will be able to crowd themselves in among the multitudes of the saints at the right hand of the Judge, and so go to heaven undiscovered. Nor is there any hope that God will alter his mind, or that he will repent of what he hath said.[57]

Edwards wanted to deny his listeners any crevices in which to hide or take comfort. The teachings they may have heard from time to time that questioned or directly contradicted the orthodox story were mere rationalizations, Edwards said, born of sinners' wishful thinking and deluded hopes.[58] None of

56. Walker, *Decline of Hell*, 26–27, 42–45, observes the close connection between this argument and the doctrine of Christ's infinite vicarious suffering for man's expiation.

57. Edwards, "The Future Punishment of the Wicked Unavoidable and Intolerable," in *Works*, IV, 258.

58. Edwards argued that the concept of a "humane" God is a delusion that grows out of man's desire to avoid justice, or God's judgment. Incapable of loving God for what He is, that is, loving Him for His perfections, His holiness and intrinsic loveliness, they try to love Him for what He can do for them, for the benefits He can confer. Yet if such men dared to see the real God who reigns in heaven, Edwards wrote, there would be only hatred for Him, since He will punish sinners severely. A situation so full of anxiety is evaded by the deluded view that God is kind, benign, and humane, a God that not just a saint can love but that any man can love, since it is a love offered in response to rewards, real or imagined, based solely on self-love, not on qualities and properties in God that have nothing to do with what God may do for the individual. In Edwards's

these devices will be of any use on the awful day. Even courage will evaporate, and the hearts of the damned will "become like wax before the furnace." Fortitude will not help to bear the pain. The souls of the condemned will sink, "utterly and totally sink, without the least degree of remaining comfort, or strength, or courage, or hope."[59]

In a series of sermons delivered in 1738, which were not of the imprecatory type at all, Edwards nevertheless concluded with a summary description of hell:

> In that dark world there are none but those whom God hates with a perfect and everlasting hatred. He exercises no love, and extends no mercy to any one object there, but pours out upon them horrors without mixture. . . . He has no other use for [hell] but there to testify forever his hatred of sin and sinners. . . . [They] shall have no pity from [the saints and angels] or from any one, for hell is looked on only with hatred, and with no pity or compassion.[60]

These were the main elements of his belief. If the horrors of hell were not visible for all eternity, then its most important purpose would be lost, namely the magnification of God's glory in the execution of His justice. Edwards shared creatively in the Augustinian tradition that defined evil as the privation of God's goodness. As he noted many times in discussions of evil, hell is the greatest exemplar, the prototype, of the catastrophic effects that necessarily follow when God withdraws from mankind. The inferno reveals as nothing else can humanity's dependence upon God's goodness for ensuring that every moment of existence on earth and in heaven is not sheer hell.[61]

Edwards did not believe that any person could be argued or reasoned into accepting the truth even of man's dependence upon common grace, which is what holds the normal created world together in relative peace, let alone be convinced by rational argument of the workings of special grace. Yet he made it a tenet of his theology that an unquestioning appreciation of the need for reprobation and hell was an essential sign of the regenerate state. Speaking from his own experience, Edwards took it as a certain rule that "a love to divine things for the beauty and sweetness of their *moral* excellency, is the first

thinking, genuine love for God must be irresistible and can never be optional and calculated. See *Religious Affections*, ed. Smith, 243–244.

59. *Ibid.*, 260.

60. *Charity and Its Fruits*, ed. T. Edwards, 516–520.

61. Since World War I, and especially since Buchenwald and Auschwitz, many modern theologians, both Jewish and Christian, have revitalized religious discussion of those abysmal moments in history when God appears to have turned His back on man.

beginning and spring of all holy affections."[62] Hell was a divine creation, although it was full of the most horribly unimaginable *natural* evils. Along with heaven, as a manifestation of God's justice hell exemplified the highest reach of moral perfection, the beauty and sweetness of which is apprehended only by the elect. The wicked in this life may have, and devils and damned souls do have, a great sense of the glory of God, to be sure; they know something of God's infinite greatness, majesty, and power. But they lack altogether a sense of the beauty and amiableness of God's holy justice. "A sight of the awful greatness of God, may overpower men's strength, and be more than they can endure; but if the moral beauty of God be hid, the enmity of the heart will remain in its full strength, no love will be enkindled, all will not be effectual to gain the will, but that will remain inflexible."[63] Gracious regeneration, however, brings about unalterable convictions of the truth of Scripture concerning "the evil of sin against so glorious a God; and also the truth of what it teaches concerning sin's just desert of that dreadful punishment which it reveals."[64] The basic principle of Edwards's logic on these matters he himself stated succinctly enough: "He who sees the beauty of holiness, must necessarily see the hatefulness of sin, its contrary."[65] People can show their hatred of sin in various ways, Edwards said, by "lamenting it, and mourning for it, and taking great pains, and undergoing great difficulties to prevent or remove it," and finally, "by approving God's vengeance for it." Though vengeance is not proper in men to show their hatred of sin, it is proper for "the Supreme Lord and Judge of the world." The "honor of [the] greatness, excellency and majesty of God's being, requires that sin be punished with an infinite punishment."[66]

In a sermon delivered late in his life and representing his maturest views, Edwards reiterated even more pointedly than in *Religious Affections* the importance of disinterested consent of the heart to God's sovereign justice as a test of true conversion. "A true Submission of the Heart and Will, to the Justice and Sovereignty of God, is therefore . . . something peculiar to true Converts, being something which the Devils and damned souls are, and ever will be far from."[67] Yet the devils and the damned know everything else about God that finite creatures can know. "The Wicked, at the Day of Judgment, will see every Thing else in Christ, but his Beauty and Amiableness. . . .

---

62. *Religious Affections*, ed. Smith, 254. My italics.
63. *Ibid.*, 264–265.
64. *Ibid.*, 302.
65. *Ibid.*, 274.
66. Miscellanies, no. 779, printed in *Works*, I, 585–586.
67. *True Grace Distinguished*, 18. The sermon was delivered in 1752 before the Presbyterian synod of New York, convened at Newark, New Jersey.

Therefore, 'tis a Sight or Sense of this that, is the Thing, wherein does fundamentally consist, the Difference between those Things in which the saving Grace of God's Spirit consists, and the Experience of Devils and damned Souls. This is the Foundation of every Thing else that is distinguishing in true Christian Experience."[68]

Much has been made of Edwards's sensitivity to the beauties of nature. He could write about them with considerable charm. In a manuscript note singled out by Perry Miller, who included it as an appendix to his edition of Edwards's *Images or Shadows of Divine Things*, Edwards mused on the hidden harmonies and "sweet mutual consents" that underlie the beauty of the world, and which represent spiritual things. "It is very probable," he wrote,

> that that wonderful suitableness of green for the grass and plants, the blues of the skie, the white of the clouds, the colours of flowers, consists in a complicated proportion that these colours make one with another. . . . The gentle motions of waves, of [the] lily, etc., . . . is agreeable to other things that represent calmness, gentleness, and benevolence, etc. The fields and woods seem to rejoice and how joyfull do the birds seem to be in it. How much resemblance is there of every grace in the field covered with plants and flowers when the sun shines serenely and undisturbedly upon them, how a resemblance, I say, of every grace and beautiful disposition of mind.

The note concludes with a sudden and unexpected thought. The reason why almost all people, no matter how miserable, love life and resist death, Edwards suggested, is that "they cannot bear to lose sight of such a beautiful and lovely world."[69]

That the physical world was an emanation of grace was a truth fully understood, perhaps, only by the regenerate. But its physical beauty was there for all to see, and Edwards did not pretend that the unregenerate were somehow excluded from this perception. Similarly, God's obvious gifts to humankind, such as the joys of human love, could be appreciated by all. God's goodness and beauty were self-evident in many things in this world, and one did not have to be a Christian to see them and love them. Redemption, then, was not made evident in the soul merely by an appreciation of the beauty and amiableness of those things that most people love easily. The test of faith for Edwards was whether a person could love the difficult parts of God's creation and thus take delight in the beauty and order of the whole, including hell and damnation. It was a true test because no act of willpower, no conscious effort, could bring about the requisite change in the soul. One had to be given the unique

---

68. *Ibid.*, 35.
69. *Images or Shadows*, ed. Miller, 135.

alteration in perceptions that suddenly transformed what was ordinarily detestable and fearful into something beautiful; this gift, of course, could only come from God Himself. Through grace, God took a small number of souls into His heart, so to speak, and united their perceptions and inclinations with His own. Thereafter, hell lost not its terror, but its ugliness and chaos and its capacity to cause men to avert their eyes from it and to fear and blame God for its existence.

The Opposition

It is impossible to know what influences determined Edwards's youthful doubt concerning the reprobation and eternal punishment of the wicked, or even to know for certain what writings in particular, after his conversion, he took as representative of the core of opposition to the orthodox conception of hell. By the 1740s, when Edwards was reading rather widely in liberal theology and secular moral philosophy, works implicitly undermining the traditional teaching about hell were ubiquitous, and the question of sources becomes less interesting. It may be worthwhile, however, to speculate about the decade prior to 1727, before Edwards was called to the pastorate at Northampton, Massachusetts. During this period Edwards had access most of the time to the Yale library where, after about 1718, there were several modern works that could have introduced him to the issues and arguments in the controversy over the existence and nature of hell and related subjects. The greatest single mine of arguments, pro and con, especially as related to the problem of theodicy, was in Pierre Bayle's *Historical and Critical Dictionary*, the four-volume English translation of which was sent to Yale as part of the Dummer gift. Edwards was definitely aware of this work (though we do not know the degree of his familiarity), and he probably would have viewed it as the product of a defender of orthodox Calvinism.[70] Bayle's articles on "Manicheanism," "Origen," "Paulicians," "Spinoza," and so on, were enor-

70. Few of Edwards's specific discussions of hell mention authors by name until the 1750s, when he directly rebutted William Whiston's *The Eternity of Hell Torments Considered . . .* (London, 1740). See Bryant and Patterson, eds., "List of Books Sent by Dummer," in *Papers in Honor of Andrew Keogh*, ed. Staff of Yale Univ. Lib. Early in his "Catalogue" of reading (MS, Beinecke Lib., Yale Univ.) Edwards made a short list of "Books to be enquired for." In addition to "the best geography," "the best history of the world," and so on, he wanted to get "the best historical Dictionary of the nature of Bayle's dictionary." This entry was made in the early 1720s. Ebenezer Pemberton, the Boston minister, at his death in 1717 owned at least one volume of Bayle, and the Harvard library owned a French edition (Rotterdam, 1720) before 1725. Bayle's *Dictionary* is mentioned several times in Edwards's "Catalogue" later when he hears of new editions, supplements, etc.

mously erudite, brilliant, and comprehensive treatments of the issues relating to the problem of evil and hell, and it does not seem improbable that Edwards knew at least some of them.

Another possible influence upon Edwards at this early stage was the third earl of Shaftesbury, though in this case, too, we are faced with the same tantalizing uncertainty as with Bayle's dictionary. In Edwards's youthful list of twenty-one rules of style to be followed in philosophical arguments, number 15 stated: "Oftentimes it suits the subject and Reasoning best to Explain by way of objection and answer after the manner of Dialogue like the Earl of Shaftesbury."[71] Internal evidence in Edwards's writings also suggests that he knew some of the books of Shaftesbury's *Characteristics* fairly early, and in about 1722 there is a direct mention of Shaftesbury in Edwards's "Catalogue" of reading.

The complex theological and philosophical tangles concerning providence and the afterlife that are meticulously reviewed in Bayle are not present in Shaftesbury's *Moralists* (1709), the dialogue that Edwards was most likely to have read in this period, but Shaftesbury's effect upon naive adherents to the doctrine of hell was as subversive as Bayle's. Like his friend Bayle, Shaftesbury waged a campaign against religious superstition, and with urbanity and illuminating wit argued that Calvinistic pessimism about human nature discouraged the development of virtue, creating the ironic situation that religion, which should be the mainstay of morals, was in fact the enemy of moral improvement. Only by some modification of religious doctrine could the cause of virtue and religion be made one. The basic modification required, according to Shaftesbury, was the recognition of the supreme goodness and excellence of God and of the perfection of His creation, which necessarily excludes all slavish obedience and the kind of "mercenary" religion founded only on fear of punishment and hope of reward. "What therefore can be worse done in the cause of a Deity than to magnify disorder, and exaggerate (as some zealous people do) the misfortunes of virtue, so far as to render it an unhappy choice with respect to this world? They err widely who propose to turn men to the thoughts of a better world by making them think so ill of this."[72]

There is no inherent malice in the design of the universe, Shaftesbury argued, and the goodness of God is as evident in the present life as in any future state proposed by religion. God does not do ill so that good may follow; rather His work is good through and through if we can but perceive the order, reason, and beauty of it. All of nature, including human nature, is essentially

71. See above, chap. 1, n. 1. The reference to Shaftesbury was not discovered until William P. Upham translated Edwards's shorthand. See Upham, "Short-Hand Writings of Edwards," Mass. Hist. Soc., *Procs.*, 2d Ser., XV (1902), 514–521.

72. Shaftesbury, *Characteristics*, ed. Robertson, II, 59.

good and shows evidence of benevolent design. Thus religion must be reformed to eliminate from its eschatology the "building of a future state on the ruins of virtue"; this tactic, Shaftesbury said, betrays both religion and God. "By making rewards and punishments the principal motives to duty, the Christian religion in particular is overthrown, and its greatest principle, that of love, rejected and exposed."[73] In sum, where the doctrine of future rewards and punishments was not outrightly destructive, it was superfluous. What was needed, Shaftesbury believed, was a campaign to improve the level of morals in this world rather than preoccupation with the perfect justice of the next.

We are on more certain ground when we come to Edwards's knowledge of Bishop John Tillotson's proposals concerning the eternity of hell's torments. Edwards unquestionably became familiar at some point with the controversy over Tillotson's sermon on this subject, preached before the queen in 1690, for Edwards directly referred to it in one of his own sermons on hell.[74] With the exception only of *The Whole Duty of Man*, Tillotson's sermons were probably the most widely read Anglican writings in America prior to 1735. He was admired equally in the northern and southern colonies, and Edwards, like virtually every other serious reader at the time, appears to have devoured his books.[75] Tillotson is representative of a trend toward the general softening of Calvinist teaching insofar as it had a grip on the Anglican church, and a

73. *Ibid.* The rejection of mercenary religion and the criticism of the doctrine of hell for contributing to it were, of course, not new with Shaftesbury. Cf., for example, Thomas Browne's *The Religio Medici* . . . (London, 1643), ed. C. H. Herford, Everyman's Library (London, 1906), 58: "That terrible term [hell] hath never detained me from sin, nor do I owe any good action to the name thereof. . . . [God's] Mercies make me ashamed of my sins, before His Judgements afraid thereof. . . . I can hardly think there was ever any scared into Heaven; they go the fairest way to Heaven that would serve God without a Hell."

74. Edwards, "Eternity of Hell Torments," in *Works*, IV, 275. Edwards also quoted from Tillotson in his *Discourses on Various Important Subjects*, 11, referring to him as "one of the greatest divines," though the two men were in disagreement on most issues. Tillotson is also mentioned very early in Edwards's "Catalogue" of reading. The commonplace book of John Hancock (1671–1752, the grandfather of the signer of the Declaration of Independence), which runs from 1687, when he was at Harvard College, to the middle of the 18th century, quotes frequently from Tillotson, and extracts in particular parts of the sermon on the eternity of hell torments, probably in about 1720. See p. 175 in Hancock's book, which is in manuscript in Houghton Library, Harvard Univ.

75. My assertion about the widespread reading of Tillotson is based on a survey of dozens of early American library lists. In the fourth Silence Dogood essay (*New-England Courant* [Boston], May 14, 1722), Benjamin Franklin implied that the New England clergy cribbed their sermons from Tillotson. The Reverend Benjamin Colman in Boston quoted Tillotson more than any other author, it has been said. See Clayton Chapman, "The Life and Influence of Reverend Benjamin Colman, D.D. (1673–1747)" (Ph.D. diss., Boston University, 1948), 273. William Byrd II also often read him. The copyright to Tillotson's sermons was sold by his widow for £2,500, the largest sum that had ever been paid up to that time for an English book. See Charles Smyth, *The*

figure so important and interesting that we must give him extra space in this review of the opponents of orthodoxy. He emphasized God's mercy more than His justice and is generally recognized as a central figure in the transformation of the image of God from an inflexible and wrathful judge to that of a benevolent ruler.[76] The fundamental principle behind Tillotson's conception of the Deity and of religion in general was his belief that the interpretation of Scripture and revelation must be governed "by what is agreeable to those natural notions which we have of God," which meant that faith required only unfaltering trust in God's goodness and benignity.[77] Speaking of predestination and eternal decrees, Tillotson wrote:

> I am as certain that this doctrine cannot be of God as I am sure that God is good and just, because this [doctrine] grates upon the notion that mankind have of goodness and justice. This is that which no man would do, and therefore cannot be believed of infinite Goodness. If an apostle, or an angel from heaven, teach any doctrine which plainly overthrows the goodness and justice of God, let him be accursed. For every man hath a greater assurance that God is good and just than he can have of any subtle speculations about predestination and the decrees of God.[78]

The contraposition of "subtle speculations" and personal "assurance" is typical of Tillotson's moderate and "reasonable" approach.[79]

Tillotson's 1690 sermon on the eternity of hell, which was still producing waves in America as late as 1740, was itself far from unsubtle, however. Like all of Tillotson's work, it is marked by a kind of suave cleverness. The sermon purported to be a defense of the doctrine of the everlasting misery of the damned, but in the course of presenting his argument Tillotson deliberately

---

Art of Preaching: A Practical Survey of Preaching in the Church of England, over Twelve Centuries (London, 1964 [orig. publ. 1940]), 103.

76. Cf. Norman Sykes, *From Sheldon to Secker: Aspects of English Church History, 1660–1768* (Cambridge, 1959), 176–181: "There can be no doubt of the widespread vogue of this doctrine of Divine Benevolence. Tillotson's sermon on the text 'And His commandments are not grievous,' became the general theme of his age." There is more information on the subject in Sykes's article "The Theology of Divine Benevolence," *Historical Magazine of the Protestant Episcopal Church*, XVI (1947), 278–291. I have in preparation a study of Tillotson's influence in America.

77. Quoted in O'Higgins, *Anthony Collins*, 46, from Tillotson's *Sixteen Sermons Preached On Several Subjects and Occasions* . . . (London, 1700), III, 74.

78. Quoted in Sykes, "Divine Benevolence," *Hist. Mag. Prot. Episcopal Church*, XVI (1947), 290–291, from *The Works of the Most Reverend Dr. John Tillotson* (London, 1752), II, 509. Cf. the comment in the *Dictionary of National Biography*: "Hitherto the pulpit had been the great stronghold of puritanism, under Tillotson it became a powerful agency for weaning men from puritan ideas."

79. Davies, "Debate on Eternal Punishment," *18th-Cent. Studies*, IV (1970–1971), 257–276, stresses particularly the role of "reasonableness" as contributing to the softening of the orthodox scheme.

subverted most of the traditional defenses as being inadequate for their purpose. This procedure left standing only Tillotson's own defense, which was,
in fact, a mitigation of the orthodox teaching. The doctrine of hell was thus
sabotaged by indirection. On the one hand, Tillotson strongly reinforced the
position of those who asserted that *aionion* could only be interpreted as
meaning "eternal"; that is, he affirmed that God definitely *threatened* eternal
punishment, the terror of which, he said, was "the sting of sin." If people
were "once set free from the fear and belief of this, the most powerful
restraint from sin would be taken away." But, at the same time, Tillotson
denied that God necessarily was obliged to follow through on this threat in
every case of mortal sin. Tillotson agreed with Origen in holding that the
pains of hell were possibly rehabilitative for some persons, at least, and that it
was in God's power to reprieve sinners even after their condemnation, should
He so choose and depending upon circumstances. On nearly every other point
—such as the preexistence of souls, the interpretation of *aion*, the doctrine of
universal salvation including the devil, and so on—he was utterly at odds
with the Greek father, but this general congruency with orthodoxy did not
protect him from considerable vilification by those who deemed his thinking
to be heterodox on the subject of hell.[80]

80. Tillotson's famous sermon was published separately in London in 1690 and subsequently
in various collections of his sermons. Jean LeClerc defended it publicly and was himself flirting
with various forms of the heretical Origenist doctrine that projected a universal restoration of
souls. See Walker, *Decline of Hell*, 188–196, on LeClerc. A defense of Tillotson that originally
appeared in LeClerc's *Bibliothèque Choisie*, VII (Amsterdam, 1705), 289–360, was translated
into English and appended to Francis Hutchinson's *The Life of . . . John Tillotson, Archbishop of
Canterbury* (London, 1717), and to the second edition of Tobias Swinden's *Nature and Place of
Hell* (London, 1727). A well-known direct reply to Tillotson was William Lupton's *The Eternity
of Future Punishment Proved and Vindicated . . .* (Oxford, 1708). During the Great Awakening,
George Whitefield committed the serious tactical error of charging that Tillotson knew no more of
Christianity than Mahomet, a slander that contributed to turning the Harvard faculty sharply
against the evangelist. "Monstrous Reflections," they said, "upon the great and good Archbishop
Tillotson (as Dr. Increase Mather Stiled him)." See *The Testimony of the President, Professors,
Tutors and Hebrew Instructor of Harvard College in Cambridge, against Mr. George Whitefield,
and His Conduct* (Boston, 1744) and Whitefield's *Three Letters from the Reverend Mr. G.
Whitefield . . . wherein he vindicates his asserting that Archbishop Tillotson knew no more of
true Christianity than Mahomet* (Glasgow, 1740). Since Tillotson had helped Mather in his nego-
tiation over the renewal of the Bay Colony charter, his memory was all the more sacred in Massachusetts. Excerpts from the relevant publications by Whitefield and the Harvard faculty are
printed in Richard Hofstadter and Wilson Smith, eds., *American Higher Education: A
Documentary History*, I (Chicago, 1961), 62–74. Whitefield's sermon "The Eternity of Hell
Torments" (see n. 8 above) took issue with Tillotson's 1690 sermon. God's "truth," Whitefield
said, "will be as much impeached and called in question, did he not inflict his punishments, as it
would be, if he did not confer his rewards" (*Sermons*, 311). It seems certain that Wigglesworth's
Duration of the Punishment is indebted to Tillotson in its argument, though he concludes differently than the English bishop. We know that as late as the 1750s Wigglesworth was recommend-

Tillotson's consistent goal was to preserve a moderate image of God's justice and goodness. This meant that he felt impelled to discard some of the more improbable or extreme defenses of the hell doctrine. Thus, with regard to the claim that all sin is infinite because it is an offense against an infinite object (namely God) and therefore deserves infinite punishment—an argument that we have seen was almost universally relied upon by the apologists for hell's eternity—Tillotson was critical. He pointed out, as had other critics before him, that this teaching made the evil and demerit of all sins equal, "for the demerit of no sin can be more than infinite." If the demerit of all sins is equal, then there is no reason for the degrees of punishment in the next world that are asserted in Scripture. Such degrees are essential to any notion of justice. Moreover, Tillotson continued, if it can be said that a sin is infinite because it is committed against God, who is an infinite object, by the same token it could be claimed that the least punishment inflicted by God is infinite. This would make all punishments from God as well as all sins against Him equal, a conclusion that Tillotson called palpably absurd.[81]

Finally, Tillotson argued, the very conception of the penal relation between the sinner and God, which is based upon an analogy to certain political crimes on earth such as lèse majesté, is erroneous. "The person against whom a fault is committed makes it to be greater when it is directly against that person, and not when it regards him only indirectly. All the crimes that are committed in a kingdom are opposed to the will of the prince, yet they are not all crimes of high-treason." If one goes along with orthodox reasoning on the subject, atheism should be a greater crime than any other breach of divine law. In addition, our notions of proper justice on earth include taking into account the circumstances of each crime, the malice of the behavior, the ill consequences of the action, and so on. Such circumstances "do much more aggravate the sin, than the object against which it was committed. Justice requires the weakness of the sinners to be consider'd, as well as the person against whom the sin is committed."[82]

Despite the power of these objections and the wide attention they received, the orthodox clergy, like Edwards, continued to use the old argument for the infinity of sin, without answering Tillotson directly. Edwards's sermon "The Eternity of Hell Torments" relied almost entirely on this traditional argument

---

ing Tillotson to Harvard students, though he warned them at the same time against Tillotson's heresies. See Shipton, *Sibley's Harvard Graduates*, V, 553. Swinden's *Nature and Place of Hell*, the second edition of which contained Tillotson's sermon in an appendix, was in the Harvard library very soon after it was published in 1727, and there is internal evidence in Wigglesworth's lecture that he used Swinden.

81. I am quoting from the reprint of Tillotson's sermon appended to Swinden, *Nature and Place of Hell*, 2d ed., 374.

82. *Ibid.*, 376.

in endeavoring to prove that "it is not contrary to the divine perfections to inflict on wicked men a punishment that is absolutely eternal." Edwards did reply directly, however, to Tillotson's main thesis, that God's threats as manifested in Scripture are not necessarily to be fulfilled in all cases, by observing: "There is an inviolable connection between threatenings and execution." God would not have threatened if He did not foreknow. Second, Edwards argued, Tillotson's proposal leads to the belief that God "was obliged to make use of a fallacy to govern the world. . . . Is it not greatly to be wondered at, that the great Archbishop Tillotson, who has made so great a figure among the new fashioned divines, should advance such an opinion as this!"[83]

Tillotson was at the fount of much of what Edwards found objectionable in eighteenth-century liberal Christianity, particularly the practical moralism that was allowed to take precedence over devotion to God and over the strict principle of divine sovereignty. Edwards saw the eternal punishment of hell in terms of unwavering retributive justice. He scarcely mentioned its deterrent value on earth, which after all was a lesser consideration for a true Christian, as it was even for a man of high secular virtue, such as Shaftesbury. Tillotson, on the other hand, although a member of a hierarchical church and an aristocratic society, believed "the measure of penalties" should not always be taken from "the quality and degree of the offence," or from the rank of the object against which the offense was committed, but rather from a prudential consideration of what degree of punishment is necessary to "secure the observation of the law, and deter men from the breach of it." Whoever considers, Tillotson wrote, "how ineffectual the threatening even of eternal torments is to the greatest part of sinners, will soon be satisfy'd that a less penalty than that of eternal sufferings, would to the far greatest part of mankind have been in all probability of little or no force."[84] On the basis of *raison d'état*, then, Tillotson held that if there could be a punishment still more terrible than eternal vengeance, it would not be unreasonable for God to make use of it, provided it achieved its end. Abstract and Scholastic considerations of justice were not at issue at all, simply the "wisdom and prudence [of] . . . the lawgiver." But—and here was the nub of Tillotson's innovation—these attributes of God must be considered adaptable to the situation; threats were one tactic among many that the Supreme Ruler could draw upon when necessary, no less than reprieves, to bring about the goal of a moral society.

Most often it is the Calvinist God, not the Anglican, that has been consid-

---

83. "Eternity of Hell Torments," in *Works*, IV, 267, 275. Tillotson's suggestion was not new. It had already been broached in the patristic period, since in *The City of God* Augustine attacked an analogous argument (XXI, xxiv).

84. Swinden, *Nature and Place of Hell*, 2d ed., 379–381.

ered unpredictable and unknowable in His workings. Edwards's defense of the eternity of hell was based, however, primarily on the undeviating constancy and regularity of divine law in morals as in physics. In the course of a lifetime of theological contemplation, Edwards moved further and further away from the idea of unique and altogether problematic interventions by God, and closer to belief in inflexible divine government founded on fixed laws and intrinsic relations between things. "Late philosophers seem ready enough to own the great importance of God's maintaining steady and inviolable the laws of the natural world. It may be worthy to be considered, whether it is not of as great, or greater importance, that the law of God, that great rule of righteousness between the supreme moral governor and his subjects, should be maintained inviolate."[85]

According to Tillotson's reasoning, any opportunity for mercy that God could find He would make use of. If God should remit and abate His threatened punishments, Tillotson remarked in a notable sentence, He would be "not worse but better than his Word," for there is an important difference between promises and threats: "He who promiseth passeth over a right to another, and thereby stands obliged to him in justice and faithfulness to make good his promise. . . . But in threatenings it is quite otherwise. He that threatens keeps the right of punishing in his own hand, and is not obliged to execute what he hath threatened any further than the reasons and ends of government do require."[86] For Edwards, on the contrary, all analogies to human conceptions of mercy were beside the point. "It is an unreasonable and unscriptural notion of the mercy of God," Edwards wrote, "that he is merciful in such a sense that he cannot bear that penal justice should be executed." "This is to conceive of the mercy of God as a passion to which his nature is so subject that God is liable to be moved, and affected, and overcome by seeing a creature in misery, so that he cannot bear to see justice executed; which is a most unworthy and absurd notion of the mercy of God, and would, if true, argue great weakness."[87] In other words, in Edwards's eyes, any abatement or remission of threatened punishments would make God not better but worse than His word.

When Edwards wrote these lines, sometime before 1740 in all likelihood, it was probably not yet completely evident to him that the survival of the doctrine of hell would depend not upon the metaphysics of infinity, the exegesis of *aion*, or the psychological question of the incorrigibility of sinners, but in large part upon the degree of authority in moral theology that could properly be granted to the sentiment of compassion or pity. Long before the

---

85. Miscellanies, no. 779, printed in *Works*, I, 582–611, under the title, "Concerning the Necessity and Reasonableness of the Christian Doctrine of Satisfaction for Sin."

86. Swinden, *Nature and Place of Hell*, 2d ed., 391–392.

87. "Eternity of Hell Torments," in *Works*, IV, 267.

growth of a scientific cosmology decisively reduced the traditional conceptions of hell and heaven to religious myths, the doctrine of hell was already
under sharp attack by humanitarians, who were otherwise not doubters or
skeptics, for the difficulties it raised concerning the very nature of God.

Two other books in the Yale library of *circa* 1718 pertained directly to the
nature and duration of hell and must be mentioned, though there is only a
slight possibility that Edwards was aware of them. Both of these titles date
from the middle of the seventeenth century but were first available at Yale in
John Dunton's two-volume *The Phenix: or, A Revival of Scarce and Valuable
Pieces from the Remotest Antiquity to the Present Times* (London, 1707–
1708), which also came to the college as part of the Dummer gift. Dunton was
comparatively well known in America as a bookseller, a compiler, and an
editor. Probably few people in America knew, however, that *The Phenix*
contained heterodox material.[88] The first volume of *The Phenix* included,
among other works, George Rust's *A Letter of Resolution Concerning Origen
and the Chief of His Opinions*, published anonymously in London in 1661;
volume two contained Samuel Richardson's *A Discourse of the Torments of
Hell. The Foundation and Pillars Thereof Discovered, Searched, Shaken and
Removed*, dating from 1658.[89] These two short sallies against the encamp-
ments of rigid orthodoxy were quite different in nature. Richardson's book
was a product of the religious openness and experimentation of the Commonwealth period, and the author, who was some sort of sectarian, made up for
the absence of academic polish in his work by his bluntness, fervor, and
native perspicacity. Rust, on the other hand, was a brilliant student and
disciple of Henry More, and after holding a fellowship at Christ's College,
Cambridge, became bishop of Dromore, dying prematurely in that office.
Aside from the cloak of anonymity that Rust wrapped around his authorship,
he protected himself from charges of heterodoxy by claiming to expound
Origen's ideas solely for the enlightenment of a friend, who needed learned
assistance in sifting the evidence concerning the controversy over the nature
and duration of the future life. Although we have no evidence that Edwards
ever opened *The Phenix*, there may be some advantage in sampling these two
works for what they can tell us about the challenges to Calvinist orthodoxy
that were available to the curious, even in New England.[90] Indeed, so much

88. For bibliographical notes pertinent to Dunton's relations with New England, see Fiering,
"Transatlantic Republic of Letters," *WMQ*, 3d Ser., XXXIII (1976), 642–660.

89. The attribution to Rust of the *Letter Concerning Origen* has been questioned by Walker,
Decline of Hell, 125. Rust's authorship was earlier sanctioned by Marjorie Hope Nicolson, who
wrote a short introduction for the Facsimile Text Society reprint of the book (New York, 1933),
which is the edition I have used. Walker mentions Richardson but does not treat the book in any
detail.

90. The presence of Richardson's tract in the Yale library was perhaps not so much of an

heterodox speculation about hell was stirred up among Calvinists in England in the middle of the seventeenth century that it seems highly probable that reverberations were felt in New England into the next century.

Half of Richardson's book consisted of contradictory quotations collected from dozens of recognized religious authorities, Catholic, Protestant, ancient, and modern, his purpose being to demonstrate the confusion and inconsistencies that surrounded the doctrine of hell. Even William Ames's *Marrow of Divinity*, the very measure of orthodoxy, was cited as stating that as to "the place of hell, and manner of torture there the Scripture hath not pronounced anything distinctly." Yet despite such disavowals, Richardson noted, many theologians pretend to know all about hell. In Richardson's eyes, most of what was taught concerning the punishment of the wicked was fabrication in that it lacked specific scriptural authority.

> The learned agree not upon which Scripture to ground their Hel-torments upon; for that place one of them alledge to prove it, another of themselves deny it. . . . See ye not the great doubting and uncertainty they are at amongst themselves? . . . It is very strange that in a thing so signall of which they say they see it in the Word of God, that they can no way agree concerning it. O ye learned in the seven liberal sciences . . . tell us in as much as ye speak contraries, as yea and nay, which of you we are to believe.[91]

Richardson spoke as a plain man, outside of the aura of learning and scholarship, who grounded his opinions on what he saw as simple truths. "Their dreams of hell," he said, are "a device of man without Scripture, . . . uncertain brain-sick fancies, for the imaginations of men have no end."[92]

It is particularly remarkable that long before Bayle, Richardson denied that the fear of the torments of hell was in practice an effective "preserver against sin." The greatest sinners sometimes believe in hell, he said, but they dissociate from themselves the consequences of their actions: "They hope it doth not belong to them; or they hope to repent and lead new lives, before they die." Moreover, like Bayle later, Richardson observed that the lives of many pagans are morally exemplary, which proves that hell is not a necessary inducement to virtue. "Experience teacheth, that the fear of hell, though at first it startleth and frighteth men, yet that is soon over, and is no preserver against sin." On

---

anomaly as it may seem, since Francis Brinley (1632–1719), judge of the Court of Common Pleas of Rhode Island, who occasionally lived in Boston, owned a copy in 1713 when he cataloged his library. See Brinley, "An Account Taken of My Books . . . March 27. 1713," *New England Historical and Genealogical Register*, XII (1858), 75–78. *The Phenix* was in James Logan's library in Philadelphia, as well as at Yale. See Wolf, *Library of James Logan*, 140.

91. Richardson, *Discourse on Hell*, 52.

92. *Ibid.*, 90.

the contrary, Richardson argued, the fear aroused by the preaching of eternal torments causes sin. If the natural man does hate God, as Edwards was later to assert, Richardson believed that he hated Him because of the "evil and hard thoughts of God" brought about through the teaching of eternal torment. Fear, Richardson said, distracts and discourages the soul. It "unfits and disableth the soul to every good work to God or man." Whereas hope comforts and enlarges the soul, fear of hell "provokes the soul to envy and unbelief, and hinders subjection to God."[93]

Like the objections to eternal torment raised by Peter Sterry and Jeremiah White, who were writing in the same period,[94] Richardson's leading argument was that the orthodox teaching (insofar as it could be reconciled into a coherent doctrine) was incompatible with a humane conception of God. "We do see men shew more kindness to a rebellious and disobedient child than he deserveth; may not God do the same, so much is God greater than man, so much greater is his mercy, love, and goodness, than that in man, yea than that is or ever was in all men." It is hard today to appreciate how radical it was in 1658 to declare: "I cannot admit to think any thing that is cruel to be in God. . . . Look above and hearken to the sweet voice above in the region of love . . . , there is no voice comes from Heaven but love, peace, and goodwill to man."[95] All of Richardson's positive beliefs, however, are not easy to determine. He seems to have held to the doctrine of the annihilation of the wicked (p. 63), which was the Socinian belief, though he also referred to Origen's hypothesis that after a thousand years all men and even the devil will be saved.[96]

Rust's *Letter Concerning Origen* was hardly the only source of information available on the opinions of that great church father. Latin editions of Origen's works were a necessary part of any solid library in patristics. Harvard, of course, had such editions. Cotton Mather cited him often, and tutor Henry Flynt owned a copy of the London 1660 English translation of Origen's

93. *Ibid.*, 103–104.

94. Walker, *Decline of Hell*, 104–121, discusses these two important figures at length. Cf. his statement on p. 111: "Compassion for the suffering of sinners, and the projection of it into God, are almost unique in the theology of that age." White was one of Cromwell's chaplains. His *Restoration of All Things: or, a Vindication of the Goodness and Grace of God* . . . , published posthumously in London in 1712 and reprinted in Philadelphia in 1844, is a masterpiece of 17th-century universalist literature. It is notable that White combined his universalism with theological determinism. Just as Arminianism was compatible with various beliefs concerning punishment in hell, so was predestinarianism.

95. Richardson, *Discourse on Hell*, 171, 190.

96. There were refutations of Richardson by Nicholas Chewney, *Hell, with the Everlasting Torments thereof Asserted* . . . (London, 1660); Jo. Brandon, το πυρ το αιωνιον: or, Everlasting Fire No Fancy . . . (London, 1678); and Thomas Lewis, *The Nature of Hell, the Reality of Hell-Fire, and the Eternity of Hell-Torments* . . . (London, 1720). The last was a response to a 1720 reprinting of Richardson's book.

polemic against Celsus.[97] Moreover, Book XXI of St. Augustine's *City of God* was mostly a refutation of the errant notions of Origen and others concerning the punishment of the wicked, which gave Origen's ideas on hell particularly widespread currency among the learned. It is perhaps significant, however, that when Tobias Swinden wrote his *Enquiry into the Nature and Place of Hell* (1714), he chose as his target the *Letter Concerning Origen* rather than any other source. Rust succeeded better than anyone else at the time, it seems, in distilling Origen's thinking about the afterlife into simple rubrics, while adding to it his own sympathetic understanding. The effect was a powerful solvent of the orthodox position.

Again and again Rust cited as the proper standard of interpreting divine doctrine the criterion that was also behind Tillotson's and Shaftesbury's reasoning: What would a good and just man do in like circumstances? God's actions, he said, must not be "to govern the world with less justice than an ordinary upright man would."[98] The fundamental idea behind this standard, as Ernst Cassirer noted about the Cambridge Platonists and their circle in general, was that of the autonomy and immutability of the transcendent notions of goodness and justice, which even God cannot change and which, in fact, He must be completely identified with. Rust was repelled by theologians who resolved the "problem of multitudes" by easy references to "the pleasure and sovereignty of God, who being the Creator and Lord of all men, may (they say) dispose of them how and where he pleases." The consequence of such talk, Rust observed, was that mankind ended up by wishing God did not exist or at least would not concern Himself in the affairs of men. "If they were as zealous Patrons of the more excellent *Attributes* of God, as they are peremptory Assertors of his *absolute Will* and *Power* . . . they would . . . render his Existence and Government in the world . . . desireable to all men."[99] When one considers, Rust continued, that according to the accepted teaching, entire peoples of the world who are ignorant of or opposed to the Gospel are considered to exist for no other purpose but ultimate condemnation, can it be affirmed with any "reasonable confidence" that "the goodness and providence of a wise minde did preside over their generations?" Is it enough to answer, Rust asked, that God can do as He pleases with "his own voluntary handy-work?" If God exists at all, Rust asserted, "he is infinitely good and wise as well as powerful and uncontrollable," and therefore one

97. The titles in Flynt's library have been compiled by the Rev. Edward T. Dunn of Canisius College, who generously permitted me to see the list. The Yale library catalog published by Thomas Clap in 1743 also included works by Origen. On Mather, see David Levin, *Cotton Mather: The Young Life of the Lord's Remembrancer, 1663–1703* (Cambridge, Mass., 1978), 120.

98. Rust, *Letter Concerning Origen*, 29.

99. *Ibid.*, 31–32.

expects to find in any of his interventions on earth the evidence of those first attributes.[100]

For Rust, or for Origen, the divine attribute of compassion was a theological factor that had to be taken into account throughout every step of one's reasoning about the Creation and last things. Assuming it is true that God did discover along the way (to His surprise and disappointment) that man in the exercise of his divinely given freedom had committed some transgressions, beginning with Adam's original misstep, and that these transgressions inevitably entailed terrible punishments, "infinitely more sharp and dolorous" than all the good sinners would enjoy from God: under such circumstances, Rust argued, God's response, "out of His great compassion," would certainly be simply then and there to annihilate these sinners, or "rather his Wisdome would have judg'd it more decorous never to have made them. For assuredly he needed them not in any respect, least of all as they were miserable." The problem with annihilation, however, as a human theory about how God might deal with errant mankind, is that the act would be a kind of admission from God that He had freely created such beings "as he could not continue in being with consistency with his own attributes." Since God cannot be liable to such disparagement, it is necessary to assume instead that He never creates a being for whom a just punishment would be a condition such that the person subject to it would far more prefer non-existence, i.e., a state of never having been created, to his present existence.[101]

Rust's conclusion was in direct contradiction to the conventional teaching, explicit in Edwards and others, that the state of hell, even the *poena damni* alone, is far worse than death, and that in hell the sufferers wish only for annihilation, and wish even that they had never been created. "Without doubt," Edwards wrote, "the misery of the least of sinners that are damned is as terrible or more terrible than no existence and such that those that endure it would choose rather to cease to be and be in a state of eternal non-existence. . . . But the affliction of a state of existence must be very great, as we see by experience, to be thus."[102] Edwards also disagreed with Origen's idea that God did not "need" the misery of the damned, for "the awful majesty of God remarkably appears," Edwards wrote, "in those dreadful and amazing punishments which he inflicts on those who rise up against him."[103]

In Rust's and Origen's view, the only purpose of divine punishment is reformatory. Punishment is justified, therefore, only when it is "profitable" to the punished. Those who fail to be improved by the lessons of this life, such

100. *Ibid.*, 32–33.
101. *Ibid.*, 72–73.
102. Miscellanies, no. 418.
103. Edwards, "Wicked Men Useful in Their Destruction Only," in *Works*, IV, 306.

as "obstinately wicked men" and the unreclaimable devils, must indeed expect "fiery vengeance," for they will be cast by the righteous hand of God into a lake of "slow-consuming fire and sulphureous stench. . . . A sad pitiable Fate and torture unsufferable."[104] But God's punishments, like those commonly imposed by human beings, have in them still something of "that *End* for which they are inflicted. They are *Curative* and for the Emendation of the party suffering." To imagine, on the contrary, that persons who are not beyond the power of redress and recovery shall be kept in torture for ever and ever "is to fix so harsh a Note upon the mercy and equity of the righteous Judge of all the world, that the same temper in a man we should for ever exsecrate and abominate."[105] Hence, it is probable that all people, even the worst, will be refined and reformed by the fires of hell and eventually given eternal bliss. To St. Jerome's criticism of Origen's hypothesis—that it implied "the devils should become angels again, and Judas a saint!"—Rust answered for Origen: "What difference is there in the distance betwixt a devil made an angel, and an angel made a devil? I am sure," Rust went on, "the advantage is on the ascending part rather than on the descending; for the mercy and compassion of God to all the works of his hands may reasonably be supposed to help them up though undeserving."[106]

Whatever Edwards's specific reading in heterodox literature in the 1720s, there can be little doubt that by the time of the Great Awakening he was well aware of the several alternatives to the strict Calvinist position and that his preaching of the eternity of hell torments was an intentional affirmation of the orthodox teaching, not simply, as one historian described it, a tenuous reflection of "the mind-set of colonial New England."

Edwards's Reply to Whiston and Others

Edwards's desire to vindicate the orthodox teaching on the eternity of hell punishments did not diminish after the Great Awakening or after his expulsion from the Northampton pulpit in 1750. On the contrary, dedicated more than ever to refuting the arguments of the deists, the liberals, and the diluters of all stripes, Edwards's most sustained treatment of the problem of hell was written in about 1755 in two long entries in his private notebooks.[107] His particular target was William Whiston's *Eternity of Hell Torments*, because, as Edwards

---

104. Rust, *Letter Concerning Origen*, 74.
105. *Ibid.*, 75–76.
106. *Ibid.*, 130.
107. Miscellanies, nos. 1348 and 1356. These have been coalesced in various printed editions as an essay on "The Endless Punishment of Those Who Die Impenitent." It is significant that these definitive statements on hell were written at approximately the same time that Edwards was

had transcribed into his "Catalogue" of reading in 1754, Whiston's book ("according to William Dodwell's two sermons" against it) " 'has indeed collected together all the objections of atheists deists and Socinians against this article intermixed and enlarged with some surprizing Novelties of his own.' " The New England minister found in Whiston a useful compendium of the principal objections.

Inevitably, most of Edwards's reasoning had direct reference to scriptural proofs. He asked, for example, if "God intends finally to deliver all mankind from misery," and if "to suppose the contrary (viz., the everlasting continuance of the torments of hell) is so extremely derogatory to God's moral character, and represents him in such black and odious colors, and as so cruel a being," then why did not Christ and His apostles, when speaking of future punishment, clearly reveal this alleged "glorious doctrine of such a universal eternal salvation?"[108]

But Edwards also engaged in some ingenious psychological reasoning that attempted to bring out the inherent inconsistencies of the opposing view, and this approach is of more interest to us here. A great number of surprising paradoxes resulted, Edwards showed, from the humanitarian argument that repentance and salvation remained a possibility even in hell and from the position that the "design of the pains of hell be that of kind and benevolent chastisement, to bring sinners to repentance, and a yielding to God's authority, and compliance with the divine will."[109] To begin with, this teaching implied that people are continued in a state of probation during their time in hell. Yet the misery of hell is so oppressive, Edwards pointed out, and the removal from positive inducements to repentance so complete, there would seem to be less probability that repentance would occur in hell than on earth.[110] Moreover, if the damned know they will eventually be granted eternal happiness, which means they are not truly under trial or in a state of probation, then what is to restrain them from their former course of life, including the expression of wickedness in all forms while they are in hell?

In addition, Edwards observed, even the enemies of the doctrine of eternal punishment assume that the punishment will be for a long time, if not eternal. Yet if, in fact, the sinner is all this time a free agent and continues willfully and perversely to refuse to repent—for this must be assumed under the probatory theory, since it is "unreasonable to suppose that they will be continued

---

working on *Original Sin* and *Two Dissertations* (*True Virtue* and *The End for Which God Created the World*). All four problems were closely related in Edwards's system.

108. "Endless Punishment," in *Works*, I, 613.

109. *Ibid.*, 614.

110. In hell, Edwards said, "there are no prophets, or ministers, or good men, to admonish [the damned], to reason and expostulate with them, or to set them good examples. . . . They are left wholly to the company of devils, and others like them." *Ibid.*, 632.

under their torments after they are brought to repentance"—how great must be their wickedness and hardness of heart! "They must therefore frowardly go on in their rebellion, enmity and opposition to the great God, whose power they feel in their misery; who continues with the greatest peremptoriness to command them to forsake their sins, and submit to him immediately without delay." Now if this is truly the case, Edwards said, "and they shall go on in such wickedness, and continue in such extreme obstinacy and pertinaciousness, for so many ages (as is supposed, by its being thought their torments shall be so long continued), how desperately will their guilt be increased! How many thousand times more guilty at the end of the term, than at the beginning!"[111]

It followed from the probatory theory of hell, Edwards maintained, that the condemned would be much more the proper objects of divine severity after a term in hell than before it. And if their misery should be augmented and "lengthened out much longer to atone for their new contracted guilt; they must be supposed to continue impenitent, till that second additional time of torment is ended; at the end of which their guilt will be risen higher. . . . At this rate, where can there be any place for an end of their misery?"[112]

It can be seen, even from this one example, that Edwards differed crucially from the "merciful doctors" and the optimists about the psychology of rehabilitation from sin. In line with a powerful tradition in Augustinian Protestant thought, Edwards believed that the foundations of all personal reform are laid instantaneously in the soul, just as justification by divine grace occurs in a moment, though the process of sanctification may be lifelong. Those who argued for a hell that was less than eternal were usually believers in the Pelagian or Arminian psychology of the will, which threw most of the responsibility for reform upon the individual himself rather than upon God. They saw moral improvement as an incremental process without a definite beginning. Edwards anticipated no moral changes in hell, because without a foundation of grace in the heart sinners would remain exactly as they were forever.[113] But those who did foresee a process of reformation in hell were caught in a dilemma. In terms of their own psychology, Edwards pointed out,

111. *Ibid.*, 620. Cf. Walker, *Decline of Hell*, 213*ff*, for discussion of the question of whether the damned continue to sin in hell.

112. "Endless Punishment," in *Works*, I, 620. A Harvard student in 1733 answered in the negative his master's degree *quaestio*, "Will the damned be punished for sins they have committed in hell?" See Young, "Subjects for Master's Degree in Harvard," Mass. Hist. Soc., *Procs.*, XVIII (1881), 119–151. But at the Yale commencement of 1750 the master's degree candidate Lyman Hall responded in the affirmative to the *quaestio*, "*An Damnatorum Miseria fuerit in aeternum progressiva?*" (Is the misery of the damned progressive through all eternity?)

113. On 18th-century theories of moral reform, including Edwards's, see Fiering, "Franklin and the Way to Virtue," *Am. Qtly.*, XXX (1978), 199–223.

it must be supposed that the extraordinary physical and mental torment of hell, enormously greater than anything experienced on earth, would immediately bring about repentance in a free willed person. Who would tolerate such torture if he were free to reform himself and thereby avoid it? It follows, then, that under the Pelagian theory there would be no hell of any significant duration whatsoever.

Assuming, however, that such quick repentance did not occur, and that God remained aloof insofar as He did not infuse a new and holy will into these crushed souls, what could in fact be expected of them? "The sinner continuing obstinate in wickedness under such powerful means to reclaim him, for so long a time, will be so far from being more and more purged," Edwards asserted, "or brought nearer to repentance, that he will be as it were, infinitely farther from it. Wickedness in his heart will be vastly established and increased. For, it may be laid down as an axiom, that the longer men continue wilfully in wickedness, the more is the habit of sin established, and the more and more will the heart be hardened in it." And it may be laid down as a second axiom, Edwards continued, "that the greater and more powerful the means are, that are used to bring men to reform and repent, which they resist, and are obstinate under, the more desperately are men hardened in sin, and the more the principle of it in the heart is confirmed." Hell would not be a reformatory, but a training ground for sin, where every application of pain would deepen bitterness, hate, and resentment. And the goal of reform would move ever farther off, for it may be posited as a third axiom of penal psychology, Edwards suggested, that "long continuance in perverse and obstinate rebellion against any particular kind of means, tend to render those particular means vain, ineffectual, and hopeless."[114] Without the aid of grace, without a spark from the Holy Spirit, however it may be transferred, nothing can be expected from merely negative punishment. The only result will be greater and greater accustomedness to the continuous ill treatment of hell.

> After the damned in hell have stood it out with such prodigious and devilish perverseness and stoutness, for ages of ages, in their rebellion and enmity against God, refusing to bow to his will under such constant severe, mighty chastisements, attended all the while with offers of mercy, what a desperate degree of hardness of heart and fixed strength of habitual wickedness will they have contracted at last, and how inconceivably farther will they be from a penitent, humble, and pure heart, than when first cast into hell![115]

114. "Endless Punishment," in *Works*, I, 620. At the Yale commencement of 1748 Daniel Lyman responded in the negative to the master's *quaestio*, *"An Damnati Favorem Dei cupiant?"* (Do the damned wish for God's favor?)

115. "Endless Punishment," in *Works*, I, 621.

Since it was a basic component of Edwards's theology that conversion consisted in a change of will from resistance to (or even hatred of) God to love and positive desire for Him, accompanied by a new sense of the divine beauty, coercive techniques appeared to Edwards to be singularly useless if true inner conversion is the end in view. Fear cannot of itself create love. "Torments inflicted," Edwards wrote, "have no tendency to bring a wicked man to repentance directly and properly, if by repentance we mean an alteration of the disposition, and appetites, and taste of the mind." The experience of pain creates an aversion to the source of the pain; hence one may become afraid to gratify certain appetites, but this does not destroy the appetite, or change one's inclinations. Only "external" compliance will be gained if "the heart in its relish and inclinations" remains averse. Thus, "it is not granted," Edwards wrote, "that even long continued pains and practice will gradually raise an habitual love to virtue." The pains of the damned may "more and more convince them of the folly of their negligence and fearlessness in sin," but their suffering "will not show them the beauty of holiness, or the odiousness of sin, so as to cause them to hate sin on its own account."[116]

This reasoning brought Edwards to a remarkable conclusion that turned the tables on the humanitarians, at least insofar as one was willing to accept his premises and his interpretation of the scriptural texts. Under the assumption that God has completely abandoned the damned, "shut them out as dogs," thrown them away, as it were, which was Edwards's belief, God appears indeed to be a horrendously ruthless judge. After the day of judgment, He takes no more pains with sinners whatsoever and feels no pity for them; it is as if they are completely forgotten. This is terrible enough. But, ironically, those who conceive of God as a merciful and benevolent ruler even over the domain of hell actually make of Him something worse, Edwards implied. We know that only a day, indeed, a moment, in the fiery furnace would suffice to make any person "wholly comply with all the pains and outward self-denial requisite in order to a universal external obedience to the precepts of the word of God, rather than have those torments renewed and continued for ages." The remembrance of this brief torment would be sufficient to outweigh all of the most lively and attractive temptations on earth. If it is God's compassion that is operative in hell, rather than His judgment, and if the whole design of it is

---

116. *Ibid.*, 628. The question of whether torture can itself bring about a genuine and lasting change of heart has been widely discussed in the 20th century in several contexts. Walker, *Decline of Hell*, 68, cites William Sargant, *Battle for the Mind: A Physiology of Conversion and Brainwashing* (London and Garden City, N.Y., 1957), and observes, "There is little doubt that prolonged pain does, in most patients, produce a neurotic state of high suggestibility in which religious or other conversion can be easily achieved." In the 18th century the problem of personality change was discussed mainly as part of the theory of habit. See Fiering, "Franklin and the Way to Virtue," *Am. Qtly.*, XXX (1978), 199–223.

an expression of His "Infinite mercy and bounty," why then, Edwards asked, "does he take such dreadful measures" to reach His end? "Will no other do? Cannot infinite wisdom find out some gentler method to bring to pass the same design?"[117] Edwards carried these questions no further, for the unstated conclusion was altogether objectionable to him. In the hands of the benevolists God appears not as an inflexible, harshly legalistic judge, but as a kind of sadist, who personally turns the thumbscrews for age upon age with the alleged intent of accomplishing a change of heart that could have been effected in an instant. Here again, Edwards seems to have preferred the inflexible—even, perhaps, impersonal—governor to the benevolent God with humane traits. For it seems that the entire conception of the divine attribute of mercy becomes confused and distorted if it is made a part of the punishments of hell. "The degree of misery and torment that shall be inflicted [in hell]," Edwards argued, is alone "evidence that God is not acting the part of benevolence and compassion, and only chastising from a kind and gracious principle and design."[118] The terrible punishment of hell is not an expression of God's "goodness" in any sentimental sense, nor can the meaning of hell be measured according to moral criteria suitable for human life on earth.

The truth is, no compromise solution whatsoever could have been satisfactory, since as Edwards succeeded in demonstrating, the tendencies of humanitarianism were fundamentally incompatible even with various sweetened conceptions of the inferno. The whole quest for a humane God could not be sustained in conjunction with a scriptural theology. The only choice left for the humanitarians was the one historically taken: the rejection of the entire idea of a hell.

Edwards knew his opponents well: "The same disposition and habit of mind, and manner of viewing things, that is indeed the main ground of the cavils of many of the modern freethinkers, and modish writers, against the extremity and eternity of hell torments, if given way to, and relied upon, would cause them to be dissatisfied with almost any thing that is very uncomfortable in a future punishment." Even the infliction of minor pain of any kind would be unacceptable. "In short, it will be found, that there will be no satisfying the infidel humor, with any thing that is very contrary to men's inclinations: any thing that they are very averse to bear, they would be averse to believe."[119] Nearly everyone in the eighteenth century felt the need for the promise of an afterlife that would compensate for the harsh injustices witnessed in this world. Since few people accepted Shaftesbury's position—that divine moral government is either evident on earth or does not exist

117. "Endless Punishment," in *Works*, I, 628.
118. *Ibid.*, 631.
119. *Ibid.*, 642.

at all—the doctrine of future rewards and punishments was necessary to preserve the picture of God's moral government over the world of mankind. Edwards himself believed that "in this world there is no such thing as a regular, equal disposing of rewards and punishments of men according to their moral estate. . . . In this world . . . all things are in the greatest confusion." It followed that if God did govern the world, there must be rewards and punishments later.[120] Given the pessimistic assessment of earthly conditions, hell and heaven were essential articles of faith, since they alone vindicated God's rule. Even for those who found the doctrine of eternal torment unpalatable, the desire remained to establish at least a compromise hell that would satisfy faith. Edwards was expert, however, at forcing upon the opposition all-or-nothing alternatives—provided, that is, they were content still to think within a framework of orthodox theology. Once accept any part of the idea of an afterlife in hell, and it was impossible, Edwards demonstrated, to escape its extreme implications.

Supposing, for example, that one assumed hell was penal or retributive and not probative or reformatory, but the punishments, rather than lasting eternally, would be sustained only until justice was satisfied. Thereafter, the damned, well chastised for their crimes, would be translated to eternal happiness with the rest of mankind. These suppositions, Edwards showed, offered merely the appearance of a more moderate doctrine, for the question still remains unresolved: Are the damned answerable for their wicked conduct while in hell or not? It must be assumed, Edwards maintained, that the damned continue sinning all the time of their punishment. "None can rationally imagine, that God would hold them under such extreme torments . . . after they have thoroughly repented, and turned from sin, and are become pure and holy, and conformed to God, and so have left off sinning."[121] If they are assumed to be answerable and accountable "for all that wickedness that is acted by them during their long state of suffering for the sins of this life," and must be punished for that wickedness as much as it deserves, then it follows that another period of suffering and punishment will begin after the first one is ended. The outcome again would be the perpetuity of the sinners' incarceration in the prison of hell.

If the damned were not held accountable for the wickedness they commit while in hell, and were allowed free rein to vent their rage against God for their pain, this condition would only further increase and confirm their habitual sin, so that they would conclude their punishment more deeply wicked than when they began. But is it not unlikely, Edwards asked, that God would

120. Miscellanies, no. 864, printed in Works, I, 565–582.
121. Ibid., 638.

then bring such souls to confirmed and eternal holiness and happiness, without any trial?[122]

Thus, Edwards attempted to foreclose any hope of the remission of sins after one's life on earth is past. Not only did this stance preserve the deterrent value of hell in its most rigorous form, it also kept the Christian's eyes focused on the religious and ethical openness and promise of the present life, rather than on the essentially intractable afterlife. As James Carse has emphasized in his chapter on Edwards's hell preaching, Edwards wanted "to make it understood by all that with death each person has lost the last chance to change the final balance of his life. After death there are no more chances." Or, in Edwards's words, "The only opportunity of escaping is in this world; this is the only state of trial wherein we have any offers of mercy, or there is any place for repentance."[123] Interestingly, both the doctrine of eternal torment and its opposite, the complete rejection of the idea of an afterlife, lead to the same conclusion: one's worthiness is either proven on earth, or not at all. Edwards compelled his followers to accept a crisis psychology. Every moment of a person's life might be the last, and then, without doubt, whether there is a hell or not, one's standing in eternity is fixed, one way or the other.

Moreover, for one living in the midst of an optimistic century Edwards understood with remarkable depth that even existence on earth, with its sordid trials, is not so far removed from the traditional images of hell, especially when conditions on earth are interpreted as typical or symbolic of God's designs and nature. Edwards was as opposed to the sentimentalization of the hardships and cruelty of life on earth as he was to the sentimentalization of hell. The benevolist conception of God was not only incompatible with the dogma of hell, it also did not fit the somber realities of the everyday world as Edwards saw them. The humanitarians, he said, would go so far as to deny even the existence of the "innumerable calamities that come to pass in the world, through the permission and ordination of divine providence," if such calamities were not universally known and incontestable facts. Edwards claimed that if before they had ever occurred these calamities were proposed in "theory," or as "matters of faith, [they] would be opposed as exceedingly inconsistent with the moral perfections of God; and the opinions of such as asserted them would be cried out against, as in numberless ways contrary to God's wisdom, his justice, goodness, mercy, etc." Edwards cited specifically

the innumerable calamities that have happened to poor innocent children, through the merciless cruelty of barbarous enemies; their being

122. *Ibid.*, 639.
123. Carse, *Edwards and the Visibility of God*, 156–158; Edwards, "Eternity of Hell Torments," in *Works*, IV, 275–276.

gradually roasted to death at the fire by Indians, shrieking and crying for
their fathers and mothers; the extreme pains they sometimes are tormented to death with, by some terrible diseases which they suffer; the
calamities that have many times been brought on whole cities, while
besieged, and when taken by merciless soldiers, destroying all, men,
women, and children, without any pity; the extreme miseries which have
been suffered by millions of innocent persons, of all ages, sexes, and
conditions, in times of persecution, when there has been no refuge to be
found on earth; yea, those things that come to pass universally, which all
mankind are subjects of, in temporal death, which is so dreadful to
nature, and which the human nature which God has made is so extremely
reluctant to.[124]

Given these facts, Edwards believed that the scriptural revelation of hell was
reliable and even though it is offensive to human sensibilities, was a better
indicator of the truth about God than the "seemings" of men.[125] As he had
said, what people are very averse to bear, they are equally averse to believe.
Hell is "terrible, and so seems shocking to the inward apprehension of their
minds." People call hell "shocking to common sense," but it is "no otherwise
so," Edwards said, "than as it is very opposite to common inclinations."[126]

124. "Endless Punishment," in *Works*, I, 642. In *Original Sin*, ed. Holbrook, 410, Edwards
took issue with the mitigation of infant damnation offered by Isaac Watts, who had suggested that
condemned infants suffer only temporal death, or annihilation, not eternal punishment. Edwards
replied that when one thinks of the torments sometimes borne by "poor little infants" in this
world, not much is gained by Watts's proposal. All of these softenings of the orthodox doctrine,
Edwards believed, relieve "nothing but one's *imagination*." They do not at all "relieve one's
reason." In other words, the problem of theodicy exists even without the doctrine of hell, because
of the natural evils experienced on earth. Edwards apparently felt that the doctrine of hell, rather
than obscuring the issues, clarified them. Watts wrote on the title page of his personal copy of
Edwards's *Sinners in the Hands of an Angry God*: "A most Terrible sermon, w[hi]ch should have
had a word of Gospell at the end of it, tho I think tis all true." Ola Elizabeth Winslow, *Jonathan
Edwards, 1703–1758: A Biography* (New York, 1940), 192.

125. Humanitarianism produces its own form of moral blindness. Two centuries of humane
rejection of hell may have contributed to Allied paralysis in doing almost anything to relieve the
plight of the Jews and others in Belsen, Auschwitz, and Treblinka. George Steiner in *Language
and Silence: Essays on Language, Literature, and the Inhuman* (New York, 1967), 159, has
written: "To *believe* the reports on Auschwitz . . . , to credit the statistical facts before such credence had become irrefutable and generally shared throughout the surviving world, was to yield
in some measure to the monstrousness of the German intent. Skepticism . . . had its part of
humane dignity and self-respect." A similar form of dignity and self-respect was certainly part of
the rejection of hell in the 18th century. Believing in hell was somehow to sanction it, to give in to
supposed clerical darkness. Yet, it is worth remembering that a theology that includes a hell cannot fail to have ever at its core the recognition of the persistence of evil in the world. The gospel
of humanitarianism seems to lack the intellectual categories to deal with evil when it is met, except in terms of the vain hope of eliminating it or episodically crusading against it.

126. "Endless Punishment," in *Works*, I, 642. There is a brilliant statement of the humanitar-

The Problem of Pity

It is safe to assume, I think, that the "common inclinations" Edwards had in mind were not only the personal dread and fear of physical pain, but also pity and compassion, or the allegedly innate and God-given aversion in most human beings to witnessing or inflicting pointless pain on others. Since the middle of the seventeenth century, philosophical interest in the sympathetic emotions had been growing steadily, until by the middle of the eighteenth century the question of the nature and significance of these emotions emerged as a subject of prime importance.[127]

The problem of pity, or compassion—the words were used interchangeably—was discussed in two main contexts, moral and theological. With regard to the former, the questions were about human nature and about ethics. To what extent may it be said that compassion is an autonomous and irreducible mechanism in human psychology? Was pity, as Hobbes said, simply an extension of the instinct of self-preservation, derivative from fear—the "imagination or fiction of future calamity to ourselves, proceeding from the sense of another man's calamities"—and thus lacking in moral authority? Was compassion, in any case, to be kept constantly subordinate to considerations of reason and prudence? Answered in the affirmative, this was the message of the entire Classical moral tradition.[128] In the context of theology, similar questions were asked about God. One, an old Scholastic problem that revived in the eighteenth century, was, In what sense can it be said that God has

---

ian position in Joseph Haroutunian's classic work, *Piety versus Moralism*, 30: "The new standards of justice and equity made it impossible to accept the facts of life as revelations of the will of God. It was no longer possible to accept events as divine decrees unless they measured up to the ethical principles which had come to constitute the standards of righteous human intercourse, and to which even the Creator and the Ruler of the universe had to conform. . . . Like the King in England, God had to justify His rule in and through His respect for the 'natural rights' of His subjects. . . . Sovereignty became permissible only when it was used for the comfort and the happiness of those on whom it was exercised."

127. See above, chap. 4, n. 109.

128. Cf. Plato, *The Republic*, X, 605–606, which warns against giving way to pity, and the well-known Stoic value of *apatheia*. John Ferguson, *Moral Values in the Ancient World* (New York, 1958) gives many examples of the expression of pity among the ancients, but he notes that it always existed in defiance of other greater values. See also James Jerome Walsh, *Aristotle's Conception of Moral Weakness* (New York, 1963). The Classical treatment of compassion was closely tied to a distinctly masculine conception of virtue. Even in the 17th century the Neostoics demeaned "womanish" emotions. The abandonment of Latinate culture is related to the inclusion of women in the world of learning, as Walter J. Ong has pointed out (see, e.g., Ong, *Rhetoric, Romance, and Technology: Studies in the Interaction of Expression and Culture* [Ithaca, N.Y., 1971], chaps. 1, 5, 11). There may also be a relationship between these developments and the new sanctioning of compassion as a moral force.

passions in any way comparable to the human sympathetic emotions?[129] And, more important, Among the attributes of God, how are His mercy and His justice balanced? In a widely known Origenist piece, *The State of Separate Souls* (London, 1735), written by Marie Huber and published anonymously, the author attempted to prove that God's justice and His goodness are falsely erected as antithetical notions. Goodness, Huber said, is "the Center of Justice" and its antecedent, whereas "severity" is not an essential part of the divine nature. The intention of God's punishments, therefore, is "always the Benefit and Advantage of those that are the Subjects of it." Huber set it down as an "incontestable" axiom about God that His "boundless Benignity . . . can never cease to will and actually do good to every Creature."[130]

These two general issues, the one pertaining to the place of pity in human nature, the other to its place in divine nature, were consciously wedded by the humanitarians, so that the answer to one stood or fell with the other. An unmerciful God would be likely to produce creatures for whom the character of virtue would be rigorous, severe, and unbending. On the other hand, a benevolent and compassionate God would implant in man natural impulses toward pity and compassion, impulses that He would put there only because He hoped to see reflected in humankind those sentiments that prevailed in His own nature. Conversely—and the following reasoning was at the very core of the philosophical and theological justification of the humanitarian movement —one can also begin with the evidence of human nature alone, and from the undeniable tendencies toward benevolence, sympathy, and compassion seen there, accurately judge God's intentions. In other words, the grand design of the universe, which the enterprise of natural theology, hand in hand with natural philosophy (or physical science), sought to uncover in the seventeenth and eighteenth centuries, was revealed authoritatively in certain of the characteristics of human psychology no less than in the motion of the planets. There

129. The paradox of God's passions, especially the nature of His love in comparison to human love, had been widely discussed already in the patristic period. A Harvard College commencement *quaestio* in 1723, answered in the negative by the master's candidate Thomas Smith, read: *"An dantur in Deo affectus Vere & proprie dicti?"* (Are there affections in God, truly and properly speaking?)

130. Huber's book was anonymously published in both French and English. My attribution comes from Walker, *Decline of Hell*, 40–41. The original French work was entitled *Sentiments différents des quelques Théologiens sur l'état des âmes séparées des corps* . . . (1731). I have quoted from the 50-page review and abstract in *Present State of the Republick of Letters*, XVI (1735), 326–358, 411–437, of the English translation, *The World Unmask'd: or, the Philosopher the Greatest Cheat* . . . *to Which Is Added, The State of Souls Separated from Their Bodies: Being an Epistolary Treatise, Proving by a Variety of Arguments, Deduced from Holy Scripture, That the Punishments of the Wicked Will Not Be Eternal* . . . (London, 1735). It is highly probable that Edwards had read all of the volumes of the *Republick of Letters*. On this point, see Fiering, "Transatlantic Republic of Letters," *WMQ*, 3d Ser., XXXIII (1976), 659.

could be no greater sanction for the reform of society along humanitarian lines than the discovery of the innate humanity of man, for this was a revelation equivalent to anything in Scripture, and, indeed, it was argued, was supported by much of Scripture. The argument for the natural goodness of human nature was on no one trait made more dependent than on the evidence of mankind's irresistible tendencies toward sympathy, pity, and compassion for others. Thus, on the exact status and nature of compassion hung questions of the greatest philosophical import.

In *The Religion of Nature Delineated*, William Wollaston summarized current thinking about the significance of compassion:

> There is something in *human* nature resulting from our very make and constitution . . . which renders us obnoxious to the pains of others, causes us to sympathize with them, and almost comprehends us in their case. It is grievous to see or hear (and almost to hear of) any man, or even any animal whatever, in *torment*. This *compassion* appears eminently in them, who upon other accounts are justly reckoned amongst the *best of men*: in some degree it appears in *almost* all. . . . It is therefore according to *nature* to be affected with the sufferings of other people and the contrary is *inhuman* and *unnatural*.[131]

Wollaston was writing in the intellectualist tradition and therefore qualified carefully the authority that might be attributed to this voice of nature. "Sympathy," he said, "ought not to be over-ruled, if there be not a *good* reason for it. On the contrary, it ought to be taken as a *suggestion* of nature, which should always be regarded, when it is not superseded by something superior; that is, by *reason*."[132]

Francis Hutcheson went even further than Wollaston in crediting the voice of the sympathetic emotions. His *Inquiry into the Original of Our Ideas of Beauty and Virtue* (London, 1725) was in many ways the culmination of the trend that made the emotions of compassion and pity authoritative in human nature. He was greatly indebted to Henry More, Richard Cumberland, Nicolas Malebranche, and Shaftesbury, among the moderns. God has shaped "the very frame of our nature" to feelingful benevolence, Hutcheson said. He considered this fact to be a great testimony to the divine element in human affairs. There is, he said, a "determination of our nature to study the good of others; or some instinct, antecedent to all reason from interest, which influences us to the love of others." The influence of compassion on human behavior is a leading trait that "strongly proves benevolence to be natural to

---

131. *Religion of Nature Delineated*, 139–140. Edwards read Wollaston's work in about 1734. See pp. 132–138, above.

132. *Religion of Nature Delineated*, 165.

us." Hutcheson reiterated the by then commonplace example, how "every mortal is made uneasy by any grievous misery he sees another involv'd in." Sounding much like Malebranche, whose work he knew well, Hutcheson wrote: "How wonderfully the constitution of human nature is adapted to move compassion. Our misery and distress immediately appears in our countenance . . . and propagates some pain to all spectators. . . . We mechanically send forth shrieks and groans . . . : Thus all who are present are rouz'd to our assistance."

Hutcheson made a particular point of disqualifying the authority of rational deliberation when human suffering confronts our senses. Considerations of reason are out of place when we witness human agony. Under such circumstances, the measure of the good person is to be found in the instantaneity of response, the unthinking, unreasoned animal (or spiritual) act of the virtuous soul. "Notwithstanding the mighty reason we boast of above other animals," Hutcheson wrote, "its processes are too slow, too full of doubt and hesitation to serve us in every exigency, either for our own preservation . . . , or to direct our actions for the good of the whole."[133] Hutcheson's *Inquiry* established implicitly an opposition between rational justifications for the infliction of pain and the divine authority of natural and instinctive compassionate feeling. Such an opposition inevitably redounded into the debate over the nature and existence of hell.

George Turnbull, a Scottish disciple of Hutcheson, directly exposed the crucial issue:

> Nothing can be more absurd than the doctrine which has sometimes been advanced; that goodness in God is not the same as goodness in men, but something of quite another kind and which we understand not. . . . The true notion . . . of the divine benevolence must be learned by considering what it is in man. And by augmenting the idea of a good man to boundless perfection, we arrive at the nearest conception that is possible for us to frame of the goodness of an all-perfect mind.[134]

133. *Inquiry into Beauty and Virtue*, 132, 137–140, 143, 176–177, 182, 195, 215–217, 245.

134. Turnbull, *Principles of Moral Philosophy*, II, preface. In vol. I, Turnbull wrote: "Indeed, it is as certain as that we have intelligent powers, and a moral sense implanted in us, that our Creator must have intelligence, and benevolent, generous affections towards public good. For if the contrary is supposed, then we are more perfect than our maker; then have we in our nature a better, a more noble disposition than our Author" (p. 204). Edwards read Turnbull in 1753. Cf. also, e.g., David Hartley, *Observations on Man, His Frame, His Duty, and His Expectations* (London, 1749): "It must be the will of an infinitely benevolent being that we should cultivate universal unlimited benevolence" (quoted by Sidgwick, *Outlines of Ethics*, 221). It is remarkable that the obscure Samuel Richardson had argued similarly as early as 1658: "It is not agreeable to the God of nature, to go contrary to the law of nature, that he hath written in mankind; there is planted in man an universal love to man, especially to their offspring, be they obedient or disobe-

According to Turnbull's reasoning and that of many other writers, human understanding of God's moral qualities is to be derived from what is known of human nature. If human nature is optimistically viewed as being irresistibly compassionate, then in God, too, compassion will be a quality so overwhelmingly important that eternal torment becomes unthinkable as a form of divine punishment.

This threat to the doctrine of hell was sufficiently serious by 1741 to lead Edward Wigglesworth, the Hollis Professor of Divinity at Harvard, to pronounce on it. He turned to the subject after reading some pamphlets from England that defended "Universal Redemption" on the basis, Wigglesworth said, of a "dangerous Deduction" from the consideration of divine mercy. Wigglesworth's tack was to distinguish sharply the divine attribute from its human counterpart. "When we speak of the Mercy of Men," he said, "we intend by it a compassionate painful sense of the Miseries we see others groaning under . . . , which excites us to endeavour to prevent those Miseries . . . and to deliver them from, or to relieve and comfort them under those miseries." God gave men and women this instinctive trait, that is, a "Readiness to shew Mercy to all that are in Misery" because human wisdom "reaches but a little way." If mankind was left to its "own Liberty in this Matter," many "Mischiefs both of a private and publick Nature" would result. In this area, man could not be trusted with freedom, for our "Disposition to Acts of Kindness and Mercy is many times too feeble," and our "angry Passions are not seldom too strong," for us to be "left to our own Discretion to shew Mercy, or to refuse it, when, and where we please."

The nature of God, however, is different. Wigglesworth, like Augustine and Edwards, denied that divine and human responsiveness to suffering are analogous. In order to give "a more lively affecting Sense of the Greatness of the Mercy of God," it is true the Scriptures represent the divine virtue as identical with the human, as though in God mercy is "attended with all that inward Commotion and uneasy Sensation, which we experience in ourselves upon the Appearance of an Object of Pity." But it is a grave mistake, Wigglesworth insisted, to use this scriptural rhetorical device as the basis of attributing the "Imperfections of human Passions to the Divine Nature." God experiences no "inward Disturbance or Uneasiness at the Misery of Creatures." Such emotions would be inconsistent with His absolute perfections, and "an Interruption of his perfect Happiness." Moreover, God is "absolutely free and

---

dient; what bounds of love is there in parents to their off-spring, when in misery, and to others in misery and want? Sure no man doth desire any man nor creature to indure the torments they speak of one year, much less their own offspring; how then may I, or can I, think so of God, to be lesse pitifull, lesse mercifull then cruell man to his off-spring? We are all his off-spring. . . . Sure God exceeds man in goodness." Richardson, *Discourse on Hell*, 169.

unconfined in his Acts of Grace and Mercy." He is not subject to the involuntariness or the passivity of any passion. In the end, Wigglesworth could offer no more to his auditors than the thought that men cannot question the divine government. We must simply accept as an unquestionable truth that "Mercy and Justice are both alike dear and essential to him."[135]

Wigglesworth espoused without criticism or modification, it should be noted, the pervasive claims of the benevolists concerning the function and significance of compassion in human nature. This fact should not be surprising when even so shrewd a critic as David Hume failed to probe beneath the superficial evidence. After reviewing the familiar facts—"that the very aspect of happiness, joy, prosperity gives pleasure; that of pain, suffering, sorrow communicates uneasiness. . . . Tears and cries and groans, never fail to infuse compassion and uneasiness"—the great philosopher remarked in a footnote:

> It is needless to push our researches so far as to ask, why we have humanity or a fellow-feeling with others. It is sufficient, that this is experienced to be a principle in human nature. We must stop somewhere in our examination of causes; and there are, in every science, some general principles, beyond which we cannot hope to find any principle more general. No man is absolutely indifferent to the happiness and misery of others. The first has a natural tendency to give pleasure, the second, pain. This every one may find in himself. It is not probable, that these principles can be resolved into principles more simple and universal.[136]

Another of the truisms of the benevolist school, in addition to the great weight given to compassion and sympathy, was the related belief, in Hume's words, that "absolute, unprovoked, disinterested malice has never, perhaps, place in any human breast."[137] Hutcheson had expressed the same opinion earlier.[138] For both men this notion followed from the conviction that human nature is instinctively benevolent and that a person will act that way unless this tendency is impeded or overridden by self-interest.[139]

In the middle of the eighteenth century, Jonathan Edwards appears to have been almost alone among philosophers of his sophistication in the skepticism

135. Wigglesworth, *Sovereignty of God*, 6–12.

136. Hume, *Enquiry Concerning the Principles of Morals*, ed. Selby-Bigge, 219n–220n. Edwards read Hume's *Enquiry Concerning the Principles of Morals* in 1755.

137. Hume, *ibid.*, 227.

138. "Human Nature seems scarce capable of malicious disinterested Hatred, or a sedate Delight in the Misery of others, when we imagine them no way pernicious to us, or opposite to our Interests." Selby-Bigge, ed., *British Moralists*, par. 96.

139. Hobbes also rejected the possibility of pure malice, but for a different reason than Hutcheson or Hume did, namely, that all human actions are governed by considerations of self-interest. Hutcheson and Hume held that men are governed either by self-interest or altruism, i.e., social interest. There was no room in the middle for disinterested malice.

with which he confronted the benevolist gospel.[140] These new teachings con-
flicted with the dogma of Original Sin and with the orthodox doctrine of hell.
Rather than taking refuge in the mere reaffirmation of the old Calvinist arguments about the sovereignty of God, Edwards waded into the humanitarian
tide, attempting to reverse its direction by force of psychological insight.
Edwards took it as his basic premise that natural men, those who are unregenerated by divine grace, are dominated in all of their actions by self-love,
or by direct derivations from self-love. Like Hobbes, the Jansenists, his
Calvinist predecessors, and a number of other pessimistic interpreters of
human nature in the previous century, Edwards was impressed above all by
the perniciousness of the natural tendencies in human nature, not their benignity. What was commonly called *natural* benevolence Edwards interpreted
as only the fragile restraint of God's common grace. Self-love alone, he said,
if it were the sole governing principle in the heart and lacking divinely given
restraint, would "dispose one to delight in anothers misery, because self-love
seeks its own comparative happiness or to diminish its comparative misery,
which is obtained in the depression of others." This comment was written in
about 1733, and it contained the germ of Edwards's basic critique of the
theory of the moral autonomy of pity or compassion: that these sympathetic
emotions, rather than being autonomous, nearly always function in relation to
certain other human emotions or tendencies, both as perceived in others and
as experienced within oneself.

Sounding perfectly Hobbesian, Edwards continued: "Self love will delight
in cruelty and putting others to pain because it appears to it as an exercise of
power and dominion." Power over others is expressed by being able freely to
afflict them, for everyone puts their own comfort and happiness first and will
only give them up if forced to. The more one is afflicted by another and
unable to resist or escape, the more the oppressor has demonstrated his power,
Edwards observed, because the greater the oppression is, the greater the
"incitement to the sufferer to shew his liberty, if he had it, in delivering
himself." Of course, except in the case of devils, who are indeed unrestrained
by God, all of this was purely theoretical, based on the hypothetical situation
in which self-love is the sole motivating principle.[141] But it should be remembered that the consideration of devils and angels allowed theologians to con-
trive psychological models, as it were, that isolated for separate examination

140. Dr. Samuel Johnson in England was another who was impatient with the prevailing assumptions about pity. "Pity is not natural to man. Children are always cruel. Savages are always
cruel. Pity is acquired and improved by the cultivation of reason" (James Boswell, *Life of Samuel
Johnson* [July 20, 1763], quoted in Henry Darcy Curwen, ed., *A Johnson Sampler* [Cambridge,
Mass., 1963], 243). Earlier, Bishop Joseph Butler, like Edwards, had introduced many qualifications that punctured some of the more excessive primitivist assumptions.

141. Miscellanies, no. 534.

various problems pertaining to human nature. According to tradition the devil is an inveterate and spontaneous enemy of God and of all goodness. "When he sinneth," Tobias Swinden wrote, "he sinneth from himself. He is not tempted to it by any other, but sinneth directly from the malicious depravity of his own will."[142] The devil is malicious without any superior "interest" behind it. He is perversity itself. For Edwards this represented a real and constant potentiality of man.[143]

Self-love for Edwards was the constant, or a hydra with many heads. The kind and social affections were the variables; they were essentially evanescent and had to be studied as such.[144] Nevertheless, Edwards did come to accept increasingly that "pity is an affection natural to men."[145] As he read more widely in eighteenth-century moral philosophy, the evidence appeared to be overwhelming. He made it his purpose, however, to elucidate its limitations, a tactic that would deny to the benevolist philosophers the vaunted claim that pity is representative of innate virtue or a proof of the goodness of human nature. Edwards also intended to remove from the arsenal of the opponents to the orthodox doctrine of hell the argument that the natural compassion of mankind was evidence of a divine benevolence that could never tolerate the administration of eternal torture.

Pity, Edwards pointed out, is no proof of benevolence or love to others, for people may pity those they have no love to, as long as they do not hate them. And even when one does hate the sufferer, pity is still possible, provided the

142. Swinden, *Nature and Place of Hell*, 2d ed., 280.

143. When it is remembered that the marquis de Sade began to write only a generation later, Edwards's convictions do not seem farfetched. "The utmost possible depravity we can in imagination conceive," Bishop Butler had remarked, "is that of disinterested cruelty" (*Sermons*, in Gladstone, ed., *Works of Butler*, II, 24). One of the problems of the age for the defenders of the orthodox doctrine of hell, as we have noted, was demonstrating that God and the saints and angels in heaven, calmly and disinterestedly contemplating the torture of human souls in hell, were not paradoxically in the role of devils. William Blake would later make this exact charge, condemning to hell for their lack of forgiveness all of the clergy who preached the traditional doctrine. In the preface to his *Sermons*, Bishop Butler took Shaftesbury to task for asserting that "it is malice only, and not goodness, which can make us afraid." In reality, however, Butler replied, "goodness is the natural and just object of the greatest fear to an ill[willed] man. Malice may be appeased or satiated; humour may change, but goodness is a fixed, steady, immovable principle of action. . . . Danger of future punishment (and if there be danger, there is ground of fear) no more supposes malice, than the present feeling of punishment does." Edwards, of course, agreed completely with Butler. On disinterested cruelty in man, see the profound comments of Dorothea Krook, *Three Traditions of Moral Thought* (Cambridge, 1959), 115*ff*. Edwards did not investigate disinterested evil, which in theory does not spring from self-love or self-interest. To this extent he may himself have been a prisoner of his century. In the 17th century the "mystery of iniquity," such as the devil's inexplicable rebellion, was a subject of greater interest, as it would become again in the 19th century in Melville.

144. Hutcheson argued contrarily that goodwill is the constant.

145. Miscellanies, no. 821, printed in Townsend, ed., *Philosophy of Edwards*.

sufferer's misery "goes beyond" one's hatred. In short, pity, according to Edwards, "is a painful sensation in us arising from the sight or sense of misery in others that is disproportionable to our disposition towards them." Rather than being a specific revelation of God's moral standards, the phenomenon of pity is actually one corollary of a more general psychological rule: "Wherever there is a disproportion between our disposition towards others and the state we see them in, it has a tendency to excite uneasiness in us, let that disposition be what it will."[146] In cases where pity is not involved, the same rule applies: when we see those happy that we do not love, or when their happiness exceeds our love, or when their misery is less than our hatred, we feel envy. On the other hand, Edwards continued, "when we see those miserable that we don't hate, or when their misery exceeds our hatred, or when their happiness is less than our love, it excites our pity." In all cases, however, the emotion is relative to the self. Far from being an absolute moral standard, pity is no better than envy with regard to its origins in self-love, though as compared to envy it is socially more acceptable and useful.

In many instances, Edwards reflected, "the workings of a man's heart are so mysterious that it . . . may be difficult to give an account how such and such things should arise from self-love." But he took it as an article of faith that however much a natural man may appear to love others " 'tis some way or other as appendages and appurtenances to himself." A spiritual man, on the other hand, "loves others as of God, or in God, or some way related to Him."[147]

The specific application of Edwards's general rule was fairly obvious. Pity is proportional to the sense of the goodness or wickedness of the sufferer. When we know of horrid things committed by some person, let us say torture inflicted on an innocent child by a monster of cruelty who pays no regard to shrieks and cries, "when we hear or read of such things, we have a sense of the evil of them. . . . Hence it seems just, and not only so, but every way fit

146. Miscellanies, no. 821. In his conception of the dynamic relationship between pity, on the one hand, and love or hate toward the sufferer, on the other, Edwards was partly anticipated by Hobbes. But Hobbes did not introduce a psychological rule of equivalent generality to Edwards's. See Hobbes's *Human Nature, or the Fundamental Elements of Policy. Being a Discovery of the Faculties, Acts, and Passions, of the Soul of Man* . . . , in William Molesworth, ed., *The English Works of Thomas Hobbes of Malmesbury*, IV (London, 1840), 44–45. Similarly, Hutcheson had already noted that pity is extinguished in certain cases: (1) when the sufferer is imagined evil (though, he said, "it is almost impossible for us to be unmov'd, even in that Case"); (2) when "advantage," i.e., self-interest, leads us astray; (3) when we are overcome by a sudden passion of hatred or anger (though "when the Passion is over, [pity] often returns"); and (4) when "Another disinterested View may even in cold blood overcome Pity; such as Love to our Country, or Zeal for Religion" (Selby-Bigge, ed., *British Moralists*, par. 156). Edwards took the same evidence and interpreted it quite differently.

147. Miscellanies, no. 821.

and suitable, that God should inflict a very terrible punishment on persons who have perpetrated such wickedness. . . . The reason is that we have a sense of the evil of their conduct."[148] For the Christian to overcome his inability to accept the reality of the eternal misery of hell, an adjustment in sensations is required so that the right proportions are reached. Objections to hell arise, Edwards wrote, because of "a want of a sense of the horrible evil of sin. . . . We hant sense enough of the evil of sin to stir up indignation enough in us against it to balance the horrour that arises from a sense of the dreadfullness of [the condemned person's] suffering[.] This makes us pity the sufferer and this raises objections against God."[149] There can be little doubt that Edwards's description of the psychological process required before one could fully accept the doctrine of hell was drawn from personal experience. A sense of "the horrible evil of sin" and the "beauty of vindictive justice" went together.[150]

Edwards's reflections on the sympathetic emotions and their meaning were largely a reaction to Hutcheson. Edwards's personal notes reveal that in the 1750s he pored over Hutcheson's *Inquiry* and his *Essay on the Nature and Conduct of the Passions and Affections with Illustrations on the Moral Sense* (1728),[151] learning from and agreeing with much of it, but also looking for openings to turn Hutcheson's own reasoning and evidence against his naturalistic and generally optimistic conclusions. Edwards's best observations about pity were usually no more than twists or modifications of what could be found in Hutcheson in whole or in part. Hutcheson wrote: "To a sedate temper, no misery [of others] is farther the occasion of joy, than as it is necessary to some prepollent happiness in the whole."[152] Edwards commented on this passage:

> It would be worth while particularly to examine this matter, and inquire, whether there be not something in the natural sense of desert, which God has implanted in creatures that are moral agents which tends to acquiescence in the pains or suffering of the ill-deserving, not merely from a natural desire of good to ourselves or others, or good to the universal system, but as what a sense of desert naturally tends to, as a gratification of that sense.[153]

148. Edwards, "Eternity of Hell Torments," in *Works*, IV, 268. See also Miscellanies, no. 866.

149. Miscellanies, no. 866.

150. Miscellany 866, written in the first person, reveals something of this personal development. See also Edwards, "Eternity of Hell Torments," in *Works*, IV, 268: Natural men fail to see "the suitableness of eternal punishment to the evil of sin; they see not that eternal punishment is proportionable and no more than proportionable to the demerit of sin."

151. Edwards used the third edition of the latter title.

152. *Nature and Conduct of the Passions*, 77.

153. Miscellanies, no. 1356, printed in *Works*, I, 641.

In other words, compassion may be directly balanced in our emotional structure not only by larger considerations of justice and reason but also by the God-given "sense of desert." The saints in heaven, we can assume, have this sense very strongly.[154]

Hutcheson noted, as did Edwards later, that "our desire of the positive good of others, is weaker than our aversion to their misery."[155] Edwards made a point of emphasizing that the aversion to the misery of others, or compassion, thus operates independently of benevolence, which detracts from compassion's claim to virtue.[156] Yet Hutcheson was not aiming at that conclusion. The Scottish moralist wanted to stress only that the universal measure of innocence, if not of virtue, is that one does not increase the misery in the system in general, and that men do not "positively condemn those as evil, who will not sacrifice their private Interest to the Advancement of the positive Good of others, unless the private interest be very small, and the publick good very great."[157] Edwards, of course, insisted on higher standards than these for determining innocence.

But as to what constituted virtue, Edwards and Hutcheson were agreed in an abstract and formal way: the "sacrificing all positive interests, and bearing all private Evils for the publick Good: And in submitting also the interests of all small systems to the interests of the whole."[158] Their agreement broke down over the question of the degree of affection that is due to God, whom Edwards made the absolute summation of "the whole," and to whom all systems and all private affections are subordinate. On this point Hutcheson shilly-shallied at length, but ultimately condemned the theological approach: "Men may use names as they please, and may chuse to call nothing virtue but what is intended chiefly to evidence Affection of one kind or other toward the Deity. . . . But let them not assert, against universal experience, that we

154. See my analysis of Edwards's notion of the "sense of desert" in chaps. 2 and 3, above. Edwards's idea of this sense as a counterweight to compassion was probably influenced by Bishop Butler's discussion of it in his "Dissertation of the Nature of Virtue," appended to the *Analogy of Religion*, which Edwards read in 1752.

155. Hutcheson, *Illustrations on the Moral Sense*, 318.

156. The difference between the merely involuntary response of compassion and an act of true benevolence, or what might be called philanthropy, was also stressed by Dr. Samuel Johnson. Compassion of this sort, Johnson said, "if ever it be felt at all from the brute instinct of uninstructed nature, will only produce effects desultory and transient; it will never settle into a principle of action, or extend relief to calamities unseen in generations not yet in being" (*The Idler*, no. 4, quoted in Curwen, ed., *Johnson Sampler*, 243). For the benevolists, however, it was the purity or disinterestedness of involuntary compassion that was important, whereas benevolence or philanthropy in Johnson's sense is extremely liable to adulteration from motives of self-love, such as pride and vanity.

157. Hutcheson, *Illustrations on the Moral Sense*, 319.

158. *Ibid.*

approve no actions which are not thus intended toward the Deity." For it is plain, Hutcheson reaffirmed, that "a generous compassionate heart, which, at first view of the distress of another, flies impatiently to his relief, or spares no expence to accomplish it, meets with strong approbation from every observer, who has not perverted his sense of life by school-divinity, or philosophy."[159] The exercise of human compassion retained for Hutcheson its crucial revelatory significance, even in the face of contrary theological reasoning.

Edwards's *Dissertation on the Nature of True Virtue*, published posthumously, was in large part directed against Hutcheson and the other benevolists, and contained Edwards's final comments on the problem of pity. Edwards accepted here, again, that pity is an affection natural to mankind, and that it has some similarity to virtue in that it is general in its exercise, rather than particular; that is, a compassionate soul responds supportively to *any* other human in distress. More limited "particular instincts," on the other hand, such as familial and parental love, and sexual love, which were also often cited as evidence of human sociality, are by comparison extremely selective in their exercise. But at its root, Edwards insisted, pity, too, was "owing to a particular instinct." The rarity of a "truly virtuous pity" must be acknowledged, Edwards said. Generalizations about *all* mankind are not admissable. The pity that arises from a "truly virtuous divine principle of general benevolence to sensitive beings" is not of the type that we find "natural to mankind in common."[160]

In his effort to depreciate the significance and authority of pity as a natural moral element in human character, Edwards presented three arguments, which he intended to have a cumulative effect. First, he observed, despite some of the claims made by secular moralists, a generalized concern for physical suffering is not necessarily present in the usual forms of pity and compassion. Most compassionate responses are highly specific. Most people are hardly moved at all by the thought of the total anguish of mankind throughout the ages. Pity seems, in fact, to be tied directly to present sensations. "Some would be moved with pity by seeing a brute-creature under extreme and long torments," Edwards noted, "who yet suffer no uneasiness in knowing that many thousands of them every day cease to live, and so have an end to all their pleasure."[161]

Second, true benevolence, as virtually all moralists admit, means properly the desire that others will be happy. Yet pity is so far from benevolence or from real goodwill on the part of men that its concern is only with extreme

---

159. *Ibid.*, 332–333.

160. *True Virtue*, ed. Frankena, 80.

161. *Ibid.* Hobbes had dismissed all pity as reducible to fear and self-love. Edwards accepted that *some* pity was a genuine irreducible emotion roughly analogous to virtue, but he sharply contained and limited its significance in human nature.

pain. We may greatly pity those who are deeply suffering whose "positive pleasure" we could be "very indifferent about." As Edwards had argued earlier, a man may be "much moved and affected with uneasiness" at the sight of someone in pain, "who yet would be affected with no sensible joy in seeing signs of the same person's enjoyment of very high degrees of pleasure."[162] Sympathy with the pains and happiness of others, in other words, does not necessarily run the whole spectrum of the other person's experience, but may be confined to only one place on the scale.

Finally, Edwards returned to the psychological law that hitherto he had stated only in his private notebooks. Pity is not only generally independent of positive benevolence, it is also perfectly compatible with true malevolence, or with "such ill will as shall cause men not only not to desire the positive happiness of another, but even to desire his calamity." We feel pity only toward the sufferings of those whose calamity goes beyond our hatred. "A man may have true malevolence towards another, desiring no positive good for him, but evil; and yet his hatred not be infinite, but only to a certain degree. And when he sees the person whom he thus hates in misery far beyond his ill will, he may then pity him: because then the natural instinct begins to operate."[163] Where malevolence leaves off, pity begins. Edwards thus tried to demonstrate that pity is essentially a relative feeling, the subjective expression of what constitutes *excessive* suffering in another, not an absolute standard of goodness, and not necessarily deserving of universal approbation. Under this assumption, the stupendous hatred toward the damned that is felt in heaven would always be great enough to overbalance the natural instinct to pity. And the challenge to the orthodox doctrine of hell arising from the natural fact of compassion is diverted into the question of why men do not hate sin more, rather than of why God seems to lack mercy.

Compassionate humanitarianism, then, Edwards regarded as a "particular instinct" rather than as a form of true virtue. The main function of pity, by God's design, is simply the preservation of mankind. It does not reveal the inherent redemption of human nature outside of the Christian dispensation. It cannot be used as a weapon against the doctrine of hell. It shows us only, Edwards said, that God did not intend to make life on earth, be it ever so sinful, one of punishment; and that God had "made a merciful provision of relief in extreme calamities."[164]

When we review the evidence compiled here on Jonathan Edwards's relation to the doctrine of hell, several different leads point to the conclusion that Edwards's obsession with hell was inseparable from his overwhelming sense

162. *Ibid.*, 81.
163. *Ibid.*, 82.
164. *Ibid.*, 83.

of sin. It was the weight of sin that he must have felt personally to a nearly un-
bearable degree and that he urgently wanted his brethren to feel, although Edwards himself apparently lived with the joyful sense of his own salvation.[165]
Sin and hell went together in his experience and they were linked in theory.
Most of what he had to say about hell turned on the matter of sin. It was the
enormity of sin that justified hell; the enormity of sin that was revealed in the
conversion experience; the enormity of sin that cancelled out psychologically
all pity for the damned; and the enormity of sin that made hell preaching an
urgent concern if his listeners were to be rescued from their perilous condition. Yet by 1750 sin was also a highly metaphysical and elusive quality in
theories of human nature, which is nowhere more apparent than in Edwards's
treatise *Original Sin* and in *The Nature of True Virtue*, both written at almost
the same time in the middle 1750s. If Edwards succeeded in defending the
orthodox conception of hell (within the terms of the religious argument), the
same cannot be said of his defense of the doctrine of sin, and without a
convincing conception of sin all teaching concerning hell was dubious.

165. In his autobiographical "Account" (see n. 20, above), Edwards wrote: "I have often . . .
had very affecting views of my own sinfulness and vileness. . . . I have had a vastly greater sense
of my own wickedness, and the badness of my heart, since my conversion, than ever I had before.
It has often appeared to me, that if God should mark iniquity against me, I should appear the very
worst of all mankind; of all that have been since the beginning of the world to this time: and that I
should have by far the lowest place in hell." Hopkins, *Life of Edwards*, in Levin, ed., *Jonathan
Edwards*, 36–37.

Morality and Determinism

The knowledge of ourselves
consists chiefly in right apprehensions concerning
those two chief faculties of our nature, the understanding
and will. *Both are very important: yet the science of the latter*
must be confessed to be of greatest moment; inasmuch
as all virtue and religion have their seat more
immediately in the will, consisting more
especially in right acts and habits
of this faculty.[1]

If Edwards was to make a convincing case for the superiority of Christian virtue over the concepts of moral virtue proclaimed in the eighteenth century by secular philosophers, he had to demonstrate that his theology, which would necessarily provide the foundation for such a Christian virtue, was not in itself antithetical or offensive to conventional ideas of morality. Thus, while Edwards defended the doctrine of Original Sin, he also attempted to show that its existence did not preclude the achievement of a degree of civic morality. As we have seen, he maintained that through merely natural understanding, plus self-love, minimal virtue was attainable, despite the Fall. He needed to show, too, that the orthodox doctrine of an afterlife with reward and punishment was an enhancement of natural morality, despite Shaftesbury's complaint that disinterested virtue was undermined by such teaching. Edwards was also able to argue against Hutcheson that the only proper and lasting foundation of virtue is an inner disposition that, on the model of Christian charity, consents to being in general—in effect, God—rather than to any more restricted, earthly end, no matter how universal.

If there were other such obstacles to be overcome in the course of establishing a system of morality that would be compatible both with Calvinist religious principles and with the concepts of secular philosophy, none was potentially more of an impediment to Edwards's goals than the widespread

1. Edwards, *Freedom of the Will*, ed. Ramsey, 133.

belief that strict adherence to the doctrine of divine sovereignty, including predestination, vitiated moral accountability in both human and divine affairs. If it is true that "freedom of the will" must be presupposed before one can think of human beings as moral agents who can legitimately be held responsible for their wrongdoings, then the religious system to which Edwards was committed was clearly unsuited to practical life, and Edwards's ambition of formulating a new religious ethics would be defeated. Edwards was certainly not prepared to give up his belief in absolute divine governance and predestination, including the doctrine of physical influx of the Holy Spirit at conversion, but he also was not convinced that such determinism, when properly conceived, interfered with conventional moral institutions. Indeed, he turned the argument around and asserted that any other assumption would be detrimental, not only to Christian virtue but even to natural morality.

The New England Background

Questions concerning the nature of the will—its relation to the faculty of understanding or intellect, to passions and emotions, to the theory of universal natural causation, to divine omnipotence and absolute decrees, to divine foreknowledge, to inclinations, habits, and choice, to the Fall of Man and the origin of evil, to the highest good and the apparent good, and to moral responsibility—were continuously subjects of discussion in the seventeenth century and, of course, for centuries before, going back to the church fathers. But at different times and in different places, certain issues appear to have been more important than others, although nearly all of the many questions about "the will" or "willing" were more or less connected to each other. Edwards's 1754 *Enquiry into the Modern Prevailing Notions of that Freedom of Will, Which is Supposed to be Essential to Moral Agency, Vertue and Vice, Reward and Punishment, Praise and Blame*, possibly the most elaborate treatise on the subject written in the eighteenth century, is remarkable for its extensiveness and for the variety of controverted questions it considers in both theology and philosophy. But also notable is the particular emphasis of the work evidenced in its title, the problem of accountability, which had not been a matter of central concern in the seventeenth century.[2] Edwards's father,

2. The problem of causality (imputability) in relation to punishment (accountability) was not entirely ignored over the centuries and had been discussed by the ancient philosophers, but Edwards's work represents an acute concern with the subject, which began with Hobbes's work. Richard McKeon, "The Development and Significance of the Concept of Responsibility," *Révue Internationale de Philosophie*, XI (1957), 7–10, observes that it was not until the mid-19th century that one can find philosophic explorations of the concept of "responsibility" as such. The word itself may have been first used, curiously, by Alexander Hamilton in *Federalist* no. 64. The

Timothy, in 1694 had asked as his master's *quaestio* whether the so-called liberty of indifference was the essence of free will. Scores of such *quaestiones* and theses concerning the will had been debated at Harvard in the seventeenth century, but few of them, if any, expressed worry that the traditional forms of religious determinism brought into doubt the meaningfulness of reward and punishment, praise and blame. Something had happened by the mid-eighteenth century to bring the topic Edwards addressed into the limelight.

Debates over the will, in sum, took many forms, occurred in a variety of contexts, and were fought out on a number of different levels. What was taken for granted in one period was actively under suspicion in another. The sheer multitude and complexity of answers that could be given to the old question of how the will is related to the intellect, or how the act of willing is related to knowledge or knowing, is exemplified in a 1703 article in the popular *Athenian Oracle*, "How does the Understanding Move the Will?" Eight different answers were recounted, ranging from the assertion that the two faculties can be distinguished conceptually but are in fact "one and the same Thing," to the opinion that "the Will depends not any way on the Intellect, and consequently is not mov'd by it." In between were stated such opinions as that "the Intellect and the Will are two different Faculties, yet there is such a Dependance between them, that the one can do nothing without the other, and they communicate mutual Assistance," and the belief that " 'tis not needful that the Intellect shew the Will its Object; but the Man's seeing it, is sufficient to cause him to move himself by his Will towards the Good he apprehends."[3]

Edwards inherited from seventeenth-century Protestant Scholasticism a number of his ideas about will—many more certainly than he got from reading John Locke's *Essay Concerning Human Understanding*—and it will be useful, first, to sketch this legacy. The diverse schools of thought at Harvard in the seventeenth century, where one finds reflected most of the major divisions in the wider republic of letters, may be reduced to three primary groups: Thomist-intellectualist; Scholastic-voluntarist; and Augustinian-voluntarist. In most if not all cases, contrary to what is sometimes asserted, the sophisticated defenders of these positions had a unified view of the human psyche and human functioning and did not fall into the kind of naive hypostatization of the faculties that Locke and others later attacked. A "faculty" of the mind was understood to be a power or capacity, and the study of the will meant the

---

term "responsible," as distinguished from "responsibility," was used earlier, but "accountable" was more common.

3. *Athenian Oracle*, 415–421. This answer in the *Oracle* was possibly written by John Norris of Bemerton. The introductory sections of Anthony Collins's *A Philosophical Inquiry Concerning Human Liberty* (London, 1717) contain a brief review of the controversy over the will, with quotes from dozens of authors, ancient and modern.

study of the act of willing, election, or choice. There was, however, the problem that the same word "will" could be used to describe several different kinds of psychological phenomena. Three different terms in Aristotle's ethics —*hekousion*, meaning voluntary actions; *boulesis*, meaning that tendency of the soul that regards the end or goal; and *proairesis*, meaning preference or choice—were translated into English as the word "will" or its cognates.[4]

A good representation of the Thomist-intellectualist view is found in a notebook originally belonging to a Harvard student named William Partridge, which came into Edwards's possession in about 1718.[5] The will, Partridge copied, is a human disposition or quality by which man freely desires the good known by the intellect.

Thomist-Intellectualist

> Even as the understanding is occupied in the knowledge of good and bad; so the will is busied in desiring of that [which] is good, but known by the understanding, whence the rational appetite is called, [whereby] it is differenced from the sensitive appetite, [which] proceeds not from the understanding, but from the sense. . . . The understanding shows to the will, [what] is to be embraced and [what] to be rejected: then the will desireth and governeth [those] inferior faculties, to wit, the sensitive and locomotive appetite. . . . The good [which] the will desireth is either good really or apparently, for as the understanding judgeth, so the will desireth: Sometimes it judgeth that good [which] is evil . . . ; so the will [in that case] desireth [what is] part of man's misery. Here the rule is: the error of the will follows the error of the judgment.[6]

The understanding shows to the will what is to be embraced or rejected. The will itself is never culpable in the case of moral error, since it only follows the judgment of the intellect. The will as the rational appetite is supposed to govern the lower sensitive appetites, although it may happen that unruly vehement appetites from below will obscure rational judgment and thus influence choice wrongly. The will by its nature (or, better, man by his nature) always desires the good, but the power of willing relies on intellect to determine what is good in any given case.

The intellectualist position was often represented by the dictum that the choice of the will is determined by the last judgment of the practical intellect. For those belonging to this school of thought, the will itself was assumed to be inherently blind, lacking in cognitive function entirely, moving only as an

---

4. For 18th-century awareness of this problem, see Grove, *System of Moral Philosophy*, ed. Amory, 157–158.

5. See chap. 1, nn. 55 and 56, above.

6. Partridge may have been copying from Henry Gutberleth's *Physicae, hoc est, naturalis philosophiae* (Herborn, 1613; 2d ed., 1623).

aspect of intellect. The will is the intellect as acting, the conative side of human rationality. Without information from the intellect, "the will is not the will, but a confused appetite."[7]

Intellectualists were generally untroubled by the problem of free will. Although opponents charged that the dependence of the will on the intellect is a curtailment of the absolute liberty of will that is man's special inheritance, the intellectualists defined freedom in terms of man's rationality. Through reason, human beings, like the angels and even God, are enabled to act by "counsel," not "coaction" (in the terminology of the time), and are thus lifted above the bondage of animals, who are governed by biological instincts and lower appetites. Because of his capacity for understanding, man is self-actuating and spontaneous, a voluntary creature who is free insofar as he is guided by persuasion of mind rather than external constraints or inner compulsions. In this tradition, it should be noted, one could not speak of the will itself as being free, since willing is only a power of the mind dependent upon understanding for meaningful action. But one could assert that the mind is free and that the individual is self-determining as a whole person.

What happens, however, when a person succumbs to the government of his passions or his sensitive appetites? Was intellectualism a schema that applied only to angels, or to Adam before the Fall? Can the human being in a corrupted state, governed by concupiscence, still be considered free? The intellectualists generally maintained that the "slave of the passions" is not free in the highest sense, but still his actions are voluntary and morally accountable in that he continues to be moved by internal forces, intrinsic to his rational nature, and not by outside coercion. The Fall was believed to have darkened the understanding so that again and again the intellect represents inferior objects to the will as good objects of choice. But despite this impairment in the understanding and the failure of the will to be altogether subservient to the intellect, the Fall did not restructure the whole psychological relationship between will and understanding. Fallen man, although corrupted, is still expected to govern himself by rational appetite (that is, by a will obedient to right reason) and is culpable for his misdeeds. Only those lacking altogether in rational understanding were considered blameless—idiots, young children, madmen, and brutes.

Defining freedom by the two conditions of rational deliberation and the absence of external constraints on thought and action, the intellectualists saw no irreconcilable problems in ascribing responsibility for actions. Neither the dictatorial rule of the intellect over the will, nor the aberrant breakdown of internal order and the temporary domination of lower appetites, was considered grounds for non-accountability.

7. Thomas E. Davitt, *The Nature of Law* (St. Louis, Mo., 1951), quoting Albert the Great.

With regard to theology, God's foreknowledge and omnipotence, as well as his decrees, were as problematical for this conception of human freedom as for all others. But as Pierre Bayle had said, the revelation of hell is itself the greatest proof of human freedom, for without it, hell would be a punishment (without hope of reformation) for a wrong that could not have been avoided. In other words, divine punishment itself implies freedom, however understood.[8] Moreover, if one leaves aside the special problem of justice in God's condemnation of sinners in the afterlife, divine prescience and government are not necessarily a problem in human affairs. In a world assumed to be controlled by God, where every action is the result of divine will, determinism becomes a universal constant that can be ignored for practical purposes, since it applies to all events whatsoever: the criminal's vicious deed, his apprehension in the name of the law, the judge's sentence, the movement of the executioner's axe. Difficult problems of responsibility may be raised, on the other hand, when a different sort of determinism is proposed, such as naturalistic theories of environmental causation, which enable one to argue that society is partly responsible for a criminal's misdeeds because it allowed him to be exceptionally neglected in his development from infancy to adulthood. But such theories were only just coming into fashion in Edwards's day. In the eighteenth century justice was administered without compunction, despite the theology of predestination and God's sovereignty, as long as it was assumed that the person under trial knew right from wrong, that is, was a moral (rational) agent. Edwards himself defined a moral agent in these intellectualist terms, although, as we will see, such a definition was probably inconsistent with his analysis of the nature of the will. A moral agent, he wrote, has "a moral faculty, or sense of moral good and evil, or of such a thing as desert or worthiness of praise and blame, reward or punishment; and a capacity . . . of being influenced in his actions by moral inducements or motives, exhibited to the view of understanding and reason, to engage in conduct agreeable to the moral faculty."[9]

The Thomist-intellectualist school was in the majority among both Protestants and Catholics. The leading competing point of view, the Scholastic-voluntarist, also had its origins in the Middle Ages, if not earlier, and is often associated with the name of Duns Scotus. The Scholastic-voluntarists maintained that human beings retain a freedom of will beyond even the freedom of unconstrained intellectual judgment and action. It was questionable, according to this group, that human freedom could be distinguished from the free-

Scholastic voluntarist

8. Bayle's point is noted in James O'Higgins, *Determinism and Freewill: Anthony Collins' "A Philosophical Inquiry Concerning Human Liberty"* (The Hague, 1976), 14.

9. *Freedom of the Will*, ed. Ramsey, 165.

dom (or lack of it) of animals if one went along with the intellectualists. For the choices of animals, too, when they are not subject to external constraints, are governed by internal necessities only, rather than mechanical causation.[10] Man's freedom, then, must consist in a liberty to will in opposition to any preceding influences from the soul. Any internal necessities, including those of reason, may be considered restrictions on freedom nearly as much as external compulsions. The freedom that on earth was alleged to be unique to man was typically illustrated by the story of Buridan's ass. This poor creature, placed equidistantly between two loads of hay perfectly equal in their attractive power to sensitive appetite and indiscernible one from the other by intellect, died of starvation because it was unable to find any basis for making a choice. According to the voluntarists, human beings would also starve to death in such a situation if the intellectualist model of choice is correct. Hence the need to attribute to the human psyche an imperial will that can move of itself, or not move, as it chooses.

On the deepest level, as a scholar has recently explained, the Scholastic-voluntarists believed that it is man's nature as a creature to be able to find ultimate happiness only in God, the highest good; consequently, the will of a person, his or her intellectual inclination, is always oriented toward this end. Consciously or unconsciously, every other possible object of desire is known to be only a limited good that can confer but partial happiness. To this universe of objects which are less than God, man is ultimately indifferent, for none of these lesser things can be seen as "necessary to happiness." Hence the will is not necessitated in relation to any of them. Animals lack this so-called "liberty of indifference" because they lack innate knowledge of God.[11]

In the sixteenth century the Jesuits became the main defenders of the liberty of indifference. Through the tremendous influence in the next century on both Catholics and Protestants of Francisco Suarez's *Metaphysical Disputations* (1597), which argued the case for the self-determining will, this form of voluntarism was frequently espoused and, along with other opinions, taught even at Harvard College in the seventeenth century.[12]

10. Aristotle in his Eudemian ethics had contrasted external causation with internal causation and included appetites and reason in the latter without differentiation. In other words, the actions of animals could also be construed as voluntary. See Harry Austryn Wolfson, "St. Augustine and the Pelagian Controversy," in Wolfson, *Religious Philosophy: A Group of Essays* (Cambridge, Mass., 1961), 172–173; this essay originally appeared as "Philosophical Implications of the Pelagian Controversy," American Philosophical Society, *Procs.*, CIII (1959), 554–562.

11. O'Higgins, *Determinism and Freewill*, 16. O'Higgins also realizes that the "liberty of indifference" has been diversely interpreted.

12. For a review of the debates at 17th-century Harvard, see Fiering, *Moral Philosophy at Seventeenth-Century Harvard*, chap. 3. On Suarez's teaching see Thomas Urban Mullaney, *Suarez on Human Freedom* (Baltimore, 1950). The Jesuit position was sometimes referred to as Molinism.

There were a number of subtle variations in the Scholastic-voluntarist position, but to review them all here would involve us in needless complexity. One important distinction stands out, however, and needs to be mentioned if we are to understand the eighteenth-century debate. Some disputants held that the will had "liberty of exercise" only, which meant the liberty simply to act or not to act, in effect a liberty to suspend action, but not a liberty to choose its own objects. Others argued, more radically, that the will had both liberty of exercise and liberty of specification, that is, the option not only to act or not to act, but also the ability to bypass the intellect altogether in supplying the objects of choice. In Humphry Ditton's *A Discourse Concerning the Resurrection of Jesus Christ*, for example, which Edwards read in the 1720s, the author argued for both liberty of specification and exercise:

> The Resolutions of the Understanding, even the most sound and positive ones, impose no manner of Necessity on the Will: For even the *last Dictate* itself is but one of the Prerequisites to Action, and leaves the Will an intire and perfect Dominion over its own Act; which it may therefore either proceed to exert, or may suspend and forbear, by its own native Liberty. . . . Our liberty extends here, not only to acting or not acting, but also to the exerting of specifically different or contrary Acts: We can chuse or refuse, chuse this or the contrary, as well as chuse or suspend the Act of Choice.[13]

It can be seen that Scholastic-voluntarism implicitly assigned to the will some cognitive functions, and particularly so when liberty of specification was claimed as well as liberty of exercise. Ditton was aroused partly by the threat of Hobbesianism, and, as we will see, the dangers posed by materialist determinism led a number of writers to refurbish Suarezian notions of freedom for eighteenth-century use.

Finally, we come to the Augustinian-voluntarists, for whom the concept of will encompassed not just the idea of a mental faculty but also the entire tendency or orientation of the personality. The term "heart" was used almost interchangeably with that of "will," since the meaning of "will" was enlarged to include the whole soul. "The Heart in the Scripture is taken for the whole rational Soul," wrote the Puritan theologian John Owen. For the heart has the capacity to "see, perceive, to be wise, and to understand; and on the contrary, to be blind and foolish; sometimes such as belong properly to the Will and Affections, as to Obey, to Love, to Fear, to Trust in God."[14]

13. Humphry Ditton, *A Discourse Concerning the Resurrection of Jesus Christ* . . . , 3d ed. (London, 1722), 90.

14. John Owen, Πνευματολογια: or, *A Discourse Concerning the Holy Spirit* (London, 1674), 181, hereafter cited as Owen, *Pneumatologia*.

The Augustinians were explicitly determinist with respect to the doctrine of predestination and God's direct influence on human destinies, but anti-determinist, in a sense, with respect to the intellectualist thesis that the will follows the last dictate of the understanding. In other words, the Augustinians denied the dependence of will on understanding—the will is free in its relations with the other faculties of the higher soul—but insisted instead on the will's utter submissiveness to innate or infused propensities, such as the habitude of concupiscence or the influence of divine grace. Because in this scheme the will as *proairetic*, as the actualizer of choice, was minimized, one could hardly speak in terms of the will as *agent* at all. Hence it is not surprising that the Augustinians identified the will with the passions and affections, particularly love. The will functioned as *patient* (that which is acted upon) more than as agent. It is clear that the Augustinian-voluntarists were less concerned about the philosophical implications of Scholastic theories of freedom than they were about the religious heterodoxies (if such they may be called) of Pelagianism and Arminianism; hence their emphasis on man's essential helplessness and his dependence on divine aid.

According to Augustinian-voluntarists, a person's will or heart must be oriented either toward God or toward self. In his *Treatise Concerning Religious Affections* Edwards spoke of a fountain with many channels running from it representing "the various faculties, principles and affections of the human nature." "If there be sweet water in the fountain, sweet water will from thence flow out into those various channels; but if the water in the fountain be poisonous, poisonous streams will also flow out into all those channels. So that the channels and streams will be alike, corresponding one with another; but the difference will lie in the nature of the water."[15]

Yet this group of voluntarists also often asserted that human beings have the capacity to achieve a unique degree of freedom. This was not, however, the freedom of the intellectualists, which came simply from taking thought or exercising reason, or the freedom of the Suarezians, which required a self-determining will, but the freedom that results from obedience to divine law and unity with the will of God. It is the freedom described by Luther in his famous address on Christian liberty, the freedom from servitude to sin and material lusts. The Augustinian-voluntarists' main concern was not with the kind of liberty that some considered to be an essential precondition of virtuous action, but with the liberty that *resulted* from virtue. They gloried in the bond-

m Luther

15. *Religious Affections*, ed. Smith, 150–151. Edwards wrote in the same paragraph: "As from true divine love flow all Christian affections, so from a counterfeit love in like manner, naturally flow other false affections. In both cases, love is the fountain, and the other affections are the streams." On the unity of affections and will, see *ibid.*, 97. On the two opposed loves, see also Edwards, *Original Sin*, ed. Holbrook, 231.

age of the will to divine grace and claimed that this bondage paradoxically conferred the only liberty worth having.

A good representative of Augustinian-voluntarism is Theophilus Gale, whose *Court of the Gentiles*, published in England in 1677, was one of the best-known books in New England and read by Edwards sometime before 1746.[16] Gale's compendious work attempted to do many things, but two of its most important functions were to bring Cornelius Jansen's *Augustinus* to the attention of English readers and to attack Pelagianism.[17] "Such therefore as the disposition of the Wil is," Gale wrote, "such wil the action prove as to its goodness or pravitie. The bent of the Wil is as a Pondus that carries the whole Soul either to good or bad: when the deliberation and intention of a bended Wil concurs in a good matter for a good end, the action is good. . . . So many degrees as there are of sanctified Wil in any Act, so many degrees there are of a moral Good therein."[18]

In the tradition of the Reformed pietists and the Jansenists, Gale, like Edwards later, denied that ostensibly moral acts, such as those of the pagans, constituted real virtue. "There is no real moral virtue but what is supernatural."[19] And in the achievement of real virtue, the human will "is a mere passive, though vital, instrument as to the reception of divine influences, albeit it be active as to its own operation." "Al[l] virtue and Beatitude come from free Grace: he that is not acted by divine Grace, is necessarily acted by carnal lust."[20]

Liberty under these circumstances does not consist "in having a varietie of objects to adhere to, and take complacence in," but in an individual's absorption in God. Volition can either exist as a means to an end or be directed itself to the highest end. Everything is willed either for itself or for some other end. For Gale, the love and will (they are the same) of a virtuous person must terminate in God as the only end worth desiring entirely for its own sake. Such a love confers freedom the more it approaches to God, for the soul thereby takes on more of the characteristics of the very standard of all free-

16. Edwards cited Gale in *Religious Affections* and in his Miscellanies. Gale, the leader of an important English dissenting academy, left a large part of his library to Harvard College. He is discussed in Fiering, *Moral Philosophy at Seventeenth-Century Harvard*, chap. 6.

17. "None have been more bold and successful in the Roman Church, for the overthrowing this proud Pelagian idol, than pious and great Cornelius Jansenius, and his Sectators. . . . It is, or ought to be the great wonder of pious souls, that in this Age, wherein so many Professors of the Reformed Religion have turned their backs on the Doctrine of Free-Grace, and imbibed so many Pelagian infusions, which are the very vital spirits and heart of Antichristianisme, God has raised up, even in the bosome of Antichrist, Jansenius and his Sectators. . . . O! what matter of admiration will this be unto al Eternitie?" Gale, *Court of the Gentiles*, Pt. III, 147.

18. *Ibid.*, Pt. IV, 60.

19. *Ibid.*, 74.

20. *Ibid.*, 92, 151.

dom, God Himself. "Herein consists the Libertie of al Creatures, . . . that we are thereby made more free in the service and fruition of God; by subjecting our selves and al inferior goods to God, . . . we gain dominion over our selves and al things else."[21]

The Augustinian-voluntarists placed particular emphasis on the complementarity, rather than the contrariety, of freedom and necessity. Power to sin, the free choice of evil, according to this analysis, is a diminution of liberty, not an increase of it. Jesus' impeccability, the impossibility of his sinning, "far from destroying libertie," is the perfection of it. "The sweetest and highest libertie is to have no power to sin." Thus, "the connexion between Pietie and Libertie" in man "is so intimate, as that indeed they have one and the same beginning, progresse, and consummation."[22] Obviously, the "blessed necessity" to do good, as exemplified by God or Jesus, was not the sort of necessity that removed the basis for praise and blame or moral accountability in general. Therefore, the Augustinians, like the intellectualists, did not believe that the postulation of a self-determining, causally unbound will was a prerequisite for holding human acts morally accountable, or deeming them praiseworthy or blameworthy.

To summarize, for many centuries, although there were religious and philosophical doctrines and dogmas that could be interpreted as being completely inimical to human freedom, such that individuals could not be held morally responsible for their actions, all schools of thought protested that no such nihilistic fatalism was implicit in their beliefs. The absolute liberty of willing that the Scholastic-voluntarists claimed was essential to the dignity of human nature was rejected by the other schools (those that claimed only a relative freedom of willing) as being illogical, impious, untrue, and, most important, unrequired.[23] St. Augustine did not shrink even from the accusation that he was a fatalist in the pagan mode, provided such fatalism was not associated with astrology. God determines all, but man remains a free agent.[24]

---

21. *Ibid.*, 23.

22. *Ibid.*, 90, 76.

23. Wolfson, "Augustine and the Pelagian Controversy," in Wolfson, *Religious Philosophy*, introduces the distinction between relative and absolute freedom of willing.

24. Wolfson, *ibid.*, maintains that Augustine's teaching was simply "a Christianization of the pagan Stoic doctrine of fate" (p. 176). Dugald Stewart remarked that it is not surprising so many church confessions assert both divine government and human freedom, for the ancient Stoics, who were professed fatalists, also believed in free agency and defended both notions together, providing a model for this kind of paradoxical assertion. Hamilton, ed., *Works of Stewart*, I, 575.

Hobbes

A major and unprecedented change in the elements of the free will debate occurred in the 1650s with Thomas Hobbes's publications and later with Spinoza's. For the first time in the Christian era an entirely naturalistic determinism was argued that made no effort to differentiate sharply the causation of human behavior from that which interconnected the world of mere physics. For Hobbes, the various defenses of human liberty—cause by counsel, the self-determining will, or the imitation of divine love—were all equally nonsensical. Human liberty referred only to the absence of external constraints, not to any emancipation from the chain of universal, natural, physical causation, and Hobbes accepted, too, without demurrer, that such a causal system brought into question some of the traditional justifications for reward and punishment and praise and blame.

It is highly improbable that Edwards ever read a word by Hobbes, even though he occasionally referred to Hobbesian ideas. (Hobbes's thought was more widely broadcast by the huge number of works written to refute him than it could ever have been by direct transmission.) But it is impossible to make sense of what happened in the eighteenth century that led to Edwards's *Freedom of Will* without understanding something of Hobbes's effect on British thought. Moreover, Edwards's theory of the will resembles Hobbes's in many of its features (partly through the influence of Locke, who had borrowed heavily from Hobbes), but there were also decisive differences, such as Edwards's deep convictions about supernatural infusions of grace (a type of "cause" that Hobbes could hardly accept), and Edwards's belief in "moral necessity" as distinguished from "natural necessity."

Although Edwards's *Enquiry into the Modern Prevailing Notions of Freedom of Will* was written almost exactly a century later than Hobbes's *Of Liberty and Necessity*, the ghost of Hobbes could not be easily exorcised. On at least five occasions in his *Freedom of Will* Edwards referred to Hobbes, always to make the same point, which was that even if his own ideas, or Calvinist notions on the will in general, did sound like Hobbesian materialist determinism, he did not care, for truth is truth wherever it is found. Edwards noted that Daniel Whitby, one of his chosen opponents in *Freedom of Will*, attempted to discredit Calvinism by claiming that its doctrines, in defining liberty as merely the power of doing what one wills, were the same as Hobbes's.[25] He also noted that Isaac Watts, another opponent, charged that the religious determinists (such as Edwards) "introduce Mr. Hobbes's doctrine of fatality and necessity, into all things that God hath to do with."[26]

25. *Freedom of the Will*, ed. Ramsey, 191–192.
26. *Ibid.*, 375. Edwards was quoting from Watts's *An Essay on the Freedom of Will in God, and in Creatures* (London, 1732).

Edwards anticipated that *Freedom of Will* would be received by those who "valued themselves on the supposed rational and generous principles of the modern fashionable divinity" with the "usual exclamations" about "the 'fate' of the heathen, 'Hobbes' necessity,' and 'making men mere machines.' "[27] It was clearly with some impatience that toward the end of his book he expostulated: "As to Mr. Hobbes' maintaining the same doctrine concerning necessity; I confess, it happens I never read Mr. Hobbes. Let his opinion be what it will, we need not reject all truth which is demonstrated by clear evidence, merely because it was once held by some bad man. . . . If Mr. Hobbes has made a bad use of this truth, that is to be lamented: but the truth is not to be thought worthy of rejection on that account."[28]

Hobbes discarded the ancient Scholastic notion of the will as a distinctive rational appetite and reduced all human motivation to variations on sensitive appetite (basically the quest for pleasure) and its alternative, fear. The "alternate succession of appetite and fear during all the time the action is in our power to do or not to do" is all that can be meant by "deliberation" in Hobbes's view. And in deliberation, the last appetite or the last fear before acting is what is ordinarily called "will." So-called "willing," then, is only the last act of this rather mindless deliberation. Any action that follows from such deliberation may be called voluntary. Those acts that spring from passions or appetites directly, without deliberation (for example, impulsive or impetuous acts), are not called voluntary, "for they proceed not from, but are the will." The will itself, which is identical to human passions, affections, and appetites, cannot be called voluntary, as though it would be possible to will to will. "A man can no more say he will will, than he will will will, and so make an infinite repetition of the word *will*; which is absurd." Will to do is appetite; will to omit is fear. The causes of appetites and fears are potentially many, including threats of punishment and promises of rewards to follow from any actions. Thus willing may be influenced by ideas, opinions, and other mental phenomena.[29]

In a short treatise, *Of Libertie and Necessitie* (London, 1654), written in reply to an attack on his determinist system by John Bramhall, the bishop of Londonderry, Hobbes introduced a number of key distinctions that are also later found in Edwards's *Freedom of Will*. An action is free, Hobbes argued, if one is free to do the thing one does, whatever it may be; that is, that which one may do, if he has the will to do it, or forbear, if he has the will to forbear

27. *Freedom of the Will*, ed. Ramsey, 430.

28. *Ibid.*, 374. Edwards went on to say that in his opinion the Arminians were in greater agreement with Hobbes than the Calvinists were, because the former reject orthodox conceptions of Original Sin, infused grace, the necessity of supernatural illumination, and the doctrine of justification by faith alone.

29. Thomas Hobbes, *Human Nature*, in Molesworth, ed., *Works of Hobbes*, IV, 68–70.

it, is a free action. But such freedom does not exclude a necessity governing the willing or not willing. "The question therefore is not, whether a man be a *free agent* that is to say, whether he can write or forbear, speak or be silent, according to his *will*; but whether the *will* to write, and the *will* to forbear, come upon him according to his *will*, or according to anything else in his own power. I acknowledge this *liberty*, that I *can* do if I *will*; but to say, I can *will* if I *will*, I take to be an absurd speech."[30]

Hobbes dismissed the distinction between liberty of specification and liberty of exercise, and also that between natural and moral efficacy, as Scholastic jargon. But he wisely avoided attempting to delineate too finely the exact nature of causation in human actions. His argument included points in favor of both psychological determinism (that every human action is motivated by a preceding psychic cause) and metaphysical determinism (that everything that happens in the universe is part of an ineluctable cause and effect sequence). It is not alone God's foreknowledge and omnipotence, not the stars, not any simple chain or concatenation, not the last dictate of the understanding, and not "the physical or moral efficacy of causes" that individually influence election, but "the sum of all things which now being existent, conduce and concur to the production of that action hereafter, whereof if any one thing now were wanting, the effect could not be produced."[31] Hobbes indicated that he did not find it objectionable for this "concourse of causes" to be called the decree of God, since everything in existence has been set and ordered by God, the eternal cause of all things. As for the last dictate of the understanding, Hobbes emphasized that though it may be part of the cause of an action, it cannot be the whole cause. It may be said to produce the effect necessarily only in the same way that "the last feather may be said to break a horse's back, when there were so many laid on before as there wanted but that one to do it." It is a mistake, he observed, to think of any one "simple chain or concatenation" as the cause of an action, rather than an "innumerable number of chains, joined together, not in all parts but in the first link of God Almighty."[32] It

30. Hobbes, *Of Libertie and Necessitie*, *ibid.*, 240. In Scholastic discussion the liberty to do as one willed, in effect freedom from constraint in one's actions, was often called "liberty of spontaneity." This type of freedom was contrasted with liberty of indifference or liberty of volition, which referred to liberty in choosing. Philosophers of the 20th century make the same distinctions using different words. J.M.E. McTaggart distinguished between "freedom of self-direction," which is liberty of spontaneity, and "freedom of indetermination," which is liberty of volition. Maurice Mandelbaum speaks of "freedom in action" and "freedom in choice." See Mandelbaum, "Determinism and Moral Responsibility," *Ethics*, LXX (1959–1960), 204–219.

31. *Libertie and Necessitie*, in Molesworth, ed., *Works of Hobbes*, IV, 246.

32. This enormous complexity in the causation of human choices makes prediction virtually impossible, we may observe, and to that extent gives the illusion of freedom; and insofar as prediction is the beginning of control, may even be said to give the reality of it.

should be noted, too, that not only the final "willed" action is necessitated, but also all of the preliminary propensions that preceded the action.

Hobbes, like Edwards, did not hesitate to use the word "free" to describe all actions that result from "deliberation," even though the ultimate choice of the agent might have been conditioned or caused by prior events. It could be said, then, that for Hobbes the process of deliberation is the criterion of freedom, which is, in effect, to say that all sentient creatures, those capable of an alternation in their appetites or passions, are free agents. The boundaries of the order of free creatures were extended down the chain of being to include most animals, it would seem, and rationality was thus abandoned as a measure of freedom. Children, after a certain degree of awareness is reached, and madmen, too, could be considered free agents. It is notable that Hobbes, like the intellectualists and the Augustinian voluntarists, did not concede that the term "free agent" could have no applicability in his system. He, too, believed that freedom (restrictively defined) and necessity are compatible. "Liberty," Hobbes maintained, "is the absence of all the impediments to action that are not contained in the nature and intrinsical quality of the agent."[33]

The general question that in the next century was most urgent to Edwards, as indicated by the full title of his *Freedom of Will*, was put earlier to Hobbes by Bramhall. Indeed, the modern concern with the reconciliation of necessity with reward and punishment, praise and blame, probably dates from the formulation of the issue in the exchange between Hobbes and Bramhall. If Hobbes's doctrine is true, Bramhall said, the laws prohibiting any action will be unjust; consultations in vain; admonitions to people of understanding of no more use than to children, fools, and madmen; praise, dispraise, reward and punishment, all in vain.[34] Hobbes's reply to some extent relied on his own contractual theory of government and his positivist conception of the law, but he also was able to make a number of telling logical points. Regarding the justice of laws prohibiting criminal actions, and the appropriateness of punishment, under conditions when it is assumed that all actions are necessitated, Hobbes, like Edwards later, argued simply that laws are directed against the will or desire to break the law, not against "other precedent causes of action."
"What *necessary* cause soever precede an *action*, yet if the action be *forbidden*, he that doth it *willingly* may justly be punished." He observed, too, that both the existence of the law and the existence of condign punishments for infractions of the law are facts that themselves enter into the complex of precedent causes and thus serve as deterrents to crime. "The intention of the law," Hobbes argued, "is not to grieve the *delinquent*, for that which is past,

33. *Libertie and Necessitie*, in Molesworth, ed., *Works of Hobbes*, IV, 273.
34. *Ibid.*, 252.

and not to be undone; but to make him and others *just*, that else would not be so, and respecteth not the evil act *past*, but the *good to come*." Without this good intention for the future on the part of judges, "no past act of a delinquent could justify his killing in the sight of God."[35] The execution of a criminal is justified only by its deterrent effect on others.

As for consultations, admonitions, and so on, it is consultation "that *causeth* a man, and *necessitateth* him to *choose* to do one thing rather than another." To argue that such persuasions are vain under a system of determinism is to say that causes themselves, which necessitate effects, are in vain. One hopes that admonition will enter into the conditions that motivate the action or the forbearance of the action. People misconceive the meaning of necessity, Hobbes pointed out, by assuming that there is some sort of fixed sequence that will occur no matter what interventions take place. But for any action for which there is a necessity that it shall be done, or for any effect that shall necessarily come to pass, there are also causes that are "necessarily requisite as a means to bring it to pass," and such causes are often consultation, admonition, and other interventions.[36] Praise and blame have utility in a similar fashion to law, punishment, and admonition, and hence are not incompatible with the principle that all actions are necessitated. Moreover, it is a simple empirical fact that necessitated actions are often considered praiseworthy, as when we praise the deeds of a person who is believed to be so good by nature that he or she could do nothing less. Hobbes did not invoke the traditional example of praise of God and angels, who are necessarily good, but his point was the same.

It should be observed about Hobbes's system that it had basically metaphysical, not empirical, foundations. He made no pretense of being able to trace the sequence of causes and effects in human behavior, as though one were studying the impact and consequence of a collision of billiard balls, where all the vectors and forces could be analyzed and results accurately predicted. His most fundamental principle was the axiom that every effect must have a sufficient cause, which is not unlike Leibniz's principle of sufficient reason and Edwards's position. A sufficient cause, Hobbes argued, is also a necessary cause, for it is *impossible* by the definition of "sufficient" that a sufficient cause will not produce the effect that follows. If a sufficient cause cannot but produce the effect, it also produces it necessarily. Thus, whatever is produced is produced necessarily.[37]

In the writing of history, we may observe, it is also assumed that every

35. *Ibid.*, 252–253. Hobbes did not maintain that it was morally just to condemn a person in a determinist system, but simply that it was practical and useful. Edwards, however, defended reward and punishment on grounds other than mere utility.

36. *Ibid.*, 255. Cf. n. 156, below.

37. *Ibid.*, 274–275.

event has a sufficient cause, even though we dare not claim to know enough about historical causation to predict what will happen next. The principle of the sufficient cause is applied retrospectively. After the event we search for a pattern of causes from which it seems the event had necessarily to follow. However, both in human psychological experience and in historical events, the present is usually experienced as a moment of contingency, when we are free agents who can bring about undetermined, unnecessitated effects. Hobbes did not believe that this testimony from experience called for an abandonment of the doctrine of necessity. When we see and know the passions or temptations that move us, Hobbes commented, we are often willing to acknowledge "necessity." "But when we see not, or mark not the force that moves us, we then think there is none, and that it is not *causes* but liberty that produceth the action." Our ignorance, Hobbes wrote, ought not to be the occasion of giving up the "certain truth, that there are certain and *necessary causes* which make every man to *will* what he willeth, though he do not *yet conceive in what manner* the will *of man* is caused."[38] It seems evident that Hobbes was, in large part, expounding an article of faith; indeed, it was the new scientific faith, based on materialism and the principle of universal causation, that Galileo's great discoveries in mechanics could be expanded to include the world of humanity.

One final observation of Hobbes's deserves notice, for it was also to be a major argument in Edwards's *Freedom of Will*. If it were true, Hobbes said, that what men will is ungoverned by necessary causes, it would follow that they could frustrate God's purposes, His decrees, even His prescience, and then God might "*foreknow* such things shall be, as shall never be, and *decree* that which shall never come to pass."[39] It is the doctrine of necessity, therefore, that is essential to religious institutions, not the doctrine of free will. But the popular belief was otherwise, and defenders of liberty, like Samuel Clarke, felt that free will was an essential presupposition of religion and morals and, like the doctrine of hell, had to be believed by the common people lest anarchy ensue.

The Clarke-Collins Debate

In Samuel Clarke's famous Boyle lectures of 1704 and 1705, published as *Demonstration of the Being and Attributes of God* (1705) and *Discourse Concerning the Unchangeable Obligations of Natural Religion, and the Truth and Certainty of the Christian Revelation* (1706),[40] he directed much of his

38. *Ibid.*, 265, 270.
39. *Ibid.*, 278.
40. The bibliographical history of these popular and influential works is complicated by the

energy against Hobbesian materialism and what Clarke viewed as Hobbesian nihilism. He also recognized as a major anti-religious evil of his time the spread of Hobbesian and Spinozistic type determinism, that is, the promulgation of a metaphysics and a moral psychology that appeared to annul human responsibility and undermine human dignity. Hobbes's work was a threat to the entire inherited religious and philosophical structure.

Although prior to Hobbes there was a significant free will debate (perhaps more often theological than philosophical), the questions and concerns, as we have noted, were typically of a different nature. Earlier, man's unique place in the natural order was rarely questioned; a liberty of choice, considered necessary to make morality meaningful, was universally believed in; even the debates between Augustinians at the extreme end of determinism and Jesuits at the extreme end of libertarianism took place within certain accepted limits regarding divine government and human responsibility. The Calvinists had consistent difficulty with the theology of foreordination, but in the end the problem remained simply a troublesome divine mystery.[41]

Hobbes changed all this. What he did, in effect, was to bring determinism into bad repute, even though a moderate and carefully qualified Aristotelian-Thomist determinism had been majority opinion for centuries. Prior to the seventeenth century, as some of the defenders of determinism (including Edwards) were quick to point out, atheism had been associated mainly with radical freedom of will, because such a combination was found historically in Epicureanism. On the other hand, the most religious, the most theistic, and the most respected of the ancient sects, the Stoics, were acknowledged fatalists. Determinism, therefore, did not seem to be particularly threatening. After Hobbes, however, to avow even a traditional determinist point of view was to be suspected of holding an opinion that led inevitably to atheism and materialism.

When Clarke entered the lists with his Boyle lectures he contributed to the dialectic that ensued by arguing for what seemed to be a more extreme liber-

---

publication in 1711 of the two books together under a single title that merged words from each: *A Discourse Concerning the Being and Attributes of God, the Obligations of Natural Religion, and the Truth and Certainty of the Christian Revelation*. There were four editions of this combined volume by 1716. See James P. Ferguson, *The Philosophy of Dr. Samuel Clarke and Its Critics* (New York, 1974).

41. The careful balancing of God's will and man's will in the following quote from Owen, *Pneumatologia*, 273, is representative of 17th-century Puritanism and also of Edwards and others in the 18th century: "The Will in the first *Act* of Conversion . . . *acts* not but as it is acted, moves not but as it is moved, and therefore is *passive* therein. . . . The Acting of Grace in the Will in our Conversion is *antecedent* unto its own acting; though in the same instant of time wherein the Will is *moved*, it moves, and when it is *acted*, it acts it self, and preserves its own Liberty in its exercise." This unity of acting and suffering is possible because the Holy Spirit "in his Power and Operation is more intimate . . . unto the Principles of our Souls than they are to themselves."

tarian position than had been typical of Protestantism at any earlier time.[42] A few years later in 1717, when the known deist and materialist Anthony Collins published his *Philosophical Inquiry Concerning Human Liberty*, which undertook to refute Clarke along the lines of Hobbes's determinism, and Clarke answered him in the same year,[43] the subject became increasingly "politicized," so to speak. Although the issue was inherently resistant to simple formulas, and many views entered into the discussion, it seems that one of the reasons the free will position was growing in popularity was that it appealed to men who saw it as the most effective answer to materialism, atheism, and nihilism. Thus, when Edwards undertook at mid-century to restate the arguments for necessity, he was opposing not just a fashionable Arminian theology, which after all was nothing new in 1754, but also a relatively recent philosophical aversion to determinism in some quarters. To argue for determinism, Edwards discovered, was to run the risk of being classified with Hobbes, Spinoza, and Collins.

Writing early in the nineteenth century, Dugald Stewart was struck by how much in "his view of the subject, and, indeed, in the very selection of his premises," Collins's *Philosophical Inquiry* "anticipated" Edwards's major work on freedom of will.[44] Collins ("one of the most obnoxious writers of his day to divines of all denominations," according to Stewart) was no less eager than Edwards to "reconcile his metaphysical notions with man's accountableness and moral agency," Stewart noted, and the similarity in the work of the two men was such, Stewart believed, that Clarke's reply to Collins in 1717 was "equally applicable" to Edwards's book. Believing that Clarke's defense of freedom was irrefutable, Stewart "regretted" that Clarke's *Remarks* on Collins's *Inquiry* "seem never to have fallen into the hands of this very acute and honest reasoner," that is, Edwards.[45] The implication was, of course, that if Edwards had read Clarke's *Remarks* on Collins he could never have written such an errant book as his *Enquiry into Freedom of Will*.

Stewart was probably correct in his belief that the Clarke-Collins debate of 1717 shaped much of the argumentation thereafter, but Edwards's work on the will was sharper, more consistent, and far more copious than Collins's. In addition, because of Edwards's well-formulated occasionalist theory of causa-

---

42. Clarke's theory of free will was actually somewhere in the middle, since an even more extreme libertarian position was advanced a little earlier by William King, archbishop of Dublin, in *De Origine Mali* (Dublin, 1702); this work was published in English as *An Essay on the Origin of Evil*, trans. Edmund Law (London, 1731).

43. Samuel Clarke, *Remarks upon a Book, Entituled, "A Philosophical Enquiry Concerning Human Liberty"* (London, 1717).

44. The "coincidence" was so close, Stewart believed, that the outline of the plan of Collins's book could serve as the preface to Edwards's. Hamilton, ed., *Works of Stewart*, I, 307.

45. *Ibid.*

tion, he was immune to some of the most effective blows Clarke was able to deliver against Collins's system, a fact that Stewart failed to notice. Yet there were stronger arguments in Clarke's work than in that of any of the adversaries Edwards set up for himself in his *Freedom of Will*, and as we will see, it is questionable that Edwards came fully to grips even with the arguments that he found in Clarke's *Demonstration*. If he had also read Clarke's *Remarks* on Collins, he would have been stiffly challenged, and, at the least, his work on the will would have been more squarely in the mainstream of debate.[46] That he did not get around to reading Clarke's attack on Collins is one instance when Edwards's provincial location was responsible for a treatise a little less relevant than it might have been otherwise.[47]

Since many of the elements in the Clarke-Collins debate are encountered again in Edwards's *Freedom of Will*, which we will be turning to below, there is no need to review this exchange in detail. Only a few points need to be brought out. Collins appraised the problem much as Edwards did later. He believed that arguments of logic strongly supported determinism, but men defended the free will position in spite of such arguments because they feared that determinism subverted moral accountability and therefore reward and punishment, praise and blame, religion and laws. If it could be shown, he reasoned, that the doctrine of necessity is truly compatible with accountability, all people would willingly accept it.[48]

Like Edwards, too, Collins maintained that the intellectualist principle held by many libertarians—that the will follows the last judgment of the understanding and that people always choose what appears to be the better of two alternatives—is already a determinist psychology that "yield[s] up the question of liberty to their adversaries, who only contend, that the will or choice is always determin'd by what seems best."[49]

Edwards, however, had a much better comprehension of the philosophy of morals than Collins, who, like his close friend Locke, saw virtue and vice primarily in terms of social conventions and hedonism.[50] Collins believed, too, like Hobbes, that it was only necessary to justify punishment on the

---

46. Edwards did make the following reference in his "Catalogue" in *ca*. 1750: "A Philosophical Enquiry Concerning Liberty & Dr. Samuell Clark's remarks on this Book. These two advertised at the End of Dr. Clark's Scripture Doctrine of the Trinity." But there is no evidence he ever got the book and read it. The "Catalogue" is in the Beinecke Lib., Yale Univ.

47. It seems that Edwards also never read the Leibniz-Clarke correspondence *(A Collection of Papers, Which Passed between the Late Learned Mr. Leibnitz, and Dr. Clarke in the years 1715 and 1716 . . .* [London, 1717]), which Clarke himself edited for publication after Leibniz's death and where he also descanted at some length on his philosophy of the will.

48. Collins, *Inquiry Concerning Human Liberty*, 24. This edition is conveniently reprinted in facsimile in O'Higgins, *Determinism and Freewill*.

49. *Ibid.*, 111.

50. *Ibid.*, 90.

grounds of deterrence and the protection of society. When a man "does a crime *voluntarily*, and his punishment will serve to deter others from doing the same, he *is justly punished for doing what* (thro' strength of temptation, ill habits, or other causes) *he could not avoid doing*."[51] Edwards held, on the contrary, that retributive punishment, too, could be justified in a determinist universe, and he was unwilling to think of punishment solely in utilitarian terms, even with the doctrine of necessity.

Throughout almost the entire length of his book, Collins never mentioned Clarke as either an opponent or a supporter of any of his ideas. But on almost the last page, he made bold to cite some of the material in Clarke's *Demonstration* as an example of how "those who assert liberty in words, deny the thing, when the question is rightly stated." Clarke's use of the principle that the will is governed by the judgment of intellect and, more specifically, his analysis of "moral necessity" as contrasted with "physical necessity" unwittingly reinforced the determinist thesis, Collins believed. And Clarke's "authority," Collins said, "is equal to that of many others put together, and makes it needless to cite others after him."[52]

Clarke's reply, provoked by Collins's use of his name, was much fuller than the brief analyses of will in his Boyle lectures, and it seems, too, that he introduced a rather different theory than he had presented in the *Demonstration*. If one cannot say that he settled the question in his own favor (it is clear the philosophical controversy over freedom and determinism can never be put to rest), he did succeed in exposing the weaknesses in Collins's work. Perhaps more important, he so organized the issues that readers found themselves faced with a real choice of sides or of philosophical and religious commitments, with determinism presented as much the inferior. Collins, he said, probably did not even know what "he has all this time been pleading for."[53] In Collins's necessitated world, Clarke said,

> a sort of a Machine of Government might be carried on, by such Weights and Springs of Rewards and Punishments, as Clocks and Watches (supposing them to feel what is done to them) are rewarded and punished withal; yet in truth and reality, according to this Supposition, there is nothing intrinsically good and evil, there is nothing personally just or unjust, there is no Behaviour of rational Creatures in any degree acceptable or unacceptable to God Almighty.

Clarke believed that in the world system implied by determinism, "superstition and bigotry" flourish, for only by "persuading Men to look upon them-

51. *Ibid.*, 95.
52. *Ibid.*, 111–112.
53. Clarke, *Remarks*, 44.

selves as rational Creatures, and [implanting] in their Minds rational Notions of Religion" can these errors be rooted out.[54]

According to Clarke's formulation of the doctrine of liberty, the alternatives are stark: either man is like a clock or a watch, that is, wholly a patient (that which is acted upon), or he is a true agent, an actor, with the power of self-motion. Neither side can be finally proved, but "if there be no such thing in nature as a *Self-moving* or *Active Power* or *Principle of Beginning Motion*, (which is the Essence of *Liberty*;) then there is, in the Motions of the Universe, an infinite progression of dependent Effects without any [first] Cause at all; an infinite progression of passive Communications, without any Agent, without any thing Active at all in Nature."[55] The alternative view is to believe (Clarke, like Hobbes, was proposing an act of faith) that there is a first cause, some original self-moving power, namely God, and if one believes that God is a true agent (His freedom is entailed by the recognition of His existence) then one can believe, too, that God has bestowed on mankind a similar power of liberty. The argument for determinism based on the principle of universal causation is "entirely founded upon the *Supposition*," Clarke said, "that there neither is nor can be in Nature any such thing as a Self-moving Power at all."[56] But all of life—Clarke argued that animals, too, were free—belied this supposition.[57] Clarke's very rhetoric created an atmosphere that made determinism a shameful ideology.

Clarke defined will as the only real source of action. Everything else is passive. Reasons and motives, any mental occurrences ("abstract notions" in Clarke's terminology), cannot move a human body any more than they can ring a bell. They may be the occasion for action, but the immediate and efficient cause can only be a real substance, and this active substance is that in which "the Principle of Self-Motion inheres."[58] The will is not the last judgment of the understanding, although that event may be called will; the will is the action that follows the judgment, if, in fact, such action does follow. In any case, if action does follow it is not necessitated in a *physical* way by any prior event. Will, for Clarke, is like the mystery of life itself. One might call it spirit, although he does not use that word. The notion is both primitive and yet very sophisticated at the same time. "When we say, in vulgar speech, that Motives or Reasons Determine a Man; 'tis nothing but a mere Figure or Metaphor. 'Tis the *Man*, that freely *determines himself* to act."[59]

54. *Ibid.*, 45.
55. *Ibid.*, 30.
56. *Ibid.*, 28.
57. "Every *Action*, every Motion arising from the Self-Moving Principle, is *essentially free*" (*ibid.*, 27). Men differ from animals in having consciousness of good and evil, not in being free.
58. *Ibid.*, 26.
59. *Ibid.*, 11.

Clarke's major difference from Edwards, as will be seen, was not that one was a believer in free will and the other a determinist. Edwards, as it happens, comfortably borrowed from Clarke's *Demonstration* some of Clarke's best anti-Hobbesian ideas. The difference was that Clarke believed the distinction between physical (or efficient) causation and mental causation (psychic, final, formal, or whatever) was absolutely basic, whereas Edwards was an occasionalist like Malebranche and Hume and reduced all causation, no matter what the kind and no matter what the *substances* involved, simply to a pattern of invariable sequence. Clarke had accused Collins of believing "that Moral Necessity and Physical Necessity do not differ intrinsically in their *own Nature*, but only with regard to the Subject they are applied to,"[60] as though Collins was some sort of an occasionalist or a materialist. It is not at all clear, however, that Collins had gotten that far in his understanding of causation; but Edwards definitely had. Edwards therefore could say, like Hobbes, that there is only one kind of causation, but rather than Hobbes's physical efficacy it is the neutral causation of invariable sequence; and, at the same time, Edwards could also agree with Clarke that there are two kinds of necessity (one allowing for moral responsibility, the other not); they differ not in the essential nature of the causality involved (as Clarke would have it) but only in the nature of the ingredients involved in the causal relationship. Edwards did not deny that "natural necessity is wholly inconsistent with just praise and blame."[61] But he did assert, in contrast to Clarke, that moral necessity is real necessity (and in that respect like natural necessity as Hobbes had said) and yet of such a nature that it does not impair the ascription of responsibility to actions. These subtle differences will all be addressed more fully below.

Edwards's Early Notions

Edwards's theory of the will combined diverse elements from the past: Augustinian principles such as those held by Gale, many seventeenth-century Puritans, and Malebranche; certain metaphysical and psychological ideas resembling those expounded by Hobbes, Locke, and Collins; and the orthodox tenets of Calvinism on foreordination. As was the case with other elements in his philosophy, Edwards had formulated or adopted most of the essential ideas in his theory of the will before he had reached the age of twenty-five.

Three beginning principles stand out as the foundation stones upon which his later thought was built: (1) a rigorous belief in the law of universal causation, held to as a matter of logic independent of theological commitments to

60. Clarke, *Remarks*, 15.
61. *Freedom of the Will*, ed. Ramsey, 350.

divine sovereignty and providence; (2) an Augustinian-voluntarist conception of the will, which removed it almost entirely from association with intellect and identified the will with non-rational appetites, passions, affections, dispositions, and inclinations; and (3) the belief that the evident praiseworthiness of necessarily good beings, such as Jesus Christ, the holy angels, and God Himself, proves that merit is compatible with moral necessity and, similarly, that blame is compatible with "necessitated" evil, properly defined.

It will be useful, perhaps, to take up these principles one by one before examining the later development of Edwards's thought on the will and the accretions to it. The French historian of philosophy Georges Lyon remarked years ago that Edwards's work is "essentially a philosophy of causality" and that the idea of cause is the pivot of his whole system. However that may be, it is a subject that has not received systematic attention.

The young Edwards took it as a fixed law of nature, imposed by God, that every event has a cause, by which he meant that every existing thing is preceded by another that it follows upon in a regular way. Edwards believed that this principle is not only a metaphysical and logical necessity, but is also psychologically dictated. "All our reasoning, with respect to Real Existence," he said, "depends upon that natural, unavoidable and invariable disposition of the mind, when it sees a thing begin to be, to conclude certainly, that there is a *Cause* of it." The assumption that anything can "make itself" is a contradiction that the mind, Edwards believed, "do what we will, will forever refuse to receive, but will perpetually reject." Therefore, when we observe the beginning of a thing, we "intuitively know there is a cause of it. . . . This is an innate principle, . . . the soul is born with it—a necessary, fatal propensity."[62]

The interpretation of events in terms of efficient causality is more than an inescapable psychological propensity, however. Although Edwards was an occasionalist and not a mechanist—that is, he saw the ordering of events in causal sequence as an arbitrary arrangement of God's, upheld by Him from instant to instant—he did not view the real world as unknowable. Human perception of causality has a metaphysical foundation. In an early note on the justice of God's decrees, Edwards observed that mankind ought to have no great complaint about such decrees *just because they are foreordained,* for even if we suppose a world without God, "things would happen as fatally as they do now." The supposition that there could be a perfect contingency in the will of man, enabling a person to will one thing and not another "perfectly by chance," Edwards considered to be "an impossibility and a contradiction."

62. "Notes on the Mind," no. 54, in Howard, *"The Mind" of Edwards*. Alexander Fraser, Locke's editor, has noted that Locke left "causality in the abstract" as a necessary principle of reasoning "almost untouched" in his discussion of innate ideas and maxims, but then relied on it, with some inconsistency, in his proof for the existence of God. *Essay Concerning Human Understanding*, ed. Fraser, Bk. I, chap. lxx; Bk. II, 307n.

There has to be some "cause or reason," Edwards argued—he did not distinguish between causes and reasons—why things are one way rather than another. Hence, he concluded, "seeing things do unavoidably go fatally or necessarily" with or without God, why consider divine determination of events to be an injustice to humanity?[63]

Human beings fit into the universal system of causal sequence because all human actions and choices are conditioned by prior events, mental or other. We do not find in Edwards's earliest writings any explicit set of distinctions between kinds of necessity or causation, but he seems to have believed from the beginning that the habitual tendency of a person, his preponderant disposition, sufficiently narrows the real choices open to him to such an extent that in most cases what he will do is quite predictable. In other words, although it may be in one's *power* to do many things, in the sense that there appears to be no inherent reason why the person could not decide to do a whole range of possible things other than what he does do, the actual choice will always reflect the agent's prevailing inclinations. "There are many things that are entirely in our power, of which things yet it may be said, that 'tis an impossibility they should be, because of our dispositions."[64]

The word "impossibility" seems too strong for the kind of predictability or moral certainty that Edwards had in mind. But his thinking at this point seems to have been influenced once more by Samuel Clarke, for Edwards's example of such an impossibility was very much like Clarke's. "It is altogether in a man's power," Edwards wrote, "when he has a cup of poison offered to him, whether he will drink it or no; and yet by reason of the man's internal disposition, the ideas and notions of things that he then has, it may be an impossibility that he should will to drink it."[65] In Clarke's *Demonstration of the Being and Attributes of God: . . . in Answer to Mr. Hobbs, Spinoza, and Their Followers: Wherein the Notion of Liberty Is Stated, and the Possibility and Certainty of It Proved*, the 1704 Boyle lectures, the author wrote: "A

63. Miscellanies, no. 51. Regarding Edwards's occasionalism, see *ibid*., no. 629, quoted in chap. 2, n. 93, above. Edwards also adhered to the traditional notion of the continuous creation. See, e.g., *ibid*., no. 125a: " 'Tis certain with me, that the world exists anew every moment, that the existence of things every moment ceases and every moment is renewed." Both of these ideas were prominent in the work of Malebranche as well as other Cartesians. Edwards's theories in this vein are presented at length in *Original Sin*, ed. Holbrook, 397–404.

64. Miscellanies, no. 70. Henry More had pointed out earlier that belief in human freedom does not imply that one believes men are *always* free. The soul can degenerate so far, More pointed out, that "it may be as certainly known what she will do upon this or that occasion, as what a hungry Dog will do when a Crust is offered him; which is the general condition of almost all men in most occurrences of their lives." On the other hand, the soul may also be "so *Heroically good*, though that happen in very few, that it may be as certainly known as before what she will do or suffer upon such or such emergencies." *Immortality of the Soul*, Bk. II, chap. iii, secs. 16–20.

65. Miscellanies, no. 71.

Man entirely free from all Pains of Body and Disorder of Mind, judges it unreasonable for him to Hurt or Destroy himself; and, being under no Temptation or External Violence, he *cannot possibly* Act contrary to this Judgment; not because he wants a *Natural Power* to do so, but because it is absurd and Mischievous and *morally Impossible* for him to Choose to do it."[66]

In his controversy with Hobbes, Bishop Bramhall had made a similar distinction between natural causes, on the one side, and moral efficacy arising from prior dispositions, on the other, but Hobbes had denied there was any real difference between the two. It is important to remember about Edwards, in any case, that although he opposed Clarke on the free will question, he made use of the idea of moral necessity, exactly as Clarke had formulated it, in order to protect his system from a Hobbesian-type materialistic determinism. In all of his later argumentation on the will, Edwards adhered unwaveringly to the maxim propounded by Clarke in his first Boyle lectures: "*Moral Necessity*," Clarke said, "is evidently consistent with the most perfect *Natural Liberty*." In other words, so-called moral necessity does not abrogate accountability and satisfies most of the criteria for what is called freedom or liberty.

Although it would seem obvious that the relationship between a person's predispositions or habitual tendencies and any particular choice is one of high probability rather than strict certainty, let alone logical necessity, by the early 1730s Edwards was maintaining that the prior conditions in one's psyche and the choices that follow are as strictly related as mathematical propositions. Thus, he illustrated, "a man may have it in his power to sell his estate and give the money to his poor neighbour, and yet the case may be so at the same time he may have so little love to his neighbour and so great a love to his possessions and the like that he certainly will not do it. There may be as much of a connection between these things in the qualities and circumstances of the man and his refusing to give his estate to his neighbour, as between any two theorems in mathematics."[67] The implications of this reasoning for religion were always immediately brought out by Edwards. Men have it in their power to come to Christ, to love God, to join the faith, but they *will* not because they are not so inclined. Is God to be held responsible for their ultimate condemnation, when they could be differently inclined if they desired to be? The problem, as Edwards saw it, is only that they do not really desire to be different, not that they cannot be.[68]

The second principle of reasoning about will that we find in Edwards from the beginning is the Augustinian notion that the verb "to will" describes not

66. Clarke, *Demonstration of the Being and Attributes of God*, 163. It was this passage that Collins cited as evidence that Clarke, too, was an unwitting determinist.

67. Miscellanies, no. 573.

68. This kind of reasoning regarding the process of conversion was commonplace in 17th-

just a singular form of intellection, the understanding as it is expressed in action, so to speak, but many forms of appetition and conation, whether expressed in immanent or transient acts and whether rational or non-rational.[69] Although the traditional type of "will"—rational appetite toward the greatest apparent good—may occasionally be operative in human motivation, and may have been predominant in Adam before the Fall, this form of willing is hardly representative of all human volition. Willing for Edwards comprehended all forms of election, including feeling this or that toward something in a decisive way. Edwards accounted it nonsense for a person to say, for example, that he or she really wishes to reform, to give up drinking, let us say, or gambling, but "can't" do it. In Edwards's terms, the person can reform if he or she really wills to. What is lacking is only genuine willingness. At the exact moment of choice there can be no such thing as conflict within the will. "The world has got into an exceeding wrong and confused way of talking about will and power," Edwards wrote. "They say, man can will such a thing, and man can't will it; which is a dreadful confusion. When we say a man can't will such a thing, the notion that is raised in our mind by such an expression is, that the man might heartily and truly desire to will it, but could not will it; that is, he truly willed to will it, but could not will it."[70] But there can be no will to will. There is only the action verb indicating what, in fact, the orientation of the will is: submitting, resisting, loving, hating, cleaving, fleeing, desiring, and so on. One's acts ordinarily reveal the disposition, tendency, inclination, or habitus of the soul, and all of these terms of conation are synonymous with the will.

In contrast to Edwards, Locke wanted to keep the meaning of "willing or volition" fairly restricted, and he cautioned against the use of "expressions

---

century Puritanism. John Owen, for example, spoke of a "natural impotency" and a "moral impotency." The former is weakness of mind, such that one *cannot* receive spiritual truth. Moral impotency is present when the mind cannot receive the things of the spirit only because "unalterably it *will not*; and that because from the unsuitableness of the Object unto its Will and Affections, and the Mind by them, they are Foolishness unto it." But on the last day, men shall be judged for the "obstinacy of their Wills and Affections." Owen, *Pneumatologia*, 224.

69. The distinction between immanent and transient acts was related to that between action and passion. In metaphysical terminology, the patient or sufferer receives the act of the agent or doer or actor. Immanent action has no patient different from the agent; it is confined within the agent, as a person forms ideas or loves himself. Transient action has an external object as a patient. Edwards used these terms, and many others, as part of his Scholastic inheritance.

70. Miscellanies, no. 71. Edwards later developed the notion of "indirect willingness," which was like the 17th-century idea of "woulding," meaning good intentions. Indirect willingness can give the illusion of conflict in the soul because people are predisposed, through a prejudice in their own favor, to think highly of these impotent motions of the will, but, Edwards said, "indirect willingness . . . can't at all excuse for the want of that good act of will that is required." Miscellanies, no. 1153, in Townsend, ed., *Philosophy of Edwards*, 169–170, and *Freedom of the Will*, ed. Ramsey, 354.

that do not enough keep up the difference between the *will* and several acts of the mind that are quite distinct from it." "I find the will often confounded with several of the affections," Locke continued, "especially *desire*, and one put for the other; and that by men who would not willingly be thought not to have had very distinct notions of things, and not to have writ very clearly about them." The reference to "distinct" and "clear" notions indicates that Locke's target here was Malebranche. Edwards, like Malebranche and unlike Locke, did "confound" the affections with "willing," including the affection of desire.[71]

The most basic division in this psychology is that between the redeemed will and the corrupt or concupiscent will, the will infused with spiritual grace and the will without it. These two opposing orientations of will are describable solely in terms of dispositions, tastes, or pleasures. Men "should be most highly affected with the highest excellencies, and less affected with the lower excellencies; . . . the mind should have the sweetest taste and most quick and exquisite delight of those things that are truly most delightful, and a lower delight and slower relish of those things that in themselves are less delightful"; Edwards continued at length in this vein, all to illustrate the consequences of the Fall.[72] We have already noted his belief that it is "the absence of the influence of God's Spirit" that allows sinful self-love and "a vile and odious disposition" to rule. Without a dominant inclination to holiness, which must be supplied by free grace, human strivings are necessarily depraved. Yet God is present in all inclinations, even the corrupt, at least as a secondary cause. " 'Tis by God's continual and immediate influence, every moment, . . . that all the exercises [and] actings of the powers or inclinations of our souls are performed. . . . An inclination is nothing but God's influencing the soul according to a certain law of nature."[73]

In addition to these fundamental, comprehensive inclinations or dispositions that may be called will, there are also particular, immediate responses to what pleases, also called will. "The Will is no . . . different from Inclination," Edwards wrote, other than that what is commonly called "Will" is only the "Mind's Inclination, with respect to its own Immediate Actions."[74] Edwards put much care into defining precisely what governs immediate choices, partly because he was stimulated, no doubt, by Locke's agonized discussion

71. Locke, *Essay Concerning Human Understanding*, ed. Fraser, Bk. II, chap. xxii, sec. 30. Edwards, *Freedom of the Will*, ed. Ramsey, 139, and *Religious Affections*, ed. Smith, 96–99. Edwards worked out the implications of this psychology most fully in *Religious Affections*, and, indeed, his theory of the passions and affections is so central to his reasoning about the free will problem that one finds implicit in the volume on the affections some of the essential ideas that appeared later in *Freedom of the Will*.

72. Miscellanies, no. 34.

73. *Ibid.*, no. 301.

74. "Notes on the Mind," no. 60, in Howard, *"The Mind" of Edwards*.

in the second edition of the *Essay*, in which Locke himself moved much closer to the Augustinian view.[75] But Edwards was also motivated by the need to find his own way amidst the competing and nearly equally powerful theories of Clarke and Malebranche.

The intellectualist view was that the will follows the last dictate of the understanding and that the understanding judges in terms of its conception of the greater good, or what Edwards called "the degree of good represented by idea." In contrast to this, Edwards argued that an adequate analysis of the process of choice must take into account not only the rationally conceived value of the object of choice but also the psychological conditions, the nature of the perceptual process, and the capacity of the stimuli to make one incline this way or that. The first distinction that had to be made was that between any form of intellectual judgment—and here one could note that not only the *degree of good* of the object enters into the calculation but also the *degree of judgment* in each case, its strength, certainty, and so on—and "the Deepness of the sense of goodness; or the clearness, liveliness and sensibleness, of the goodness or sweetness." In other words, it is not so much the effect of good on the reason that inclines the person, but, as Edwards said, "Good, as it is thus most clearly and strongly present to the mind."[76] It is the arousal power or the attractive power of the impression or the idea that matters in choice. As Edwards observed in another section of his "Notes on the Mind," there are at least two ways of apprehending good: "having a clear and sensible idea of any good" (sense) and "judging that there is good" (intellect).[77] With regard to the act of faith, it is "the dictate of the understanding, in conjunction with the clearness and liveliness of the idea that determines the will."[78] The effect of divine grace, of course, is to add another dimension to the merely "speculative and notional understanding" of the things of God, so that they become lively and exciting, which causes the will to move toward them.[79]

The dictum that the acts of the will are guided by "Good, as mentally or ideally existing" could still be sustained, according to Edwards's reckoning, provided it is understood that "Good" means only "that which agrees with the inclination and disposition of the mind."[80] Good is defined as that which is

---

75. Locke almost entirely rewrote his analysis of the will as it appeared in the first edition of the *Essay*. See the discussion in Fraser's introduction to the *Essay Concerning Human Understanding* and the notes to Bk. II, chap. xxii.

76. "Notes on the Mind," no. 60, in Howard, *"The Mind" of Edwards*.

77. *Ibid.*, no. 21.

78. Miscellanies, no. 212. See chap. 3, pp. 126–127, above.

79. Cf. Miscellanies, no. 540: "Distinguish between meer speculative and notional understanding and that which implies a sense of heart, or arises from it, wherein is exercised not meerly the faculty of understanding, but the other faculty of will or inclination of the heart."

80. "Notes on the Mind," no. 60, in Howard, *"The Mind" of Edwards*.

desired by the individual, and the choice of the apparent good in any given case is not necessarily based on intellection.

The will as a constant disposition (which is like a habit or inclination) and the will as immediate choice (which is an act or exercise) are linked, because moment to moment choices generally reflect one's prevailing ideas of what is good, that is, agreeable. A change in the disposition of the soul, Edwards wrote, "is the very same as the causing that for the future the mind shall have more lively ideas of such a sort of good." Conversion is "nothing but God's causing such an alteration with respect to the mind's ideas of spiritual good."[81]

Perhaps the main emphasis in Edwards's analysis of the will at this stage was that human inclinations and choices are not, and cannot be, governed by rational will. The attraction to objects that promise to afford pleasure and the aversion to those that promise pain, which are the forces that generally rule human choices, are not properly spoken of as being subordinate to acts of will; choices based on what is agreeable or disagreeable *are* the will in action, and the moral and religious problem is somehow to help mankind to take pleasure in the better things rather than the worser. "Pleasure and pain," Edwards wrote in his "Notes on the Mind," "have their seat in the Will, and not in the Understanding. The Will, Choice, etc. is nothing else, but the mind's being pleased with an idea, or having a superior pleasedness in something thought of, or a desire of a future thing."[82]

Like Malebranche, Edwards believed that the appetites and inclinations, not reason, are the mechanisms of divine ordering of human affairs in a fallen world. The rational will of the intellectualists, which arises from rational judgment, is capable of calculating what one's best interests are in the long run. Therefore, a person can *desire to love* God, in a sense, because the intellect foresees imminent condemnation. But the inclination of the soul is not directed by rational conclusions; rather it is "the liveliness and intenseness of the idea, or sensibleness of the good of the object presented to the mind" that determines choice. In the integrated state of man before the Fall, intellectual will and appetites are in concurrence—man sees the ultimate good and takes his greatest pleasure in it. But in the fallen state, one takes pleasure in lesser goods and the discoveries of rational will hold little appeal. Moreover, Edwards noted that the rational will is easily perverted in its judgments of what is best for the person. In the gracious state, although sinful inclinations

81. Miscellanies, no. 284. As we have noted above, p. 127, n. 51, Edwards believed that God caused this alteration by direct intervention, physical infusion, not persuasion. Cf. Miscellanies, no. 665: "The effect that is wrought by grace is on the will it self to incline and bring it to a compliance. The very first effect of saving grace that touches the will is to abolish its resistance and to incline the will."

82. "Notes on the Mind," no. 67, in Howard, *"The Mind" of Edwards.*

may persist, the total inclination of the person is found "by composition of inclinations[;] the excess of one above the other is the inclination of the man." In a perfected state, the rational will apprehends the absolute good and desires it because the will recognizes that that good is best for oneself, and at the same time the appetites are moved by the inherent supreme loveliness of the object. In the fallen state, any and all of these components can be in error or be misdirected.

Long before Edwards had fully clarified his thinking on the problem of free will, he took note of the traditional observation that certain kinds of psychological necessity (at least in practice, if not in theory) were compatible with praise and blame. There is "the greatest and most absolute necessity imaginable," he wrote in his Miscellanies, "that God should always will good and never evil." Similarly, it was impossible for Jesus Christ to will sin.[83] These examples illustrated for Edwards that liberty and necessity can agree, and also that moral merit of the highest kind is consistent with necessity.[84] Moreover, Edwards recognized the obvious practical fact that throughout the ages legal action against criminality has been taken without concern over whether or not the punishable acts were "determined." The mere fact that an action is voluntary and is an "ill action" is enough to justify punishment.[85] A criminal might plead, "I didn't want to commit the murder, but I was driven to do it by defects in my moral environment (or by passion, or by temperamental characteristics)." Such considerations, if they indicated repentance on the part of the accused, might lead to some degree of mercy, but the act remains justifiably punishable because, as Edwards would say, the agent's will was in the act; it was a voluntary act.

The justification of reward and punishment based on practical experience became somewhat more complicated, however, when predestination to eternal hell was brought into the picture. Edwards clung to the essential principle that necessity and liberty (and therefore personal responsibility) are not incompatible. As he put it in one of his early notes, "It is no contradiction to say that we can do such a thing when we please, and yet that 'tis an impossibility that

---

83. Miscellanies, no. 31.

84. See also, *ibid.*, no. 116a. The point that God and the angels are praiseworthy was already noted in the Hobbes-Bramhall debate and by many others before Edwards, including Collins. In the excellent introduction to their edition of Edwards's *Freedom of the Will* (Indianapolis, Ind., 1969), Arnold S. Kaufman and William K. Frankena refer to the view "that a man may be fully determined in thought, feeling, and action by circumstances beyond his control, and may yet be morally responsible for his choice or action" as the "compatibility thesis." See also, for discussion in current philosophical terms, Paul Helm, "John Locke and Jonathan Edwards: A Reconsideration," *Journal of the History of Philosophy*, VII (1969), 51–61.

85. Miscellanies, no. 363.

[doing that thing] should be what we please,"[86] but it remained questionable that this principle was entirely applicable to God's relation to mankind. The analogy with the praise given to angels or with the condemnation of criminals in courtrooms broke down, because in neither of these cases is the praiser or the judge at the same time the creator of the agent. Can God be morally justified in the condemnation of sinners that He has made? Edwards struggled with this problem throughout his life, and it was a constant difficulty for Calvinists in general in the eighteenth century. The whole purpose of Edwards's treatise on the will could be reduced to the one task of solving the paradox of man's being responsible for his own condemnation despite his subjection to God's decrees.[87] It would be absurd to say that Edwards succeeded in dissolving this theological mystery (all of his solutions seem to be sophistical), but his work contributed to clarification, at least, of the philosophical problems.

The Libertarians (or Arminians)

Edwards saw it as his main philosophical task, as we have noted, to demonstrate that determinism, even in the form of the Calvinist absolute decrees of God, was not inconsistent with praise and blame, and reward and punishment, or, in effect, with merit and demerit. But along the way he also devoted many pages to exposing the weaknesses of the various arguments antagonistic to determinism.[88] Edwards took the offensive against the free will position, even though his primary purpose was to put forth an effective statement of religious determinism and then to show that such determinism did not vitiate moral judgment of actions and moral responsibility.

Edwards concentrated above all on destroying the so-called liberty of indifference, which, although it had a long history, was probably the weakest of the arguments for freedom. He also attacked, not so successfully, Samuel Clarke's concept of freedom of intellect, as it was presented in Clarke's first Boyle lecture, and several other vaguer ideas about the self-determining power of the will. By artificially collecting all of the advocates of liberty into a single group, called by Edwards "the Arminians," he was able to charge the group as a whole with inconsistencies among themselves without necessarily exposing adequately the fallacies of each of the libertarian arguments taken alone. The freedom claimed by the Scholastic-intellectualists, for example, was al-

---

86. *Ibid.*, no. 71.

87. See also, *ibid.*, nos. 573 and 761.

88. The demonstration that punishment and psychological necessity are compatible would itself be a major blow against the libertarian position, for many writers argued that the very existence of moral responsibility, i.e., the fact that men are held punishable for past deeds, constitutes convincing evidence that men do act freely somehow.

together different from and even contradictory to the freedom claimed by the Scholastic-voluntarists like Suarez, although both of these schools were opposed in principle to determinism. Probably no single individual held all of the arguments for free will that Edwards opposed, nor was there a self-conscious "Arminian" group based on the criterion of free will alone. Not only were there diverse arguments for free will, there were also a number of grounds on which one could turn against determinism, which itself was not a single, unified concept.

Edwards did not confront squarely some of the arguments for freedom then current, particularly Clarke's. When, at the beginning of *Freedom of Will*, Edwards briefly summarized and categorized the arguments for liberty, he significantly left out an argument such as Clarke's in the *Demonstration*. Edwards spoke of (1) liberty as "a self-determining power in the will, or a certain sovereignty the will has over itself, and its own acts"; (2) liberty as "indifference," namely, "that the mind, previous to the act of volition be, *in equilibrio*"; and (3) liberty as "contingence," not in the "common acceptation" of that word, but as "opposed to all necessity, or any fixed and certain connection with some previous ground or reason."[89] All of these examples tended to focus either on the idea of "*the* will," rather than on that of choice or action, or on the question of whether the grounds of choice could be so framed in theory that one could speak of a human liberty beyond merely liberty from external constraint.

The liberty of indifference was not a difficult argument for Edwards to undermine. It was an argument weakened throughout its history by its attribution to "the will" (as some sort of separate entity) of a power to make gratuitous choices independent of rational grounds.[90] In Isaac Watts's version, according to Edwards, the will can be moved by "no motive at all" and can act "altogether without motive, or ground of preference." Edwards considered this belief inherently inconsistent. If the will does actually make a choice, it expresses a preference, which means that it is no longer indifferent. At most, one could say that the mind, or a person, is indifferent before the choice is made. But it is impossible, Edwards wrote, for the will to be indifferent "*when* it chooses."[91]

It is true, Edwards said, that if in the view of the mind two or more things are perfectly equal, neither one of which preponderates or has a prevailing influence upon the mind, there is no basis for choice. But, in fact, there is

---

89. Edwards, *Freedom of the Will*, ed. Ramsey, 164–165.

90. Edwards cited Isaac Watts's *Essay on Freedom of Will* as an example. Jean LeClerc was one of the most prominent defenders of the liberty of indifference at the turn of the century.

91. Edwards, *Freedom of the Will*, ed. Ramsey, 195–196.

always a discernible basis for choice, or the mind can invent one. Suppose one is asked, to take a classic example, to put a finger on one square of a chessboard when no extrinsic circumstances dictate a preference. Edwards analyzed the steps as follows: (1) a general determination to touch one of the squares; (2) another "*general* determination [of the mind] to give itself up to accident, in some certain way," for example, by determining to touch the square that happens to be most in view, or that the eye is most fixed upon at that moment; (3) a "*particular* determination to touch a certain individual spot."[92] Throughout the process, the mind never proceeds in "absolute indifference," but is continually influenced by "a preponderating inducement," often simply that of achieving the assigned purpose of touching one square. Even the "accident" that is allowed to serve as the basis of the particular choice is not uncaused. When one casts a die, the specific manner of its falling is called accidental, yet no one supposes that "there is no cause why it falls as it does." Similarly, "the involuntary changes in the succession of our ideas, though the cause may not be observed, have as much a cause, as the changeable motions of the motes that float in the air, or the continual, infinitely various, successive changes of the unevennesses of the surface of the water. There is nothing in the world more constantly varying, than the ideas of the mind," and therefore more apparently accidental.[93]

Edwards's analysis of the process of choice in apparently indifferent matters singled out, as he said, not the mind's determination with relation to the *objects* of choice themselves, which are equal for all intents and purposes, but the mind's determination with relation to "the *acts to be done* concerning these objects." Rather than the mind finding any differentiation in the objects, the choice in such a case is made from "foreign considerations," that is, on the basis of a preference irrelevant to any value in the objects. Moreover, Edwards observed, although a state of indifference with reference to the objects may exist in general before the choice is made and at a time when the choice is still relatively distant, once one becomes directly concerned in a

---

92. *Ibid.*, 199. If Edwards did read Collins's *Inquiry Concerning Human Liberty*, the evidence for it would lie right here, for Collins's analysis of the process of choosing one out of two or more hen's eggs, among which there is no perceivable difference, was very much like Edwards's later. That things are equal in themselves, Collins pointed out, does not mean that they will be equal to the will. "All the various modifications of the man, his opinions, prejudices, temper, habit, and circumstances are to be taken in and consider'd as causes of election no less than the objects without us among which we chuse." Collins then analyzed the steps in choosing as follows: (1) "a will to eat or use an egg"; (2) "a will to take but one"; (3) the choosing or taking, which is done "most commonly, according as the parts of our bodies have been form'd long since by our wills or by other causes to an habitual practice, or as those parts are determin'd by some particular circumstances at that time" (pp. 47–48). Collins did not mention specifically the will to give oneself up to accident.

93. Edwards, *Freedom of the Will*, ed. Ramsey, 200.

choice between the several objects, particular differences may come to mind that do provide the basis for a preference.[94]

Edwards also took up the question of liberty of indifference in a theological context. The Leibniz-Clarke correspondence had brought to the forefront of discussion the question of whether God ever exercises His will in a state of indifference. Although Edwards never read this famous exchange of letters, at least two of his principal sources in *Freedom of Will*, Andrew Baxter, author of *Enquiry into the Nature of the Human Soul* (1730), and Isaac Watts, surely had. Watts maintained, like Clarke, that in some instances God may act without rational ground for preference, as when "there is a perfect indifference and equality as to fitness, or tendency to attain any good end." There are instances, Watts proposed, when "there is absolutely no difference between various possible objects of choice, which God has in view," or when the differences are so insignificant that they are of no consequence.[95] For example, God may have exercised such a liberty of indifference when He chose where to place the first created matter in the immensity of space, or when He decided which of two identical atoms to locate in one spot rather than another. Edwards dealt with the first example by arguing that before the creation of matter, space (and time) were meaningless concepts.[96] With regard to the second example, Edwards replied that it would be "infinitely unlikely" that two particles could be exactly identical in dimensions and quantity of matter. But even if God did create two particles alike to this degree, they would still be distinct with regard to their circumstances, such as "place, time, rest, motion, or some other present or past circumstances or relations." In any case, if God determines "that there should be the same figure, the same extension, the same resistance, etc. in two different places . . . he has some reason."[97]

Edwards espoused, probably without knowing it, Leibniz's principle of sufficient reason, namely, "that nothing happens without a reason why it should be so, rather than otherwise."[98] He also would have agreed with a second Leibnizian axiom, the identity of indiscernibles. Leibniz used both of

94. *Ibid.*, 201. On pp. 320–323, Edwards discussed liberty of indifference in a different sense, where indifference meant apathy, and he asked, How could virtue consist with a cold and detached heart? It is not clear, however, what Edwards read that interpreted liberty of indifference in such a sense.

95. *Ibid.*, 384–385.

96. Although Edwards may have been a believer in Newtonian absolute space and time in his youth, it is clear from his reply in this case that he had abandoned the notion in favor of a doctrine of relative space and time, such as was advanced more prominently by Leibniz. See H. G. Alexander, ed., *The Leibniz-Clarke Correspondence* . . . (New York, 1956), *passim*.

97. Edwards, *Freedom of the Will*, ed. Ramsey, 388.

98. Alexander, ed., *Leibniz-Clarke Correspondence*, 16. The similarities to Leibniz have also been noted by Ramsey in his introduction to Edwards's *Freedom of the Will*.

these principles in his debate with Clarke. Clarke responded that though it may be true that nothing exists without a sufficient reason, "this sufficient reason is oft-times no other, than the mere will of God," and gave the example later used by Watts of God's indifference in the setting of the creation. To ask why God did not create everything a year sooner, or why matter was not placed somewhere else in space than it was, with the same relative position of bodies among themselves being preserved, Leibniz answered, is to maintain that God has willed something without any sufficient reason. "This is falling back," Leibniz wrote, "into the loose indifference, which I have confuted at large, and showed to be absolutely chimerical even in creatures, and contrary to the wisdom of God, as if he could operate without acting by reason."[99]

A stronger argument for freedom of willing, perhaps, was the notion of liberty of suspension, which Locke among others believed in.[100] This position had much in common with the old Scholastic "liberty of exercise" (also known as liberty of contradiction), which posited that although the will, being blind, is dependent upon the intellect for the provision of objects toward which it may be directed, it can decide without the intellect to suspend action. The will, for the most part, Locke wrote, is determined by the greatest and most pressing uneasiness, but not always: "For, the mind having in most cases, as is evident in experience, a power to *suspend* the execution and satisfaction of any of its desires . . . is at liberty to consider the objects of them, examine them on all sides, and weigh them with others." In this, Locke averred, "lies the liberty man has. . . . This seems to me the source of all liberty; in this seems to consist that which is . . . called *free-will*."[101] Locke expressly indicated that this power of suspension was called free will "im-

99. Alexander, ed., *Leibniz-Clarke Correspondence*, 20, 27, 32. "Where there is any difference in the nature of things," Clarke wrote, "there the consideration of that difference always determines an intelligent and perfectly wise agent. But when two ways of acting are equally and alike good, . . . to affirm in such case, that God cannot act at all, or that 'tis no perfection in him to be able to act, because he can have no external reason to move him to act one way rather than the other, seems to be denying God to have in himself any original principle or power of beginning to act." Leibniz answered, "In things absolutely indifferent, there is no foundation for choice, and consequently no election, nor will; since choice must be founded on some reason, or principle." Mere will, without any motive, "is a fiction."

100. Cf. Leibniz, in Alexander, ed., *Leibniz-Clarke Correspondence*, 57–58: "Our will does not always exactly follow the practical understanding; because it may have or find reasons to suspend its resolution till a further examination." Heereboord and Descartes had also argued for the liberty of suspension.

101. *Essay Concerning Human Understanding*, ed. Fraser, Bk. II, chap. xxii, secs. 47 and 57. See also sec. 53: "I desire it may be well considered, whether the great inlet and exercise of all the liberty men have, are capable of, or can be useful to them, and that whereon depends the turn of their actions, does not lie in this,—That they can suspend their desires, and stop them from determining their wills to any action, till they have duly and fairly examined the good and evil of it."

properly," for he was essentially a determinist (albeit a troubled one), and he clearly did not mean for the power of suspension to be excluded somehow from the natural concatenation of causes by which human beings are moved. He seems to have meant only that people have the power to sustain deliberation for as long as seems necessary to make an intelligent choice, that is, as he said, to suspend the *execution* of the will. This is to claim only the traditional belief that man is a rational creature and that the voluntariness of his behavior consists in his ability to take thought before he acts.[102]

Edwards pointed out with reference to the liberty of suspension—which he described as the belief "that liberty consists in a power of the mind to forbear or suspend the act of volition, and keep the mind in a state of indifference for the present, till there has been opportunity for proper deliberation"—that the act of suspension is itself an act of volition and is based on some prior consideration that determines it.[103] The power of suspension, then, confers no more liberty upon the will than any other choice or act, if by liberty one means the possibility of non-motivated choice. Yet the emphasis in the idea of liberty of suspension was on the control of impulsive choice, not on the possibility of non-motivated choice. Although it is sometimes assumed that Locke must have been Edwards's target in his attack on the liberty of suspension, it seems improbable that he was, for Locke made no great claims about the so-called power of suspension.[104]

102. Locke's vacillation on the problem of the will is well known and well documented.

103. *Freedom of the Will*, ed. Ramsey, 209–210. Collins, *Inquiry Concerning Human Liberty*, 38, made exactly the same point: a man "is not less determin'd to will, because he does often suspend willing or chusing in certain cases; for *suspending to will*, is itself an *act of willing*; it is willing to defer willing about the matter propos'd."

104. Collins did explicitly associate Locke with this teaching, which perhaps gives support to Ramsey's comment in his introduction to Edwards, *Freedom of the Will*, 61: "Now, the striking and puzzling thing about Edwards' *Inquiry* is that, with all this before him in Locke, he nevertheless introduces the theory of suspension quite anonymously, or as if it were a formulation or possible objection he himself has made up. . . . Why does Edwards not single out John Locke for refutation? . . . Is this not an extraordinary reticence?" My belief is that Edwards did not single out Locke because the argument for the power of suspension was extremely common, and that Locke did not mean to imply by it that the will was somehow autonomous. Locke's point was simply the undeniable one that man has at least the liberty to deliberate intelligently before he acts. Many commentators on Edwards's theory of the will have noted his rebuttal in "Notes on the Mind," no. 70, to Locke's theory of motivation (introduced in the second and all subsequent editions of the *Essay Concerning Human Understanding*) that, as Edwards put it, "Uneasiness, in our present circumstances, . . . always determines the Will." Edwards pointed out simply that if a person is comfortably seated, and it is proposed to him that he get up and move, his "voluntary refusal is an act of the Will, which does not arise from any uneasiness in his present circumstances certainly." It is not often noticed, however, that Locke also included "satisfaction in one's present state" as a motive, which makes Edwards's example somewhat pointless. Isaac Watts used the same example as Edwards's in arguing against Locke's emphasis on "uneasiness." See the re-

The liberty of suspension posited that the will had liberty of exercise but not specification. Another form of free will teaching denied liberty of exercise, or contradiction, to the will but posited that the will could freely guide action by directing the *attention* of the mind. It may be argued, Edwards wrote, that although the will follows the understanding, yet the acts of the will are not necessitated "because that conviction and notice of the understanding is first dependent on a preceding act of the will, in determining to attend to, and take notice of the evidence exhibited." By first attending to something, "the mind obtains that degree of conviction which is sufficient and effectual to determine the consequent and ultimate choice of the will." But the act of attention itself, the decision to attend or not to attend, which precedes the action of the will, is not itself necessary or determined.[105] "Attention" as a subject of psychological study had been somewhat scanted by Locke because it was a mental phenomenon generally out of line with his emphasis on the passivity of mind in the acquisition of knowledge. John Norris, however, in an exchange of letters with the aging Henry More, proposed that free agency depends upon "the Degrees of *Advertency* or *Attention* which the soul uses." The liberty of the soul consists, Norris wrote, "in her having an *immediate Power* to *Attend* or not *Attend*, or to attend *more* or *less*."[106] Most later proponents of this argument were probably borrowing from Norris, although Norris's mentor, Malebranche, had also emphasized "attention." Edwards responded to it exactly as had More: the preceding act of will in determining the mind to attend or consider is still an act of will, just as the decision to suspend choice is an act of will, and acts of the will do not occur without a motive, whether the motive be a prevailing habit or a momentary preponderating inducement. But here, too, one may question whether Edwards gave due recognition to the freedom conferred by the power of attention as a prelude to choice.

We have noted that the major debate over the will at seventeenth-century Harvard College, which was a microcosm of the larger European debate, concerned the question of whether liberty is properly seen as an attribute of intellect or of will.[107] The Scholastic-intellectualists, it should be remem-

---

view of Watts's *Essay on Freedom of Will* in *Present State of the Republick of Letters* (Oct. 1732), 271.

105. *Freedom of the Will*, ed. Ramsey, 220–221.

106. "Letters Philosophical and Moral, to Dr. Henry More, with the Dr.'s Answers," appended to Norris, *Theory and Regulation of Love*. The letters were exchanged in 1685 and 1686.

107. See, e.g., John Norris's formulation: We agree "there must be . . . some Principle of free Agency in Man. All that does or can fall under debate, is what is the *primary* and *immediate* subject of this free Agency. Now this being a *Rational* perfection, must be primarily subjected either in the *Understanding* or in the *Will* (or to speak more accurately), either in the Soul as *Intelligent*,

bered, were themselves determinists in their description of the process of willing because it was a basic tenet of their psychology that choice follows the last dictate of the practical intellect. But this dependence of the will on the understanding did not, in their estimation, deprive the person of freedom. Rationality itself conferred freedom.

If we are to have a correct understanding of Edwards, it is essential to recognize that he was bound to reject Scholastic-intellectualism on religious grounds alone, if not philosophical. Intellectualism was inconsistent with the belief among Reformed pietists that God converts the will directly and that regeneration consists, among other things, in a new will or disposition infused physically by the Holy Spirit, an event that takes place without the meditation of intellect, although illumination of the intellect will also occur.[108] Moreover, the Augustinian sentimentalist psychology to which Edwards adhered, in which "the affections are no other, than the more vigorous and sensible exercises of the inclination and will of the soul," divorced the will from its traditional link to intellect. As Edwards wrote in the preface to *Freedom of Will*, "The knowledge of ourselves consists chiefly in right apprehensions concerning those two chief faculties of our nature, the *understanding* and the *will*. Both are very important: yet the science of the latter must be confessed to be of greatest moment; inasmuch as all virtue and religion have their seat more immediately in the will, consisting more especially in right acts and habits of this faculty."[109] Like William Ames a century earlier, Edwards was fighting a battle on two fronts: one against intellectualism, which led so easily to moralism and to human pride, and the other against Molinist notions of an autonomous will, which made nonsense of Calvinist doctrine.

"Some of the chief of the Arminian writers," Edwards noted, are willing to grant that the acts of the will "have some connection with the dictates or views of the understanding,"[110] and he pointed to one of his chief libertarian

---

or in the Soul as *Volent*. That the latter cannot be the *Root of Liberty* will be sufficiently clear, if this one Proposition be fully made out, *viz*. That the Will necessarily follows the Dictate of the Understanding, or that the Soul necessarily Wills as she Understands." Norris, *Theory and Regulation of Love*, 4th letter to More. See also Fiering, *Moral Philosophy at Seventeenth-Century Harvard*, chap. 3.

108. The importance of this issue for Edwards can hardly be overstressed. The belief that "there is a *Real, Physical Work* of the Spirit on the Souls of Men in their Regeneration," as John Owen put it, was the pietists' transubstantiation and equally divisive. For the other side, compare Grove, *System of Moral Philosophy*, ed. Amory, 226: Can God determine the will to action "by a positive, immediate, and irresistible influx?" It is called "*physical premonition* or *predetermination*" in distinction from that which is *moral*, and influences the Will by an address or application to the Understanding. . . . Whoever was the author of this ill-favoured opinion, he has had too many followers, as well among the Protestants as among the Romanists." Cf. also, Edwards, *Religious Affections*, ed. Smith, 138–141. See chap. 3, n. 51, above.

109. See n. 1, above. For Aristotle, virtue consisted in a habit of the practical intellect.

110. *Freedom of the Will*, ed. Ramsey, 217.

opponents in *Freedom of Will*, Daniel Whitby, as an example, as well as to Samuel Clarke and George Turnbull.[111] In his attack on Whitby, Edwards found it relatively easy to show, first, that Whitby accepted the traditional teaching that "the acts and determinations of the will always follow the understanding's apprehension or view of the greatest good to be obtained, or evil to be avoided." Second, Edwards argued that Whitby therefore must also accept that

> every determination of the will, in choosing and refusing, is necessary. . . . For if the determination of the will, evermore, in this manner, follows the light, conviction and view of the understanding, concerning the greatest good and evil, and this be that alone which moves the will, and it be a contradiction to suppose otherwise; then it is *necessarily* so, the will necessarily follows this light or view of the understanding, not only in some of its acts, but in every act of choosing and refusing.[112]

Thus, it could be concluded that the will is not self-determining, but depends on an antecedent cause, in this case the acts of the understanding.

Whitby's own intellectualist psychology, Edwards exulted, "utterly abolishes" his "whole scheme of liberty of will," and all of Whitby's "exclamations against the doctrine of the Calvinists, as charging God with manifest unrighteousness, unfaithfulness, hypocrisy, fallaciousness, and cruelty," which "over, and over, and over again, numberless times" are set forth in his book, are "enervated and made vain." As Edwards saw it, it was not the Calvinists alone who lived in a predestinate world of causal necessities—Whitby did, too, whether he liked it or not.[113]

To summarize for a moment, we have seen that Edwards could demonstrate that the so-called liberty of indifference was confused nonsense; that the liberty of suspension was reducible to a form of intellectualism; and that most of the other libertarians were acknowledged adherents to intellectualism, which in fact was a psychology that could not be separated from psychic determinism. As Edwards pictured the opposition in *Freedom of Will*, the libertarians were caught in a dilemma. The notion of an autonomous will was inherently untenable, but as soon as one accepted that the will or choice is dependent upon prior mental acts or present inducements, determinism seemed to be inescapable. But was there no more that could be said for human freedom than could be found in Molinism or in various other naive notions of the self-determining will?

111. On Whitby and on Edwards's other antagonists in the *Freedom of the Will*, see the helpful summaries in Ramsey's introduction.

112. *Ibid.*, 218–220. Collins had followed the same strategy in refuting the intellectualists.

113. *Ibid.*, 222. See also, p. 261.

The major question, the question that lay at the center of much of the free will debate, was whether intellectualism in all of its forms is necessarily determinist, yet it was a question that Edwards never fully confronted. The Thomist view, and the one propounded widely in academic argument, was that the government of reason, or more broadly, government by intellect, which is the prerogative of human beings alone of creatures on earth, is the ultimate in human liberty and is, in fact, sufficient to release man from the chain of causation that controls the rest of nature. Man is free insofar as he is rational, or a creature capable of intelligent deliberation. The most effective expositor of this view that Edwards encountered was undoubtedly Samuel Clarke, who essayed to defend freedom of volition in his first Boyle lecture, the *Demonstration of the Being and Attributes of God*, cited by Edwards in *Freedom of Will*, and then again in his correspondence with Leibniz and in his pamphlet debate with Anthony Collins.

"Dr. Samuel Clarke," Edwards wrote, in order "to evade the argument to prove the necessity of volition, from its necessary connection with the last dictate of the understanding, supposes the latter *not to be diverse from* the act of the will itself."[114] As Edwards understood Clarke, the Boyle lecturer was gratuitously transferring the locus of freedom from the dependent will to the autonomous intellect and making choice a function of intellect itself, rather than thinking of it as an activity sequential to and separate from cognition. Just as the Hobbesians, the Augustinians, and the sentimentalists were, in diverse ways, merging volition into appetite, instinct, affections, and passions, Clarke was assimilating volition to the process of intellection. There was, in fact, nothing new in Clarke's argument. Rather, he introduced a corrective to the tendency of philosophers and psychologists to reify the powers of the mind in discussion until these powers take on the characteristics of independent fiefdoms. In the seventeenth century William Ames wrote, borrowing from Thomas Aquinas, "Intellect and will differ neither from the rational soul nor from one another essentially, but only differ formally or by a formal notion, namely with respect to intrinsic operation. Will is intellect as external, for the purpose of possessing and making what it knows. Intellect is will as immanent, for the purpose of understanding."[115] Harvard commencement theses from 1675 and 1684, respectively, made the same point: "The faculties of the rational soul are distinguished from the soul only notionally," and "Intellect and will are the soul as understanding and as willing."[116]

---

114. *Ibid.*, 222.

115. "Gulielmi Amesii Theses Physiologica," in the college notebook of William Partridge, Beinecke Lib., Yale Univ.

116. *"Facultates animae rationalis Ratione tantum differunt ab Anima"*; *"Intellectus & Voluntas sunt anima intelligens & volens."* Theses, in Comitus publicis, 1660–1753, MS, Harvard Univ. Archives.

It may be significant that in responding to Clarke's suggestion Edwards was singularly obscure:

> If the dictate of the understanding be the very same with the determination of the will or choice, as Dr. Clarke supposes, then this determination is no *fruit* or *effect* of choice: and if so, no liberty of choice has any hand in it: as to volition or choice, it is necessary; that is, choice can't prevent it. If the last dictate of the understanding be the same with the determination of volition itself, then the existence of that determination must be necessary as to volition; inasmuch as volition can have no opportunity to determine whether it shall exist or no, it having existence already before volition has opportunity to determine anything. It is itself the very rise and existence of volition. But a thing, after it exists, has no opportunity to determine as to its own existence; it is too late for that.[117]

Edwards seems to have meant by this statement that if volition does in fact take place, then it is conditioned by the determination of the intellect, which is necessarily prior to the volition. But Clarke's point was that it is not correct to assume that the determination of the intellect is prior to the volition. The *mind* may be, in the terminology of the time, spontaneous and self-governing, even if the "will" is not.

In attempting to rebut Clarke, Edwards was guilty of the tactic mentioned earlier: he attributed to Clarke what the "Arminians suppose" and then argued that Clarke was inconsistent. Thus, Edwards wrote:

> If liberty consists in that which Arminians suppose, viz. in the will's determining its own acts . . . and being without all necessity; this is the same as to say, that liberty consists in the soul's having power and opportunity to have what determinations of the will it pleases or chooses. And if the determinations of the will, and the last dictates of the understanding be the same thing, then liberty consists in the mind's having power to have what dictates of the understanding it pleases, having opportunity to choose its own dictates of understanding. But this is absurd; for it is to make the determination of choice prior to the dictate of understanding, and the ground of it; which can't consist with the dictate of understanding's being the determination of choice itself.[118]

But can it not be said that the mind does have what ideas it pleases, leaving aside the question of whether these elements of understanding are to be considered dictates or not?

In the same disingenuous fashion Edwards raised a final objection: "Be-

117. *Freedom of the Will*, ed. Ramsey, 222.
118. *Ibid.*, 222–223.

sides, if the dictate of the understanding, and determination of the will be the same, this confounds the understanding and the will, and makes them the same. Whether they be the same or not, I will not now dispute; but only would observe, that if it be so, and the Arminian notion of liberty be just, then all liberty consists in a self-determining power in the understanding, free of all necessity."[119] Why did Edwards speak here of the "Arminian notion of liberty," rather than confining his criticism to Clarke's notion of liberty? By enlarging the issue to the Arminian notion of liberty, Edwards could then go on to reduce Clarke's suggestion to absurdity. The understanding becomes independent of "any evidence or appearance of things, or anything whatso-ever that stands forth to the view of the mind, prior to the understanding's determination. And what sort of liberty is this!" Edwards asked, which con-sists "in an ability, freedom and easiness of judging, either according to evidence, or against it; having a sovereign command over itself at all times, to judge, either agreeably or disagreeably to what is plainly exhibited to its own view." The implications of Clarke's position, according to Edwards, are that "persuasive reasoning, arguments, expostulations, and such like moral means and inducements" are useless, since the understanding is alleged to be sover-eign over its own determinations.[120] Surely Clarke would not have agreed with this interpretation of his argument.

If one turns from Edwards's text to that section of Clarke's *Demonstration* concerned with liberty, will, and intellect, a rather extraordinary discovery is made about Edwards's management of the debate and his use of sources in this case. Clarke's declared purpose was to refute the naturalistic determinism of Hobbes and Spinoza, for whom efficient, physical causation was the sole model of sequential relations between events. Clarke took it as a matter of faith that it was possible for God, who is Himself free, to endow man with a comparable liberty.[121] He also took particular care from the beginning to assert a principle that Edwards consciously avoided facing: "As to the Pro-priety of the Terms, whether the Will be properly the Seat of Liberty or not, it is not now to the purpose to inquire: The Question being, not where the Seat of Liberty is; but whether there be *at all* in Man any such Power, as a Liberty of Choice and of Determining his own Actions."[122] After Hobbes, as Clarke saw it, the challenge to moralists was no longer that of locating and properly defining freedom, but of proving that man was free in any sense at all that left room for moral responsibility.

Clarke then addressed the specific issues. Does the proposition that the will

119. *Ibid.*, 223.
120. *Ibid.*, 223–224. See also, p. 331.
121. Wolfson, "Augustine and the Pelagian Controversy," in Wolfson, *Religious Philosophy*, traces this idea ultimately to Philo.
122. Clarke, *Demonstration of the Being and Attributes of God*, 142.

is determined by the last judgment of intellect destroy liberty? Clarke answered that the assumption that it does is only a "necessity upon supposition." After the choice is made, it is supposed that there was no real alternative to it, "just as if one should affirm, that everything which is, is therefore Necessary to Be, because when it Is, it cannot but Be."[123] But the last judgment of the understanding in any given case, does not *have to be* the last judgment; the termination of deliberation, whenever that occurs, is itself the free act of choosing. This act of choice is what Clarke had in mind when he said that the last judgment of the understanding "is the very same with the *Act of Volition*." This clarification removed the easy leap of criticism that treated all acts of will as necessitated because they are directly caused by the dictate of the understanding.

Let us assume, however, Clarke said, that the last judgment of the understanding is really "a different Thing from the Act of Volition, and that the One *Necessarily* produced the other." What is the nature of this "necessity"? It was at this point that Clarke introduced the distinction between "moral" and "natural" necessity, a distinction that was absolutely essential to Edwards's own defense of moral merit and demerit in a determinist system. Yet it is remarkable that Edwards nowhere mentions Clarke's name in connection with the distinction, even though Clarke is the probable source of the idea in Edwards's work.[124] The reason for Edwards's reticence in identifying Clarke with this notion is obvious. In the *Demonstration*, Clarke used the distinction to defend the principle of liberty! Moral necessity, he said, is "*no Necessity* at all, in the Sense of the Opposers of Liberty.*" Moral necessity is "consistent with the most perfect *Natural Liberty*."[125] For Edwards, however, using exactly the same concept, moral necessity was real necessity, enough necessity at least, Edwards believed, to serve as a bulwark of the Calvinist doctrine that individual human character is predestined.

That Edwards and Clarke could use the very same idea for contrary purposes is revealing of the inherent obscurity or ambiguity in the notion of "moral necessity." Clarke adopted it because it was a barrier against Hobbesian materialistic determinism. Moral necessity was a kind of spiritual influence that seemed compatible with human liberty and responsibility. Edwards adopted it because otherwise there would be hardly any difference between his argument in *Freedom of Will* and Hobbesianism. Like Clarke, Edwards was concerned about preserving the concept of moral accountability, not

123. *Ibid.*, 162.
124. Although the distinction between moral and natural necessity was not entirely new, Clarke's formulation was original enough to make it highly likely that the *Demonstration* was Edwards's source. Earlier Scholastic debates between Jesuits and Thomists over moral determination *vs.* physical determination concerned the means of God's control over His creatures.
125. Clarke, *Demonstration of the Being and Attributes of God*, 163.

only in human affairs but above all in connection with divine predestination. For Edwards, the concept of moral necessity was useful because it gave the appearance of systematic uniformity and universality to his determinist argument, yet without the drawbacks of Hobbesianism. For Clarke, moral necessity was useful as a loophole in the determinist argument, one that made freedom a reality; for Edwards it was supposed to be the plug that kept out false notions of liberty. Clarke emphasized the mental or spiritual, that is, the *moral*, character of moral necessity; Edwards the *necessity* part of it. Moral necessity is compatible with freedom, Clarke said; moral necessity is *necessity*, Edwards said, but a unique type that is compatible with accountability.

Motives

Moral necessity was another name for what might today be called psychological or mental causes as distinguished from physical or organic causes. Reasons and purposes would certainly fit in the first category as would many other kinds of culturally formed "causes," whether conscious or not, such as commitments, obligations, concerns, passions, habits, faiths, beliefs, attitudes, and so on. Because human beings live in a world of "culture," which elevates them above a life of mere biological instincts and appetites and induces them to satisfy needs and goals far beyond those required solely for physical survival, it might be argued that they are free as no lower animal is. Human beings live in a world of choice. On the other hand, mental phenomena are not random in normal people; we recognize sequences, even possibly laws, which give human behavior a degree of regularity. Psychological causes of this sort, even though they determine actions, seem to be compatible with freedom and responsibility.

To take a different kind of case, it has often been held that lunatics are not responsible for their actions, which is, in effect, to assume that their behavior is governed by some sort of natural necessity, and yet not simply by chemical or biological causes. The madman's actions are unconventional, erratic, and unpredictable, but he is seen as being less free for all this caprice than someone who is in possession of his faculties. In other words, such criteria as rationality, intellectual coherence, intelligibility, and reasonableness are the marks of actions governed by moral necessity of the sort that is consistent with liberty. Compulsive or obsessive behavior is probably controlled by psychological, not organic, causes, but such behavior is unintelligible to reason, and hence seems more appropriately considered a form of natural necessity than moral necessity. It seems, then, that one of the ambiguities lurking in the concept of moral necessity is that it may be interpreted to mean either psychological causes in general, whether rational or irrational, or rational causes only. The question that has to be considered about Edwards's use of the concept of moral necessity is whether he interpreted it in contradictory ways so that he could both preserve his determinist hypothesis and also maintain that his theory provided for the freedom that makes moral choice meaningful.

We have come to accept in the twentieth century that there may be many levels of explanation for a human event. The question of why someone does a particular act may be answered satisfyingly in a number of different ways.[126] We may rely on expressed reasons, look for hidden motives, assign biological causes, and so on. Although Hobbes wanted to find efficient causes for all human behavior, he believed in determinism as a metaphysical principle and made no attempt to list exhaustively all the kinds of causes that might influence behavior. It was the principle itself that mattered. Malebranche also referred to the complexity of human motivation, which made fully adequate analysis forever impossible.

> The Effects of Pleasure, and of all the Sensations of the Soul, have a thousand several Dependencies on the actual Dispositions of the Mind. The very same Weight has not always the same Effects. . . . Different degrees of Light, Charity, Concupiscence, and the different degrees of Liberty, are perpetually combining infinite ways, with the different degrees of actual Pleasures; which Pleasures are operative, but according to their relation to the Dispositions of the Mind and Heart; 'tis manifest that no finite Mind can with any certainty pronounce of the Effect a particular Grace ought to produce in us. . . . 'Tis impossible for any finite Mind to discover what passes in the Heart of Man.[127]

Edwards, too, like Malebranche, believed that choice was influenced by an incomprehensible multitude of both unrecognized causes and conscious reasons, and this whole complex of inducements—appetitive, emotional, cognitive, and spiritual or supernatural—Edwards called simply "motives." He could ostensibly adopt the form of the intellectualist paradigm of choice—the will is moved by the last judgment of the practical intellect—while changing its contents totally. It is true that "in some sense," Edwards wrote, "the will always follows the last dictate of the understanding. But then the understanding must be taken in a large sense, as including the whole faculty of perception or apprehension, and not merely what is called reason or judgment." The dictate of reason, Edwards said, is but "one thing that is put into the scales."[128]

126. See R. S. Peters's very clarifying study, *The Concept of Motivation* (London, 1958).

127. Malebranche, *A Treatise of Nature and Grace* bound with *Search after Truth*, trans. Taylor, 31.

128. *Freedom of the Will*, ed. Ramsey, 148.

By "motive," Edwards explained, he meant "the whole of that which moves, excites or invites the mind to volition, whether that be one thing singly, or many things conjunctly. Many particular things may concur and unite their strength to induce the mind; and when it is so, all together are as it were one complex motive."[129] Every act of the will is excited by some motive, Edwards believed, for if there is no motive, the mind in willing or choosing would have to do so without any end or purpose; it would aim at nothing and seek nothing. "And if it seeks nothing, then it don't go after anything, or exert any inclination or preference towards anything. Which brings the matter to a contradiction; because for the mind to will something, and for it to go after something by an act of preference and inclination, are the same thing."[130]

Psychological motives are also classifiable as causes, according to Edwards's definitions, albeit "moral causes" rather than "natural." But moral causes are causes in "as proper a sense," Edwards argued, "as any causes whatsoever." A cause, then, Edwards defined as "any antecedent, either natural or moral, positive or negative, on which an event, . . . so depends, that it is the ground and reason, either in whole, or in part, why it is, rather than not; or why it is as it is, rather than otherwise."[131] A cause, in other words, is a determining antecedent; so once Edwards had established that choices are always governed by motives, and that motives are causes, the determinist conclusion was inescapable. There was still the question raised by Clarke, however, as to whether "moral causes" could rightly be called "necessary" and, if they are determining, in what sense. By leaving the exact nature of "motives" relatively unexplored, Edwards avoided facing the problem of whether the complex of psychological preconditions and inducements that govern choice are all equally necessitating. Freedom, Edwards said, is simply being able to do what one wills to do, or being able to do what one is motivated to do. Some kinds of motivation, however, namely irrational motives, do seem to limit freedom. If this is so, then one must come back to the old idea that it is not simply being able to do what one wants to do that is the criterion of liberty, but also the participation of reason in the action. Yet this criterion Edwards could not accept.

As an occasionalist, Edwards did not have to worry about one kind of dis-

129. *Ibid.*, 141. Edwards, following Locke, apparently did not recognize unconscious motives, however: "Whatever is a motive . . . must be something that is extant in the view or apprehension of the understanding, or perceiving faculty. Nothing can induce or invite the mind to will or act anything any further than it is perceived, or is some way or other in the mind's view." Yet certain mental processes that we now associate with the unconscious were well understood, such as rationalization.
130. *Ibid.*, 225.
131. *Ibid.*, 180–181.

tinction that might be drawn between natural and moral causes, namely that the former are efficient causes and the latter teleological. The difference between moral and natural necessity "does not lie so much in the nature of the connection," Edwards wrote, "as in the two terms connected." Both are subsumed under the single idea of causation. But the cause in moral necessity "is of a moral nature; either some previous habitual disposition, or some motive exhibited to the understanding. And the effect is also of a particular kind; being likewise of a moral nature; consisting in some inclination or volition of the soul, or voluntary action."[132]

As in Malebranche and Hume, "cause" for Edwards meant only fixed sequence, or, as he said, a cause is "any antecedent with which a consequent event is so connected, that it truly belongs to the reason why the proposition which affirms the event, is true; whether it has any positive influence, or not." The word "effect," Edwards said, he used to describe the "consequence of another thing, which is perhaps rather an occasion than a cause, most properly speaking."[133] But certain questions remained: whether one could truly say that mental events are caused; whether choosing, or willing, is connected to preceding mental events in as strict and invariable a sequence as physical phenomena in nature; and whether rationality in behavior indicated a different kind of moral cause than irrationality? Clarke believed that the substance of freedom was implicit in the soul of man and denied that in moral necessity there was any connection at all that could be called an efficient cause.

Habits and Moral Necessity

It is a strange quirk in Edwards's argument for determinism that he sometimes spoke, as Malebranche and Clarke had, not in terms of real necessity governing choice, but of the probability that a person's choice would be of a certain kind. Edwards sometimes presented "necessity" in terms such as the following: Given all that we know about a person's preponderating inclinations, we can anticipate with a fair degree of certainty that he or she will choose thus

132. *Ibid.*, 158. In addition, Edwards perceptively observed, "the word 'nature' is often used in opposition to 'choice'; not because nature has indeed never any hand in our choice; but this probably comes to pass by means that we first get our notion of nature from that discernible and obvious course of events, which we observe in many things that our choice has no concern in; and especially in the material world. . . . So men make a distinction between 'nature' and 'choice'; as though they were completely and universally distinct. Whereas, I suppose none will deny but that choice, in many cases arises from nature, as truly as other events. But the dependence and connection between acts of volition or choice, and their causes, according to established laws, is not so sensible and obvious."

133. *Ibid.*, 181; see also for explication, pp. 152–154.

and so. We have already noted Edwards's use of Clarke's example of the moral necessity involved when a healthy person refuses (that is, chooses not) to commit suicide. In the logic of twentieth-century science, all "causal" sequences are interpreted in terms of probabilities of greater or less degree, but in Edwards's day there was a great difference (and to some extent there still is) between an anticipated event in human affairs that is highly probable and an anticipated event in nature that is absolutely certain. If by moral necessity Edwards most of the time meant little more than high probability, then Clarke's interpretation of moral necessity, that it is not really necessity at all, would seem to be more correct than Edwards's.

We cannot come to a satisfactory understanding of the meaning of moral necessity for Edwards without first giving some attention to the theory of habit, which was for centuries everywhere in the West the keystone of moral psychology.[134] Edwards's ideas on the subject were relatively conventional, although much about the theory of habit was controversial, and there were opposing schools of thought.

A habit was understood to be an acquired power of the soul that gave a person facility and consistency in some activity. Aristotle had spoken of both intellectual habits and practical habits. Moral habits were of the latter sort. In sharp contrast to the usual modern understanding of the term "habit," the idea as it was used in moral philosophy had no connotation of merely autonomic behavior, such as a mechanical rut or routine that one cannot "kick." The habit of virtue, for example, is a conscious, intelligent, internal disposition that underlies and gives rise to virtuous acts. Of the relation between acts and habits (actual versus habitual behavior), it was commonly said that acts come before habits in time, because only by repetition of acts can a habit be acquired, but the habit precedes the act in the order of nature in the sense that facility in the action is achieved only after possession of the habit. Almost all of the points mentioned here were open to dispute, but a particular area of controversy concerned the permanence of habits, both in a state of disuse and even more when acts antithetical to the habit are performed. In what sense could one be said to have a habit that is not manifested in acts? And how can the mere repetition of external acts result in the establishment of an internal disposition? Does a habit become qualitatively different from the acts that lead to its formation, or is a habit never anything more than the accumulation of acts, a mere quantitative fact?

134. Although the idea of habit has been the most enduring of psychological concepts, with clear beginnings in Aristotle and continuous use thereafter in theories of memory, association, and behavioral conditioning, the literature on the history of the idea and its importance is relatively small. For a short review of the idea of habit in the early 18th century, with some attention given to Jonathan Edwards, see Fiering, "Franklin and the Way to Virtue," *Am. Qtly.*, XXX (1978), 199–223.

So pervasive was the theory of habit in Western moral thought that it is hardly surprising to find it became intertwined with certain notions in Christian theology. The innate depravity of mankind after the Fall was thought of in terms of moral habit as was the renewed state of the saved, although these habits, rather than being acquired through iteration of acts, were assumed to be infused directly by God. The infused habit of grace is permanent, for from the beginning it was not dependent upon acts. Thus, the perseverance of the saints could be attributed to the indelible habit of holiness and virtue bestowed by grace.[135]

In terms of the prevailing theory, it is not hard to see how Edwards could argue that acts related to particular habits follow necessarily from those habits. Although different terminologies were used, roughly it can be said that a habit was comparable to a disposition or inclination of the psyche that leads a person consistently to behave in a particular way. Edwards saw this relationship as one of varying or graduated regularity. Sometimes the connection between a habit and its acts is loose, because the habit is not deeply embedded; in other cases, Edwards believed, the habit is so fixed that one can truly speak in terms of a necessary connection between the disposition and the act equivalent to the necessity of a proposition in logic.

Moral necessity, Edwards wrote, refers to that "necessity of connection and consequence, which arises from such *moral causes*, as the strength of inclination, or motives" and the volitions or actions that follow. Moral causes include "habits and dispositions of the heart."[136] Moral necessity "*may*" be as absolute as a natural necessity, Edwards observed, as in some cases when "a previous bias and inclination, or the motive presented" is "so powerful, that the act of the will may be certainly and indissolubly connected therewith."[137] But the influence of motives or habits is not always so.

> When motives or previous bias are very strong, all will allow that there is some difficulty in going against them. And if they were yet stronger, the difficulty would be still greater. And therefore, if more were still added to their strength, to a certain degree, it would make the difficulty so great, that it would be wholly impossible to surmount it. . . . Therefore it must be allowed, that there may be such a thing as a sure and perfect connection between moral causes and effects.[138]

---

135. Cf. Owen, *Pneumatologia*, 411–415: The new nature of the regenerate arises "not from *precedent Actions* of Holiness, but is the Root of them all. Habits acquired by a multitude of Acts . . . are not a *new* Nature." Such habits are no more than "a readiness for Acting from Use and Custom." Holiness, however, is "a gracious supernatural Habit."

136. *Freedom of the Will*, ed. Ramsey, 156.

137. *Ibid.*, 157. My italics.

138. *Ibid.*

Thus, only when the prevailing motives and inducements are overwhelming can one speak of real necessity. In such a case, however, we may ask, can a person still be held responsible for his actions?

The opposite of moral necessity to do something is "moral inability" to do it, which in Edwards's terminology refers to the want of inclination. "When a person is unable to will or choose such a thing, through a defect of motives, or prevalence of contrary motives, 'tis the same thing as his being unable through the want of an inclination, or the prevalance of a contrary inclination, in such circumstances, and under the influence of such views."[139] Edwards's examples of moral inability reveal how much his concept of moral necessity was really a form of psychological predictability or probability rather than true metaphysical or logical necessity:

> A woman of great honor and chastity may have a moral inability to prostitute herself to her slave. A child of great love and duty to his parents, may be unable to be willing to kill his father. A very lascivious man, in case of certain opportunities and temptations . . . may be unable to forbear gratifying his lust. A drunkard, under such and such circumstances, may be unable to forbear taking of strong drink.

Finally,

> A strong habit of virtue and great degree of holiness may cause a moral inability to love wickedness in general, may render a man unable to take complacence in wicked persons or things; or to choose a wicked life, and prefer it to a virtuous life. And on the other hand, a great degree of habitual wickedness may lay a man under an inability to love and choose holiness; and render him utterly unable to love an infinitely holy Being, or to choose and cleave to him as his chief good.[140]

That most of these examples seem tautologous was the result of the existing confusion in the theory of habits. If the acts define the habit, then it is a purely analytic statement to say that the drunkard cannot refuse a drink. A person who cannot refuse a drink is by definition a drunkard. If, on the other hand, the habit has a psychological reality independent of acts, then the statement describes one of the properties of the habitual trait of drunkenness.

Edwards attempted to deal with this confusion by distinguishing between "*general and habitual* moral inability" and "*particular and occasional* moral inability." The former referred to "a fixed and habitual inclination, or an habitual and stated defect, or want of a certain kind of inclination." In this condition, the habit is so deeply established that it is no longer definable

139. *Ibid.*, 159–160.
140. *Ibid.*, 160.

in terms of the acts to which it gives rise. A particular or occasional moral inability, on the other hand, is an "inability of the will or heart to a particular act, through the strength or defect of present motives, or of inducements presented to the view of the understanding, on this occasion." Thus, if a person takes a drink against good advice, it may be only an occasional weakness, possibly an inchoate habit, but not yet a chronic state. In any case, as was evident in Edwards's large treatise on *Original Sin*, he believed that a general inability, or better, a general inclination to sin, could exist without its being manifested consistently in particular acts, since particular acts can be influenced by transient causes and occasions that give rise to a choice inconsistent with the preponderant habit.[141] In both cases, however, the choice is determined, whether it be by the prevailing habitual inclination or by a passing excitation or inducement. There is always some motive. Yet one may well ask at this point, is not this very possibility of alternate choices a meaningful liberty of will? To say, as Edwards seems to, that whether a person is governed in his choice by the general inclination or by the particular inducement makes no difference with regard to his freedom, since in either case his choice is determined by a motive, is what Clarke called a "necessity upon supposition." Because a choice has been made, it is assumed by the determinist reasoner that the choice was necessitated by prior conditions. Some choice had to be made, even if the choice was a refusal to make a choice, and that choice must be caused. Yet, as Isaac Watts put it in one of his philosophical essays, the question is not whether one is free to do neither of two absolute alternatives — let us say, to take a drink or not take it — but whether one is genuinely free to do either.[142] Both of the possible choices will be governed by motives, a prevailing habit or a preponderating inducement, reasons or causes, but is it inevitable, prior to the choice, that one rather than the other will be chosen? Edwards could only give two answers to such a question: (1) the strength of the habitual disposition makes it highly probable what the choice will be; (2) the choice, whatever it is, will be "caused" by antecedent events. It is easy to see, however, that the first answer does not describe real necessity; and the second, by focusing only on the fact that the individual choice, whatever it may be, is necessitated or determined, avoids the crucial question of whether the power of election *between* the two alternatives is preserved. As

141. *Ibid.*, 160–161. Cf. Edwards, *Religious Affections*, ed. Smith, 118–119: "The degree of religion is rather to be judged of by the fixedness and strength of the habit that is exercised in affection, whereby holy affection is habitual, than by the degree of the present exercise: and the strength of that habit is not always in proportion to outward effects and manifestations, or inward effects, in the hurry and vehemence, and sudden changes of the course of the thoughts of the mind."

142. [Isaac Watts], *Philosophical Essays on Various Subjects* . . . (London, 1733), 290.

we noted earlier, Edwards failed to explore the question of whether the locus of freedom might lie in the intellect that governs choosing or willing;[143] he concentrated instead on the absence of freedom in the act of choosing itself. In Edwards's broad definition of motive, it is true that this act cannot occur without a motive.

Merit and Psychological Necessity

We have already noted Edwards's conviction that, practically speaking, if one simply observes what society does rather than what philosophers say, there is no evident incompatibility between the assumption of psychological determinism and moral approbation, disapprobation, or even reward and punishment. Edwards took it as his main task in *Freedom of Will* to deal with the question of whether the Calvinist system, with its determinist doctrines, implicated God in an ordering of the world that was morally unacceptable to reasonable men.[144] It seems evident that the most difficult paradoxes arise when one moves from the issues raised by psychological determinism alone to those posed by theological determinism. As we indicated earlier, in ordinary judicial affairs, however men may assign blame and punishment to the actions of others, it is always assumed that no one involved in meting out punishment is also in any way part of the cause of the punishable action.[145] Nevertheless, whatever Edwards's failures were to untie this formidable knot, he succeeded in *Freedom of Will*, perhaps more than anyone else had before him, in demonstrating that determinism is for the most part irrelevant to the dispensing of praise and blame and reward and punishment, assuming always, of course, that the agent has liberty of spontaneity (that is, that there are no external constraints). This achievement is independent of the question of

143. Edwards would say that this "solution" only pushes the question back to the question of what has governed the choice in the intellect.

144. Edwards argued that logically there is no difference between the problems of freedom that arise when one assumes simply the existence of divine prescience and foreknowledge and when one assumes the existence of absolute decrees of predestination. There is as much liberty or absence of liberty with divine foreknowledge as there is with divine decrees, and therefore Calvinists are no more burdened with the problem than any other Christian denomination. See *Freedom of the Will*, ed. Ramsey, 261–266.

145. It is currently fashionable to speak of all of society as being the cause of the assassin's deed, which puts society in the same moral predicament as God in the traditional theological conundrum. Can society justifiably punish the murderer when it has itself created the moral and environmental conditions that nurtured the murderer and led him to commit his crime? This kind of social causation is privative just as God's "creation" of sinners was usually assumed to be privative.

whether determinism is a valid hypothesis or not. Indeed, by showing that justifiable praise and blame and reward and punishment are relatively unaffected by one's notions of liberty, Edwards set up a roadblock against the argument frequently used in the eighteenth century that human beings must have freedom of will in order to make reward and punishment justifiable. Edwards effectively separated the two issues, the one concerning determinism, the other concerning responsibility.

Edwards's most important contribution to the debate over the compatibility of merit and psychological necessity was the forcefulness of his argument that if the virtue of a person resides in the strength of his virtuous habits or inclinations, then the closer those habits come to making all consequent acts utterly necessitated, the greater is the merit, rather than the contrary. In the gradation of habits toward absolute control, a person is the more praiseworthy or the more blameworthy to the degree that he is irreversibly inclined to virtue or wickedness respectively. An uncertain virtue is not as rewardable as certain virtue, nor is only partial wickedness as condemnable as total wickedness. Liberty of will with regard to choice between moral good and evil would seem to make one less virtuous and less praiseworthy, if such liberty means hesitation and uncertainty in choosing the morally right course of action.[146]

Edwards particularly addressed the false belief that a "moral inability" relieves the agent of blame. According to this reasoning, if a drunkard says with apparent "sincerity" that he would like to reform but cannot, and indicates the depths of his inability to change, he thereby becomes less culpable than the drinker who is closer to reform because his tendency to drunkenness is weaker. In effect, such reasoning erroneously made moral difficulty comparable to natural difficulty. Since it is universally accepted that a natural impediment excuses, and a partial natural handicap partially excuses, this argument implied, by analogy, that the greater the moral inability the more excusable the wickedness.[147] But a moral inability, Edwards argued, is no more than a strong disinclination to act in a requisite way, and it is precisely inclinations that deserve moral judgment. It is an opposition of will, and men are properly held responsible above all for what they will, that is, for their voluntary acts. If disobedience to a moral command is excusable merely on the grounds of the inability of a person to obey because of the strength of his

146. It is usually the case, however, that a manifest struggle against temptation resulting in victory is more praised than an unconflicted victory. This fact led to an interesting discussion in the 18th century on the question of whether self-denial is the essence of virtue. Benjamin Franklin, among others, was a contributor to it. See Labaree *et al.*, eds., *Franklin Papers*, II, 19–21. Edwards commented on it in *Original Sin*, ed. Holbrook, 205.

147. Edwards, *Freedom of the Will*, ed. Ramsey, 297.

or her contrary inclinations, "then wickedness always carries in it that which excuses it," Edwards observed.

> 'Tis evermore so, that by how much the more wickedness there is in a man's heart, by so much is his inclination to evil the stronger, and by so much the more therefore has he of moral inability to do the good required. His moral inability, consisting in the strength of his evil inclination, is the very thing wherein his wickedness consists; and yet according to Arminian principles, it must be a thing inconsistent with wickedness; and by how much the more he has of it, by so much is he the further from wickedness.[148]

Such misconceptions, Edwards pointed out, result from confusion between how *actions* are properly morally evaluated and how *dispositions* are properly morally evaluated. Jesus remains praiseworthy even though it was morally impossible for him to sin, because moral value lies above all in constancy of dispositions, not in particular acts. Moreover—and this was Edwards's most effective insight—the virtuousness or viciousness of dispositions must be evaluated solely on the basis of their essential nature without relation to alleged causes or origins. To say, for example, that Jesus' holy disposition was caused by God's will is completely irrelevant to moral evaluation. Moral appraisal of internal inclinations or dispositions is of a different order than that used in judging outward actions, Edwards pointed out, although the two are easily confused. It is a "very plain dictate of common sense," Edwards wrote, that the moral good or evil of "outward actions, and sensible motions of the body . . . don't lie at all in the motions of themselves; which taken by themselves, are nothing of a moral nature." The essence of all the moral good or evil in such actions "lies in those internal dispositions and volitions which are the cause of them." What happens then typically, Edwards observed, is that having become used to judging *external actions* with reference to prior causes, people unwarily come to speak of volitions and "*internal exercises* of their inclinations*" in the same way, as though volitions, too, must be seen as an effect of a prior cause and the cause itself judged. It is obvious, however, that if internal dispositions and inclinations are seen as effects, then one is caught in the fallacy of explaining evil or good acts by infinite regression of causes. "If the essence of virtuousness or commendableness, and of viciousness or fault," Edwards wrote,

> don't lie in the nature of the dispositions or acts of mind, which are said to be our virtue or our fault, but in their cause, then it is certain it lies

---

148. *Ibid.*, 309. Natural defects in the understanding may excuse one from blame, Edwards wrote, but "insufficiency of motives will not excuse."

nowhere at all. . . . If the vice of a *vicious* act of will, lies not in the nature of the act, but the cause; so that its being of a bad nature will not make it at all our fault, unless it arises from some faulty determination of ours as its cause, or something in us that is our fault; then for the same reason, neither can the viciousness of that cause lie in the nature of the thing itself, but in *its* cause. . . . And thus we must drive faultiness back from step to step, for a lower cause to a higher, in infinitum: and that is thoroughly to banish it from the world, and to allow it no possibility of existence anywhere in the universality of things.[149]

There is no escape from the conclusion, as Edwards saw it, that either the agent is responsible for his voluntary acts or nobody is. Moral evil, Edwards summed up, "consists in a certain *deformity* in the *nature* of certain dispositions of the heart, and acts of the will; and not in the deformity of something else, diverse from the very thing itself . . . supposed to be the cause of it."[150] A person is responsible for his or her character under all circumstances. To prove that person has a virtuous or a vicious character simply intensifies the goodness or the badness of their deeds; it does not vitiate the worth of a good deed, or excuse the evil of a bad one.

Action and Passion

Almost the very last question that Edwards considered in *Freedom of Will* was perhaps the most fundamentally important, the practical one of whether it can be said that determinism contributes to "atheism and licentiousness."[151] Broadened slightly, this question could rightly be seen as the central consideration behind all the wrangling over free will in the seventeenth and eighteenth centuries. Which belief—determinism or libertarianism—contributes more to moral betterment and reform? According to the libertarians, determinism "saps the foundations of all religion and virtue, . . . [and] renders vain all means and endeavors."[152] By appearing to eliminate the significance

---

149. *Ibid.*, 337–338.

150. *Ibid.*, 339. Edwards wrote to his friend the Rev. John Erskine in Scotland on Aug. 3, 1757: "I think that the notion of liberty, consisting in a *contingent self-determination of the will*, as necessary to the morality of men's dispositions and actions, is almost inconceivably pernicious, and that the contrary truth is one of the most important truths of moral philosophy, that ever was discussed." Reigning wicked dispositions of heart, the failure of men to convert, Edwards wrote, "These things are very much, for want of being thoroughly instructed, in that great and important truth, that *a bad will, or an evil disposition of heart, itself, is wickedness*. It is wickedness, in its very being, nature and essence." Printed *ibid.*, 465–470.

151. *Ibid.*, 420–422.

152. *Ibid.*, 420.

of personal effort and the possibility of real options, leaving all to the chain of causes, the doctrine of necessity seems to result ultimately in passivity.[153]

Edwards, Collins, and other determinists replied that, on the contrary, the doctrine of liberty creates the greatest danger, for it "overthrows all connection, every degree, between endeavor and event, means and end." If men are to be held responsible only for what they are conscious of freely choosing, they will end up excusing wicked inclinations, a vicious nature, and evil dispositions as things they have had no control over forming in themselves. Insofar as people can claim that their deeds and particular actions were necessitated by these preexisting states, they will be able "to justify the vilest acts and practices." "How naturally," Edwards wrote, "does this notion of the sovereign self-determining power of the will, in all things, virtuous or vicious, . . . tend to encourage men to put off the work of religion and virtue, and turning from sin to God." Relying only on the power of self-determination, men tend to make excuses for themselves when they find they are unable to overcome evil habits.[154]

Edwards believed it was historically demonstrable that during the period when people in Britain and America generally accepted Calvinist beliefs virtue and piety abounded, whereas in his own time, when Arminianism was in the ascendancy, vice, luxury, profaneness, and wickedness prevailed, despite the new doctrines. " 'Tis remarkable," he sneered, "that this happy remedy (discovered by the free inquiries and superior sense and wisdom of this age) against the pernicious effects of Calvinism, . . . should on so long a trial, be attended with no good effect."[155]

It is a curious fact that each side in the dispute charged the other with having encouraged passivity. The libertarians feared Islamic fatalism and apathy;[156] the determinists feared irresponsible self-indulgence. In order to compensate for the moral dangers and errors seen in the opposition, the libertarians stressed man's independence of fate, destiny, and inherited character, a position that can easily lead to excesses of pride and to false confidence, and that did eventuate in a crushing Victorian emphasis on "will-power." Personal

153. *Ibid.*, 422. Calvinist doctrines, it was said, "undermine the very foundation of all religion and morality, and enervate and disannul all rational motives, to holy and virtuous practice."

154. *Ibid.*, 421.

155. *Ibid.*, 422.

156. Leibniz wrote, "There is a *fatum mahometanum*, a *fatum stoicum*, and a *fatum christianum*. The Turkish fate will have an effect to happen, even though its cause should be avoided; as if there was an absolute necessity. The stoical fate will have a man to be quiet, because he must have patience whether he will or not, since 'tis impossible to resist the course of things. But 'tis agreed, that there is a *fatum christianum*. . . . Those who submit to it . . . have not only patience like the heathen philosophers, but are also contented with what is ordained by God, knowing he does everything for the best." Alexander, ed., *Leibniz-Clarke Correspondence*, 58.

character itself became something believed to be easily manipulated through rational will.

> Manlike he stood by man's free will
> And power to effect each thing he would,
> Did reason but pronounce it good.[157]

The determinists, on the other hand, reacted against the easy self-acceptance they saw as the prime danger in libertarianism by adopting the severely judgmental attitude that people are wholly to blame for who they are under any and all circumstances. They challenged the human spirit by producing guilt rather than by demanding willpower.

In both cases, what each group feared in the other did not come to pass. Rather than self-indulgence, the libertarians developed willpower; rather than apathy, the determinists were energized by their guilt. It seems that either determinism or libertarianism can be used as an instrument of moral reform, although, as Edwards believed, there are perhaps greater spiritual dangers in libertarianism. The determinists retained a better sense of what is and what is not within a person's power for effecting self-transformation. They understood that will can only do so much; it is necessary also sometimes to wait for outside blessings.[158] The wisdom in the Calvinist doctrine of conversion is particularly evident in its emphasis on the intricate blending of acting and suffering.[159]

Edwards demanded of men both action and passion, agency and patience, and he specifically noted that "the soul may be both active and passive in the same thing in different respects, active with relation to one thing, and passive with relation to another."[160] Certainly the will has the peculiarity in Edwards's psychological schema of being both active in relation to directing the body and passive in relation to emotions like love. Willing or choosing may be seen as either active or passive, or as both. One of the major differences between accountability in the eyes of God and accountability in the eyes of men is that in the case of the latter, people are legally punished only for active willing, whereas God holds men punishable for their passive willing, too, that

157. Herman Melville, *Clarel*, I, xxxvii, 30–34.

158. I am much indebted to Leslie H. Farber, *The Ways of the Will: Essays toward a Psychology and Psychopathology of Will* (New York, 1966) for an understanding of the limitations of rational or active willing.

159. "In efficacious grace we are not merely passive, nor yet does God do some, and we do the rest. But God does all, and we do all. God produces all, and we act all. For that is what he produces, viz. our own acts. God is the only proper author and fountain: we only are the proper actors. We are in different respects, wholly passive, and wholly active." Edwards, "Concerning Efficacious Grace," in *Works*, II, 580.

160. *Freedom of the Will*, ed. Ramsey, 157.

is, for their affections and passions as well as for their deeds. To some extent, Edwards's analysis of the will silently shifted back and forth between these two kinds of will. The theological criterion was transported into the terrain of secular ethics.[161]

God has promised salvation to man, Edwards wrote, if man fulfills two conditions, both of which are within his power. First, are "those acts which consist and are compleat in the meer immanent exercise of the will, or inclination it self. Such are the internal breathings of love to God." These internal dispositions, habitudes, volitions, or whatever, are in man's power, Edwards insisted, "because when we say a thing is not in any one's power we mean that he can't do it if he will, but this is absurd," for in the case of immanent acts of the will "the willing is the doing, and the doing of 'em consists in the willing of 'em." The second kind of condition to which salvation is promised are "those actions . . . that are the effects of will, and depend upon it," which flow from it, which are properly called voluntary actions." This kind of condition a person "may be said properly to have in his own power in the vulgar and more ordinary use of such an expression." To say that something is in a person's power means that the person can do that thing if he or she wills to. Edwards was convinced, apparently, that the "vulgar" distinction between a person's power over transient acts and power over immanent acts of will was false in the sense that one bears no less responsibility for immanent acts of will than transient ones. "A man has it in his power in the voluntary actions of his life, universally and steadfastly and faithfully to obey God's commands and cleave to and follow Christ through all difficulties and trials, tho it be certain that without love to God and faith in Jesus Christ no man will do it."[162] Love, then, is the precondition, or rather is the very immanent act of will, required for salvation. But everyone knows that it is impossible to will to love. One cannot force a passion.[163] As the etymology of the words indicate, passions and emotions come to pass in us involuntarily. In courts of law men and women are held responsible only for their active willing, for what they do in the world, but not for hating or loving, resenting or desiring, because human beings cannot deliberately generate such things as loves and hates. We are held responsible for controlling and governing passions and affections, but not for producing them. Legally, people are punishable for their passions only if they act on them criminally.

God is different, however, Edwards supported the profound theology that held people equally responsible for their passive willing and their active will-

161. Cf. Kaufman and Frankena, eds., *Freedom of the Will*, xxxi: Edwards "writes as if he believed that the criteria of blameworthiness appropriate on the Day of Judgment are the same as those appropriate in the criminal court."

162. Miscellanies, no. 573.

163. See the discussion in Farber, *Ways of the Will*, 1–25.

ing. Indeed, the distinction was practically ignored. The same word "will" could be used to describe the effort of moving a little finger and the disposition to love God, even though the latter is the kind of willing that has to be given to one and cannot be brought about simply by effort. Such a theology can be extremely effective in engendering a personal crisis, which may then be the furnace in which the new metal is cast. The call for men to *feel* differently than they have hitherto and to redirect their loves lest they be severely judged, although it seems to be an impossible demand—for one is asked by it to alter actively what has to happen passively—can bring about extraordinary change, a conversion. Psychoanalysts and other curers of souls in the twentieth century use a similar spiritual logic. They force the patient back on himself, making him (or her) take responsibility in totality for who he (or she) is—inclinations, hidden desires, resentments, and all. The alternative, after all, is to allow the patient to blame causes outside—parents, society, or God—which has the effect of hardening one's faults rather than correcting them. The patient, like the seeker of redemption, must adopt the paradoxical belief that he can change himself by the passive action of assuming responsibility or guilt (what the Puritans called conviction of self), which means taking full possession of undesirable affections and passions that one knows cannot be changed merely by will. The patient and the seeker both accept that they are *justly* suffering for who they are by admitting in the end that the most despised elements in their personalities are, in effect, the product of deliberate choice *as well as being at the same time* the result of outside forces. By this process of humiliation and remorse, health and salvation may be gained.

The acceptance of responsibility for even those qualities in ourselves which we had no power to will into existence may be a means to moral regeneration and health, a fact that Edwards certainly understood. But did it also follow that divine punishment by damnation was justifiable because of a failure in passive willing? These internal acts of will, passions and dispositions, are within each person's power, Edwards said, and people are as responsible for them as for outward acts. The only constraints on will, after all, are ourselves. It is arguable, however, that while useful as a therapy, it is unjust for people to be held responsible *and punished* for what they feel, since these kinds of internal "acts" are not within personal control. They are determined, as Edwards said, but they are more like a form of natural necessity than moral, if the distinction be allowed. Edwards's argument that a determinist system is compatible with reward and punishment may be valid only for transient acts of will, that is, those outward acts that are truly within a person's power in the vulgar sense, which means that the determinism of passive volitions does in fact relieve men of responsibility for their worst crimes in the heart. Yet, as Edwards said, it is internal nature that above all will be judged and must be judged for what it is in itself, without regard to origins or causes. The only way out of the dilemma is the miracle of conversion, which alters passive willing through the transmission of the Spirit. But how can one actively seek conversion, which is a passive process?

"It is certain," Edwards wrote, "that [in] every sinner that becomes good there is a last moment of his being bad, and a first moment of his [be]ing good, a last moment of his being in a state of damnation and a first moment of his being in a state of salvation." There is no way to get to heaven small step by small step. " 'Tis said that a sinful [man] begins to use himself to act the matter of virtue, and after a while it became habitual to him." Edwards responded to this proposal:

> It may become habitual to him [if] he did; but it can't become habitual to him to act as he never did before, by the means of his using himself to it. When [was the] time when the man first began to act from a truly virtuous principle? I suppose that it was [the] time that the man first acted true virtue. But [what made] him so to act true virtue, or from a truly virtuous principle . . . ? Suppose there is a person most profligate and vicious in his life, who afterwards leaves his old courses and reforms. . . . I ask, how this man became better than he was before, in his first beginning to reform; how came he by that virtue from which he acted when he first began to reform?[164]

The belief in free will leads men to assume that it is easy to reform oneself step-by-step through acquired habits. Yet is the first step, the one that creates the inclination to go on and take the subsequent steps in self-reform, freely acquired, or is it given, that is, determined? Edwards believed that hope for humankind must rest not on the assumption that men and women can remake themselves by arbitrary action of will, but on a sense of dependence upon divine intervention in human character.

164. Miscellanies, no. 73. See also Fiering, "Franklin and the Way to Virtue," *Am. Qtly.*, XXX (1978), 199–223.

7

Moral Theology

And it may be asserted in general,
that nothing is of the nature of true virtue,
in which God is not the first and the last.[1]

Jonathan Edwards's dissertation on the nature of true virtue, his most comprehensive statement on ethics, has two principal parts, as we have already noted. The first may be called a metaphysics of morals and constitutes his synthetic ethics and his moral theology. The second and more empirical part is critical ethics, and mainly relates to the debates among the naturalistic moral philosophers of his time. The questions Edwards was asking in each of these parts are quite different.

The first part consists of only two short chapters, hardly more than twenty-five highly concentrated pages in all, and addresses the problem of determining the metaphysical or ontological foundations of true virtue. This is a question that Edwards assumed could be answered on the basis of deductive reasoning alone, largely without regard to the practical matter of whether such virtue, whatever it may be, is possible on earth and without regard also to the psychological nature of such virtue or of the means by which it may be known. Neither the epistemological question of how we know a good act when we see it, nor the psychological question of how good actions are motivated, is considered in this first section.

The kind of metaphysical problem that Edwards examined in the first part of *True Virtue* was rarely explicitly investigated by the British moralists of the eighteenth century, who were mostly concerned with the psychology and epistemology of ethics and tried to use the inductive method as consistently as they could. In order to find a context for the first part of *True Virtue* one must turn to the philosophical epoch in which Edwards's thought was embedded,

---

1. Edwards, *True Virtue*, ed. Frankena, 26. This work was originally published posthumously in Boston in 1765, along with *Concerning the End for Which God Created the World*, under the inclusive title *Two Dissertations*.

the post-Cartesian rationalism of the late seventeenth century and the work of such figures as Spinoza, Leibniz, and Malebranche.

The second part of *True Virtue*, however, meshed very closely with the interests of the British moralists, as we have seen. Here Edwards descended from moral theology and considered those "other qualities, other sensations, propensities and affections of mind, and principles of action, that often obtain the epithet of virtuous, and by many are supposed to have the nature of true virtue."[2] In this second part Edwards did attempt to delineate both the motives of moral conduct—leaving aside spiritual influences—and the basis of natural moral judgments, in order to demonstrate the inadequacies of all natural morality when measured by the highest standards. He investigated the place of self-love, instincts, and habits, the meaning and function of conscience, and the concept of a moral sense, among other things, and grappled with the central problem of determining the actual relation of reason and of sentiment to moral experience.

On the naturalistic level Edwards recognized a difference between the foundation of moral *choices* in personal actions and the foundation of moral *judgments*; at the level of the highest virtue, however, such a distinction was invalidated in his thinking. At the natural level a person may "know" what is right, in a sense, and yet do wrong; wrongdoers may have a proper moral standard and yet not have the right moral temper. At the level of true virtue it is impossible for a person to truly relish the beauty of general benevolence and its harmonious order without also having that temper himself.[3] In the first part of Edwards's treatise, virtue is examined "in the eyes of him that perfectly sees all things as they are," namely, God.[4] In the second part, virtue is examined in the eyes of men. Except for what may be brought in incidentally, I intend to concentrate in this chapter only on the synthetic elements of Edwards's ethics, his moral theology. Some of Edwards's ideas in this area have been adumbrated already in the preceding chapters, but they have not been given systematic treatment.

The geometrical method of Edwards's first chapter in *True Virtue*, entitled "Shewing Wherein the Essence of True Virtue Consists," has rarely been noticed. This method is indicative of the quest in the post-Cartesian period to establish a strictly deductive ethics, which even Locke believed was possible. Henry More's *Enchiridion Ethicum* had a list of *noemata*, which were, in effect, his axioms, and in the early editions of the *Inquiry into Beauty and Virtue* Hutcheson attempted to develop a highly mathematized calculus of

2. *True Virtue*, ed. Frankena, 27.

3. *Ibid.*, 12.

4. *Ibid.*, 27.

virtue. Perhaps even closer in method to Edwards was Spinoza's *Ethics*.[5] After Edwards defined what true virtue most essentially consists in, he drew from this definition apodictically a series of eleven corollaries.[6] These corollaries are basically geometric in nature, having to do with the logical extension and elaboration of the elements in the basic definition or axiom.

True virtue, according to Edwards, "consists in *benevolence to being in general*." Or, in different words, it is that "consent . . . of heart to Being in general, which is immediately exercised in a general good will."[7] The main elements in this definition are the heart, or the will, which may also be described as the habitude or permanent disposition of the inner man; benevolence; and being in general. We have already frequently encountered the heart-language of seventeenth- and eighteenth-century ethics, and there is little more to be said about it, except to note once more Edwards's adherence to the school of thought that rooted virtue in the "qualities and exercises of the heart, or those actions which proceed from them" (2).

"Benevolence" requires a little more attention. Edwards observed that both Holy Scriptures and most Christian divines, as well as "the more considerable Deists," assert that virtue "most essentially consists in love" (4). This love is generally interpreted as benevolence or "kind affection."[8] The one point that needs to be stressed is that for Edwards, this benevolence, as in the traditional Protestant theory of holy affections, must consist in a "benevolent temper or . . . habit or frame of mind" (5). Edwards thought of a moral habit

5. Allen, in *Jonathan Edwards*, quotes from Spinoza's ethics: "35. God loves Himself with an infinite intellectual love." "36. The intellectual love of the mind towards God is that very love whereby God loves Himself." "37. The good which every man who follows after virtue desires for himself he will also desire for other men, and so much the more the proportion as he has a greater knowledge of God" (pp. 320–321). See the similar axioms from Leibniz in chap. 1, n. 88, above. On p. 36, however, Allen erroneously speaks of Edwards as moving from "Platonic rationalism, even Spinozism, to the Augustinian conception of God as unconditioned and arbitrary will." In fact, the process was exactly the reverse. The direction of Edwards's thought, under the influence of Samuel Clarke, was away from arbitrariness. Of course, Edwards knew little more of Spinoza than the name. In the 18th century Spinozism, like Hobbesianism, was synonymous with atheism.

6. The division of the corollaries into 11 is entirely my doing. I have ignored Edwards's numbering, which is erratic, and imposed my own, and also changed the order of Edwards's propositions as I found necessary and convenient for clear presentation.

7. *True Virtue*, ed. Frankena, 3. Hereafter, page references to this volume will appear in parentheses in the text.

8. Both Butler and Hume denied that benevolence was alone an adequate description of virtue. In particular, a full definition of virtue must include qualities not related to loving other persons, such qualities as are sometimes known as duties to oneself, and it must take into account the importance of usefulness or utility as a moral criterion. Since Kant, it has also been common to point out that although *virtue* may be a matter of goodwill or benevolence, *morality* requires also a sense of duty or obligation.

in this context not in terms of the accumulation of small acts, which then magically metamorphose into an indelible character, but as an inherent and permanent disposition of the soul, which in the case of conversion was divinely infused rather than acquired. The habit of virtue, in Edwards's thought, was fruitful in acts but could not be derived from acts or reduced to them.[9]

It is significant that in the two definitions of true virtue given just above Edwards treated the term "benevolence" as being interchangeable with "consent of heart." As we will see, when speaking of the foundations of true virtue Edwards did not mean by "benevolence" simply willing and doing good to another, since the term used in that sense would be inapplicable to the affections felt toward God. "Consent," as in consent of heart, is the more exact term in Edwards's thought, since its connotation more clearly includes both intellectual union (as in the old term in logic, "consentaneity") and affection, without the suggestion of condescension that clings to benevolence.[10]

Finally, the object of benevolence or love, "being in general," calls for comment. We know that in the English translations of Malebranche at the end of the seventeenth century the phrase "being in general" was frequently used; that *ens commune* was a subject of Scholastic discussion for centuries prior to Edwards's writing; and that Shaftesbury's "great Whole" and related expressions are closely allied to Edwards's notion. It is easy to speak in broad terms about the concept of being in general, but without more detailed research into seventeenth-century Protestant Scholasticism and Platonism it is impos-

9. See Fiering, "Franklin and the Way to Virtue," *Am. Qtly.*, XXX (1978), 199–223.

10. As Leo Spitzer has shown, the word "consent" relates to concord and harmony, suggesting a kind of objective union quite separate from doing good. See Spitzer, *Classical and Christian Ideas of World Harmony*, 102–107. In James Tyrrell's *Brief Disquisition of the Law of Nature*, a widely known condensation of Cumberland's *Laws of Nature* that was prepared with Cumberland's approval, we see a description of consenting union that is more intellectualist than Edwards's use of "consent": "The voluntary acknowledgment and consent of our minds to the perfections of the divine nature and actions, include the agreement and concurrence of our chief faculties, viz. the understanding and will, therewith. . . . When our acknowledgment and high esteem of the divine attributes move us to the imitation thereof, we must needs thereby arise to those high degrees of charity, or the endeavour of the greatest publick good which we observed God to prosecute; and such charity imparts not only exact justice to all, but that overflowing bounty, tenderness and sympathy with others, beyond which human nature cannot arrive; because these not only harmoniously consent with the like perfections in God, but also cooperate with him, to the improvement of the finite parts of the rational system." Tyrrell and Cumberland, writing years earlier than Edwards, were less concerned than the American about the degeneration of religious piety into utilitarianism: "Our benevolence, by giving [God] glory, love, reverence and obedience, thereby fulfills all the duties of humanity towards those of our own kind, which answers both the Tables of the moral and natural law; and in this consent of our minds with the divine intellect, consists that compleat harmony of the universe of the intellectual beings." James Tyrrell, *A Brief Disquisition of the Law of Nature, According to the Principles Laid Down in the Reverend Dr. Cumberland's . . . Latin Treatise on That Subject . . .*, 2d ed. (London, 1701 [orig. publ. 1692]), xxxii–xxxiii.

sible to speak very precisely about Edwards's ontological theories, since we lack knowledge of their immediate historical background. One can relate Edwards's theory of being to Thomas Aquinas, because there are libraries of volumes on Thomas's theories, but Edwards obviously was not a direct intellectual descendant of St. Thomas.[11] Fortunately, however, one can gain a fairly complete understanding of Edwards's moral thought without a full comprehension of his metaphysics.

For Edwards, as for Malebranche earlier, God is being, He who is, He whose essence is to exist, and He who is absolutely self-sufficient.[12] God is also properly designated "being in general," because God's being is itself the cause of all created essences. All existence, all being, derives from God, who is the one self-sufficient being. It seems clear that Edwards meant by "being in general" the transcendent God *plus* His ordered creation. Similarly, St. Thomas had said that God is not contained in *ens commune* (being in general), but transcends it.[13] Edwards's concept of being in general included all of what is now called "nature" as well as God, who is above nature. Edwards sharply contrasted benevolence to being in general with benevolence to "particular things within a limited, and as it were a private sphere" (2). Particular loves are not a bridge to universal love, but a bar to it. In Edwards's ethics there is no moving from particulars to generals, either from particular objects of love to general benevolence to being, or from individual acts to a permanent spiritual habitude. On the contrary, universal benevolence, that is, full consent to being, is the necessary and proper basis or precondition of all virtuous love for particular things. It seems probable that "being" was for Edwards, as for Malebranche, an intellectual *given* that required no defense. It is the necessary substratum of all knowledge whatsoever. The prima facie apprehension of being also means that all human beings innately know God in some sense; God is a necessary part of intellectual experience, although we are not always conscious of this knowledge and it varies in degree from person to person.[14]

11. On the difficulties of defining precisely the meaning of "being in general" in Edwards's thought, see the excellent discussion in Schafer, "Concept of Being in the Thought of Edwards," 135–141.

12. Cf. Beatrice K. Rome, *The Philosophy of Malebranche: A Study of His Integration of Faith, Reason, and Experimental Observation* (Chicago, 1963), 136–137.

13. Cf. St. Thomas Aquinas, *The Division and Methods of the Sciences*, ed. Armand Maurer (Toronto, 1958), xx.

14. Cf. Malebranche, *Search after Truth*, trans. Sault, Bk. III, chap. iv, 24: "The clear, intimate, necessary Presence of God (I mean the Unlimited, Infinite, and General Being) with the Mind of Man, acts with more Force upon it, than the Presence of all Finite Objects. It is impossible that it [*the mind of man*] should absolutely lay aside that general Idea of Being, because it cannot subsist out of God. Perhaps some may urge, that it may wander from it, because it may think on those particular Beings; but they would be mistaken: For when the mind considers any

One other property of true virtue that Edwards emphasized and that is central to his ethical theory is beauty. Although we have already commented on Edwards's concept of beauty at some length,[15] a word more must be said about it before we can examine his moral *noemata* or corollaries. True virtue and *moral* beauty are synonymous in Edwards's late thinking. Virtue is itself a form of beauty, and moral beauty is virtue. By "virtue" everyone means something beautiful, or rather, "some kind of beauty or excellency" (1), Edwards believed. "Virtue is the beauty of those qualities and acts of the mind that are of a moral nature, i.e., such as are attended with desert or worthiness of praise or blame." Beauty is connected with desert or justice, which has certain formal aesthetic qualities, but virtue is also "the beauty of the qualities and exercises of the heart, or those actions which proceed from them" (1).[16] As in the case of true virtue, true beauty by definition can be found only in the whole system. Particular beauties, no less than particular loves, are necessarily deficient and partial. True virtue, Edwards wrote, is the quality "belonging to the heart of an intelligent being, [that] is beautiful by a general beauty, or beautiful in a comprehensive view, as it is in itself, and as related to every thing with which it stands connected" (3). As in the work of Shaftesbury and Hutcheson, beauty was featured by Edwards because the analogy to aesthetics emphasized the point that a true moral response (like a religious conversion) must be an involuntary and disinterested perception, free of any calculation in relation to self-interest. The true appreciation of

---

Being in particular, it is not so far from removing from God, that it rather draws near, if I may so speak, to some of his Perfections, in removing from all others: However, it removes from them in such a manner, that it never wholly loses the sight of them. . . . They are always present to the Mind, but the Mind only perceives them in an inexplicable Confusion, because of its smallness, and the greatness of its Idea of Being. We may chance sometimes not to think on ourselves; but I believe we cannot subsist one Moment without thinking on Being; and even at that very time when we fancy we think on nothing, we are of necessity full of the wandering and general Idea of Being. . . . This Idea of Being, so great, so vast, so Real and Positive as it is, is yet familiar to us, and touches us so little because of its familiarity, that we almost believe we do not see it, that we do not reflect upon it, that we afterwards judge there is but little Reality in it; and that it is only form'd by the confused mixture of all particular Ideas: Though on the contrary, it is in that alone, and by that alone, that we perceive all Beings in particular." See Edwards's short essay "Of Being," probably written in the 1720s, conveniently printed in Townsend, ed., *Philosophy of Edwards*, 1–20.

15. See pp. 80–82, 110–118, above.

16. Cf. Edwards's *End for Which God Created the World*, in *Works*, II, 206: "Moral beauty especially consists in the disposition and affection of the heart." As we have already seen, there are two kinds of consent or agreement that evoke aesthetic or quasi-aesthetic responses: true moral beauty, consisting of concord and union of heart and mind, both within oneself and with others; and natural agreement, or secondary beauty, which has no "will, disposition, or affection" in it but consists only in uniformity and consent of "nature, form, quantity, etc." See *True Virtue*, ed. Frankena, 28.

beauty is not acquisitive or utilitarian, although beauty might hold out the "promise of happiness," in Nietzsche's and Stendhal's phrase.[17] In the first two chapters of *True Virtue* Edwards was concerned primarily with moral or spiritual (i.e., primary) beauty, which emerges uniquely in the loving relations of intelligent, purposeful beings: human beings, angels, and God. As we noted in our earlier discussions of beauty, secondary beauty is derivative from this primary beauty and is natural, whereas primary beauty is an attribute of the supernatural alone.

The Corollaries of True Virtue

Given these preliminary definitions, we can turn to Edwards's gnomic deductions from them.

1. Virtuous benevolence, since it has "an ultimate propensity to . . . the highest good of being in general," will "seek the good of every individual being unless it be conceived as not consistent with the highest good of being in general" (8). In other words, a general love includes the love of particulars, but it also includes a principle of discrimination, the ordering or grading of particular loves based on their relation to the ultimate love of being in general.

2. When the good of a particular being is in conflict with the highest good of being in general, the good of the former "may be given up for the sake of the highest good of being in general" (8). Cumberland, Shaftesbury, and Butler all enunciated similar rules regarding the subordination of parts to the interest of the whole, and the concept is, of course, an ancient tenet of Natural Law.[18] The common welfare may sometimes require the suppression of the interests of one individual. In Edwards's case, however, the emphasis is more on theological goods than social goods. This rule allowed for the divine penal

---

17. See above, chap. 3, n. 36. Edwards held, as we have seen in chap. 5, that the desire for happiness is a constant in human nature, that happiness cannot be removed as the goal of human striving. That beauty promised joy or happiness was also a tenet of Thomism.

18. Cf., for example, St. Thomas Aquinas, *The Summa Contra Gentiles*, trans. English Dominican Fathers (London, 1928), Bk. III, chaps. xvii–xx: "All things are subordinate in various degrees of goodness to the one supreme good, that is the cause of all goodness: . . . all things are subordinate to God as preceding ends under the last end. . . . The particular good is directed to the common good as its end: for the being of the part is on account of the whole: wherefore *the good of the nation is more godlike than the good of one man*. Now the supreme good, namely God, is the common good, since the good of all things depends on him: and the good whereby each thing is good, is the particular good of that thing, and of those that depend thereon." Moreover, "a thing partakes of the good, in so far as it is like to the sovereign goodness, which is God. Therefore all things, by their movements and actions, tend to a divine likeness as their last end. . . . It is clear that the last end of all things is to become like God."

justice of hell as well as for earthly justice.[19] Moreover, Edwards believed that this rule was valid not merely because it is prudential or socially useful, but because it is a law of God that has the intuitive force of self-evidence in the experience of the regenerate.

3. "If there be any being statedly and irreclaimably opposite, and an enemy to being in general, then consent and adherence to being in general will induce the truly virtuous heart to forsake that enemy, and to oppose it" (8-9). As we observed in Edwards's theory of hell punishment, the saint and the angel are necessarily in full consent or agreement with God in cutting off sinners and devils from divine benevolence, and on this basis the glorified in heaven may rejoice in the eternal torture of the rejected in hell. But it is possible to be even more specific about the graded love of particulars as it emanates from general love.

4. "That object who has most of being, or has the greatest share of existence, other things being equal, so far as such a being is exhibited to our faculties, will have the greatest share of the propensity and benevolent affections of the heart" (9). This puzzling statement is easily open to misinterpretation. By "most being" or "greatest share of existence," Edwards did not mean physical mass, spatial extension, or numerical quantity in any conventional sense. He did accept, however, the Neoplatonic tradition that spoke of ranks and orders of being based on degrees of divinity, perfection, holiness, or closeness to God.[20] There is an ordering of angels and an ordering of earthly

19. Cf. Shaftesbury, *Characteristics*, ed. Robertson, I, 246: "Now, if the whole system of animals, together with that of vegetables, and all other things in this inferior world, be properly comprehended in one system of a globe or earth, and if, again, this globe or earth itself appears to have a real dependence on something still beyond, as, for example, either on its sun, the galaxy, or its fellow-planets, then is it in reality a part only of some other system. And if it be allowed that there is in like manner a system of all things, and a universal nature, there can be no particular being or system which is not either good or ill in that general one of the universe; for if it be insignificant and of no use, it is a fault or imperfection, and consequently ill in the general system."

20. The following is one beautiful example of this kind of thinking out of many similar statements in the Neoplatonic tradition: "Every degree of Being to the least, the narrowest, and obscurest Point, hath Being it self in its amplitude and *majesty* in it, without which it could not be. Every thing that is in any kind or degree, hath the *Throne* of Being set up in it, with God the supream King, and Fountain of Beings, sitting upon it, and filling it with the train of his Glories. . . . Being it self, in its universal Nature, from its purest heighth, by beautiful, harmonious, just degrees and steps, *descendeth* into every Being, even to the lowest shades. All ranks and degrees of Being, so become like the mystical steps in that scale of Divine Harmony and Proportions, *Jacobs Ladder*. Every form of Being to the lowest step, seen and understood according to its order and proportions in its descent upon this *Ladder*, seemeth as an *Angel*, or as a Troop of Angels in one, full of all Angelick Musick and Beauty. Every thing as it lieth in the whole piece, beareth its part in the Universal Consort. The Divine Musick of the whole would be changed into Confusion and Discords, All the sweet proportions of all the parts would be disordered, and be-

things, with man at the pinnacle of earthly creatures. But these distinctions did not extend so far into human affairs that one could also presume to rank any one person in relation to another person. It is true the saint will necessarily love and prefer other saints over those who are unregenerate, but it is a serious misinterpretation of Edwards to assume that the theory of degrees of being was a theory applicable to human society taken alone.[21]

In addition to Neoplatonic theories of graded being, Edwards may also have been influenced by certain related Scholastic concepts, some of which were explicitly quantitative. Aristotle had spoken of each specific essence in the hierarchy of intelligibility as having a certain quantity of being, and he drew an analogy between definitions of essences and numbers. For essences, like numbers, can be related to each other quantitatively. This idea was developed by Thomas Aquinas and, undoubtedly, by many others. The modern historian Étienne Gilson describes the idea as follows: "Numbers are greater and smaller than other numbers; they make up an order and a hierarchy of larger and smaller quantities in which every particular number has its own place determined by purely quantitative relations of *plus* and *minus*. In a universe in which essences are like numbers, beings must necessarily constitute a hierarchy, and since being and the good are convertible, a hierarchy of 'quantities' of being is, by the same token, a hierarchy of degrees of goodness; that is, a hierarchy of perfection."[22] This interpretation of St. Thomas seems to match the presuppositions of Edwards's thinking exactly.[23]

---

come disagreeable, if any one, the least, and least considered part, were taken out of the whole. Every part is tyed to the whole, and to all the other parts, by mutual and essential *Relations*." From Peter Sterry's *A Discourse of the Freedom of the Will* (London, 1675) excerpted in Vivian De Sola Pinto, *Peter Sterry: Platonist and Puritan*, 151–152.

21. See Edwards, *An Humble Inquiry into the Rules of the Word of God, Concerning the Qualifications Requisite to a Compleat Standing and Full Communion in the Visible Christian Church* (Boston, 1749), 71.

22. Étienne Gilson, *Elements of Christian Philosophy* (New York, 1960), 192–193. Gilson continues: "Thomas joins the fundamental conception of the universe developed by Dionysius, in which the creative power of God flows down in a continuous stream of creatures, imparting to each of them, from the highest angelic hierarchy down to the humblest of minerals, such light and being as it is able to receive according to its kind."

23. Malebranche stressed hierarchy and order, but without emphasizing quantities: "God, who is the Universal Being, includes within himself all Beings after an intelligible manner; . . . all these intelligible Beings, which have a necessary Existence in God, are not equally perfect; it is evident [therefore,] that there must be an immutable and necessary Order among them . . . , an immutable and necessary Order, by reason of the relations of Perfection which are among the same Beings." Like Edwards, Malebranche held that God loves Himself with a necessary love and for that reason must love better in Himself that which includes and represents more perfection than that which includes less. The same "immutable Order which has the force of a Law in respect to God himself, has visibly the force of a law in relation to us" (*Search after Truth*, trans. Sault, 467). On Edwards's meaning of the term "being," cf. Elwood, *Philosophical Theology of Edwards*, 99. "Only persons, endowed with perceptive and reflective powers, are capable of par-

There is one other sense in which the notion of degrees of being may be understood. When he spoke of metaphysical hierarchies, Edwards sometimes had in mind the degree of charity or benevolence in the soul. Under the influence of gracious benevolence, as Edwards explained in *Charity and Its Fruits*, the soul is "enlarged to the comprehension of all . . . fellow-creatures" and goes forth "in the exercise of holy love to the Creator, and abroad upon the infinite ocean of good, and [is], as it were, swallowed up by it, and [becomes] one with it."[24] The measure of being is thus the extent of one's disinterested love. A virtuous person will love other beings in direct proportion to the lovingness of these others. Greatness of being, on the one hand, and goodness on the other, ordinarily correspond in the hierarchy of perfection.[25] If benevolence expands the individual's being, selfishness contracts it, shrinks existence by confining awareness and love to oneself, and shuts out divine being. The natural man, locked in self-love, would therefore rank lower in the quantitative hierarchy of being than the person who is regenerate.

5. The degree of true virtue that exists in benevolent propensity of heart to being in general is to be measured not only in proportion to the greatness of being of the object, but also in proportion to the greatness of being of the benevolent agent. "One who loves being in general, will necessarily value good will to being in general. . . . But if he sees the same benevolence in two beings, he will value it more in two, than in one only. Because it is a greater

---

ticipating in the wisdom and love of God wherein His true glory and beauty consist. God's 'communication is really only to intelligent beings' since they alone 'are the consciousness of the world.' This statement from the 'Miscellanies' blends in with the earlier 'Notes on the Mind,' in which [Edwards] had affirmed that 'perceiving being only is properly being.' " Yet Edwards definitely did not use the term "being" exclusively with reference to intelligent creatures. Being encompassed the entire creation.

24. Edwards, *Charity and Its Fruits*, ed. T. Edwards, 227–228.

25. Alfred Owen Aldridge, in "Jonathan Edwards and William Godwin on Virtue," *American Literature*, XVIII (1946–1947), 308–318, and in *Jonathan Edwards*, 149–159, compares Edwards and Godwin in relation to this hierarchy principle. Godwin knew Edwards's book on *True Virtue* and believed he was in agreement with Edwards when he asserted that love of the happiness of the greatest number of intelligent beings is virtue (*An Enquiry Concerning Political Justice and Its Influence on General Virtue and Happiness* [London, 1793]). Both Edwards and Godwin believed, according to Aldridge, that "our love is always to be proportioned to the magnitude of its object in the scale of being." In both cases, Aldridge maintained, the consequence of this principle can be discrimination about the "worth" of individuals in ultimate terms and the breakdown of the principle of human equality. Godwin presented the hypothetical case of Fénelon and his chambermaid trapped in a burning room with the possibility of saving only one, and decided that the principles of virtue dictated that Fénelon ought to be the one saved, because he was the greatest potential benefactor of mankind. Aldridge's discussion is not irrelevant to Edwards's ethics, but its effect is to minimize the great difference between Godwin and Edwards (even though Godwin himself may not have recognized the difference). Edwards was talking in ontological terms, not utilitarian, and would have been squarely opposed to Godwin's distinctions.

thing, more favourable to being in general, to have two beings to favour it, than only one of them. For there is more being that favours being: both together having more being than one alone" (12). This idea was apparently intended to provide a rationale for the divine creation of a multitude of souls and to demonstrate more fully the glory of the work of redemption. God's delight in numbers of beings, as well as in the quantity of being, explains why He did not rest content with His love for the Son and its reciprocation and went on to create the world. As Edwards wrote in his *Dissertation Concerning the End for Which God Created the World*, the companion piece to the *Dissertation on the Nature of True Virtue*, "It seems to be a thing in itself fit and desirable, that the glorious perfections of God should be known, and the operations and expressions of them seen by other beings besides himself. . . . It is a thing infinitely good in itself that God's glory should be known by a glorious society of created beings."[26]

At the same time, it was also necessary to preserve the principle of hierarchy in individual quantities of being, so that the love to God of one angel is not equated with the love to God of one toad. It is not numbers alone that matter. If one being is as great as two, or has as much existence in itself as two, Edwards wrote, with the same degree of benevolence as the two combined, "it is more favorable to being in general, than if there were general benevolence in a being that had but half that share of existence. As a large quantity of gold, with the same quality, is more valuable than a small quantity of the same metal" (12).[27] Pure metal, with minimal dross, is most desirable. God does not want existence to be wasted. A smaller vessel filled to the brim is preferable to one that is large but half filled.

The love of how many saints, one wonders, is equivalent to the love of one seraph? By what celestial scale are these things weighed? I am not familiar with more detailed speculations by Edwards on these questions, and the answer, in any case, would not be directly relevant to Edwards's ethics. His essential purpose in these corollaries was to establish and emphasize the principle of order or hierarchy in the entire system of being. Edwards wanted to make it perfectly clear that *benevolence to man* was not God's primary purpose in the creation of the universe, nor is it His foremost end in sustaining the world from moment to moment. God's end is His own glory, and human beings are given an opportunity to participate in this glory through consent of

26. *End for Which God Created the World*, in *Works*, II, 205–206.

27. In a footnote to *True Virtue*, ed. Frankena, 9, Edwards explained: "That which is great has more existence, and is further from nothing, than that which is little. One being may have every thing positive belonging to it, or every thing which goes to its positive existence (in opposition to defect) in an higher degree than another; or a greater capacity and power, greater understanding, every faculty and every positive quality in a higher degree. An archangel must be supposed to have more existence, and to be every way further removed from nonentity, than a worm."

heart to being in general. The creation is not subordinate to man's finite ends; man must subordinate himself to the infinite purposes of the Creator. If a hypothetical disinterested arbiter was introduced, Edwards wrote, whose office was to determine "how things shall be most fitly and properly ordered in the whole system, or kingdom of existence, including kings and subjects, God and his creatures," such a judge would be bound to decide that the "degree of regard should always be in a proportion, compounded of the proportion of existence, and proportion of excellence, or according to the greatness and goodness considered conjunctly. . . . As the Creator is infinite, and has all possible existence, perfection, and excellence, so he must have all possible regard." A disinterested arbiter would determine "that the whole universe, including all creatures, animate and inanimate, in all its actings, proceedings, revolutions, and entire series of events, should proceed from a regard and with a view, to God, as the supreme and last end of all: that every wheel, both great and small, in all its rotations, should move with a constant, invariable regard to him as the ultimate end of all; as perfectly and uniformly, as if the whole system were animated and directed by one common soul."[28]

Nevertheless, Edwards warned, it should not be thought that God is indifferent to man and has no love specifically for His creatures. For God's love may be understood in both a larger and a narrower sense. God's primary love, by which He communicates His own fullness in general—His knowledge, His holiness, His happiness, and so on—existed before the Creation, it is true. But "after the creatures are intended to be created, God may be conceived of as being moved by benevolence to these creatures." Therefore, it is an error to "set in opposition" or to consider as "the opposite parts of a disjunction" God's love for Himself and for His creatures. These two loves "are rather to be considered as coinciding one with the other, and implied one in the other. But yet God is to be considered as first and original in His regard; and the creature is the object of God's regard consequentially, and by implication as it were comprehended in God."[29]

6. Just as God's first love is to Himself, a fact that establishes His self-sufficiency, so the primary object of true virtue or of virtuous love is being in general, *not* benevolent being. This point cannot be stressed too much. True virtue consists of love to Him who *is*, to being itself, not to the God who is benevolent to man. Both a pure ontology and a pure religious psychology

28. *End for Which God Created the World*, in *Works*, II, 201–202. Edwards's reference to "one common soul" animating the whole universe was a daring allusion to the *anima mundi*, which had been a central notion in radical metaphysics since the 16th century. Gassendi's *Syntagma philosophicum* (1658), which was known in New England, contained a historical account of the doctrine (cf. J. S. Spink, *French Free-Thought from Gassendi to Voltaire* [London, 1960], 96 and *passim*). Edwards's phrase "as if" makes his usage perfectly orthodox.

29. *End for Which God Created the World*, in *Works*, II, 209.

demand this ordering of loves. At the level of moral psychology, Edwards wanted nothing to do with a prudential love for God. Although on several occasions he explicitly rejected the "willing to be damned for the glory of God" doctrine, his fundamental axiom of ethics, that true virtue consists in the consent of heart to being in general, in fact entailed that very teaching. Edwards was as intent as Fénelon had been to establish the principle that religious virtue presupposes disinterested purity of heart in devotion to God.[30]

However, true virtue in man, as in the excellence of God, includes two loves. In addition to the primary love to being in itself, there is another *secondary* object of virtuous propensity of heart, which is not simply being in general, but "benevolent being." Benevolence, in other words, necessarily loves benevolence, and love to being in general necessarily involves love to being's love for itself. This love of God's love to Himself (and to the whole creation) must be secondary to avoid a circular definition of virtue. The foundation of virtue remains love to being in general, but it follows from this primary principle that when anyone "under the influence of general benevolence, sees another being possessed of the like general benevolence, this attaches his heart to him, and draws greater love to him, than merely his having existence: because so far as the being beloved [i.e., the beloved being] has love to being in general, so far his own being is, as it were enlarged; extends to, and in some sort comprehends being in general" (9–10). By loving the trait or attribute of *benevolence to being* as it is found in another, one is also loving being in general, because all benevolence or love enlarges one's own being and becomes unified with being in general. The broader one's love, the broader one's being. Hence, benevolence to benevolence is shown to be logically deducible from love to being in general; the secondary principle follows from the primary.

7. Loving a being on the basis of that being's benevolent propensity to love being in general "necessarily arises from pure benevolence to being in general, and comes to the same thing." He that has "a simple and pure good will to general existence, must love that temper in others that agrees and conspires with itself. A spirit of consent to being must agree with consent to being. That which truly and sincerely seeks the good of others, must approve of, and love that which joins with him in seeking the good of others" (10). This statement has obvious political as well as theological meaning. Edwards's first principle

30. "The most proper evidence" that any love to a created being (including oneself) arises from "that temper of mind wherein consists a supreme propensity of heart to God," is the "agreeableness" of that love, in kind and degree, to "God's end in our creation, and in the creation of all things." There should be a "coincidence," Edwards wrote, in "manner, order, and measure" between our love and "the manner in which God himself exercises love to the creature in the creation and government of the world," and the way in which God subordinates the creature's happiness to Himself "as his own supreme end." Edwards, *True Virtue*, ed. Frankena, 24.

of psychology, as we have seen, was that the natural man loves love to himself and hates hate to himself. The regenerate soul, on the other hand, in an ordered fashion, loves love to others and hates hate to others. Edwards would be the first to say that the natural man, too, may love love to others, but if so that love is based on the recognition of the usefulness, direct or indirect, of such love to himself. In the case of the regenerate, the love of love to others is free of such concerns because it is based primarily on shared love to being in general, not on love to benevolence. One stands to benefit, perhaps, from benevolence, but not from being in general.[31]

It may not be altogether coincidence that Rousseau prepared his first draft of *The Social Contract* in 1755, the very year in which Edwards is believed to have written *True Virtue*. The logic of community and concord, whereby the sum of disinterested individual wills in a polity forms the sole legitimate will for all and the moral authority in the community, had already been stated fairly completely by Richard Cumberland in the preceding century and had become a very available idea by the time of Edwards's writing. But Edwards differed from both Cumberland and Rousseau in insisting that a true "general will" is possible only with the aid of divine grace. Nonetheless, for all three men the process is similar whereby individual wills transcend self-interest and merge in their common devotion to the good of all.

In *The End for Which God Created the World* Edwards stated these principles more clearly perhaps than he had anywhere else in his work.

> In God, the love of himself, and the love of the public are not to be distinguished, as in man, because God's being, as it were, comprehends all. His existence, being infinite, must be equivalent to universal existence. In God, the love of what is fit and decent, or the love of virtue, cannot be a distinct thing from the love of himself. Because the love of God is that wherein all virtue and holiness does primarily and chiefly consist, and God's own holiness must primarily consist in the love of himself.

31. Natural conscience and pure love to others function differently. In the latter case there is a union of heart with others, and a "kind of enlargement of the mind, whereby it so extends itself as to take others into a man's self." There is by implication "a disposition to feel, to desire, and to act as though others were one with ourselves." Approval and disapproval of conduct is not from uneasiness but from "a sense" of the primary beauty of true virtue, and this sense, of course, comes only from unity with being in general, not from the instinct toward self-unity. Natural conscience, Edwards held, is "private" in nature; true virtue, on the contrary, is "public." The first—"an inclination to agree with ourselves"—is a natural principle; the second—"an agreement or union of heart to the great system, and to God the head of it, who is all and all in it—is a divine principle." Both processes, though infinitely different, usually concur in practical life. *Ibid.*, 62–63. See above, chaps. 3 and 4.

The unity of self-love and general love in God is, of course, unique, but a useful comparison may be drawn to human affairs. The proper relation between the individual and the whole in the divine ordering of the universe, which is perfect in the case of God, and the basis of Natural Law in politics and society are connected. For the same reason that "public affection in the creature is fit and beautiful," Edwards wrote, "God's regard to himself must be so likewise. . . . If God's holiness consists in love to himself, then it will imply an approbation of, and pleasedness with the esteem and love of him in others; for a being that loves himself, necessarily loves love to himself." Man's love to himself, and his love of love to himself, separate him from God and from his fellow men. This is the first principle of sin. God's love to Himself and His love of love to Himself, on the contrary, unite all being in a community of love, and decisive participation in this great underlying consensus is the first principle of salvation.[32]

Edwards was in close agreement with the benevolist moralists, he himself observed, in placing "public affection or general benevolence" at the pinnacle of virtue. And Edwards and the benevolists agreed also that "if the essence of virtue lies primarily in this, then the love of virtue is itself virtuous. . . . Because if a man truly loves the public, he necessarily loves love to the public." For Edwards, it followed from these axioms that God, whose love for the public is superior to all others, ought to be the first object of virtuous love.[33] Hutcheson did not draw the same conclusion, and it was on this point that Edwards and he most sharply divided. In his careful discussion of "How far a Regard to the Deity is necessary to make an Action virtuous,"[34] Hutcheson commented: "We must disapprove that Temper, which, upon Apprehension of the perfect Goodness of the Deity, of his innumerable Benefits to Mankind, has not stronger affections of Love and Gratitude toward him, than those toward any other Being. . . . Positive virtue toward the Deity must go farther than a resolute abstaining from offence, by engaging us with the greatest vigor, to do whatever we apprehend as positively pleasing, or conducive to those ends in which we apprehend the deity delights."[35] So far Hutcheson and Edwards were in accord. But after this concession to religious motivation, Hutcheson concluded: "The bare absence of the idea of a deity, or of affections to him, can evidence no evil; otherways it would be a crime to fall asleep, or to think of any thing else. . . . Nay, that temper must really be very deficient in goodness, which ever needs to recall the thoughts of a divine

32. *End for Which God Created the World*, in *Works*, II, 217.

33. *Ibid.*

34. Hutcheson, *Illustrations on the Moral Sense*, Treatise II of the *Nature and Conduct of the Passions and Affections*, 3d ed., 307–339.

35. *Ibid.*, 320.

command and its sanctions, or even the thoughts of the interests of greater societies or systems, before it can be engaged into any particular acts of kindness."[36] In sum, Hutcheson believed that if one's heart is in the right place, considerations of love to God can only be secondary or peripheral as far as virtue is concerned. Mankind are agreed in their approval of certain kinds of good actions whether or not God is part of the end of the action. "This notion of making all virtuous affections to be only directed toward God," Hutcheson wrote, "is not suggested to Men by anything in their Nature, but arises from the long subtle reasoning of men at leisure, and unemployed in the natural affairs of life."[37] Hutcheson was willing to concede that love of God *ought to be* man's highest end in moral conduct, but he also pointed out that no human estimation of what constitutes virtue requires it and that no one in practical life applies such a standard.[38]

How far Hutcheson's ethical theory was deficient on its own grounds Edwards tried to show in the second part of *The Nature of True Virtue*, which we have already examined. The first part of *True Virtue* is not really commensurable with secular ethics. Edwards was concerned here with the metaphysical foundations of all value, and not simply with human moral experience. He was attempting to look at the question of virtue from the standpoint of the last and highest value, which must be, ultimately, union with God. He sketched a verbal picture in his conclusion to *The End for Which God Created the World* that captures all of his moral idealism and religious devotion, and which also reveals something of the vast canvas on which his thought must be displayed:

> Let the most perfect union with God be represented by something at an infinite height above us; and the eternally increasing union of the saints with God [be represented] by something that is ascending constantly towards that infinite height, moving upwards with a given velocity, and that is to continue thus to move to all eternity. God, who views the whole of this eternally increasing height, views it at an infinite height. . . . The time will never come when it can be said it [i.e., the body of the saints] has already arrived at this infinite height. . . . [Still] God aims at that

36. *Ibid.*, 334.

37. *Ibid.*, 339.

38. Edwards admitted that for virtue to be authentic "every particular exercise of love to a creature" does not have to "sensibly arise from any exercise of love to God, or an explicit consideration of any similitude, conformity, union or relation to God, in the creature beloved." "It is sufficient to render love to any created being virtuous, if it arise from the temper of mind wherein consists a disposition to love God supremely" (*True Virtue*, ed. Frankena, 24, 23). This answer brings out clearly how extremely important the idea of a permanent inward habitude or disposition to God was in Edwards's theory of virtue. Without this elusive quality of soul, there was little to choose between him and Hutcheson. In other words, almost all that stood between Hutcheson and Edwards was the theory of gracious regeneration.

which the motion or progression which he causes, aims at, or tends to.
. . . As he is the first author of [all creatures'] being and motion, so he is
the last end, the final term, to which is their ultimate tendency and aim.[39]

The basis of true moral aspiration is the dynamic circle of love that governs
the universe. One is either flowing to God as part of this consenting unity or
swimming against the stream in self-interested dissent. It should hardly need
stating that what was considered dissent in the social and political realm on
earth could well be—and most of the time in Edwards's eyes probably was—
consent to God's will. There was certainly not the slightest suggestion in his
thought that those who conformed merely to the tendency of things on earth
would be exempted from ultimate damnation.

Edwards's last four corollaries refer to the meaning of beauty in relation to
virtue and are helpful particularly in revealing, in a general way, more about
the peculiar psychology of true virtue.

8. "Spiritual beauty" consists of benevolence or love to benevolent being
and is, therefore, another name for the secondary object of virtuous love (see
corollary number 6, above). Spiritual beauty consists of those "various qualities and exercises of mind" that proceed from love to benevolent being and of
"the external actions which proceed from these internal qualities and exercises" (11). Like the secondary object of virtuous love, it is analyzable into
love to being in general.

9. "As all spiritual beauty lies in these virtuous principles and acts, so it is
primarily on this account they are beautiful, viz. that they imply consent and
union with being in general." The beauty of virtue, or rather, the true beauty
of true virtue, is grounded in consent or love to being in general.

10. Spiritual beauty, as defined above, is the object not only of benevolence
or well-wishing, but also of complacence or delight.[40] The first or primary
object of virtuous *benevolence* is being itself; the secondary object of virtuous
benevolence is spiritual beauty, which, as defined, is an attribute of benevolence to benevolent being. However, the primary object of virtuous *complacence* is not being, but spiritual beauty (or benevolence to benevolence). In
other words, complacence or delight, the appreciation of the beauty, occurs
first in the holy man's loving response to benevolence. If complacence did not
come first, it could be suggested that the response was egoistic, a calculating
benevolent love springing from hope of personal gain. But, no, complacence,
or disinterested esteem and appreciation, is primary in the man of true virtue

39. *End for Which God Created the World*, in *Works*, II, 256–257. The image is Malebranchean, but also Neoplatonic in general.
40. The distinction between love of complacence (i.e., complacent, or better, complaisant
love) and love of benevolence (i.e., benevolent love) was a traditional Scholastic notion. See
chap. 3, n. 50, above.

when he confronts true benevolence. In response to being in general, however, which transcends both spiritual beauty and benevolence or goodness, and is the highest name of God, complacent love is not the primary form of response. Benevolence is first. Being in general is not beauty and is not delightful, and therefore it cannot be the basis of complacence. Spiritual beauty, and a holy response to it (that is, a love of complacence), comes in only when, at the second level, God's benevolence to benevolence is perceived. His love to Himself then becomes the measure of all spiritual beauty.

Yet the question may arise, How can a person have benevolence to God? As Hutcheson wrote, "That word carries with it some supposal of indigence, or want of some good in the object."[41] To some degree, Edwards's term "consent" got around this difficulty, as we have noted, but he also gave the matter a detailed response in chapter two of *True Virtue*. Benevolence, Edwards said, is exercised not only in seeking to promote the happiness of another, but also in "rejoicing in his happiness." Benevolence implies sympathetic identification. When a favor has been bestowed upon us by another who has little need of our repayment, we show our gratitude mainly by rejoicing in the other's prosperity. Second, though we cannot give anything to God that we have independently of God—for we have nothing independently of God—we can still be "instruments of promoting his glory, in which he takes a true and proper delight" (16). In short, people can and ought to feel benevolent love to God, properly understood. He that has true virtue, Edwards wrote, consisting first of all in benevolence to being in general, and secondarily in benevolence to virtuous being, "must necessarily have a supreme love to God, both of benevolence and complacence. And all true virtue must radically and essentially, and as it were summarily consist in this" (15).

Continuing, Edwards took issue directly with Hutcheson's vacillation toward the doctrine that God is the proper end in any true system of ethics. "There seems to be an inconsistence in some writers on morality," Edwards noted. Although they do not

> wholly exclude a regard to the Deity out of their schemes of morality,
> . . . [they] mention it so slightly, that they leave me room and reason to
> suspect they esteem it a less important and a subordinate part of true
> morality: and insist on benevolence to the created system, in such a
> manner as would naturally lead one to suppose they look upon that as by
> far the most important and essential thing in their scheme. But why
> should this be? If true virtue consists partly in a respect to God, then
> doubtless it consists chiefly in it. If true morality requires that we should
> have some regard, some benevolent affection to our Creator, as well as

41. Hutcheson, *System of Moral Philosophy*, 70.

to his creatures, then doubtless it requires the first regard be paid to him; and that he be every way the supreme object of our benevolence (17).

Given Edwards's presuppositions about the divine infusion of true virtue, this issue with Hutcheson was moot, in any case. True virtue was attainable only with the aid of regenerating grace, which irresistibly pointed one toward God as the practical object of love. Edwards's final corollary made this rule clear.

11. It is impossible for one to "truly relish" the beauty of true virtue, consisting in general benevolence, "who has not that temper himself." But if one has the temper he will "unavoidably be pleased" with the same temper in another (12) and, of course, be pleased, above all, with God's benevolence. The determinist note in this last corollary, similar to that found in Hutcheson's theory of the moral sense, should not be overlooked. The regenerate soul is unavoidably determined by God in its holy responses. There is no coaction, of course, because the will and affections are themselves fundamentally re-oriented. In both Hutcheson and Edwards this determinism is a translation into philosophical terms of the concept of the perseverance of the saints.

Edwards's great purpose in the first two chapters of *True Virtue* was to give philosophical substance to his religious beliefs. In his *Thoughts Concerning the Revival* (1742) one can find stated in scriptural terms nearly all of the basic ideas he later included in the first section of *True Virtue*. God leads His children in a manner that "natural men cannot have," Edwards wrote in the earlier book, "by inclining them to do the will of God, and go in the shining path of truth and Christian holiness, from an holy heavenly disposition, which the spirit of God gives them." God teaches the saints their duty in a "gracious manner" and a "higher manner" than "any natural man is capable of while such."

> The spirit of God enlightens them with respect to their duty, by making their eye single and pure, whereby the whole body is full of light. The sanctifying influence of the spirit of God rectifies the taste of the soul, whereby it savours those things that are of God, and naturally relishes and delights in those things that are holy and agreeable to God's mind, and like one of a distinguishing taste, chuses those things that are good and wholesome, and rejects those things that are evil; for the sanctified ear tries words, and the sanctified heart tries action, as the mouth takes meat.[42]

42. *Thoughts Concerning the Revival*, 233.

Edwards and Malebranche

The essential point to be remembered about Edwards's metaphysics of virtue is his belief that the foundation or ground of true virtue is not love to *good* in general, as Hutcheson said, but love to *being* in general. The problem with the utilitarian view, Edwards observed, is that to define virtue only in terms of benevolence to benevolence, which is what Hutcheson's position amounts to, makes virtue itself "the foundation or first motive of that love wherein virtue originally consists, or wherein the very first virtue consists; or, it supposes the first virtue to be the consequence and effect of virtue. Which makes the first virtue both the ground and the consequence, both cause and effect of itself" (7). Although from an analytic point of view there may be nothing wrong with this circularity—one has to start somewhere—Edwards's theological concerns demanded that ethics be set upon a foundation in eternity, with God as the creator of all. In Hutcheson's theory, Edwards said, "we never come to any beginning or foundation; it is without beginning, and hangs on nothing" (7). If we begin with God, as we must, being is the primary term, with love and goodness as acts, attributes, or perfections of divine being.

Nicolas Malebranche sometimes expressed himself differently, in that he spoke more of *good in general* than *being in general*, but in fact his differences with Edwards on this point were verbal, not substantive. Edwards's intent was anticipated, for example, in the opening of the ninth dialogue in Malebranche's *Dialogues on Metaphysics and Religion*, where one of the characters observes: "How difficult it is to separate the notion of Being in general from the ideas of particular finite beings! How difficult it is not to attribute to God anything of that one feels in oneself! We are always ascribing human attributes to God; naturally we tend to limit the Infinite."[43] Edwards's stress on love to being as the essence of true virtue not only rejected utilitarian ethics, it also established that the world was not created out of sentimentality. The structure of the created moral universe, Edwards believed, is based on strict relations of fitness and order, with virtue taking its place in this order not merely as a human affection, but as a metaphysical category in its own right, expressing a certain fixed relation to God. "When our love is regulated by virtue," Malebranche wrote in words that are indistinguishable from Edwards's, "we love God; for when we love according to these Rules, the impression of love that God continually produces in our hearts inclines us toward him, and is neither diverted by free-will, nor changed into self-love.

---

43. Malebranche, *Dialogues on Metaphysics and Religion*, trans. Ginsberg, 225. Dialogues eight through ten generally expound a metaphysic quite like Edwards's. It is unlikely that Edwards knew Malebranche's *Dialogues* in any form, but as I have argued in chap. 1, above, it seems to me a certainty that he read Malebranche's *Search after Truth* early in life.

The mind then does only, with the greatest freedom, follow this impression that God gives it."[44]

But virtue is not only to love God, Malebranche continued, it is also "to love as God does; who only loves himself, and his works, because they relate to his perfections, and He loves these works proportionably to the relation they have to these perfections. . . . To love according to the rules of virtue, is to love God only; and to love God in every thing, is to love every thing so far as it partakes of his goodness and perfection, since that is to love them in proportion to their amiableness. In short, 'tis to love by the impression of the same love by which God loves himself."[45] Malebranche's implied "rules of virtue" could be no different from Edwards's corollaries.

For both men, God is not a humanitarian who can be identified with sentimental human criteria. Edwards's conception of hell and reprobation makes this perfectly evident, and it is apparent also in his metaphysics of true virtue, which begins with being rather than benevolence. "God is neither good, compassionate, nor patient in the vulgar sense of these terms," Malebranche had also stressed. God possesses these qualities only in a context of reason. "The immutable order is the law of God, the inviolable rule of His will." God "cannot prevent Himself from loving things in proportion as they are worthy of love." It follows, Malebranche continued, that "God cannot will that His creatures should not love in accordance with His immutable order. . . . He cannot will that we should love best what least deserves to be loved." The order of divine perfections constitutes God's law. When God acts on man through His love, He creates in man a love like His own. God cannot, therefore, will that "our love, which is but the effect of His love, should be contrary to His, or should tend towards that to which His love does not tend." On the rationale for punishment of sin, Malebranche and Edwards had an identical position. "A man whose heart is disordered through the bad use he makes of his liberty comes under the order of justice which God owes to his divine perfections, if this sinner is unhappy in exact proportion to his unruliness. . . . God loves order irresistibly. Therefore, He inevitably punishes those who offend against it."[46]

The extraordinary thing about Edwards's ethics, A. Owen Aldridge has commented, "which Edwards does not seem to have realized himself," is that he has "prescribed" for true virtue in man a standard exactly equivalent to

---

44. Malebranche, *Search after Truth*, trans. Sault, Bk. V, chap. v, 38.
45. *Ibid.*
46. Malebranche, *Dialogues on Metaphysics and Religion*, trans. Ginsberg, 221–224. Cf. Edwards's Miscellanies, no. 779: "The justice of God obliges him to punish sin. . . . Suffering is suitable and answerable to the quality of sinful dispositions and actions; it is suitable that they that will evil, and do evil, should receive evil in proportion to the evil that they do or will. . . . When sin is punished, it receives but its own, or that which is suitably connected with it."

that which he has "ascribed" to God.[47] But of course Edwards did realize exactly what he was doing, and so did Malebranche. For both men, it was precisely the unity of theology or Christian ontology with ethics that was of vital importance. Both Malebranche and Edwards believed that they were not only ascribing and prescribing, but also describing those very laws by which the universe is governed. The standard was indeed divine, infinite, and unattainable. But it held out the opportunity for continuous ascent toward union with God.

We have already stressed sufficiently the metaphysical rationalism of Edwards's later thought, which is so much akin to Malebranche's and Samuel Clarke's. The naive claim heard so often that Edwards restored the arbitrary, inscrutable *Deus absconditus* of early Calvinism must be corrected on two counts: first, such a God was not featured in any of the tenets of Calvin or his immediate disciples; and second, Edwards's God is preeminently a God of order who acts on the inherent fitness and suitability of the relations of things. If Edwards is properly designated a Puritan, in his theology he was the most rationalist of the Puritans, for the laws by which Edwards's God governs are beyond even the contractual or covenantal; they are the expression of what is inherently right. In the operations of grace, as in all of His actions, God is of course absolutely free, in the sense that His laws are unconditioned; but He acts in a context that He Himself has predetermined will be far from capricious. God's supernatural interventions in the world, like the processes of higher mathematics, are recondite, esoteric, and subtle, but they are not irrational or arbitrary. Except in the rarest of rare cases—such as the original creation of matter out of nothing—God operates by fixed, self-consistent, and orderly principles.[48]

The inherent rationalism of Edwards's universe is nowhere better revealed

47. Aldridge, *Jonathan Edwards*, 137.

48. See pp. 93–103, above. Although Perry Miller arrived at a conclusion similar to this, his analysis of the foundations of Edwards's metaphysical rationalism is generally ahistorical. Miller's third chapter in *Jonathan Edwards*, entitled "The Objective Good" (pp. 71–99), which revolves around Edwards's theory of causation and Newton's physics, contains a number of dubious statements that are the result of looking at both Edwards and Newton in an intellectual vacuum. Descartes, More, Malebranche, Leibniz, Clarke, and others might as well not have lived and written at all. The implicit rationalism in Newton's physics that, according to Miller, Edwards brilliantly sniffed out, was itself the result of prior *philosophical* speculation. If Newton had not lived at all, Edwards's metaphysics would hardly have been different. Everything Edwards ever said about causation and the order of the universe was already to be found in the philosophical speculation of the Cartesians before Newton published a word, and much of it can be found in writings that preceded Descartes. More generally, it seems to me to be a fundamental error to assume that Edwards's thought is a deduction from natural philosophy rather than from a priori principles, that is, ontology, or philosophical theology.

and illuminated than in his discussion in *True Virtue* of the nature of the response to the beauty of virtue. Edwards noted, first of all, that the beautiful is always an end in itself. It must be "immediately pleasant to the mind" and directly gratifying. Things that are agreeable for their usefulness, that is, for what they can bring beyond themselves, are not beautiful. Beauty is not the result, then, of uncovering "the relations" of a thing, looking for its consequences, or whatever. Edwards compared the immediacy of the sensation of beauty to tasting honey.[49] The pleasurable response does not depend on "any reasonings." It is, Edwards said, the direct result of "the frame of our minds" (99).

Almost all of this analysis of aesthetic response was quite traditional and could be found in the thirteenth century, if not before. But Edwards departed from tradition and united his thinking with various forms of seventeenth-century speculation when he spoke of beauty as being an objective relation between the "frame of our minds" and certain characteristics of the perceived world. Edwards gave this relation a theological content, but that specific content is only incidental to the analysis: "They who see the beauty of true virtue do not perceive it by argumentation on its connections and consequences, but by the frame of their own minds—or a certain spiritual sense given them of God—whereby they immediately perceive pleasure in the presence of the idea of true virtue in their minds, or are directly gratified in the view or contemplation of this object" (99). In contrast to Hutcheson, Edwards did not consider this relation to be arbitrarily imposed by the Creator. Edwards denied that God could have, had He wanted to, made the ugly beautiful and the beautiful ugly. In other words, some of the secular moralists were more voluntarist in their theology than Edwards! The frame of mind or inward sense of beauty that characterizes the regenerate, Edwards said, is not given by God "arbitrarily, so that if he had pleased he might have given a contrary sense and determination of mind, which would have agreed as well with the necessary nature of things" (99). Unlike Descartes, Edwards did not even suggest that if God had wanted to He could have made two plus two equal five.

Those gifts given by God to His creatures must consist with the nature of things, Edwards said. Any other basis for moral beauty than the consent of being to being would introduce an absurd self-contradiction into the universe. In giving to regenerate humankind that "temper of mind" that loves being in general (and loves love to being in general), God

> gives that which is agreeable to what is by absolute necessity his own temper and nature. For, . . . God himself is in effect being in general;

---

49. Like Thomas Aquinas, Edwards would probably have denied, however, that the sensations of taste, touch, or smell can be beautiful in themselves, since they are unable to take on form and, thus, unlike perceptions of sight and hearing, cannot be united in some way with intellect.

and without all doubt it is in itself necessary, that God should agree with himself, be united with himself, or love himself: and therefore, when he gives the same temper to his creatures, this is more agreeable to his necessary nature, than the opposite temper: yea, the latter would be infinitely contrary to his nature (100).

Not only metaphysical contradictions but also practical ones would arise if God had, for example, made hate to universal being, rather than love, the basis of goodness and beauty. Social discord would result, and human nature would be inconsistent with itself, for mankind would be inclined to what would bring it utter unhappiness, namely misery in general. "He that loves a tendency to universal misery, in effect loves a tendency to his own misery: and as he necessarily hates his own misery, he has then one inclination repugnant to another. . . . If men loved hatred to being in general, they would in effect love the hatred of themselves; and so would be inconsistent with themselves, having one natural inclination contrary to another" (102). Of course, some natural men are inconsistent with themselves in exactly this way, and in the case of devils it is a permanent condition.

The spiritual sense, then, is neither a subjective experience, nor a personal "inspiration" or enthusiasm. It is a sense in the closest correspondence with the nature of things. "It is the representation of the moral perfection and excellency of the divine Being" (102), and a source of true ideas about God. It is an integral part of a complex of divine laws by which God necessarily governs Himself as well as the universe.

Likewise, the natural moral sense, which the secular philosophers isolated, is a necessary concomitant of fixed relations in the universe and is not arbitrary or subjective in its responses. The operation of the moral sense, Edwards believed, when it is not corrupted, parallels that of the spiritual sense and approves of the same things that a spiritual and divine sense approves of. The natural moral sense is limited, however, by its foundation strictly in intellect rather than sentiment (despite the contrary claims of its proponents), which keeps it from being *necessarily* effective in practical life. Knowing in the natural man does not imply doing or living. Nevertheless, the natural moral sense and the spiritual sense can and do work together in approving "the uniformity and natural agreement there is between one thing and another" (104), although the spiritual sense has entirely different grounds and moves with a different kind of approbation. For Edwards, then, God governs Himself and His creation by wisdom or reason above all, not by arbitrary will and not by benevolent inclinations.[50]

50. My insistence that Edwards was a metaphysical rationalist does not contradict my argument that Edwards's psychological theory of the regenerate was sentimentalist. Opposingly, Edwards explained the moral psychology of the natural man in intellectualist terms. In the realm of

Edwards and Utilitarian Ethics

It has not been uncommon in twentieth-century treatments of Edwards to feature the practical side of his philosophy or theology and to argue that, like Benjamin Franklin and like Cotton Mather in his alleged character as a "do-gooder," Edwards preeminently valued moral expression in action and subordinated piety, or devotion, to it. This interpretation has the advantage for historians of fitting Edwards neatly into the prevailing thesis about what happened to Puritanism in the eighteenth century.[51] A. Owen Aldridge drew support for such a view of Edwards from Benjamin Franklin himself, who was "one of the few observers of American religion," Aldridge noted, "to have taken the trouble" to point out Edwards's concern with doing good. When Franklin was rebuked by his devout sister, Jane Mecom, for ignoring church worship, Franklin replied that in Edwards's *Thoughts Concerning the Present Revival*, the evangelical leader himself had particularly emphasized that the Christian life requires "moral duties, such as acts of righteousness, truth, meekness, forgiveness and love towards our neighbours" and that these "are of much greater importance in the sight of God, than all the externals of worship."[52] It is not surprising that Franklin of all people would prefer to read Edwards this way, since it coincided so closely with his own theories. Why not bring Edwards over to his side if he could?

The idea that virtue, Christian or secular, is reducible to benevolence or to practical good actions of any kind, whether considered in terms of charity or of usefulness, had great force in the eighteenth century. It appears nowhere

---

grace, human conceptions of reason and logic do not prevail, although they do in all natural relations. For clarification on this point, see pp. 89–103, above.

51. Aldridge, *Jonathan Edwards*, 32, 78: Edwards "was vitally concerned with practical ethics as well as with abstract moral excellence." "The ethical element is strong in Edwards. . . . It is almost misrepresenting him to ignore such passages as the following from *Religious Affections*: 'In order to men's being true Christians, it is necessary that they prosecute the business of religion, and the service of God, with great earnestness and diligence, as the work to which they devote themselves, and make the main business of their lives. All Christ's *peculiar people*, not only do good works, but are *zealous of good works*.' Edwards insisted that Christian practice is not only 'the greatest evidence that *others* can have of the sincerity of a professing Christian,' but also the chief sign to the individual himself." Aldridge also quotes from John E. Smith's introduction to his edition of Edwards's *Religious Affections*: "It is no small irony that a skillful and vigorous defense of the primacy of practice in religion should have found expression in a treatise on religious *affections*" (Aldridge, *Jonathan Edwards*, 78–79). Alan Heimert, *Religion and the American Mind from the Great Awakening to the Revolution* (Cambridge, Mass., 1966), 112, refers to the "primacy of a social vision" in Edwards's thinking (p. 103), and interprets Edwards's concept of "love to being in general" as "heartfelt love of the beautiful society and active longing after its establishment."

52. Aldridge, *Jonathan Edwards*, 32. Franklin's letter, dated July 28, 1743, is in Labaree *et al.*, eds., *Franklin Papers*, II, 384–385.

more unmistakably than in George Turnbull, that collector of fashionable philosophical notions at mid-century, whose *Principles of Moral Philosophy* (1740) Edwards read in 1752. "Benevolence is the root of piety. . . . Benevolence does really, in the nature of things, include in it all that is good and worthy. . . . We have no clear conception of any moral attribute in the Supreme Being, but what may be resolved up into goodness or benevolence."[53] Utilitarian ethics and utilitarian theology were closely wedded, each supporting the other in a single closed circle.[54] It was widely held that God's perfection was principally in His benevolence and that man is closest to the divine when he imitates this divine character. The circularity came in most obviously when moralists argued, as they commonly did, that God's goodness was proved by the benevolent nature of man, for only a benevolent Creator would have given man a natural inclination to doing good; at the same time, in the next breath it was maintained that man *must* be naturally benevolent, for if he were not, God would be revealed as a malicious deity, which is a dogmatically unacceptable conception of the Creator. "We are placed in this world not to retire from it," Turnbull wrote,

> but to be active in it, and to exert ourselves to promote publick happiness. And indeed to suppose, that the virtue required of us is any thing besides such a temper of mind as prompts and excites to doing good in the world, is to suppose our excellence to consist in separating ourselves from our kind, and living independently of them. It is to place it in something that cannot make us like God, whose moral perfection consists in the continual exertion of his goodness.[55]

Although some interpreters of Edwards might argue that Edwards, too, believed that true virtue consists ultimately in doing good in the world, I am inclined to think that Edwards identified Turnbull and his ilk as the archenemy. As early as the 1720s Edwards showed signs of opposition to both theological and ethical utilitarianism, and, indeed, anti-utilitarianism is the main key to a profound understanding of *The Nature of True Virtue*. Whatever traces of utilitarianism may be found in Edwards's thought must be discounted, I believe, as either momentary carelessness in expression or concessions to the regular need felt by his auditors for conventional moral exhortation.[56] Edwards's

53. Turnbull, *Principles of Moral Philosophy*, II, 354.

54. I am defining "utilitarian" here simply as the belief that virtue is essentially a matter of doing good in the world, in the sense of bringing about good consequences in terms of human happiness.

55. Turnbull, *Principles of Moral Philosophy*, II, 342.

56. Cf. Allen, *Jonathan Edwards*, 196–197: Edwards was not willing "to lay supreme emphasis on moral practice as the test of the Spirit's presence and power. . . . From this mode of escape he had shut himself off by placing conscience, together with the greater part of the moral sphere

most cogent statements suggest that he cared primarily about internal states and exercises, not results or consequences in the world in and for themselves. And he embraced this position not simply because he believed that a good tree will yield good fruit, that is, that the right internal state would necessarily issue in good deeds—which, though it may be true, was incidental to his reasoning—but because purity of soul was ontologically of supreme importance for him and preceded any strictly ethical considerations.

On this matter Edwards sometimes took stands astonishingly contrary to the prevailing winds, opposing common social expectations to a degree that may not be found again in American letters before Thoreau's similar refractoriness. In a note in his "Miscellanies," written when he was twenty years old, Edwards espoused the position he would maintain to the end of his life. The subject of this private note was "Devotion":

> As for the other thing that is said, that there may be a degree of Devotion that may hinder one from being Usefull to the Rest of the Universe, I suppose they will not Dislike Devotion if it Only hinders one for but half a minute and makes one much more usefull, ever after, I mean if it only makes us useless During our life upon Earth, and much more Usefull to Eternity afterwards, not that I believe that a man would be less usefull Even in this World, if his Devotion was to that Degree as to keep him all his lifetime in an extasie.[57]

From the standpoint of eternal salvation, in other words, why all this fuss about doing good for a few score years on earth?

Moreover, Edwards understood what to many in the eighteenth century was already incomprehensible, namely that, conceived in the right framework, even religious "extasies" are not simply useless. Above all, he believed it was already a fatal concession to the materialistic spirit of the age to accept that the ethical measure of all experience is usefulness. In *Thoughts Concerning the Revival*, the same work that Franklin had quoted to his sister, Edwards affirmed:

> The work of God in the conversion of one soul, considered together with the source, foundation, and purchase of it, and also the benefit and eternal issue of it, is a more glorious work of God than the creation of the whole material universe. . . . More happiness and a greater benefit to man, is the fruit of each single drop of such a shower, than all the

---

of human life, under the control of God's common grace, which carries with it no saving efficacy."

57. Miscellanies, letter "tt."

temporal good of the most happy revolution in a land or nation amounts to, or all that a people could gain by the conquest of the world.[58]

So much for the value of worldly reforms and revolutions in relation to piety.

About a dozen years later, in *The Nature of True Virtue*, Edwards reiterated this essential theme of his moral theology in a statement we have already once quoted: "If there could be a cause determining a person to benevolence towards the whole world of mankind, or even of all created sensible natures throughout the universe, exclusive of union of heart to general existence and of love to God—not derived from that temper of mind which disposes to a supreme regard to him, nor subordinate to such a divine love—it cannot be of the nature of true virtue."[59] Benevolence to the entire universe cannot be equated with true virtue if essential piety is missing. Nothing that Edwards said, certainly, *excluded* good works as an important element in the Christian life. Indeed, so firmly did Edwards adhere to the notion that conversion unified the soul, that he denied it was possible for regeneration to occur without resulting in Christian practice. It would be an absurd distortion to say that he had abandoned the Amesian ideal of practical piety and "living to God" in favor of some sort of *vita contemplativa*. By their fruits you shall know them, obviously. But it is the completely evidential or reflex position of good works that must be noted in Edwards's thought. Edwards espoused an ethics of internal self-perfection (attainable only with the aid of divine grace), not an ethics of happiness, social harmony, or benevolence. Being good was for him distinguishable from doing good in any conventional sense. He was more on the side of Mary than Martha.

Edwards would surely have sympathized with Thoreau's attitude in *Wal-*

58. *Thoughts Concerning the Revival*, 84. Comments like this from Edwards bring into serious doubt some of the assertions in Heimert's volume, mentioned in n. 51 above, about the thrust of Edwardsianism.

59. *True Virtue*, ed. Frankena, 78–79. The manuscript index to his Miscellanies that Edwards must have worked on as late as the 1750s includes this entry: "Devotion. Virtue consists primarily in it. 962. 963." Miscellanies nos. 127, 141, 243, 1080, and 1218 also relate to this question. Cf. no. 127: "The highest end and happiness of man is to view God's excellency, to love and receive expressions of his love; and that therefore their greatest business is to meditate [on] and use means to understand God's bounty, and to express suitably their love." In the 17th century Michael Wigglesworth was torn between devotion and doing good. The latter was much *easier*, but God demanded the former. Wigglesworth wrote in his diary on Nov. 9, 1653: "An Atheistic irreverent frame seizeth upon me; and whilest God is bidding me see his glory I cannot see it; vile and unworthy conceptions concerning god come into my mind. I cannot desire heaven because 'tis a place where I shall see and wonder at and acknowledge the glory of god for ever; But I rather desire a heaven where I might be doing for god [rather] than only thinking and gazing on his excellency. Blind mind! Carnal heart!" Morgan, ed., "Diary of Wigglesworth," Col. Soc. Mass., *Trans.*, XXXV (1951), 372.

den: "As for Doing-good, that is one of the professions which are full. . . . Probably I should not consciously and deliberately forsake my particular calling to do the good which society demands of men, to save the universe from annihilation; and I believe that a like but infinitely greater steadfastness elsewhere is all that now preserves it."[60] God is not a benevolent humanitarian, and neither must this new credo be declared the absolutely highest virtue for man. By Thoreau's day the weight of conventional moralism cried out for such a response, whereas Edwards's resistance was prophetic. Both men understood the cardinal point, however, that good works are always susceptible to the corruptions of superficiality and hypocrisy and can never in themselves be germinal of any profound change in human nature. "There are a thousand hacking at the branches of evil to one who is striking at the root," Thoreau wrote. "Philanthropy is almost the only virtue which is sufficiently appreciated by mankind. Nay, it is greatly overrated. . . . The kind uncles and aunts of the race are more esteemed than its true spiritual fathers and mothers."[61]

The solitary purity of the devout, it should be remembered, is in fact the only yardstick by which in the end all the good deeds in the world can be measured. Practically speaking, without models of disinterested love, that is, without individuals who have cultivated internal purity and exercises first of all, there would be no measure for discriminating the true from the false among all the acts that pass for benevolence in the world. We recognize the hypocrite, or the vanity of the do-gooder, because we have a concept of sincerity in mind that serves as a standard. Can that concept be embodied in the world, or is it a mere fiction? Thoreau's essential message was no different from Edwards's in *Religious Affections*. Thoreau wrote: "Goodness must not be a partial and transitory act, but a constant superfluity, which . . . is unconscious. This is a charity that hides a multitude of sins."[62] For Edwards, true virtue is the spontaneous overflowing of a purified soul, just as God's so-called "goodness" is such a superfluity rather than self-conscious benevolence in human terms. Edwards made a special point of denying that we can properly speak of God's "goodness" as though it were a separate attribute from His inclination to glorify Himself. God's primary inclination is to exhibit His perfection and to cause His excellence to be exercised.[63] Love to being in general, Edwards argued, is the essence of true virtue, and this internal habit or disposition produces an enormous superfluity of love, out of which, subordinately, love for the particular beings in the creation will flow.

60. *Walden*, ed. Brooks Atkinson (New York, 1950), 65.

61. *Ibid.*, 68.

62. *Ibid.*, 69.

63. Cf. Miscellanies, no. 1218, in Townsend, ed., *Philosophy of Edwards*.

Although, as we have seen in chapter 4, Edwards accepted some forms of self-love as the inescapable condition of human action, the thrust of his faith was toward a purity of deed that excluded self-love. On the one hand, he was a realist about human nature. On the other, he hoped for a possession of soul by divine infusion that would make the devout believer a pawn in God's economy of salvation. This latter hope became fully explicit only in the writing of Edwards's disciple Samuel Hopkins, who revived the "willingness to be damned" criterion of holiness. This criterion in some form will always emerge in religious minds that crave purity of intention and find even the promise of reward in heaven to be an obstacle in their quest for total renunciation or mortification of self-interest.

Edwards's solution to the problem of self-love was not to hold out the possibility of greater and greater renunciation of self, until self-regard is annihilated altogether. Rather, he formalized the relations between God and man at the ontological level, through the doctrine of fittingness and suitability, until what mattered was no longer the specific quality of one's intention. In the end, it is the conformity of a human heart, disposition, or sentiment to God's nature, the *convenientia* of man to God, that is decisive, and this relationship exists at a level beyond any person's mere intentions. This is the purity of geometry or mathematics rather than of psychology or chemistry. "How doth all the world congratulate, embrace, and sing to a sanctified soul," Edwards wrote when he was about twenty years old.[64] It was a theme that he did not outgrow. A few years later he speculated that "Holiness of heart doth of its own nature and tendency, considered abstractedly from any immediate guidance of the Holy Spirit, keep men from errors in judgment about religion and directs them to truth; . . . holiness is as a touchstone whereby they try doctrines; and . . . they have a distinguishing taste and relish, more and more perfect as they have more holiness." Holiness is a touchstone because, Edwards continued, as the sanctified mind is "let into the spiritual world" and has those "ideas" (in the sense of objects of knowledge) that an unsanctified mind is "not capable of,"

> it easily perceives what ideas are harmonious, and what not; for nothing else is requisite in order to seeing the proportion of ideas but clearness, or having the ideas themselves clear; but the holy mind does and safely may reject for false, everything in divinity that is not harmonious. The soul distinguishes as a musical ear; and besides, holiness itself consists in spiritual harmony; and whatever don't agree with that, as a base to a treble, the soul rejects.[65]

64. Miscellanies, letter "a," the first he wrote.
65. Miscellanies, no. 141, written in about 1722. Edwards added as a corollary the thought that "as the harmony in the mind will keep it from embracing unharmonious spiritual things, so will

The soul is either in tune with God or it is not. The problem of self-love and impurity of motive in general is to some degree bypassed by this description. Harmony with God is inward rather than a correspondence in practical outward exercises, and from this regenerate condition acts and feelings in conformity with divine law will surely emanate.

Much of the evidence for the belief that Edwards is properly interpreted as a theologian who placed great emphasis on external morality for its own sake (as opposed, let us say, to the interpretation that he is best seen as a theologian with primarily mystical leanings) rests on his discussion in *Religious Affections* of the "twelfth sign."[66] One finds in this discussion many statements that bear up Aldridge's point of view. "There is a sort of external religious practice, wherein is no inward experience," which is of "no account" in the sight of God, Edwards says. But there is also "what is called [religious] experience, that is without practice, being neither accompanied, nor followed with Christian behavior; and this," Edwards says, "is *worse* than nothing."[67] Protestants traditionally feared and detested monkish, otherworldly contemplation. "Christian practice," Edwards wrote, "is the sign of signs . . . which confirms and crowns all other signs of godliness."[68] Many more such expressions in *Religious Affections* appear to testify to a commitment in Edwards toward doing good equal to that felt by anyone else in the age. Yet I think this conclusion is drawn too hastily from Edwards's careful words in *Religious Affections*. Edwards's discussion of the "twelfth sign," it should be noted, is not in the least concerned with the *definition* of virtue, or even with the definition of grace and holiness. It is occupied with what constitutes valid *evidence* for these states of being. The problem in interpreting Edwards is not whether gracious inward states will actually issue in many forms of holy practice, for, of course, they do, as Edwards himself insisted. Such a belief was integral to the Puritan tradition of "practical theology" represented by Ames and Mastricht. The question is, rather, what is Edwards primarily concerned with, inward states or doing good in the world? And on this matter it seems to me that he is overwhelmingly preoccupied with the former, assuming, as he does, that when the heart is right everything else will take care of itself. It is notable, too, that a close reading of the last part of *Religious Affections* makes clear that Edwards's emphasis on "practice" had mostly to do with the *testing* and *trials* of truly gracious affections. When real conversion

---

an embracing things generally and notably unharmonious . . . effectually keep harmony or holiness out of the mind." For the medieval background to the idea that grace brings into harmony the discordant parts of the soul, see Spitzer, *Classical and Christian Ideas of World Harmony*, 50–55.

66. I do not think that Edwards can properly be called a mystic, but the term is sometimes useful to set off his thinking against utilitarian views.

67. *Religious Affections*, ed. Smith, 452. My italics.

68. *Ibid.*, 444.

has occurred, and the heart is transformed, this fact should be evident in one's ability to withstand temptation, persecution, and other trials of the soul. The heart is proven in practice, and, as Edwards says, this is the highest proof there can be. Edwards also stressed, in discussing the "twelfth sign," that regeneration is unification of the soul, such that it becomes "exceeding absurd, and even ridiculous, for any to pretend that they have a good heart, while they live a wicked life, or don't bring forth the fruit of universal holiness in their practice."[69] In this sense, too, external practice is completely inseparable from inward states. Yet Edwards did not intend to *equate* the external with the internal, for the proposition is not reversible. It is by no means exceeding absurd for a person with a wicked heart to exhibit in his actions what appears to everyone to be the fruit of universal holiness. In short, the entire meaning and value of Christian practice is derived from the inward condition or habitude of the soul, not from any autonomous or independent criteria, such as promoting the general welfare.

To express this point slightly differently: Edwards explicitly denied that outward Christian practice could ever completely exhaust, encompass, or express the fullness of the inward condition of holiness. At most, good works can be only a *sign* or a minor part of the whole; the whole is itself grounded in love to being in general, not in benevolence to man or any other practical exercises. Good deeds are but one aspect of an inner gracious condition that is itself the one essential thing in virtue and holiness.[70] There is relatively little exhortation to good works in Edwards's published writing precisely because he assumed that real good works were not detachable from a regenerate state. In *Religious Affections* he brought out the important *evidential* value of works.[71] But nowhere did he make the mistake of asserting that holiness or virtue is equivalent to works, may be defined by works, or is reducible to works, for it was exactly that type of opinion he was dedicated to opposing.[72]

Edwards's emphasis on love to God as the preeminent criterion of virtue is so marked that it has led to an interpretation of his thought quite the opposite

---

69. *Ibid.*, 428.

70. Cf. *ibid.*, 422–423 particularly.

71. For a discussion of Edwards's doctrine of "signs" in *Religious Affections*, with an emphasis different from that presented here, see John E. Smith, "Jonathan Edwards: Piety and Practice in the American Character," *Journal of Religion*, LIV (1974), 166–180.

72. Edwards would have been comfortable not only with some of Thoreau's opinions but also with those of the 17th-century Jesuit Louis Lallemant, as he is described in Aldous Huxley's *The Devils of Loudun* (New York, 1952), 87–88: "All this explains why most would-be good works are ineffective to the point of being almost bad. If hell is paved with good intentions, it is because most people being self-blinded to the inner light, are actually incapable of having a purely good intention. For this reason, says Lallemant, action must always be in direct proportion to contemplation. 'The more inward we are, the more we may undertake outward activities; the less inward,

of that just considered. More than one critic has observed that Edwards's theory of true virtue, by setting up what seems to be a nearly unattainable criterion of goodness and by dismissing as inferior and counterfeit the achievements of natural morality, leaves a vacuum as it were between true virtue and the devil. Reinhold Niebuhr, for example, cited Edwards in connection with religious writers who in their yearning for the absolute draw the contrast between the divine and the human so starkly that "all lesser contrasts between good and evil on the human and historic level are obscured." "Sin finally becomes disobedience to God and nothing else" and loses all "social significance."[73] It is a criticism not unlike that which Niebuhr launched against pacifism: in condemning all violence the pacifist gives up the chance to do at least some intermediate good by working within the terms and conditions of the real world, debased as it may be. In the eighteenth century, one of Edwards's most perceptive critics, the Reverend William Hart of Saybrook, Connecticut, who had been an opponent of the evangelical party since the Great Awakening, commented that in *True Virtue* Edwards demeaned ordinary virtuous actions to the status of secondary morality and thus set natural moral virtue in such a light as to "disgust enlightened and virtuous men and perplex the simple."[74] Edwards's moral theory, it would seem, left mankind with no graded set of moral values to apply to everyday choices. It is important, after all, to distinguish degrees of self-love or degrees of benevolence, so

---

the more we should refrain from trying to do good.' Again, 'one busies oneself with works of zeal and charity; but is it from a pure motive of zeal and charity? Is it not, perhaps, because one finds personal satisfaction in this kind of thing, because one does not care for prayer or study, because one cannot bear to stay in one's room, cannot stomach seclusion and recollectedness?' A priest may have a large and devoted congregation; but his words and works will bear fruit 'only in proportion to his union with God and his detachment from his own interests.' The appearances of doing good are often profoundly deceptive. Souls are saved by the holy, not by the busy. 'Action must never be allowed to be an obstacle to our union with God, but must rather serve to bind us more closely and lovingly to Him.' . . . Without the selfless inwardness which is the condition of inspiration, talent is fruitless, zeal and hard work produce nothing of spiritual value. 'A man of prayer can do more in a single year than another man can accomplish in a whole lifetime.' Exclusively outward work may be effective in changing outward circumstances; but the worker who wishes to change men's reactions to circumstances—and one can react destructively and suicidally to even the best environment—must begin by purifying his own soul and making it capable of inspiration. A merely outward man may work like a Trojan and talk like Demosthenes; but 'an inward man will make more impression on hearts and minds by a single word animated by the spirit of God' than the other can do by all his efforts, all his cleverness and learning."

73. Reinhold Niebuhr, *Moral Man and Immoral Society: A Study in Ethics and Politics* (New York, 1941), 67.

74. William Hart, *Remarks on President Edwards's Dissertations Concerning the Nature of True Virtue* . . . (New Haven, Conn., 1771), quoted in Holbrook, *Ethics of Edwards*, 117. Holbrook's chapter " 'True Virtue' and Its Early Critics" is very useful for studying the historical response to Edwards's ethical thought. See also for the climate of the time, Haroutunian, *Piety versus Moralism*.

that the hateful and malicious person is not found equally objectionable with the well-meaning good citizen and neighbor who may be unredeemed in religious terms. If God does not care about degrees of goodness at the natural level, but only about saintly holiness, what happens to religion's support for a basic level of moral observance in society? Edwards's concept of being, Hart said, is so abstract as to be "neither wise nor foolish, neither morally good nor evil, neither self-existent nor created[,] and dependent upon neither God nor a creature. It has no relation to the benevolent mind."[75] In 1890 Alexander Allen raised a similar objection: "The ethical principle of Edwards is defective in grounding morality in the immeasurable, incomprehensible essence of God. The landmarks disappear by which the good in itself may be recognized."[76]

These criticisms of Edwards make a valuable point about the socially harmful consequences that can follow from a moral theology too far elevated above moral philosophy, but they fail to take the measure of Edwards's moral thought in its entirety. Edwards assumed, we can surmise, that in a world already obsessed with the secular pursuit of conventional virtue and moral respectability, religion had to play a different and higher role than that of strengthener of practical morals. Edwards accepted, and even contributed significantly to, the belief that the elements of Judaeo-Christian morality have fixed, natural foundations rooted in the rational structure of the world. The laws of morality are discoverable by natural intellect and conscience and are even manifested in natural instincts and affections. Divine revelation and the workings of grace do not contradict these facts, although they serve to put natural morality in proper perspective. Natural morality takes care of itself, so to speak. Religion or theology, by contrast, reveals God's highest expectations of man in the realm of morals and points to forms of virtue beyond the discoveries of natural men and beyond their attainment.

If one looks only at Edwards's description and definition of *true* virtue, the criticisms just mentioned have some validity. But if one takes into account more than Edwards's moral theology and looks also at his discussions of the strengths and weaknesses of natural morality in both theory and practice, it is evident that his thought can hardly be said to have undermined society's concern for conventional rectitude. It is not correct, then, to argue that because Edwards elevated true virtue to the level of devotion to the infinite, there is no human scale left by which to measure degrees of good and evil on earth. A natural standard for morality continues to exist.

As a recent writer has pointed out, we unfortunately have only the one word "morality" to describe a wide range of ethical behavior and achievement, which results in a certain amount of confusion. The extremes are often

75. Hart, *Remarks on Edwards's Dissertations*, quoted in Holbrook, *Ethics of Edwards*, 114.
76. Allen, *Jonathan Edwards*, 317.

in conflict. There is a demand for self-sacrificing, positive goodness, for a transcendent love for others on the order of Edwards's concept of true virtue, as well as a demand for strictly observed judicial limits, for the reciprocity of restraint in the self-interest of all, for civil justice based solely upon outward conduct rather than special internal virtue. The possession of virtuous goodness alone, it is sometimes said, does not necessarily indicate that one is also moral, in the sense of possessing a set of unbreakable restraints. "A pure heart . . . may sorrowfully send legions of heretics to the stake,"[77] just as Edwards looked with complacency on the condemnation of legions to eternal torment. Several such divisions within the meaning of morality may be introduced, including the traditional one between scriptural moral law and Christian charity. Edwards failed to investigate these diverse meanings in a systematic fashion, but with the exception of his omission of any extensive discussion of the concept of duty or obligation, his work is fairly comprehensive in its attention to the full spectrum of morality.

True and Counterfeit Virtue

The central problem Edwards confronted as a theologian of morals, as we have indicated on several occasions earlier, was that of wresting back from the secular philosophers the traditional distinctive attributes of Christian virtue that the philosophers had silently appropriated and camouflaged for their own use. In the face of the gradual but unmistakable cracking and weakening of the millennium-old foundations of moral and civil authority in the West (which had been embedded in religious principles), philosophers between 1650 and 1760 undertook to reestablish and rebuild morality and government on new foundations without direct dependence on the waning influence of religion. This tremendous feat was successfully accomplished by the end of the eighteenth century and has served our civilization well, without fundamental change in many respects, since that time. But Christian, or Judaeo-Christian, values were, in one guise or another, so profoundly intermixed in the new secular order that an identifiably and avowedly Christian thinker like Edwards was challenged not only to combat the secularizing wave but also to distinguish precisely wherein nominally Christian ethics was in any way superior to secular ethics. Like Christianity, the Shaftesbury-Hutcheson gospel was optimistic without being naive about human nature; it was inward and affective without being antinomian; it was benevolent without being parochial; it stressed purity and disinterest without reverting to eremitism or withdrawal; and it was zealous and infectious without being dangerously militant or uto-

---

77. Allen Wheelis, *The Moralist* (New York, 1973), 53 and *passim*.

pian. It presided over the greatest psychological revolution in modern times through its sponsorship of the widespread movement that sanctioned the full exercise of the passions and affections in the moral life, an emphasis that had formerly been characteristic of Christian definitions of virtue only. And attendant upon this naturalization of "feeling," or along with it, had come the pervasive force of humanitarianism, which upheld an irreversible commitment to the relief of unnecessary pain and misery, a commitment based on the self-evident rightness of the emotion of compassion.

Because of these facts, Edwards's dissertation on true virtue, though very short in length, was his most ambitious book and, in terms of the problem it was confronting, the most difficult he could have undertaken to write. His works on the will and on religious affections posed far easier problems for him. He came to them with preexisting—one might even say, ready-made—answers that had firm roots in the seventeenth century, if not before. But the problem of distinguishing true "Christian" ethics from its imitations in eighteenth-century secular philosophy was an altogether new difficulty that had only come into focus in the course of Edwards's own lifetime. This was not at all the familiar and well worked-over problem of distinguishing Christian from pagan virtue or from Hebraic virtue, and Edwards knew it. Secular benevolist philosophy in Britain, like Edwards's own moral theology, was a direct descendant of seventeenth-century Puritan piety. Two branches of the same tree were set against each other. Edwards's defense of specifically Christian virtue may be a unique work in American thought, for it neither takes refuge in strictly doctrinal or dogmatic definitions of what constitutes true virtue (it does not simply quote Paul on charity, as though repeating Scripture could solve the modern problem), nor adopts the liberal view that secular counterparts are good enough for all practical purposes. Moreover, Edwards did not attempt to show the merely *practical* value of religion to state and society—a matter that had become controversial since Bayle and Shaftesbury had claimed that atheists could make perfectly good citizens—but rather the theoretical and logical necessity of devotion to God in any adequate system of morals.

In chapter seven of *True Virtue* Edwards undertook to explain why what was obvious to him had yet deceived others, that is, why the new moral philosophy, in its different secular varieties "which have not the essence of virtue, have yet by many been mistaken for true virtue" (85). Edwards found several reasons for this general error. Since the argument of this chapter of Edwards's is so close to the central problem behind the composition of *True Virtue*, it will be worth our while to look at it in some detail.

First, Edwards noted, the natural affections and principles that are featured in secular morality do truly have "something that belongs to the general nature of virtue" (85). In particular, natural morality and true virtue have in common "the tendency and effect of benevolence," although in natural morality the benevolence is deficient, because it is invariably a private benevolence that "falls short of the extent of true virtuous benevolence." The pity and compassion, the benevolence and gratitude, and so on, of natural morality resemble true virtue, but they lack its specific distinguishing nature and essence. The essential defect of these expressions of natural morality is that they are private in nature, which means that the "temper of benevolence to being in general" is absent. Natural virtue appears beautiful, despite its limitations, only because people tend to view things in a narrow context. Natural morality is beautiful only within its "own private sphere" (86–87). God is mistakenly excluded from the assessment, "as though he did not properly belong to the system of real existence, but was a kind of shadowy, imaginery being," and the private system takes on the "image of the universal" and appears, falsely, to be true virtue.[78] Man's typically limited perspective leaves him open to the illusion that there is true virtue in the world.

In addition, when an individual is benevolent to a large number of people, such conduct is easily confused with true virtue because people fail to see that this benevolence is simply an extension of private affections, founded in self-love and differing from it only in the quantity of objects loved. Although self-love is "necessary to society," everyone recognizes that it must be subordinated to and regulated by a more extensive principle, or else a person may become "a common enemy to the general system." But this undeniable truth is usually ignored when private affections embrace "a system that contains millions of individuals." From Edwards's point of view, as we have noted, a love to anything less than universal, no matter how extended, existence can bear no greater proportion to the infinite whole than self-love alone, although men prefer to believe that somehow benevolence to large numbers of people brings one closer to the whole (88).

Second, natural morality resembles true virtue not only in its tendency toward benevolence but also in its complacence and delight in, and approbation of, virtue. True virtue consists "in a sense and relish of the essential beauty of virtue." Natural virtue, particularly the approbation of conscience, acts "from a sense of the inferior and secondary beauty which there is in virtue, consisting in uniformity; and from a sense of desert, consisting in a sense of the natural agreement of loving and being loved, shewing kindness and receiving kindness" (89). Similarly, natural virtue may share with true

---

78. Holbrook, *Ethics of Edwards*, 69–70, n. 61, has pointed out that in Edwards's view natural morality is like a type that merely foreshadows the antitype of true virtue. This idea seems to me to be correct, for although Edwards may not have been explicit on the point, it is the best way of expressing the relationship of natural morality to true virtue as Edwards tried to shape it. However, this parallel to typology, while it brings unity to Edwards's thought, does not serve to clarify the relationship philosophically.

virtue a disapprobation of vice, from "a natural opposition to deformity and disproportion." The approbation of conscience is the more readily mistaken for truly virtuous approbation, Edwards argued, because God has so arranged the constitution of the world that "when conscience is well informed and thoroughly awakened," it agrees with true virtue "fully and exactly" as to the object approved, though not as to the "ground and reason of approving." As I have indicated in earlier chapters, natural conscience, according to Edwards, remains intellectualist and cannot taste and relish the beauty of true virtue; it cannot participate, as it were, in the loving relations of virtue. Natural conscience is also deficient in that what it *knows* of right and wrong is independent of any inducement or incentive to live a holy life. In the case of true virtue, moral knowledge and conduct are integrated.

Third, by the force of habit (that is, the association of ideas), emotions rooted in self-love may take on a life of their own and appear to be disinterested responses to evil and wickedness. Thus, people dislike those things in the world that they have always connected with "hurtfulness, malignancy, perniciousness," and they approve of things that they have always connected mentally with profit, pleasantness, and utility. "This approbation of virtue and dislike of vice, is easily mistaken for true virtue" (90), even though the underlying basis of the approbation is self-interest. Because of the strong association of ideas, the same things are approved of that true virtue might approve of.

Fourth, the exercise of the natural instinct of pity, which Edwards did not consider an intrinsic virtue, but rather a mechanical contrivance of human nature, can create the appearance of virtue.[79] Moreover, from a sympathetic relation to natural pity, men feel complacence in the virtues of humanity, mercy, tenderness of heart, and so on, and find the contrary behavior very odious. Compassion is all the more deceptive, Edwards wrote, because unlike self-love, it is an affection that "respects others, and resembles benevolence," although in Edwards's terms it falls far short of true virtue (90).

Fifth, many of the traits of natural virtue have "a true negative moral goodness," Edwards believed, in the sense that they contain "the negation or absence of true moral evil." Natural morality is, after all, evidence that one is not entirely sunken into depravity, and it shows the absence of "that higher degree of wickedness, which causes great insensibility, or stupidity of conscience" (91). Sin is not only committed "against a spiritual and divine sense of virtue, but is also against the dictates of that moral sense which is in natural conscience." To lack even natural morality signifies unusually great corruption. In both natural and true virtue, self-love, "the source of all the wickedness that is in the world" (95), is the enemy when it is not kept within strict

79. For Edwards's close analysis of the nature of pity and compassion, see chap. 5, above.

bounds. Natural virtue is proof at least that selfishness has been contained to some degree. For a really corrupt person can become so habituated to indulgence of self-interest that he loses all sense of ill desert with regard to it. In effect, his conscience stops operating. Therefore, natural virtue is a relative or negative moral good, for men can sink much lower (92).

Natural morality is also like true virtue in that it tends to "restrain vice" (94). Natural affection keeps us from acts of injustice against those closest to us, which if allowed to occur would be "real wickedness." "Pity preserves from cruelty, which would be a real and great moral evil." Self-love itself, although no part of true virtue, may function to keep people from committing great wickedness and is often an inducement leading them to seek virtue. Self-love plays the paradoxical role of restraining people from the worst crimes and being at the same time at the very foundation of sin. As came to be widely believed in the eighteenth century, God gave mankind self-love to fall back on as a prop to virtue when the purer inclinations fail. Edwards was prepared to accept this conclusion, provided it was not in any way confused with the foundations of true virtue.

Sixth, natural moral principles and affections resemble and may be mistaken for true virtue in that they often tend to have the same effects as the exercise of true virtue. Common morality tends to the good of mankind, as do the natural affections of pity, gratitude, and parental affection; similarly, true virtue tends to the good of mankind. But simple usefulness in the world does not make an action truly virtuous, Edwards maintained, so the resemblance is merely superficial. Self-love, for example, is exceedingly useful and necessary, as are natural appetites like hunger and thirst, but no one would claim that the latter have the nature of true virtue.[80]

Finally, natural virtue is mistaken for true virtue because we usually give the same names to those affections that are truly virtuous as to those that are purely natural. Edwards believed, for example, that in addition to natural compassion, there is "a truly virtuous pity, or a compassion to others under affliction or misery" that springs from universal benevolence, rather than natural instinct (95). But the expression of real universal benevolence, that is, true virtue, does not *depend on* the particular instinct of compassion for its response. The true virtue of universal benevolence is sufficient in itself to respond with pity to another in calamity. The pity that is an expression of

---

80. Edwards was here casting a glance at Hume's argument in the *Enquiry Concerning the Principles of Morals* that "*utility*, in all subjects, is a source of praise and approbation: That it is constantly appealed to in all moral decisions concerning the merit and demerit of actions: That it is the *sole* source of that high regard paid to justice, fidelity, honour, allegiance, and chastity: That it is inseparable from all the other social virtues, humanity, generosity, charity, affability, lenity, mercy, and moderation: And in a word, that it is a foundation of the chief part of morals, which has a reference to mankind and our fellow-creatures." Hume, *Enquiry Concerning the Principles of Morals*, ed. Selby-Bigge, par. 188.

grace is an outgrowth of that pure benevolence that seeks another's good and leads us to desire his deliverance from evil. This kind of pity, Edwards argued, is "far more extensive than the other. It excites compassion in cases that are overlooked by natural instinct; and even in those cases where instinct extends, it mixes its influence with the natural principle, and guides and regulates its operations. And when this is the case, the pity which is exercised may be called a virtuous compassion" (95). As there is a unique virtuous compassion that is the fruit of grace, so there is a unique "virtuous gratitude," a unique virtuous love of justice, a unique virtuous sense of desert, and a unique virtuous or "sanctified" conscience (96).

A difficult question, and one we need not debate here, is whether Edwards's primary, objective, ontological foundation for virtue is philosophically or even theologically tenable. Even granting a belief in the efficacy of divine grace to transform human nature, one could still ask whether Edwards in *True Virtue* has described anything real or simply been led on by terminology. And the naturalistic minded critic could well ask whether Edwards has in fact described in practical terms a type of human being that is in any way morally superior to the ideal figure implicit in the Shaftesbury-Hutcheson gospel, who is in no need of special grace as Edwards understood it. "It cannot surely but seem *natural*," Shaftesbury wrote, "that the particular mind should seek its happiness in conformity with the general one, and endeavour to resemble it in its highest simplicity and excellency."[81]

Yet at the very least, Edwards's accomplishment in *True Virtue* was impressive in range. He greatly devalued the currency of everyday morality, which is always subject to the inflationary forces of pride, self-righteousness, and complacency. With scarcely a reference to the Gospel or to any conventional religious authority, Edwards attempted through force of metaphysical reasoning alone to shift the whole scale of moral valuation that had become established in his day. He pushed the measure of true value up to the skies and exposed the average social coinage for what it is: mostly vanity interlarded with a few God-given instincts. Edwards's effort, in short, kept alive a transcendental standard of virtue or, at minimum, kept alive the possibility of aspiration toward a transcendental standard of virtue that is not strictly identified with institutionalized Christianity. Edwards's critical philosophy in the second portion of *True Virtue* was essential to this achievement, for without it, his moral theology alone would have appeared to be not so very far from Shaftesbury. It is this combination of a rationally derived metaphysics of morals and an acute critique of the presumptions of natural morality that gives Edwards's *True Virtue* its permanent stature.

81. *Characteristics*, ed. Robertson, II, 106.

Appendix

Although most of Edwards's early manuscript notes have received their share of attention from historians, there is one set that has been relatively neglected, his outline of a projected work on the "Natural History of the Mental World, or of the Internal World." This outline addresses directly many of the central concerns of moral philosophy in the seventeenth and eighteenth centuries, indeed, of philosophy in general, including logic and epistemology, and reveals impressively the extent of Edwards's involvement with the problems of secular philosophy in his time.

It seems obvious from internal evidence that the outline was written considerably later than Edwards's famous "Notes on the Mind." Number 25 of the outline, for example, refers to the "moral sense," a term that was not in current use until after the publication of Francis Hutcheson's first book in 1725. Yet the "Notes on the Mind," which are for the most part lengthy philosophical notes rather than topics for a book, have been mistakenly conflated with this later list. The confusion began with Sereno Dwight's printing of the two numbered lists as though they were a single work, and, even more peculiarly, his printing of the "Natural History of the Mental World" *before* the "Notes on the Mind" even though Dwight himself said in a concluding footnote to the "Natural History" that these numbered articles *followed* the "Notes on the Mind" in Edwards's manuscripts. Unfortunately, both manuscripts are lost, and we have only Dwight's printed transcription of them to work with.

Many of the same questions occur in the "Notes on the Mind" as are found in the outline for a "Natural History," but the later work is somewhat more concerned with moral psychology and less with metaphysics, reflecting, I believe, the general direction of the development of Edwards's philosophical interests. There is no direct evidence for assuming that this book project was still an important part of Edwards's writing plans when he was stricken at the height of his powers at age fifty-four. It may represent an outline long before abandoned. But whatever the case, there can be no doubt that Edwards was perfectly equal to tackling a project of the difficulty outlined here and that if he had gone on to write this book, it would have been one of the great works of eighteenth-century moral thought.

The copy presented here is taken from Sereno E. Dwight, ed., *The Works of President Edwards* (New York, 1830), I, 664–668.

TITLE. The Natural History of the Mental World, or of the Internal World: being a Particular Enquiry into the Nature of the Human Mind, with respect to both its Faculties—the Understanding and the Will—and its various Instincts, and Active and Passive Powers.

INTRODUCTION. Concerning the two worlds—the External and the Internal: the External, the subject of Natural Philosophy; the Internal, our own Minds. How the Knowledge of the latter, is, in many respects, the most important. Of what great use, the true knowledge of this is; and of what dangerous consequence errours, here, are, more than in the other.

Subjects to be handled in the Treatise on the Mind.

1. Concerning the difference between Pleasure and Pain, and Ideas, or the vast difference between the Understanding and the Will.

2. Concerning Prejudices; the influence of Prejudice to cloud the mind. The various sorts of prejudices in particular, and how they come to cloud the mind; particularly Prejudices of Interest—the true reason why they cloud the judgment.—Prejudices of Education and Custom. Their universal influence on wise, and learned, and rational, as well as other men; demonstrated from fact and experience—of their insensible influence, how it is insensible on great men.—How difficultly a people are got out of their old customs. In husbandry, how difficult to persuade that a new way is better.—Another prejudice, is the general cry, and fashion, and vogue, of an age. Its exceeding strong influence, like a strong stream, that carries all that way. This influence on great men. Prejudices of People, in favour of individual great men, to the contempt of others.—Again, the voice of men in power, riches, or honourable place.—How some Churches would laugh at their ceremonies, if they were without them.—How a man's being rich, or in high place, gives great weight to his words.—How much more weighty a man's sayings are, after he becomes a Bishop, than before—another prejudice is from ridicule, or an high strong overbearing contemptuous style.

3. Either after, or before, this, to have a dissertation, concerning the exceeding vanity, blindness and weakness of the mind of man.—What poor

fallible creatures men are. How every man is insensible of his own; thinks himself best.—Concerning the Pride of men; how ready to think they shall be great men, and to promise themselves great things.

4. How some men have Strong Reason, but not Good Judgment.

5. Concerning Certainty and Assurance. How many things, that are demonstrations in themselves, are not demonstrations to men, and yet are strong arguments; no more demonstrations than a boy may have, that a cube of two inches may be cut into eight cubes of one inch, for want of proper clearness, and full comprehension of the ideas. How assurance is capable of infinite degrees.—How none have such a degree, but that it might be heightened—even of that, that two and two make four. It may be increased by a stronger sight, or a greater clearness of ideas. Minds of clearer and stronger sight, may be more assured of it, than those of more obscure vision. There may be beings of a thousand times stronger sight than we are. How God's sight only, is infinitely clear and strong. That, which is demonstration at one time, may be only probable reasoning at another, by reason of different degrees of clearness and comprehension. It is almost impossible, that a long demonstration should beget so great assurance, as a short one; because many ideas cannot be so clearly comprehended at one time, as a few. A very long demonstration may beget assurance, by a particular examination of each link of the chain, and so by recollection, that we were very careful and assured in the time of it; but this is less immediate, and less clear.

6. Why it is proper for Orators and Preachers to move the Passions—needful to show earnestness, etc. how this tends to convince the judgment, and many other ways is good and absolutely necessary.

7. Of the nature of the Affections or Passions—how only strong and lively exercises of the Will, together with the effect on the Animal nature.

8. In treating of Human Nature, treat first of Being in general, and show what is in Human Nature, necessarily existing from the nature of Entity. And then, concerning Perceiving or Intelligent Beings, in particular, and show what arises from the nature of such. And then Animal Nature, and what from that.

9. Concerning Enthusiasm, Inspiration, Grace, etc.

10. Concerning a two-fold ground of Assurance of the Judgment—a reducing things to an Identity or Contradiction, as in Mathematical demonstrations, —and by a natural, invincible inclination to a connection, as when we see any Effect to conclude a Cause—an opposition to believe a thing can begin to be without a Cause. This is not the same with the other, and cannot be reduced to a contradiction.

11. Difference between Natural Appetites and Rational Desires.

12. Whether any difference between the Will and Inclination. Imperate acts of the Will, nothing but the prevailing Inclination, concerning what

should be done that moment. So hath God ordained that the motions of the Body should follow that.

13. Concerning the Influence which Nearness, or Remoteness, of Time has in Determining the Will, and the Reason of it.

14. Concerning Speculative Understanding, and Sense of Heart. Whether any difference between the Sense of the Heart, and the Will or Inclination. How the Scriptures are ignorant of the Philosophic distinction of the Understanding, and the Will; and how the Sense of the Heart is there called *Knowledge*, or *Understanding*.

15. Of what nature are Ideas of what is Internal or Spiritual. How they are the same thing over again.

16. Concerning Liberty, wherein it consists.

17. Concerning the prime and proper foundation of Blame.

18. How far men may be to blame for their Judgments; or for Believing, or Not Believing, this or that.

19. Concerning great Prejudices from the ambiguous and equivocal use of Words—such as Liberty, Force, Power, etc. How from this many things seem to be, and are called, Natural Notions, that are not so.

20. Concerning Beauty and Deformity, Love and Hatred, the nature of Excellency or Virtue, etc.

21. Whether or no Self-Love, be the ground of all Love.

22. Concerning the Corruption of Man's Nature. How it comes to be corrupt. What is the positive cause of corruption.

23. How greatly things lose their influence on the mind, through persons being used to them; as Miracles, and the Evidence of the Being of God, which we daily behold. The greatest Demonstrations—most plain and direct Proofs. Use makes things fail of their influence on the Understanding, so on the Will and Affections—things most satisfying and convincing—things otherwise most moving.

24. Consider of what nature is that inward sensation, that a man has when he Almost thinks of a thing—a name or the like—when we say it is *at our tongue's end.*

25. Concerning Moral Sense: what moral Sense is Natural.

26. How Natural men have a Taste of, and Delight in, that External Beauty, that is a resemblance to Love.
[End of first series]

27. Sensitive Appetites: How far they consist in some Present Pain, attended with the idea of Ease, habitually connected, or associated, with the idea of such an object—Whether the sight of Food excites the appetite of one who is hungry, any other way.

By what means persons come to long after a particular thing; either from an idea of Pleasure, or the Removal of Pain, associated.

Not immediately after the Thing itself, but only the pleasure, or the removal of pain.

28. Judgment. Wherein an Act of the judgment consists, or an Assent to a thing as true, or a Dissent from it as false. Show it to be different from mere Perception, such as is in the mere presence of an idea in the mind; and so not the Perception of the Agreement and Disagreement of Ideas.

29. Sensation. How far all acts of the mind are from Sensation. All ideas begin from thence; and there never can be any idea, thought, or act of the mind, unless the mind first received some ideas from Sensation, or some other way equivalent, wherein the mind is wholly passive in receiving them.

30. Separate State. How far the Soul, in a Separate State, must depend on Sensation, or some way of passively receiving ideas equivalent to Sensation, in order to conversing with other minds, to the knowing of any occurrence, to beholding any of the works of God, and to its farther improvement in knowledge.

31. Sensation. Whether all ideas, wherein the mind is merely passive, and which are received immediately without any dependence on Reflexion, are not ideas of Sensation, or External ideas. Whether there be any difference between these? Whether it be possible for the Soul of man, in this manner, to be originally, and without dependence on Reflexion, capable of receiving any other ideas than those of sensation, or something equivalent, and so some external idea? And whether the first ideas of the ANGELS, must not be of some such kind?

32. Angels. Separate Spirits. How far the Angels and Separate Spirits, being in some respects *in place*, in the Third Heaven, where the body of Christ is; their removing from place to place; their coming down from Heaven, then ascending to Heaven; their being with Christ at the Day of Judgment; their seeing bodies; their beholding the Creation of the Material Universe; their having, in their ministry, to do with the bodies of men, with the body of Christ, and other material things; and their seeing God's works of Providence, relating to the Material Universe;—how far these things necessarily imply, that they have some kind of Sensations like ours; and, Whether these things do not show that, by some laws or other, they are united to, some kind of Matter?

33. Concerning the great Weakness and Fallibility of the Human Mind, in its present state.

34. Concerning Beauty.

35. How the Affections will suggest words, and expressions, and thoughts, and make eloquent.

36. The manifest analogy between the Nature of the Human Soul and the Nature of other things. How Laws of nature take place alike. How it is Laws, that constitute all permanent being, in created things, both corporeal and spiritual.

37. Wherein there is an agreement between Men and Beasts. How many things, in Men, are like instincts in Brutes.

38. Whether the mind perceives more than One object, at a time.

39. How far the mind may perceive, without adverting to what it perceived; as in the winking of the eyelids, and many other like things.

40. How far there may be Acts of the Will, without our adverting to it; as in walking, the act of the will for each individual step, and the like.

41. The agreement between Objects of Sight, and Objects of Feeling; or Visible Magnitude and Figure, and Tangible Magnitude and Figure, as to Number and Proportion.

42. How far Imagination is unavoidable, in all Thinking; and Why?

43. Connection of Ideas. Concerning the Laws by which Ideas follow each other, or call up one another, in which one thing comes into the mind after another, in the course of our thinking. How far this is owing to the Association of ideas; and how far, to any Relation of Cause and Effect, or any other Relation. And whether the whole may not be reduced to these following: *Association of Ideas*; *Resemblance of some kind*; and that *Natural Disposition* in us, when we see any thing begin to be, to suppose it owing to a Cause.— Observe how these laws, by which one idea suggests and brings in another, are a kind of mutual attraction of ideas.—Concerning the importance, and necessity, of this mutual attraction and adhesion of ideas—how rarely our minds would serve us, if it were not for this. How the mind would be without ideas, except as suggested by the Senses. How far Reasoning, Contemplation, etc. depend on this.

44. How far the Love of Happiness, is the same with the Faculty of the Will? It is not distinct from the mere Capacity of enjoying and suffering, and the Faculty of the Will is no other.

45. Whether it be possible for a man to love any thing better than himself; and in what sense it is so.

46. Example. To enquire, What are the true reasons of so strong an inclination, in mankind, to follow Example. How great its influence over men, in their opinions, their judgment, their taste, and the whole man. How by this means, at certain times, a particular thing will come to be in great vogue, and men's passions will all, as it were, be moved at once, as the trees in the wood, by the same wind, or as things floating with the tide, the same way. Men follow one another like a flock of sheep. How sometimes the vogue lasts an age, at other times, but a short time; and the reason of this difference.

47. In what respects men may be, and often are, ignorant of their own hearts; and how this comes to pass.

48. Concerning the Soul's Union with the Body, its Laws, and Consequences.

49. One section, particularly to show wherein Men differ from Beasts.

50. In how many respects the very Being of Created things depends on Laws, or stated methods, fixed by God, of events following one another.

51. Whether all the Immediate Objects of the mind, are properly called Ideas; and what inconvenience and confusion arises from giving every Subjective Thought that name. What prejudices and mistakes it leads to.

52. In what respects Ideas, or thoughts, and judgments, may be said to be *Innate*, and in what respects not.

53. Whether there could have ever been any such thing as Thought, without External Ideas, immediately impressed by God, either according to some law, or otherwise. Whether any Spirit, or Angel, could have any Thought, if it had not been for this. Here particularly explain what I mean by *External Ideas*.

54. How words came to have such a mighty influence on thought and judgment, by virtue of the Association of Ideas, or from Ideas being habitually tied to words.

55. How far, through Habit, men move their bodies without thought or consciousness.

56. Whether Beauty, (Natural and Moral,) and the pleasure that arises from it, in ourselves or others, be not the only object of the Will; or whether Truth be not also the object of the Will.*

*The preceding articles were set down from time to time at the close of the work, in two series; the first, ending with No. 26. [Dwight's note]

Bibliographical Note

A recent bibliography reveals that since 1899 about 165 dissertations have been written that deal in large part with Jonathan Edwards. At least an equal number of books and articles on Edwards have been published, and Edwards's own writings, including much that is still in manuscript at the Beinecke Library at Yale University, are massive. I have read no more than a small portion of this huge literature and can only hope that I have not overlooked those parts of it that, had I read them, would have decisively altered the interpretations presented in this book.

In the early stages of my research, when everything about Edwards was new to me, I learned and profited from studies that later I regarded more critically. In the list below, I have tended to mention only what now seems important. But in general, this list is rather arbitrarily selective, and I am sure I have omitted a number of useful studies purely out of inadvertence. Moreover, this brief bibliography does not repeat all of the references found in the footnotes and should be thought of rather as a supplement to the annotation found in the text.

There are several good starting points for discovering the existing literature about Edwards. An extensive list of nineteenth-century materials may be found in William Peterfield Trent *et al.*, eds., *The Cambridge History of American Literature*, I (New York, 1917), 432–438, and the annotated bibliography in Clarence H. Faust and Thomas H. Johnson, eds., *Jonathan Edwards: Representative Selections, with Introduction, Bibliography, and Notes* (New York, 1935) continues to be enormously useful. More recently, the secondary literature has been surveyed by Everett H. Emerson, "Jonathan Edwards," in Robert A. Rees and Earl N. Harbert, eds., *Fifteen American Authors before 1900: Bibliographic Essays on Research and Criticism* (Madison, Wis., 1971), 169–184, and some recent studies (or excerpts from them) are gathered in David Levin, ed., *Jonathan Edwards: A Profile* (New York, 1969). Also valuable as a review of work on Edwards is William S. Morris, "The Reappraisal of Edwards," *New England Quarterly*, XXX (1957), 515–525. The list of dissertations on Edwards, mentioned above, is in Richard S.

Sliwoski, "Doctoral Dissertations on Jonathan Edwards," *Early American Literature*, XIV (1979–1980), 318–327.

Thomas H. Johnson, *The Printed Writings of Jonathan Edwards, 1703–1758: A Bibliography* (Princeton, N.J., 1940) is the authoritative guide to the early editions of Edwards's writings. Since 1940 there have been a number of major additions to the printed corpus described by Johnson: *Images or Shadows of Divine Things*, ed. Perry Miller (New Haven, Conn., 1948); Harvey G. Townsend, ed., *The Philosophy of Jonathan Edwards from His Private Notebooks* (Eugene, Ore., 1955), which consists primarily of selections from Edwards's "Miscellanies"; and, most important, the Yale University Press edition of Edwards's works, originally under the general editorship of Perry Miller and now guided by John E. Smith. Six volumes in this excellent series had appeared as of 1979, all with substantial introductions that are themselves major contributions to the literature. I have made particular use of *Freedom of the Will*, ed. Paul Ramsey (1957); *Religious Affections*, ed. John E. Smith (1959); and *Original Sin*, ed. Clyde A. Holbrook (1970). *Scientific and Philosophical Writings*, ed. Wallace E. Anderson (1980) unfortunately appeared after my manuscript was already in the hands of the copy editor. Two other volumes in the Yale series, one containing Edwards's apocalyptic writings and the other his evangelical tracts written in connection with the Great Awakening, are not germane to this book. Also available in a modern edition is *The Nature of True Virtue*, ed. William K. Frankena (Ann Arbor, Mich., 1960). Sereno E. Dwight's *The Life of President Edwards* (New York, 1830) remains uniquely indispensable as both an early authoritative biography and as a major source of Edwards documents found nowhere else.

Many volumes are still forthcoming in the Yale edition. Most relevant to this book will be the volume on Edwards's moral thought, edited by Paul Ramsey, and Thomas Schafer's edition of Edwards's philosophical and theological notebook, the "Miscellanies." Individual numbers of Edwards's "Miscellanies" have appeared in some of the early editions of Edwards's writings, notably *Miscellaneous Observations on Important Theological Subjects* . . . (Edinburgh, 1793) and *Remarks on Important Theological Controversies* (Edinburgh, 1796), and Harvey Townsend printed a good number in *The Philosophy of Jonathan Edwards*, although not always in perfectly accurate transcriptions.

I relied primarily on Edwards's "Miscellanies" for understanding the chronological development of his thought, since they are written in numerical sequence and can be at least roughly dated. For this purpose I was fortunate to have been given access to Thomas Schafer's definitive transcripts. The original manuscript of the "Miscellanies" and Schafer's transcripts are housed at the Beinecke Library, Yale University, along with most of the other surviving

Edwards manuscripts. For the serious researcher on Edwards, there is no substitute for spending a summer at the Beinecke.

Of the more general book-length studies of Edwards's thought, I regard Alexander V. G. Allen's *Jonathan Edwards* (Boston, 1889) as still one of the best comprehensive accounts, maybe *the* best, although it contains errors and outrageous prejudices. Alfred Owen Aldridge's *Jonathan Edwards* (New York, 1964) is learned and interesting, as one expects from a scholar of Aldridge's varied accomplishments, and is much less impressionable and eulogistic than the usual treatments of Edwards, but it errs on the side of cynicism. Conrad Cherry's *The Theology of Jonathan Edwards: A Reappraisal* (Gloucester, Mass., 1974 [orig. publ. Garden City, N.Y., 1966]) is by far the most solid and accurate account of Edwards's theology. Also excellent are Roland André Delattre, *Beauty and Sensibility in the Thought of Jonathan Edwards: An Essay in Aesthetics and Theological Ethics* (New Haven, Conn., 1968) and Clyde A. Holbrook, *The Ethics of Jonathan Edwards: Morality and Aesthetics* (Ann Arbor, Mich., 1973), although each of these volumes contains a central thesis that I am unable to agree with. Finally, I profited from reading Douglas J. Elwood's *The Philosophical Theology of Jonathan Edwards* (New York, 1960), although the author attempts to explain Edwards by making use of essentially twentieth-century concepts. Such a procedure is allowable up to a point, but Elwood's book, like a number of other studies of Edwards's thought that I have omitted here, does not adequately establish the intellectual context within which Edwards was working.

The most influential general book on Edwards in the last twenty-five years has undoubtedly been Perry Miller's *Jonathan Edwards* (New York, 1949). Rhetorically brilliant but utterly misleading in content, Miller's *Edwards* can only be judged an unaccountable lapse in the scholarship of one of the greatest of American historians. Miller appears to have relied primarily on intuition in writing about Edwards, rather than on dogged research.

Turning now to the literature pertinent specifically to some of the topics treated in this book, Edwards's early education and intellectual development deserve first consideration. The only comprehensive assault on the many problems posed by the fragmentary evidence that survives is William Sparks Morris, "The Young Jonathan Edwards: A Reconstruction" (Ph.D. diss., University of Chicago Divinity School, 1955). Morris points to the importance of seventeenth-century Protestant Scholastic literature for understanding early American philosophy, particularly the Latin works of Franco Burgersdyck and Adrian Heereboord, the latter of whom was influenced by Descartes. On the available books, see Arthur O. Norton, "Harvard Text-Books and Reference Books of the Seventeenth Century," Colonial Society of Massachusetts, *Transactions*, XXVIII (1935), 361–438; Norman S. Fiering, "Solomon Stoddard's Library at Harvard in 1664," *Harvard Library Bulletin*, XX (1972), 255–269; Samuel Eliot Morison, *Harvard College in the Seventeenth Century*, 2 vols. (Cambridge, Mass., 1936); Perry Miller, *The New England Mind: The Seventeenth Century* (New York, 1939); Richard Warch, *School of the Prophets: Yale College, 1701–1740* (New Haven, Conn., 1973); Anne S. Pratt, "The Books Sent from England by Jeremiah Dummer to Yale College," in *Papers in Honor of Andrew Keogh, Librarian of Yale University*, prepared by the staff of the Yale Library (New Haven, Conn., 1938), 7–44; Thomas Goddard Wright, *Literary Culture in Early New England, 1620–1730* (New Haven, Conn., 1920); Jonathan Edwards, "Catalogue," MS, Beinecke Library, Yale University; James S. Caskey, "Jonathan Edwards' 'Catalogue'" (B.D. thesis, Chicago Theological Seminary, 1931); and Thomas H. Johnson, "Jonathan Edwards' Background of Reading," Colonial Society of Massachusetts, *Transactions*, XXVIII (1935), 193–222. Additional information on Edwards's reading may be found in Howard C. Rice, Jr., "Jonathan Edwards at Princeton: With a Survey of Edwards Materials in the Princeton University Library," *Princeton University Library Chronicle*, XV (1953–1954), 69–89, which lists fifteen books owned by Edwards, and in Stanley T. Williams, ed., "Six Letters of Jonathan Edwards to Joseph Bellamy," *New England Quarterly*, I (1928), 226–242.

For an understanding of Protestant Scholastic literature, pre- and post-Cartesian, the following studies are helpful: Ernst Bizer, "Reformed Orthodoxy and Cartesianism," *Journal for Theology and the Church*, II (New York, 1965), 20–32; Paul Dibon, *La Philosophie néerlandaise au siècle d'or. L'Enseignement philosophique dans les universités à l'époque précartésienne, 1575–1650* (Paris, 1954); Keith L. Sprunger, *The Learned Doctor William Ames: Dutch Backgrounds of English and American Puritanism* (Urbana, Ill., 1972); John W. Beardslee III, ed. and trans., *Reformed Dogmatics: J. Wollebius, G. Voetius, F. Turretin* (New York, 1965); Matthias Nethenus, Hugo Visscher, and Karl Reuter, *William Ames*, ed. and trans. Douglas Horton (Cambridge, Mass., 1965); Heinrich Ludwig Julius Heppe, *Reformed Dogmatics . . .* , ed. Ernst Bizer, trans. G. T. Thomson (London, 1950); and Thomas Arthur McGahagan, "Cartesianism in the Netherlands, 1639–1676; the New Science and the Calvinist Counter-Reformation" (Ph.D. diss., University of Pennsylvania, 1976). Also useful for background on a related subject is F. Ernest Stoeffler, *The Rise of Evangelical Pietism* (Leiden, 1965, 1971). In *Moral Philosophy at Seventeenth-Century Harvard: A Discipline in Transition* (Chapel Hill, N.C., 1981), I have tried to bring together a diverse collection of data that might help to explain Edwards's starting point.

The most intensive work on Edwards's early intellectual development has been done in connection with the problem of discovering the sources of his metaphysical idealism. The exact dating of the earliest Edwards manuscripts is a closely related question. Some of the pertinent early studies are: Egbert C. Smyth, "Some Early Writings of Jonathan Edwards. A.D. 1714–1726," American Antiquarian Society, *Proceedings*, N.S., X (1895), 212–247, and "Jonathan Edwards' Idealism," *American Journal of Theology*, I (1897), 950–964; William P. Upham's analysis of Edwards's shorthand, Massachusetts Historical Society, *Proceedings*, 2d Ser., XV (1902), 514–521; H. N. Gardiner, "The Early Idealism of Jonathan Edwards," *Philosophical Review*, IX (1900), 573–596; and John H. MacCracken, "The Sources of Jonathan Edwards's Idealism," *Philosophical Review*, XI (1902), 26–42. More recent investigations include: Wallace E. Anderson, "Immaterialism in Jonathan Edwards' Early Philosophical Notes," *Journal of the History of Ideas*, XXV (1964), 181–200, and George Rupp, "The 'Idealism' of Jonathan Edwards," *Harvard Theological Review*, LXII (1969), 209–226.

The background in both Continental and British philosophy against which Edwards's youthful thought must be viewed is revealed in such works as: Georges Lyon, *L'Idéalisme en Angleterre au XVIIIe siècle* (Paris, 1888); Clarence Gohdes, "Aspects of Idealism in Early New England," *Philosophical Review*, XXXIX (1930), 537–555; Leroy E. Loemker, *Struggle for Synthesis: The Seventeenth Century Background of Leibniz's Synthesis of Order and Freedom* (Cambridge, Mass., 1972); W. von Leyden, *Seventeenth-Century Metaphysics: An Examination of Some Main Concepts and Theories* (New York, 1968); Richard A. Watson, *The Downfall of Cartesianism, 1673–1712: A Study of Epistemological Issues in Late 17th Century Cartesianism* (The Hague, 1966); John W. Yolton, *John Locke and the Way of Ideas* (London, 1956); as well as in such standard histories of philosophy as John Herman Randall, Jr., *The Career of Philosophy*, I: *From the Middle Ages to the Enlightenment* (New York, 1962) and Harald Höffding's *A History of Modern Philosophy: A Sketch of the History of Philosophy from the Close of the Renaissance to Our Own Day*, trans. B. E. Meyer, I (New York, 1950 [orig. publ. 1900]).

Edwards's relationship to the Cambridge Platonists has long been a matter of interest, and there are a number of good anthologies and secondary studies of this school. Many of these are cited in Fiering, *Moral Philosophy at Seventeenth-Century Harvard*, chapter 6. Emily Stipes Watts, "The Neoplatonic Basis of Jonathan Edwards' 'True Virtue,'" *Early American Literature*, X (1975), 179–189, pays particular attention to the influence of Henry More's *Enchiridion Ethicum . . .* (London, 1667).

Locke's influence is considered in some of the titles already mentioned and is given special attention in Claude A. Smith, "Jonathan Edwards and 'The Way of Ideas,'" *Harvard Theological Review*, LIX (1966), 153–173, and in Leon Howard, *"The Mind" of Jonathan Edwards: A Reconstructed Text* (Berkeley and Los Angeles, Calif., 1963). Rufus Suter, "The Conception of

Morality in the Philosophy of Jonathan Edwards," *Journal of Religion*, XIV (1934), 265–272, sharply distinguishes Edwards's ethics from the belief that "the material welfare of the people as a whole" is the highest moral good and that the "proclivity of an act to beget this universal welfare" is true virtue.

A few of the studies useful for comprehending the American philosophical context in general are: I. Woodbridge Riley, *American Philosophy: The Early Schools* (New York, 1907); Herbert W. Schneider, *A History of American Philosophy* (New York, 1946, 1963); Elizabeth Flower and Murray G. Murphey, *A History of Philosophy in America*, I (New York, 1977), which contains an excellent fifty-page essay on Edwards; Joseph Ellis, *The New England Mind in Transition: Samuel Johnson of Connecticut, 1696–1772* (New Haven, Conn., 1973); Herbert and Carol Schneider, eds., *Samuel Johnson, President of King's College: His Career and Writings*, 4 vols. (New York, 1929); and Norman Fiering, "Early American Philosophy vs. Philosophy in Early America," Charles S. Peirce Society, *Transactions*, XIII (1977), 216–237, and "President Samuel Johnson and the Circle of Knowledge," *William and Mary Quarterly*, 3d Ser., XXVIII (1971), 199–236.

Access to the moral philosophy of eighteenth-century Britain has been made remarkably easy by two excellent anthologies: L. A. Selby-Bigge's classic work, *British Moralists, Being Selections from Writers Principally of the Eighteenth Century*, 2 vols. (Oxford, 1897), reprinted in one volume in a Library of Liberal Arts edition (Indianapolis, Ind., 1964), and D. D. Raphael's companion anthology, *British Moralists, 1650–1800*, 2 vols. (Oxford, 1969). The topical indexes in both of these works could not be improved upon. The serious historian will not rest with the excerpts in Selby-Bigge or Raphael but will want to go on to read the classic works in entirety. Both of these anthologies contain complete bibliographies of contemporary works in moral philosophy. Leslie Stephen's two-volume *History of English Thought in the Eighteenth Century* (New York, 1927 [orig. publ. 1876]), although now over a century old, remains essential reading for those interested in the context of Edwards's thought. Basil Willey, *The English Moralists* (London, 1964) also provides a useful overview. Of the British moralists, Edwards's relation to Francis Hutcheson has been examined specifically in A. Owen Aldridge, "Edwards and Hutcheson," *Harvard Theological Review*, XLIV (1951), 35–53, and in his book *Jonathan Edwards*. Aldridge generally looks at Edwards in the light of the British philosophical tradition.

There are numerous valuable treatments of the third earl of Shaftesbury and of Hutcheson. In my dissertation, "Moral Philosophy in America, 1700 to 1750, and Its British Context" (Ph.D. diss., Columbia University, 1969), 95–189, I attempted to treat both of these men in relation to the development of American moral thought. Other works on Hutcheson's influence in America are Caroline Robbins, " 'When It Is That Colonies May Turn Independent:'

An Analysis of the Environment and Politics of Francis Hutcheson (1694–1746)," *William and Mary Quarterly*, 3d Ser., XI (1954), 214–251, and David Fate Norton, "Francis Hutcheson in America," *Studies on Voltaire and the Eighteenth Century*, CLIV (1976), 1547–1568. Of the many essays on Shaftesbury's ideas, two by Ernest Tuveson are particularly pithy and accurate: "The Importance of Shaftesbury," *ELH: A Journal of English Literary History*, XX (1953), 267–299, and "Shaftesbury on the Not So Simple Plan of Human Nature," *Studies in English Literature, 1500–1900*, V (1965), 403–434. R. S. Crane's "Suggestions toward a Genealogy of the 'Man of Feeling,' " *ELH: A Journal of English Literary History*, I (1934), 205–230, is also valuable for understanding the sentimentalist tradition in which Edwards was a participant.

The literature on the rationalist tradition in eighteenth-century Britain and America is much sparser. John Locke, it is usually assumed, drove out Continental rationalism, aided by the achievements of Isaac Newton. Changes in ideas or modes of thought seldom proceed so neatly, however. Traces of the impress of Cartesianism remained, perhaps more even in America than in Britain. On Cartesianism in England, see Marjorie Nicolson, "The Early Stages of Cartesianism in England," *Studies in Philology*, XXVI (1929), 356–374; Sterling P. Lamprecht, "The Rôle of Descartes in Seventeenth-Century England," *Studies in the History of Ideas*, III (1935), 179–240; and Charlotte S. Ware, "The Influence of Descartes on John Locke," *Révue Internationale de Philosophie*, IV (1950), 210–239. The influence of Nicolas Malebranche has not been thoroughly investigated, although there is reason to believe it was profound. The subject has been approached primarily in studies of John Norris of Bemerton, who was a declared disciple of Malebranche and an author with a significant readership in the American colonies.

The most important rationalist in early eighteenth-century moral philosophy, and a major figure in every respect, was Samuel Clarke, the Boyle lecturer and friend and interpreter of Newton. Until only a few years ago, despite Clarke's indisputable importance, not a single book-length study of the man had been written, other than contemporary eulogies. We are fortunate now to have two competent books on Clarke, although neither of these has been reviewed in the United States, perhaps because one volume was published by a vanity press and the other by a small English publisher: James P. Ferguson, *The Philosophy of Dr. Samuel Clarke and Its Critics* (New York, 1974), and by the same author, *Dr. Samuel Clarke: An Eighteenth Century Heretic* (Kineton, Warwick, England, 1976).

On the permutations of the idea of self-love in the seventeenth and eighteenth centuries, the best introduction is Arthur O. Lovejoy's *Reflections on Human Nature* (Baltimore, 1961), a set of lectures fully representative of the author's masterly skill at combining erudition and philosophical precision.

For clarification of the idea of self-love, few modern works can compete with Bishop Joseph Butler's *Fifteen Sermons* (London, 1726), which have been reprinted in two excellent editions of Butler's *Works*, one edited by W. E. Gladstone, 2 vols. (Oxford, 1896) and one edited by J. H. Bernard (London, 1900). F. B. Kaye's introduction and notes to his superb edition of Bernard Mandeville, *The Fable of the Bees: or, Private Vices, Publick Benefits*, 2 vols. (Oxford, 1924) is a mine of information on the eighteenth-century debate concerning the place of self-love in morality. There is also, of course, a large body of secondary literature on Mandeville that is addressed to the problem of self-love. J. E. Crowley, *This Sheba, Self: The Conceptualization of Economic Life in Eighteenth-Century America* (Baltimore, 1974) and Joseph A. Conforti, "Samuel Hopkins and the New Divinity: Theology, Ethics, and Social Reform in Eighteenth-Century New England," *William and Mary Quarterly*, 3d Ser., XXXIV (1977), 572–589, discuss the issues in an American context.

Relatively little has been written on the doctrine of hell in the eighteenth century, but D. P. Walker's *The Decline of Hell: Seventeenth-Century Discussions of Eternal Torment* (Chicago, 1964) has obvious bearing on what came later. Although much too broad in scope to be useful for certain kinds of historical details, William Rounseville Alger, *A Critical History of the Doctrine of a Future Life* (New York, 1867) is a neglected masterpiece. It is especially valuable when consulted with its prodigious companion work, Ezra Abbot's *Literature of the Doctrine of a Future Life* . . . (New York, 1867), a bibliography. Paul C. Davies, "The Debate on Eternal Punishment in Late Seventeenth- and Eighteenth-Century English Literature," *Eighteenth-Century Studies*, IV (1970–1971), 257–276, is one of the few studies focused specifically on the eighteenth-century problem. My own essay, "Irresistible Compassion: An Aspect of Eighteenth-Century Sympathy and Humanitarianism," *Journal of the History of Ideas*, XXXVII (1976), 195–218, deals more generally with the humanitarian opposition to the doctrine of eternal torment than does chapter 5 in the present book. Norman Sykes, "The Theology of Divine Benevolence," *Historical Magazine of the Protestant Episcopal Church*, XVI (1947), 278–291, is a good introduction to humanitarian developments in the Anglican church.

Finally, on Edwards's theory of the will, many of the accounts one finds in general studies of Edwards are not entirely accurate. Given that Edwards was himself ambiguous on certain points, there will probably always be some disagreement. The best investigations, whatever the conclusions they arrive at, effectively clarify the issues. Arthur E. Murphy, "Jonathan Edwards on Free Will and Moral Agency," *Philosophical Review*, LXVIII (1959), 181–202, is particularly incisive and clarifying. Also helpful is Arnold S. Kaufman and William K. Frankena's introduction to their edition of Edwards's *Freedom of the Will* (Indianapolis, Ind., 1969). There are, of course, dozens of essays by philosophers on the problem of the will that can be helpful to the student of Edwards, even though these essays may evince no particular interest in Edwards. Two that I profited from are: Maurice Mandelbaum, "Determinism and Moral Responsibility," *Ethics*, LXX (1959–1960), 204–219, and Rem B. Edwards, "Is Choice Determined by the 'Strongest Motive'?" *American Philosophical Quarterly*, IV (1967), 72–78. For the specific historical background to Edwards's treatment of the problem of the will, see Fiering, *Moral Philosophy at Seventeenth-Century Harvard*, chapter 3.

Index